THE ARCHAEOLOGY OF CANTERBURY
NEW SERIES

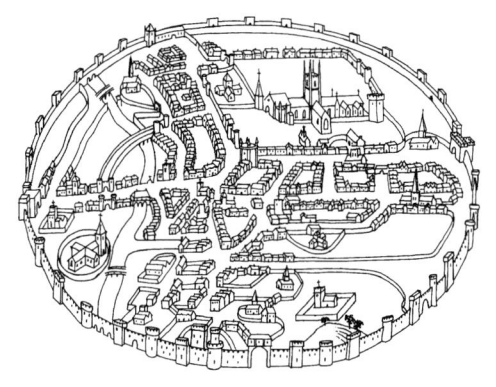

THE ARCHAEOLOGY OF CANTERBURY

New Series

VOLUME IV

HIGHSTEAD NEAR CHISLET, KENT EXCAVATIONS 1975–1977

Paul Bennett, Peter Couldrey and Nigel Macpherson-Grant

with contributions by

Tim Champion
and
Paul Arthur, Joanna Bird, Paul Craddock, Brenda Dickinson,
Ian Freestone, Pan Garrard, Peter Garrard, Marion Green, Stephen Greep,
Alex Gibson, Kay Hartley, Elizabeth Healey, Martin Henig, Mike Heyworth, Anthony King,
Don Mackreth, Andrew Middleton, Stuart Needham, Valery Rigby, John Shepherd,
Maggy Taylor, Isobel Thompson and Michael Tite

Published by Canterbury Archaeological Trust Ltd
2007

Produced by Canterbury Archaeological Trust Ltd
Printed in Great Britain by Lanes Ltd

This publication was funded by English Heritage

© Canterbury Archaeological Trust Ltd

The moral right of the contributors to be recognised as the
authors of their contributions has been asserted by them
in accordance with the Copyright, Designs and Patents Act 1988

ISBN 978-1-870545-11-2
British Library Cataloguing-in-Publication Data
A catalogue record for this book is available from the British Library

CONTENTS

Foreword (Barry Cunliffe) ix
List of figures xi
List of plates xv
List of tables xvii
Acknowledgements xix
Preface xxi

PART 1: INTRODUCTION (Paul Bennett)
Highstead in its setting 1
Geology 1
Previous discoveries 1
Aerial photography 5
Survival and retrieval 8
Organisation of the report 8
The archive 8

PART 2: THE EXCAVATED EVIDENCE (Paul Bennett and Nigel Macpherson-Grant)
Summary of the excavated sequence 11
    Period 1: Mesolithic to Late Neolithic 11
    Period 2: *c.* 900–600 B.C. 11
    Period 3A: *c.* 600–500 B.C. 11
    Period 3B: *c.* 500–400 B.C. 12
    Period 3C: *c.* 400–125/100 B.C. 12
    Period 4A: *c.* 100–50 B.C. 12
    Period 4B: *c.* 50–25 B.C. 14
    Period 4C: *c.* 25 B.C.–A.D. 50 14
    Period 4D: *c.* A.D. 50–75 14
    Period 5A: *c.* A.D. 75–150 14
    Period 5B: *c.* A.D. 150–250+ 15
Period 1: Mesolithic to Late Neolithic 15
Period 2: *c.* 900–600 B.C.
    Summary 16
    Enclosure B70 16
    Enclosure A24 25
    Enclosure A260 31
    Other Period 2 features 32
    Discussion 32

Period 3: *c.* 600–100 B.C.
    Period 3A summary 34
    Enclosure A118 35
    Enclosure B70 35
    Enclosure B144 37
    Isolated pits 37
    Discussion 37
    Period 3B summary 39
    Penannular house gullies 39
    Post-built structures 41
    Possible cremation burials 49
    Isolated post-pits 49
    Undated rectangular buildings 51
    Pits and hearths 51
    Enclosure ditch B70 62
    Discussion 62
    Period 3C 65

Period 4: *c.* 100 B.C.–A.D. 75
    Introduction 65
    Period 4A summary 65
    Enclosure B139 67
    Ditch B8 67
    Ditches B17, B18 and B20 67
    The post-hole row 67
    The isolated pit 69
    Discussion 69
    Period 4B summary 69
    Enclosure B3 69
    Ditches B10 and B312 71
    The isolated pit 71
    Discussion 71
    Period 4C summary 71
    Enclosure B7 71
    Discussion 75
    Period 4D summary 75
    Enclosure B1 75
    Enclosure B5 78
    Pit complex B15 78
    Early field system, Area A 78
    Pits, Area A 79
    Discussion 81

Period 5: *c*. A.D. 75–250+
- Introduction 81
- Period 5A summary 81
- Enclosure B1 83
- Ditches south-west of Enclosure B1 83
- Possible building 85
- Ditches B14 and B495 85
- Pits, Area B 85
- Field system, Area A 86
- Area C 93
- Discussion 93
- Period 5B summary 93
- Pit A274 93
- Area B late field ditch 95
- Enclosure B21 95
- The post-pit alignment 95
- Cropmarks 95
- The hypocausted building 95
- Evidence for later occupation 98
- Discussion 98

PART 3: THE POTTERY (Peter Couldrey, Marion Green, Nigel Macpherson-Grant and Isobel Thompson)

The Late Bronze Age/Early Iron Age pottery (Peter Couldrey)
- Introduction 101
- Fabrics 101
- Forms 103
- Decoration types 112
- Surface treatment 114
- Chronology 115
- Technology 156
- Continental influence 167
- Catalogue of illustrated vessels from Periods 2 and 3 171

The Late Iron Age pottery (Peter Couldrey and Isobel Thompson) 176
- Flint-tempered pottery from Period 4 (Peter Couldrey) 176
- Grog-tempered pottery (Isobel Thompson) 189

The Roman pottery (Marion Green)
- Summary 214
- Pottery from Ditch B164 216
- Pottery from Ditch B1 and Pit complex B15 225
- The Early Gaulish and other imported finewares (Valery Rigby and Marion Green) 233
- The amphorae (Paul Arthur) 237
- The samian (Maggy Taylor, Joanna Bird, Brenda Dickinson) 242
- The Roman and Romano-British finewares 244
- The mortaria (Kay Hartley) 245

PART 4: OTHER FINDS

Flints (Elizabeth Healey) 251
    Raw materials 251
    Reduction strategies 251
    Retouched pieces 254
    Discussion 256

Evidence for metalworking
    Mould fragments (Stuart Needham) 258
    Possible polishing stone (Nigel Macpherson-Grant) 265
    Scientific examination of vitrified and other debris associated with
    metallurgy (Ian Freestone) 266
    Crucible (Stuart Needham) 266
    Perforated pottery slabs (Nigel Macpherson-Grant) 267

Evidence for salt production
    Examination and analysis of fired clay from Pit B215 (Mike Heyworth) 268
    Later prehistoric briquetage from north-east Kent (Nigel Macpherson-Grant) 269

The small finds
    Objects of copper alloy (Martin Henig) 270
    Objects of iron (Martin Henig) 273
    Roman brooches (Don Mackreth) 274
    Roman glass (John Shepherd) 275
    Weaving implements (Nigel Macpherson-Grant and Stephen Greep) 276
    Object of antler (Stephen Greep) 278
    Objects of stone (Pan Garrard, Paul Craddock and Ian Freestone) 278

The Bones
Human (Peter Garrard) 279
Mammal and bird bones (Anthony C. King) 279

PART 5: DISCUSSION (Tim Champion)

The importance of Highstead 283
    Later prehistoric chronology 283
    Late Bronze Age and earliest Iron Age 284
    Early Iron Age 289
    Late Iron Age and Roman periods 291
    The development of the landscape 292
    Conclusions 293

PART 6: SUMMARY (Paul Bennett)

Summary 295
Résumé 295
Zusammenfassung 296

APPENDIX I: The Beaker pottery (Alex Gibson) 299
APPENDIX II: The scientific examination of part of a decorated Iron Age bowl
(Andrew Middleton and Michael Tite) 301

ABBREVIATIONS 303
BIBLIOGRAPHY 305
INDEX 323

FOREWORD

The publication of the excavation of the multi-period settlement site at Highstead near Chislet is a matter for celebration. Highstead, with its long sequence of occupation spanning the first millennium B.C. and early first millennium A.D., was excavated under difficult conditions between 1975 and 1977 in those pioneering days when rescue archaeology was in its infancy. It is a story well told by Paul Bennett in his preface and is a stark reminder of how hand-to-mouth archaeology was in the era before developer-funding. What the small dedicated team managed to recover during the course of those three punishing years was little short of remarkable. More remarkable still has been the dogged determination of the Canterbury Archaeological Trust to see the project through to the completion of full academic publication.

The value of Highstead is two-fold. It is a type-site for Late Bronze Age and Iron Age settlement in eastern Britain and it provides a pottery sequence without parallel in the region which demonstrates not only the *longue durée* development of ceramic technology throughout the first millennium but also the mobility of ideas – and of course people – between the Continent and Britain. It is no exaggeration to say that Highstead calls for a complete reassessment of connectivity in the Channel–North Sea zone.

Paul Bennett, in his preface, says that this report is 'unashamedly old fashioned'. If by this he means it is designed to be used rather than to impress, he is right. There is an unfortunate tendency these days to produce either superficial, colourful accounts bereft of necessary detail or tortured constructions muddling interpretation with observation. The Highstead report is crisp, well structured and a delight to use. The facts are logically presented and easy of access, and there follows a splendid interpretative essay succinctly placing the site in its national and international context. What more could one want?

Highstead will immediately, and deservedly, take its place as one of the classic type-sites for British prehistory. It is a monument to those who battled with the frozen ground during the bitter winter of 1975–6 and to the authors who dedicated themselves to bringing this report to fruition. The archaeological community will forever be in their debt.

Barry Cunliffe
February 2007

LIST OF FIGURES

Fig. 1	Site location	2
Fig. 2	Geology of the Highstead area	2
Fig. 3	Archaeological finds around Highstead	3
Fig. 4	Neolithic/Early Bronze Age transition: main features and finds	3
Fig. 5	Excavated features, soil stains and cropmarks	4
Fig. 6	Phased plan of excavated features	9
Fig. 7	Principal features, Period 2	12
Fig. 8	Principal features, Period 3A	12
Fig. 9	Principal features, Period 3B	13
Fig. 10	Principal features, Period 4A	13
Fig. 11	Principal features, Period 4B	13
Fig. 12	Principal features, Period 4C	13
Fig. 13	Principal features, Period 4D	14
Fig. 14	Principal features, Period 5A	14
Fig. 15	Principal features, Period 5B	15
Fig. 16	Period 2. Enclosure B70, plan of excavated features, reconstructed enclosure layout and detail section of rampart and ditch	17
Fig. 17	Period 2. Enclosure B70, ditch sections	18
Fig. 18	Period 2. Features within and immediately outside Enclosure B70	21
Fig. 19	Period 2. Detail of features within Enclosure B70	22
Fig. 20	Period 2. Detail of features outside Enclosure B70	23
Fig. 21	Period 2. Enclosure A24, with location	26
Fig. 22	Period 2. Enclosure A24, pits A5 and A181 and Gully A191	31
Fig. 23	Period 2. Enclosure A260, pits A100, A124, A270, A129 and A130	32
Fig. 24	Period 3A. Enclosure ditch A118 with location	34
Fig. 25	Period 3A. Features within Enclosure B70	36
Fig. 26	Period 3A. Enclosure ditch B144, pits B244 and B12, with location	38
Fig. 27	Period 3B. Area B, features described in the text	40
Fig. 28	Period 3B. Buildings B16 and B26	42
Fig. 29	Period 3B. Buildings B308 and B311	43
Fig. 30	Period 3B. Structure B35 within Enclosure B70	44
Fig. 31	Period 3B. Structure B260	45
Fig. 32	Period 3B. Structures B329, B196 and B159	46
Fig. 33	Period 3B. Structure B200	48
Fig. 34	Period 3B. Structure B200, internal features	49
Fig. 35	Period 3B. Structures B111 and B29, plan and post-hole profiles	50

Fig. 36	Period 3B. Pits and hearths	53
Fig. 37	Period 3B. Hearths	55
Fig. 38	Period 3B. Hearths and fire pits	56
Fig. 39	Period 3B. Clay-lined pits	58
Fig. 40	Period 3B. Pits	60
Fig. 41	Period 4 features	66
Fig. 42	Period 4A. Enclosure B139	68
Fig. 43	Period 4B. Enclosure B3	70
Fig. 44	Period 4C. Enclosure B7	72
Fig. 45	Period 4C. Late modifications to Enclosure B7	74
Fig. 46	Period 4D. Enclosures B1 and B5 and Pit complex B15	76
Fig. 47	Period 4D. Area A field ditches	80
Fig. 48	Period 5 features	82
Fig. 49	Period 5A. Features south-east of Enclosure B1	84
Fig. 50	Period 5A. Sections through pits B186, B13 and B268	86
Fig. 51	Period 5A. Northern and southern field ditches, Area A. Period 5B pit A274, Area A	88
Fig. 52	Period 5A. North-eastern field, Area A	90
Fig. 53	Period 5B. Enclosure B21, Ditch B165 and post-pit alignment	94
Fig. 54	Period 5B. Area C hypocaust structure	96
Fig. 55	Sites mentioned in the Late Bronze Age/Early Iron Age pottery report	119
Fig. 56	Enclosure B70. Pottery distribution in ditch fill	122
Fig. 57	Pottery from Ditch B70, levels 1, 2 and 3	123
Fig. 58	Pottery from Ditch B70, level 3	124
Fig. 59	Pottery from Ditch B70, level 4	125
Fig. 60	Pottery from ditch B70, level 4	126
Fig. 61	Pottery from Ditch B70, level 5	127
Fig. 62	Pottery from Ditch B70, level 5	128
Fig. 63	Pottery from Ditch B70	129
Fig. 64	Pottery from Ditch B70	130
Fig. 65	Pottery from Ditch B70	131
Fig. 66	Pottery from Ditch B70	132
Fig. 67	Period 2 pottery from Enclosure A24	133
Fig. 68	Period 2 pottery from Enclosure A24, Post-pit 145 and Pit A18	134
Fig. 69	Period 2 pottery from Pit A152 and Pit A2	135
Fig. 70	Period 2 pottery from Pit A3, Pit A4 and Gully A191	136
Fig. 71	Period 2 pottery from Pit A4	137
Fig. 72	Period 2 pottery from Pit A5, Pit A8, Pit A50, Pit A155 and Pit A180	138
Fig. 73	Period 2 pottery from Pit A227, Post-pit A19, Pit A47, Pit A153, Pit A179 and Pit A187	139
Fig. 74	Period 2 pottery from Post-pits A158, A163, Post-hole A143 and Pit A100	140
Fig. 75	Period 2 pottery from Pit A129	141
Fig. 76	Period 2 pottery from Pit A130	142
Fig. 77	Period 2 pottery from Hollow A208	143
Fig. 78	Period 2 pottery from Pit B317	144
Fig. 79	Period 2 pottery from Pit B317	145
Fig. 80	Period 2 pottery from Pit B79, Pit B80 and Pit B81	146
Fig. 81	Period 2 pottery from pits B84, B97 and B92 and Period 3A pottery from enclosures A118 and B144	147
Fig. 82	Period 3A pottery from Pit B12	148

Fig. 83	Period 3A pottery from Pit B12	149
Fig. 84	Period 3A pottery from Pit B244	150
Fig. 85	Period 3A pottery from pits B71, B131 and Post-hole B68	151
Fig. 86	Period 3A pottery from post-holes B49, B36 and Pit B270	152
Fig. 87	Period 3B pottery from gullies B16, B26 and B325	152
Fig. 88	Period 3B pottery from Pit B189, Hearth B188, Pit B174, Pit group B200A, Structure B200 and Pit B226	153
Fig. 89	Period 3B pottery from pits B177, B203, Hearth B207 and post-pits B196 and B197	154
Fig. 90	Period 3B pottery from pits B215, B314 and B133	155
Fig. 91	Period 3B pottery from pits B154 and B166	156
Fig. 92	Period 3B pottery from Pit B114	157
Fig. 93	Period 3B pottery from Pit B271	158
Fig. 94	Period 3B pottery from Pit B124	159
Fig. 95	Period 3B pottery from pits B147, B168, B195, B214, B119, B126, B172 and Hearth B132	160
Fig. 96	Period 3B pottery from hearths B180 and B228, pits B247, B128, B146 and B218	161
Fig. 97	Period 3B pottery from pits B245 and B248	162
Fig. 98	Period 3B pottery from Pit B266	163
Fig. 99	Period 3B pottery from Pit B266	164
Fig. 100	Period 3B pottery from Pit 267, post-holes B38 and B40, Pit complex B15 and unstratified	165
Fig. 101	Late Iron Age pottery from earlier features	184
Fig. 102	Late Iron Age pottery from Period 4 features	185
Fig. 103	Late Iron Age pottery from Period 4 features	186
Fig. 104	Late Iron Age pottery from Period 4 features	187
Fig. 105	Late Iron Age pottery from Period 4 and Period 5 features	188
Fig. 106	Late Iron Age pottery from unstratified and Period 5 features	188
Fig. 107	Late Iron Age grog- and shell-tempered pottery from unstratified and Period 5 features	189
Fig. 108	'Belgic' grog-tempered pottery from Period 4A	194
Fig. 109	'Belgic' grog-tempered pottery from unstratified, Periods 4A–B and 4D features	195
Fig. 110	'Belgic' grog-tempered pottery from Period 4C features	196
Fig. 111	'Belgic' grog-tempered pottery from Period 4C features	198
Fig. 112	'Belgic' grog-tempered pottery from Period 4C features	199
Fig. 113	'Belgic' grog-tempered pottery from Period 4D features	200
Fig. 114	'Belgic' grog-tempered pottery from Periods 4D and 4D-5A features	202
Fig. 115	'Belgic' grog-tempered pottery from Period 4D–5A features	203
Fig. 116	'Belgic' grog-tempered pottery from Period 4D–5A features	204
Fig. 117	'Belgic' grog-tempered pottery from Period 4D–5A features	206
Fig. 118	'Belgic' grog-tempered pottery from Period 4D–5A features	207
Fig. 119	'Belgic' grog-tempered pottery from Period 4D–5A features	208
Fig. 120	'Belgic' grog-tempered pottery from Periods 5A–5B features	210
Fig. 121	'Belgic' grog-tempered pottery from Periods 5A–5B features	211
Fig. 122	'Belgic' grog-tempered pottery from Periods 5A–5B features	212
Fig. 123	Period 5B, unstratified or intrusive 'Belgic' grog-tempered pottery	213
Fig. 124	'Belgic' grog- and-chalk-tempered pottery from Period 4 features	214
Fig. 125	'Belgic'/Early Roman pottery from Ditch B164 and supplementary contexts	218

Fig. 126	'Belgic'/Early Roman pottery from Ditch B164 and supplementary contexts	219
Fig. 127	'Belgic'/Early Roman pottery from Ditch B164 and supplementary contexts	220
Fig. 128	Early Roman pottery from Ditch B164	222
Fig. 129	Early Roman pottery from Ditch B164 and Grave A119A	223
Fig. 130	Roman pottery from Ditch B1, Pit complex B15 and supplementary contexts	224
Fig. 131	Roman pottery from Ditch B1, Pit complex B15 and supplementary contexts	228
Fig. 132	Roman pottery from Ditch B1, Pit complex B15 and supplementary contexts	229
Fig. 133	Roman pottery from Ditch B1, Pit complex B15 and supplementary contexts	230
Fig. 134	Roman pottery from Ditch B1, Pit complex B15 and supplementary contexts	232
Fig. 135	Roman pottery from Ditch B1, Pit complex B15 and supplementary contexts	233
Fig. 136	Roman pottery from Ditch B1	234
Fig. 137	Roman pottery from Pit complex B15	235
Fig. 138	Early Gaulish finewares	237
Fig. 139	Roman amphorae and stamps	240
Fig. 140	Decorated samian	244
Fig. 141	Mortaria and stamps	248
Fig. 142	Mortaria	250
Fig. 143	Flint cores, choppers and scrapers	252
Fig. 144	Flint scrapers	253
Fig. 145	Flints with marginal retouch, piercers, axes and a fabricator	255
Fig. 146	Flint arrowheads, leaf-shaped points, a knife and a blade	256
Fig. 147	Flints with marginal retouch and a hammerstone	257
Fig. 148	Pin mould fragments	259
Fig. 149	Pin mould fragments	261
Fig. 150	Miscellaneous clay refractory fragments and crucible	262
Fig. 151	Form of pins and comparisons	263
Fig. 152	Perforated stone polisher	265
Fig. 153	Perforated pottery slabs	267
Fig. 154	Objects of copper alloy	271
Fig. 155	Objects of iron	272
Fig. 156	Objects of iron	273
Fig. 157	Copper alloy brooches	275
Fig. 158	Roman glass	275
Fig. 159	Fired clay spindlewhorls	276
Fig. 160	Loomweights	277
Fig. 161	Antler weaving comb	278
Fig. 162	Antler handle	278
Fig. 163	Quernstones	279
Fig. 164	Beaker sherd from Pit complex B15	299

LIST OF PLATES

Pl. I	Air photograph showing Highstead before excavation or the start of quarrying	5
Pl. II	Air photograph showing Highstead before excavation or the start of quarrying	6
Pl. III	Air photograph showing cropmarks south-west of Highstead Area A	6
Pl. IV	Air photograph showing cropmarks south-west of Highstead Area A	6
Pl. V	Air photograph showing Highstead Area B during excavation	7
Pl. VI	Air photograph: showing Highstead Area B during excavation	7
Pl. VII	Period 2: Enclosure ditch B70, section	19
Pl. VIII	Period 2: Enclosure ditch B70, entrance	19
Pl. IX	Period 2: Enclosure A24	25
Pl. X	Periods 4 and 5: Enclosure ditch B1 and later post-pits	77
Pl. XI	Period 5: Hypocausted structure, Area C	98
Pl. XII	Period 5: Hypocaust extension, Area C	99
Pl. XIII	Period 2 pottery: abundant flint grits adhering beneath a flat base	158
Pl. XIV	Period 3B pottery: rusticated surface	167
Pl. XV	Period 3B pottery: bowl with burnished surface over the shoulder and rustication beneath	167
Pl. XVI	Period 2 pottery: detail of cordon applied to storage jar	168
Pl. XVII	Period 2 pottery: Late Bronze Age/Early Iron Age cup	169

LIST OF TABLES

Table 1	Distribution of fabrics in Periods 2 and 3	102
Table 2	Association of form and decoration in Periods 2 and 3	113
Table 3	Styles of decoration in Periods 2 and 3	115
Table 4	Classification of surface treatment in Periods 2 and 3	115
Table 5	Seriation of forms in features of Periods 2 and 3	116
Table 6	Continental chronologies	118
Table 7	Relationship between surface treatment and average wall thickness of plain convex forms during Periods 2 and 3	121
Table 8	Percentage distribution of styles of decoration during Periods 2 and 3	122
Table 9	Distribution of types of surface treatment during Periods 2 and 3	166
Table 10	Distribution of wall thickness during Periods 2 and 3	169
Table 11	Association of flint-tempered forms and fabric during Period 4	177
Table 12	Association of form and decoration during Period 4	177
Table 13	Distribution of forms from Area B in Period 4	181
Table 14	Distribution of fabrics from Area B during Period 4	182
Table 15	Distribution of grog-tempered forms from areas A and B	190
Table 16	'Belgic' forms at Highstead	192
Table 17	Ditch B164, Period 4D: fabric quantification by sherd count and Vessel Rim Equivalent	215
Table 18	Comparison of Canterbury-type sandy wares at Highstead (B1, B15) with kiln site assemblages from the town	226
Table 19	Canterbury-type coarse sandy ware. Summary of forms occurring at Highstead as represented by Ditch B1 and Pit complex B15. Quantification by Vessel Rim Equivalent	227
Table 20	Enclosure ditch B1 and Pit complex B15, Period 5A. Fabric quantification by sherd count and Vessel Rim Equivalent	236
Table 21	Early Gaulish and other imported wares	238
Table 22	Early Gaulish and other imports. Areas A and B	239
Table 23	Amphorae quantified by sherd count	240
Table 24	Amphorae. Areas A, B and C	241
Table 25	Samian. Form quantity and date range	243
Table 26	Roman and Romano-British finewares. Areas A, B and C	246
Table 27	Mortaria	247

Table 28	Mortaria. Areas A, B and C	249
Table 29	Composition of the flint assemblage	251
Table 30	Contexts containing material possibly associated with metalworking	266
Table 31	Numbers of identified bones	280
Table 32	Minimum number of animals	280
Table 33	Epiphyseal fusion for ox in Period 5	280
Table 34	Bone/teeth ratios	280

ACKNOWLEDGEMENTS

The Trust is grateful to the late Mr John Harbour, tenant of the site and to Messrs Robert Brett and Sons Ltd, the gravel extractors for permission to work on the sites during their operations. Mr Harbour also gave free access to his collection of flints found in the vicinity of the excavations.

We are also grateful to Christopher Young (then of the Ancient Monuments Inspectorate, and now English Heritage) and Barry Cunliffe, for their interest in the work and to the Manpower Services Commission for a substantial grant towards the cost of the Job Creation Programme team. We are particularly keen to express our thanks to all those who worked on the site some thirty years ago.

Peter Couldrey is grateful to many people who helped during his study of the ceramics. In the time that has elapsed since the initial work on the material, they have probably forgotten they had any involvement. Stuart Needham and Tim Champion both answered specific questions and offered encouragement. Information was generously provided by Peter van den Broeke on Dutch Iron Age pottery and Jean Bourgeois on Belgian ceramics. While they are not responsible for any mistakes in the final report, their advice has steered him away from several pitfalls.

It is now possible for us to extend thanks to Valery Rigby and Justine Bayley who arranged (all those years ago) for work to be carried out on various aspects of the prehistoric pottery. Thanks are also belatedly extended to the Cambridge University Committee for the use of aerial photographs and to Jon Rady and David Dobson for their task in transposing the photographic data, to Andrew Savage for producing the pottery photographs and to Mark Duncan, Laurie Sartin, Dave Lees, Gill Hulse, and Cathy Tutton for their work on the finds illustrations. Above all in the finds department, thanks are extended to Pan Garrard for her on-site conservation work and for undertaking the heroic task of washing and marking the bulk of the 14,500 sherds recovered from the excavation. Jane Elder, Janet Strugnell and Maureen Oliver are thanked for typing successive texts.

For the last lap of the project the authors would like to thank the many contributors to this report. We are particularly grateful to Elizabeth Healey, Stuart Needham, Isobel Thompson, Marion Green and Tim Champion for their extreme patience and the generous and prompt way that they and other contributors have updated their reports and to Barry Cunliffe, Ann Clark and Sarah Jennings for their continued support, help and advice.

Personal thanks are extended to Peter Atkinson for expert assistance with updated and new figures, to Peter Clark for his comments on an early draft of the text and to Peter Couldrey, Jane Elder and Mark Duncan for editorial support and design to bring the work to publication. I am doubly grateful for the forbearance of many, not least English Heritage, the principal funding body and fellow authors, Nigel Macpherson-Grant and Peter Couldrey who have waited patiently for this finished product.

Paul Bennett

PREFACE

When Tim Tatton-Brown took up his post as the first Director of Canterbury Archaeological Trust at the beginning of October 1975, one of the first things he was told was that there was a site 8 miles north-east of Canterbury which needed urgent attention. It was a hilltop site where topsoil had been stripped in the late summer and where there was clearly a mass of archaeological features cut into the top of the 30 m. gravel terrace. He was also shown some air photographs taken in the early 1960s by Professor J.K. St Joseph, of a mass of cropmarks on the gravel terraces (Plates I–IV), and it was clear to him that a 'Mucking' type site had been revealed, only this time it was on the south side of the Thames Estuary where no large gravel terrace sites had to his knowledge been excavated.

When he first visited the site in October he was dismayed to find that a drag line and conveyor were eating away at the terrace (Site A) at an alarming rate. Working with a small team, initially only at weekends, a start was made excavating sections across some of the most obvious features. After negotiations with Messrs Robert Brett and Sons Ltd who were operating the site, a slightly larger operation was mounted from the middle of November with Nigel Macpherson-Grant as Site Director.

In March 1976 Nicholas Erskine-Riall took over from Nigel and by the end of May work moved north of the Highstead to Chislet road to a new area (Site B) that had just been stripped of topsoil by Bretts. Soon after commencement of the new site Tim was offered a flight in a light aircraft from Lydd airport to photograph the site (Plates V and VI). Work on the new site remained under the supervision of Nicholas and continued until March 1977.

From the beginning, site work was undertaken with very little money, but plenty of volunteer enthusiasm. Work on Site B benefited from grant of £500 from the Ancient Monuments Inspectorate of the Department of the Environment and a rather more substantial grant from the Manpower Services Commission (Job Creation Programme), with a small team of hitherto unemployed young people taken out each day from Canterbury to work on the site.

Even at the best of times, gravel subsoils are not the friendliest of environments for archaeologists. The Highstead gravels were frozen solid in the arctic winter of 1975–6, with icy winds blowing directly from the Urals for bone chilling weeks and rock hard in the glorious, memorable, but blistering, long summer that followed. If the conditions were not problematical enough, the job was made all the more difficult by exuberant machine clearance of the site and the truncation of deposits and features by bulldozer during topsoil stripping. Added to this was widespread trampling and obscuring of large parts of the site by machine tracking, all before the arrival of a small (very small) archaeological team. Although the full-timers were joined occasionally by volunteers and for longer periods by the youngsters supported by the Manpower Services Commission, the core team comprised but three individuals, Nigel Macpherson-Grant, Peter Keeling and Nicholas Erskine-Riall and it was arguably a shortage of experienced manpower that was the greatest problem of all. The team experienced a major disaster in the closing week of the excavation when part of an important collection of pin-mould fragments and materials associated with metalworking was stolen. Full credit must be given to the core members of the team, who survived both the rigours of climate and of late night sessions in the Gate Inn at Boyden Gate, where they received lodgings from the landlord and his wife. I am pleased to report that these most excellent hosts are still resident at the time of writing. With the passing of time, memory fades, but the many kindnesses given to the team by Mr and Mrs Chris Smith, all those years ago, remain keenly and enjoyably recollected.

On completion of the fieldwork, the task of compiling an archive of the excavation records initially fell to Nicholas Erskine-Riall and the processing and spot-dating of the finds to Pan Garrard and Nigel Macpherson-Grant respectively. Later still, Nigel took on the task of bringing the work to publication, assisted by Peter Couldrey, Isobel Thompson and Marion Green, responsible for prehistoric, Late Iron Age and Roman pottery respectively.

Although the project was supported by a small grant from English Heritage, the greater part of the work was undertaken without payment, in whatever spare time was available to the specialists. Nigel and others, most notably David Dobson and Mark Duncan, drew illustrations for the report as and when funds could be found for the work. Given the size of the undertaking and the importance of the site, particularly the ceramic sequence, this was immensely regrettable. Other funded work consistently hampered and delayed the project and finding money to maintain continuity of work was very difficult indeed. There were months, even years, when little progress was made. Time passed, until eventually, a sustained effort by Nigel Macpherson-Grant in 1989 saw the production of a draft report, in three volumes.

Sadly, the format in which the report was compiled and its colossal size, meant that it could not be published without major editing and revision. The draft report languished in purgatory for almost ten years, until English Heritage generously agreed to provide an editorial grant to bring the work to publication. Much of the initial work on the draft text was undertaken by Jane Elder but since 2000 the present writer has been struggling to bring an edited version of the report to press. Pressure of time and other commitments has meant that the editing of the report has been at best slow and at worst, full stop. Most of the work has been undertaken in early mornings, Christmas holidays and during fieldwork seasons in Libya.

This report is unashamedly old-fashioned; it is more an archive report than an up to date thematic analysis of data. Thirty years ago, when the results of the excavation were being assessed, the most exciting and important product of the work was the quite extraordinary collection of prehistoric pottery. This was at a time when few large scale open area prehistoric excavations had taken place in the county and when our knowledge of prehistoric pottery assemblages particularly of the Late Bronze Age and Early to Middle Iron Age was based on excavated evidence from elsewhere in the South-east or on the Continent. Although for various reasons the features may not have been precisely or completely excavated, well recorded, stratigraphic relationships made it possible perhaps for the first time in Kent to develop from excavated evidence a distinctly east Kentish ceramic sequence. Although this report does not (and never could) provide a key for unlocking the development of prehistoric ceramics in the extreme south-east, the assemblage, even today, so many years after the excavation, provides a broad foundation upon which others may build a more comprehensive understanding. From the outset then, this report was intended to highlight the pottery sequence and we have attempted to keep to those original aims and intentions. Far from apologizing for an out of date presentation, we regret the delays which have bought this long-awaited report to press at least twenty-five years later than we all would have wished.

The rescue excavations at Highstead, undertaken between 1975 and 1977 will have been published some thirty years after the site was first stripped for gravel extraction. Despite the passage of time, the results of the work are still of great value to archaeologists and stand as a monument to the efforts of all those who have contributed to the volume.

Paul Bennett
April 2005

PART 1: INTRODUCTION

Paul Bennett

Highstead in its setting (Fig. 1)

Highstead in the parish of Chislet, is located 10 km. north-north-east of Canterbury and 2 km. south of the A299 Thanet Way at TR 214 662. The village stands in an exposed position on the south-eastern edge of a small plateau that stretches north-westward towards Herne Bay. The settlement's immediate neighbours are Ford, set in a small stream valley to the south-west and astride the former Roman road between Canterbury and Reculver (on the coast approximately 3.5 km. to the north), and Boyden Gate and the hamlet of Marshside, set below the 5 m. contour to the south-east and east. As its name suggests, Marshside lies on the edge of the former Wantsum channel now infilled. Beacon Hill (the site of an Armada beacon) where the subject site was discovered overlooks the northern arm of the former seaway with commanding views north to Reculver and the outlet of the channel, south-east to the junction of the river Stour with the seaway (Stourmouth) and east toward Richborough and the eastern mouth of the seaway. This strategic, if exposed, position was clearly appreciated throughout all periods of Highstead's history.

The main focus of prehistoric and later settlement appears to have been confined to the eastern end of a narrow plateau, essentially defined by the modern 30 m. contour. To the west this plateau broadens, and is level, only gradually rising towards the north-west. The south-western side of the hilltop is indented by small coombs which lead into a fairly deep stream valley. At its south-eastern end the plateau is almost cut in two by small valleys, creating a relatively steep-sided 'headland' to north and south, with a more gentle but still steep eastern slope running down to the Wantsum Channel.

Geology (Fig. 2)

The underlying geology of the excavated sites is shown on the 1:50,000 geological survey as Head Gravel underlain by the upper part of the Palaeocene Thanet Beds. The Thanet Beds were not directly exposed during the excavation, since most of the excavation area was confined to the eastern edge of the 30 m. Head Gravel bed. However, excavation on the down-slope parts of Area A often produced much loamier, sandier soils with a lower gravel content, the sand probably being derived from the underlying Thanet Beds. The Head Gravel is probably a Pleistocene solifluxion deposit possibly derived from a pre-existing river terrace. There is also photographic (Pl. I) and excavated evidence for ice-wedge polygons, particularly on Area A. These were detected during the excavation by their irregular course and fills of fine compact pale grey silt.

Previous discoveries (Figs 3 and 4)

Discoveries prior to the 1975–7 excavations were mostly confined to chance finds made either during quarrying (notably by Dr Armstrong-Bowes) or field walking, particularly by Mr Harbour, the tenant farmer of the site.

The earliest recorded chance finds are of Palaeolithic date and comprise a small number of flint tools including two hand-axes recovered during quarrying activities in the 1920s.[1] A smaller corpus of later Mesolithic flints (c. 7000–4000 B.C.) also collected at this time,[2] perhaps attests exploitation of the area by occasional groups of hunter-gatherers. Neolithic flints in the same collection,[3] including a polished axe fragment, suggest some form of occupation

---

1. T. Armstrong-Bowes collection, Herne Bay Museum, Nos 215 and 234.
2. Herne Bay Museum Collection, Nos 360–361.
3. Herne Bay Museum Collection, Nos 360, 361, 359 and 323.

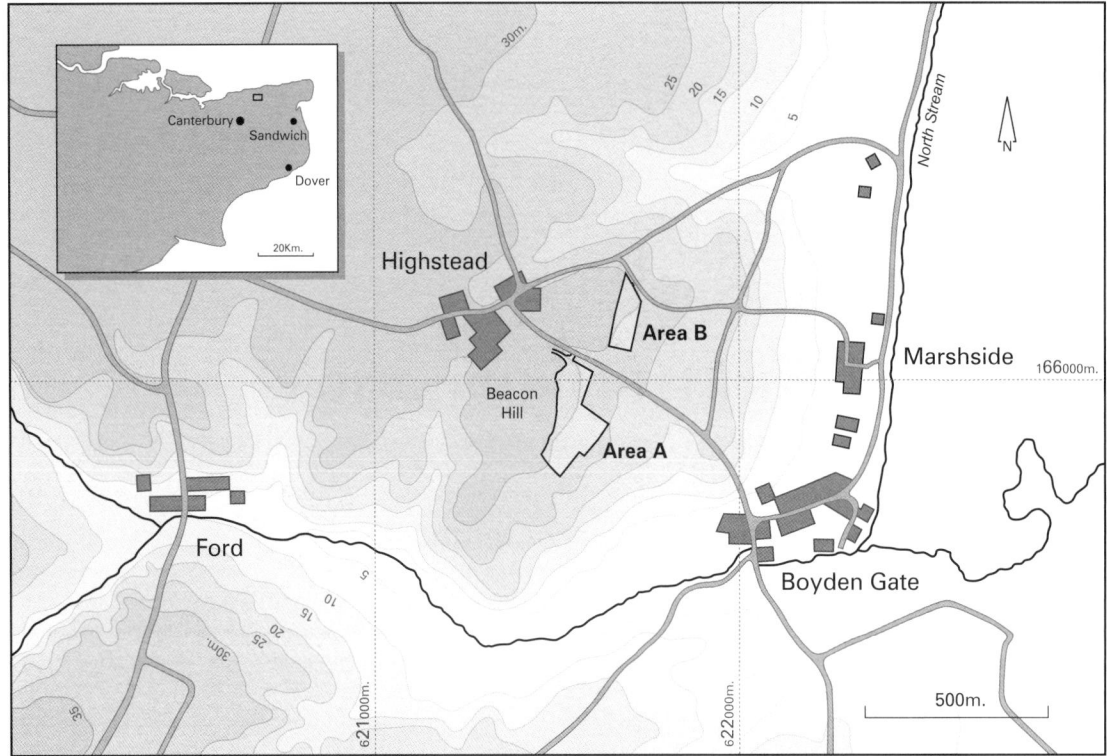

Fig. 1. Site location.

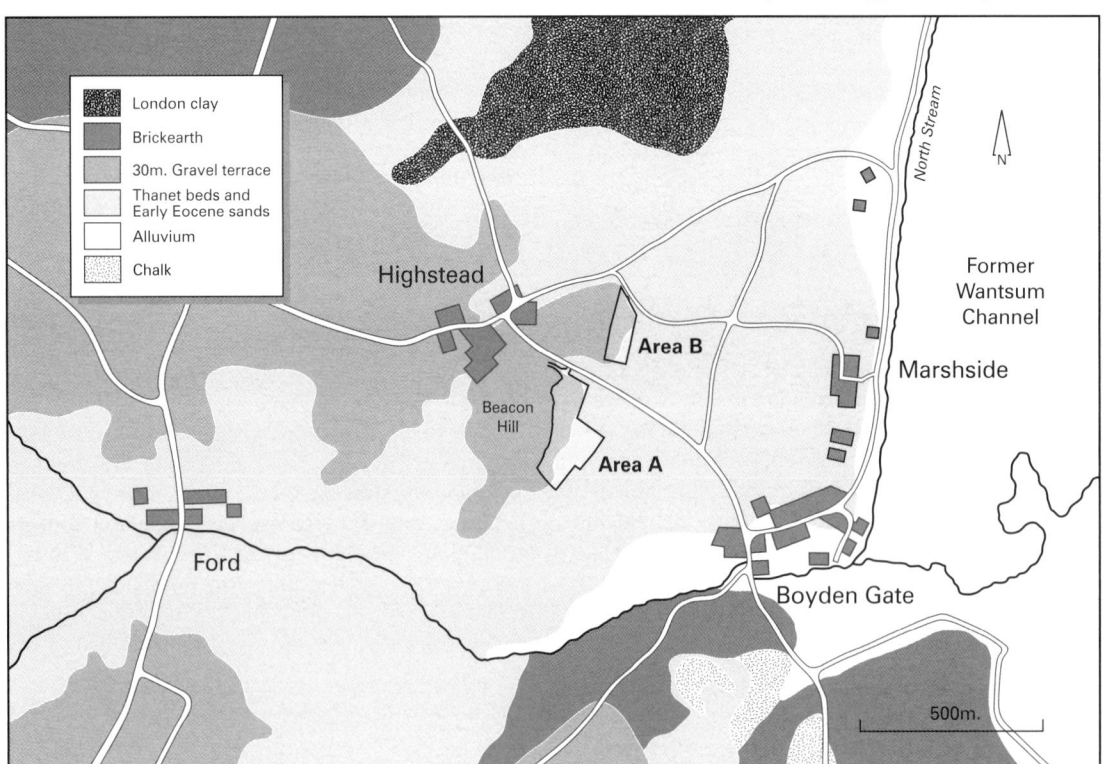

Fig. 2. Geology of the Highstead area.

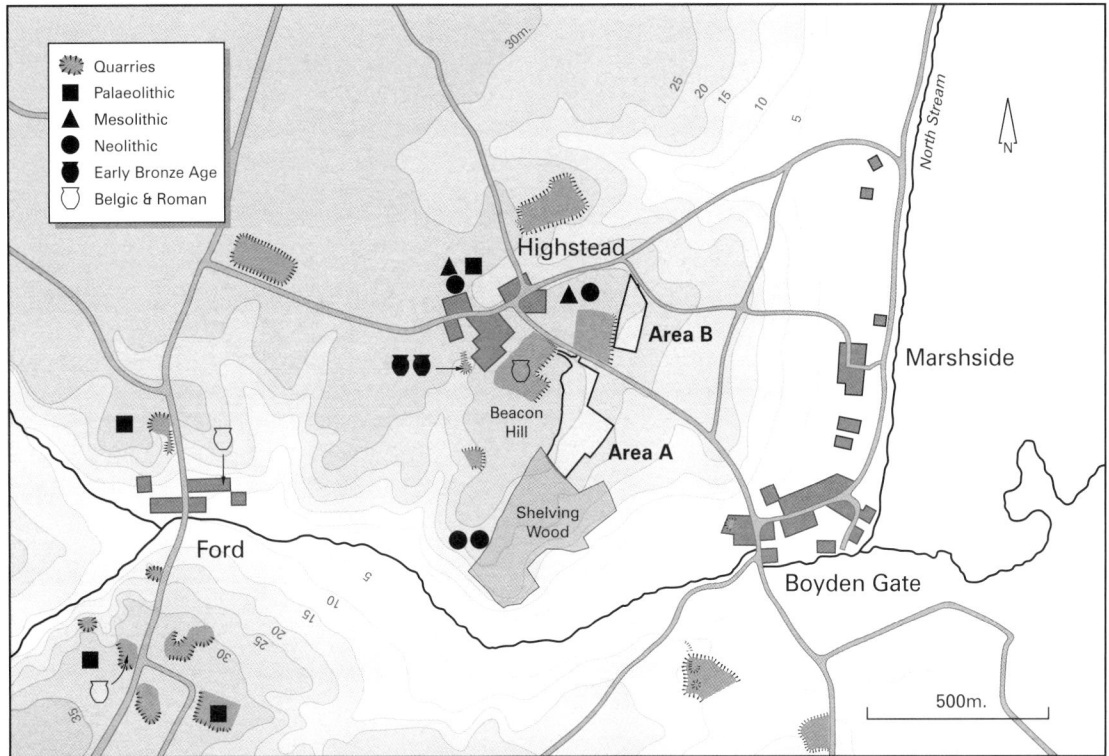

Fig. 3. Archaeological finds around Highstead.

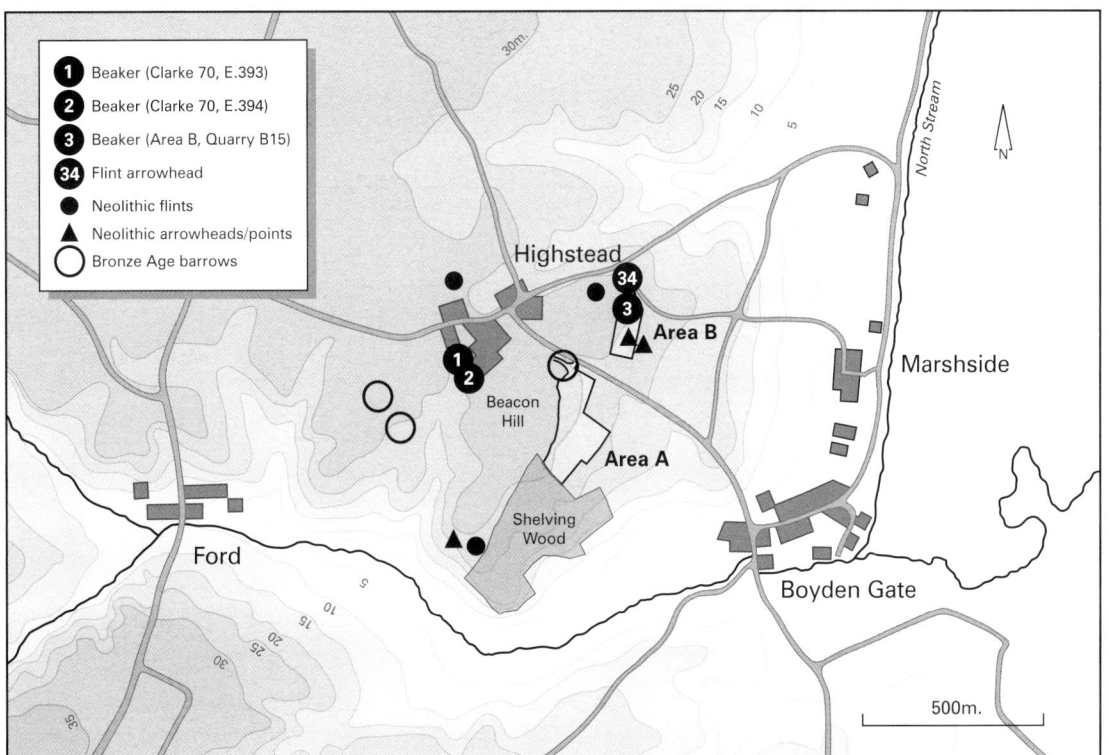

Fig. 4. Neolithic/Early Bronze Age transition: main features and finds.

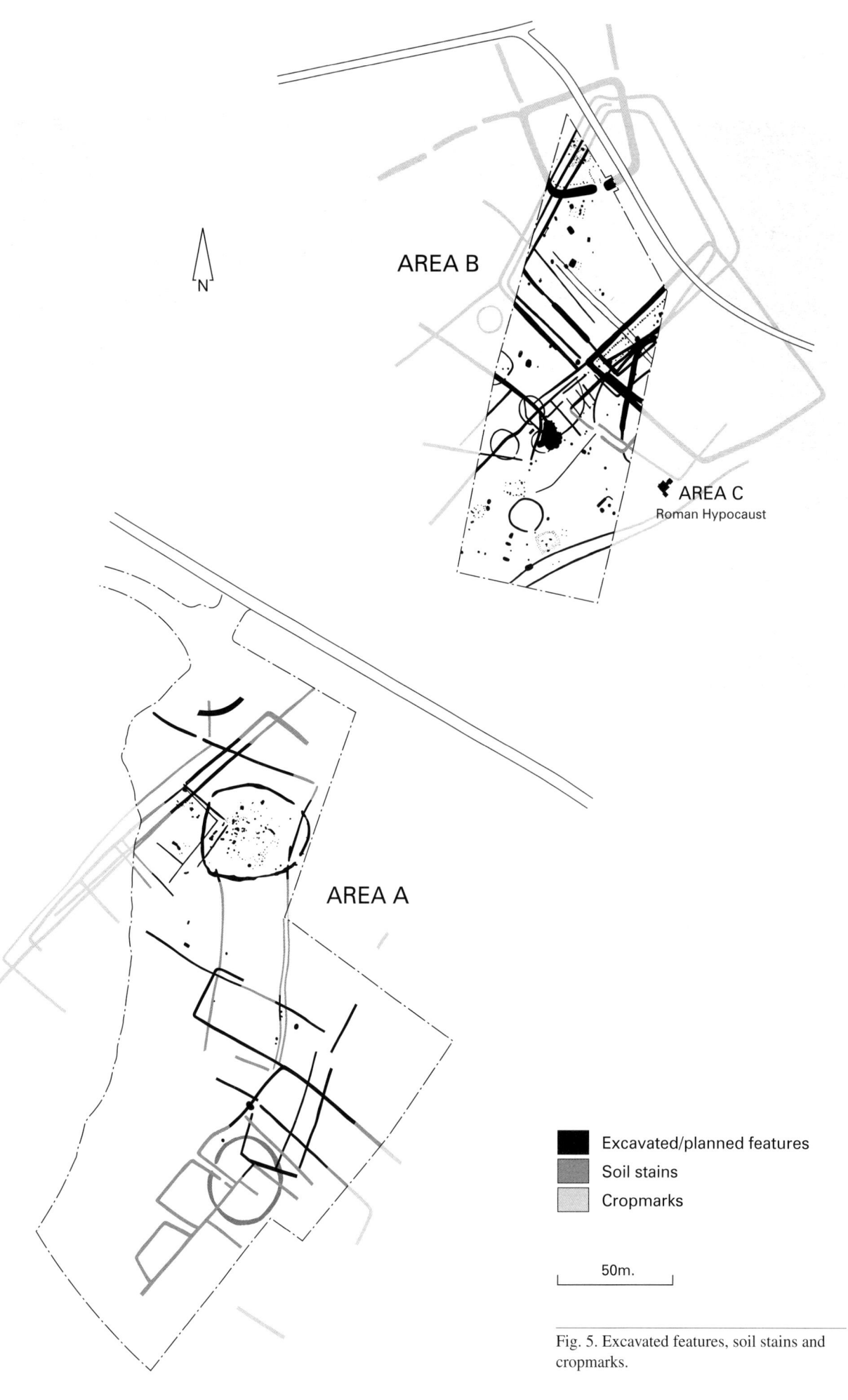

Fig. 5. Excavated features, soil stains and cropmarks.

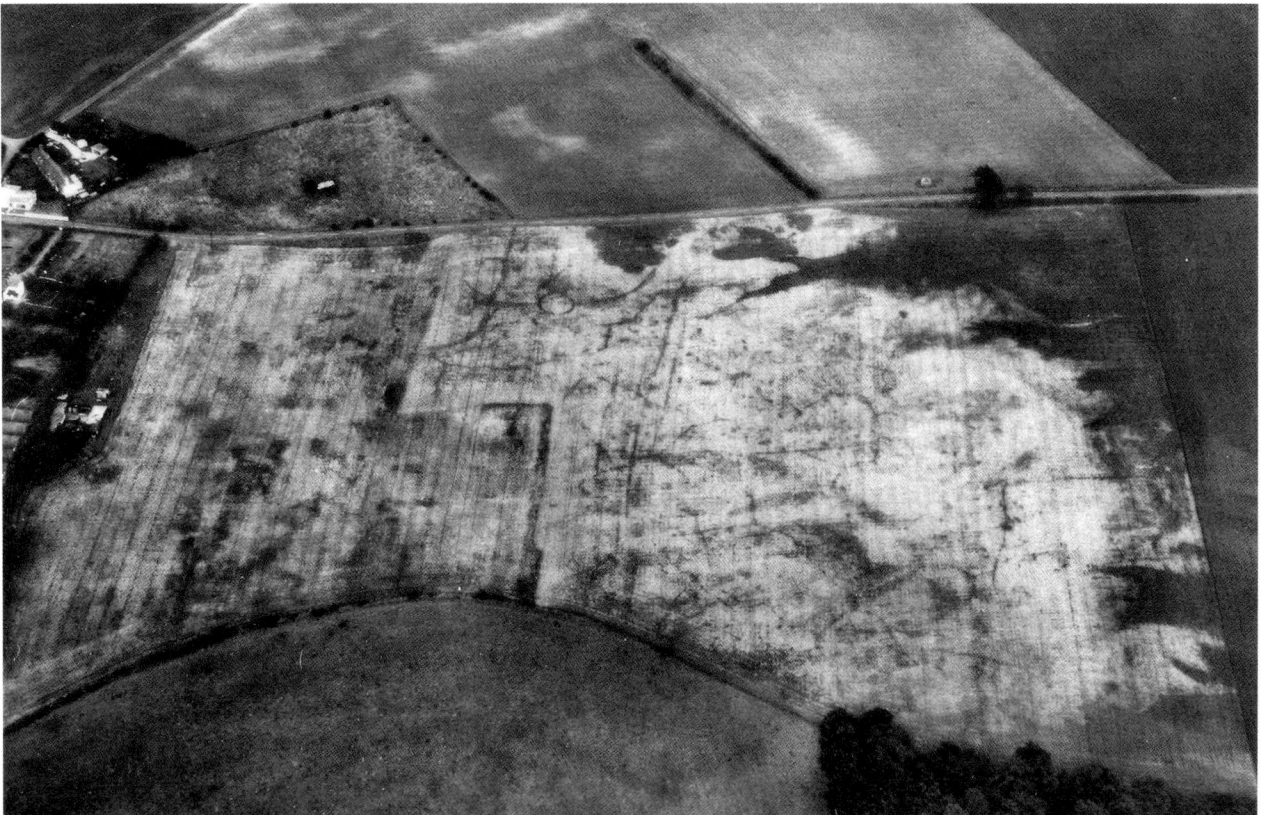

Pl. I. Air photograph showing the area before excavation or the start of quarrying, looking north-east (Cambridge University Committee for Aerial Photography).

on the plateau during the period *c.* 4000–2000 B.C. Early Bronze Age activity is represented by Beaker pottery that may have originally been associated with one or more burial mounds (Abercrombie 1912, nos 34–5; Jessup 1930, 91; Clarke 1970, nos 393–4, 485 and Appendix I). A possible Late Iron Age ('Belgic') cremation burial is recorded from this general area[4] but no precise provenance is available. Roman burials and a stone slab bearing an inscription have been recorded to the south-west of Highstead near the Archbishop of Canterbury's manor of Ford[5] and an isolated Roman cremation burial is known south of Highstead village immediately west of the present excavations (Area A).[6] The remains of a small hypocausted structure was excavated by members of the Canterbury Archaeological Society in the summer of 1974, east of Highstead village (Area C) and an edited version of a report on that work by the late Dr Frank Jenkins is published here (p. 97–9).

Aerial photography (Fig. 5)

A series of air photographs taken before and during the 1976 excavations has assisted with the interpretation of aspects of the excavated sequence by providing additional parch and soil mark evidence for features within or near the excavated areas (Pls I, II, V and VI). Other cropmarks located immediately south-west of Highstead and mostly confined to the flat plateau and headlands of the gravel terrace above the 30 m. contour are more difficult to fit within a chronological narrative. Notable in these air photographs (Pls III and IV) are dark 'inlets' and a 'coastline' of coombes bordering the plateau to the south and south-west. Here at least two possible undated ring-ditches and a number of linear features are visible together with a fine web of sub-polygonal periglacial features and irregular dots and patches representing solution hollows and ancient 'tree-throws'.

---

4. Herne Bay museum collections, No. 362.
5. British Museum Collections, 1934.1-11-1.
6. British Museum Collection, 1903.218–9, 11–15.

Pl. II. Air photograph showing the area before excavation or the start of quarrying, looking north-west (Cambridge University Committee for Aerial Photography).

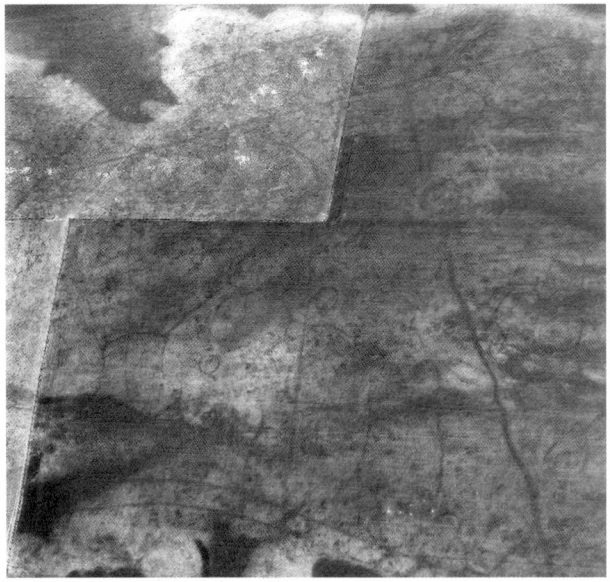

Pl. III. Air photograph showing cropmarks south-west of Highstead Area A, looking south-west (Cambridge University Committee for Aerial Photography).

Pl. IV. Air photograph showing cropmarks south-west of Highstead Area A, looking north-east (Cambridge University Committee for Aerial Photography).

Pl. V. Air photograph showing Highstead Area B during excavation, looking west.

Pl. VI. Air photograph showing Highstead Area B during excavation, looking north-west.

Survival and retrieval

The gravel subsoil at Highstead was a poor environment for the preservation of human and animal bone, shell and metal and such materials that were recovered and are reported on below must be taken to be indicative and not statistically representative.

A significant number of features contained *in situ* burnt clay, either as hearth bases or as the fired linings of possible storage pits. Many feature fills contained burnt material, including carbon. The burnt clay was not subjected to dating by archaeomagnetism, nor were the linings sampled for further analysis. Similarly samples of carbonised materials were not taken for dating by radiocarbon and feature fills were not sieved manually or by flotation for the retrieval of artefacts or ecofacts. The excavation provided evidence for metalworking, particularly for the period 900 to 600 B.C. and from features widely separated across areas A and B. Not only were features containing metalworking waste not sieved for the retrieval of fine residues, but a significant proportion of the material recovered was stolen before it was subjected to specialist analysis and only a small proportion of the original corpus is reported on in detail (pp. 258–65).

The absence of a sampling strategy for study of the palaeo-economy and early metal and saltworking industries (Periods 2 and 3B) is immensely regrettable given that many features contained potentially important residues. More regrettable is the absence of C14 dates for the earlier prehistoric features since with pottery alone it has only been possible to provide a broad chronological framework for the early periods. Like many salvage excavations of the early 1970s, this situation was the product of lack of manpower, funding, facilities and time, and the infancy of disciplines and methods of working that are now commonplace on most archaeological excavations.

Organisation of the report

This report is in five parts: an introduction; the structural narrative; the pottery; the other finds; and a discussion of the importance of the Highstead excavations.

The narrative has been subdivided into five periods, with Periods 3, 4 and 5 further divided. Each period or sub period opens with a summary of the evidence, followed by detailed descriptions of features set out, where possible, in groups. Each feature is individually described with specific reference made to pottery or other finds recovered from the feature fills. A discussion of each period or sub period follows. Reference is made to pottery recovered from the period or sub-period features with specific mention of distinctive traits in fabric, shape and decoration and implications for manufacture and function.

The finds have been reported in two parts: pottery and other finds. The pottery report provides a detailed review of selected groups of recovered material by period, commencing with the earliest. The report on the other finds provides reports on the flints, metalworking debris, salt production, other small finds and the small corpus of human and animal bones.

The fifth and final section of the report comprises a discussion of the importance of Highstead by Professor Tim Champion. The discussion provides broad parallels for the principal prehistoric discoveries and highlights Highstead's contribution to our knowledge of the early and later Iron Age of Kent.

The archive

An archive containing original site records has been compiled. With over 500 sherds of illustrated Late Bronze and Early Iron Age pottery, and as many 'Belgic' and Roman pieces, individual sherd descriptions have usually not been published and are held in the archive. Exceptions are three groups recovered from Enclosure B1, Ditch B164 and Pit complex B15 (*see* pp. 216–33) The full archive, including the draft report in three volumes, has been deposited with Canterbury Museums.

Fig. 6. Phased plan of excavated features.

Key for plans

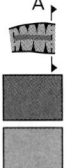 Excavated feature with section

 Planned feature

 Soil stain

Crop mark

 Cut by a later feature

Cutting an earlier feature

 Hearth

Key for sections

Loam

 Clay

 Gravel

 Burnt flint

 Charcoal flecks/lenses

 Burnt clay lumps

 Pot sherds

PART 2: THE EXCAVATED EVIDENCE

Paul Bennett and Nigel Macpherson-Grant [7]

Summary of the excavated sequence

Excavations in advance of gravel extraction on the 30 m. (100 ft) gravel terrace near Highstead village, were undertaken in two areas. Area A lay to the south of the village and a modern road linking Highstead to Boyden Gate. Area B was to the north of the road and east of the village, occupying slightly elevated ground with commanding views of the northern arm of the Wantsum channel to the north-east and east. A third limited excavation, Area C, was undertaken by the Canterbury Archaeological Society in 1974, immediately east of Area B.

Period 1: Mesolithic to Late Neolithic

Worked flints recovered from the excavated areas and in the immediate vicinity before and during the excavation indicated that the site was perhaps sporadically occupied over a long period beginning in the Mesolithic. The latest dated lithic pieces were of a Late Neolithic flintworking tradition. There was little or no contemporary flintwork recovered from Period 2 features or later activity.

Period 2: *c.* 900–600 B.C. (Fig. 7)

The earliest settlement activity at Highstead was represented by three enclosures, one located in Area B and two in Area A. The earliest of the three was a subrectangular enclosure (B70), defined by a substantial ditch. Only part of the southern side of the enclosure, including a rampart palisade and an entrance causeway flanked by post settings was excavated; the enclosure plan was determined by air photography. A firm construction date for the enclosure was not established, but the primary ditch fills yielded a small number of pot sherds dated early in the period *c.* 900–600 B.C. Occupation was attested within and immediately outside the enclosure. Cropmarks indicated a possible annex to the north of the enclosure and an associated causewayed ditch to the west.

During Period 2, an oval-shaped enclosure (A24) with four entrance causeways and a central building was established in Area A. Modification to the enclosure was apparent, including the construction of a second structure to replace the first and the formation of an internal division within the enclosure. A second enclosure (A260) was located by air photography and mapped as a soil stain during gravel extraction south-west of enclosure A24 in Area A. The enclosure ditch was not excavated, but an associated feature contained Period 2 dated material. Between the two enclosures in Area A, a cluster of features containing Period 2 pottery suggested a third occupation focus.

Evidence for metalworking was present immediately outside and within Enclosure B70 and within Enclosure A24. The pottery exhibited close affinities to material in the lower Thames valley and on the continent. All Period 2 features were broadly dated by the pottery to *c.* 900–600 B.C.

Period 3A: *c.* 600–500 B.C. (Fig. 8)

Two enclosures (A118 and B144) only partially within each excavated area, and a small number of pits in Area B, were broadly dated to Period 3A on the basis of recovered pottery. Period 3A was the least certain of the prehistoric phases and

---

7. The following account is based on the draft report compiled by Nigel Macpherson-Grant in 1989 (*see* p. xxii).

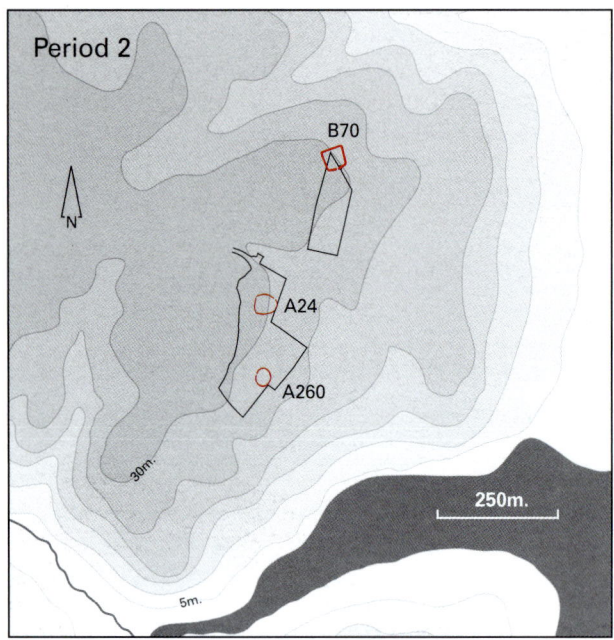

Fig. 7. Principal features, Period 2.

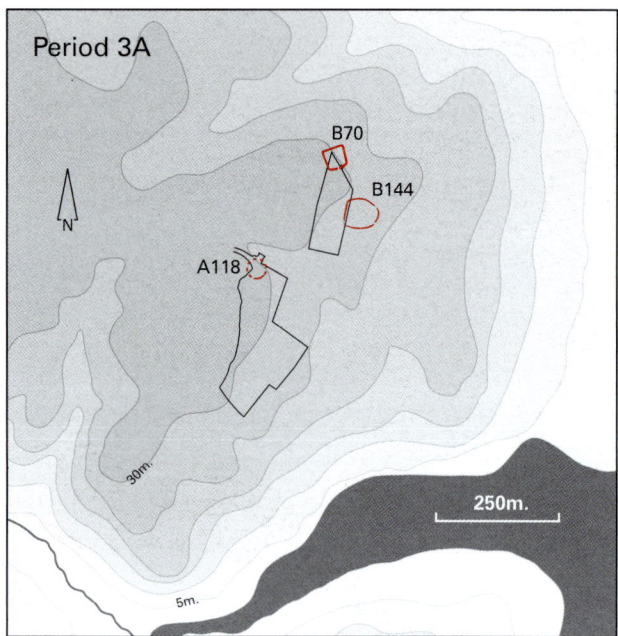

Fig. 8. Principal features, Period 3A.

may represent occupation that was broadly contemporary with the latest phase of Period 2 or the earliest phase of Period 3B. Although the Period 3A ceramic assemblage contained elements characteristic of both Period 2 and 3B, there was sufficient difference to indicate that this group of features formed a separate occupation phase in perhaps a near continuous period of settlement activity on the north-eastern part of the Highstead plateau. Throughout this period the new ceramic styles demonstrated continental contact continuing from Period 2 without interruption.

Period 3B: *c.* 500–400 B.C. (Fig. 9)

A distinct change of settlement type and pattern occurred in Period 3B. In Area B, a group of at least five curvilinear house gullies, all with south or south-east facing doorways, was found together with two circular huts defined by earth-fast posts, two rectangular buildings also of post-hole construction and three possible granary-type structures indicated by post-holes. A series of pits, some perhaps used for grain storage and others containing evidence of salt production, pottery manufacture and metalworking, were also associated with this occupation phase. An unusual multi-post structure (B200) may be associated with the buildings of this period. Two possible cremation burials were located outside the south-east facing entrance of the structure. The change from an 'enclosed' to an 'open' form of settlement evidenced by a move away from the building of enclosures was accompanied by an apparent increasing emphasis on continental affinities, demonstrated by the pottery styles which, during Period 3B, were now rarely found outside east Kent.

Period 3C: *c.* 400–125/100 B.C.

In Area A occupation appeared to terminate before 500 B.C. (at the end of Period 3A) and did not resume until *c.* 50 B.C. (Period 4C). In Area B a near-continuous occupation sequence, spanning a period of 550 years from *c.* 900 B.C., came to an end in *c.* 400 B.C. and did not resume again until the late second or early first century B.C. (Period 4A). Period 3C therefore represents abandonment of the eastern part of the Highstead plateau for settlement lasting perhaps 250 years in Area B and 450 years in Area A.

Period 4A: *c.* 100–50 B.C. (Fig. 10)

The earliest feature post-dating abandonment was represented by elements of two small enclosures or fields defined by three ditches located in the north-eastern corner of Area B. The north-eastern enclosure was cut by two parallel ditches and a row of post-holes representing major modifications to the arrangement. An absence of pits or other domestic features suggested that the contemporary occupation focus

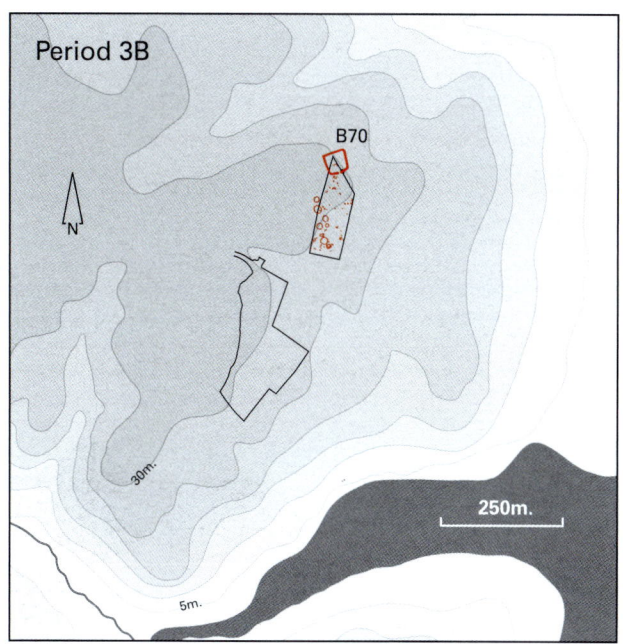

Fig. 9. Principal features, Period 3B.

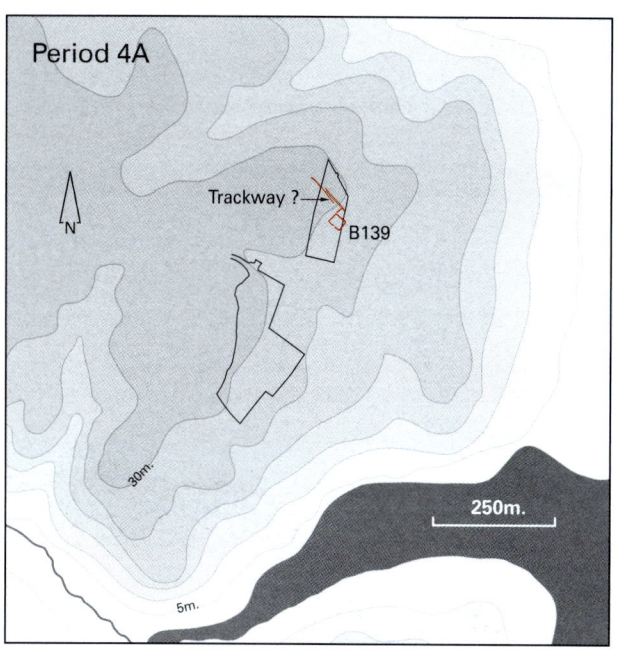

Fig. 10. Principal features, Period 4A.

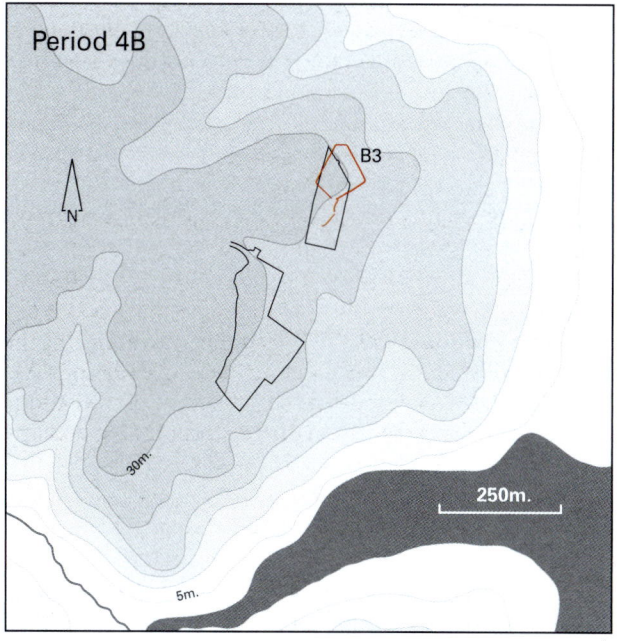

Fig. 11. Principal features, Period 4B.

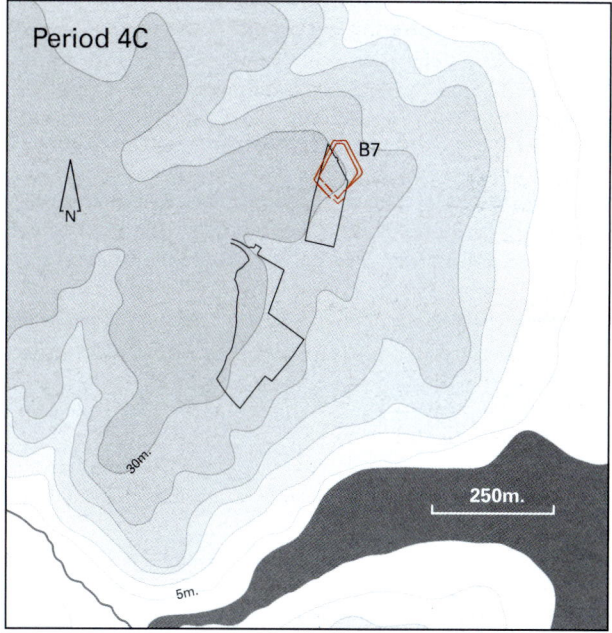

Fig. 12. Principal features, Period 4C.

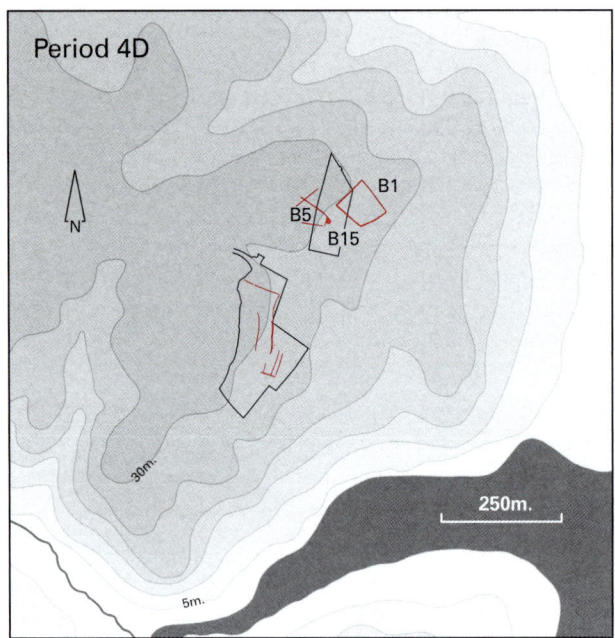

Fig. 13. Principal features, Period 4D.

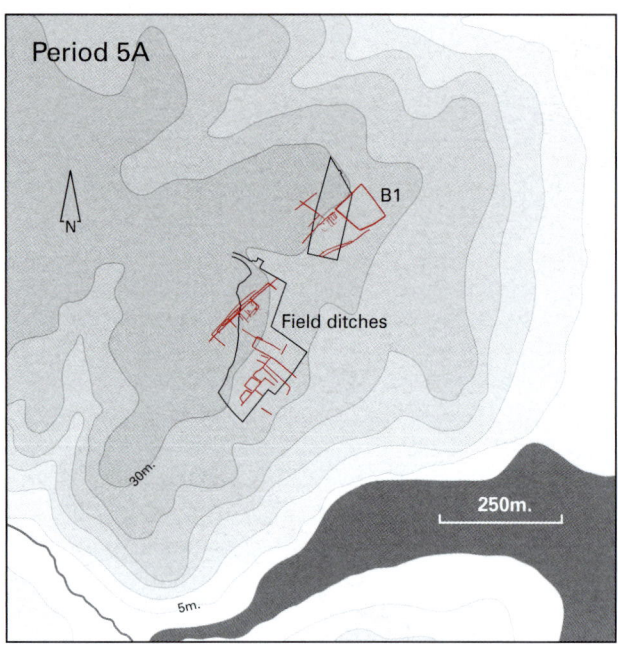

Fig. 14. Principal features, Period 5A.

lay outside the excavation and that this part of the plateau perhaps underwent a change of use following protracted abandonment, from domestic occupation to one associated with a field system.

Period 4B: *c.* 50–25 B.C. (Fig. 11)

In Period 4B the earlier field system in Area B was replaced by a polygonal enclosure (B3) with an entrance at its southern corner. The enclosure yielded no traces of internal features and the small quantities of ceramic material recovered from the ditch fills suggested an occupation focus outside the excavated area. A pair of curving discontinuous ditches located outside the entrance may have formed a contemporary outwork.

Period 4C: *c.* 25 B.C.–A.D. 50 (Fig. 12)

In the last quarter of the first century B.C., Enclosure B3 was reconstructed to approximately the same plan as its predecessor but with a reduced internal area (Enclosure B7). Perhaps of contemporary construction was a set of outer ditches. A possible outer entrance was identified at the southern corner of the earthwork and two entrance causeways in the inner south-west side. The enclosure plan was reconstructed from cropmarks identified on air photographs.

Period 4D: *c.* A.D. 50–75 (Fig. 13)

During Period 4D, Enclosure B7 was superseded by a new subrectangular enclosure, B1. Only the south-west corner of the new enclosure fell within the excavated area; the enclosure plan was established from cropmarks. A second contemporary irregular-shaped enclosure was established to the south-west (B5). Immediately east of the entrance was a group of intercutting pits (B15).

In Area A reoccupation of this part of the plateau occurred after a gap of over 400 years, with the establishment of long, narrow north–south aligned fields, bounded to the north and south by single, but more substantial, east–west aligned ditches.

Period 5A: *c.* A.D. 75–150 (Fig. 14)

Before the end of the first century A.D. Enclosure B5 had been replaced by a field system, Enclosure B1 remained in use. To the south-east of the field system an area of intercutting pits was cut by slots and post-holes taken to represent a fenced enclosure possibly containing a building. At least three large pits at widely separated locations were dated by their contents to the period. A pair of parallel aligned curving ditches, located in the south-east corner of the excavation, was also tentatively dated to the period *c.* A.D. 75–150.

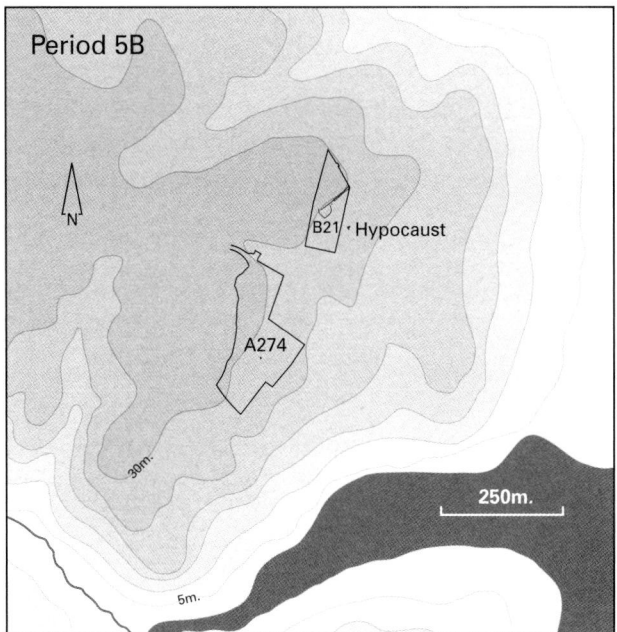

Fig. 15. Principal features, Period 5B.

In Area A, a field system established during Period 4D was replaced by more extensive boundaries laid out on a new orientation. Two groups of fields were identified, one in the northern part of the excavated area and one to the south (mainly reconstructed from cropmarks). In the second phase the easternmost field of the northern system was found to contain a large number of pits, post-holes and at least four burials.

In Area C three pits were found to pre-date a hypocausted structure, constructed in Period 5B.

Period 5B: *c.* A.D. 150–250+ (Fig. 15)

By the mid second century Enclosure B1 appears to have gone into disuse. The infilled north-western ditch of the enclosure was recut. The new ditch extended as a single straight boundary well to the south-west of the former enclosure. A small enclosure adjoined the ditch to the south, using the ditch as its north-west side and an enigmatic row of closely-spaced post-pits, perhaps for a stout fence, adjoined the straight boundary on its south-east side. No other related features were identified within the excavation, but cropmarks indicated that the new boundary may have formed the south-west side of a large polygonal enclosure.

In Area C, to the east of Area B, the masonry footings of a hypocausted building were uncovered by volunteers from the Canterbury Archaeological Society. Two heated rooms and a stoke-house of a potentially much larger building, perhaps constructed in the early to mid second century, were found. The heated rooms were probably in disuse by the mid third century, although some form of activity, perhaps indicating re-use or more likely robbing of the structure, may have continued into the early fourth century.

No excavated features in Areas A or B contained material post-dating the mid third century, but stray finds of later third- and fourth-century date recovered from topsoil in those areas, clearly indicated that occupation of the hilltop, perhaps at some distance from the present site, probably continued well into the fourth century.

Period 1: Mesolithic to Late Neolithic

Period 1 activity was indicated solely by flintwork recovered from Areas A and B and from adjoining fields. The corpus contained material of Mesolithic to Later Neolithic (non-Beaker) flintworking traditions (pp. 251–8).

The flint assemblage derived from three principal collections: material recovered from Area A by the excavation team; similarly collected material from Area B; and surface finds collected by the late Mr Harbour in fields adjoining the excavated areas. Taken together, the collections clearly indicated widespread multi-period activity across the high-level gravel spur overlooking the northern mouth of the Wantsum sea channel. The earliest dated flintworking tradition was of Mesolithic date, this mainly present in the general collection and therefore of imprecise provenance. Earlier and Middle Neolithic implements were also represented together with a Late Neolithic tradition.

Despite the various collection zones there was no recognisable concentration of flints of a specific period in an area. It was therefore impossible to suggest a focus of settlement prior to Period 2.

The combined collections represent a palimpsest of occupation debris extending across an area which enjoyed an elevated location looking out across the Wantsum sea channel to the east and the mouth of the sea channel to the north-east. To the south was a small valley with a fresh water stream flowing into the Wantsum and to the north and east a relatively flat and fertile landscape dominated by London Clay, Head Brickearth and closer to the coast, Gault Clay. The elevated location provided good views on all sides and a territory rich in resources. The wooded valleys, freshwater spring, tidal marshes and sea channel, all must have provided a stimulus for intermittent or near continuous occupation well before the beginning of the first millennium B.C.

Period 2: *c.* 900–600 B.C.

Summary

The earliest excavated settlement evidence on Beacon Hill, Highstead probably dates from the Late Bronze or Early Iron Age and comprised parts of three substantial enclosures, one in Area B (B70) and two in Area A (A24 and A260). Arguably the earliest of the enclosures was B70. The enclosure, approximately 0.25 hectares in extent, was unusual in that it appears to have been built for strength and possibly defence. Located in the northern corner of Area B, the rectangular earthwork was defined by wide deep ditches interrupted by a single gated and revetted entrance causeway to the south and by palisade pits cut to retain the front of an internal bank. Only a small number of potsherds dated early in the period *c.* 900–600 B.C. was recovered from the primary fills of the ditch and a firm construction date was not established. Erosion and partial infilling of the enclosure ditches, perhaps following rampart collapse, appears to have taken place soon after construction with the resultant deposits capped by debris from an associated occupation focus outside and close to the enclosure entrance. Contemporary occupation within the enclosure was attested, with pottery recovered from features within the enclosure being identical to the range of wares recovered from outside and within the fills of the enclosure ditch. One of a number of pits outside the enclosure (B80), produced an exceptional group of fragmentary clay moulds used mainly for the manufacture of bronze pins (pp. 258–65). Metalworking debris was also present within the enclosure and in contemporary fills within the enclosure ditch.

Broadly contemporary with Enclosure B70 but perhaps established later, was Enclosure A24 in Area A. The enclosure, constructed for domestic use, was oval-shaped, defined by a shallow ditch and an unrevetted bank. The circuit was pierced by four symmetrically placed entrance causeways and a hut was located roughly at the centre of the enclosure. Modifications to the enclosure were apparent, including the construction of a second hut to replace the first, an internal division of the enclosure, perhaps for the penning of domesticated animals, the blocking of at least one entrance causeway and the construction of a fence to supplement or replace part of the enclosure boundary. Evidence for metalworking activity was also attested.

A third enclosure (A260) was identified in Area A to the south-west of Enclosure A24. The circular-shaped earthwork with at least one west-facing entrance was identified as a cropmark and mapped following topsoil stripping, but remained unexcavated. A small cluster of features located between the two enclosures suggested a third focus of Period 2 occupation in Area A.

Enclosure B70

Ditches (Fig. 16)

Only part of the southern side of the enclosure fell within the northernmost corner of the excavated area. All remaining elements of the enclosure plan have been extrapolated from air photographic evidence.

Two lengths of ditch (B70) forming the south side of the enclosure were located either side of a 3.5 m. wide causeway. The western ditch, traced for 19 m. on an east–west alignment, returned to the north-west to form the western side (south-west corner) of the enclosure. The western ditch was sectioned in two locations: at the terminal adjacent to the causeway (Sections C and D) and at the south-west corner of the enclosure (Section E). The ditch, with rounded terminal against the causeway was between 3.5–4 m. wide and 2 m. deep. The eastern ditch, aligned approximately north-west to south-east was traced for a distance of 5 m. into the main section (Sections A and B). The ditch, with squared terminal against the causeway, was 4.6 m. wide and 1.92 m. deep. Both ditches deepened quite quickly from the terminals, with ditch profiles essentially taking a broad open 'u' shape, changing to a v-shaped profile at depth. All profiles were exaggerated by weathering and appear not to have been recut.

Ditch fills (Fig. 17, sections A–E and Pl. VII)

Five consistent bulk fills were identified in three separate sections. With some exceptions however, the artefacts were recorded as falling within horizontal spits, measured as depths from the surface, and cannot be related to individual stratigraphic units with certainty. In this summary, reference is made to layer numbers corresponding to those recorded on the drawing of Section C. The pottery report refers to horizontal levels (p. 132) and the relationship between the two, when referring to finds from specific layers, is regarded as a best fit.

Layer 1 was a primary deposit of sandy silt and gravel which appeared to relate to the weathering of the ditch sides soon after construction of the bank and ditch. The layer provided forty sherds of pottery of which thirty may derive from a single vessel (Fig. 57, No. 1), dated early in the period *c.* 900–600 B.C.

Layer 2 was a secondary deposit of clean gravel interleaved with sand. The material, of varying thickness, may have derived from further weathering of the ditch sides. The deposit was thickest at Section D and it is suggested that the layer may have been formed in this location as a consequence of early rampart collapse. This layer appears to have contained no finds.

Layer 3 was a deposit of gravel and sand discoloured by dark loam. The layer, present in all sections, was very

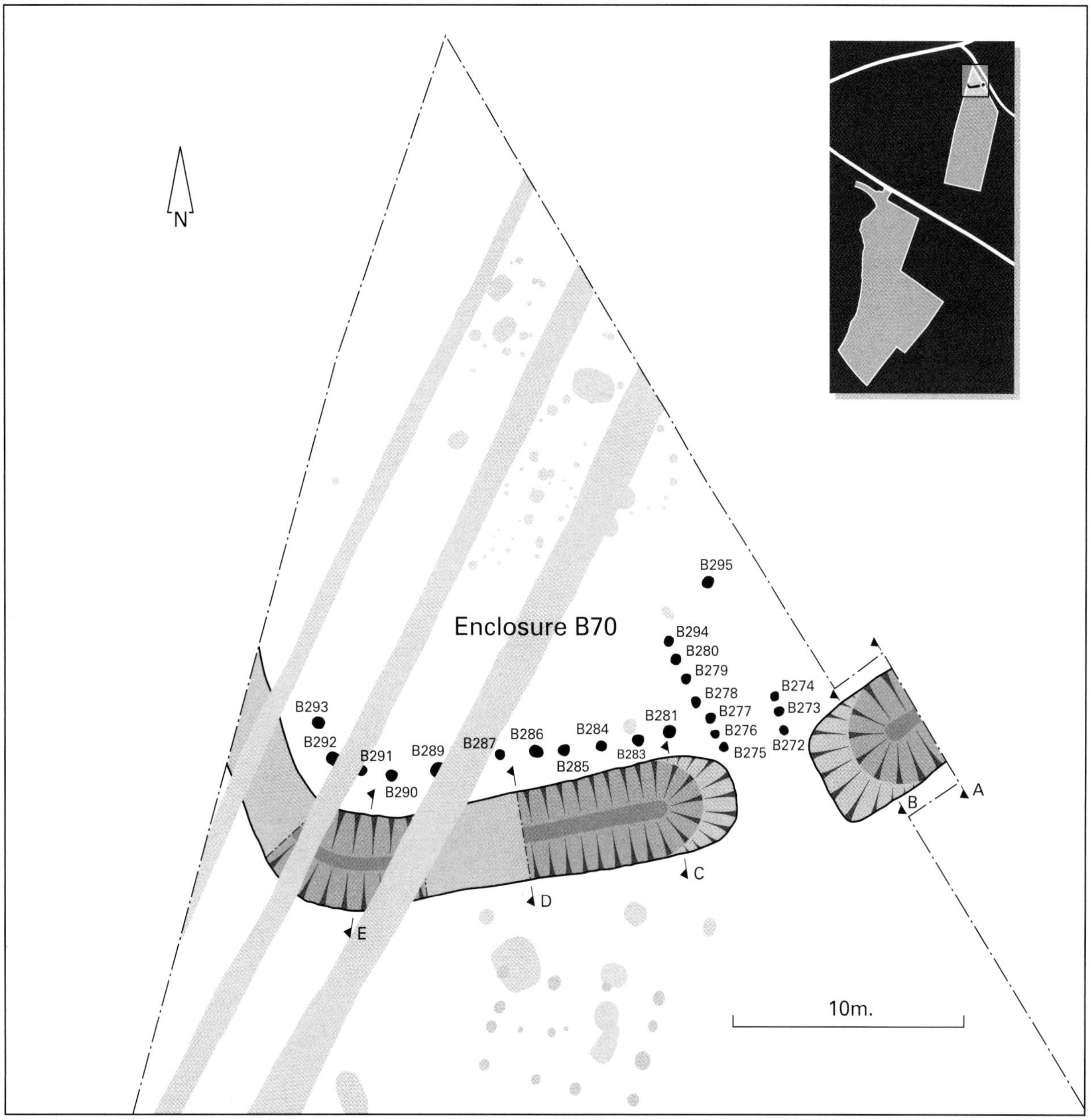

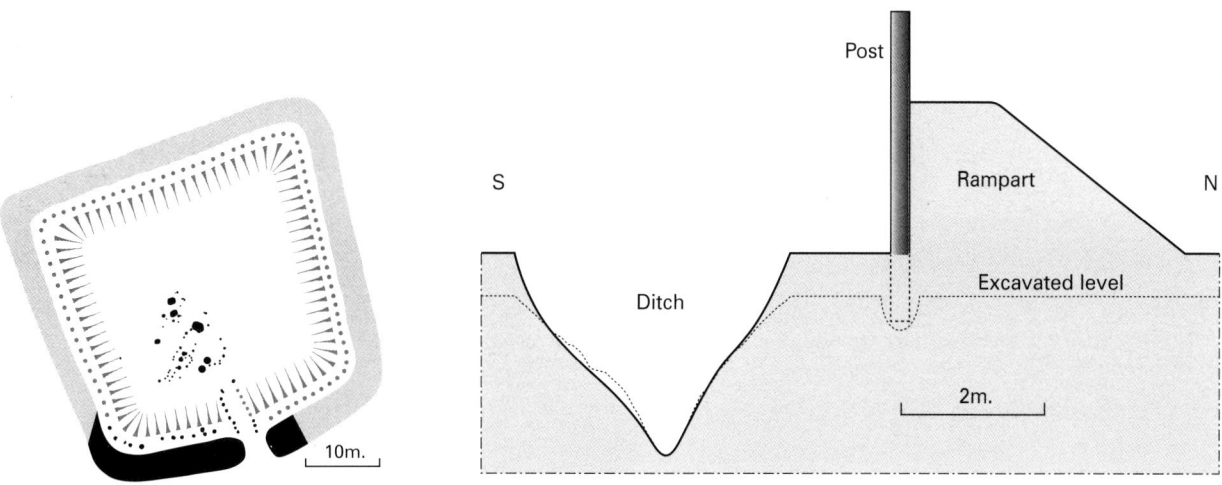

Fig. 16. Period 2. Enclosure B70, plan of excavated features (*above*), reconstructed enclosure layout and detail section of rampart and ditch (*below*).

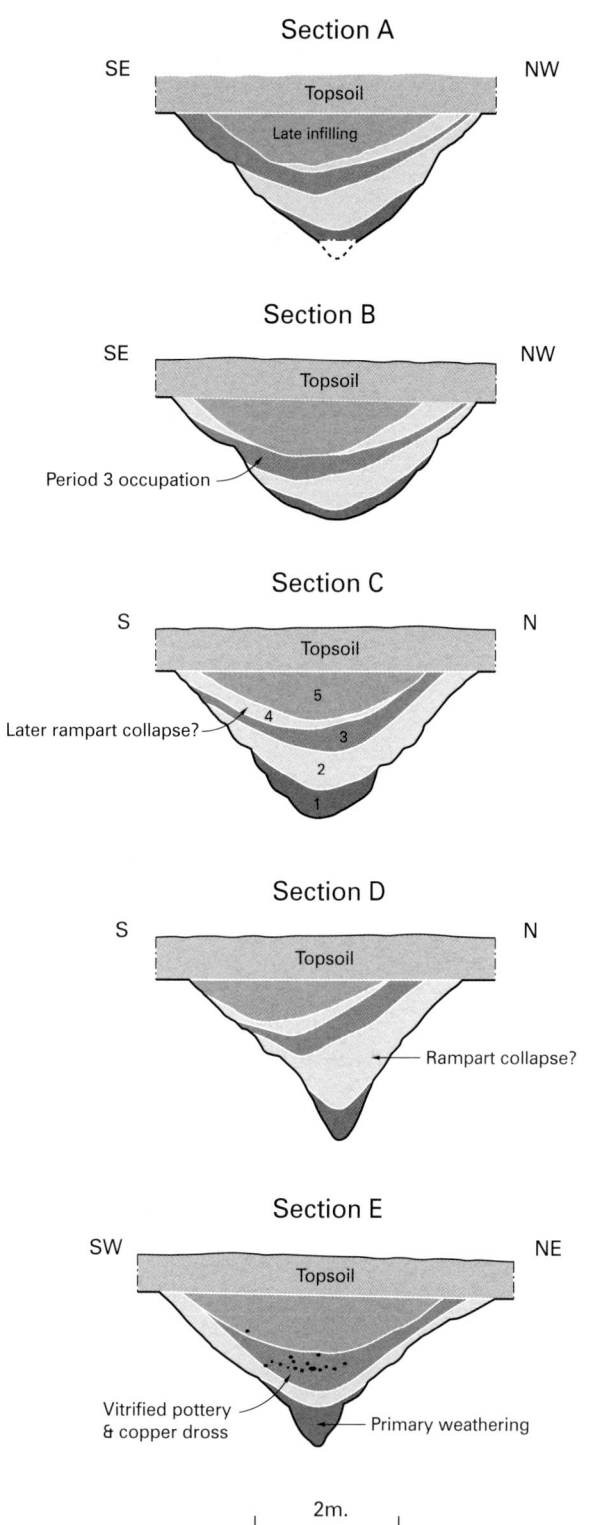

Fig. 17. Period 2. Enclosure B70, ditch sections.

distinct. In the south-west corner of the enclosure at Section E, the material contained significant amounts of burnt clay, carbon and debris, perhaps discarded from occupation outside the enclosure. Much of the pottery from Levels 2 and 3 (Figs 57, Nos 2–14; Fig. 58) probably derived from this layer (Fig. 56), which also produced vitrified clay, perhaps a bi-product of metalworking, fragments of perforated pottery slabs also perhaps associated with metalworking (pp. 267–8) and two spindlewhorls (Nos 37–8, p. 276). The pottery recovered from Layer 3 has been dated to the period c. 900–600 B.C.

Layer 4 was a thin deposit of clean gravel and sand which may derive from the rampart mass perhaps following the decay and collapse of timberwork associated with the rampart front and revetment of the causewayed entrance. This layer appeared to contain no finds.

Layer 5 was a bulk fill of dark brown gravelly loam found capping the ditch below topsoil. Most of the pottery from Levels 4 and 5 (Figs 59–62) probably came from this layer. Most belonged to Period 2, with some Period 3 forms in Level 4 and with material from Periods 3–5 in Level 5. A few sherds of later Iron Age and Roman pottery recovered from the uppermost fill suggests that a remnant of the monument may still have been visible at that time.

The ditch fills and dated contents clearly indicated that the earthwork was exceptionally long-lived and that by inference the enclosure would have been a dominant feature in the landscape and perhaps in near continuous use from 900–400 B.C.

Palisade post-pit

A row of eleven post-pits (B281, B283–7, B289–B293) forming a palisade was located some 0.70–1.50 m. north of and parallel to the western ditch. The post-pits, cut to a depth of between 0.26–0.38 m. were on average 0.50 m. in diameter. All fills were similar, being of medium brown loam, with little gravel. No finds were recovered from these fills.

Entrance post-pits (Pl. VIII)

Two parallel rows of post-pits defined an entrance passage 2.40 m. wide. A row of some seven post-pits (B275–80, B294) formed the west wall of the passage. The eastern wall was defined by only three post-pits set close to the ditch terminus (B272–4) and an isolated pit (B295) located at some distance north of the alignment. The entrance post-pits were on average 0.40 m. in diameter and 0.37 m. deep. The majority contained a single fill of medium brown loam, with little gravel; B274 had rather more stone than other post-pits; B275 had virtually no gravel content; in B278–80, B294 the gravel was noticeably confined to the base only. The fill of B294 was of dark brown loam and gravel. No finds were recovered. The dimensions of the palisade posts increased

Pl. VII. Period 2. Enclosure ditch B70, section D, looking east. Scale 2 m.

Pl. VIII. Period 2. Enclosure ditch B70, entrance, looking west. Scale 2 m.

marginally towards the entrance. Of the western entrance wall post-pits, B277, at the 'junction' with the palisade, was the deepest at 0.40 m., a requirement possibly dictated by the need for structural strength at the sharp bank corner.

Enclosure plan (Fig. 5; Fig. 16, inset plan; Pls V and VI)

Parch marks identified in a series of air photographs indicated that the enclosure was roughly rectangular in plan, measuring internally 45 m. north–south, by 50 m. east–west, enclosing an area of some 0.25 hectares in extent.

Within the enclosure, to the rear of the palisade, was a 7 m. wide zone void of features, thought to represent the footprint of a rampart. Even allowing for later erosion and spreading of the rampart tail, it is unlikely that the rampart would have originally been less than 5 m. wide at its base. This would suggest that occupation space within the enclosure would have been between 1116 and 1400 square metres in extent.

Access into the enclosure appears to have been through a gated entrance in the south side and a narrow 2.50 m. wide passage extending presumably for the full width of the rampart. The lack of continuous posts flanking the passage tentatively suggests that the rampart tapered steeply from front to back and as would be expected the highest part of the rampart carrying a parapet walk and needing support would have been against the main palisade.

The recovered data indicates that up to 160 vertical timbers were required to form the structure of the palisade and entrance. Whilst the rampart was probably 'faced' with split timbers set horizontally behind the uprights to retain a loose gravel bank, there was no evidence for revetment to the rear, suggesting that the rampart tail may have been unsupported and angled to achieve stability. A rampart width of at least 5 m. has been suggested and this perhaps indicates a modest height for the rampart and palisade. The timber and earthmoving required to form the enclosure must have represented a significant investment of human and natural resources, implying that the enclosure was of special status. The siting of the enclosure on the elevated edge of a promontory, with advantageous views on all sides but particularly across the Wantsum sea channel to the east, also suggests that the enclosure was built as much to be seen as to provide a commanding view.

Occupation within and outside Enclosure B70 (Fig. 18)

Evidence for occupation within and outside the enclosure post-dated the weathering of the ditch edges (Layer 1) and a possible early episode of rampart collapse (Layer 2). The natural gravel and sand subsoil at Highstead is poorly cemented and erosion and infilling of the enclosure ditches by natural processes was probably rapid. There was no evidence to suggest that the ditch was cleaned or recut, so the presence in the base of the ditch, west of the causeway of a large slump of gravel (Fig. 17, Section D), suggested that despite apparently robust construction the rampart gave way in at least one location soon after construction. Although the ditch was not cleared of debris, there is no reason to believe that the breach was not repaired and the rampart palisade maintained throughout Period 2.

Capping primary silts and deposits considered to represent collapsed rampart were gravels and sands containing a high proportion of sandy loam mixed with carbon, burnt clay flecks, fired clay fragments and a small quantity of metalworking debris (p. 266). This distinct layer (Layer 3), present in all five ditch sections was particularly well-defined and up to 0.30 m. thick at the south-west corner of the enclosure (Fig. 17, Section E). The entire deposit yielded six perforated clay slabs (including Fig. 153, Nos 47–50), copper dross and vitrified clay fragments (p. 268) and a large collection of pottery sherds (probably including most of Fig. 57, Nos 2–14; Fig. 58) dated *c.* 900–600 B.C.

Features within the enclosure

A cluster of features of Period 2 and later date was excavated within the enclosure, but set some way back from the enclosure ditch. The absence of features within approximately 7 m. of the internal edge of the ditch suggested that the rampart footprint extended at least that far. As no feature within the enclosure was cut more than 0.50 m. below the existing surface of subsoil, it is possible that other features may have been cut into the rampart tail, but were perhaps removed by ancient weathering and modern agricultural practices. Surviving features comprised two possible hearths or fire pits, two clay-lined pits, two shallow pits and a possible structure defined by post-holes.

Hearths

Hearth B53 was subrectangular, measuring 0.70 by 0.60 m. and cut to a depth of 0.11 m. into the gravel subsoil. The feature contained the fragmentary remains of a very hard burnt clay lining, in places 1–2 cm. thick and a fill of dark brown black sandy loam mixed with carbon, burnt clay and fire-crazed gravel. Although the hearth provided no datable finds it was cut by a Period 3 post-hole (B54) and has therefore been tentatively assigned to Period 2.

Hearth B69 was located some 4 m. to the south-west of B53. This subrectangular feature, 0.45 by 0.35 m., cut 0.10 m. into the subsoil, contained a single fill of fire-reddened clay embedded with burnt flints, and provided no datable finds. The feature was cut by a Period 3 post-hole (B68) and has been tentatively dated to Period 2.

Clay-lined pits

Pit B84 was rectangular (Fig. 19), measuring some 1.10 by 0.90 m. and cut to a depth of 0.38 m. The pit, located

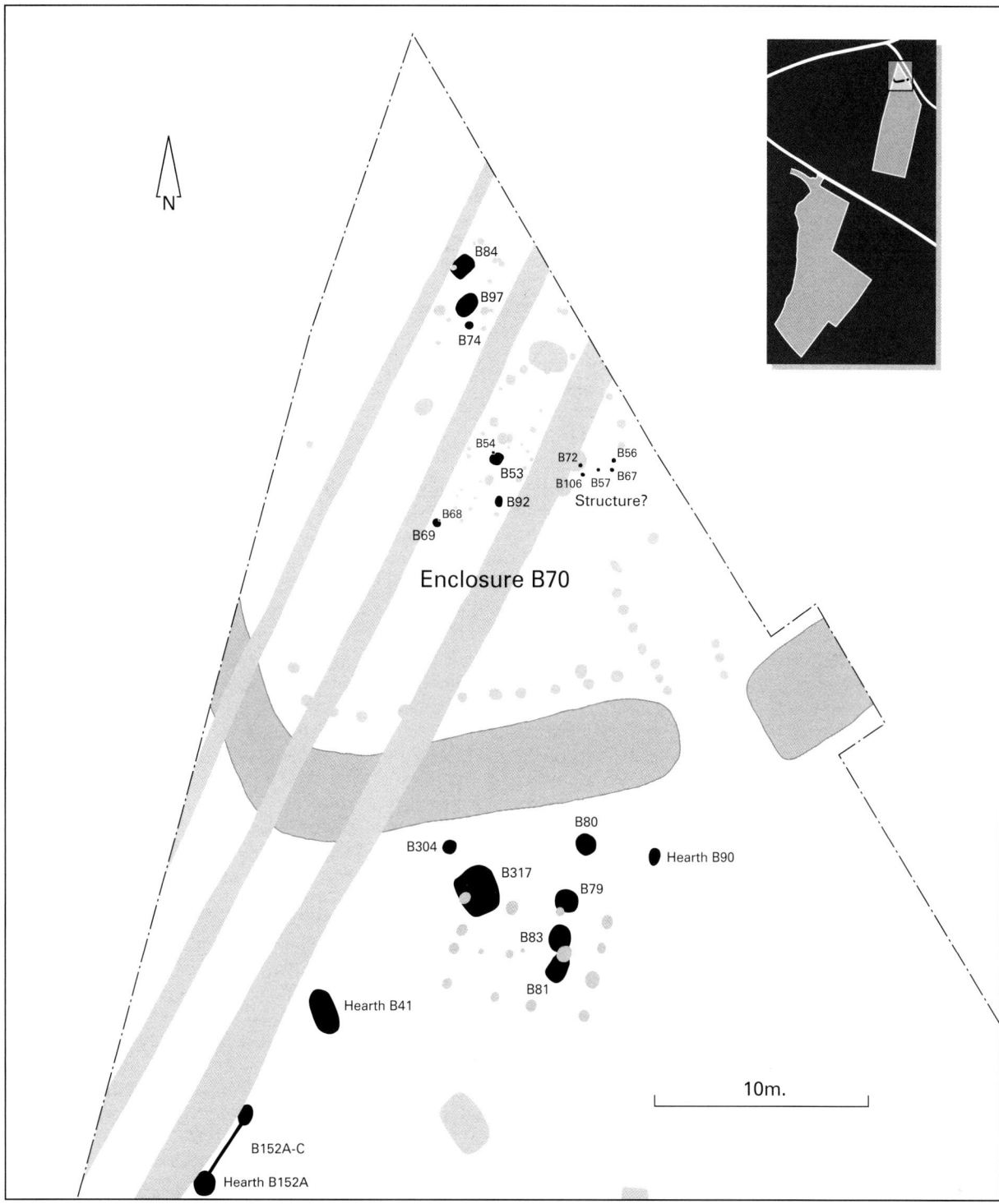

Fig. 18. Period 2. Features within and immediately outside Enclosure B70.

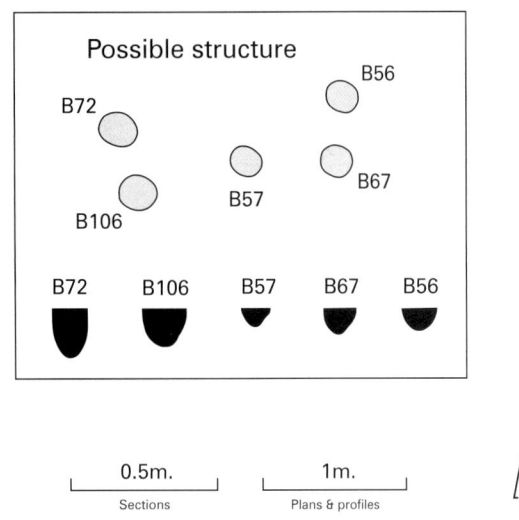

Fig. 19. Period 2. Detail of features within Enclosure B70.

some 9 m. north of hearths B53 and B69, contained the well-preserved remains of a brown clay lining on average some 1–3 cm. thick. The fill was of dark brown sandy loam and gravel with charcoal and burnt clay flecks capped by mid brown gravelly loam containing twenty sherds of flint-tempered pottery dated c. 900–600 B.C.

Pit B92 was an oval-shaped feature measuring approximately 1 m. by 0.80 m. The pit, barely 0.05 m. deep, contained a remnant pale brown clay lining and a carbon rich dark brown gravelly loam fill. The fill provided lumps of burnt clay together with twenty-three flint-tempered sherds (including Fig. 81, Nos 272–4), dated 900–600 B.C.

Pit B97 was oval-shaped, 1 m. by 0.80 m., cut 0.22 m. deep. The pit contained a bi-partite fill of weathered gravel capped by a deposit of dark brown loam with sparse gravel flecked with charcoal and contained thirty-one sherds of flint-tempered pottery (including Fig. 81, Nos 268–70) dated c. 900–600 B.C.

Pit B74 was located immediately south of Pit B97. The circular pit, 0.35 m. in diameter, was 0.15 m. deep. The fill of dark brown loam and gravel provided a single fragment of a perforated clay slab (No. 52, p. 268).

The possible structure (Fig. 19)

A group of five post-holes (B56–7, B67, B72 and B106) located to the east of the hearths and some 10 m. north of the enclosure entrance were tentatively interpreted as a structure. The post-holes, on average 20–25 cm. in diameter, and cut 12–32 cm. deep with near identical fills of gravel and loam, appear to form a rectangular structure 1.5 m. long and 0.50 m. wide. The dating of the possible structure is uncertain. Post-hole B72 was cut by a Period 3 feature (B71) and although post-hole B67 yielded two sherds of flint-tempered pottery, a date cannot be assigned. The function of the structure is unknown.

Features south of the enclosure

A cluster of features was excavated immediately outside the enclosure to the south-west of the enclosure entrance. The features comprised three possible hearths or fire pits and five pits. To the south-west of the feature cluster was a pit and a hearth linked by a long, narrow, clay-lined gully.

Hearths

Two possible hearths located outside the enclosure were defined by fire-fractured and heat discoloured gravel linings and fills of fire-crazed gravel and loam flecked with carbon and burnt clay.

Hearth B41 (Fig. 20, plan and section) was rectangular with a bowl-shaped profile and rounded ends, measuring some 2.05 by 1.10 m. and was cut to a depth of 0.20 m. The fill of the hearth yielded twenty flint-tempered sherds dated c. 900–600 B.C. together with copper dross and a fragment of a perforated pottery slab (p. 268).

Hearth B90 (Fig. 20, plan and section) was oval shaped, measuring some 0.80 by 0.55 m. and had been cut to a depth of 0.16 m. The fill of dark brown gravelly loam flecked with

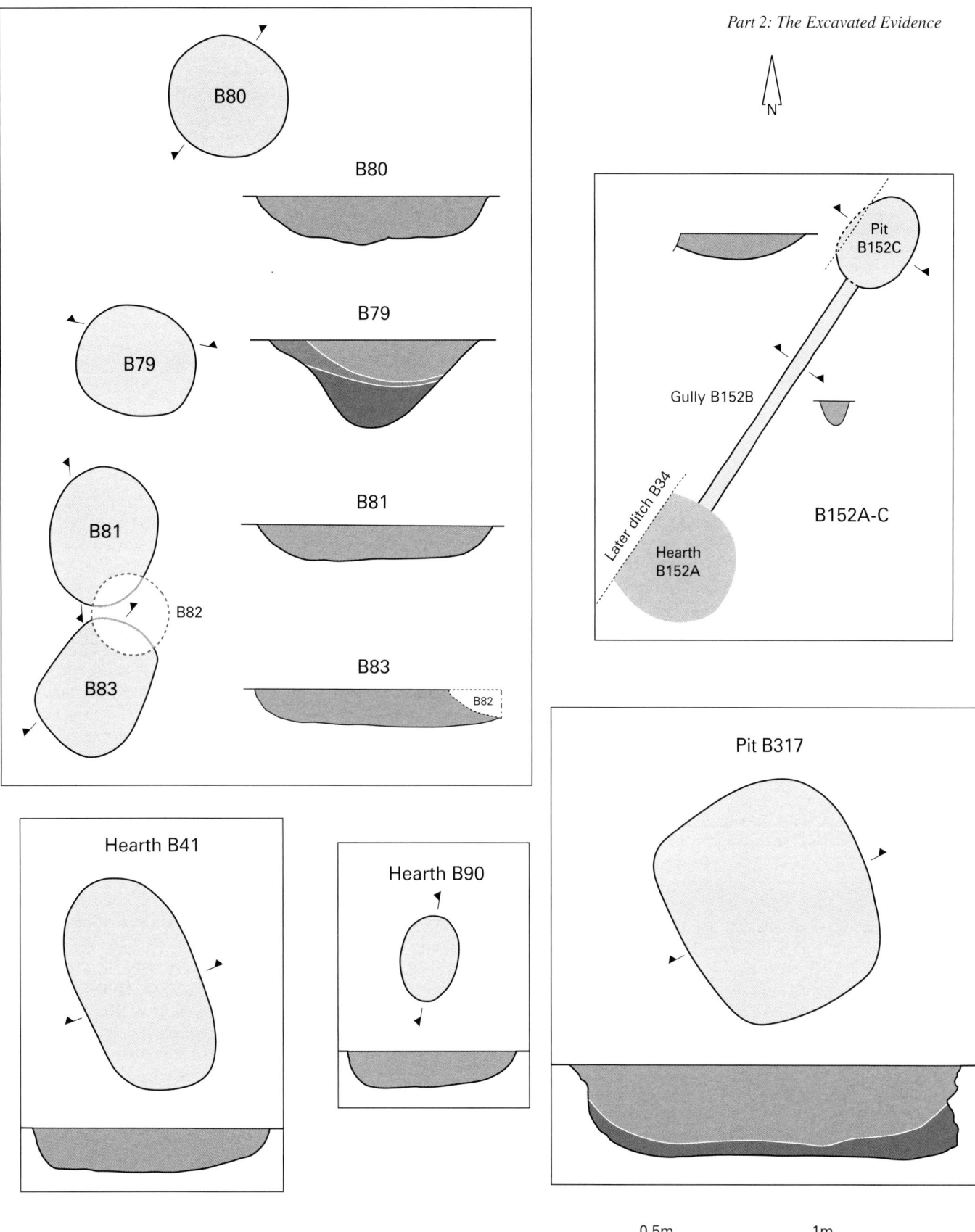

Fig. 20. Period 2. Detail of features outside Enclosure B70.

carbon and burnt clay, capping traces of a fired orange-red clay lining, provided three flint-tempered sherds.

Pits

Six pits, located immediately south of the enclosure have been dated to Period 2. Four closely-spaced pits were located in an arc just outside the western terminal of the enclosure entrance (B79, B80, B81, B83). The remaining pits (B317 and B304) were located to the west of the group.

Pit B79 (Fig. 20, plan and section) was circular with a diameter of approximately 0.90 m., cut to a depth of 0.40 m. The pit contained a primary fill of black-brown pebbly loam flecked with charcoal and burnt clay, capped by successive lenses of clean gravel and an upper fill of medium brown gravelly loam. The basal fills yielded no finds, but the upper loam provided thirty flint-tempered sherds (including Fig. 80, Nos 252–4) dated *c*. 900–600 B.C. together with a fragment of a perforated pottery slab (Fig. 153, No. 45).

Pit B80 (Fig. 20, plan and section), located at close proximity to the enclosure ditch, was circular, 1 m. in diameter and 0.22 m. deep. The pit contained a single fill of black brown gravelly loam flecked with charcoal and burnt clay. The fill provided a substantial corpus of 258 sherds of flint-tempered pottery (including Fig. 80, Nos 255–63) dated *c*. 900–600 B.C., together with pin mould debris (p. 264–5), a fragment of perforated pottery slab (Fig. 153, No. 46) and a perforated stone, possibly a polisher (Fig. 152, No. 43: p. 265–6). The pin-mould debris, stone polisher and perforated pottery slab represented the best evidence recovered from the site for metalworking. The pit contained not only mould fragments associated with the manufacture of copper alloy pins, but also for a blade-like implement perhaps a sword, rapier or spear-head. A separate fragment from a tubular casting, perhaps for a spearhead or an axe-like tool (p. 260 and p. 265) was also recovered.

Pit B81 (Fig. 20, plan and section) was circular, approximately 1.25 m. in diameter and 0.16 m. deep. The pit, filled with a single deposit of gravelly loam with lenses of clean water-washed sandy gravel, contained burnt flints and a corpus of sixty-three flint-tempered sherds dated 900–600 B.C., but also contained a rusticated sherd which may suggest a later Period 3A date for the pit.

Pit B83 (Fig. 20, plan and section) was subrectangular measuring 1.20 by 0.92 m. Cut to a depth of 0.16 m. the feature was filled with a single deposit of dark brown gravelly loam containing small lumps of burnt clay and nine flint-tempered sherds tentatively dated to the period *c*. 900–600 B.C.

Pit B317 (Fig. 20, plan and section) was roughly square, measuring 2.10 by 1.90 m. and was cut to a bowl-shaped profile 0.40 m. deep. The pit contained a lower fill of charcoal, ash and burnt clay, capped by black-brown clay-loam with burnt clay and provided a substantial corpus of 293 flint-tempered sherds, (including Figs 78–9, Nos 227–51), together with fragments of two perforated pottery slabs (including No 54, p. 268) and copper dross (p. 266).

Pit B304, located to the west of the pit group, close to the external edge of the B70 enclosure was oval shaped, approximately 0.80 m. in diameter and 0.14 m. deep. The pit, filled with mid brown gravelly loam, burnt clay and fired flints, provided no datable finds. The proximity and similarities of fill to others in the group indicated a possible Period 2 date for the feature.

Isolated features (Fig. 20)

Three linked features (B152A–C) were located to the south-west of the hearths and pits previously described. The features (a hearth, a gully and a pit) may also have been associated with metalworking.

Hearth B152A was represented by a circular patch of fire-reddened, heat-fractured natural gravel approximately 1.10 m. in diameter. The burnt natural gravel may have been located beneath a feature subjected to intense heat, perhaps a furnace or a smithing hearth. Adjoining but not cutting the hearth was a 2.50 m. long gully (B152B) aligned north-east to south-west. The gully, on average 0.13 m. wide, cut with u-shaped base and vertical sides to a maximum depth of 0.12 m., was lined with fire-reddened clay. At the northeast terminus of the gully was a contemporary pit (B152C). The pit, 0.90 by 0.60 m., cut to a maximum depth of 0.12 m., was filled with a single deposit of mid brown gravelly loam containing burnt flints, flecks of carbon and burnt clay and fragments of vitrified clay. An identical deposit filled the gully.

Although the features provided no datable finds (an intrusive iron double-spiked loop of Roman date was recovered from the context, p. 273), the presence of burnt materials including fire-fractured flints and vitrified clay, together with the location close to Enclosure B70 suggests that the features may be associated with Period 2 industrial activity.

The function of the gully, with its fired clay lining, is difficult to determine, but appeared to have been designed to transfer liquid from a hearth (of which only the sub-base survived) to a pit located 2.50 m. distant. Vitrified clay was recovered close to the junction of the gully and the pit. The common fills of both features indicated that they had perhaps been backfilled at the same time. It is tentatively suggested that the gully may have formed a quenching trough used during the working of metal.

Cropmarks adjoining the B70 enclosure
(Fig. 5, Pls V and VI)

Reconstruction of the shape of the B70 enclosure was based on cropmark data extracted from photographs taken at the

Pl. IX. Period 2. Enclosure A24, looking north-east.

time of excavation. In addition to the enclosure boundary ditch, three separate cropmarks were identified. Of these two stains were ditches attached to the corners of the enclosure on its north side. The marks appear to continue the line of the east and west sides of the enclosure so precisely that they may indicate the presence of a contemporary northern extension or annexe to the enclosure. A third linear cropmark aligned north-east to south-west was identified springing from the north-west corner of the enclosure. The feature appeared to comprise of three lengths of ditch separated by two causeways, with the entire soil stain extending for some 75 m. This third ditch may have been for a field boundary perhaps established late in the life of the enclosure or even at a time when the enclosure was derelict but still extant and visible in the landscape. A great many periglacial features are present in this area and it is not impossible that at least part of this third feature may have been of natural origin. What can be certain however is that settlement features extend well to the north and west of the excavation.

Enclosure A24 (Fig. 21, Pl. IX)

During Period 2 a second enclosure (A24) was established in Area A some 300 m. to the south of B70. The entire enclosure fell within the area of excavation and most identified features were excavated. The enclosure, set on the 30 m. contour, on ground dipping gently to the east, was defined by a single ditch, interrupted by at least four separate entrances; two to the east and two to the west. The enclosure was subcircular with long axis aligned approximately east to west. The entrances were symmetrically placed in the 'corners' of the enclosure. A bank almost certainly accompanied the enclosure ditch, although it is unlikely to have served a defensive function.

During the life of the enclosure one entrance was blocked and part of the circuit repaired or replaced by a possible fence. Within the enclosure were concentrations of features associated with hearths or fire pits, possibly representing two separate domestic structures of different phases. In addition, groups of pits and rows of post-holes possibly indicated functional subdivisions of the enclosure. A small number of features provided metalworking debris.

Enclosure ditches (Fig. 21)

Four separate continuous lengths of ditch were cut to form an oval-shaped enclosure measuring some 44.10 m. east–west by 36.80 m. north–south.

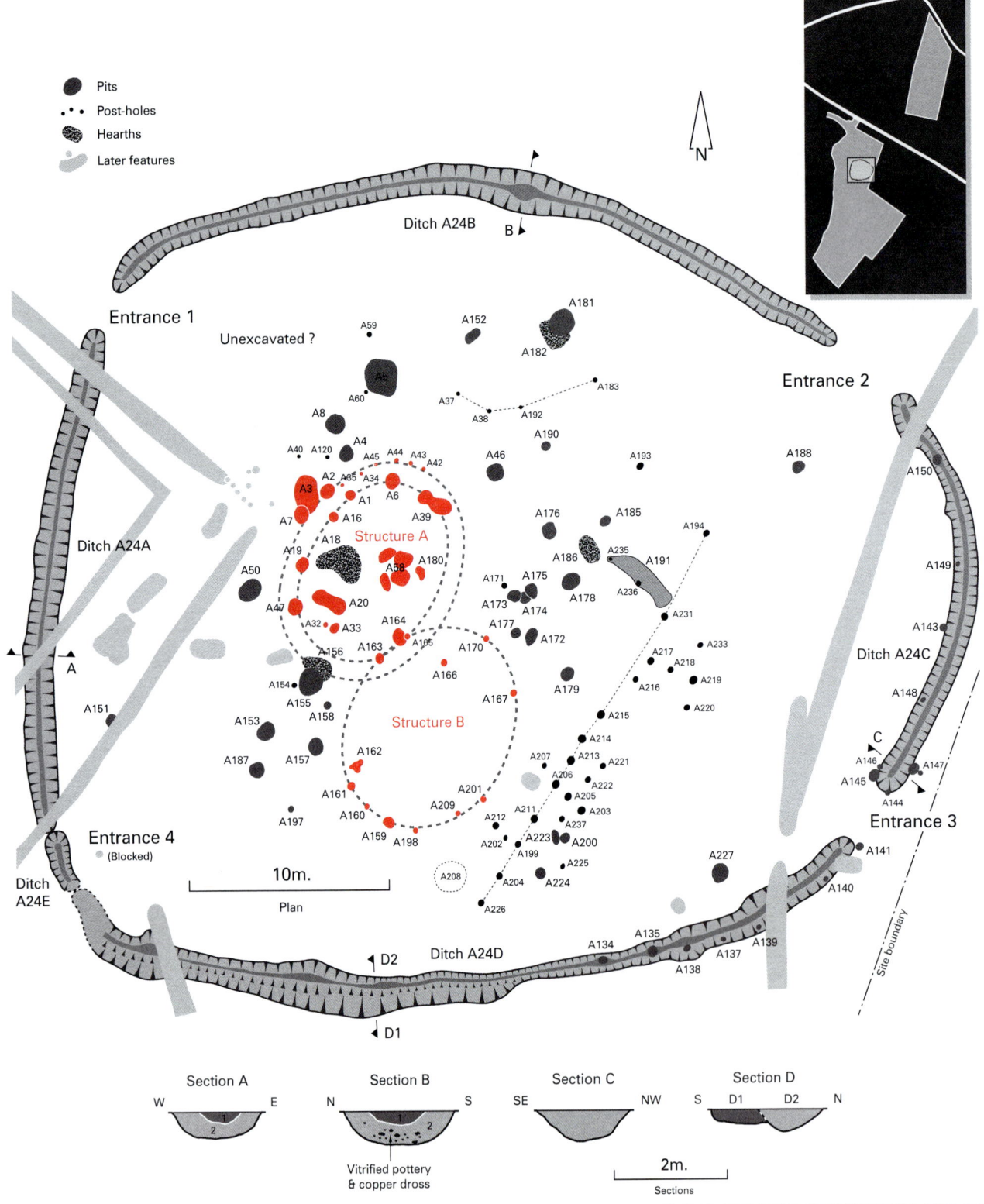

Fig. 21. Period 2. Enclosure A24, with location (inset).

The western ditch (A24A), some 24.20 m. long, on average 1.60 m. wide and 0.45 m. deep, was cut with rounded terminals giving onto Entrance 1 to the north and Entrance 4 to the south. The ditch fills of compact loam and gravel overlying a chocolate brown sandy loam and gravel, yielded pottery dated to the period 900–600 B.C.

The northern ditch (A24B) was 36.30 m. long with rounded terminals facing Entrances 1 and 2. The ditch was cut to an average width of 1.20 m. and depth of 0.40 m. The ditch fills of compact loam and gravel yielded pottery and a copper alloy knife blade (p. 270). Mid way along the ditch was a concentration of burnt material including fire-fractured flints, burnt clay, vitrified pottery and copper dross from metalworking (p. 266).

The eastern ditch (A24C) was some 18.55 m. long, with rounded terminals giving onto Entrance 2 to the north and Entrance 3 to the south. The ditch was on average 1.25 m. wide and cut to an average depth of 0.50 m. The fill of medium brown gravelly loam flecked with charcoal and burnt clay, yielded pottery dated 900–600 B.C. and an intrusive iron spearhead of Roman date (Fig. 155, No. 14; p. 273).

The southern ditch (A24D) was some 38.80 m. long with rounded terminals giving onto Entrance 3 to the east and Entrance 4 in the west. Entrance 4 was blocked by the cutting of a later ditch (A24E). The original ditch was of irregular width. The eastern half was 0.60 m. to 1 m. wide and approximately 0.20 m. deep. The western half was 0.45 to 1.95 m. wide and between 0.40 and 0.60 m. deep. Although no difference in ditch fills was noted, it is likely that the western part of Ditch A24D was recut when Ditch A24E was formed to block the entrance. Few finds were recovered from the ditch fills.

The combined ditch fills yielded 397 flint-tempered sherds with most of them recovered from the northern ditch A24B. The assemblage (including Fig. 67, Nos 138–49; Fig. 68, 150–67) has been dated to *c*. 900–600 B.C. The general ditch fills also yielded a complete pyramidal loomweight (No. 44) and a fragment of a second loomweight bearing the marks of a suspension cord on the inner surface (No. 45). The first loomweight is dated by type to before *c*. 500 B.C. (p. 276). An iron object (p. 274) was considered to be intrusive.

Enclosure entrances

Enclosure A24 was provided with four symmetrically placed entrances, represented by gaps in the surrounding ditch. The north-western entrance (1) was approximately 2 m. wide and the north-eastern entrance (2) was 4 m. wide. There was no indication of a gate structure for either of these openings.

The south-eastern entrance (3) was 2.60 m. wide. Two post-holes (A141, A144) located either side of the opening may have formed part of an entrance structure or part of a late fence (*see* below). The post-holes, on average 0.40 m. in diameter and cut to depths of 0.45 and 0.40 m. respectively, were filled with a similar gravelly loam containing no finds. A third post-hole (A145) 0.40 m. in diameter and cut 0.45 m. deep with a fill of dark brown loam flecked with burnt clay was located in the south-west corner of the western terminal of Ditch A24C. This post-hole, which contained no finds, may also have formed part of a gate structure for Entrance 3.

The south-western entrance (4) originally at least 3 m. wide was blocked by a later section of ditch (A24E). The blocking ditch, at least 4.50 m. long (but probably part of a much longer recut of Ditch A24D), was cut to an average width of 1 m. and depth of 0.40 m. The ditch had a rounded north terminal, which butted the southern terminal of Ditch A24A. Ditch A24E fills yielded no datable finds.

The enclosure bank

A lack of features immediately to the rear of the enclosure ditches suggested that a bank no more than 3–5 m. wide at its base, accompanied each length of ditch. The bank was not revetted and did not have a defensive function but was perhaps planted with a hedge to exclude animals from a domestic space or pen them in when it was required. The four entrances formed by causeways in the enclosure ditch and gaps in the bank may have required no formal gate structure. As none of the causeways was particularly wide, a prefabricated hurdle would no doubt have sufficed to seal each entrance. If a gate structure did exist at Entrance 3 then it is likely that such a structure was formed when a possible late fence was erected to strengthen or replace the western bank and ditch arrangement. It is equally possible that the fence was continuous and partly constructed to block the causeway at Entrance 3 at that time.

The late fence

Three post-holes interpreted above as part of the possible gate structure at Entrance 3 (A141, A144, A145) may have formed part of a late fence replacing or strengthening the eastern side of the enclosure. The fence post-holes were cut through partially filled ditches, A24C and A24D to form a fence almost 40 m. long, perhaps interrupted by the south-eastern entrance. Six post-pits were identified cutting Ditch A24D to the west of Entrance 3. From west to east these post-pits A140, A139, A137, A138, A135 and A134 were on average 0.40 m. in diameter and cut 0.30 m. deep. The post-pits were regularly spaced on average 2 m. apart. Five post-pits were identified cutting the edge of Ditch A24C to the north of Entrance 3. From south to north these post-pits (A147, A148, A143, A149 and A150) were on average 0.40 m. in diameter and cut to an average depth of 0.20 m. The post-pits set at intervals of approximately 3 m. were filled with a dark brown sandy loam containing few datable finds. Single sherds of flint-tempered pottery were recovered from Post-pits A137 and A143. Post-pit A147 contained two flint-tempered sherds, a vitrified sherd and copper dross (p. 266).

The enclosure interior

The interior of Enclosure A24 was almost entirely excavated. The majority of features recorded were confined to a central position within the enclosure with large areas to the east and west void of remains. Concentrations of features, mainly post-holes but also pits, occurred around three possible hearths or fire pits. Analysis of the feature clusters tentatively indicated that two structures occupied the centre of the enclosure at different times. There was also some evidence for fenced divisions of the enclosure and for metalworking.

Domestic structures (Fig. 21)

A concentration of post-holes, post-pits and stake-holes recorded west of centre within the enclosure were almost certainly associated with a domestic structure or structures. Insufficient detail survived however to provide a coherent reconstruction and only a tentative interpretation of the evidence has been attempted here.

Structure A

The northern side of a possible structure was indicated by an arc of six post-holes and post-pits (A47, A19, A16, A1, A6 and A39A). The pits and post-holes, set between 1 and 3 m. apart, may have formed part of an internal frame or eaves support for the northern side of a circular hut. An isolated post-pit (A164) may have formed part of the southern side of an oval-shaped frame of maximum dimensions 9.50 by 7 m. The pits and post-holes between 0.30 m. and 1 m. in diameter and between 0.10 and 0.40 m. deep were generally filled with a gravelly mid brown loam. All of the pits apart from A39A provided finds, each yielding between one and ten sherds of flint-tempered pottery dated *c*. 900–600 B.C. (including Post-pit A47 Fig. 73, No. 207 and Post-pit A19: Fig. 73, No. 206). Post-pit A6 contained a copper alloy ring (p. 270).

Possibly associated with the frame timbers was an arc of six small post-holes (A35, A34, A45, A44, A43, A42) surviving only against the north side of the possible structure. The posts, set on average 0.30 m. apart and approximately 1 m. beyond the frame posts, were taken to represent a short section of hut wall. They were between 0.80 and 0.35 m. in diameter, cut to a depth of between 0.10 and 0.20 m. and were generally filled with brown gravelly loam. Only post-hole A43 yielded finds (three sherds of flint-tempered pottery).

One post-pit, A164, at the south-east corner of the structure, was cut by a post-hole, A165, thought to form part of a later structure (Structure B) possibly built to replace Structure A.

Features within Structure A

A burnt patch of natural gravel (A18), possibly indicating a hearth and a group of six pits and a post-hole were identified within the footprint of the possible hut.

Hearth A18 comprised an irregular patch of burnt natural gravel extending across an area 2 m. north–south by 2.5 m. east–west. No trace of a hearth structure was found. The irregular nature and substantial size of the burnt area may indicate that more than one hearth was represented by the stain.

Pit A20, located a short way south-west of the hearth was 1.70 m. long and 0.70 m. wide. The rectangular feature with rounded ends, aligned approximately east–west and cut to a maximum depth of 0.40 m., was filled with a pale brown gravelly loam which provided no datable finds.

Pit A33, a short way to the south was 0.60 m. in diameter and 0.20 m. deep. The pit, filled with mid brown loam and gravel, contained no datable finds.

A group of five small, shallow pits, on average 0.70 m. in diameter and up to 0.40 m. deep, were located in a cluster in the western half of Structure A (A58, A58A, A58B, A58C and A180). All five pits contained dark brown clay loam and gravel, flecked with carbon and burnt clay. Four pits were void of finds, but Pit A180 provided seven flint-tempered sherds including a near-complete small vessel (Fig. 72, No. 202) and substantial fragments from a second (Fig. 72, No. 203). A single post-hole (A32) 0.25 m. in diameter and 0.20 m. deep was also within the footprint of Structure A. The post-hole, filled with dark brown gravelly loam, provided no datable finds.

Structure B

A second possible structure was represented by an incomplete circle of ten post-pits and post-holes (A163, A165, A170, A167, A201, A209, A198, A159, A160 and A161). The posts were taken to form the outer wall of a hut approximately 10 m. in diameter. One post-hole for Structure B (A165) was found to cut a post-pit for Structure A (A164). No other stratigraphic link between the two buildings was established, but on the strength of this one relationship, Structure B has been taken to post-date Structure A. The posts and post-pits of Structure B were between 0.18 and 0.56 m. in diameter, cut between 0.18 and 0.36 m. deep. Only Post-pit A163 provided datable finds comprising four flint-tempered sherds (including Fig. 74, No. 220) dated *c*. 900–600 B.C.

Features within Structure B

Only two features fell within the proposed footprint of Structure B: a pit (A162) against the putative west side of the hut and a post-hole (A166) against the north side. The pit, approximately 0.65 m. in diameter and 0.20 m. deep, was filled with a mid brown gravelly loam yielding two flint-tempered sherds. The post-hole (A166) 0.28 m. in diameter and 0.15 m. deep, filled with dark brown gravelly loam provided no finds.

Other features within the enclosure

Three possible hearths, a clay-lined gully and thirty-one pits were identified within the western half of the enclosure. A group of twelve pits was located to the east of structures A and B; a further nine pits lay to the north and north-east of structure A and nine pits were recorded to the west of structures A and B.

Hearths

Three possible hearths were located in the western half of the enclosure. All three comprised patches of burnt orange natural subsoil with fire-fractured flints.

Hearth A156 comprising a patch of burnt orange ground and fire-crazed gravel fell within the postulated footprint of Structure A and was cut by a later pit (A155). The hearth and pit probably post-dated Structure A.

Hearth A182 was located in the northern part of the enclosure, perhaps close to the internal bank. The circular patch of fired ground, some 2 m. in diameter was cut by a later pit (A181) containing metalworking debris.

Hearth A186, located to the east of Structures A and B, was oval shaped, 2.30 by 0.90 m. in extent.

Clay-lined pits

Five of the pits identified within the enclosure contained a clay lining, perhaps suggesting that they may have been used for food storage. Four of these pits lay in an intercutting group adjoining the north side of Structure A (A3, A7, A2 and A4). The fifth pit (A178) lay at some distance east of Structure A.

Pit A3 was oval shaped some 1.90 by 1.20 m. with a bowl-shaped profile, cut to a depth of 0.40 m. The base of the pit contained traces of a yellow clay lining and was capped by consecutive fills of dark brown loam, flecked with carbon and burnt clay and by dark brown loam and gravel. The pit fill provided twenty-one flint-tempered sherds (including Fig. 70, Nos 180–82) dated *c.* 900–600 B.C. The pit was cut by a later clay-lined pit (A7).

Pit A7 was circular, 1 m. in diameter and cut to a maximum depth of 0.60 m. The base and sides of the pit were lined with traces of unburnt and burnt clay. The pit fill of dark brown gravelly loam provided six flint-tempered sherds.

Pit A2 was 0.90 m. in diameter and had been cut to a bowl-shaped profile 0.50 m. deep. The base of the pit contained a clay lining which extended up the sides of the pit for a maximum height of 0.20 m. The pit fill of dark brown loam with carbon and burnt clay flecking and burnt flints yielded thirty-three flint-tempered sherds (including Fig. 69, Nos 172–9) dated *c.* 900–600 B.C.

Pit A4, located a short way east of the group, but almost certainly formed part of it, was 1 m. in diameter and 0.50 m. deep was lined with clay and filled with light brown gravelly loam. The pit fill provided 169 flint-tempered sherds (including Fig. 70, Nos 183–7 and Fig. 71, No. 188) dated *c.* 900–600 B.C. Amongst the vessels represented was a large storage jar (No. 188).

Pit A178 was located 4 m. north-east of Structure B. Roughly circular, 0.90 m. in diameter and 0.24 m. deep, it contained a clay lining which covered half of the base and the sides up to a height of 0.16 m. It was filled with dark brown gravelly loam mottled with burnt clay and provided three flint-tempered sherds.

Other pits and post-holes

Twenty-six other pits were found within the enclosure. Five pits were located to the west of Structures A and B (A155, A157, A153, A187 and A50). A second group of ten pits (A174, A175, A173, A177, A172, A179, A176, A46, A190, A185) was located to the north-east of Structures A and B. Associated with this group of pits were a clay-lined gully (A191) and six post-holes. A group of four pits was located north of Structure A (A8, A5, A152 and A181). Two of these (A5 and A181) provided evidence of metalworking. A nearby row of four post-holes (A37, A38, A192 and A183) was identified as a possible fence. Three other unrelated post-holes were recorded nearby. The eastern part of the enclosure was largely void of features. A row of up to ten post-holes (A226, A204, A199, A211, A206, A213, a214, A215, A231 and A194) may have been used for a fence and a further twelve formed no coherent pattern. Five pits (A200, A223, A224, A227 and A188) were located to the east of the fence line, though most of this area was largely devoid of features. One pit (A151) was located in the western quarter of the enclosure.

Pits west of Structures A and B

Pit A155, located against the south-west side of Structure A was approximately 1.30 m. in diameter and cut to a bowl-shaped profile 0.50 m. deep. The pit, found cutting Hearth A156 and probably post-dating Structure A, was filled with laminated deposits of dark and light brown gravelly loam. The fill provided ten flint-tempered sherds (including Fig. 72, No. 201) dated *c.* 900–600 B.C.

Pit A157, located a short way south, was 0.57 m. in diameter, cut 0.35 m. deep. The fill of light brown gravelly loam flecked with charcoal and burnt clay provided three flint-tempered sherds.

Pit A153, located to the west, was 0.80 m. in diameter and 0.40 m. deep. The pit fill of gravel and light brown loam, heavily flecked with charcoal and burnt clay, provided fifty-four flint-tempered sherds (including Fig. 73, Nos 209–10) dated *c*. 900–600 B.C.

Pit A187 was 0.88 m. in diameter and 0.32 m. deep. The pit, filled with a deposit of light brown clay loam and gravel, flecked with burnt clay, provided seven flint-tempered sherds (including Fig. 73, Nos 212–14) dated *c*. 900–600 B.C.

Pit A50, located to the west of Structure A at slight remove from the previous pits was 1 m. in diameter and 0.30 m. deep. The pit fill of mid brown loam and gravel contained thirty-one flint-tempered sherds (including Fig. 72, No. 200) dated *c*. 900–600 B.C.

Pits north-east of Structures A and B

Pits A174, A173, A175, A177 and A172 formed a tightly clustered group to the north-east of Structure B. They were all subcircular, between 0.55 and 0.95 m. in diameter and between 0.17 to 0.45 m. deep. Their fills of light and dark brown gravelly loam, contained a few sherds of flint-tempered pottery. Pits A173 and A175 were found to cut Pit A174 suggesting that they were not all contemporary and perhaps represent a bi-product of longer term occupation.

Pit A179 lay to the south-east of the group. The pit, 0.70 m. in diameter and 0.20 m. deep, contained a fill of grey brown loam and gravel providing eight flint-tempered sherds dated *c*. 900–600 B.C.

Pit A176 lay to the north-east of the group. The pit, 0.70 m. in diameter and 0.16 m. deep, contained a fill of grey brown sandy loam and gravel which provided no datable finds.

Pit A46 was located to the north-west of the group, east of Structure A. The pit, 0.90 m. in diameter and 0.18 m. deep, was filled with dark brown gravelly loam containing no datable finds.

Pits A185 and A190 lay to the north-east of Structures A and B. They were approximately 0.45 m. in diameter and 0.10 m. deep. Both pits contained dark brown gravelly loam with no datable finds.

Gully and post-holes east of Structures A and B

Gully 191 (Fig. 22, plan and sections) lay to the east of the group of pits. The irregular gully, 3.70 m. long and on average 0.50 m. wide, was aligned roughly north-west to south-east, and cut to a u-shaped profile 0.20 m. deep. The gully, lined with yellow clay, was filled with mid brown gravelly loam containing five flint-tempered sherds (including Fig. 70, Nos 189–91) dated *c*. 900–600. The shape of the feature suggested that it may have been formed from two or more separate pits that were joined and lined with clay. The function of the gully was not determined but it is possible that it was cut to hold water, perhaps as a trough.

Six post-holes were recorded on the fringes of the eastern group of pits (A202, A212, A207, A193, A235 and A236). Two of the post-holes were found to cut the fill of Gully A191. The post-holes, of identical size, being 0.20 m. in diameter and 0.18 m. deep, were filled with brown gravelly loam, but provided no datable finds. The remaining post-holes, located across a wide area were between 0.30 and 0.15 m. in diameter and 0.20 and 0.11 m. deep. All were filled with gravelly loam and none of the six posts contained datable finds.

Pits north of Structure A

Pit A8 was located close to a group of clay-lined pits. It was 0.90 m. in diameter and of bowl-shaped profile, cut to a depth of 0.20 m. The fill of mid brown gravelly loam flecked with burnt clay provided twenty flint-tempered sherds (including Fig. 70, Nos 198–9) dated *c*. 900–600 B.C.

Pit A5 (Fig. 22, section) was a large shallow, bowl-shaped feature, 2 m. by 1.70 m. in extent, cut to a maximum depth of 0.40 m. The fill comprised a basal fill of dark brown gravelly loam with burnt clay, capped by light brown sandy loam and gravel and an upper fill of dark brown gravelly loam heavily flecked with carbon and burnt clay. The lowest fill provided no datable finds, but the capping deposit yielded fifteen flint-tempered sherds (including Fig. 70, Nos 192–7) dated *c*. 900–600 B.C. and copper dross (p. 266).

Pit A152 was a rectangular feature 1 m. by 0.65 m. in extent cut with rounded ends and a bowl-shaped profile 0.24 m. deep. It contained a single fill of light brown sandy loam filled with burnt flint and containing charcoal and burnt clay. The pit fill provided six flint-tempered sherds (including Fig. 69, Nos 170–71) dated *c*. 900–600 B.C.

Pit A181 (Fig. 22, section) was located further north-east of Structure A almost 5 m. from the northern enclosure ditch (A24B). The bowl-shaped pit, 1.40 m. in diameter and 0.50 m. deep, found cutting Hearth A182, was filled with a basal deposit of mid brown loam and gravel containing burnt clay, charcoal and burnt flint. Capping the primary layer was a lens of weathered natural sand and gravel. The lens was surmounted by successive deposits of light brown and mid brown loam, the uppermost containing burnt clay and charcoal and a lump of copper dross (p. 266). Five sherds of flint-tempered pottery recovered from the pits fills (including Fig. 68, No. 169) have been dated to *c*. 900–600 B.C.

Post-hole row

An arc of four post-holes (A37, A38, A192 and A183) located south of pits A152 and A181, were tentatively interpreted as a possible fence line. The posts were between 0.16–0.27 m. in diameter, 0.08–0.20 m. deep and filled with dark to mid brown gravelly loam. The post fills provided not datable finds.

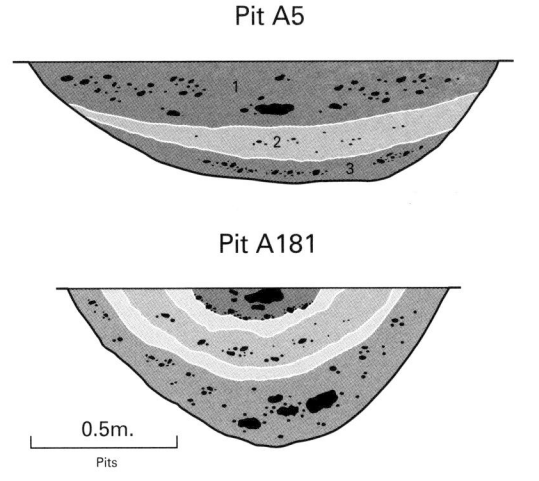

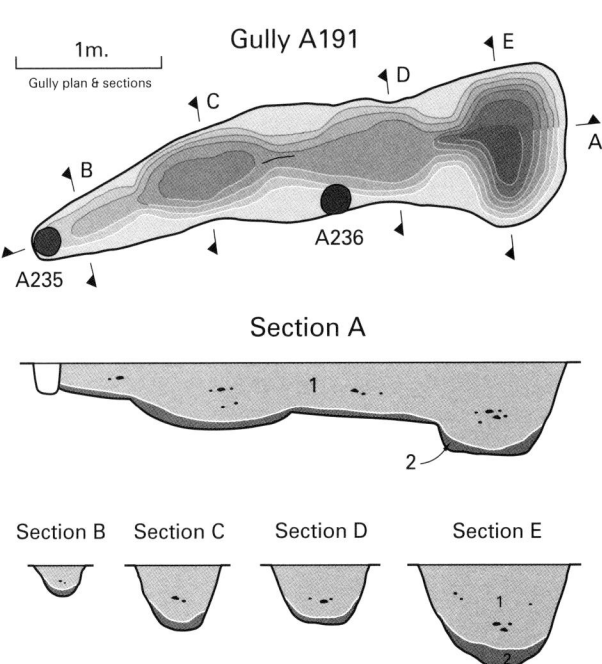

Fig. 22. Period 2. Enclosure A24, pits A5 and A181 and Gully A191.

Four other post-holes, cut for an unknown purpose, were located north of Structure A. The posts (A40, A120, A60 and A59) were of similar size and depth to the post row and contained no datable finds.

The eastern part of the enclosure

The eastern part of the enclosure was largely void of features. One possible interpretation for this absence was that the area may have been used as an animal pen or paddock, separated internally from the domestic space by a 10 m. long north-east to south-west aligned fence (A226, A204, A199, A211, A206, A213, A214, A215). Two post-holes (A231 and A194) approximately on line with the fence may indicate that the boundary extended for a distance of at least 21 metres. The posts, between 0.22 and 0.42 m. in diameter and 0.11–0.40 m. deep, were generally filled with mid brown gravelly loam. A single sherd of flint-tempered pottery was recovered from Post-hole A213.

To the east of the fence was a scatter of post-holes (A225, A237, A205, A203, A222, A221 A216, A217, A218, A220, A219 and A233). The group formed no coherent pattern or alignment. The posts, of varying diameter (0.22–0.42 m.) and depth (0.11–0.40 m.), contained no datable finds.

A group of three small subcircular pits (A200, A223 and A224) was located east of the fence. The pits 0.45–0.68 m. in diameter and cut between 0.22–0.40 m. deep yielded no datable finds.

Two isolated pits were examined in the eastern part of the enclosure.

Pit A227 was located close to the southern enclosure ditch and some 7 m. west of Entrance 3 and is likely to have been cut through the enclosure bank. The pit, a circular feature 1.10 m. in diameter, cut 0.28 m. deep, contained a brown loam and gravel fill flecked with carbon and burnt clay. The pit fill yielded copper dross (p. 266) and the rim of a jar (Fig. 73, No. 205) dated c. 900–600 B.C.

Pit A188, located some 6 m. south-west of Entrance 2 was subcircular, 0.58 m. in diameter and cut to a depth of 0.22 m. The fill, of brown loam and gravel, provided no datable finds.

The western quarter of the enclosure

The western quarter of the enclosure was void of features save for one pit (A151) located some 8 m. north of Entrance 4 and 2.50 m. east of the western enclosure ditch. The pit, probably cut into the enclosure bank, was 0.60 m. in diameter and 0.30 m. deep, filled with light brown loam and sandy gravel and provided no datable finds.

Enclosure A260 (Fig. 23)

Enclosure A260 was located at the southern end of Area A. Identified as a cropmark and a soil stain during topsoil stripping, the feature was mapped but not excavated. Other features (elements of a Roman field system, p. 92) were found to have cut the enclosure. The speed of gravel extraction in this part of the site precluded major fieldwork activities save for the making of a plan of exposed soil stains before quarrying activities removed all trace of them. A few features were sample excavated during a hectic and intense period of activity, but the A260 enclosure was not one of them.

The enclosure was oval shaped, 35 by 30 m., with long axis aligned north–south. An enclosure ditch 1.25–2 m. wide was indicated by the soil stain together with a single western causewayed entrance approximately 3 m. wide. The fills of the enclosure ditch were of mid brown gravelly loam except in the north-west side of the circuit, north of the entrance, where quantities of burnt orange and unburnt yellow clay were in evidence.

Pit A100

Pit A100, located immediately outside Enclosure A260, a short way north of the enclosure entrance, was circular, 0.80 m. in diameter, cut to a depth of 0.34 m. The pit fill of dark brown gravelly loam, contained substantial quantities of burnt clay similar to the fill of an adjacent section of the A260 enclosure ditch and yielded five flint-tempered sherds, including Fig. 74, No. 222 tentatively dated *c.* 900–600 B.C. The similarities of fill within the pit and within part of the adjacent enclosure ditch, tentatively suggested that the infilling of the ditch and of the pit were contemporary events.

Other Period 2 features (Fig. 23)

A group of five pits located outside the A24 enclosure in Area A have been dated by finds evidence to Period 2. The pits (A124, A129, A130, A269 and A270) were located some 65 m. south of Enclosure A24 and may represent an entirely separate focus of domestic activity. There was one isolated pit, two clay-lined pits and two post-pits.

The isolated pit

Pit A124 was an isolated circular feature, 0.76 m. in diameter and 0.35 m. deep. Its fill of mid brown gravelly loam provided three flint-tempered sherds.

Storage pits

Pits A129 and A130 were located within 1 m. of each other, approximately 70 m. south of the A24 enclosure. Both pits were circular 0.50 and 0.30 m. in diameter respectively, cut to depths of 0.30 and 0.10 m. Both pits were filled with a stone-free chocolate-brown clay loam containing the remains of jars. Both had been damaged by soil stripping for the quarry. That from A129 was fragmentary (Fig. 75, No. 223) but that from A130 (Fig. 76, No. 224) substantially complete, suggesting that it may have been buried deliberately. The

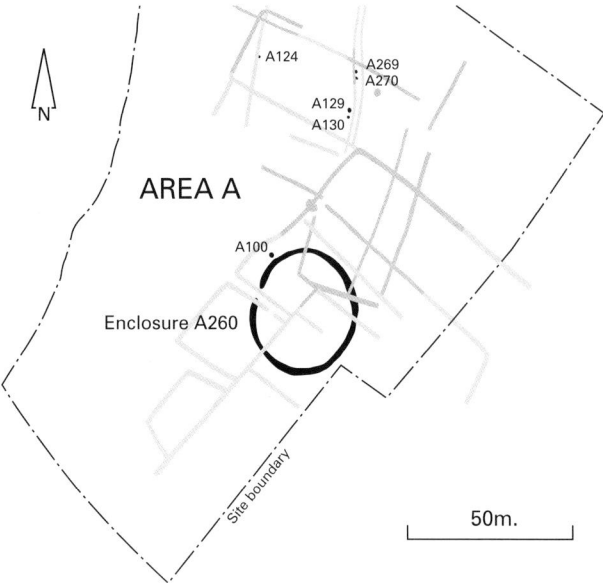

Fig. 23. Period 2. Enclosure A260, pits A100, A124, A270, A129 and A130.

presence of the possible storage pits may indicate an undetected domestic structure in this location.

Post-pits

Pits A269 and A270 were also located in close proximity to one another and some 10 m. north of the previously described pits.

Pit A269 was oval shaped of dimensions 0.80 by 0.40 m., cut to a depth of 0.73 m. The feature was filled with a single deposit of charcoal rich dark brown loam containing large burnt and unburnt flints forming a packing around the edge of the pit possibly to support a substantial post 0.30 m. in diameter. The pit fill provided three flint-tempered sherds of Period 2 date.

Pit A270 was D-shaped of dimension 0.90 m. by 0.48 m., cut to a depth of 0.70 m. The fill, also of charcoal rich dark brown loam, contained flint packing for a post approximately 0.30 m. in diameter. The pit yielded three flint-tempered sherds of Period 2 date. The existence of two flint-packed post-pits in close proximity to one another suggested the presence of a building.

Discussion

The earliest settlement activity at Highstead, dated to the period 900–600 B.C., was characterised by the building of enclosures. The earliest of the enclosures, B70, occupying the 30 m. contour at the north-east edge of the plateau, with deep ditches, palisade and gated entrance causeway, appears to have been constructed early in the period to fulfil a non domestic function. Although only the south-western extremity of the feature fell within the excavation, cropmark evidence provided the remaining elements of a rectangular ditched enclosure containing internally approximately 0.25 hectares. The lack of features immediately inside the enclosure ditch and the presence of substantial post-holes for palisade and causewayed entrance, clearly indicated the presence of a rampart some 5–7 m. wide. Allowing for the rampart mass, available space within the enclosure may have been no more than 1400 square metres and probably considerably less. Construction of the earthwork would have required considerable investment in time, labour and natural resources and is therefore more likely to have been built by a community for common use. Long distance views across the surrounding countryside would have been obtained from the rampart and conversely, set high in the contours, the earthwork would have been conspicuous for miles around. The enclosure entrance faced south towards an inlet of the Wantsum Channel which may have provided a sheltered landing place for those using the plateau.

The size and complexity of the earthwork sets the B70 enclosure apart from the adjacent enclosures of which two have been dated to Period 2 (A24 and A260) and at least two others fall just outside the period (B144 and A118). Although it has not been possible to create a more refined chronological sequence for enclosure building than pottery alone will allow, it is likely that some were in contemporary use and it is not impossible that others may exist nearby. Whereas the B70 enclosure may have been the product of a community, each enclosure may have been built by a family or extended family, representing an agricultural focus – a farm within perhaps a landscape of farmsteads.

Enclosure A24 may provide a model example with 'farmhouse' and yard surrounded by a modest ditch and bank arrangement, with bank perhaps surmounted by a close grown hedge. Access into the enclosure would have been through one of a number of gateways each closed by perhaps a simple hurdle. Two phases of activity were identified within Enclosure A24 with two possible structures, one perhaps replacing the first at the centre of the enclosure, together with fence lines, pits and some evidence for metalworking. There was in addition evidence of repair or strengthening of the eastern side of the enclosure and the blocking of at least one entrance.

Feature concentrations and postulated fence lines provided tantalising clues to the use of space within the enclosure. The eastern and western quarters of the enclosure were relatively free of features and it is tempting to postulate that both areas may have been open yards or paddocks with each area accessed by a pair of gateways. Whilst it may be assumed that the eastern quarter may have been used for domestic purposes, given the immediate proximity of the domestic hut, the eastern 'yard' may have performed a separate function, possibly for the penning of animals. This space may have been separated from the domestic building by a fence of regularly spaced posts. The southern end of the fence is likely to have been set against a presumed internal enclosure bank. The northern terminus however is more difficult to determine and there is no evidence to suggest that the fence line extended to intersect the opposite internal bank and form a secure space.

Although survival of animal (and human) bones and shell was exceptionally poor, the few bones that were recovered from the occasional Period 2 feature (only twenty-one bones, pp. 279–81) indicated the presence of ox, sheep and horse.

If viewed in a pastoral landscape, with farm enclosures built to keep domesticated animals in and perhaps wild animals out, Enclosure B70 takes on special significance. Located to provide advantageous views over the surrounding countryside (particularly the northern mouth of the Wantsum Channel) and to be visible from a distance, it is tempting to view the earthwork as perhaps a 'mini hillfort' and a focus of political power. Alternatively the earthwork may have been constructed as a place of refuge, to provide emergency protection during periods of crisis. If constructed for defence or strength it is difficult to reconcile the early possible rampart collapse and the general non clearance of ditches, particularly near the only entrance giving onto the enclosure; the most vulnerable part of a defensive earthwork. That occupation traces are present within the enclosure (and immediately outside it) suggests that it was used soon after construction and perhaps used on a regular and long term basis. A further alternative may be that the enclosure may have been formed specifically to be seen perhaps as a totem or emblem of the community occupying the plateau and its environs.

Whatever, the precise function of the B70 enclosure the size and complexity of its defences set it apart from nearby domestic-scale enclosures. Perhaps too small to offer long term protection for a community seeking refuge, it is far too elaborate for a farm compound. Most of the enclosure still remains available for study and a more definitive explanation of its function must await more detailed investigation.

Some of the most compelling evidence for metalworking in the period was recovered from features outside the entrance of the B70 enclosure. Although the hearths, some within the enclosure, may not have been used for metalworking processes, it is tempting to assume an association. The best evidence for metalworking (clay mould debris from the manufacture of bronze pins and perhaps other implements) was obtained from Pit B80 located outside the enclosure. The mould debris indicated that the objects produced were dress or cloak pins with straight shafts and simple flat disc heads (p. 263). The manufacture of other objects may also be represented, including spearheads. Casting debris was also recovered from a number of other features, including a layer of detritus thrown into the B70 ditch during this period of metalworking activity. Included among the finds from the ditch were a number of enigmatic perforated ceramic slab fragments. Similar fragments were also recovered from nearby features (Pits B79, B80, B74, B317 and Hearth B41). The perforated slabs are thought to be associated with metalworking but are of unknown function. Pit B80 additionally yielded a perforated stone, possibly a 'polisher' used perhaps in the finishing of cast bronze objects. The combined evidence clearly suggested that metalworking was being practised perhaps within and certainly outside the enclosure.

The distribution map of Late Bronze Age metalwork hoards and finds shows a strong bias towards waterways and creeks around the Wantsum seaway and along the north Kent coast (Champion 1980, figs 2–3). There is plentiful evidence for trans-Channel contact during the period, with a wide range of shared metalwork types between south-east England, north-western France and Belgium (O'Connor 1980, 225–9). Trade in scrap metal and finished products was commonplace at this time and it is therefore perhaps unsurprising that a settlement such as that at Highstead, located close to the mouth of the Wantsum sea channel, should provide evidence of metalworking and a casting method with continental affinities.

The pottery from Period 2 represents what is now regarded as a standard 'Post-Deverel-Rimbury' Decorated assemblage. It includes a wide range of forms from large jars, presumably used for storage, and cooking pots, to smaller bowls and cups. A particularly distinctive feature of the ceramic repertoire is the relatively large range of 'finewares', with thin walls and smooth, often burnished surfaces. This trait is not confined to the smaller cups and bowls, but is also in evidence in the larger jars which demonstrate instances of thin walls in hard flint-tempered fabric with slurried and burnished surfaces; suggesting that some of these were made for display as much as for use.

Almost all the pottery appears to have been of local manufacture, though no direct evidence of production was recovered. Clays were available close to the site and the full range of ceramics is likely to have been made nearby. Just one vessel, a small cup, might be regarded as an 'import', possibly from close to the Medway. While the pots might have been made locally however, the community was not isolated since shared traits reflect contact with other sites in the lower Thames valley and across the Channel in Northern France and, particularly, Belgium; supplementing the picture of widespread contacts obtained from the metalwork.

Period 3: 600–100 B.C.

Period 3 activity at Highstead has been tentatively subdivided into three phases: Period 3A (*c.* 600–500 B.C.), Period 3B (*c.* 500–400 B.C.) and Period 3C (*c.* 400–125/100 B.C.). Period 3C represents a period of abandonment.

Period 3A summary

During Period 3A a substantial enclosure (A118) was constructed in Area A. Only a small part of the enclosure was available for excavation as most of it had been destroyed by quarrying prior to the commencement of excavation; a further part lay beneath the entrance to the quarry. No other Period 3A features were located in Area A. In Area B continued occupation of the B70 enclosure was attested together with the construction of a new enclosure, B144 of which only a small part was available for excavation. Two isolated pits located to the west and south-west of the enclosure have also been dated to this period

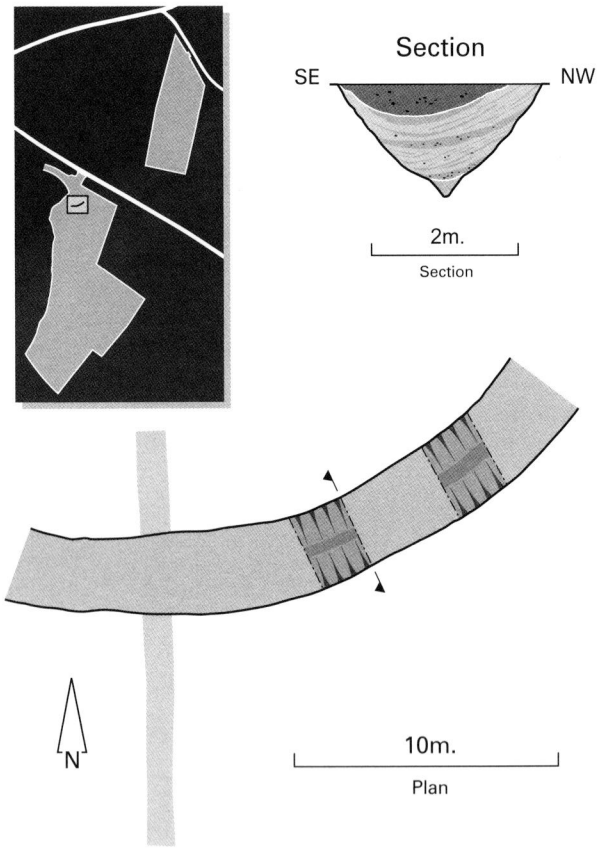

Fig. 24. Period 3A. Enclosure ditch A118 with location (*inset*).

Enclosure A118 (Fig. 24, plan and section)

The greater part of Enclosure A118 had been destroyed by quarrying prior to the commencement of excavations.

A curving 20 m. length of ditch representing the southern side of a substantial enclosure perhaps originally up to 50 m. in diameter, was mapped during a brief hiatus in quarrying activities. Two 2 m. wide sections were cut into the ditch fills. These revealed a broad open 'u' profile, 2.70–3 m. wide and 1.45–2 m. deep. The sump of the ditch with v-shaped profile was filled with fine sandy 'rapid' silt. Capping the primary deposit were bands and lenses of gravel and sandy gravel that probably accumulated as erosion products. Sealing these soils were tip lines of gravel, loam and sandy loam that may have been laid down in rapid succession from a slighted enclosure bank. Overlying the bulk deposit was a sequence of layers and lenses of sandy silt and gravel that probably accumulated over a considerable period. The uppermost ditch fill was a dark brown sandy loam, which may also have developed over an extended period. The dating of this enclosure is uncertain. The ditch fills yielded few finds, but seventeen flint-tempered sherds were recovered from the lowest fills (including Fig. 81, Nos 275–7). These are mainly Period 2 in character, but could fall within Period 3A. The enclosure's proximity to A24 might imply that the two are not contemporary. Hence its tentative allocation to Period 3A.

Enclosure B70 (Fig. 25)

Ditch fills (Fig. 17)

Capping ditch fills associated with Period 2 occupation (Layer 3) was a deposit of clean sand and gravel (Layer 4), taken to represent a bi-product of weathering of the ditch edges and perhaps the rampart. The deposits, on average 0.30 m. thick against the rampart, tapering to 0.10 m. against the leading edge of the ditch, may have gradually accumulated following decay and collapse of timberwork revetting the rampart face and causewayed entrance of the enclosure. The modest thickness of the layer suggested that a substantial unsupported bank was left standing for a protracted period, perhaps held in place by turf and vegetation. Layer 4 provided no datable finds.

Sealing Layer 4 was a deposit of dark brown, gravelly loam (Layer 5). The deposit up to 1 m. thick comprised multiple tip lines of loam and gravel representing perhaps both natural erosion and deliberate infill. Most of the pottery from this layer spans Levels 4 and 5 (Fig. 56). That from Level 4 (Figs 59–60, Nos 32–69) is attributable to Period 2, with some Period 3 forms, while that from Level 5 (Figs 61–62, Nos 70-91) contains Period 2 and 3 forms as well as Late Iron Age and Roman material. The final infilling may have been a gradual process and the back and ditch may have been visible in the landscape until late in the millennium.

Features within the enclosure (Fig. 25)

A group of four pits and a cluster of post-holes of Period 3A date were located within the B70 enclosure, at the northern corner of the excavated area.

Pits

Pit B71 was circular, 0.92 m. in diameter and 0.28 m. deep and lined with grey-green clay flecked with charcoal and burnt orange clay. The bulk fill, of mid brown loam with sparse gravel, provided twenty-five sherds of flint-tempered pottery including one base with abundant flints projecting beneath it, but these were not closely datable. The pit cut post-hole B72, associated with the possible structure attributed to Period 2 (Figs 18 and 19), and has been placed in Period 3A.

Pit B91 was adjacent to B71. This circular pit, 0.80 m. in diameter and 0.24 m. deep, contained a single fill of black-brown loam with charcoal flecking and sparse gravel. The fill provided three undiagnostic sherds of flint-tempered pottery.

Pit B46 was circular, 0.6 m. in diameter and 0.2 m. deep. The fill of mid brown gravel flecked with charcoal and orange-red burnt clay contained three undiagnostic sherds of flint-tempered pottery.

Pit B131, located to the north of the previous pits, was by far the largest of the group measuring 1.80 by 1.40 m. The oval-shaped pit, cut to a depth of 1.14 m. was filled with a laminated sequence of dark loam capped by dumps of clean gravel. The basal fills (Layers 7, 9 and 11) of banded layers of grey silted clay, burnt brown loam mixed with carbon and burnt clay, separated by lenses of clean gravel (Layers 8 and 10), contained forty-three flint-tempered sherds. Capping the early sequence was a dump of clean gravel (Layer 6) containing no finds. Sealing this were two deposits of dark brown loam, rich in carbon, burnt clay and pottery (Layers 3 and 5) separated by a lens of clean gravel (Layer 4). These layers of loam probably provided seventy sherds of flint-tempered pottery, including two sherds with rusticated surfaces. The pottery (including Fig. 85, Nos 305–16) has been tentatively dated to 600–500 B.C. Three fragments of perforated pottery slabs (p. 268) recovered from the pit fill were taken to be residual, a bi-product of perhaps metalworking activity in Period 2. The pit was capped by two dumps of discoloured gravel (Layers 1 and 2) containing burnt clay and sintred flint but with no datable finds. The nature of the laminated pit fills, with finds-rich occupation layers capped by clean gravel suggest that the feature may have functioned as a cess-pit.

Part 2: The Excavated Evidence

Highstead, near Chislet

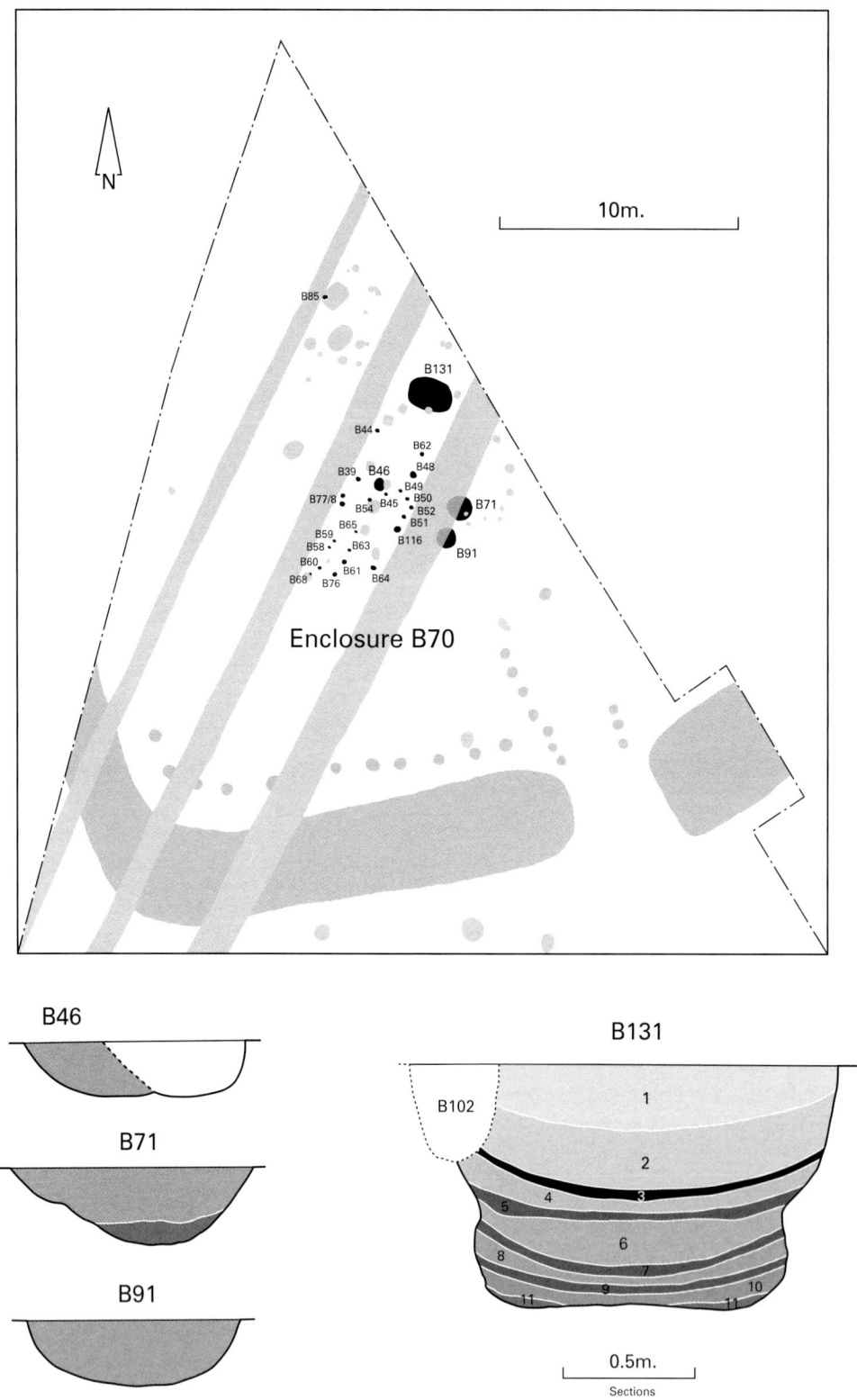

Fig. 25. Period 3A. Features within Enclosure B70.

Post-holes

A group of twenty-two post-holes was identified at the northern end of the excavated area, within the B70 enclosure. Many of the posts appeared to have been placed in rows of three or four, aligned roughly north-east to south-west (B68, B60, B58, B59; B77, B78, B39; B76, B61, B63, B65; B116, B51, B52; B49, B48, B62), the remainder (B44, B45, B50, B54, B64) appeared to have been unrelated. The post-holes were of fairly uniform size and depth, being on average 0.20–0.30 m. in diameter and 0.15–0.18 m. deep. Their fills were characterised by mid brown loam flecked with charcoal and orange-red burnt clay. They have been tentatively placed in Period 3A because two of the post-holes, B54 and B68 cut Period 2 hearths B53 and B69 (Fig. 19). Pottery of mainly Period 2 type, though not unexpected in Period 3A, was recovered from a number of the features. The fill of Post-hole B68 provided twelve sherds of flint-tempered pottery (including Fig. 85, Nos 317–18); Post-hole B76 provided twelve sherds; Post B61, three sherds. Single sherds were recovered from B49 (Fig. 86, No. 319), B50, B65, B78, B44, B54, B60, B77 and B116.

The post-holes did not appear to form a coherent pattern. Although possible alignments of up to four posts were discerned, each row about 2 m. long, the function of the post-rows remains enigmatic.

Enclosure B144 (Fig. 26)

A wide but shallow ditch (B144) located against the eastern edge of the excavation south of the B70 enclosure was interpreted as the western side of an enclosure. No further trace of the enclosure to the east was seen in air photographs. The ditch, traced against the excavation edge for 50 m. was interrupted by a possible entrance set close to a possible south-west corner for the enclosure. The ditch was for the greater part of its northerly length approximately 2.60 m. wide and 0.25–0.30 m. deep. The ditches flanking the entrance were of the same depth but were narrower, being only 1 m. to 1.20 m. wide. One possible interpretation for the variation in ditch width is that the feature was of two phases. The first phase boundary was formed with a narrow ditch and rounded terminals flanking a causeway 4 m. wide; the second phase involved a re-cutting of the northern part of the ditched circuit, but not the sections of ditch closest to the causeway, which remained unaffected by the refurbishment. The ditch fill was of medium-brown gravelly loam flecked with charcoal and orange-red fired clay. Quantities of fire-fractured flint were noted in the fill, which also yielded over eighty sherds of flint-tempered pottery dated to *c.* 600–500 B.C. (including Fig. 81, Nos 278–80), seven of which had rusticated surfaces. The field record lists vitrified pottery or copper dross from this context, but the material has been lost and the observation remains unconfirmed by analysis.

Isolated pits

Two pits located west and south-west of Enclosure B144 have been dated by pottery to Period 3A.

Pit B12 (Fig. 26, section) was 13.5 m. west of Enclosure B144 in an area heavily truncated by later features. The circular pit, 0.46 m. in diameter, with steep vertical sides 0.36 m. deep, was cut to receive a large storage vessel (Fig. 83, No. 296) which was recovered intact and *in situ* from shoulder to base (Fig. 26, section B12) with a sterile packing of mid brown gravelly loam. The fill of the storage jar, a carbon-rich dark brown sandy loam, may have yielded eighty-three sherds of flint-tempered pottery (including Fig. 82, Nos 281–95) dated 600–500 B.C., though there is some doubt about their association (*see* comments in the pottery report, p. 115). Without these additional sherds, which included rusticated forms, the storage jar would have been placed in Period 2. It is likely that the jar was deliberately placed in the pit which had been dug to contain it. It may have marked the location of a building for which no other trace was found.

Pit B244 (Fig. 26, section) was located in the south-west corner of the excavated area at some remove from Enclosure B144 and Pit B12. This subrectangular pit measuring 2.80 by 1.80 m., cut with steep sides to a depth of 0.70 m., was filled with laminated deposits of mid brown loam and gravel containing lenses of charcoal and burnt clay. The pit fill provided a collection of ninety-three flint-tempered sherds (including Fig. 84, Nos 297–303) dated *c.* 600–500 B.C. and a residual leaf-shaped arrowhead of Early to Mid Neolithic date (p. 254; Fig. 146, No. 33).

Discussion

Period 3A was the least certain of the prehistoric phases and was represented by one possible enclosure in Area A (A118) and a second in Area B (B144). Area B also produced occupation features within the B70 enclosure and a few pits with ceramic elements characteristic of both Period 2 and Period 3B.

The pottery from Period 3 sees new developments contrasting with that from Period 2. No sudden break in tradition is evident and elements of Period 2 forms and decoration continue alongside new forms for a while. This co-existence has been used to define Period 3A, though no independent dates are available to confirm this and it is not impossible that problems of residual and intrusive material may be blurring the picture.

Whilst Period 3A appears to continue a tradition established in Period 2, that of enclosure building, occupation in Period 3B was characterised by the establishment of 'open' settlement. The lack of more precise dating evidence means that the material presented as Period 3A sits uncomfortably between periods characterised by two very different forms

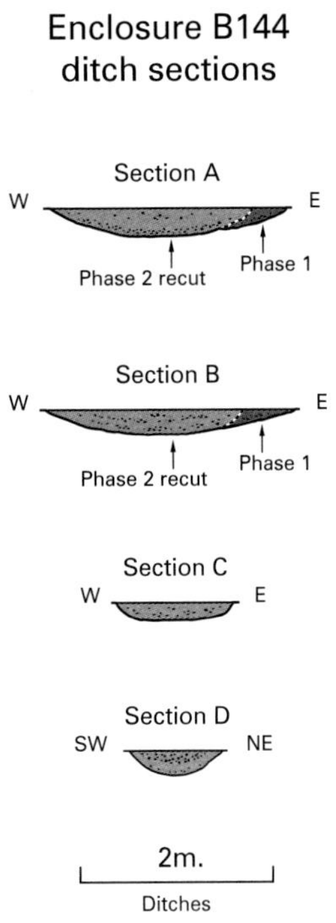

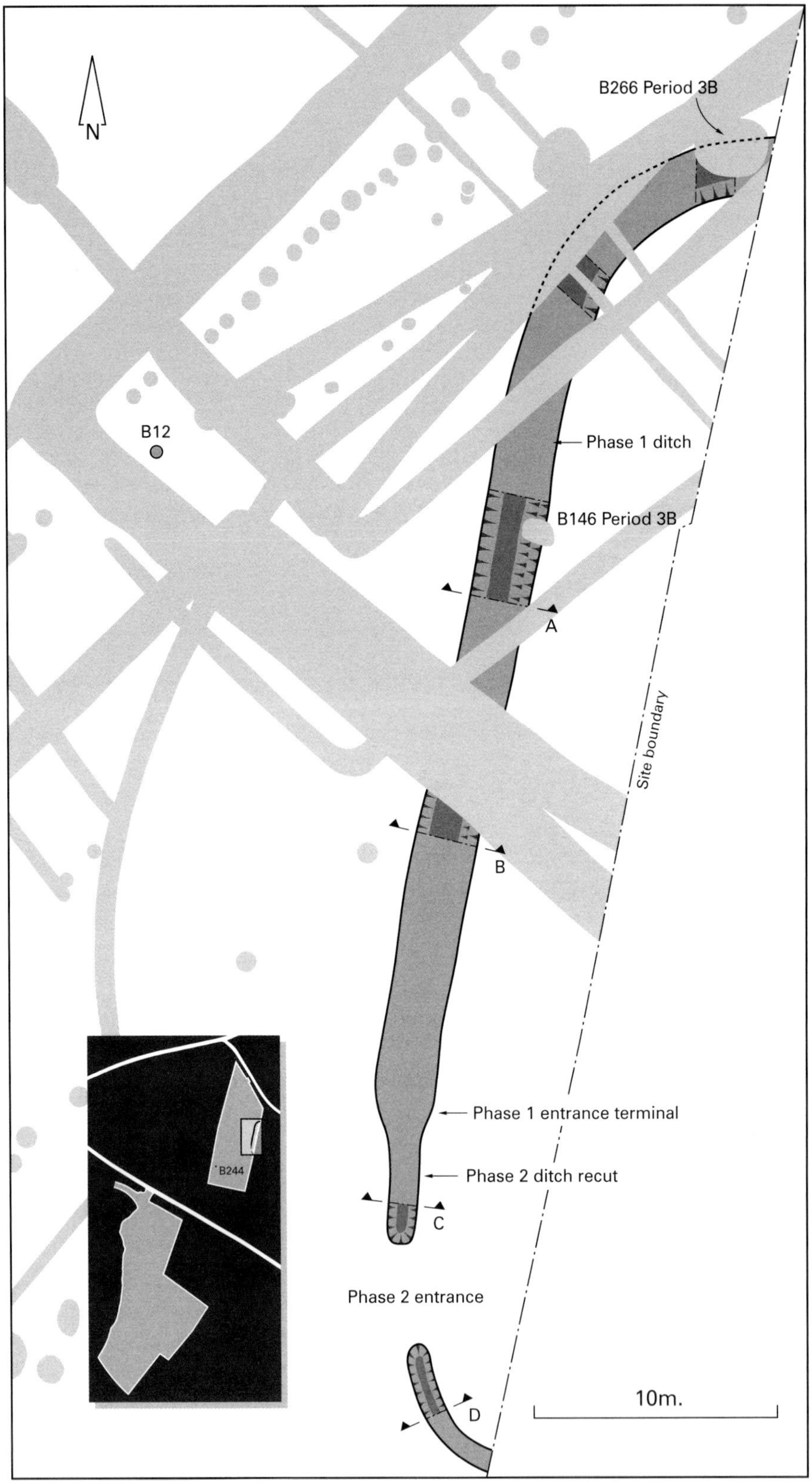

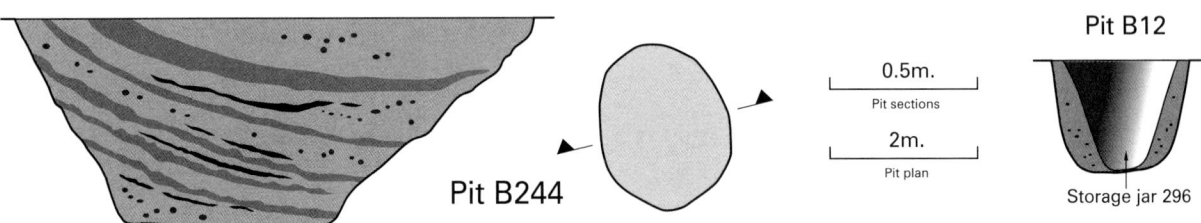

Fig. 26. Period 3A. Enclosure ditch B144, pits B244 and B12, with location (*inset*).

of settlement. In the absence of more precise dating it is suggested that Period 3A may perhaps be best regarded as the final phase of a long tradition of enclosure building that began in *c.* 900 B.C. and finally gives way to a new type of open settlement some time around *c.* 500 B.C.

Period 3B summary (Fig. 27)

Period 3B occupation was characterised by a move away from enclosures to the development of 'open' settlement. Only apparent in Area B, the period features included three building types; the footprints of five, possibly six, buildings defined by penannular gullies with entrance 'causeways' facing south or south-east; two circular buildings with earth-fast posts, three granary-type structures (two of four-post and one of five-post construction) and an enigmatic multi-post structure with south-east facing entrance. Outside the entrance were two possible cremation burials. Two small pits containing single pottery storage vessels and three isolated but substantial post-pits may indicate other buildings. Two undated rectangular structures of post-hole construction have also been included in Period 3B.

A substantial number of pits, hearths and fire-pits were identified. Amongst these were a number of clay-lined pits that may originally have been constructed for food storage. A small number of the pits and hearths provided evidence for industry, including pottery manufacture, salt working and metalworking in copper-alloy and iron. Other pits were of unknown function. The spatial grouping of the features provided some indication of the organisation of the settlement and suggested that not all the features and buildings were contemporary.

The pottery of the period includes many new forms and distinct finishes that are more closely paralleled in the Low Countries, particularly Belgium, than in other counties of southern England. The ceramic repertoire of Period 3B, dating to the period 500–400 B.C. is rarely found outside Kent.

Penannular house gullies

Five pennanular gullies, each interrupted by a south-east or south-south-east facing causeway, were located in the south-eastern quarter of the excavated area. The gullies probably mark the location of drainage gutters surrounding individual circular timber-framed domestic houses for which no structural posts were observed. The lack of structural posts associated with the circular gullies, taken together with the survival of post-holes for contemporary square and rectangular buildings nearby, suggested uniformity of construction for the houses, with structural components for each building located on the contemporary ground surface or in shallow post-holes which had not survived. Features associated with the buildings included a number of post-holes and small pits. A sixth penannular gully was identified as a cropmark a short way north-west of the group.

Building B16 (Fig. 28)

Penannular gully B16, located mid way along the west side of the excavated area, fell only partly within the excavation. The reconstructed diameter of the circuit was approximately 12 m., with a south-east facing causeway or entrance 1.50 m. wide. Unlike the other building footprints, the drainage gully did not describe a regular circle; a section of ditch east of the causeway was sharply angled and the north-east side was flattened and almost straight. Overall, the gully defining the footprint of Building B16 was subcircular. Only the northern part of the circuit was excavated, save for a fragment of surviving terminal defining the opposite side of the causeway. The profile of the gully was generally u-shaped, but in one location (section C) it had been cut to a 'v'. The depth also varied. At section A the gully was 0.50 m. wide and 0.23 m. deep; between sections B and C, it was 0.72 m. wide and 0.42 m. deep. The gully was filled with a mid brown gravelly loam, apart from section C where a deposit of sandy loam was in evidence. Twenty-nine flint-tempered sherds of pottery (including Fig. 87, Nos 331–3) of which one had a rusticated surface and all were dated to the period *c.* 500–400 B.C., were recovered from the fill. A single sherd of Dressel 20 amphora was taken to be intrusive, possibly from an intercutting Period 5A ditch (B23).

Features within Building B16

Two small pits were located within the footprint of building B16, both located north-west of the causeway.

Pit B31 was a subcircular, bowl-shaped feature measuring 0.74 m. in diameter and 0.19 m. in depth. The pit was lined with dirty yellow clay (Fig. 26, section B31, layer 3), and contained a fill of black-brown loam (layer 2) capped by a thin but dense and compact layer of burnt flint in a bedding of hard dark brown clay-loam. The pit, which provided no datable finds, may have served as a hearth base.

Pit B30, located adjacent to the house gully, was subcircular, 0.76 m. in diameter and 0.16 m. deep. The pit was filled with dark brown gravelly loam which provided no datable finds.

Building B26 (Fig. 28)

Gully B26 was roughly circular forming a footprint of maximum diameter 12–13 m. and a south-east facing entrance causeway 0.90 m. wide. Approximately one-third of the total diameter of the ditch was excavated. This was generally cut to a v-shaped profile 0.33–0.40 m. deep. Gully width varied from 0.70 m. at sections A and B to 0.50 m. wide at the

Fig. 27. Period 3B. Area B, features described in the text.

entrance (section C). The fill was of mid brown gravelly loam containing considerable quantities of burnt orange clay north of the causeway (section C). The fill provided a fragment of iron slag and six flint-tempered sherds (including Fig. 87, Nos 334–6) dating to the period *c.* 500–400 B.C.

Building B308 (Fig. 28)

Penannular gully B308 was badly truncated by later features, but has been reconstructed as having had a diameter of approximately 10 m. The gully described a circular footprint with a south-south-east facing entrance causeway 0.90 m. wide and was between 0.40–0.60 m. wide and 0.30–0.40 m. deep. Cut to a varying profile, it was filled with mid brown gravelly loam flecked with carbon and burnt orange clay which provided no datable finds.

Building B311 (Fig. 28)

Gully B311 was circular with a diameter of 16 m. and a south-south-east facing entrance causeway 1.80 m. wide. Describing the footprint of the largest of the five houses, it was on average 0.90 m. wide, was cut to a u-shaped profile 0.25 m. deep and either side of the causeway was 0.20 m. deep. The gully was generally filled with a mid brown sandy loam with sparse gravel, burnt flint, charcoal and fragments of burnt orange clay. The fill provided no datable finds and the interior of the building contained no features. A single post-pit (B190), possibly for an associated porch, was located against and outside the eastern terminal of the causeway. The post-pit 0.60 m. in diameter and 0.32 m. deep, was filled with black-brown loam and gravel which provided no datable finds.

Building B325 (Fig. 27)

Penannular gully B325 was salvage-excavated immediately in advance of gravel extraction. The building, 11.80 m. in diameter with a south-south-east facing causeway entrance approximately 0.90 m. wide, was defined by a gully 0.55 m. wide. The gully, cut to a v-shaped profile approximately 0.20 m. deep, was filled with mid brown gravelly loam flecked with charcoal and burnt clay and yielded six flint-tempered sherds (including Fig. 87, Nos 337–8) dated *c.* 500–400 B.C. There were no internal features.

Post-built structures

Perhaps of contemporary build with the penannular gullied buildings were two circular and four sub square buildings located in the northern and southern extremes of the excavated area. Of the northern group, one circular structure (B35) lay within the B70 enclosure. A possible granary building (B329) was located some way south of the enclosure and a second possible granary (B159) at greater remove to the south-east. The southern group of three structures comprised a circular building (B260), a possible granary (B196) and an enigmatic multi-post structure (B200). Isolated post-holes, post-pits and pot-pits in Area B suggested that other buildings may have been present, but left little trace. The buildings are described below by location from north to south.

Circular structure B35 (Fig. 30)

An arc of six post-pits (B40, B38, B75, B117, B36 and B35) found within the B70 enclosure, was tentatively taken to represent the northern half of the structural frame of a circular structure. The post-pits, 0.30–0.50 m. in diameter and on average 0.30 m. deep, appeared to describe part of a circle approximately 6 m. in diameter and may indicate a building in excess of 8 m. in diameter. The post-pits contained no trace of a post 'ghost', but the gravel and loam fills of three of the post-pits (B36, B38 and B117) provided thirty-eight sherds of flint-tempered pottery, one with a rusticated surface (Fig. 86, No. 320) tentatively dated to *c.* 500–400 B.C. The fill of Post-pit B40 additionally yielded a residual fragment of a perforated pottery slab (p. 268, Fig. 153, No. 51). An additional post-pit (B102) was recorded within the putative structure. This pit was of similar size and had a similar fill to those of the structural post-pits, but contained no datable finds.

Circular structure B260 (Fig. 31)

A large subcircular structure, probably a domestic house, defined by eleven post-pits was located in the south-west corner of Area B. The internal frame of the structure, approximately 5–6 m. in diameter, with longest axis north–south, comprised an oval ring of ten post-pits (B260, B260A, B264, B259, B258, B254, B251, B249, B134, B263). The post-pits, on average 0.30–0.50 m. in diameter and 0.15–0.30 m. deep, contained similar fills of compact dark brown gravelly loam flecked with charcoal and carbon. Traces of posts were not found in the fills of the pits. A centre post-pit was identified (B257), but there was no trace of an outer ring of posts or a ring-ditch, defining the outer wall of the house. A post-pit (B264A) was located outside and to the east of the frame posts. This was circular, 0.38 m. in diameter, cut 0.22 m. deep and filled with dark brown gravelly loam. A similar-sized post-pit (B252) was identified against the south-west side of the building. Neither post-pit contained datable finds, but it is tentatively suggested that they may mark the position of the outer frame wall of the house. One post-pit located against the west side of the frame (B263) may have been replaced during the life of the building. The replacement post-pit (B261) was of similar size and fill.

The post-pits provided little dating evidence. Five flint-tempered sherds were recovered from post-pits B251, B254

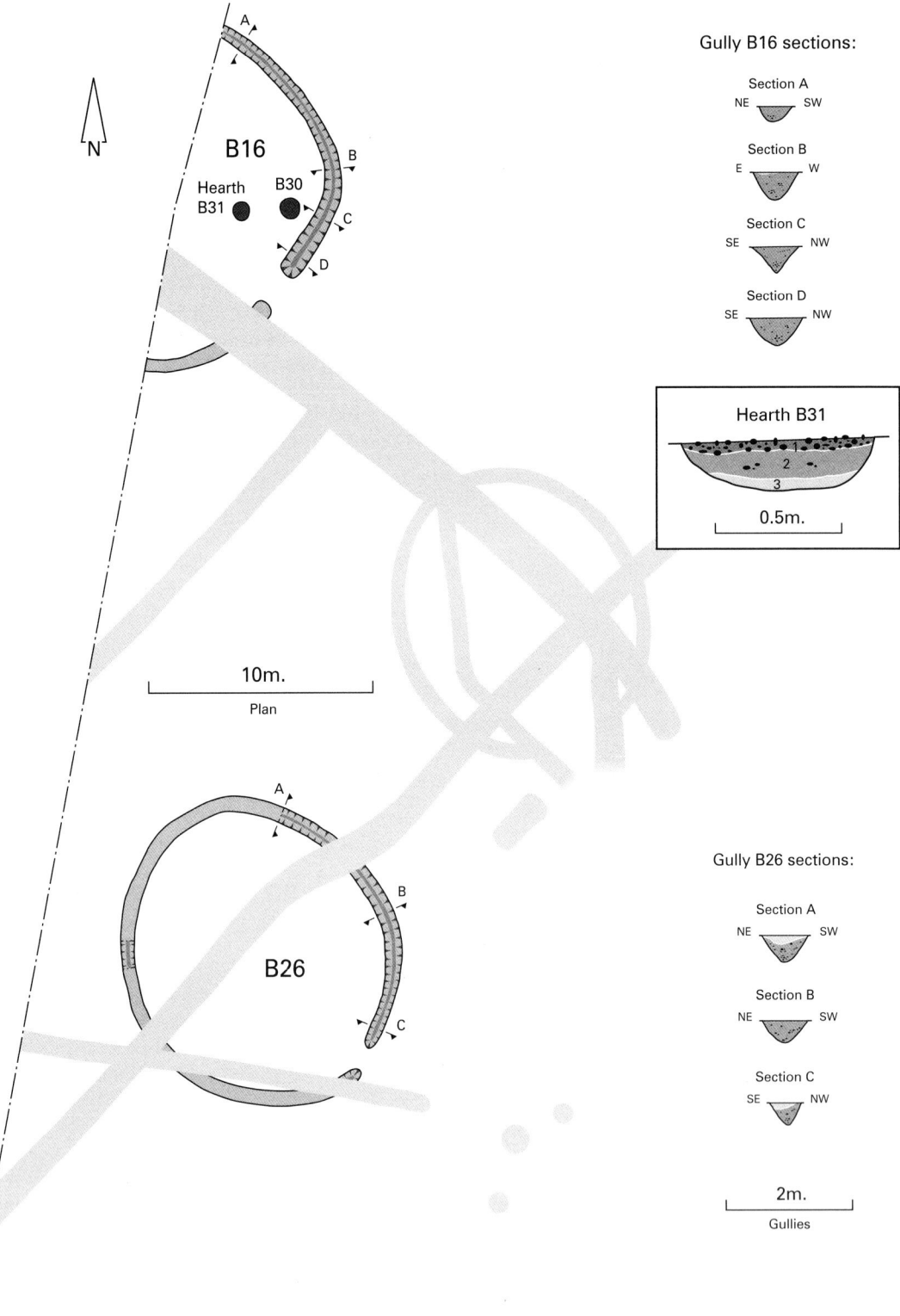

Fig. 28. Period 3B. Buildings B16 and B26.

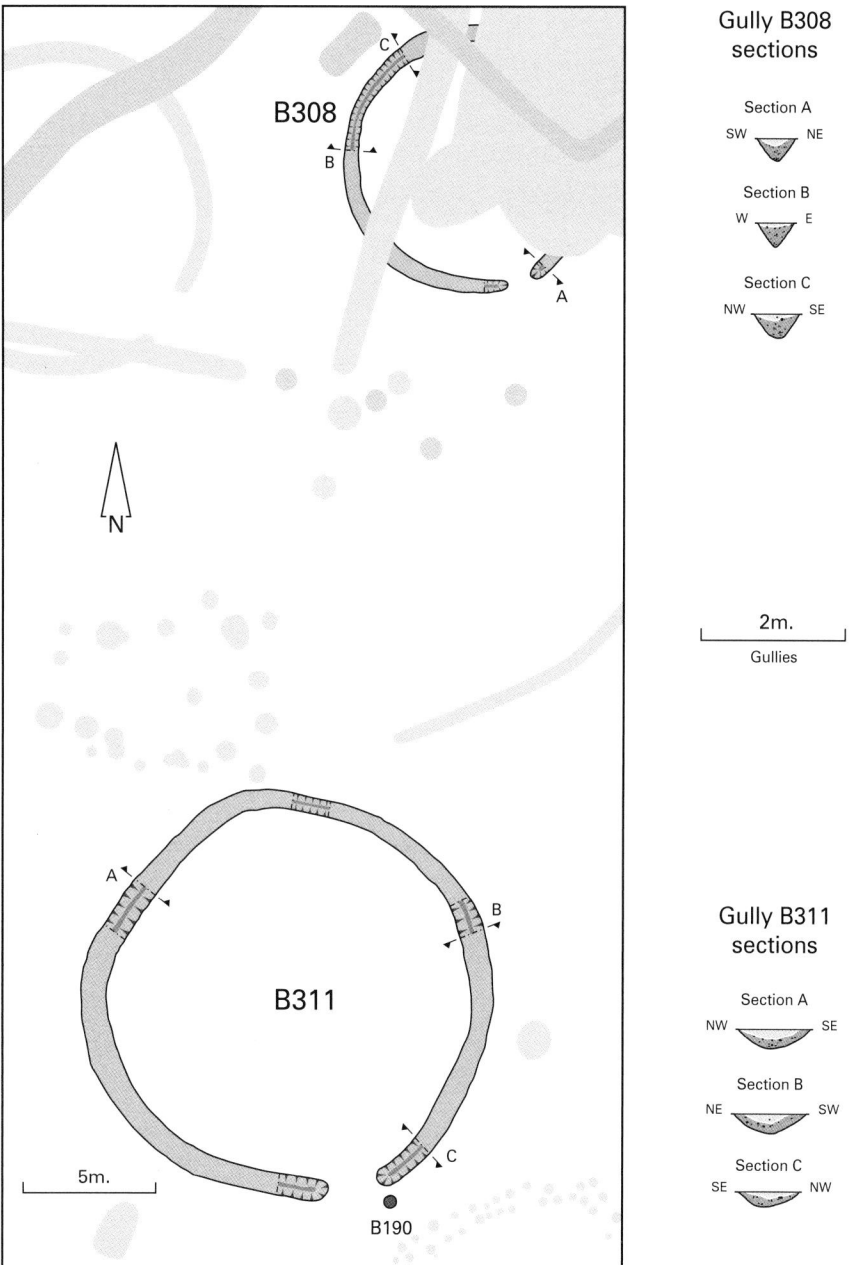

Fig. 29. Period 3B. Buildings B308 and B311.

and B257. Post-pit B264 provided eleven flint-tempered sherds, of which one was lightly rusticated, and a single, probably intrusive, grog-tempered sherd. The small group is not closely datable, but probably falls within the period c. 500–400 B.C.

A group of four features (B256, B255, B133 and B253) fell within or close to the footprint of the structure but appeared to pre-date the building. A large rectangular pit, B133 (p. 54, Fig. 36), also dated to Period 3B, located against the west side of the hut was cut by one of the frame posts of the building (B134). The remaining features are described below (pp. 59–61) and probably represent significant use of this area, within Period 3B, but before construction of B260.

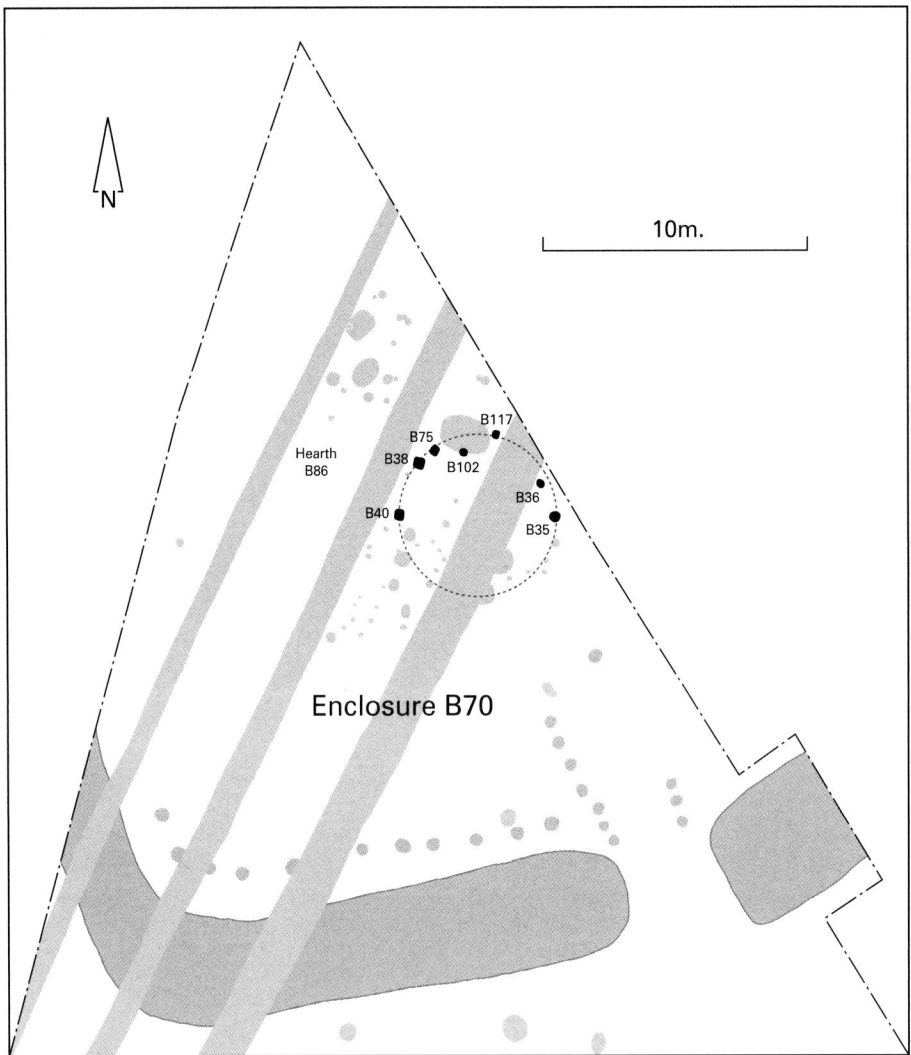

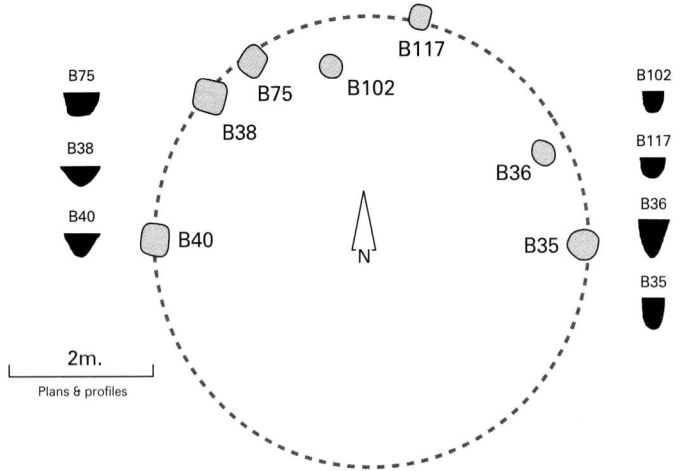

Fig. 30. Period 3B. Structure B35 within Enclosure B70.

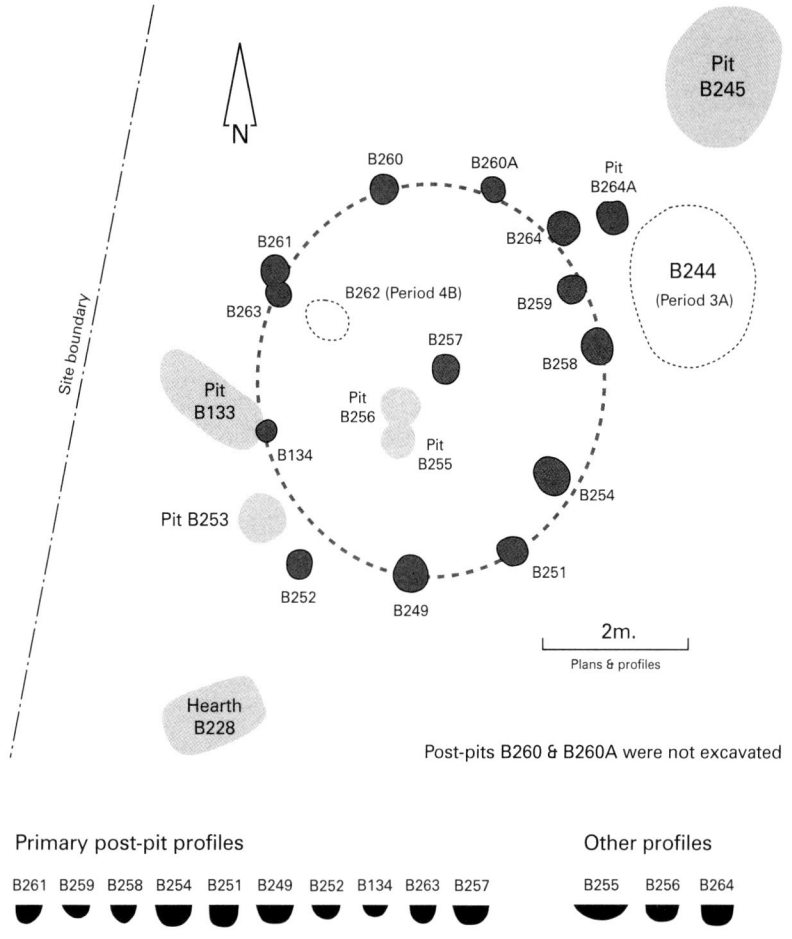

Fig. 31. Period 3B. Structure B260.

Structure B329 (Fig. 32)

A small rectangular structure defined by five earth-fast posts (B329, B333, B330, B331 and B332) was located 30 m. south of Enclosure B70. The building, possibly a small granary-type structure aligned long-axis north–south was of maximum dimensions 2.6 by 1.50 m. The constituent post-holes were of similar dimensions, being on average 0.30 m. in diameter, and 0.20 m. deep. The fill of all five post-holes was of mid brown gravel. There were no datable finds. Despite the lack of dating evidence the building appeared to be broadly contemporary with a substantial clay-lined pit (B271, below p. 59) located immediately to the north-west. The location, size and orientation of the building and pit suggest that their functions, possibly connected with grain storage, were closely related and that they were either contemporary or that one followed the other in quick succession.

Structure B159 (Fig. 32)

A second possible granary, defined by four posts (B159A–C and B185) was identified in the north-east corner of Area B in association with a scattered group of pits, some of which were clay-lined. The post-holes, forming a possible structure approximately 2 m. square, were all circular, being on average 0.48–0.56 m. in diameter and between 0.15 and 0.32 m. deep. Their fills were all similar, being of medium brown gravelly loam with flecks of burnt clay and charcoal. Only post-hole B185 yielded finds, these being three sherds of pottery, two with rusticated surfaces, dated to 500–400 B.C. The post-hole was cut through a hearth (B184), also of Period 3B date, suggesting that the building was constructed later in the period.

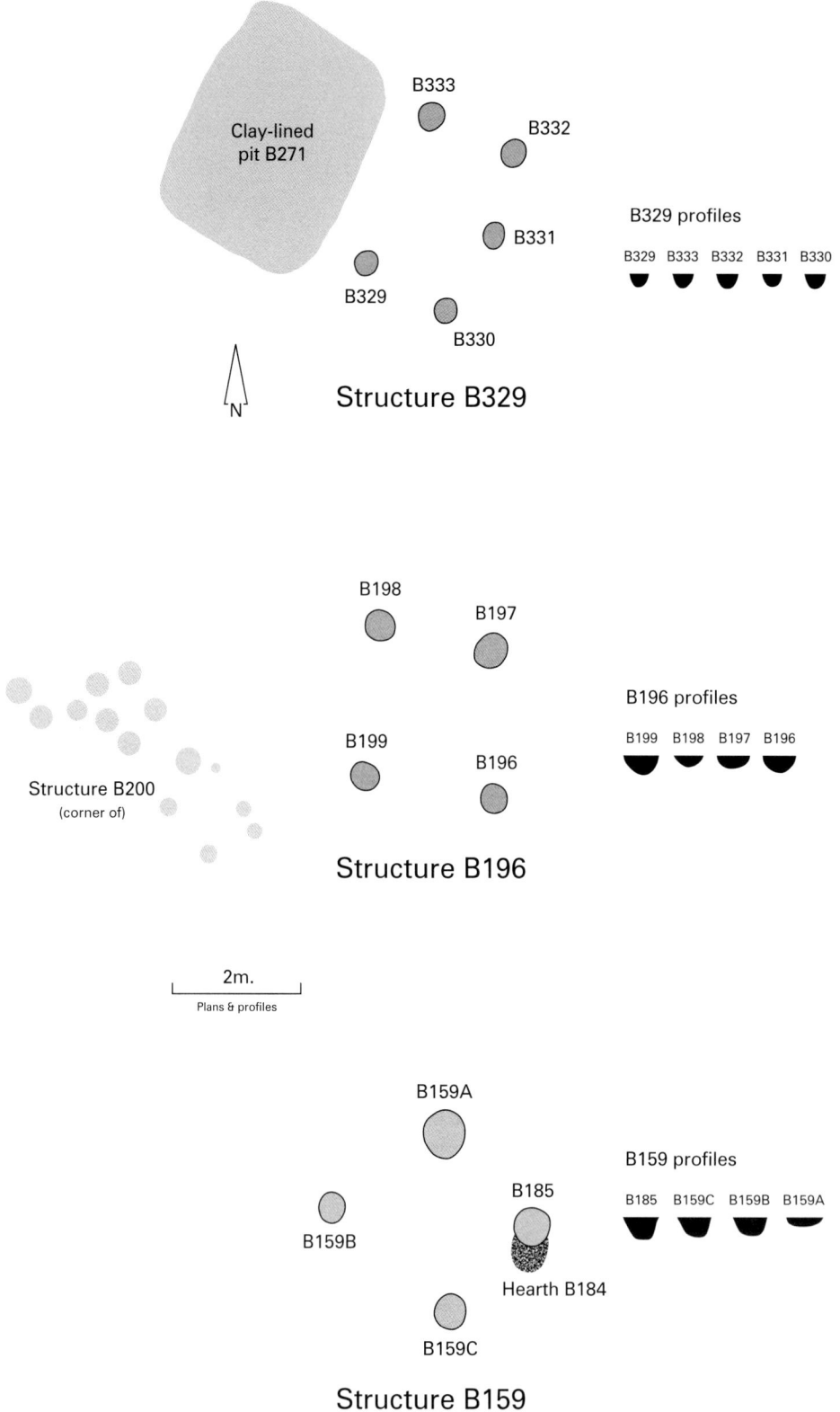

Fig. 32. Period 3B. Structures B329, B196 and B159.

Structure B196 (Fig. 32)

A third possible granary-type structure defined by four post-pits (B196, B197, B198 and B199) was tentatively identified within the southern group of buildings, 10 m. east of building B311. The square structure, of sides approximately 2.50 m. and aligned approximately north–south was provided with post-pits of similar diameter (0.50 m.) but variable depth (0.16–0.26m). The fill of all four pits was a mid brown gravelly loam flecked with charcoal and burnt clay. Post-pit B196 provided twenty flint-tempered pot sherds (including Fig. 89, Nos 368–71) and one (No. 371) joined a vessel located in a pit 28 m. to the south-west (B195). Post-pit B197 contained six flint-tempered sherds (including Fig. 89, No. 372). Pottery from both pits has been dated c. 500–400 B.C.

Structure B200 (Fig. 33)

Structure B200, comprised over ninety small post-holes, defining a possible rectangular building or enclosure aligned north-east to south-west, of maximum dimensions 9.70 by 7.70 m. A single 1.40 m. wide entrance pierced the centre of the south-east side of the structure, giving onto an interior measuring 7.35 by 5.60 m. The walls of the structure, formed by a double row of posts, set one inside the other, were between 0.70 m. and 1 m. thick. The post-hole fills were of remarkably similar mid brown gravelly loam. Overall the building was subrectangular, with rounded internal and external corners to the north-west and north-east. The opposite corners formed right angles. No single wall formed a perfectly straight line, but curved slightly, or 'bulged' as a consequence of misaligned posts. The south-east facing entrance was flanked on either side by rows of four posts, comprising the wall thickness with single posts projecting inside and beyond the threshold. A single post was set at the centre of the entrance, on line with the front face of the structure, perhaps located to restrict entry or to function as a 'stop' for a two leaf door. Wall construction, with closely-spaced double rows of posts 0.15 to 0.35 m. in diameter, set 0.10 to 0.25 m. deep, suggested that the structure may have been built with an internal and an external skin of wickerwork or hurdling. It is additionally possible that the cavity between the two skins may have been infilled with another material, perhaps clay or turf. This method of construction, taken together with a singular lack of indicative frame posts or post-pits, implies that the structure may not have been roofed, but perhaps served as a small ritual enclosure, perhaps a shrine.

Dating of the structure is based on its location, orientation and ceramic evidence (*see* p. 145). None of these is conclusive. It was located just under 3 m. outside the circular building B311, almost blocking its entrance (Fig. 27), implying that the two were not contemporary. Throughout Period 3B the circular huts, surrounded with eaves-drip gullies appear to be earlier than the buildings represented by post-holes with square and rectangular plans. The former are found on undisturbed ground, whereas post-holes for the latter are often dug into earlier pits, though still within Period 3B. Structure B200 cuts into Hearth B219 and surrounds pits B200A, B200B, B174, B175, B176, B226 and B227. Ceramic evidence suggests that Hearth B219 and the internal pits are all likely to date to Period 3B. Dating the structure itself is less certain. The pottery could fall within Period 3B or early in Period 4A, though the later sherds could be intrusive. The position of the structure B200 around the internal pits however, is unlikely to have been due to chance. It was either contemporary with them or respected their location after they had been filled.

The lack of purely grog-tempered pottery, or any 'Belgic' forms, which are plentiful in Period 4, can be taken as evidence that it preceded the second half of the first century B.C. Thus this structure is included in Period 3B, though a late Iron Age, Period 4A, date cannot be discounted altogether.

Features within Structure B200 (Fig. 34)

A number of pits and post-holes were located within structure B200, but they need not all have been contemporary. A hearth (B219) was found to have been cut by one post-hole forming the south-east jamb of the southern entrance.

Pits

Three groups of intercutting pits were found within the structure, with seven individual pits represented.

Pit B176 was the earliest of a group of three, located just within and to the north-west of the entrance to the structure. It was approximately 0.50 m. in diameter and 0.40 m. deep. The fill, of mid brown gravelly loam flecked with carbon and burnt clay, was cut by Pit B175 and contained no datable finds.

Pit B175 was cut through the fill of Pit B176 and was in turn cut by Pit B174. The feature, originally circular with a diameter of 0.40 m. and depth of 0.53 m. may have been cut to receive a post. It was filled with a homogeneous mid to dark brown gravelly loam which provided no datable finds.

Pit B174 was the latest of the three pits and cut Pit B175. The pit was oval-shaped, 0.70 m. in diameter and 0.34 m. deep and contained six layers of infill. The earliest deposits were of laminated grey clay and silt (Layers 6 and 5) capped by a band of clean gravel (Layer 4). Sealing the basal deposits were further lamina of pale brown loam (Layer 3), gravel (Layer 2) and brown loam and gravel (Layer 1). Two flint-tempered sherds (Fig. 88, Nos 348–9) tentatively dated to c. 500–400 B.C. were recovered from Layers 5 and 6.

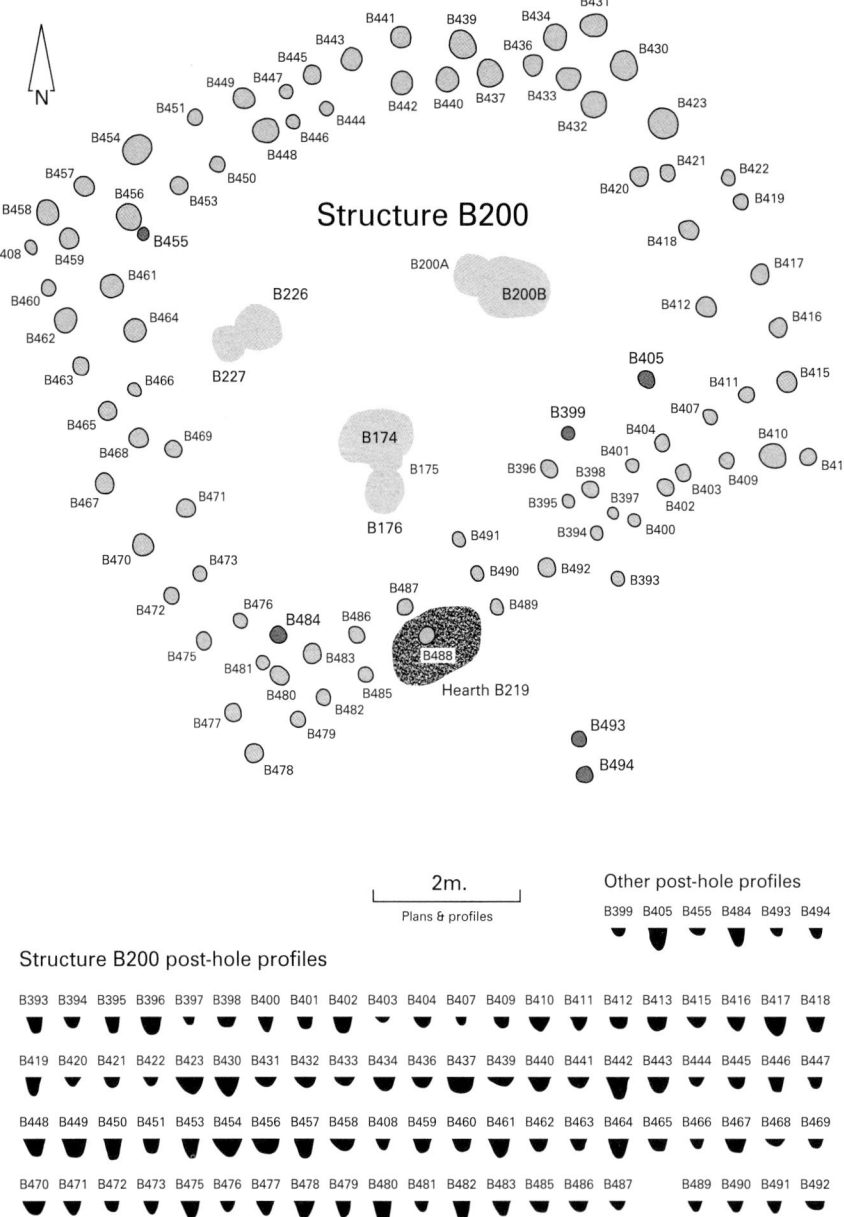

Fig. 33. Period 3B. Structure B200.

Pit B200B, a large oval pit located to the north-east of the enclosure entrance, was 1 m. by 0.8 m. in extent, cut to a depth of 0.35 m. The west end of the pit was truncated by a later post-pit (B200A). The post-pit was 0.55 m. in diameter and 0.40 m. deep. The pit and later post-pit fills of mid brown gravelly loam were excavated as a single context. The fills provided a fragment of iron slag and twenty-nine flint-tempered sherds (including Fig. 88, Nos 350–55) dated c. 500–400 B.C., of which nine were rusticated.

Pit B227 was the earlier of two pits located close to the north-west corner of the enclosure. The pit was bowl-shaped with a diameter of 0.50 m. and had been cut to a depth of 0.23 m. The fill of mid brown gravelly loam flecked with charcoal and daub, provided no datable finds.

Pit B226 was cut through the fill of Pit B227. Pit B226 was circular, 0.67 m. in diameter, and 0.35 m. deep. Its fill of dark brown gravelly loam mixed with burnt clay provided eleven flint-tempered sherds of which two were rusticated (Fig. 88, No. 360–61) tentatively dated c. 500–400 B.C.

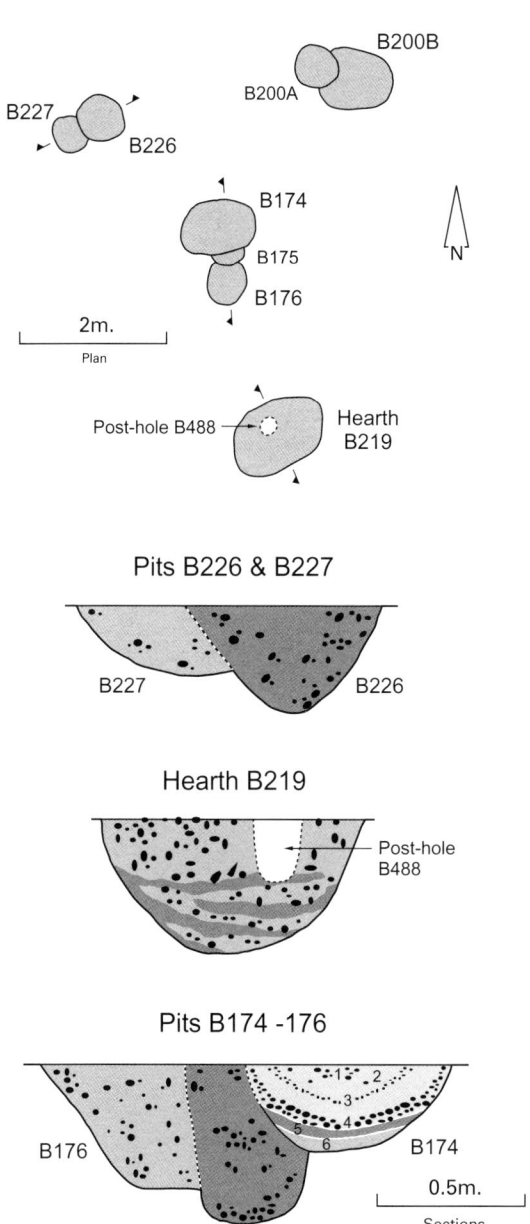

Fig. 34. Period 3B. Structure B200, internal features.

Post-holes

In addition to the two possible post-pits located within Structure B200 (B175 and B200A), four small post-holes (B484, B455, B405 and B399) were identified; one in the south-west corner of the structure, a second in the north-west corner and two set a short distance from the south wall in the south-east corner. The pits, on average 0.20 m. in diameter, cut between 0.10 and 0.25 m. deep, were located in those positions for an unknown purpose, but may have supported fittings. The fills of mid brown gravelly loam provided no finds. Two similar sized post-holes (B494 and B493), located approximately 2 m. south-east of the entrance may also have related to use of the structure.

Possible cremation burials (location: Fig. 27)

Two possible cremation burials (B166 and B173), set 3 m. apart, were located 7 m. south-east of the entrance to Structure B200. The features, set parallel to the wall of the structure may have flanked a possible approach to the entrance, their presence perhaps suggesting that Structure B200 may have been constructed for ritual use. There was, however, insufficient bone recovered from either feature to confirm interpretation as human cremation burials.

Pit B166 was oval and measured 0.37 by 0.32 m., cut with a rounded base and near vertical sides to a depth of 0.12 m. The pit had been truncated and little survived of the original fill of charcoal, grey ash and fragments of burnt bone. Insufficient survived to confirm that the bone fragments were human. The fill provided three non-joining fragments of perhaps one pottery vessel tentatively dated *c.* 500–400 B.C., of which the largest sherd has been illustrated (Fig. 91, No. 384).

Pit B173 was circular, 0.28 m. in diameter and cut to a depth of 0.12 m., with the base and near vertical sides lined with a primary deposit of dirty yellow-brown clay. The fill of the pit was entirely of charcoal and ash flecked with burnt bone. There was no accompanying vessel and insufficient fragments to prove that the burnt bone was human.

Isolated post-pits (location: Fig. 27)

Six isolated post-pits recorded in the southern half of the site may provide additional evidence for small buildings, structures or perhaps free-standing posts within the settlement.

Post-pit B202 was located south-west of Building B311 on the edge of a cluster of pits of which some contained industrial waste. The post-pit, 0.80 m. in diameter and 0.38 m. deep was filled with dark brown gravelly loam and provided no datable finds.

Post-pit B194 was found approximately 5 m. south of the entrance to Building B311. The pit, 0.90 m. in diameter and 0.28 m. deep, was filled with dark brown charcoal flecked gravelly loam. There were no datable finds.

Post-pit B178 was located 8 m. south-west of Building B308. The pit, 0.80 m. in diameter and 0.32 m. deep contained a fill of pale brown gravelly loam which yielded a ceramic spindlewhorl (p. 276) and seven sherds of pottery, five with rusticated surfaces, dated to the period *c.* 500–400 B.C.

Post-pit B218 was located 3 m. south of Building B308 close to Post-pit B178 and Hearth B180. The post-pit 0.60

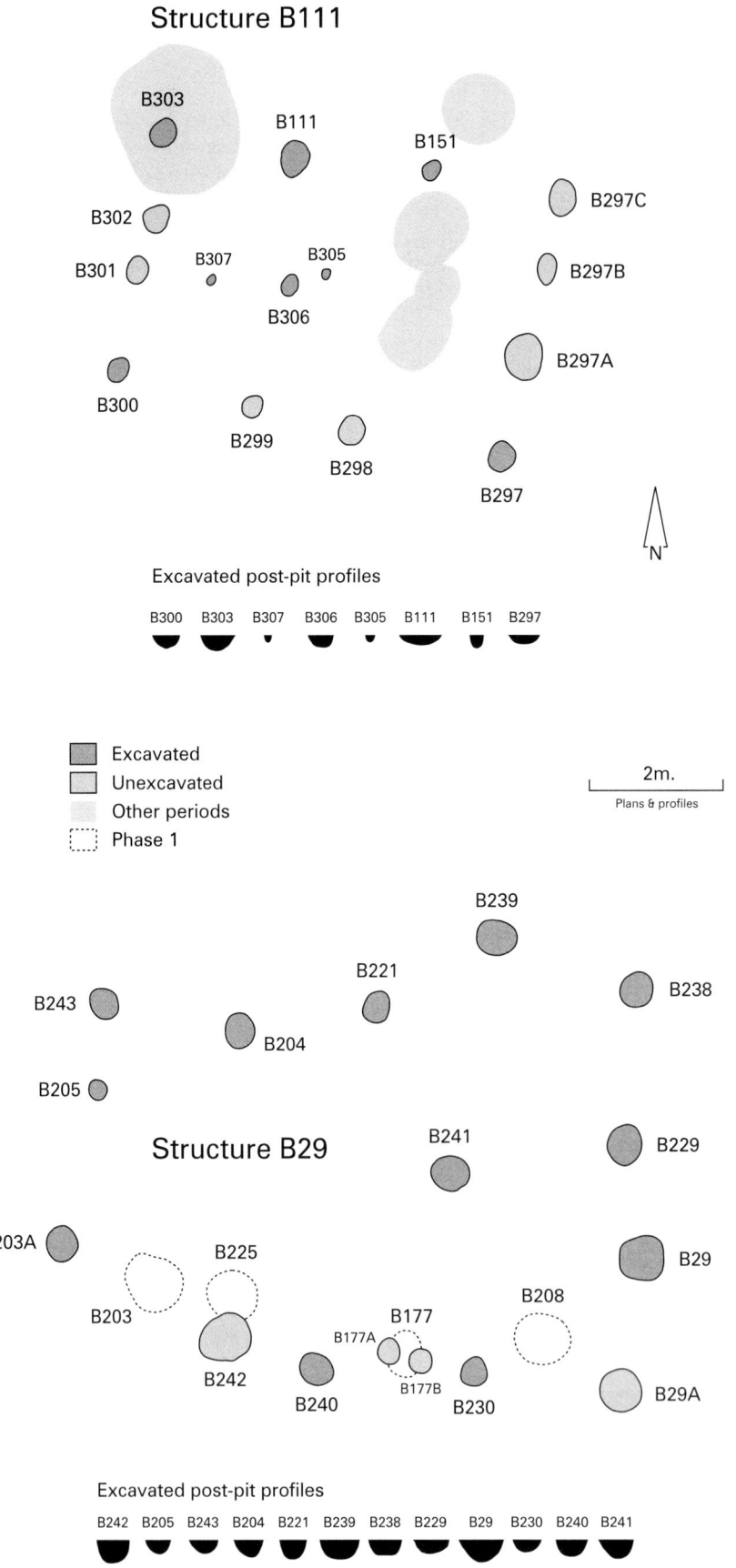

Fig. 35. Period 3B. Structures B111 and B29, plan and post-hole profiles.

m. in diameter and 0.30 m. deep contained a fill of pale brown gravelly loam, flecked with carbon and burnt clay which yielded ten flint-tempered sherds (including Fig. 96, No. 450) tentatively dated *c*. 500–400 B.C.

Post-pit B171 was an isolated feature located in the south-east corner of Area B. The post-pit 0.80 m. in diameter and 0.32 m. deep was filled with dark brown gravelly loam containing no datable finds.

Post-pit B127 was located to the north-east of Building B16, found cutting the northern corner of a Period 3B pit (B126). The post-pit was 0.60 m. in diameter, cut to a depth of 0.40 m. with near vertical sides. The fill of dark brown gravelly loam, contained no evidence for a post-pipe and no datable finds.

Undated rectangular buildings

Two buildings formed of earthfast posts remain to be discussed. Although both structures were of multi-post construction, no datable finds were recovered from any of the associated post-holes. Period 3 features were cut by post-holes associated with both buildings and at the earliest both structures must date late in the Period 3B sequence. It is not impossible that both structures may date into Period 4 or even Period 5, although given the quantities of pottery and other finds associated with later period features, it would seem unlikely that so many post-holes and post-pits would be void of finds had the buildings been constructed in periods 4 or 5. The undated rectangular buildings have therefore been tentatively assigned to Period 3B not on dating evidence but on the basis that other earthfast post buildings characterised the period, that pottery is not as frequent in Period 3 as in later periods and that feature fills for both buildings were broadly more consistent with Period 3 features than of later periods.

Rectangular structure B111 (Fig. 35)

A rectangular timber-framed building formed with at least twelve earthfast posts was located south-west of the B70 enclosure. The building set with long axis east–west, was approximately 6 m. long and 4 m. wide. The main frame post-pits (west: B300, B301, B302, B303; east: B297, B297A, B297B, B297C; north: B111, B151; south: B299, B298) were on average 0.40–0.50 m. in diameter and less than 0.20 m. deep. Post-pits south and north were set on average 2 m. apart, whilst those to the east were more closely spaced at 1.30 m. The west gable end was formed with two closely set posts at the centre of the side with equal gaps from the central posts to the corners. Overall, there appeared to be regularity and consistency in the spacing of posts, sufficient to suggest a stout, perhaps box-framed building with ridge running east–west. A south-facing door was tentatively suggested by a slightly wider gap between posts in the south-east corner of the building. Three additional posts were identified within the building (B306, B305 and B307). Post B306 may have been located as a subsidiary support for the ridge or to support a major partition within the building. The post was 0.36 m. in diameter and 0.17 m. deep. The remaining features, probably post-holes of unknown function, were 0.15 m. in diameter and 0.10 m. deep. All post-pit and post-hole fills were of mid brown gravelly loam with varying amounts of carbon and burnt clay flecking. No datable finds were retrieved from the features.

Rectangular structure B29 (Fig. 35)

A concentration of post-holes and post-pits located immediately north-west of Building B311 appeared to represent a substantial rectangular timber building aligned long axis north–south of minimum dimensions 9 by 4 m. Although a reasonable pattern of pits and posts survived to indicate south (B203A, B242, B240, B177A, B177B, B230 and B29A), west (B205 and B243) and east walls (B29 and B229). The north side of the putative structure (B204, B221, B239 and B238) was poorly defined and overall a convincing plan was not determined. The number of misaligned posts and post-pits, suggested that the structure may have been of more than one phase and that not all of the structural components of this building or buildings had survived. A single post was recorded within the structure (B241). The sizes, depths and fills of the post-holes and post–pits varied considerably, also perhaps suggesting more than one build. No single post provided any datable finds, although the dark brown gravelly loam fills of the features appeared to be more consistent with Period 3 features than features of a later date. Two Period 3B pits (B225 and B177) were cut by post-pits for Structure B29 and two further pits (B203 and B208) were located within the footprint of the structure, all beneath the southern wall line. A single hearth (B207) of Period 3B date was located under the northern wall line of the building. If Structure B29 is of Period 3B date then it must have been constructed late in the period.

Pits and hearths

Finds recovered from over fifty pits and hearths located across Area B shed particular light on the nature of settlement in the period. Some of the pits with remnants of a clay lining may have been used for food storage. A small number of both pits and hearths may have been connected with industrial activities including metalworking, pottery production and perhaps the refining, storage or transport of salt. Period 3B features recorded during the excavation of Area B have been grouped below, where possible, by functional category.

Pits with *in situ* storage jars (Fig. 36)

Two small clay-lined pits (B314 and B154), each containing substantial parts of a single, jar, may have originally been used for the storage of domestic foodstuff. The location of both pits at the northern end of the excavated area, in ground relatively free of contemporary features, may additionally suggest the presence of domestic buildings that had otherwise left no trace.

Pit B314 was located close to the main west section of the northern end of the excavated area, south-west of granary building B329. The feature was subcircular, 1.10–1.20 m. in diameter, cut with near vertical sides to a depth of 0.40 m. The pit base and sides were lined with a dirty yellow clay (Layer 2), capped by dark loam and gravel (Layer 1). The pit contained twenty-nine sherds of a jar (Fig. 90, No. 379), the base and sides of which remained *in situ* at one end of the pit. The fill additionally contained six sherds including the rim and shoulder of a smaller jar (Fig. 90, No. 378). These are tentatively dated to *c.* 500–400 B.C.

Pit B154 was located at the centre of the north end of the excavated area south-east of granary building B329. The pit, 0.31 m. in diameter and barely 0.10 m. deep had been badly truncated during topsoil clearance and before that by agricultural activities. Filling the base of the pit were 165 sherds of an inverted jar (Fig. 91, No. 383) whose base had been destroyed before excavation. In addition, there was a single rusticated sherd, evidently from a separate vessel. These pots are tentatively dated to *c.* 500–400 B.C.

Pit with evidence of salt production (Fig. 36, plan and section)

A large subrectangular pit (B215), located at the southern margin of the excavated area, 3 m. south-west of Gully B311, provided evidence of possible salt production (*see* pp. 268–9). The pit, measuring 2.50 m. by 1.60 m., aligned long axis north-north-east to south-south-west, was cut with rounded sides and bowl-shaped base, to a depth of 0.38 m. Traces of a dirty yellow clay lining (Layer 4) found adhering to the sides of the pit indicated that the feature may have originally been dug for food storage. The lowest fills capping the base of the pit were of pale brown sandy loam flecked with traces of carbon and burnt clay (Layer 3), overlain by successive lenses of brown loam, the uppermost containing burnt flint, lumps of fired orange clay and two lumps of ironworking slag (Layer 2), suggesting that other forms of industrial activity were taking place in the area. The capping fill (Layer 1) of charcoal and ash-rich dark brown loam contained a foundation of burnt flint and fired clay, which was interpreted as a hearth. The constituents of the foundation included large quantities of hard-fired, oranged-red ceramic material likely to be the remains of one or more evaporating pans (Fig. 90, No. 375). An off-white deposit found adhering to the internal surface of a number of sherds has been identified by analysis as a residue of salt production (p. 269). Only the lowest part of the hearth survived, but it is thought that the burnt flint and re-used brine pan fragments may have been used to support either end of an evaporation dish during the boiling process. As it is unlikely that salt water would have been transported to the settlement from the sea, the processing taking place was perhaps one of refining salt saturated mud or sun-dried briquettes. The hearth (Layer 1) provided 253 flint-tempered sherds, mostly fragments of one or more evaporating dishes, and the jar Fig. 90, No. 373. Beneath this were recovered six sherds, one with light rustication. From the fill in general were recovered the vessels illustrated as Fig. 90, Nos 374, 376–7. The ceramic evidence supports a Period 3B date. It is interesting to note that a pit containing evidence for pottery production (B133) also contained sherds from a salt evaporation pan (Fig. 90, No. 382) suggesting that the two pits may have been filled and used at broadly the same time. Both pits also contained metalworking waste.

Pits and hearths containing metalworking debris (Fig. 36)

In addition to the discovery of metalworking debris from the fill of two pits (B133 and B215), four other features were found to contain iron and copper-working slag (B147, B195, B214 and B155). The combined evidence recovered from widely separated contexts clearly indicated that metalworking was taking place on the site in this period.

Pit B147 was located at the southern end of the excavated area, 2 m. east of Building B311 and 5 m. north of Structure B200. The pit measured 1.50 by 1.20 m. and had sloping sides and a rounded base to a depth of 0.36 m. The pit contained the remnants of dirty yellow sandy clay lining (Layer 3), flecked with carbon and burnt clay, perhaps indicating that it may have originally served for storage. The bulk fill of the pit (Layer 2) was of dark, reddish-brown loam containing fire-fractured and burnt flint. The uppermost fill (Layer 1), was of dark brown loam and unburnt gravel from which a near complete bowl was recovered (Fig. 95, No. 423). Layer 2 provided eleven sherds of flint-tempered pottery, one of which was rusticated, together with a fragment of vitrified pottery or copper dross and flecks of copper alloy recorded in the loam fill. The pottery has been dated to *c.* 500–400 B.C.

Pit B195 was a large rectangular feature located at the southern limit of excavation, south of Building B311 and south-west of Structure B200. The pit measured 2.80 by 1.50 m. and had been cut to a depth of 0.42 m. The flat base was lined with dirty yellow clay (Layer 4) perhaps indicating previous use as a storage pit. The lower fills (Layers 3 and 2) were of mid brown and dark brown loam mixed with gravel. The capping fill (Layer 1) was of reddish-brown

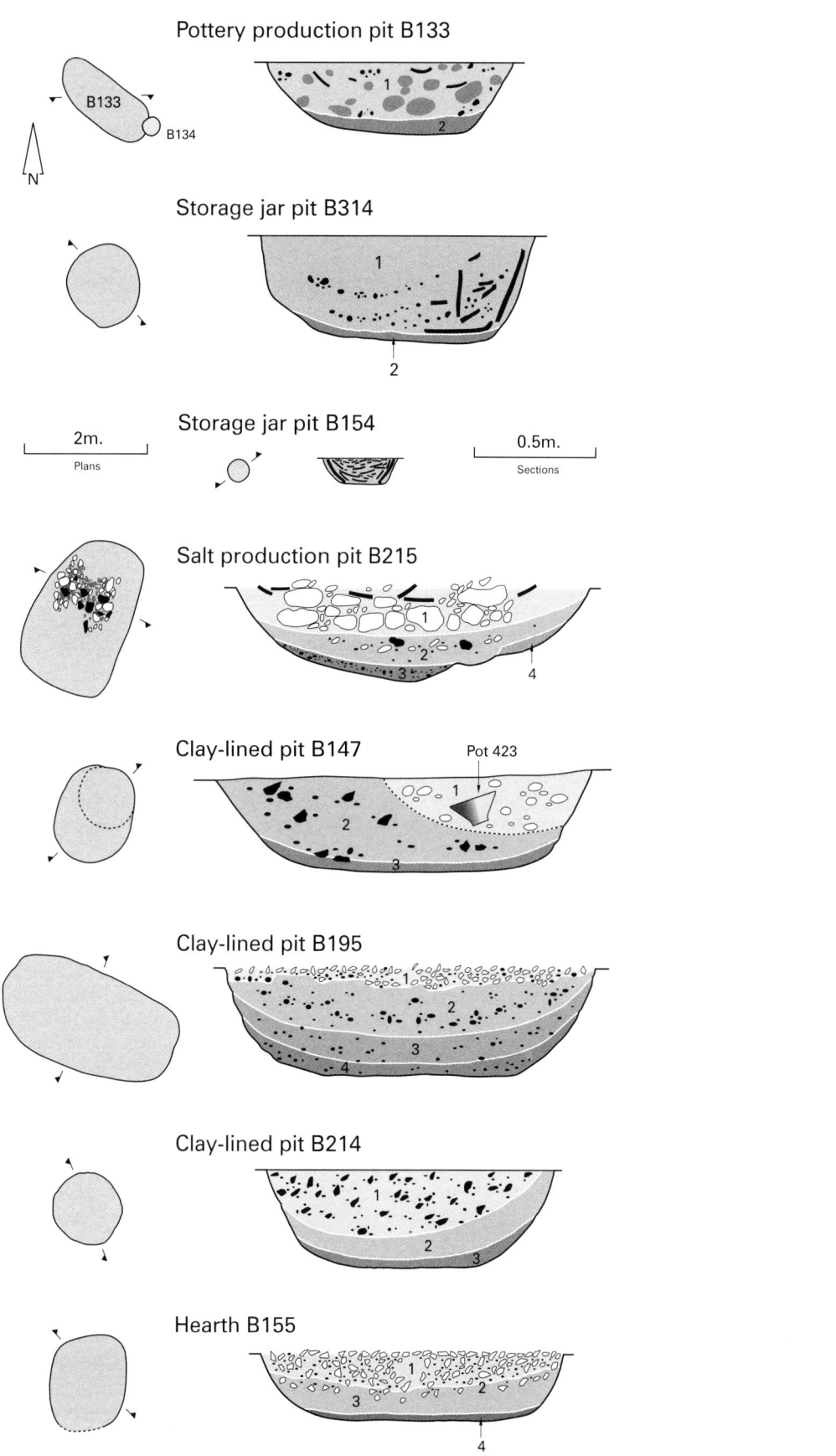

Fig. 36. Period 3B. Pits and hearths.

burnt loam and burnt and fire-fractured flint. The lower fills (Layers 2 and 3) yielded thirty-three flint-tempered sherds (including Fig. 95, Nos 425–7), one of which joined a sherd (Fig. 89, No. 371) from Post-pit B196 (the south-east post of a possible granary-type structure), located 28 m. to the east. The pottery has been dated c. 500–400 B.C. Other finds recovered from the fill were a flint hammerstone (Fig. 147, No. 48, p. 252) and fragments of iron slag. A single sherd of intrusive pre-Flavian samian ware was reported to have been recovered from the feature (p. 244).

Pit B214 lay within a small group of features, set in relatively open ground 14 m. west of the entrance to the Period 3A Enclosure B144. The pit was subsquare, measuring 1.20 by 1.10 m. and cut with sloping sides and a rounded base to a depth of 0.38 m. The base of the pit contained a deposit of pale brown clay-loam (Layer 3), possibly a remnant lining, capped by successive layers of pale brown loam flecked with carbon (Layer 2) and dark brown gravelly loam with charcoal (Layer 1). Both latter deposits provided burnt and fire-fractured flint, together with eighty-one flint-tempered sherds of which sixteen were rusticated (including Fig. 95, Nos 428–30) dating to c. 500–400 B.C. and a crucible fragment (Fig. 150, No. 44, p. 266).

Hearth B155 was located in open ground north-west of Enclosure B144, in the northern third of the excavated area. The pit was subrectangular, measuring 1.50 by 1.20 m., cut with bowl-shaped sides and flat base to a depth of 0.26 m. The pit sump was sealed by a thin deposit of sandy yellow clay, in places burnt orange and heavily flecked with carbon (Layer 4). The sides of the pit had been reddened by fire and the base of the pit was hardened by fire and compaction. Capping the basal fill was a mixed deposit of compact, burnt, reddish-brown loam, charcoal and ash (Layer 3) sealed by a thin layer of black loam and charcoal containing fire-fractured flint (2). The uppermost fill was of compact burnt flint mixed with reddish-brown loam and charcoal. The hearth provided twenty-six sherds of flint-tempered pottery, of which three were rusticated, and a fragment of vitrified pottery or copper dross. The pottery has been dated to c. 500–400 B.C.

Pit containing evidence for pottery production (Fig. 36)

Pit B133 located in the south-west corner of the excavated area, 15 m. west of building B311, contained possible evidence for pottery manufacture. The rectangular pit, 1.70 m. long, was cut to a bowl-shaped profile, 0.28 m. deep. The base of the pit was lined with grey clay flecked with burnt orange clay and charcoal (Fig. 36, section, Layer 2). The fill (Layer 1) was entirely of unfired clay lumps, a large number of sherds and gravel-free mid brown and dark reddish brown loam. The clay lumps, filled with fine fragments of burnt flint grit or temper, were taken to represent processed potting clay that had either been deliberately stored or discarded in the pit. The clay lining may indicate that the pit had been made to hold water or moisture and it is possible that B133 was a clay 'puddling' pit, used by a potter to mix, weather and store tempered potting clay. The fill of the pit contained 287 flint-tempered sherds, including a sherd possibly from a salt evaporation pan (Fig. 90, No. 382). A pit containing evidence for salt manufacture (B215) lay only 17 m. to the south-west and the presence of an evaporation pan fragment in the clay puddling pit suggests that the two activities may have been taking place at the same time. Save for three sherds (Fig. 90, Nos 380–82) the corpus comprised mainly body sherds and it is possible that the material represents the discard of pots broken during firing (although no obvious 'waster' sherds were identified). Although there is no evidence to suggest that the sherds had been collected for reprocessing as a clay temper, this possibility cannot be excluded. The pottery has been dated to c. 500–400 B.C. The pit was cut by a post-pit associated with circular Structure B260, clearly suggesting that the building post-dated the use of what appears to have been an industrial activity area broadly contemporary with the penannular gullied buildings (pp. 39–43 and p. 63).

Hearths and fire-pits

In addition to Hearth B31 within Building B16 and Hearth B155 previously described in connection with metalworking, fifteen additional features were identified as hearths or fire-pits. Two of the hearths located in the south-east corner of the excavated area were associated with a group of four large pits all with burnt sides and containing burnt materials. The four pits have been included in this category as fire-pits. Although widely distributed across Area B the hearths may be grouped. Four hearths were identified in the south-west corner of the site (B132, B233, B219 and B228) south of Building B311. Two hearths (B222 and B211) and three fire-pits (B189, B188 and B223) were identified in the south-east corner of the area. Two hearths (B207 and B180) were located between Buildings B311 and B26 and an isolated hearth (B213) to the east of Building B308. Hearth B125 (with B155 described above) was identified in a group of pits clustering around Granary B329, a single hearth (B86) was located to the west of Building B35 within Enclosure B70 and another single hearth (B184) was found to have been cut by a post-hole for Granary B159.

Hearth B132 (Fig. 25) was located in the south-west corner of the excavated area, within a group of features containing two further hearths (B233 and B288), a pit containing potting clay (B133) and the hearth used for salt production (B215). The hearth was oval in shape, measuring 1.20 by 1 m., cut with shallow sloping sides and a flat base to a depth of 0.19 m. The base and sides were compact and had been burnt by low temperature firing. The feature contained a basal fill (Layer 3) of fire-fractured gravel and reddish brown loam flecked with charcoal capped by successive layers of burnt flint in a black-brown carbon-rich loam (Layer 2) and a deposit of compact burnt flint in reddish-brown loam (Layer 1). Layer 2 contained sixteen flint-tempered sherds (including Fig. 95, No. 436) dated to *c.* 500–400 B.C. and of which two were rusticated.

Hearth B233 (Fig. 37) was located 3 m. to the south-east of Hearth B132. The feature was subrectangular with sides 1.12 by 0.75 m. long, was 0.19 m. deep and was lined with hard-fired brittle orange-red clay (Layer 2), which had been subjected to intense heat. The hearth was filled with mixture of gravel and dark loam (Layer 1). Layer 1 provided a single sherd of flint-tempered pottery with a rusticated surface dated *c.* 500–400 B.C.

Hearth B219 (Fig. 34) was cut by a post-hole (B488) associated with Structure B200. The hearth was oval, measuring 1.20 by 0.90 m. and bowl-shaped in profile, being cut to a depth of 0.44 m. The feature was filled with compact lenses of burnt and fire-fractured gravel and burnt reddish-brown loam. The uppermost fill was a capping of mid brown loam and gravel. The laminated fills provided fourteen flint-tempered sherds tentatively dated *c.* 500–400 B.C.

Hearth B228 (Fig. 37) was located in the south-west corner of the excavation, 13 m. north of hearths B233 and B132. This subrectangular, bowl-shaped feature, of dimensions 1.50 by 0.80 m. was cut to a depth of 0.17 m. The hearth, contained a basal fill of fired orange clay with burnt flint (Layer 2), capped by a thin layer of black-brown loam and burnt gravel (Layer 1). Layer 2 contained five flint-tempered sherds (including Fig. 96, No. 441) dating to the period 500–400 B.C. One was rusticated.

A group of features comprising hearths B211 and B222, a gully (B189A) and three pits containing evidence of burning, including fire scorching of the pit sides (pits B189, B223 and B188) were recorded near the south-west corner of the excavation.

Hearth B211 (Fig. 37) lay a short way south of Hearth B222 within a group of three fire-pits in the south-east corner of the site. The hearth was subcircular, 1.05 by 0.75 m. and cut to a depth of 0.18 m. The feature was filled with reddish-brown loam with burnt and fire-fractured flint (Layer 2) capped by black-brown loam and burnt flint (1). The fills yielded two flint-tempered sherds which were not closely datable.

Hearth B222 (Fig 38) was a circular steep-sided, flat-bottomed feature, 1.50 m. in diameter and 0.20 m. deep containing a lining of burnt orange and unburnt dirty-yellow clay (Layer 3), capped by successive deposits of burnt dark brown clay-loam (Layer 2) and dark brown gravelly loam (Layer 1). The fills provided no datable finds.

The earliest feature in the group appeared to be the gully. Located in an area which had been truncated during topsoil clearance, it was felt that it may have been a remnant of a more extensive feature of unknown function. Gully B189A was traced for only 3 m. and was between 0.75–0.80 m. wide, cut to a v-shaped profile 0.22 m. deep (Fig. 38, sections B, C and D). The fill, of mid brown gravelly loam

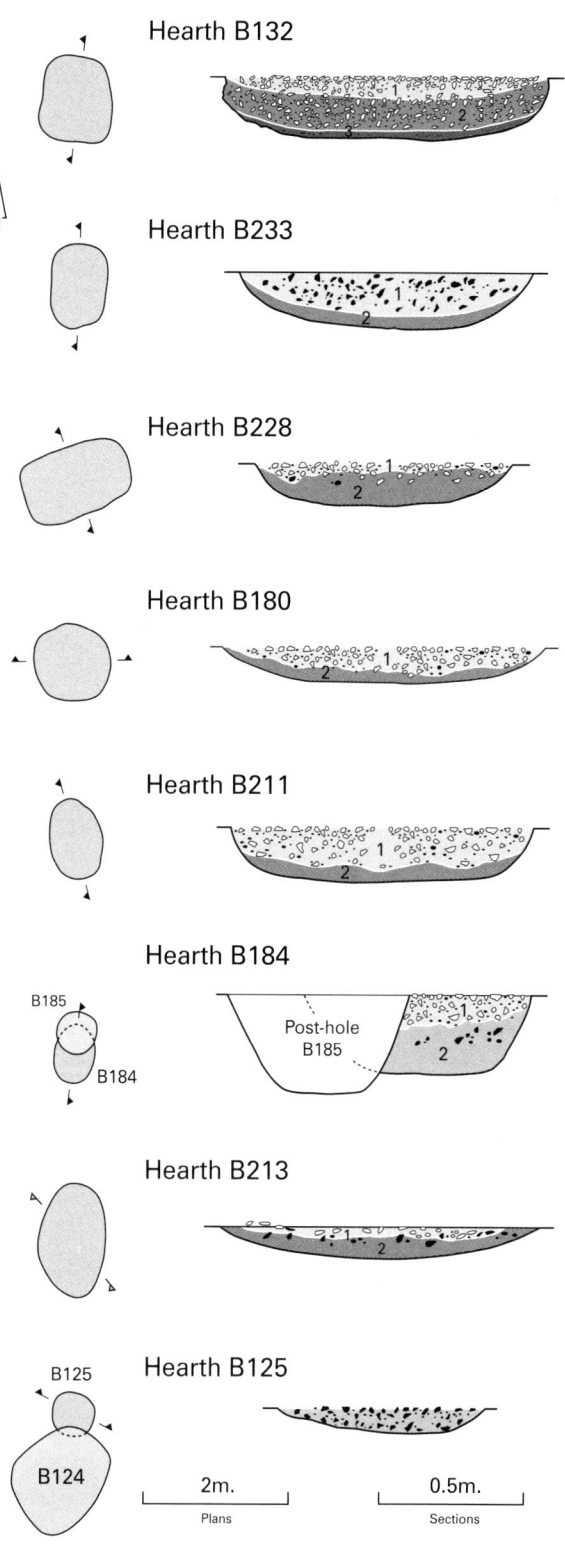

Fig. 37. Period 3B. Hearths.

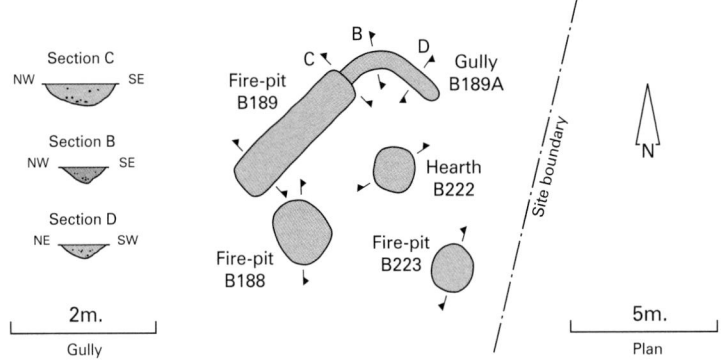

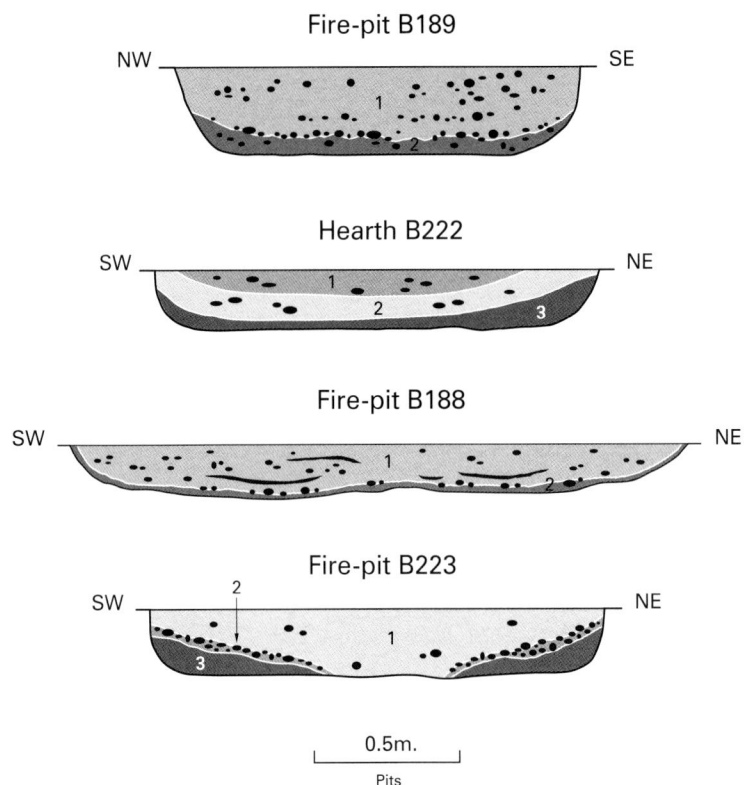

Fig. 38. Period 3B. Hearths and fire-pits.

contained only fragments of burnt clay. The gully was cut by Pit B189.

Pit B189 (Fig. 38) was a long, narrow, rectangular feature aligned long axis north-east to south-west. The pit, 5 m. long and 1.40 m. wide was cut to a depth of 0.30 m. The base and sides of the pit were burnt. The sump of the pit contained burnt flints and red-orange burnt clay (Layer 2) capped by black-brown gravelly loam containing burnt flints and red-orange burnt clay (Layer 1). One possible interpretation of the feature is that it was used as a fire-pit or trench for the firing of pots or for cooking food. The pit fills provided twenty flint-tempered sherds (including Fig. 88, Nos 345–6) dating to the period c. 500–400 B.C. None of the sherds appeared to be 'wasters' and nine were rusticated.

B188 (Fig. 38) was a large shallow oval-shaped feature some 2.10 by 1.80 m. in extent cut 0.18 m. deep. The feature had shallow sloping fire-reddened sides lined with burnt orange-red clay (Layer 2). The bulk capping fill (Layer 1) was of dark brown gravelly loam with much burnt flint and lenses of burnt clay and charcoal. The feature provided three flint-tempered sherds (including Fig. 88, No. 347) which can be accommodated within Period 3B.

Pit B223 (Fig. 38) was oval-shaped, measuring 1.55 by 1.30 m. Located against the main east section, the feature, cut with steep sides to a depth of 0.23 m. contained a basal fill of black-brown burnt clay-loam with charcoal, burnt flint and burnt orange clay (Layers 2 and 3), capped by a compact deposit of mid brown loam and gravel (Layer 1). The basal fills provided thirteen flint-tempered sherds, five with rusticated surfaces, broadly dating to the period c. 500–400 B.C.

Hearth B207 was apparently located between penannular buildings B26 and B311, but its precise position is uncertain. The site notebook records that the feature was of irregular oval shape, measuring 1.70 m. north–south by 1 m. and shallow, being barely 0.05 m. deep. The base of the hearth of burnt orange brown clay with abundant fire-fractured flints was capped by a deposit of dark brown loam containing twenty-one flint-tempered sherds (including Fig. 89, Nos 366–7) seven with rusticated surfaces, together with a residual flint scraper (Fig. 143, No. 8). The pottery was dated to the period c. 500–400 B.C.

Hearth B180 (Fig. 37) was located between building B308 and structure B29 at the southern end of the excavation. This circular feature, 1.10 m. in diameter and 0.09 m. deep was fire-scorched, with a basal fill of carbon-rich dark loam containing fire-crazed flints (Layer 2). Capping the fill was a deposit of dark brown gravelly loam and burnt flint. The lowest fill provided a flint-tempered wall sherd and, possibly a pedestal base (Fig. 96, No. 440), though there is some doubt about the provenance of the latter.

Hearth B213 (Fig. 37) located approximately 13 m. west of the entrance to the Period 3A Enclosure B144, was shallow, surviving to a depth of 0.10 m. The feature was irregular, of size 1 m. by 0.80 m., filled with fragmentary traces of a cherry-red fired lining, studded with fire-fractured flints (Layer 2), capped by a deposit of mid brown loam containing burnt flints, lumps of fired orange-red clay. Two sherds of flint-tempered pottery recovered from the fill were not closely datable.

Hearth B184 (Fig. 37) was located in the north-east corner of Area B, cut by the eastern corner post of granary-type structure B159. The hearth was subcircular, measuring 0.80 by 0.55 m. and cut 0.26 m. deep. The fill comprised a dense layer of burnt flint and charcoal (Layer 1), capping a deposit of mid brown loam with sparse gravel (Layer 2). The lower deposit may have been the fill of an earlier pit. Neither deposit provided datable finds.

Hearth B125 (Fig. 37) lay close to the western section in the northern third of the site. The hearth, cut by Pit B124, was circular, approximately 0.60 m. in diameter and surviving to a depth of 0.08 m. The fill of loam and fire-fractured flint, provided no datable finds.

Hearth B86 was located within the B70 enclosure, west of circular building B35. The hearth was roughly rectangular in shape with rounded corners measuring some 0.90 by 0.55 m. and 0.15 m. deep. It had shallow, sloping sides which were fire-reddened and a flat base. The fill of dark brown to reddish brown loam was filled with fire-crazed flint. The hearth contained two sherds of flint-tempered pottery with rusticated treatment dated c. 500–400 B.C.

Pits with clay lining (Fig. 39)

Fifteen pits were found to contain the remains of a clay lining. This clay must have been deliberately imported and some of the pits may have been used for food or even water storage. Five of these pits have already been discussed and described above (B31, a pit within building B16; B215, containing evidence for salt production; B195, B214, B147; pits containing metalworking debris). Eight of the pits may be associated with the pennanular-ditch buildings in the southern half of the site (B195, B215, B147, B212, B214, B31, B130 and B309); a second group of five mainly large pits, lay to the south of Enclosure B70 (B124, B313, B271, B114, and B153) and two outlying pits (B168 and B11) were recorded to the south-east of the second group.

Pit B212 (*not illus.*) was recorded in the site notebook located to the east of the penannular-ditched buildings immediately adjoining the west side of a clay-lined pit containing metalworking debris (B214). The pit was rectangular measuring 3 by 2 m. and was cut approximately 0.30 m. deep. It was badly disturbed by later features, but contained the remnants of a dirty yellow clay lining capped by mid brown gravelly loam which contained no datable finds.

Pit B130 was located to the north of the ring-ditch buildings, roughly at site centre. The pit was oval, measuring 0.76 by 0.65 m. and bowl-shaped, being cut to a depth of 0.23 m. It was lined with green-grey clay (Layer 2), particularly thick at the base, but fragmentary to the sides and filled with mid brown loam (Layer 1) containing large lumps of burnt orange clay and charcoal, perhaps from a dismantled domestic hearth or oven. The fills provided no datable finds.

Pit B309 was found to the north-east of Building B16 at site centre and was of substantial size, being 1.90 by 1.20 m. and cut 0.65 m. deep. The pit retained a hard yellow clay lining at the base and for three of the near vertical sides (Layer 3). The remaining side had collapsed in antiquity, perhaps as a result of weathering or water action. The lowest fill (Layer 2) was of dark brown loam with charcoal and ash. The upper fill (Layer 1) was of mid brown loam with

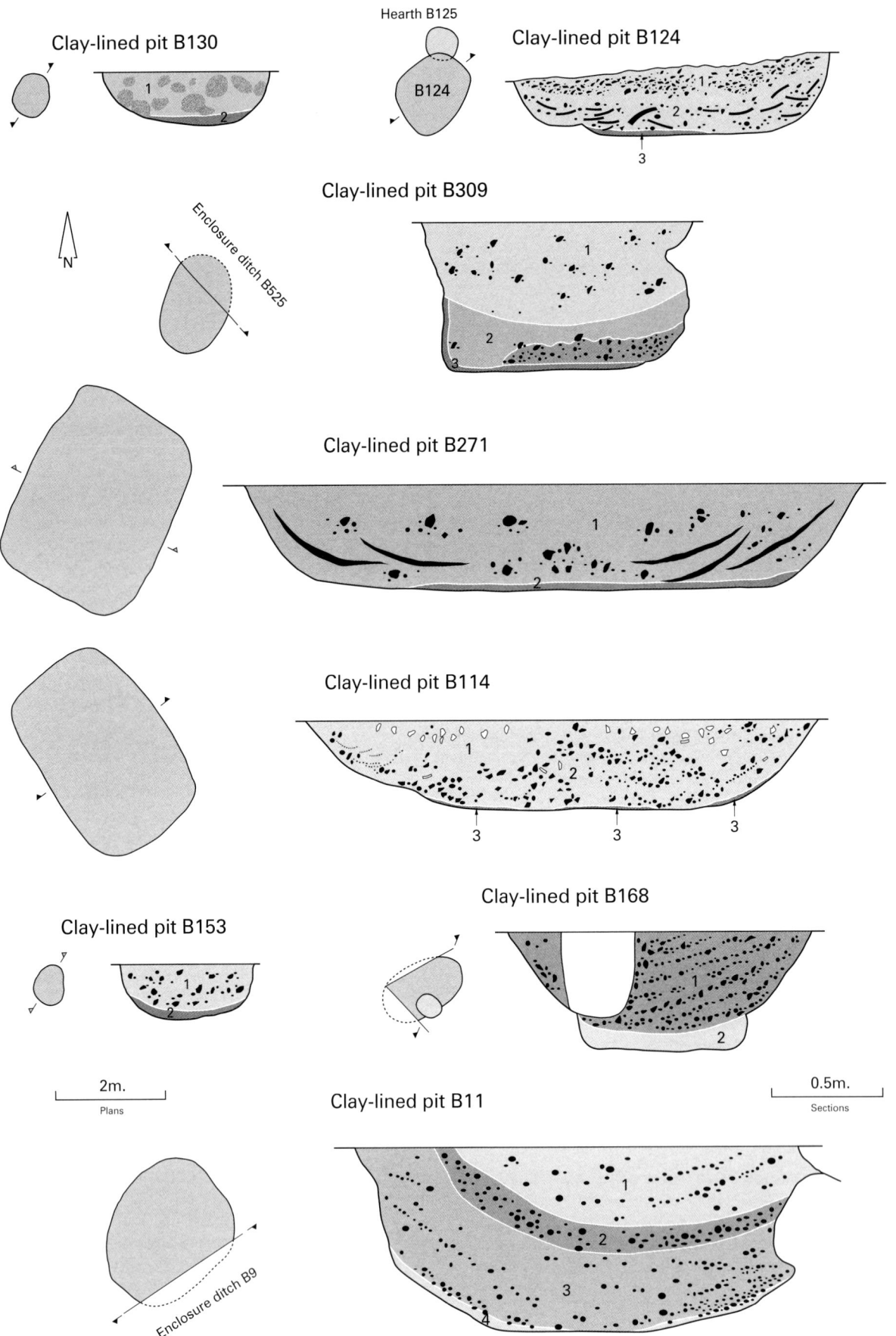

Fig. 39. Period 3B. Clay-lined pits.

charcoal flecking and lumps of burnt clay. There were no datable finds.

Pit B124 formed part of a northern group of clay-lined pits. The pit, found cutting Hearth B125, was oval, measuring 1.40 by 1.20 m. and had been cut with rounded sides and flat base to a depth of 0.35 m. Traces of a primary yellow clay lining were found at the base of the pit (Layer 3), this capped by a bulk fill of dark brown gravelly loam with pockets and lenses of charcoal and a large number of pottery sherds (Layer 2). The capping fill (Layer 1) was of mid brown loam and gravel. Layer 2 provided 449 sherds of flint-tempered pottery (including Fig. 94, Nos 403–21) dated *c.* 500–400 B.C. and of which 180 were rusticated.

Pit B313 (*not illus.*) fell within the northern group of pits. The pit was subsquare (3.20 by 2.82 m.), cut with near vertical sides to a depth of 0.37 m. A remnant yellow clay lining was recorded on the base and sides of the pit, which was otherwise filled with a single deposit of mid brown loam and gravel. The feature provided no datable finds.

Pit B271 formed part of the northern group of pits. Measuring 3.60 by 2.80 m. in extent, cut with steep sides and a flat base to a depth of 0.46 m., it was lined at its base with the remains of a compact and burnt brown-red clay lining (Layer 2). The sides were eroded by weathering, suggesting that the pit had been left open for a period of time before infilling had taken place. The fill (Layer 1) appeared to represent a single deposit of mid brown gravelly loam containing lenses of pure loam flecked with carbon and burnt and fire-fractured flint. The fill provided eighty-eight sherds of flint-tempered pottery (including Fig. 93, Nos 399–402) dated to the period *c.* 500–400 B.C. and of which twelve were rusticated. The pit was cut parallel to an adjoining possible granary structure (Building B329). Although the post-holes for the granary provided no datable finds, their proximity and alignment, argue for contemporary or successive use.

Pit B114 was the most northerly of the northern group of clay-lined pits. This pit was rectangular, 3.50 by 2.30 m. in extent, cut with shallow sloping sides and flat base to a depth of 0.40 m. Traces of a thin yellow clay lining (Layer 3) were found at the base of the pit. The sides were eroded by weathering. The fills comprised a lower deposit of gravel and mid brown loam with occasional pockets of carbon and burnt clay (Layer 2) capped by a mid brown loam and gravel containing carbon and burnt clay and fire-fractured flints (Layer 1). Layers 1 and 2 provided 171 sherds of flint-tempered pottery (including Fig. 92, Nos 385–98), thirty-eight with rusticated surfaces.

Pit B153 was located on the eastern fringe of the northern group of clay-lined pits. The pit was small, subcircular and bowl-shaped, measuring 0.70 by 0.55 by 0.24 m. It retained a lining of grey-green clay at its base (Layer 2) and was filled with mid brown gravel and loam (Layer 1) which contained no datable finds.

Pit B168 found 10 m. east of Enclosure B144 was located amongst a small group of features including one other clay-lined pit, in the north-east corner of the site. The pit was oval, measuring 1.40 by 0.90 m., cut with steep but weathered sides and a flat base to a depth of 0.53 m. The base and lower part of at least two sides retained a compact and thick lining of pale grey clay (Layer 2). The pit was filled with dark brown loam and gravel (Layer 1), laid in banded layers containing charcoal and fired clay lumps. The fill provided eighteen flint-tempered sherds (including Fig. 95, No. 424) of which two were rusticated, and a fired clay weight (Fig. 160, No. 46, p. 276). The pottery has been dated *c.* 500–400 B.C.

Pit B11 was found just outside Enclosure B144, close to the north-east corner of the excavated area. It was subrectangular of sides 2.40 by 2.10 m., cut with steep but rounded sides and slightly rounded base to a depth of 0.80 m. Traces of a yellow clay lining survived at the base beneath a basal fill of collapsed gravel from the weathered sides of the pit (Layer 4). The remaining fills comprised mid brown gravelly loam (Layer 3), a thick lens of dark brown loam with fire-fractured flints and carbon (Layer 2) and a capping fill of mid brown gravelly loam (Layer 1). The fills provided no datable finds.

Other pits

In addition to the pits categorized above, twenty-three others were identified. Like those, they appeared to fall into groups. Seven were identified in the south-west corner of the excavated area (B247, B248, B253, B255, B256, B245 and B179). A group of five small pits (B203, B225, B177, B208 and B220) were identified between buildings B311 and B26 and three larger examples (B126, B128 and B172) to the north of the penannular ditched buildings. Three others (B119, B323 and B156) were associated with a northern group of clay-lined pits and a group of five (B146, B266, B267, B6 and B270) were found to the east of the previous group.

Pit B247 (Fig. 40) was located in the south-west corner of the excavation, partly beneath the main west section. The pit was circular with a diameter of 1.40 m. and had been cut to a depth of 0.15 m. The lowest fill contained quantities of burnt orange clay mixed with burnt clay and pottery (Layer 2). The uppermost fill was of dark brown loam with little gravel (Layer 1). Both layers provided fifty-six flint-tempered sherds (including Fig. 96, Nos 442–4) dated *c.* 500–400 B.C. and of which twenty-four were rusticated.

Pit B248 was one of a group found in the south-west corner of the excavated area and was oval, measuring approximately 1.80 by 0.95 m. and cut 0.28 m. deep. The pit contained a single fill of mid brown loam and gravel, providing four flint-tempered sherds (including Fig. 97, Nos 458–9) tentatively dated *c.* 500–400 B.C.

Part 2: The Excavated Evidence

Highstead, near Chislet

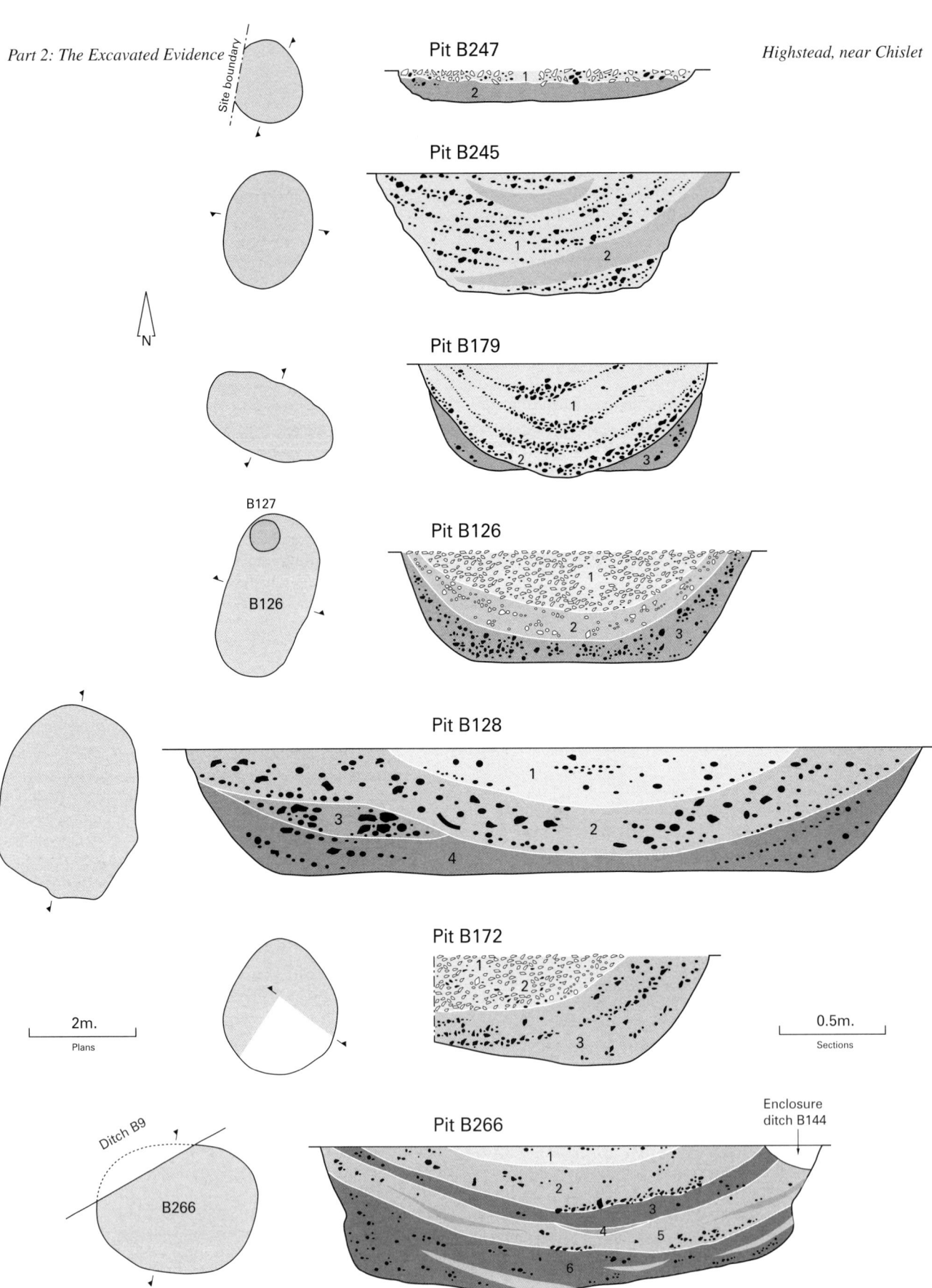

Fig. 40. Period 3B. Pits.

Pit B253 was located immediately south-west of Structure B260. The circular pit, 0.70 m. in diameter and 0.35 m. deep, was filled with dark brown gravelly loam and provided no datable finds. This pit, together with others in the immediate vicinity (B133, B255, B256 and B245) probably pre-dated Structure B260.

Pits B255 and B256 were located within the footprint of Structure B260 and were considered to pre-date it. The pits were intercutting, but it was not possible to determine which was cut first. The features were circular and of near identical size being 0.7–0.9 m. in diameter, cut to a maximum depth of 0.28 m. Both were filled with a dark brown gravelly loam and provided no datable finds.

Pit B245 (Fig. 40) was located to the north-east of Building B260. The feature was oval in shape, of size 2.20 by 1.70 m., cut with weathered but steep sides and a flat base to a depth of 0.55 m. The pit was filled with a basal deposit of eroded gravel (Layer 3) capped by a thick layer of dark reddish-brown burnt loam, charcoal, burnt flint and pottery (Layer 2). The layer was capped by an extensive deposit of mid brown gravelly loam (Layer 1). Layer 2 provided ninety-one flint-tempered sherds, fourteen with rusticated surfaces (including Fig. 97, Nos 451–7) dated c. 500–400 B.C. Two sherds of grog-tempered pottery recovered from the fill were regarded as intrusive.

Pit B179 (Fig. 40) was located to the south-west of Building B311. The feature was rectangular, measuring 2.50 by 1.35 m, cut with steep curving sides and rounded sump to a depth of 0.51 m. The pit contained a primary fill (Layer 3) of dark brown loam capped by a compact, thin layer of gravel (Layer 2) and successive banded layers of mid brown loam and gravel (Layer 3). Only Layer 3 provided finds; four flint-tempered sherds which were not closely datable.

Pit B203 was one of a row of four small pits (Fig. 35) located to the north of Building B311. The pit was subcircular, approximately 1 m. in diameter, cut 0.32 m. deep and the fill comprised a single deposit of brown gravelly loam, containing burnt flints, charcoal and burnt clay flecks. Five flint-tempered pot sherds (including Fig. 89, Nos 363–5) dated c. 500–400 were recovered from the fill.

Pit B225 was one of four small pits located to the north of Building B311. It was circular and bowl-shaped, 0.75 m. in diameter and 0.30 m. deep. The fill was a bi-partite deposit of weathered gravel capped by grey-brown loam with flints containing no datable finds. It was cut by a post-pit (B242) associated with the undated structure B29 (above, p. 51).

Pit B177 was located to the east of Pit B225. It was bowl-shaped, of maximum diameter 0.60 m., cut to depth of 0.20 m. and filled with a single deposit of dark brown loam containing flecks of burnt clay, charcoal and fire-crazed flints. The pit provided nine sherds of flint-tempered pottery (including Fig. 89, No. 362) of which two were rusticated, dated c. 500–400 B.C. The pit was cut by two post-holes (B177A and B177B) associated with the undated structure B29.

Pit B208 was the easternmost of the row of four and was circular, 0.90 m. in diameter and 0.40 m. deep. The pit had sloping sides and an irregular cut in the sump perhaps suggesting that it had been recut or that the feature may have originally contained a storage pot. It contained a single fill of dark brown loam and gravel with no datable finds.

Pit B220 was located south of Building B26 and was subcircular, 1.40 m long and 1 m. wide. Cut with sloping sides and flat base, it was filled with a single deposit of dark brown to reddish brown loam containing charcoal, yellow clay flecks and burnt and unburnt flints. The fill provided no datable finds but was cut by a post-hole (B204) associated with the undated structure B29.

Pit B126 (Fig. 40) was located within a group of pits north of the penannular-ditched buildings. It was subrectangular, 3 m. long, 1.70 m. wide, cut with steeply sloping sides to a depth of 0.50 m. The fill comprised a basal deposit of dark brown loam and gravel mixed with burnt orange clay and fire-fractured flints (Layer 3). This was capped by successive deposits of mid brown loam and gravel (Layer 2) and a final fill of compact gravel (Layer 1). Layer 3 provided thirty-five flint-tempered sherds (including, Fig. 95, No. 435), five of which were rusticated, dated c. 500–400 B.C. Pit B126 was cut by Pit B127.

Pit B127 (Fig. 40) was set within the northern end of Pit B126. It measured 0.80 by 0.60 m. across and 0.72 m. deep. It contained one fill of deep brown loam with some gravel and flecks of charcoal and fired clay. It contained no datable finds.

Pit B128 (Fig. 40) was one of a group of pits found north of the penannular-ditched buildings. This substantial feature was oval, measuring 3.50 by 2.60 m, cut with sloping sides and a flat base to a depth of 0.56 m. The pit contained a primary fill of light brown sandy loam flecked with charcoal (Layer 4), capped by dark brown loam and gravel (Layer 3). The lower deposits were sealed by mid brown loamy gravel (Layer 2) and mid brown loam with little gravel (Layer 1). The lowest deposits (Layers 3 and 4) yielded sixty-three flint-tempered sherds dated c. 500–400 B.C. (including Fig. 96, Nos 445–7), of which six were rusticated.

Pit B172 (Fig. 40) was located at the centre of the excavated area, on the eastern periphery of a group of pits north of the penannular-ditched buildings. The pit was circular, 2.25 m. in diameter and cut 0.50 m. deep. The fills comprised primary deposits of mid brown gravelly loam with tip lines of gravel (Layer 3) capped by gravel mixed with dark brown loam and burnt flint (Layer 2) and sealed by a deposit of clean gravel (Layer 1). Layer 3 provided seventy sherds of flint-tempered pottery dated c. 500–400 B.C. (including, Fig. 95, Nos 437–9), thirty-seven with rusticated surfaces.

Pit B119 comprised one of two large pits located at the northern end of the excavated area, south of Enclosure B70 (Fig. 27). B119 was rectangular, measuring 2.75 by 1.98 m., and had been cut with near vertical but eroded and weathered sides to a depth of 0.53 m. The lowest fills were of redeposited natural gravel, taken to represent the products of weathering. This material was capped by successive layers of mid brown gravelly loam and dark brown gravelly loam with charcoal, burnt clay, fire-fractured flints and pottery. The upper layers provided thirty-eight sherds of pottery (including Fig. 95, Nos 431–4) dated *c.* 500–400 B.C., seven of which had rusticated surfaces.

Pit B323 was at the end of the excavated area, about 20 m. north-east of Pit B119. It was rectangular, measuring 3.90 by 1.90 m., cut 0.49 m. deep. The fill of dark brown gravelly loam with carbon and burnt clay flecking, capped by mid brown gravelly loam, provided no datable finds.

Pit B156 was located east of storage jar Pit B154 and west of Hearth B155 in the northern half of Area B. It measured 1.20 m. in diameter and 0.25 m. deep and was filled with mid brown gravelly loam flecked with carbon and burnt clay which yielded one sherd of flint-tempered pottery with a rusticated surface, dated to *c.* 500–400 B.C. and an intrusive iron object (p. 273).

Pit B146 was one of a group of pits located in the north-east side of the excavated area, cutting the fills of Enclosure ditch B144. The pit was rectangular, measuring 1.40 by 0.90 m. and cut 0.45 m. deep. The fill of dark brown gravelly loam provided seven flint-tempered sherds, one with a rusticated surface (including Fig. 96, Nos 448–9) dated *c.* 500–400 B.C. and an intrusive possible spindlewhorl (p. 276).

Pit B266 (Fig. 40) was found cutting the fills of Enclosure ditch B144 and was cut by a later Ditch B9, close to the eastern edge of the excavated area. The pit was large, measuring 3 m. by 2.30 m. and had been cut with near vertical, but eroded, sides to a depth of 0.65 m. The lowest fill (Layer 6) was of dark brown loam and gravel containing charcoal and burnt clay. This deposit was capped by successive layers of mid brown loam (Layer 5), lenses of yellow clay and loam (Layer 4), dark brown gravelly loam (Layer 3) and mid brown loam with charcoal, burnt clay and fire-fractured flints (Layer 2). The capping fill was of grey-brown clayey loam with charcoal and burnt clay (Layer 1). All layers provided a total of 338 sherds of flint-tempered pottery (including Figs 98–9, Nos 460–93) dated *c.* 500–400 B.C. and twenty-four of which had rusticated surfaces. A bone weaving comb (p. 276) was also recovered. Three sherds of pre-conquest amphora (*see* p. 237) and one of grog-tempered pottery were taken to be intrusive, probably from the fill of Ditch B9.

Pit B267 was also in the eastern group, just to the north of B266. It was circular, approximately 1 m. in diameter, cut 0.35 m. deep. The fill of mid brown gravelly loam provided seven flint-tempered sherds (including Fig. 100, No. 494) tentatively dated *c.* 500–400 B.C.

Pit B6 was found on the eastern side of Area B, just to the north-east of Pit B267. Approximately 2 m. in diameter and 0.22 m. deep, it was filled with a uniform deposit of dark brown gravelly loam flecked with carbon and burnt clay. The fill yielded no pottery or other datable artefacts.

Pit B270 was the northernmost of the cluster of pits against the eastern side of Area B, just north-west of Pit B6. It was oval-shaped, 1.45 m. in length and 0.80 m. wide and cut to a depth of 0.22 m. Its fill comprised pale brown gravelly loam flecked with charcoal. The fill yielded no pottery or other datable artefacts.

Enclosure ditch B70

Artefacts associated with Period 3B activity was recovered from the upper fills of Enclosure ditch B70 (Layer 5). The upper fill of Ditch B70, in excess of 1 m. deep, comprised dark brown loam containing tip lines of gravel and silty loam, indicating that the material had accumulated over a considerable period, mainly, but perhaps not exclusively by weathering. Although this upper fill (Layer 5, covering Levels 4 and 5, Fig. 56) contained a high proportion of Period 2 material, pottery of Period 3B date was also recovered (Table 5) indicating that the enclosure ditch had largely been infilled by *c.* 400 B.C.

Discussion

Activity in Area A appears to end in Period 3A and there is no evidence of reoccupation in the area until the opening decade of the first century A.D. As near-continuous occupation is attested in Area B throughout Periods 2 and 3, the lack of features, or background scatter of finds of the period, suggests that arable farming was not practised, since it is reasonable to assume that across the large area investigated at least one or two field boundaries or trackways separating fields may have been present. Similarly, if arable farming was taking place one would expect a background 'noise' of material deriving from the nearby settlement, either by manual loss or as a bi-product of enriching the soil by manuring. As it is unlikely that the landscape south and east of Area B would not have been managed, then perhaps that part of the southern spur of the gravel plateau may have been used for pasture and woodland, with pasture high in the contours where the soils are thinnest and woodland on shelving ground to the south-west and south-east overlooking the valley of the Ford stream and the main stream of the Wantsum channel, respectively.

The cessation of occupation in Area A may have coincided with a transition from the building of enclosures to the establishment of open settlement; an indicator of considerable social change. If each enclosure represented perhaps the property of an individual household, then the development of open settlement suggests a change to a more collective approach to living and working – in effect, to a form of village life. Quite what prompted the change sometime between 600 and 500 B.C. is difficult to determine, but one can say that the development coincides with an apparently gradual change in pottery styles. No sudden break in tradition is in evidence and elements of Period 2 forms and decoration exist alongside new forms for a while.

Period 3B activity is characterised by the appearance of circular buildings indicated by penannular gullies and by a wide range of pits, some clay-lined and some used as hearths and fire-pits indicative of industrial activity. Some of the features contained evidence for metalworking, salt production and pottery manufacture and many occurred in groups, suggesting activity areas. Intercutting features indicated not only longevity of occupation, but internal phasing of the settlement. The penannular-ditched buildings appeared to represent the core of the early settlement and were tentatively associated with adjacent activity areas. Buildings of earthfast post construction were found to cut early features, suggesting that they were a later development. Two undated rectangular buildings, one found south of Enclosure B70 and the other near the penannular ditched buildings may be of this later period, but could conceivably be dated to Periods 4 or 5.

The penannular ditches appeared to represent the footprints of domestic houses. Few of these buildings contained internal features and no structural components, frame members or wall lines survived. The ring-ditches presumably acted as a drainage gully positioned close to and outside the wall of each building as an eaves drip for rainwater. Little can be said of the building form save that they were circular with a single entrance facing south-east, as commonly found in the Iron Age. The lack of post-holes suggests that structural elements rested on the contemporary ground surface or were set in shallow-cut emplacements. As some ground reduction had taken place across Area B, it is not impossible that all trace of such features had been removed. The circular buildings may therefore have been of light construction on average 8–10 m. in diameter. There was at least one smaller building (B308) 5–6 m. in diameter.

Two circular structures with earthfast posts were also present. One (B260) was located a short way south-east of the penannular-ditched buildings in the south-west corner of Area B. The survival of the structure so close to the penannular gullies suggests that two or more building types may be represented within the settlement, or that a lighter-weight framed building may have been succeeded by one constructed with more deeply-buried earthfast posts. That structural posts associated with Building B260 were cut through Period 3B dated features, with others close to or within the footprint of the building, suggests that the earthfast posts are late in the sequence and may post-date the penannular buildings. The second circular building was located within the B70 enclosure at some remove from the penannular buildings. It is interesting to note that both building types appeared to be of comparable size.

There were in addition three structures that may have been granaries; two were of four-post construction (B196 and B159) and one of five (B329). The buildings, at widely spaced locations, suggest that cereal production may have been a dominant feature of the local economy. Despite the acid soils and poor preservation of bone, cattle, sheep and pig were represented from Period 3 features (p. 280) and it seems likely that livestock rearing also formed a likely mainstay of settlement economy. The rare survival of a bone weaving comb recovered from Pit B266 (p. 276) implied the presence of sheep and the production of woollen cloth during the period.

Two pits (B314 and B154) contained jars which appear to have been deposited deliberately. In the case of B154, the pit was dug to just the right size to hold pot No. 383 inverted. B314 however, was larger and contained the remains of pot No. 379 at one end. These pits were situated on the southern fringes of a northern group of pits including five that were clay-lined (B114, B153, B271, B313 and B124) that surrounded Granary B329. Hearths B125 and B155 were close by. While hearths do not accompany all buildings (Building B16 had a hearth within it and Buildings B35, B26 and B311 all had one or more hearths nearby), it is tempting to suggest that two additional buildings may have existed close to these pits.

Five large post-pits also suggested the presence of structures. Two (B202 and B194) located south of Building B311 were formed to receive substantial posts. Two other post-pits (B218 and B178) were recorded to the south of Buildings B26 and B308 and an isolated post-pit (B171) was recorded well to the east of the penannular gullied buildings. The relative paucity of post-holes and post-pits other than those associated with buildings, is notable and would suggest that the features served an alternative purpose. The pairs of posts were widely separated and need not have been associated. Although the features may have been isolated survivors of more complex structures they may perhaps represent isolated supports for more temporary structures.

The final structure, B200 was of curious construction comprising of over ninety small post-holes defining a rectangular building formed with an internal and an external skin of wicker-work or hurdling; the space between perhaps infilled with soil or turf. The structure, with a south-east facing entrance, may not have been roofed and possibly served the community as a small ritual enclosure perhaps a shrine. The presence of two cremation burials (B166 and B173) nearby and located south of the enclosure entrance may support the interpretation.

There were additionally two rectangular undated post-built structures (B111 and B29) that have been tentatively included in Period 3B. The buildings, 9 m. and 6 m. long, with long axis set east–west were both 4 m. wide. The larger of the two buildings (B29) was poorly defined and a convincing plan was not determined. However, the number of related posts of differing sizes and depths suggested a complex evolution for the structure. Building B111 appeared to be box-framed with an east–west extension, internal partition and perhaps an east facing doorway. The walls of both structures were presumably of wattle and daub. The roofs were probably thatched. The function of both buildings is difficult to determine, but in the unlikely event that all the structures were broadly contemporary, then presumably the rectangular buildings were constructed for a non-domestic use. Period 3B buildings therefore comprise an interesting range of types and sizes that imply mixed function, from the lightweight circular domestic structures to those of earthfast post construction; from domestic dwellings to buildings possibly used as stores, workshops, granaries and perhaps a shrine. The construction of the buildings may also reflect chronological depth, with the range of buildings representing an evolving vernacular tradition beginning with circular surface-built structures and ending with circular and rectangular structures with earthfast posts.

The spatial distribution of pits and hearths tells us something of the organisation of the community. A group of pits and hearths in the extreme south-west corner of Area B, south of a group of penannular buildings, provided evidence for salt production, metalworking and potting, perhaps suggesting that this part of the site may have been a focus of industrial activities. That the industries may have been active simultaneously is suggested by the presence of metalworking slag in salt production pit B215 and the presence of an evaporation pan fragment in finds retrieved from potting pit B133. Five other pits and three hearths identified in the same area suggest that the zone may have been used for a variety of different activities. The construction of building B260 over a number of the pits and a hearth suggests that use of the area for industry and rubbish disposal may have been of limited duration and perhaps associated with the penannular-ditched buildings.

Pit B215, located in the south-west corner of Area B provided evidence for the processing or refining of salt. The feature contained the remains of a hearth with numerous fragments of one or more large evaporating dishes lying above it (Fig. 90, No. 375). The evidence reflects perhaps domestic scale refining of salt rather than larger scale production. Salt was an essential staple of life, particularly for the preservation of meat and fish and most communities with easy access to the sea would have been self-sufficient in the commodity. Although no evidence has yet been found, the principal salt-working sites of the period would have been situated in the tidal salt flats bordering the edge of the Wantsum seaway. Here sea salt would have been produced by natural evaporation in salt pans or by artificial evaporation by boiling. This process may not have provided a pure commodity and the salt bricks produced against the high water mark may have been further refined at the settlement in evaporation pans. The evaporating dish reconstructed as a shallow rectangular trough, externally finished with roughly horizontal fluted finger smoothing, is broadly paralleled by earlier dishes from St Mildred's Bay and Minnis Bay on the northern seaboard of Thanet (p. 269) and suggests perhaps a longer tradition of salt production and refining in east Kent.

Six other activity areas were suggested by the spatial distribution of features. A group of five features located in the south-eastern corner of the excavated area were associated with burning. There were at least two hearths (B211 and B222) and three fire-pits (B223, B188 and B189). The largest of the features may perhaps have been used for the trench-firing of pottery. The other pits and hearths may also have been associated with manufacturing of some sort. A second small group of features, two clay-lined pits (B212 and B214) and a hearth (B213), lay to the east of Building B308. One feature (B214) contained metalworking debris including a crucible fragment (p. 266), and it is tempting to associate the group of features and the building. A third group of pits and a hearth were located to the north of Building B311 (and under the footprint of later Building B29). The group of features here is perhaps best associated with Building B311 or one of its near neighbours. A further activity area was indicated by a group of clay-lined pits (B319, B130) and pits (B126, B128, B172) east of Building B16. A similar but slightly more diffuse collection of pits (B270, B6, B267, B266 and B146), and two clay-lined pits (B11, B168) lay in the eastern corner of the excavation east and south of Granary B159. A final activity area was located to the south of Enclosure B70. Here a group of pits (B323 and B119, and clay-lined B114, B153, B271, B313 and B124) and Granary B329 were located in a zone flanked by Building B111 to the north and by two possible buildings represented by pits B314 and B154 to the south.

All seven activity zones with perhaps the exception of the south-eastern group contained a range of different types of features and adjoined a potentially contemporary building. In some cases adjacent buildings were found to cut features within the activity zone or in other cases intercutting features were present, clearly suggesting longevity of settlement. Whilst many of the features were similar, some of the activities appeared to suggest a specialised function for the activity zone. The south-western group of features contained evidence for salt processing, pottery production and metalworking as well as rubbish disposal. One clay-lined storage pit was also present. The principal use of this activity zone appears to have been industrial. The south-eastern group was almost exclusively associated with processing by fire. The function of the features north of Building B311 is less clear. A mixed function of food storage and industrial was suggested for a small group of features east of Building B308 and food storage for a group of five pits east of Building B16; at least some of the pits were of a substantial size. A group of pits south and east of Granary B159 was probably used for food storage. A final group next to Granary B329 and south of Structure B11, was dominated by clay-lined storage pits including three rectangular examples. The pits and the granary suggest that this zone was used for grain storage, though the apparently deliberate burial of pots in pits B154 and B314 indicate other, less mundane activities were performed.

The pottery of the period includes many new forms, though some, such as storage jars with neck cordons (occasionally plain rather than with finger-tip impressions), continue. In general, the pottery becomes coarser, with thicker walls and the most distinctive feature is the appearance of rusticated surfaces which become common, often appearing in about half of the sherds in a single context. This trait, and several of the new forms can be found in the Low Countries, again with particular emphasis on Belgium. As well as these, we find a few painted vessels demonstrating closer links with the Marne region of France than with Belgium, a tantalising glimpse of a more complex series of cross Channel relationships which can only be elucidated with evidence from other excavations. Unlike Period 2 however when the pottery also shares traits with other sites in the lower Thames valley, during Period 3 the emphasis is on similarities with the Continent. Much of the new ceramic repertoire is rarely found outside east Kent.

At the end of Period 3B, some time around 400 B.C. after a long period of near continuous occupation (in Area B) archaeological traces of activity cease.

Period 3C

Period 3C represents an episode of abandonment that may have lasted for approximately 300 years in Area B and 450 years in Area A. No features or artefacts were recovered that could confidently be dated after 400 B.C. and before *c.* 125–100 B.C.

The excavations provided no direct evidence for the cause of this abandonment. It is of course possible that the settlement moved a short distance beyond the area of excavation, but the absence of features and pottery attributable to the period post 400 B.C. would suggest something more than a slight shift to another part of the plateau. While the cause may have been local, such as a growing lack of fertility in the soil, minor climatic change, dilapidated buildings or disease, it is worth viewing this in a broader context. Throughout east Kent and beyond, settlements which are active in the fifth or early fourth century rarely continue beyond *c.* 350 B.C. The evidence from metalwork and pottery in south-east and central southern England has long been interpreted as showing that after this time cultural affinities become insular with greatly reduced, but not absent, continental

contact (Cunliffe 1991, 405–43; Haselgrove 2001, 43–4). It is tempting to see the fortunes of the settlement at Highstead closely associated with this continental contact and that changing economic and social conditions resulted in its abandonment.

Period 4: *c.* 100 B.C. – *c.* A.D. 75

Introduction (Fig. 41)

Period 4 activity can be placed into four phases (4A–D), each representing a major episode of change, first in Area B where a palimpsest of enclosures was identified and much later in Area A where ditches associated with a possible field system were recorded. In both areas the interpretation of features and their spatial extent owed much to cropmark evidence, this determined from a number of air photographs taken before and during the excavation.

Most Period 4 features were dated by stratigraphic relationship. As many features, particularly in Area B, formed part of a complex sequence of intercutting contexts that were excavated rapidly, the pottery groups were found to contain much residual, and in a number of instances some intrusive, material. Although every effort has been made to fit excavated features into a chronological framework, the allocation of a date to each of the four phases must be considered tentative. These are as follows: Period 4A (*c.* 100–50 B.C.); Period 4B (*c.* 50–25 B.C.); Period 4C (*c.* 25 B.C.–A.D. 50) and Period 4D (*c.* A.D. 50–75).

Period 4A summary

Following an apparent period of abandonment lasting approximately 300 years, the earliest features in Area B appear to be a number of ditches collectively forming part of two adjacent north-east to south-west aligned enclosures or fields (ditches B139, B141 and B8). Only the north-west corner of the south-eastern enclosure (B139) and a single ditch representing one side of the north-eastern enclosure (Ditch B8) were positively identified and sample excavated. Other parts were tentatively indicated by cropmarks identified on air photographs. The north-eastern enclosure ditch B8 was cut by a pair of closely set parallel north-west to south-east aligned ditches (B18 and B20) and two of a row of six north-east to south-west aligned post-pits (B167, B150, B160, B138, B142 and B137) suggesting that the north-western enclosure had been modified or that both enclosures had been superseded by a new arrangement. A third north-west to south-east aligned ditch (B17) was identified to the south-west of the pair and two isolated pits,

Fig. 41. Period 4 features.

located against the southern boundary of the excavation, were dated by pottery to this period.

There was no recognisable occupation in Area A at this time, although residual pottery in later features suggests activity in the immediate vicinity.

Enclosure B139 (Fig. 42)

Two ditches set roughly at right angles to one another (B139 and B141) appeared to form the north-west corner of an enclosure or field aligned long axis north-east to south-west.

The north-eastern ditch (B141), found cutting a Period 2B enclosure (B144) appeared to be earlier than any other ditches in Area B. Traced for 21 m., it formed a junction with Ditch B139 aligned north-east to south-west. Ditch B141 was sample-excavated in one location close to the north-west corner and was found to be between 1.30–2.20 m. wide and cut 0.60 m. deep to a broad u-shaped profile. Four separate fills were noted each defined by different proportions of gravel and mid brown loam (Fig. 42, inset section). The fills, excavated as one deposit, provided a fragment of iron slag and twenty-four flint-tempered sherds (including Fig. 102, No. 16), together with some fifty-nine grog-tempered sherds (including Fig. 108, Nos 64–9) and a single sherd of grog and chalk-filled ware (Fig. 124, No. 322). The late grog-tempered pottery is regarded as intrusive, from Period 4D activity in the area.

Ditch B139 was traced for a total length of 22.50 m. The feature, sample-excavated at one location (Fig. 42, inset section), was approximately 1.70 m. wide and 0.45 m. deep. The ditch, cut to a v-shaped profile, with a central basal slot 0.20 m. wide and 0.20 m. deep, contained a bi-partite fill of medium brown gravelly loam, over a basal fill of dark brown sandy loam and gravel. A similar slot was not located in the contemporary adjacent ditch (B141) and no post-holes were observed. It is possible the slot may have been cut during an episode of maintenance. The ditch fills yielded thirty-three sherds of flint-tempered pottery (including Fig. 102, Nos 10–15) and ten sherds of grog-tempered pottery.

Ditches B139 and B141 were heavily truncated by Roman period features and a few sherds of Roman pottery present in the recovered assemblage were intrusive.

Cropmarks indicated the presence of a ditch forming a right-angled junction with Ditch B139 and perhaps a south side for the enclosure. A south-east corner, together with part of an east side, was also indicated by cropmarks forming an enclosure of maximum dimensions 22 by 28 m. with long axis north-west to south-east. An apparent gap in the line of the mark defining the southern side of the enclosure may be interpreted as a possible entrance. No trace of ditches in these locations was found during the excavation. It is possible that machine clearance of this part of Area B may have removed all trace of the features or that machine trample may have obscured them.

Ditch B8 (Fig. 42)

An adjoining enclosure or field to the north-east was indicated by a third ditch aligned north-east to south-west (B8). This feature, identified as a soil stain 26.50 m. long contined the line of the enclosure from the junction of the early ditches to the boundary of excavation. The ditch, sample-excavated in only one location (Fig. 42, inset section), where it was cut to a v-shaped profile 1.35 m. wide and 0.43 m. deep, contained a fill of medium brown sandy loam with gravel lenses and flecks of carbon and burnt clay. The fill yielded three undiagnostic flint-tempered sherds.

Ditches B17, B18 and B20

Three ditches, closely set and aligned approximately north-west to south-east, appeared to post-date Ditch B8, but were earlier than other Period 4 ditches in the area.

The southernmost ditch (B17) was traced from the western edge of the excavation for over 19 m. and ended in a rounded terminal. The ditch (Fig. 42, inset section), on average 1 m. wide and 0.30 m. deep, was filled with a dark brown gravelly loam containing five undiagnostic flint-tempered sherds and ten grogged sherds (including Fig. 109, Nos 71–2).

The second and third ditches (B18 and B20) were set roughly parallel to one another 1.50–2 m. apart and were of near identical size, being 0.75–0.80 m. wide and 0.25–0.30 m. deep (Fig. 42, inset sections). Both ditches were filled with a mid brown loam. Ditch B18 provided one flint-tempered sherd (Fig. 102, No. 9), three grog-tempered and two Romano-British sherds. Ditch B20 yielded a single sherd of undiagnostic flint-tempered ware. The broad similarities and close proximity of the two ditches suggested that they were contemporary. Ditch B17 may also have formed part of the same arrangement of ditches. As the southern of the two parallel ditches (B18) was found to cut Ditch B8, all three ditches were considered to post-date Enclosure B139.

The function of the three ditches is difficult to determine, but they may represent a short-lived boundary or boundaries perhaps for a field extending to the north, established after Ditch B8 had been backfilled and before a new enclosure (Enclosure B3) was established at the northern end of Area B, in Period 4B.

The post-hole row

Post-dating Ditch B8 was a row of six post-pits arranged in pairs (B137 and B142; B138 and B160; B150 and B167), and aligned north-east to south-west. The pits on average 0.40 to 0.50 m. in diameter were cut 0.15 to 0.50 m. deep. Although post-'ghosts' were not observed in the fills, the post-pit row, with paired posts set approximately 2 m. apart with gaps

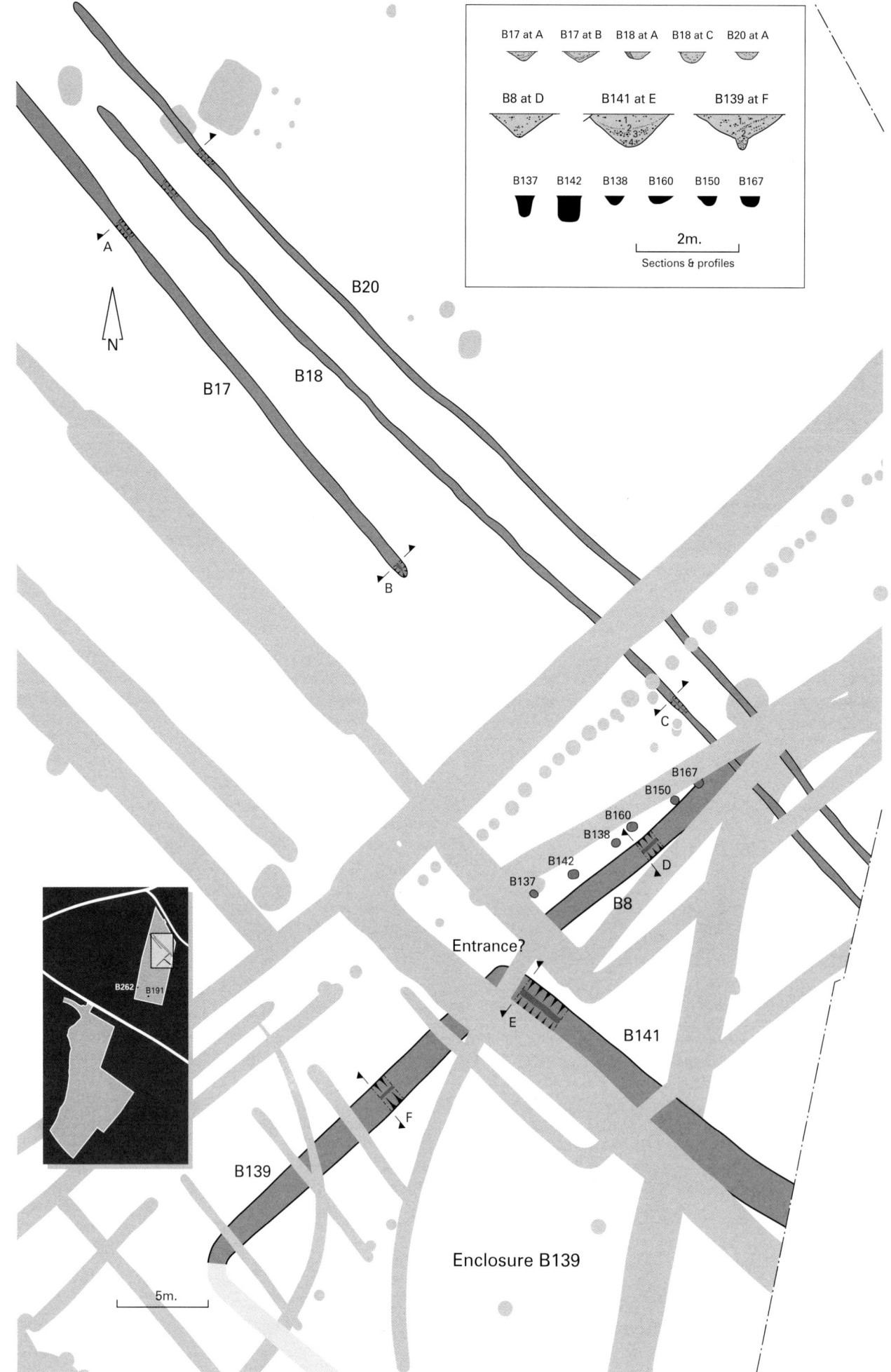

between each pair of 3 m., was interpreted as a fence line. The loam and gravel fills of all the post-pits, save for B150, provided twenty-one undiagnostic flint-tempered sherds and two Romano-British sherds.

The north-east pair of post-pits (B167, B150) was cut into the backfill of Ditch B8 and the north-easternmost post, B167, was cut by a Period 4B ditch which also cut ditches B18 and B20. The relationship suggests that the post-pit row may have been for a fence replacing Ditch B8 and may infer that Enclosure B139 and Ditch B18 may have been in use at the same time.

The isolated pit

One Period 4A feature remains to be described. This was a single pit, B191 located at the southern edge of Area B.

Pit B191 was roughly oval, measuring 1.10 by 0.60 m. and cut to a depth of 0.12 m. It was filled with dark brown gravelly loam yielding burnt flints and three sherds of flint-tempered pottery (including Fig. 102, No. 15).

Discussion

The earliest evidence for reoccupation following the end of Period 3B was represented by a small rectangular enclosure (B139) located in the north-east corner of Area B, dated by pottery *c.* 125–50 B.C. Combined evidence from the excavation and from cropmarks indicated a field enclosure measuring some 22 by 28 m. with a possible entrance in the centre of the southern side. A contemporary ditch continued the western side of the enclosure to the north, perhaps as an annex. A gap between the ditch and north-west side of the enclosure suggested an entrance giving on to the northern enclosure. Of later date were three north-west to south-east aligned ditches. The lightweight character of the features suggests that they may have been boundary ditches perhaps associated with a field extending to the north. The ditches continued beyond the excavated area; one appeared to terminate a short distance to the north-west. One of the ditches (B18) was found to cut the backfill of Ditch B8, clearly indicating that at least the north-eastern of the two enclosures was in disuse when the new ditch was cut. A row of six paired post-pits was perhaps for a north-east aligned fence linking the north-west corner of Enclosure B139 to Ditch B18. Two of the post-pits were found to cut Ditch B8 suggesting that the fence replaced that boundary and further indicated that Enclosure B139 and Ditch B18 may have been in use at the same time. The Period 4A features appeared to be aligned to the north-eastern edge of the plateau and perhaps to relict boundaries that may have still been visible in the landscape.

No pits or other signs of domestic activity could be directly linked to Enclosure B139. Only one pit containing late Period 4A ceramics was identified against the southern boundary of the excavation and at some remove from the enclosure and tentatively assigned to this period.

Period 4B summary

A major change appears to have taken place in the third quarter of the first century B.C. At this time ditches forming an early enclosure (B139) and the remains of a possible a field system (B17, B18 and B20) went into disuse and were replaced by a set of substantial ditches forming a new polygonal enclosure (B3). Situated at the northern end of Area B, three sides of the enclosure fell within the excavation, with an entrance at the southern corner. A pair of curving but discontinuous ditches located south of the entrance may have formed part of an outwork. The enclosure contained no contemporary features. Of broadly the same date was an isolated pit (B262) located in the south-west corner of Area B.

The enclosure was provided with new ditches in successive phases, but retained a consistent polygonal shape. The reconstructed shape of the enclosure and developmental sequence of boundary ditches has been established by pottery recovered from the ditches and from cropmarks identified in a series of air photographs taken before and during the excavation.

Enclosure B3 (Fig. 37)

The north-western side of the enclosure was defined by a north-east to south-west aligned ditch (B33). Approximately 45 m. of the ditch was identified by soil stain. The ditch, where sectioned (Fig. 43, inset sections), was u-shaped, on average 1 m. wide and 0.33 m. deep. The ditch fills of yellow-brown sandy gravel, capped by a single fill of medium brown sandy loam and gravel provided no datable finds.

The south-western side of the enclosure (Ditch B3) was traced for 38 m. The ditch, on average 1.30 m. wide, was cut to a maximum depth of 0.45 m. to an open 'u' profile (Fig. 43, inset sections). A rounded terminal at the south-east end of the ditch formed one side of a possible entrance. The ditch contained a bi-partite fill of pale brown sandy gravel (Layer 2) capped by medium brown loam and sparse gravel (Layer 1). The uppermost fill provided seven undiagnostic sherds, one flint-tempered and one grog-tempered.

A 28 m. length of north-east to south-west aligned ditch (B9) formed the south-eastern side of the enclosure. The ditch, on average 1.40 m. wide and 0.50 m. deep was cut to a v-shaped profile. A narrow slot observed in the base of the

Fig. 42 (*opposite*). Period 4A. Enclosure B139.

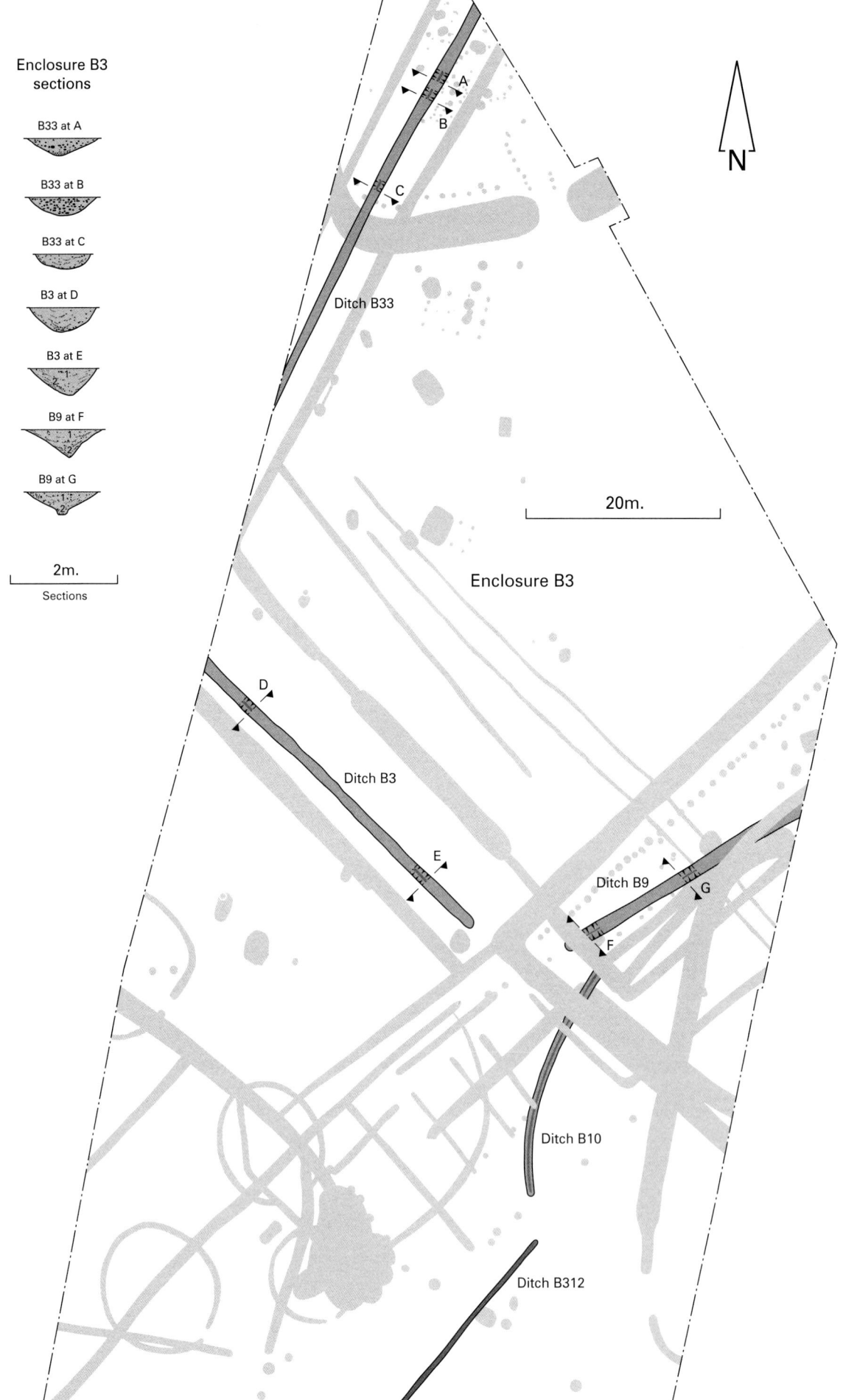

ditch, suggested that it was deepened during use (Fig. 43, inset sections). The western end of the ditch was v-shaped (section B9, F) and ended with a rounded terminal forming the eastern side of a 9.50 m. wide entrance to the enclosure. The fill of pale brown sandy gravel (Layer 2) capped by medium brown loam (Layer 1), provided eighteen flint-tempered sherds.

Ditches B10 and B312

Perhaps cut shortly after the enclosure was formed were two curving lengths of ditch (B10 and B312) that appeared to form an outwork designed perhaps to screen the enclosure entrance.

Ditch B10 was aligned approximately north–south with its surviving northern end (cut by later ditches) lying close to the eastern side of the enclosure entrance. The ditch was traced for 23 m. where a further linear soil stain indicated a separate but perhaps contemporary ditch aligned north-east to south-west. Ditch B10 was 1 m. wide and 0.50 m. deep. Cut to a u-shaped profile the ditch contained a primary lens of pale brown silt and gravel, a secondary fill of medium brown loamy gravel and a bulk tertiary fill of dark brown gravelly loam. The lowest fill provided a single sherd of grog-tempered pottery (Fig. 109, No. 73) dated to the first century B.C. Ditch B312 was not excavated.

The function of the sinuous pair of ditches was difficult to determine but the alignment and northern termination of Ditch B10, suggested a relationship with the enclosure entrance. As most ditches were probably accompanied by a bank and more likely a bank and pale or hedge, it is possible that the ditches were formed to screen the enclosure entrance or flank the west side of a field south and east of the enclosure entrance.

The isolated pit (Figs 31 and 41)

Pit B262 was located within the footprint of an earlier Period 3B circular building (B260) in the south-west corner of Area B. The oval pit, 1 m. by 0.80 m., cut 0.50 m. deep, was filled with dark brown gravelly loam flecked with carbon and burnt clay. The fill contained one Late Iron Age flint-tempered sherd (Fig. 102, No. 18) and one sherd of Dressel 1B amphora (not illustrated) dated 60–10 B.C.

Discussion

In this period a large single-ditched polygonal-shaped enclosure (B3) was constructed over an earlier arrangement of ditches forming a small enclosure and possible fields at the northern end of Area B. The new enclosure, with a southern entrance causeway and a possible outwork comprising two curving, discontinuous ditches approximately aligned north-east to south-west, was only partly within the excavated area. The excavated ditches were traced as cropmarks in adjacent fields to form an irregular pentagonal enclosure of some 0.7 hectare extent.

The enclosure occupied a north-eastern spur of the plateau, with northern and eastern sides set against the top of shelving ground. Its location provided spectacular views across the surrounding countryside, most specifically the Wantsum Channel to the east. However, although the surviving remains of the fills were truncated as a result of soil erosion and the activities of quarrying machinery, the ditches do not appear to have been defensive in character, even if originally accompanied by an internal bank and hedge. The excavated sections, although limited in scope, produced just twenty-one sherds of pottery (Table 16), and although about half the interior was examined, no evidence for contemporary buildings or pits was found. The size of the enclosure and its ditches nevertheless indicates that it performed an important function, with the cutting of replacement ditches during Period 4C, testifying to near continuous use until c. A.D. 75; quite what that function may have been is hard to determine. It is possible that its use was agricultural, though its shape is rather elaborate. Its conspicuous position and its apparent isolation suggest that it may have been built as a focal point for a more widely scattered community, perhaps as a place of common assembly

Period 4C summary

In Period 4C, Enclosure B3 was reconstructed to approximately the same plan but with a reduced internal area (Enclosure B7). Perhaps of contemporary construction was a set of outer ditches to the north-west (B32), to the south (B2) and to the south-east (B336). A possible outer entrance was identified at the southern corner. Enclosure B7 appeared to have been constructed as a double-ditched enclosure with staggered entrances on the south-west side. Cropmarks identified on air photographs helped to reconstruct the enclosure plan.

Enclosure B7 (Fig. 44)

The south-eastern ditch of the new enclosure (B7) was cut through the infilled ditch of the previous enclosure (B9). The new ditch, traced for 29 m. was on average 1.25 m. wide, but widened to 2 m. at the south-east corner of the new enclosure. The ditch, cut 0.50 m. deep to a v-shaped profile (Fig. 44 inset sections F and G), contained a primary fill of yellow-brown sand (layer 3) capped by successive deposits of dark brown gravelly loam (layer 2) and mid brown loam

Fig. 43 (*opposite*). Period 4B. Enclosure B3.

Part 2: The Excavated Evidence

Highstead, near Chislet

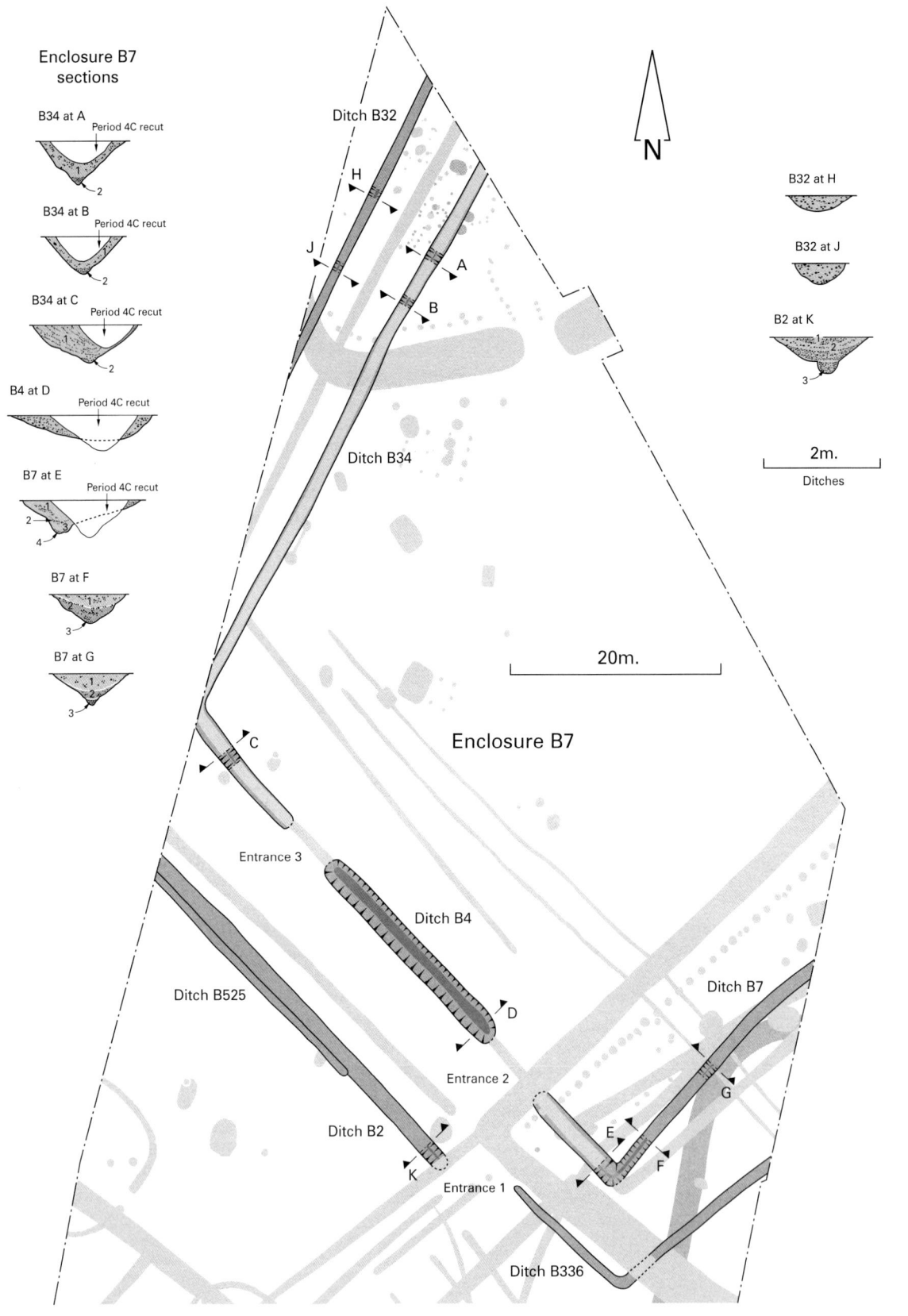

Fig. 44. Period 4C. Enclosure B7.

and gravel (layer 1).The bulk upper fills provided eighty-nine grog-tempered sherds (including Fig. 110, Nos 78–88) dating into the first half of the first century A.D.

A north-west to south-east aligned ditch (part of B7) springing from the south-east corner of the enclosure was traced for 10 m. where it appeared to terminate at an entrance approximately 6.50 m. wide (Entrance 2). This part of Ditch B7, together with other ditches forming the south-west side of the enclosure, had been truncated along their axis by a later ditch (B143) (Fig. 44, inset sections A–E, showing late Period 4C recut). The central part of the south-west side of the enclosure was defined by Ditch B4. The ditch was traced for 22.50 m. from south-east to north-west where it ended with a rounded terminal, suggesting the location of a second smaller entrance approximately 5 m. wide (Entrance 3). A separate ditch (B34) continued to the line of the western edge of the excavation where it returned on a north-east to south-west line to form the western side of the new enclosure.

Between Entrances 2 and 3, Ditch B4 was 2.40 m. wide and 0.40 m. deep, cut to an open 'u' profile with shallow sloping sides to the south-west (Fig. 44, inset section). The gravel and loam fills of Ditch B4 provided a massive 453 sherds of grog-tempered fabric (including Figs 110–12, Nos 91–95, 97–102, 105–13, 115, 119–12- and 122–3) dating from the first century B.C. into the mid first century A.D. Included in the material were 117 sherds of flint-tempered fabrics (including Fig. 104, Nos 32–37), two sherds of grog- and chalk-tempered fabric (including Fig. 124, No. 321), a fragment of an iron saw blade (p. 273) and a handle fashioned from antler (p. 278).

The south-west corner and the west side of the enclosure (to the west of Entrance 3) was defined by Ditch B34. The ditch was cut to an average width of 1.30 m. and depth of 0.65 m. (Fig. 44 inset sections), and was traced for a length of 56 m. The fill of silty sand flecked with burnt clay and carbon capped by medium brown gravelly loam provided just two sherds of grog-tempered pottery (including Fig. 112, No. 124). The line of the ditch was traced to the north-east as a cropmark where it returned to the east to form the northern and north-eastern sides of the enclosure, before returning south-east to link with Ditch B7.

Some 9 m. south-east of Ditch B7 was a soil stain for a ditch set parallel to Ditch B7. The soil stain (B336) appeared to follow a parallel line to the southern corner of the enclosure and the southernmost part of the south-western side of the enclosure set some 5 m. distant. The soil stain, extending parallel to the southernmost side of the enclosure, terminated some way short of enclosure Entrance 2 and did not continue.

Extending parallel to and 9.50 m. south of the south-west boundary was a second soil stain for a ditch. The ditch (B2) was traced for 32 m. and terminated opposite enclosure Entrance 2. The ditch sample-excavated at its terminal (Fig. 44, inset section) was on average 1.80 m. wide and 0.40 m. deep. A slot 0.38 m. wide and 0.20 m. deep cut in the base of the flat-bottomed ditch suggested the feature had received some maintenance. The basal fills of the ditch and slot, of medium brown gravelly loam (layer 3) was capped by banded deposits of medium brown loam and gravel (layers 2 and 1). Only the uppermost fills provided datable finds comprising 157 grog-tempered sherds (including Fig. 112, Nos 125–9) dating into the post-conquest period. There was also a quantity of late material, including samian ware (p. 272) and mortaria (p. 247, Table 27) dating into the mid second century and three iron objects (p. 273 and s.f. no. 119, *not illus.*). Ditch B2 was recut for the greater part of its length by a later ditch (B525) and the second-century material may have derived from that.

A possible outer ditch was found to extend some 6.50 m. to the north-west of Ditch B34. The ditch (B32), traced for 31 m., was 1 m. wide and 0.30 m. deep (Fig. 44 inset sections). Cut to a u-shaped profile, it contained a fill of light brown gravelly loam and was also traced as a cropmark (Fig. 5) where it appeared to define an outer north-west, north, north-east and south-east side to the enclosure. The cropmark converged with the south-east boundary to overlap just outside the excavated area. Ditch B32 was also traced as a cropmark to the south-west, where again it appeared to form an outer north-west boundary to the enclosure. The mark returned to the south-east, just outside the excavated area, to form an outer south-west boundary and link with excavated Ditch B2

Late modifications to Enclosure B7 (Fig. 45)

In the closing years of Period 4C the internal enclosure ditches (B7, B4 and B34) were recut. Ditches B34, B4 and the south-western arm of the southern corner of Ditch B7 were recut on line (Fig. 44 recuts in inset sections A–E; Fig. 45, inset sections A and B) and the internal ditch on the south-east side of the enclosure was recut on a new line a short way to the south-east of the previous boundary. The new ditch (B143) on all sides was of similar size and profile, being on average 1.25 m. wide, cut to a v-shape profile with rounded sump up to 0.60 m. deep. The new ditch was cut across entrances 2 and 3 to close the southern side. Ditch B143 was identified late in the excavation process and although recorded in the enclosure entrances and at the southern corner of the enclosure, elsewhere the ditch was only identified in section after excavation had taken place. The excavated sections of Ditch B143 were filled with pale brown sandy gravel providing sixteen flint-tempered sherds (including Fig. 104, No. 40). The drawn sections were recorded with similar fills. The pottery recovered from the B7 enclosure contained a quantity of material dating late in the period. The recut of the outer Ditch B2 to the south-west was identified only as a soil stain (B525) (Fig. 44) and not excavated. The soil stain was apparent only for two thirds of

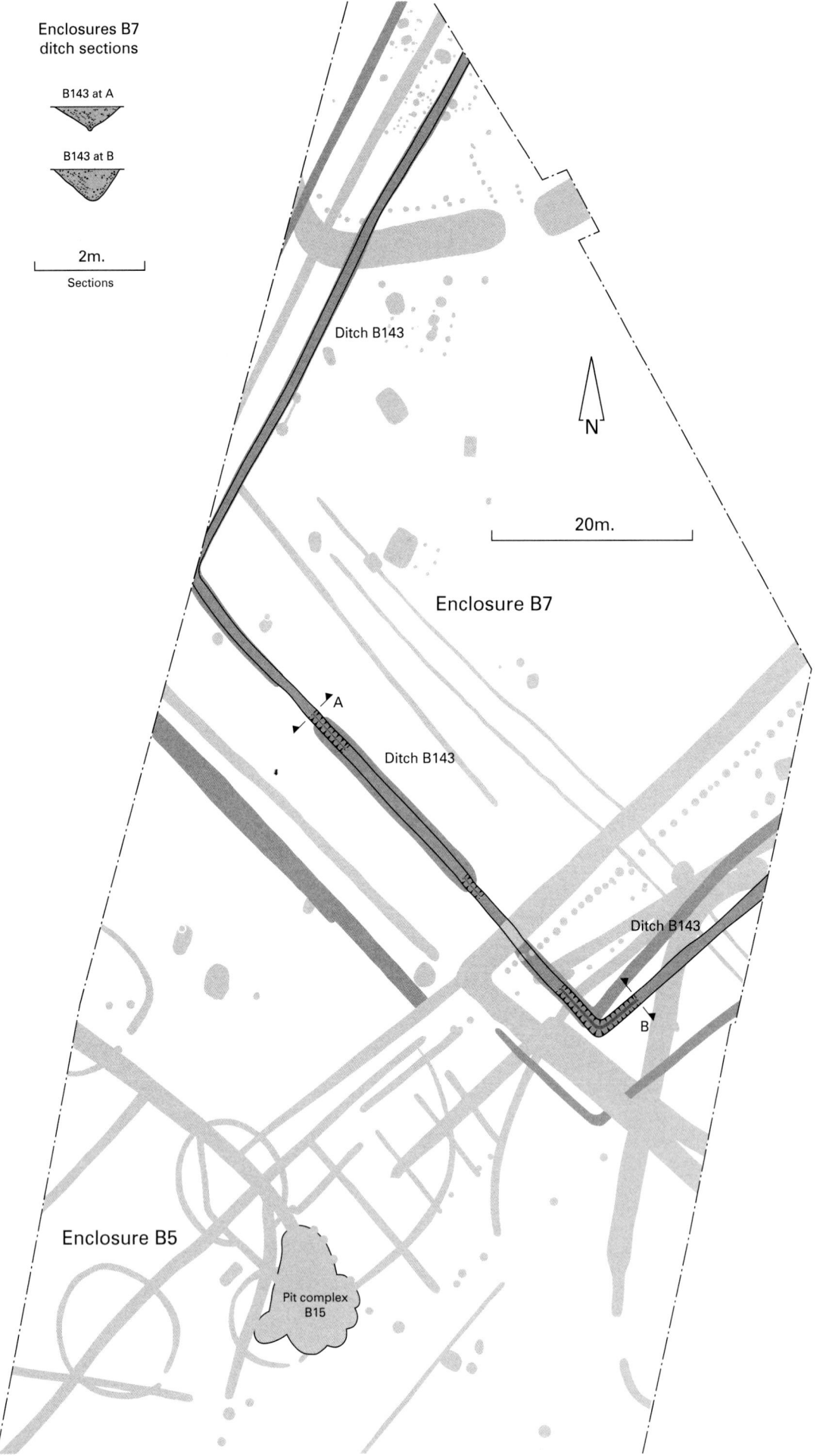

the length of Ditch B2; the south-easternmost third appears to have contained an intact backfill. Soil stain B336 (Fig. 44) defining the southern outer corner of the enclosure and Ditch B32, defining the outer north-western side, provided no evidence of having been recut and there was no indication of a replacement entrance.

Discussion

During Period 4C Enclosure B3 was entirely rebuilt. The rebuilding involved the infilling of the enclosure ditches and perhaps the levelling of associated banks. The rebuilt enclosure, B7, was more elaborate than its predecessor being provided with double ditches and a staggered entrance piercing the south-west side of the enclosure. The outer ditch was interrupted by a single entrance west of the southern corner and the inner ditch was pierced by two wide openings symmetrically located in the enclosure side.

Although the enclosure was provided with double ditches, it is not possible to say that they were cut at the same time, but it is likely that they were open simultaneously. Despite the double ditches, and perhaps double bank, one between the two ditches and one inside the inner ditch, neither of the ditches was of sufficient size and depth to suggest that the enclosure was rebuilt for a defensive purpose. The rebuilt enclosure contained no contemporary features. Such an elaborate construction is unlikely to have been formed to surround agricultural fields or to contain animals and therefore some other use is likely. In contrast to the relative paucity of finds from Enclosure B3, its Period 4B predecessor, large quantities of pottery were recovered from the ditches of Enclosure B7. Ditch B4 produced 578 sherds; B7, 108 sherds; and the terminal of B2, 173 sherds. While this may be to some extent due to sampling strategies, there is no doubt that Enclosure B7 witnessed considerable activity, while still apparently maintaining an open, empty interior. The earlier use of Enclosure B3 appears to have been maintained in B7, with the expanded ditches giving added emphasis to its function. With the evidence available interpretation is largely speculation, but it may have continued to serve as a focal point for assembly of the surrounding population.

At the end of the period, the inner ditch and at least one of the outer ditches were recut to close the south-western entrances to the enclosure, suggesting a major change or re-alignment of the enclosure late in its life.

Period 4D summary

In Area B during Period 4D, Enclosure B7 went out of use and was superseded by a new subrectangular enclosure built over its south-eastern side (B1). Only the south-west corner of the new enclosure fell within the excavated area; the plan of the enclosure was established from cropmarks. A second, probably contemporary, irregular-shaped enclosure or field with a south-east entrance (B5) was established to the south-west of the new enclosure. Immediately east of the entrance was a large area of disturbed ground (B15) thought to represent an area of intercutting pits, the earliest of which may have been of 'Belgic' or Early Roman date.

In Area A, reoccupation of this part of the plateau occurred after a gap of over 400 years with the cutting of a series of north–south aligned ditches. The ditches appeared to represent the fragmentary remains of a system of long, narrow fields, bounded to the north and south by single but more substantial east–west aligned ditches.

Enclosure B1 (Fig. 46)

Enclosure B1, located at the north-east end of Area B, overlying the eastern edge of the 30 m. gravel terrace, was laid out on approximately the same axis as its predecessor (Enclosure B7). The north-west side of the enclosure was defined by a ditch aligned north-east to south-west (B1). The ditch for the south-west side of the enclosure (B164) was aligned north-west to south-east and the two ditches formed a right-angled, south-west corner for a subrectangular enclosure of approximately some 0.64 hectare extent, the plan of which was determined by cropmarks (Figs 5 and 13).

Ditch B1 (Pl. X) was traced for a length of 48 m. and was on average 2.60 m. wide and 0.60–0.70 m. deep. Generally, the ditch was cut to a broad, open, v-shaped profile, but in places it was cut to a sharp v-shaped profile and elsewhere to a u-shaped profile, with a near flat base (Fig. 46, inset sections). Although there were variations in shape, the ditch fills comprised two bulk deposits: a primary fill of fine gravels, pale brown sand and mid brown silty clay (Layer 2), all perhaps formed as a consequence of weathering, and an upper and majority fill of banded layers of mid and dark brown loam with charcoal and gravel (Layer 1). The primary fills provided 130 flint-tempered sherds (including Fig. 105, Nos 41–4) as well as some grog-tempered and Romano-British sherds. The upper fills, excavated as a single context, yielded a wide range of local and imported Roman ceramics (342 sherds) ranging in date from the mid first to mid second century (Tables 18–20, Figs 130–36). The assemblage is notable for the range of grog-tempered wares (including Figs 118–19, Nos 230–59) and Canterbury-type kitchen coarsewares and a few sherds of samian ware including one stamp (p. 244) dating into the mid second century. The upper fills also provided three glass fragments from at least two vessels (p. 275) and seven metal objects. Of these two were of copper alloy (an unguent or ear

---

Fig. 45 (*opposite*). Period 4C. Late modifications to Enclosure B7.

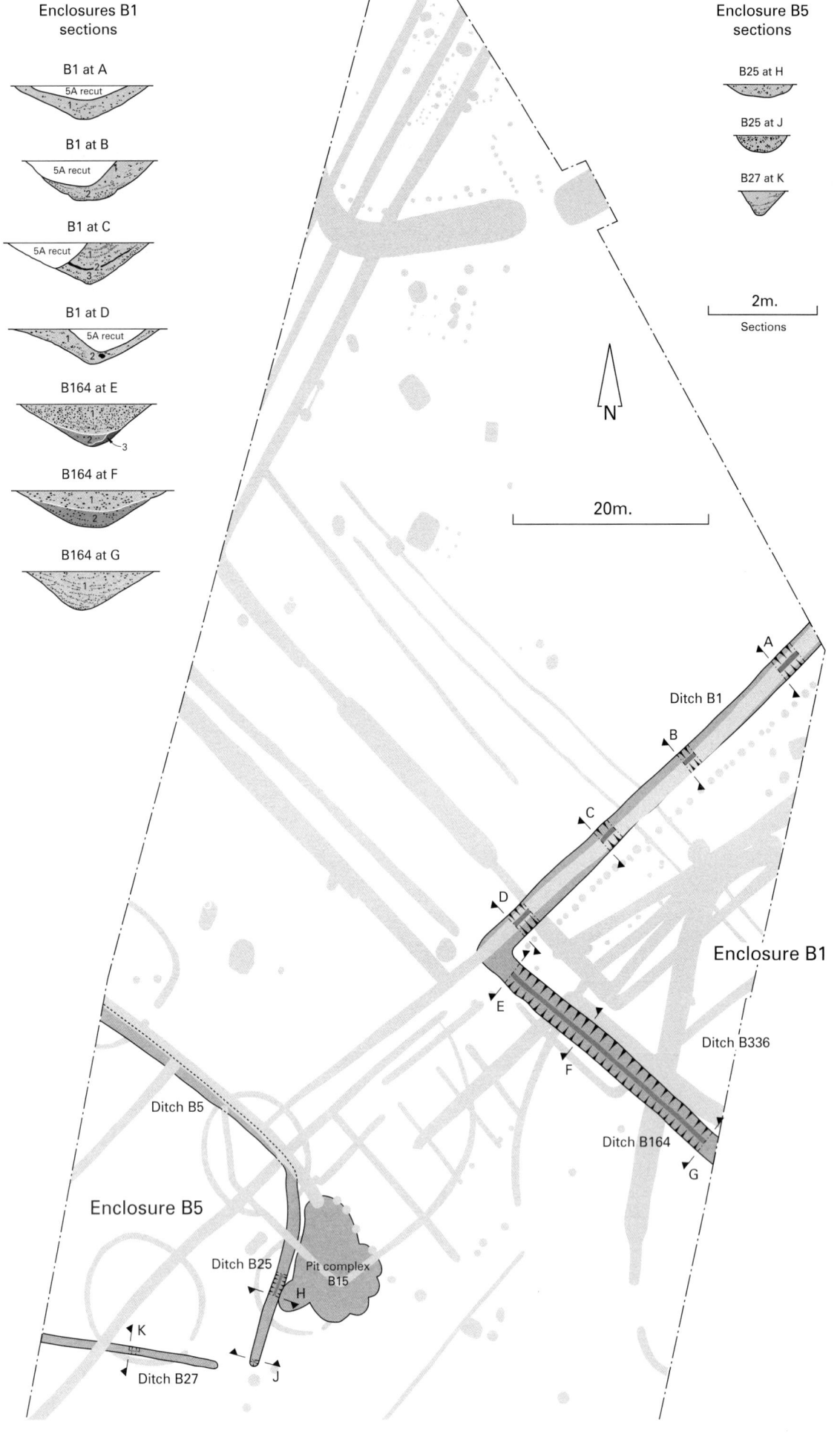

Pl. X. Periods 4 and 5. Enclosure ditch B1 and later post-pits, looking north-east. Scale 2 m.

scoop and part of a plate brooch, p. 275, Nos 8 and 34) and five were of iron (a double-spiked loop, No. 18; a coiled ferrule, No. 26; part of a horseshoe, No. 27; part of a link from a cauldron chain, No. 28 and a possible chisel, not illustrated).

Ditch B164 was traced for approximately 33 m. The width varied from 2.40–2.75 m., but the depth of the feature was consistently between 0.60–0.70 m. The ditch profile was similar to that of Ditch B1 (Fig. 46, inset sections). The fills were also broadly similar to those of Ditch B1. A primary fill of pale sandy silt, clay and fine gravel was overlain by banded deposits of brown and mid brown gravelly loam, flecked with charcoal. An upper fill of dark-to-medium brown gravelly loam completed the sequence. The primary fills of redeposited weathered soil provided 149 flint-tempered sherds (including Fig. 105, Nos 45–51); the secondary and tertiary fills, excavated as a single context, provided 419 grog-tempered sherds (including, Fig. 117, Nos 208–29), 413 'Belgic' fine sandy ware sherds and 298 sherds of local and imported wares. The bulk of the assemblage has been dated to c. A.D. 50–70 (Table 17, Figs 125–9, pp. 216–25) although some later material was present including a samian ware stamp (p. 244) dating into the mid second century. The group is notable for indigenous sandy wares.

The B1 enclosure ditches contained a huge corpus of 2159 sherds of pottery, the majority (1285) from the fill of Ditch B164. Although the bulk of the material dated from the mid first century A.D. there were small but significant groups of earlier and later material. Whilst the residual 'Belgic' and earlier Iron Age material is to be expected, the presence of quantities of later pottery requires explanation. Both ditches were excavated as bulk deposits without separation of individual fills. Ditch B1 was found to have been recut by a later Period 5 ditch (B165, Fig. 48), but the discovery was made too late in the excavation process to prevent contamination of the earlier fills. A greater quantity of later material was recovered from Ditch B164. As this ditch was not cut by later features the only explanation for the presence of material dating up to the mid second century is that the feature or parts of the feature remained open to receive rubbish until at least that time. It is also likely that part of B1 also remained visible in the landscape well into Period 5 and that some of the late material may have been introduced up to a century after the earthwork was originally constructed.

Air photographs taken before and during the excavation provided evidence of cropmarks enabling a reconstruction of the enclosure plan. Taken together with the excavated ditches, the cropmarks described a roughly rectangular

Fig. 46 (*opposite*). Period 4D. Enclosures B1 and B5 and Pit complex B15.

enclosure aligned long axis north-west to south-east, of sides measuring approximately 85 m. by 75 m.

Enclosure B1 was again sited on the very edge of a promontory with long distance views on all sides. The ditches of the enclosure were substantial and it is likely that an internal bank of some size would have accompanied the ditch. There was no evidence for a revetment. A line of posts found adjoining the ditch on its south-east side were of a later date and are not connected with Ditch B1. The lack of a revetment means that it is unlikely that the bank would have been taken to a great height and if embellished in any way it is more likely to have been planted with a hedge rather than a palisade.

Enclosure B5 (Fig. 46)

Enclosure B5, located some 34 m. south-west of Enclosure B1, set against the western boundary of the excavation, was defined by three ditches (B5, B25 and B27).

The north-eastern side of the enclosure was formed by a north-west to south-east aligned ditch (B5) cut to an open 'u' profile, and on average 1.20 m. wide and 0.35 m. deep. The ditch fill, of pale brown sandy silt capped by medium brown gravelly loam, provided a mixed group of Late Iron Age pottery, together with a smaller number of Roman coarse and fineware sherds dating into the late first century A.D. The south-eastern part of Ditch B5 was almost entirely removed by a later, Period 5A ditch (B23). Some of the later dated material recovered from the fill of Ditch B5 may derive from the Period 5A ditch.

The eastern side of the enclosure was formed by a 19 m. long north–south aligned ditch (B25). The ditch, 1.20 m. wide and cut 0.30 m. deep ended with a rounded terminal to the south, forming the east side of an entrance into the enclosure. The ditch fill of medium brown loam provided three flint-tempered and twenty grog-tempered sherds (including Fig. 114, No. 155) as well as fifty-three Roman sherds dating into the later first century A.D. The northern end of Ditch B25 was cut by two later (Period 5A) ditches (B23 and B24A).

The southern side of the enclosure was closed by Ditch B27. Aligned east–west, and traced for at least 18.50 m. into the west section, the ditch was 0.50 m. wide and 0.43 m. deep. The east end of the ditch ended with a rounded terminal for an entrance 3.30 m. wide. The brown sandy gravel fills of the ditch provided no datable finds. The feature was traced as a cropmark on the same alignment for a further 25 m.

Pit complex B15

Immediately east of Enclosure B5 was a large and irregular area of disturbed ground. The disturbance appeared to respect the line of Ditch B25, but a stratigraphic relationship was not established. The feature, of maximum dimensions 13 m. north–south by 11 m. east–west was cut with irregular lobed sides and undulating base between 0.50 and 1.10 m. deep. Individual pits were not recognised in the homogeneous fill and the feature was excavated as a single context. Although it is possible that gravel extraction may have had something to do with the formation of the extensive feature, the high proportion of Iron Age flint- and grog-tempered pottery and substantial quantities of later material dating into the mid second century A.D. (pp. 225–33, Tables 18–20; Figs 130–35, 137), suggest that this was an area of intercutting pits and perhaps other features spanning a considerable period. Although Enclosure B5 appeared to form a western boundary to the area of disturbance, and a ditch springing from the north-east corner of the enclosure (B23) may have been formed to drain water into a pre-existing cutting indicating a direct relationship between the two features, the sheer quantity of early pottery suggests that the earliest of the pits may pre-date the establishment of Enclosure B5. That the area was used intermittently for the cutting of pits and the disposal of rubbish into Period 5 is clearly suggested by significant quantities of Roman coarse and finewares recovered from the fills. The pit fills also provided the largest collection of small finds from any of the Area A or B features (pp. 270–79). Copper alloy finds included two brooches (Nos 31 and 33), a needle (No. 9), a pin (No. 3), two possible toilet probes (Nos 4 and 5), tweezers (No. 6), a barbed fish hook (No. 11) and two pieces of wire (No. 13). Objects of iron included a latch-lifter (No. 17), a socketed hook (No. 23), a T-staple (No. 29) and a fragment of binding for woodwork (No. 30). Glass fragments included a bowl rim (No. 36) and bottle, flask and jar sherds. One spindlewhorl was present (No. 40). Part of the upper stone of a Lower Greensand quern was recovered (No. 49) and two fragments of human bone (p. 279), parts of a femur and a radius of an adult aged 20–35 years. These were the only human bones recovered from the entire site. Animal bones were also recovered although not in great numbers. Those bones that did survive were in very poor condition, but a range of species were represented including ox, sheep/goat, pig and horse.

Early field system, Area A (Fig. 47)

Following a long period of abandonment, perhaps lasting over 400 years, a complex of north–south aligned ditches, flanked to the south and north by east–west aligned ditches, appeared to pre-date all other field boundaries and may form vestigial elements of an early system of fields in Area A.

An east–west aligned ditch, A249, represented a southern boundary for the field system. The ditch, traced for 22 m., was 1.80 m. wide and 0.42 m. deep. Cut to a shallow v-shaped profile, it was filled with a mid brown gravelly loam from which was retrieved a corpus of grogged and sandy wares dating from the mid to late first century A.D. An upper capping fill of darker sandy loam and gravel provided a smaller number of Roman wares, including South Gaulish samian and a mortaria sherd dating up to the early to mid second century A.D.

Adjoining the boundary to the north were three north–south aligned ditches (A252, A272 and A246).

The westernmost ditch (A252) mapped for 18 m. was 1.57 m. wide and 0.30 m. deep, filled with successive deposits of mid brown and dark brown gravelly loam. The fill yielded a fragment of quern in Millstone Grit from Northern England (p. 278).

The second ditch (A272), set parallel to the first, adjoined the southern boundary of the field system, some 16 m. to the east. The ditch, mapped for 51.50 m. was 1 m. wide and 0.20 m. deep. The fill of pale brown sandy loam and gravel yielded a single grog-tempered sherd.

The easternmost ditch (A246), located 8 m. east of the middle ditch, was traced for 44 m. It was 0.85–1.30 m. wide and 0.33–0.51 m. deep and was filled with a dark brown gravelly loam which provided grogged and fine sandy ware pottery, and an imported sherd of Gallo-Belgic *terra rubra* of the early first century A.D. A small number of Roman coarseware sherds were also recovered.

To the north of the southern arrangement of field boundaries were a further four north–south aligned ditches (A263, A294, A262 and A229).

The westernmost ditch of the group, A294, was mapped as a soil stain for approximately 6 m. but not excavated.

The easternmost ditch, A262, may have been a northern continuation of Ditch A252. Traced for approximately 10 m., the ditch, cut to a u-shaped profile, was between 0.55–0.80 m. wide and 0.25–0.38 m. deep. The fill, of mid brown gravelly loam provided a few sherds of residual Iron Age flint-tempered pottery, a number of grog-tempered sherds (including Fig. 109, Nos 74–7) and four Roman coarseware sherds dating up to the late first century A.D. The northern end of the ditch ended with a rounded terminal, defining the south side of a 3.25 m. wide causeway. The line of the boundary was continued by Ditch A229 which extended on a north–south line for a further 33 m. An east–west boundary (A117) lay a short way to the north and it is likely that the two ditches formed a north-east corner to the field system. The southern terminal of Ditch A229 cut a short section of a pre-existing ditch (A228) which may have been an earlier version of Ditch A229.

Ditch A228, aligned north–south and traced for 7.50 m., had been recut by Ditch A229. Best preserved at its northern end, the ditch was 1.20 m. wide and 0.42 m. deep, cut to an open 'v' profile. The ditch was not recorded beyond this point, but is presumed to have continued. The fill of medium brown gravelly loam with much burnt flint, provided nine early to late Iron Age flint-tempered sherds (including Fig. 103, No. 21) and an iron knife blade (Fig. 102, No. 16).

Ditch A229, between 1–1.40 m. wide and 0.30–0.50 m. deep, was cut to a u-shaped profile and was filled with mid brown gravelly loam. The fills provided some flint-tempered sherds (including Fig. 103, No. 20) and a number of grog-tempered sherds (including Fig. 114, Nos 149–54), and one sherd of imported white ware flagon dating into the second half of the first century A.D.

An isolated 18 m. length of north–south aligned ditch (A263) was located a short way north of the southern group of ditches. The ditch was of u-shaped profile, cut to an average width of between 0.60–0.95 m. and depth of 0.25–0.32 m. The fill of pale brown gravelly loam, provided a small number of prehistoric flint-tempered sherds and a single sherd of mortaria dated to the second century A.D. (Fig. 141, No. 586). The mortaria sherd was recovered from the uppermost fill and may have been deposited after the field system had gone into disuse.

A northern boundary to the field system was indicated by a discontinuous east–west ditch (A117/A117A), separated by a 3 m. wide causeway. The easternmost ditch (A117), traced for 52 m., was on average 1–1.20 m. wide and between 0.45–0.60 m. deep. The fill provided no datable finds. The boundary ditch was found to continue beyond the causeway (A117A) and was mapped but the speed of gravel extraction precluded excavation.

Pits, Area A

Three pits identified at different locations within Area A may be associated with the use of the field system.

The southernmost pit, A255 was located east of Ditch A263. The pit was subcircular, 2–2.60 m. in diameter and 0.42 m. deep. The fill, comprising carbon-rich dark brown loam capped by mid brown gravelly loam, provided two grog- and flint-tempered sherds (Fig. 104, Nos 38–9), a number of grog-tempered sherds (including Figs 113–14, Nos 136–48), sherds of 'Belgic' coarse sandy ware and a single Gallo-Belgic sherd of *terra nigra* dating from the early to mid first century A.D.

The second pit (A126) was located east of Ditch A294 and was oval, 0.85 m. in diameter and 0.36 m. deep. The fill of burnt loam, charcoal and daub, capping a yellow-brown clay lining, yielded one Iron Age flint-tempered sherd, a small number of grog-tempered sherds (including Fig. 113, Nos 130–33) and lumps of ironstone, broadly dated to the first half of the first century A.D.

The third pit (A131) was located a short way east of a causeway dividing ditches A262 and A229. The pit was rectangular, 1.40 by 0.80 m. in extent and 0.45 m. deep. The fill, of dark brown gravelly loam, contained a small number of grogged and 'Belgic' coarse sandy ware sherds dating to the first century A.D.

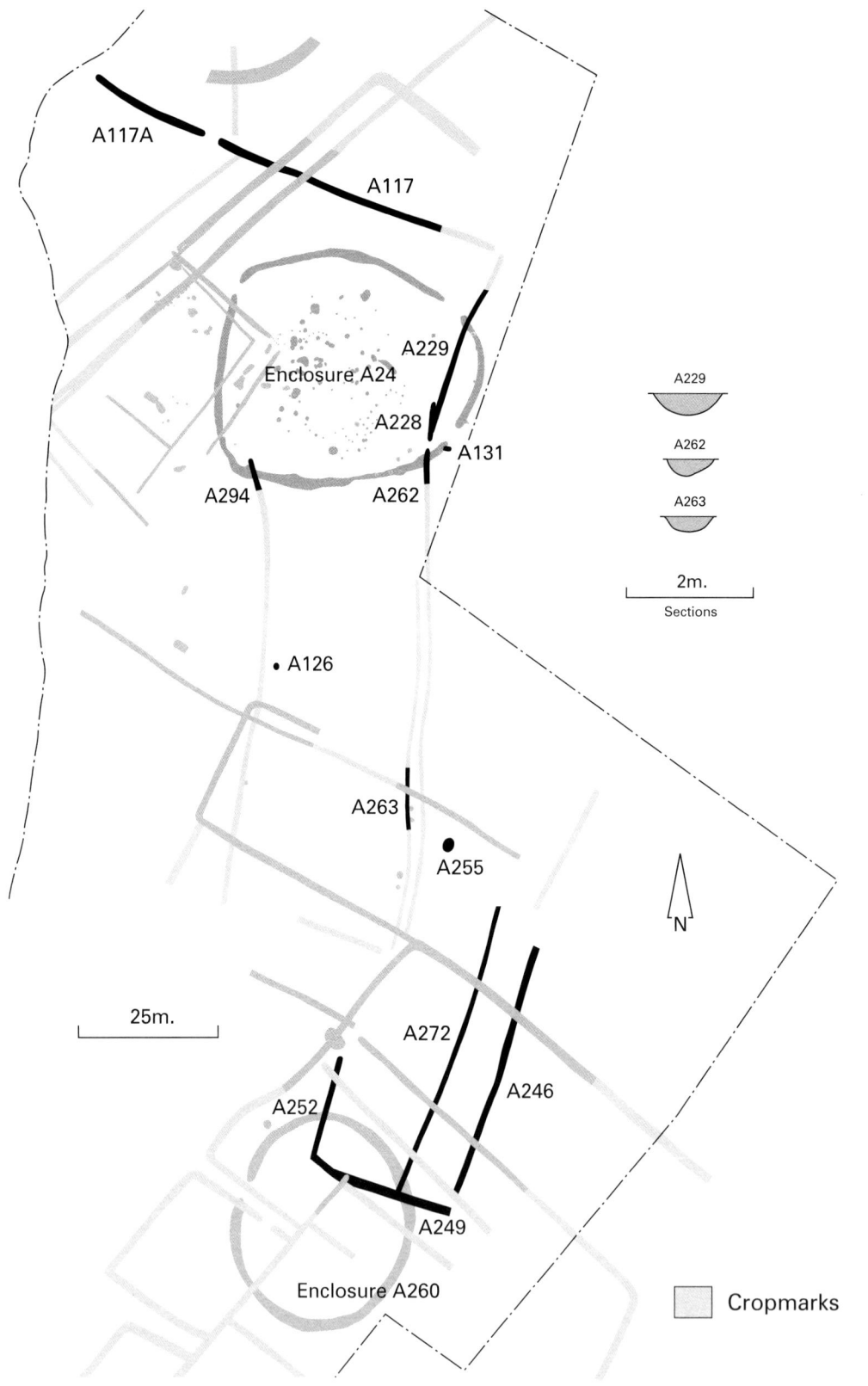

Fig. 47. Period 4D. Area A field ditches.

Discussion

In Area B, Enclosure B7 appears on pottery evidence to have gone into disuse at the end of the first quarter of the first century A.D. Sometime after this and possibly by the mid first century a new ditched enclosure (B1) was built over the southern side of B7. If the date range indicated by material recovered from the enclosure ditches is taken to represent a period of use, then the Enclosure B1 may have been long-lived. The size and depth of the enclosure ditches suggest a large accompanying internal bank and overall, given ditch size, the possible construction date and the enclosure's position overlooking the Wantsum sea channel, then the enclosure may conceivably have been built with defence in mind. No features were found within the enclosure, however, and there is no evidence to suggest either a military presence on the hilltop or that the deep ditches were cut for a defensive purpose.

Perhaps established at the same time as Enclosure B1, located to the south-west was a complex of ditches for a large field (B5). Combined evidence from the excavation and from a study of cropmarks (Pls V and VI) indicates that the field boundaries formed an irregular wedge shape aligned long axis north-west to south-east, with the narrowest part of the field to the south-east. A cropmark (Fig. 41) for a north-east to south-west aligned ditch joining the south-west corner of Enclosure B3 and intersecting with the north-east boundary of Enclosure B5 may have formed the north-west side of the field. If this was the case then the field may have been some considerable size. An entrance to the field was identified in the south-east corner of the earthwork. There were no apparent subdivisions of the field.

Adjoining the south-east side of the enclosure was a large, irregularly-shaped area of disturbed ground representing a zone of inter-cutting pits dating from the early first to the mid second century A.D. and perhaps later. As the feature was excavated as a single context it was impossible to determine with certainty the location and date of the earliest features. Despite the presence of some early material within the substantial corpus of finds recovered from the bulk fill, a connection between the construction of Enclosure B5 and the formation of the pit complex has been suggested on grounds of their spatial relationship. The western limit of disturbed ground appeared to respect the line of the enclosure boundary. The features however did not cut one another and the assignment of date for the earliest pits in the complex must remain conjectural. That pits contemporary with the use of the enclosure formed part of the larger feature is suggested by a significant corpus of pottery of the period. Whilst the presence of pits containing quantities of refuse is suggestive of domestic occupation, Enclosure B5 contained no pits or post-holes indicating the presence of occupation or buildings. The same pattern of ditches surrounding a settlement devoid of features, but containing substantial quantities of pottery was encountered with Enclosure B7 in the previous period. As in the case of B7, only a small portion of the enclosure was excavated and it is possible that settlement traces have eroded away. Nevertheless, it is possible that settlement contemporary with these enclosures lies nearby.

In Area A, resumption of occupation following protracted abandonment occurred in the period. The excavated remains comprised a series of shallow, north–south aligned ditches set between two more substantial east–west ditches, with the features perhaps forming vestigial traces of a field system some 160 by 55 m. in extent, aligned long axis north–south. The pattern of fields recorded was incomplete, but a bi-partite system of strip fields, the smallest approximately 10 m. wide (with perhaps four or more strips against the southern boundary) and the largest 40 m. wide (the western component of the complex) may be represented. The fields were of indeterminate length, but given the lack of intermediate east–west ditches, could have been up to 160 m. long. The northern and southern ditches probably formed major boundaries containing the fields. The size of the eastern and westernmost ditches suggested that they were not topographical boundaries. At least one of the field boundaries was re-cut during the life of the system and two causeways connecting fields were identified at the northern end of the complex. Three pits located within the complex but at distant locations were also dated by pottery to the period.

Although features immediately pre-dating the period were not located in Area A, the ditches of the field system did collectively contain a significant number of residual Iron Age flint-tempered sherds, possibly derived from the Periods 2 and 3 activity, or suggesting some form of later, more ephemeral, activity in the area before Period 4D.

Period 5: *c.* A.D. 75–250+

Introduction

Period 5 features and deposits date from the second half of the first century A.D. Although a few sherds of pottery post-dating the mid third century were recovered from Area B (the latest dated material from Area A was mid third century), no features may be confidently dated after *c.* A.D. 250. Only in Area C were there deposits dating into the fourth century.

Period 5 has been subdivided into two phases; Period 5A, *c.* A.D. 75–150 and Period 5B, *c.* A.D. 150–250 or later.

Period 5A summary

By Period 5A ditches defining Enclosure B5 had been infilled and replaced by a new system of ditches set at right-angles

Fig. 48. Period 5 features.

to one another continuing the line of the north-west side of Enclosure B1 to the south-west. The ditches of Enclosure B1 appear to have remained open to the end of Period 5A. A cardinal ditch continuing the line of Ditch B1 to the south-west divided a series of contemporary boundaries to the north-west and south-east. To the north-west were two ditches forming at least two or three possible fields. To the south-east were a greater number of ditches and slots representing boundaries and a possible building. Two rows of post-holes and post-pits may have been for associated fences. Additional pits may have been cut within an adjacent complex of intercutting features. At least three large pits at widely separated locations have been dated by their contents to the period together with a pair of parallel aligned curving ditches located within the south-east corner of the excavation.

In Area A, a field system established during Period 4D went out of use and was replaced by a more extensive system of boundaries laid out on an entirely new orientation.

In Area C three pits were found to pre-date a hypocausted structure constructed in Period 5B.

Enclosure B1 (Fig. 49)

The ditches defining Enclosure B1 (B1 and B164) appeared to have remained open throughout Period 5A. The continuing use of the enclosure is suggested by a significant quantity of late material in the backfill of both ditches. Although stratigraphic excavation of the ditch fills did not take place (fills were excavated as a single deposit), the large pottery assemblage recovered clearly indicated that the feature was long-lived. Whilst a significant quantity of early material suggested a possible construction date at or around the conquest, there was sufficient later material, including samian ware, Upchurch ware and local coarsewares, to indicate that rubbish disposal was taking place up to the second century, but probably no later. A small quantity of later material recovered from Ditch B1 was thought to have derived from a Period 5B ditch (B165) found cutting Ditch B1.

Ditches south-west of Enclosure B1

A complex of ditches located to the south-west of Enclosure B1 may have been established during Period 5A. The ditches post-dated Enclosure B5, but an adjacent area used for the disposal of rubbish (a complex of intercutting pits, B15) appears to have continued in use throughout Period 5A. A north-east to south-west aligned ditch (B24/B24A) continuing the line of the north-west side of Enclosure B1 (Ditch B1) separated a possible row of narrow fields to the north-west from a possible building contained within a fenced enclosure to the south-east.

Ditch B24/B24A was traced for 60 m. The ditch, sectioned in only two locations, was on average 1.10–1.30 m. wide and 0.40 m. deep. Traced as a soil stain for the greater part of its length, it ended with a rounded terminal 5 m. south-west of the corner of Enclosure B1, indicating perhaps a causeway or entrance. Where sample-excavated the ditch had shallow sloping sides, filled with a single deposit of dark brown to grey brown gravelly loam (Fig. 49, inset section). Some 20 m. to the north-east the ditch was cut with shallow sloping sides and a flat sump (inset section). The ditch fill provided residual Iron Age flint-tempered pot sherds together with grog-tempered and fine sandy ware 'Belgic' sherds, Roman sherds, including Canterbury sandy ware (Fig. 132, No. 417) and samian ware sherds dating into the first quarter of the second century A.D. The ditch was traced as a cropmark for at least another 30 m. to the south-west (Fig. 5).

Ditch B23 was cut approximately at right-angles to Ditch B24 to the north-west. The ditch cut into the backfill of the northern ditch of Enclosure B5 (Ditch B5) and was traced as a soil stain for 28 m. The intersection with Ditch B24 was not investigated and it was not possible to determine a stratigraphic relationship. The fills of both ditches were identical and it appeared that both ditches might have been contemporary. A short 5 m. long section of ditch continuing the line of B23 to the south-east also appeared to have been filled with the same material, perhaps at the same time. This south-eastern extension terminated at the edge of a complex of intercutting pits (B15) possibly indicating that it was formed to drain water into a soakaway. Ditch B23 was sectioned in two locations (Fig. 49, inset sections), close to the western baulk and close to the eastern terminus, respectively. It was 1.20 m. wide and 0.30 m. deep, cut to an open u-shape profile and filled with a pale brown gravelly loam. The fill provided a small number of grog- and sand-tempered sherds and a pair of copper alloy tweezers (p. 270). Ditch B23 was traced as a cropmark in air photographs for a further 40 m. to the north-west and may have been with Ditch B24 the north-east and south-east side of a field system, perhaps subdivided into a number of long and narrow plots. Ditch B28 set parallel to Ditch B24 and 11 m. to the north-west may have been for an internal division of the field system. The ditch, sample excavated in one location (inset section), was 1 m. wide, 0.30 m. deep and filled with pale brown gravelly loam which provided no datable finds. The intersection between ditches B28 and B23 was not excavated and a stratigraphic relationship was not established. The ditch was found to cut Period 4D Ditch B5 (Fig. 46), however, and the fills of B28 and B23 were indistinguishable. Cropmarks indicated the presence of other strip fields to the north-west.

To the south-east of Ditch B24A and set perpendicular to it was a soil stain for a north-west to south-east aligned ditch (B187). The 20 m. long feature was mapped but not excavated. This ditch may have been formed to demarcate the north-eastern boundary of the B15 pit complex.

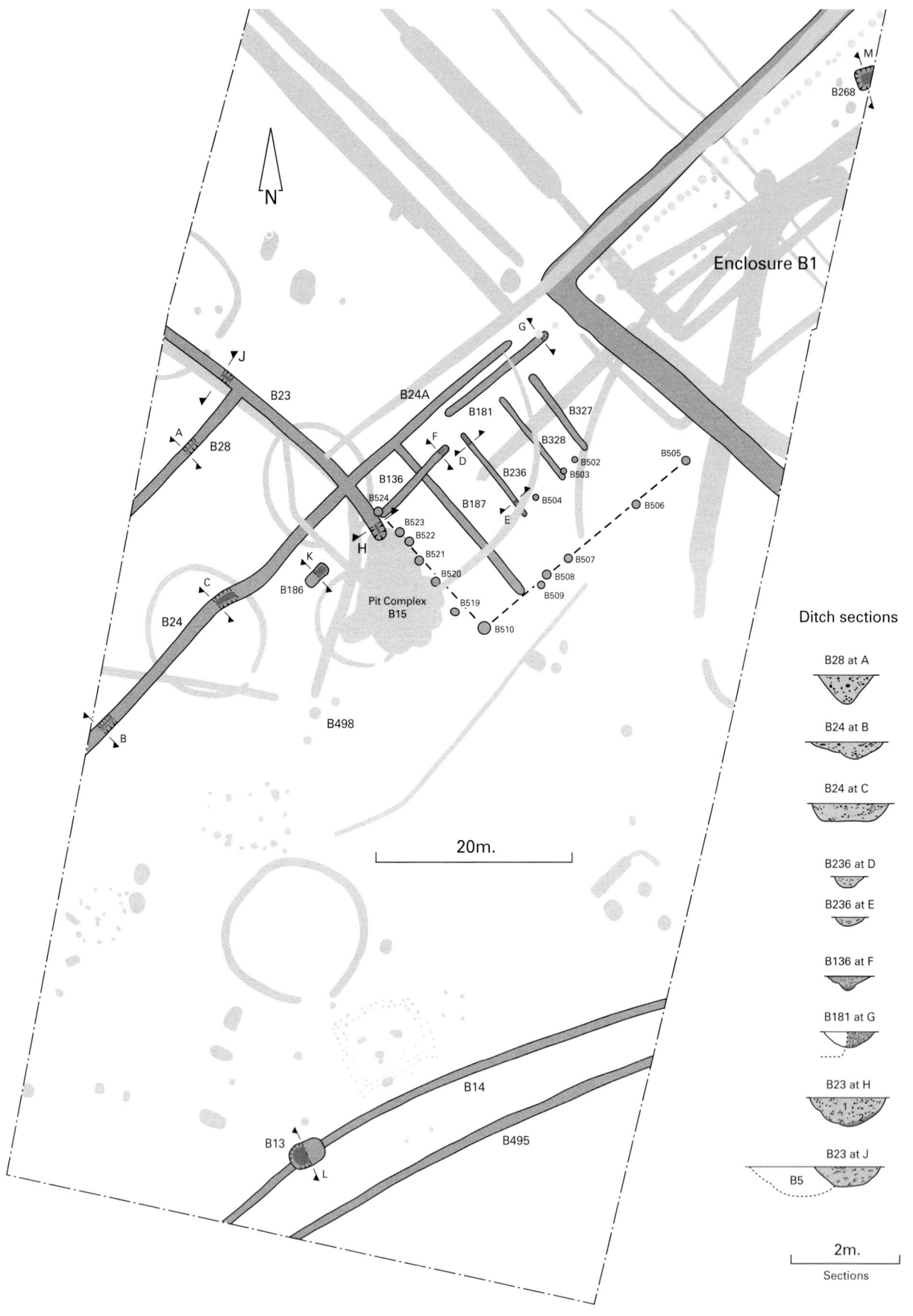

Fig. 49. Period 5A. Features south-east of Enclosure B1.

Possible building

A north-east to south-west aligned row of soil stains for at least six post-holes (B505–B510) was recorded 20 m. south-east of Ditch B24A and may have been broadly contemporary with ditches B24 and B187. A second row of six soil stains for post-holes (B519–B524) set at right-angles to B24A and the post row, cut the north-eastern edge of Pit complex B15. The rows of posts may have been formed either to fence off a rectangular block of ground between the B1 enclosure and the B15 pit complex, or perhaps formed component parts of a substantial building in this position.

The north-westernmost post stain was cut into the edge of the south-eastern terminus of Ditch B23 indicating that perhaps the ditch had been infilled when the fence or building was established. Within the area defined by the post rows, Ditch B24A to the north-west and Ditch B164 to the north-east were soil stains for five short lengths of ditch. Three parallel ditches (B236, B328 and B327) aligned north-east to south-west, set 4 m. and 2.50 m. apart and north-east of centre within the area were recorded as soil stains.

The south-western ditch (B236), sample-excavated at both ends (Fig. 49 inset sections) was 10.50 m. long, 0.50 m. wide and 0.14 m. deep. The ditch was filled with mid brown gravelly loam containing seven sherds of Central Gaulish samian ware, and eleven sherds of Roman coarseware dating to the late first century A.D. The fill also provided a copper alloy pin or stylus (Fig. 154, No. 10). The second and third ditches (B328 and B327) were mapped as soil stains 9.50 m. long and 0.60–1 m. wide, but not excavated.

Two further slots, aligned north-east to south-west, were recorded within the area. To the south-west was Ditch B136. This ditch, 9.75 m. long and 0.90 m. wide, cut or butted Post-hole B524, the westernmost post of the row of posts closing the south-western side of the area. Although the ditch was only sample-excavated at its north-east terminal it was recorded to have cut Ditch B187 indicating that B187 had been infilled when Ditch B136 was formed. Ditch B136 was filled with a grey brown clay loam with sparse gravel containing five flint-tempered and eleven grog-tempered sherds, the latter dating into the first century A.D.

The second ditch (B181) was recorded 2.60 m. north of the first, set close and parallel to Ditch B24A. The ditch, sample excavated at the north-east terminal (Fig. 49, Section B181, G), was 13 m. long, 1 m. wide, 0.30 m. deep, cut to a u-shaped profile and filled with mid brown gravelly loam containing three grog-tempered sherds dating into the first century A.D.

Soil stains for three small post-holes (B502–4) were found at the centre of the area. One of them, B503, was found to cut Ditch B328. The post-holes were not excavated.

The purpose of the arrangement of post rows and slots was difficult to determine. Whilst the rows of posts may have been for fences demarcating a rectangular area, the arrangement of slots and posts may suggest parts of an imperfectly preserved building. Whilst the post rows may indicate wall lines for a structure, the narrow shallow ditches may have been for beam slots, perhaps supporting a planked floor. As the majority of features recorded here remained unexcavated, the identification of the features as a building remains only a tentative suggestion.

Ditches B14 and B495 (Fig. 49)

Two parallel soil stains for ditches (B14 and B495) set 6 m. apart and aligned east-north-east to west-south-west were recorded in the south-east corner of Area B. Traced for 52 m., only Ditch B14 was sample excavated and was found to be 0.8 m. wide, 0.25 m. deep and filled with dark brown gravelly loam. A collection of grog-tempered sherds and Roman pottery dating from the mid to late first century A.D. was recovered. The ditch was cut by Pit B13 which yielded pottery dating up to the mid second century A.D.

A cropmark (Fig. 5) continued both ditches on a converging course to the north-east for a further 25 m., where they joined. A single ditch continued the alignment, extending parallel to a cropmark forming the southern boundary of Enclosure B1 and ending some 70 m. beyond the excavation. The ditches, perhaps two phases of a single boundary, may have been associated with a field system to the south. Given the date for Pit B13, one or both ditches may have been out of use by the mid second century.

Pits, Area B (Fig. 50)

In addition to pits likely to have been cut within Pit complex B15, three pits located at widely separated locations in Area B were probably cut during Period 5A.

Pit B13 was located at the southern end of the area, cutting Ditch B14. Roughly rectangular, measuring some 2.75 by 2.50 m. and cut only 0.18 m. deep, it was packed with 875 sherds many of them burnt. The fill was of dark brown to black loam with little gravel and much charcoal, burnt clay and burnt flint. The substantial corpus comprised, 716 sherds of grog-tempered ware, much of the collection oxidised and refired (including Fig. 121, Nos 276–82); twenty-three sherds of 'Belgic' fine sandy ware (including Fig. 125, No. 331); thirty 'Belgic' or early Roman coarse sandy ware sherds, 103 Roman sherds, including Canterbury sandy ware (Fig. 130, No. 385; Fig. 131, Nos 408, 412; Fig. 133, No. 467 and Fig. 134, No. 493) and two Central Gaulish samian ware sherds dating up to the mid second century A.D. The pit fill also provided an iron tool (p. 274).

Pit B186 was located south-east of Ditch B24 and west of Pit complex B15. The pit was rectangular, measuring 2.75 by 1.14 m. and was cut to a depth of 0.27 m. It contained a bi-partite fill of yellow to pale brown charcoal-rich loam

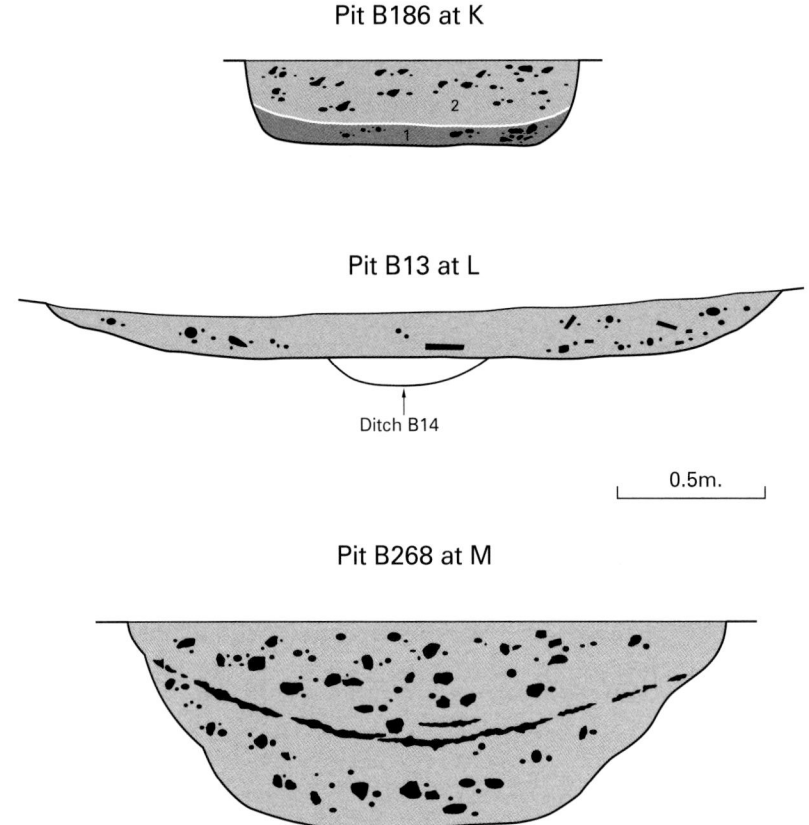

Fig. 50. Period 5A. Sections through pits B186, B13 and B268.

and dark brown charcoal filled loam providing seven grog-tempered sherds (including Fig. 122, Nos 302) and five sherds of Roman pottery dating into the second century A.D.

Pit B268, located in the north-east corner of the excavation but only partly within the excavated area, was approximately square with rounded corners, measuring 2 m. by 1.75 m. Cut to a depth of 0.68 m. the pit was filled with mid brown loam mixed with chalk and charcoal. It contained a mixture of finds including eight residual Late Iron Age flint-tempered sherds, forty grog-tempered sherds (including Fig. 121, Nos 274–5), seven 'Belgic' fine sandy ware sherds (including Fig. 126, No. 336) and eleven Roman coarseware sherds dating into the second century. The fills also provided a number of fragmented oyster shells (a rare survival) and a copper alloy awl (Fig. 154, No. 12).

Field system, Area A (Fig. 51)

A combination of evidence from a relatively small number of excavated features from soil stains rapidly mapped during gravel extraction and cropmarks plotted from air photographs has been used to identify and describe a series of field systems identified in Area A. Two field systems appear to be represented: a northern complex and a southern complex. Both sets of boundaries were aligned roughly north-east to south-west, although the southern ditches represented a rather more irregular pattern of fields. The northern complex of ditches appeared to represent a developing system of fields of at least three phases. The southern fields may also have evolved rather than been laid out in one phase.

The northern complex

The northern complex of ditches was of three phases. The earliest feature appeared to be a single north-east to south-west aligned ditch (A9), mapped, sample excavated and traced as a cropmark for a total distance of 190 m. A mapped soil stain and a cropmark indicated that the ditch was recut at least once before it was superseded by a series of ditches forming a narrow rectangular block of land aligned north-east to south-west, subdivided into four irregular-sized fields with a possible extension to the north-east. Parts of two northern fields were excavated, together with a length of ditch representing a north-east extension. The early system of ditches was overlaid by a later pattern of ditches forming a larger rectangular block, subdivided into at least two fields, east and west, the south-western field twice the size of its neighbour. A large number of post-holes, pits and other features fell within the excavated portion of the north-eastern field. A number of features, recorded to the east of the field system, may have been broadly contemporary.

Boundary ditch A9

Pre-dating the new system of fields, but post-dating a Period 4D arrangement of field boundaries (A117, etc, Fig. 47), was a north-east to south-west aligned ditch (A9), mapped as a soil stain for 45 m. across the north-west end of Area A. Outside the excavated area the feature was traced as a cropmark for a total distance of approximately 190 m. into fields beyond the limit of the quarry (Fig. 5). Within the excavation, the ditch, cut to a shallow u-shaped profile, was on average 1.40 m. wide and 0.40 m. deep. The ditch fill of mid brown gravelly loam, yielded five worn grog-tempered sherds and six sherds of Roman pottery, including one south Gaulish samian sherd.

A possible re-cut of Ditch A9 was observed against the western boundary of the excavation (Fig. 51). The ditch (A288) was mapped and traced to the south-west as a cropmark for a further 86 m., but was not excavated.

Early fields

The north-east end of a rectangular field system, aligned long axis north-east to south-west, fell within the excavated area. Four irregular-sized fields, together with a possible extension of the system to the north-east, were represented by mapped soil stains and cropmarks.

A ditch (A99) forming the north-western side of the field system was traced as a soil stain for 42 m. within the excavated area and for a further 69 m. to the south-west as a cropmark. An excavated section of the ditch was between 0.90 and 1.20 m. wide, 0.50 m. deep and cut to a u-shape profile. The ditch fill was of mid brown gravelly loam containing two grog-tempered sherds, two worn Roman coarseware sherds and part of a an iron latch lifter (p. 273).

Cut at right angles to the line of Ditch A99 was a second contemporary ditch (A12), aligned north-west to south-east. Forming the north-east side of the field system, it was traced for a length of 20 m. A contemporary ditch (also A12) returned to the south-west to form the south-east side of the field system. A soil stain for the ditch was traced for 33 m.

To the south-east the field system was reconstructed from cropmarks. The south-west end of the field system was tentatively identified together with two north-west to south-east aligned cropmarks for ditches (A290 and A291) indicating two fields. A third north-west to south-east aligned ditch fell within the excavation (A67). Ditch A67 was traced for a total length of 15 m. and formed a right-angled junction with the south-east side of the field system (Ditch A12). The ditch was 0.50 m. wide and barely 0.20 m. deep. The loam and gravel fill of the ditch contained four grog-tempered sherds and four sherds of Roman pottery broadly dated to the first two centuries A.D.

The four fields, forming a block measuring 90 m. north-east to south-west by between 20 and 24 m. north-west to south-east, were of different sizes. The south-west field was 35 by 30 m., the adjoining field to the north-east measured 20 by 30 m., the third field measured 16 by 27 m. and the north-eastern field measured 25 by 23 m.

A possible northern extension to the field system was indicated by a continuation of Ditch A99 to the north-east (A99A, Fig. 52). It is possible that A99 and A99A formed the same ditch. The junction between them was cut through by a later ditch and it was not possible to determine the relationship between the two features. Ditch A99A was traced as a soil stain for 50 m. from the north-west corner of the field system to the north-east where the soil stain returned at right-angles to the south-east (A295) to form a north-east end to a contemporary or later extension to the field system. Ditch A295 was traced for 50 m., but was not excavated.

Later fields (Fig. 51)

A later system of field boundaries was cut to replace the earlier system. The new system also on a north-east to south-west line was wider (on average 35 m.) and longer (103 m.) and divided into two fields, one much larger than the other. Only the north-east end of the new system fell within the excavated area. The remaining part was determined from cropmarks. The greater part of the smaller of the two fields fell within the excavated area (Fig. 52).

Cutting Ditch A99 at right-angles was a later ditch (A11). Traced for 24.50 m. the ditch was on average 0.80 m. wide and between 0.20 and 0.50 m. deep. The fill of dark brown gravelly loam provided one grog-tempered sherd and three sherds of Roman pottery dating into the second century. The ditch ended with a rounded terminal to the south-east which perhaps defined an entrance into the field.

The south-east side of the field was formed by Ditch A14. Traced for 22 m., it ended with rounded terminals at both ends. That to the north-east may have flanked an entrance into the field. The terminal to the south-west was exceptionally shallow and it is likely that the ditch continued to the south-west but had been ploughed out. The northern part of the ditch was approximately 0.80 m. wide and 0.30 m. deep, cut to u-shape profile. The fill of mid brown gravelly loam provided nine sherds of grog-tempered sherds and six Roman coarseware sherds dating into the second century A.D.

The south-west side of the field was defined by Ditch A68 aligned north-west to south-east and traced for a total

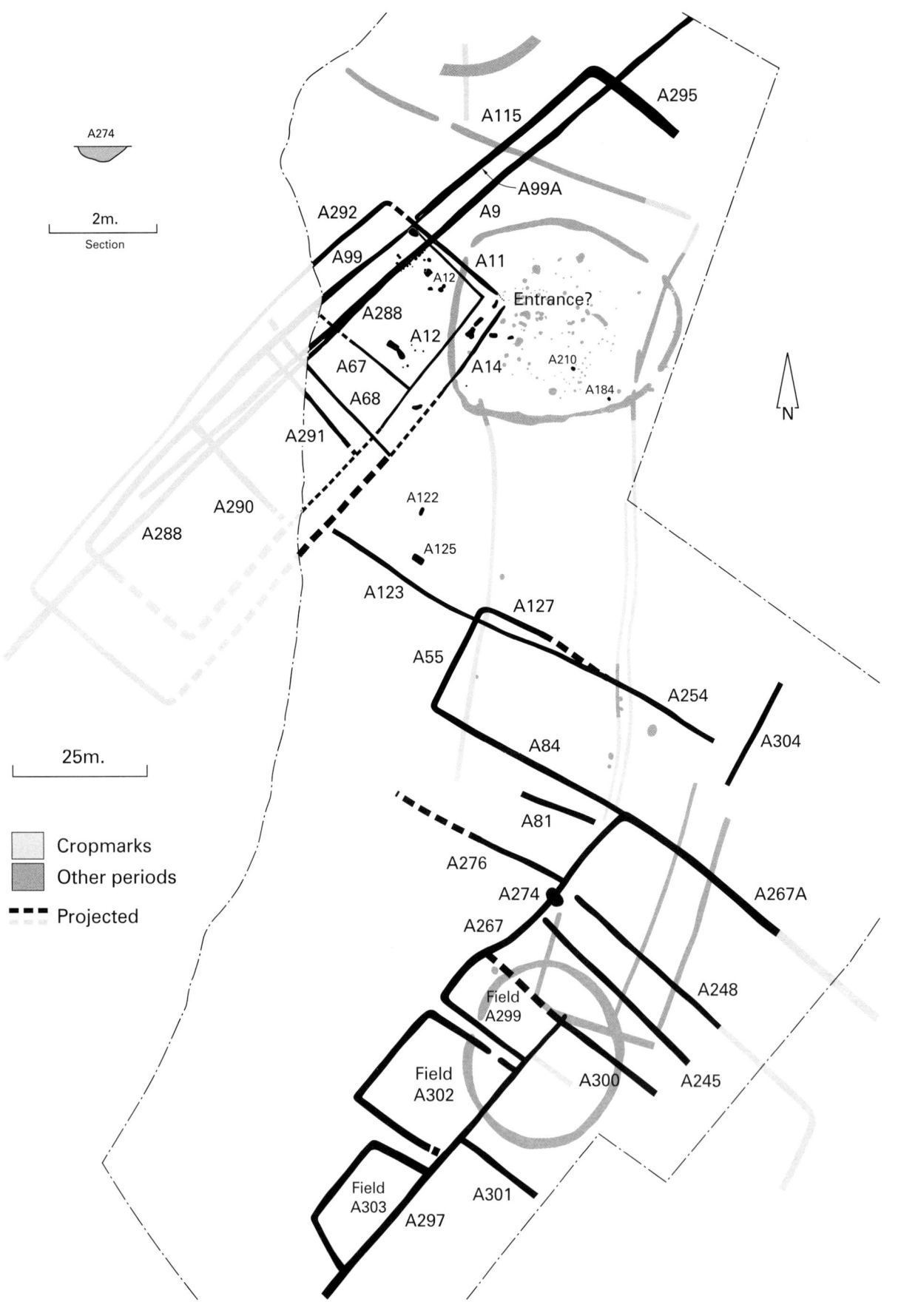

Fig. 51. Period 5A. Northern and southern field ditches, Area A and Period 5B, Pit A274, Area A.

length of 15 m. A sherd of Roman glass was recovered from the surface of the feature (p. 275). The ditch terminated on line with Ditch A14 but some 16 m. distant.

The north-west side of the northern field and of the field system was identified as a cropmark (A292) extending parallel to but 7.50 m. north-west of Ditch A99. The northern field was approximately square with sides some 36 m. long. The south-west field has been reconstructed measuring some 67 m. north-east to south-west by approximately 36 m. north-west to south-east.

No soil stains or cropmark was identified for a ditch forming the south-east side of the larger field. Although a boundary may not have existed it is more likely that it had been destroyed by past agricultural practice or had simply not been identified. The northern part of the earlier field system may have continued in use. Identified only as a soil stain and not excavated was a recut for Ditch A99A. The new ditch (A115) appeared to terminate close to the line of Ditch A11, perhaps suggesting that the features were contemporary.

Features within the later fields

A large number of features, mainly domestic rubbish pits were identified within the area bounded by ditches A292, A11 and A14. A smaller number of features lay outside the field to the south-east. Amongst the group of features in the south-east corner of the field was a possible cremation burial (A119) and three inhumation burials (A119A, A13, A36). Three concentrations of post-holes and post-pits identified in the northern and north-eastern corners of the field and centrally may have been for fences or structures. It was not possible to determine whether all features related to the later of the two fields.

Pits

Pit A52, located in the extreme northern corner of the enclosure, was approximately circular and 2 m. in diameter, cut just 0.30 m. deep into the corner of the previous field boundary (ditches A99 and A12). The feature, a wide shallow 'hollow' was filled with mid brown gravelly loam. The pit fill provided two grog-tempered sherds and three sherds of Roman pottery dating from the late first or early second century A.D.

Pit A62 was circular, cut 0.90 m. in diameter and 0.20 m. deep. Its fill of mid brown gravelly loam provided a single grog-tempered sherd and two sherds of Roman pottery broadly dating into the second century A.D.

Pit A96 was approximately 1.60 m. square. The pit was shallow, being cut to a maximum depth of 0.28 m. and filled with pale brown gravelly loam. The fill provided three sherds of grog-tempered fabric (including Fig. 120, No. 271) and a single sherd of Roman pottery dated to the mid to late first century A.D.

Pit A76 was roughly oval in shape measuring 1.10 by 0.80 m. The pit, cut to a depth of 0.31 m. and filled with dark brown gravelly loam, yielded a single 'Belgic' fine sandy ware sherd and an iron nail.

Pit A74 was circular, 0.85 m. in diameter and was cut to a depth of 0.23 m. The fill of brown loam and gravel contained a single sherd of grog-tempered fabric (Fig. 120, No. 269) and an iron nail. Pit A74 was cut by Pit A75.

Pit A75, found cutting Pit A74, was circular, 0.90 m. in diameter and 0.22 m. deep. The fill yielded a small number of fine grog-tempered sherds and two sherds of Roman pottery dated to the mid to late first century A.D.

Pit A95, located in the southern corner of the earlier field (close to the intersection of ditches A12 and A67) was oval, measuring 2.15 by 1.26 m. The pit, cut to a depth of 0.41 m. and filled with mid brown gravelly loam, contained a single sherd of grog-tempered fabric and a single Roman sherd broadly dated to the first or second century A.D. The feature was cut by Pit A87.

Pit A87, found cutting Pit A95, was rectangular aligned long axis north-west to south-east. The pit (Fig. 52, inset section) measuring 2.60 by 1.25 m. was cut with steep vertical sides to a depth of 0.85 m. The pit contained a primary fill (Layer 4) of dark brown loam capped by a bulk fill of medium brown loam and gravel (Layers 2 and 3). An upper fill of loam and gravel was also discernable (Layer 1). The primary and tertiary fills provided no finds, but the bulk intermediate fill yielded eighty sherds of grog-tempered fabric (including Figs 121–2, Nos 285–300) and a single sherd of Canterbury-type coarse sandy ware. The fill also yielded part of a spindlewhorl (p. 276). The combined contents have been tentatively dated to the early to mid first century A.D.

Pit A128 was close to the southern corner of the field. The pit, of irregular shape, measuring 2.30 by 0.90 m. and cut 0.15 m. deep, was filled with pale brown gravelly loam yielding no finds.

Possible cremation burial

A single cremation burial (A119A) was located 2 m. south of the centre field, close to the south-east edge of the field. The cremation pit, approximately 1.25 m. in diameter and 0.35 m. deep had been cut and disturbed by a later inhumation burial (A119). The fill of the cremation pit contained the greater part of a grog-tempered jar, with other sherds of the same vessel recovered from the fill of the grave (Fig. 120, No. 261). Although carbon and burnt flint was identified in the pit and pot fills, cremated bone was not recovered.

Inhumation burials

Three north-east to south-west aligned inhumation burials were recorded positioned just inside the south-east edge of the field.

Fig. 52. Period 5A. North-eastern field, Area A.

Grave A119 was located 2 m. north-west of the field boundary. The wide grave cut, measuring 2.40 by 1.10 m., was 0.32 m. deep. The grave when cut disturbed an earlier cremation burial (A119A), with sherds from a cremation urn thrown back in the grave fill together with a small number of Roman coarseware sherds. Human bone did not survive, but a complete Upchurch-type beaker (Fig. 129, No. 374) was found *in situ* at the south-west end of the grave, together with twelve iron coffin nails. The burial has been dated by the pottery to late first or early second century A.D.

Grave A13 was located a short way north-east of Grave A119. The grave, 2.40 m. long, 0.85 m. wide and 0.50 m. deep, was filled with mid brown gravelly loam. Human bones did not survive, but thirteen iron coffin nails were identified at either end of the grave. The grave fill also yielded five sherds of grog-tempered ware and a single sherd of Roman pottery dating into the second century A.D.

Grave A36 was positioned close to the north-east entrance to the field, north-east of Grave A13. It was cut 0.30 m. deep, 2 m. long and 0.70 m. wide. Human bones did not survive but a single near complete vessel in 'Belgic' grog-tempered ware (Fig. 120, No. 260) was found at the south-west end of the grave. Two iron nails, probably from a coffin were recovered from the loam and gravel fill of the grave.

Post-holes

A number of single post-holes and a post-hole and post-pit alignment were identified within the field.

At the northern end of the field were three post-pits (A116, A116A and A113) on average 0.50 m. in diameter, cut between 0.20 and 0.28 m. deep. A north-east to south-west aligned row of four post-holes (A106, A108, A112 and A114) and four post-pits (A97, A66, A64 and A65) was also identified at the north end of the field, together with an isolated post (A107) to the south-east of the alignment. Set some 5 m. south of the boundary, the post-pits were on average 0.40–0.90 m. in diameter, cut at close proximity to one another, between 0.33 and 0.50 m. deep. The post-holes were on average 0.20–0.30 m. in diameter, with an average depth of 0.22 m. Only Post-hole A114 provided any finds, this a spindlewhorl fashioned from a sherd of fine sandy ware, possibly of Early Roman date (p. 276).

A single post-hole (A96A), 0.50 m. in diameter and 0.30 m. deep filled with a fine black loam but yielding no datable finds, was found cutting Pit A96. Five seemingly unrelated post-holes were recorded in the southern corner of the earlier field (A88 and A91–4).The posts varied in size and depth and contained no datable finds.

Five post-holes were identified in the north-east entrance to the field. The post-holes (A26–A30) continued the line of the field boundary south-eastwards and may have been placed to restrict or even close the entrance. The post-holes were between 0.15 and 0.25 m. in diameter and cut to a depth between 0.15 to 0.30 m. The post-holes yielded no datable finds.

Pits outside the north-eastern field

A number of pits were located south-east of the field.

Pit A53, located close to the eastern boundary of the field (A14) and south of the eastern corner was oval-shaped, measuring 1.30 by 0.90 m., cut 0.50 m. deep. The fill of mid brown gravelly loam provided a small group of twelve grog-tempered sherds including Fig. 120, No. 268 dating from the first half of the first century A.D.

Pit A210 was located some 18 m. east of the field. The pit was oval measuring 1.10 by 0.72 m. and was cut to a depth of 0.45 m. Its fill of medium brown gravelly loam with daub and charcoal flecks, provided two sherds of grog-tempered ware.

Pit A184 (location, Fig. 51) was located south-east of the field approximately 10 m. south-east of Pit A210. Pit A184 was oval, measuring 1.80 by 1 m. and cut to a maximum depth of 0.45 m. The fill of light brown loam and gravel with lenses of charcoal-rich loam flecked with burnt orange clay, contained seventeen 'Belgic' grog-tempered sherds (including Fig. 113, Nos 134–5) and a single sherd of Central Gaulish samian ware.

Post-pit A80, located just outside of the eastern boundary of the field (A14) was circular, 0.40 m. wide and 0.15 m. deep. The fill of gravelly loam yielded nine grog-tempered sherds (including Fig. 120, No. 270) and a fragment of an iron hoe (p. 274).

Pit A122 (Fig. 51) was located south of the field a short way north of Ditch A123. The pit, oval-shaped, measuring 1.80 by 0.90 m., cut 0.20 m. deep, was filled with brown gravelly loam containing sixteen sherds of 'Belgic' grogged ware (including Fig. 121, Nos 272–3) and a number of worn Roman coarseware sherds. Fragments of burnt sandstone were also recovered from the fill.

Pit A125 (Fig. 51) was located south of Pit A122, adjacent to Ditch A123. The pit, rectangular-shaped, 2.70 by 1.30 m. and cut 0.42 m. deep, was filled with brown gravelly loam containing fourteen 'Belgic' grog-tempered sherds (including Fig. 120, Nos 262–5).

The southern complex (Fig. 51)

A well-defined pattern of ditches was recorded mainly as soil stains and cropmarks to the south-east of those previously described. Two phases of ditches were in evidence. The earliest of these (A81, A123 and A304) defined fields which were were aligned west-north-west to east-south-east and appeared to link the north-western and south-western series of ditches.

The later ditches appeared to define a pattern of long, narrow fields, flanked to the south-west by a number of irregular but probably interlinked enclosures. Reconstruction of the south-eastern complex, particularly the irregular enclosures, has relied heavily on cropmark evidence (Pls III–IV).

Boundary ditches

Ditch A81 was traced as a soil stain for a distance of 16 m. with only the south-eastern terminal of the ditch being excavated where it was 1.30 m. wide and 0.40 m. deep and cut to a shallow, open v-shaped profile. The fill of mid brown gravelly loam provided a single sherd of grog-tempered ware.

Ditch A123 was traced for approximately 89 m. with the south-eastern part of the ditch alignment (A254) indicated by a cropmark. The ditch, sample-excavated at the eastern terminus, was on average 1 m. wide and 0.25–0.50 m. deep, cut to an open 'u' profile. The fill, of light brown gravelly loam, flecked with burnt clay and charcoal, yielded a mixed corpus of three residual Iron Age flint-tempered sherds, four grog-and-flint-tempered sherds, nine grog-tempered sherds (including Fig. 121, Nos 283–4), four 'Belgic' sandy ware sherds, and one Gallo-Belgic import (micaceous *terra nigra*). The entire corpus has been tentatively dated to the first half of the first century A.D.

The south-eastern end of the fields appears to be represented by Ditch A304. This was traced as a soil stain for approximately 24 m. and not excavated. The visible traces almost certainly did not reflect its full length. It is included with this early group because of its position and alignment.

Fields

The later ditches in this area were mainly identified from cropmarks, with eight ditch lengths representing parts of perhaps three rectangular fields.

A northern field was bounded to the north-west by Ditch A55, to the north-east by Ditch A127 and the south-west by Ditch A84. The south-eastern side of the field was undefined. The field may have been at least 55 m. long (north-west to south-east) and 21 m. wide.

Ditch A55 was sample-excavated and was 0.70 m. wide, 0.50 m. deep and cut to a v-shaped profile. It was filled with a primary sand and gravel weathering deposit, capped by a bulk fill of dark brown gravelly loam. The bulk fill provided two grog-tempered sherds, one sherd of Central Gaulish samian ware and one Dressel 20 amphora sherd. The corpus has been dated into the second century A.D.

Ditch A127 was traced for only 12 m. The ditch, 0.70 m. wide and 0.40 m. deep, was cut to an open 'u' profile and filled with a dark to mid brown gravelly loam flecked with charcoal. The fill contained one grog-and-flint-tempered sherd and seven grog-tempered sherds (including Fig. 122, No. 301) dating to the first century A.D. A continuation of the northern boundary was indicated by Ditch A254. The ditch was traced for 25 m. as a soil stain, but not excavated.

Ditch A84 was traced for 84 m. and may have formed part of a continuous boundary for perhaps two fields. The ditch was on average 0.50 m. wide and 0.30 m. deep. Although sampled in two locations, the mid brown gravelly loam fill provided no datable finds.

The south-west side of a second rectangular field to the south of the first was indicated by Ditch A276. Traced for 20 m. as a soil stain and sample excavated in one location, the ditch was 0.80 m. wide and 0.35 m. deep and cut to an open 'u' profile. The fill, of mid brown gravelly loam provided eight sherds of grog-tempered ware and thirteen sherds of Roman pottery, including one Dressel 20 amphora sherd dating broadly to the second century A.D. The east side of the field was indicated by Ditch A267. The ditch, aligned north-east to south-west was traced for 34 m. and appeared to have been cut as a common boundary for at least two fields. The second field was at least 20 m. wide.

The third field shared common boundaries with both previous fields. The north-eastern side of the field was defined by a south-eastwards continuation of Ditch A84 (A267A) and the north-west side by Ditch A267. The south-western side of the field was formed by Ditch A248. This latter ditch traced mainly as a soil stain for 55 m., was sample-excavated. The ditch was on average 1.20 m. wide and cut to a broad, open 'u' profile 0.40 m. deep. The fill, of medium brown gravelly loam, provided no datable finds. The south-eastern side of the field was not determined, but the field measured at least 55 by 21 m.

A fourth field, further along Ditch A267 and sharing boundary Ditch A248 with the previous field appeared to comprise a relatively narrow strip with A245 as its south-western boundary. The width of the field was 6.50 m. at the north-western end, broadening to 8 m. towards the south-east. The south-eastern end did not survive, but the field was at least 42 m. long.

Ditch A245 was located to the south of Ditch A81 and was traced for a distance of approximately 35 m. A short section of the ditch was excavated at its north-western terminus where it was found to be 1.10–1.15 m. wide. The ditch, cut to a open 'u' profile and 0.55 m. deep was uniformly filled with dark brown gravelly loam flecked with burnt clay and charcoal containing residual Iron Age pottery, grog-tempered sherds and twenty-nine sherds of Roman coarseware, including three mortaria sherds dating up to *c.* A.D. 180 (Table 27). Two small finds were recovered: an iron socketed cleaver (p. 273) and a fragment of quernstone (p. 278).

The south-west side of a possible fifth rectangular field was represented by cropmark A300. The cropmark was traced for 32 m. The north-west side of the field may have been formed by a south-west continuation of Ditch A267. The combined evidence suggested a field approximately 20 m. wide and at least 40 m. long.

The remaining fields, reconstructed entirely from cropmarks, shared a common boundary to the south-west (A297). Two large fields may have existed to the south-east of the common boundary, separated by cropmark A301. To the north-west of boundary A297 were three small fields.

A small rectangular field (A299) measuring some 20 by 10 m., adjoined the south-west side of the fourth field. A second rectangular field (A302) lay to the south-west with a gap 2–4 m. wide separating the fields. The gap may have been a droveway giving access to the fields to the south-east. A second rectangular field measuring 24 by 21 m. was flanked to the south-west by a second possible droveway also perhaps giving access to a field to the south-east. The droveway, 3 m. wide, was flanked to the south-west by a third roughly rectangular field (A303) measuring 25 by 12 m.

Area C (Fig. 54)

Three pits (C1, C2 and C4) pre-dating the construction of a hypocausted structure were recorded in Area C.

Pit C1 was located against the south-west section of the excavated area and had been cut by the south wall of the hypocaust. The pit was circular, approximately 1.50 m. in diameter and 0.40 m. deep. The fill of mid brown gravelly loam provided a small group of pottery broadly dated to the second century A.D.

Pit C2 was located against the south-east section of the excavated area, east of the hypocausted building. It was of irregular shape, measuring 0.80 by 0.55 m. and had been cut to a maximum depth of 0.35 m. The fill provided two grog-tempered sherds and ten Roman sherds of second-century date together with an iron socketed hook (p. 274).

Pit C4, cut by the northern corner of the hypocausted structure, was roughly circular, 0.90 m. in diameter and 0.25 m. deep. The fill yielded grog-tempered and sandy wares dated broadly to the late first or early second century A.D.

Discussion

At the conquest the continuing survival of some features and the adaptation of others, showed that there was probably no significant change in status, and certainly no change in the agricultural base of the local community. Even after the conquest the commonality of boundary alignments suggests that most features formed part of a contemporary agricultural system.

Soon after the construction of Enclosure B1, the field system in Area A was reorganised and integrated into a new orientation determined by the main north-east to south-west axial ditches. The series of arable fields and several smaller enclosures, generally aligned long axis north-east to south-west were superimposed over the earlier system. The northern complex of fields was reorganised at least once in the period with the north-eastern of two late fields containing a number of pits, hollows, and post-holes and at least three graves. Immediately outside the enclosure were a number of other pits.

In Area B, the basic framework of the field system was retained but previous subdivisions were infilled. An area was used for the disposal of rubbish (Pit complex B15), tied into a growing pattern of ditched and fenced paddocks or fields.

The development of the field system in Area A and redevelopment of the more domestic zone in Area B, suggests continuous settlement and a south-westward expansion of activity beyond Area A.

Ceramic data shows that native potting traditions survived well into the late first and into the second century; grog-tempered wares were dominant together with a new fine sandy ware that almost certainly was emerging prior to the conquest. Amongst the grogged wares were conservative forms; large and small comb-finished coarsewares and finer wares including eastern Kentish variants of standardized platter forms, themselves copies of imported Gallo-Belgic fine 'tablewares'. A few native products were still hand-made but most were wheel-thrown and, like the platters and beakers, were influenced by Roman imports. The emergence of a new sandy ware, though essentially native in style, also heralds a new Roman potting tradition. Also in the corpus of pottery are Canterbury and North Kentish wares, early industries that rapidly developed to meet the requirements of an increasingly sophisticated market.

Period 5B summary

In Area A the only feature post-dating the early to mid second century was a pit (A274) found cutting one of the ditches of an earlier field system.

During this period the system of boundary ditches in Area B to the south-west of the B1 enclosure was replaced by a ditch forming a north-east to south-west aligned boundary (B165) incorporating a polygonal enclosure (B21) at its south-west terminus. To the south of the boundary and extending parallel to it was an enigmatic alignment of closely-spaced post-pits, perhaps for a stout fence.

In Area C the masonry footings of a hypocausted building were uncovered. The building, constructed in the early second century, was probably in disuse by the mid third century, although some form of activity perhaps indicating re-use or robbing may have continued into the early fourth century.

Pit A274 (Fig. 51)

In Area A there was little to suggest that activity continued into the second half of the second century, save for a single

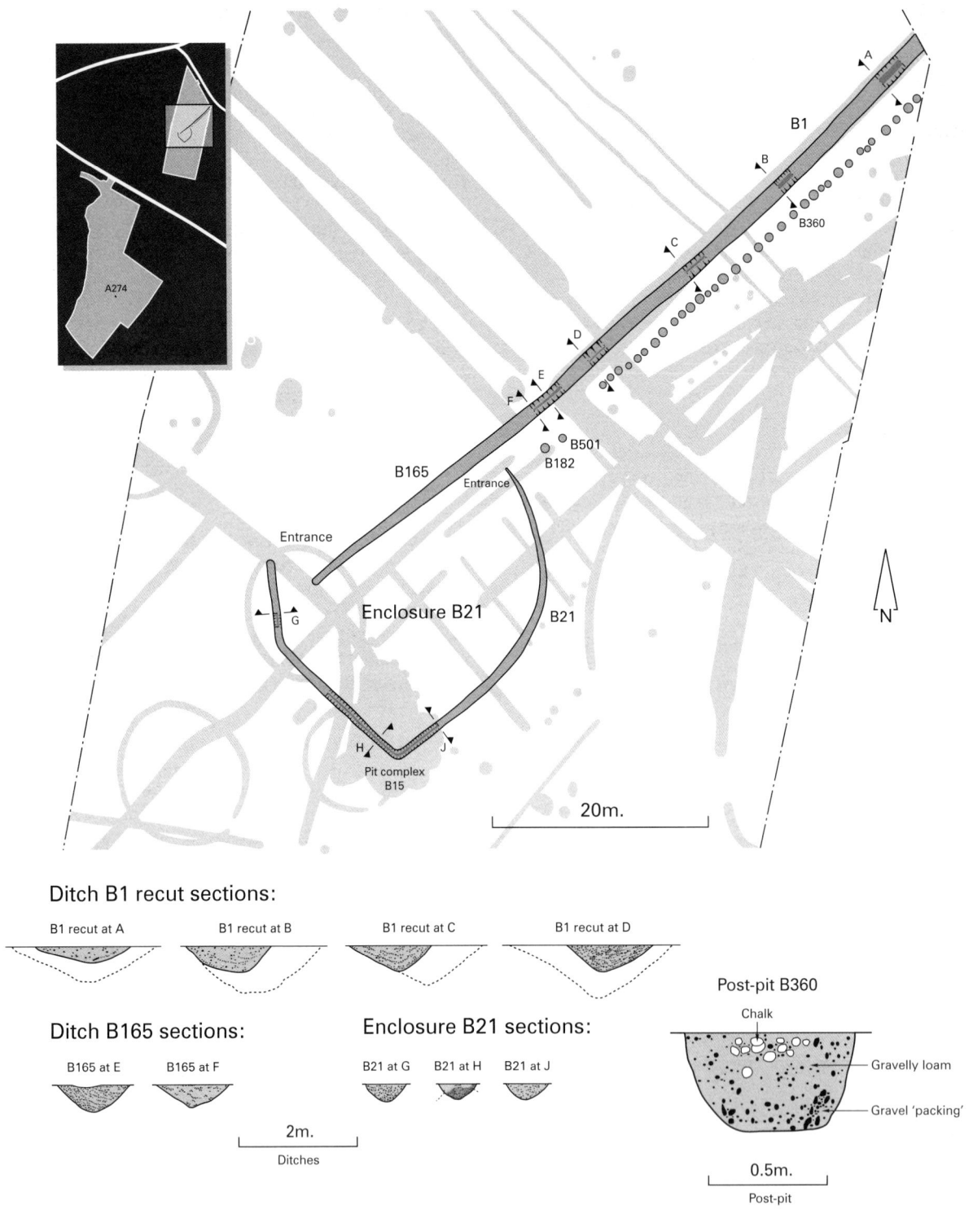

Fig. 53. Period 5B. Enclosure B21, Ditch B165 and post-pit alignment.

pit (A274) found cutting a field boundary ditch (A267) at the centre of the south-eastern field system. The pit, subrectangular with rounded corners and measuring 4.10 by 3.20 m., was cut with steep sides to a depth of 0.85 m. It was filled with a primary deposit of dark brown loam containing much charcoal, burnt clay and a substantial mass of pottery, much of it burnt and of small sherd-size. The corpus included 181 sherds of grogged ware (including Fig. 122, Nos 303–11), one 'Belgic' fine sandy ware sherd, one early Central Gaulish import (micaceous *terra nigra*), one Gallo-Belgic import (*terra rubra*) and 123 other Roman sherds, including one Dressel 20 amphora sherd and eleven samian ware sherds broadly dating from the Flavian period to the mid second century. Small finds recovered from the pit included a copper-alloy brooch (p. 274) and an iron socketed hook (p. 274, *not illus.*).

Area B late field ditch (Fig. 53)

In Area B a single ditch (B165) aligned north-east to south-west was found following the north-western side of the earlier B1 enclosure and extending some 28 m. south-west of the infilled corner of the enclosure. The ditch was on average 1.65 m. wide and 0.25 m. deep, but to the north-east it was up to 1.20 m. wide and 0.42 m. deep and to the south-west tapered to a width of 1 m. and a depth of only 0.25 m. The profile also varied from an open 'v' in the north-east to a u-shaped profile to the south-west. The fill of dark brown loamy gravel with charcoal and burnt clay flecking provided only a few sherds of grog-tempered ware.

Enclosure B21

Located at the south-west end of Ditch B165 was a ditch (B21) forming part of the south-east side of a polygonal, roughly D-shaped paddock or enclosure measuring approximately 25 m. north-east to south-west by 17 m. north-west to south-east. A 5 m. wide entrance into the enclosure existed in the south-west corner with a second entrance suggested in the north-east corner by a 2 m. wide gap between Ditch B21 and the north-western side of the enclosure (B165). The enclosure ditch, which cut through the infilled remains of a group of intercutting pits (B15), was on average 0.80 m. wide, cut to a u-shaped profile, 0.30 m. deep. The ditch fill of mid brown and grey-brown gravelly loam, provided ten residual Early to Late Iron Age flint-tempered sherds, eighteen grog-tempered sherds (including Fig. 123, No. 312), one 'Belgic' sandy ware sherd, fourteen Roman sherds, including six sherds of samian ware dating into the second half of the second century and possibly into the early third century A.D.

The post-pit alignment

Cut to the south-east of Ditch B165 was an enigmatic row of closely-spaced post-pits perhaps forming a stout fence. The post-pit row, located approximately 1.60–2 m. south-east of the ditch comprised some thirty-four pits extending from the north-east corner of the excavated area, for over 41 m. to the line of the south-western boundary of the (infilled) B1 enclosure ditch. A further two post-pits were identified in line with the rest south-west of the enclosure boundary (B182 and B501) and it is considered likely that others may have existed cutting the earlier ditch fills but were not recognised.

The fence may have originally been designed to project parallel with the field boundary to terminate at the north eastern entrance of the paddock (Enclosure B21), a distance of approximately 52 m. The post-pits were generally spaced at intervals of between 0.50–0.80 m. and were on average 0.70 m. in diameter. The largest had a diameter of 0.80 m. and the smallest 0.40 m. Most of the pits were vertical-sided with a flat base cut between 0.30 and 0.50 m. deep. All of them, including those closest to Enclosure B21, contained remarkably similar fills of mid brown gravelly loam mixed with chalk lumps. No post-'ghosts' were identified, perhaps indicating that timbers had been removed in antiquity. Twelve of the post-pits contained a total of seventeen flint-tempered sherds (including Fig. 106, Nos 58–9), but of more relevance to their date, six contained sherds of Roman pottery of the later first and second centuries and three yielded samian ware sherds dating up to the late second or early third century A.D.

Cropmarks (Fig. 5)

A number of cropmarks identified in air photographs, but not located as soil stains during the excavation were plotted to the south-west of Enclosure B1. A single cropmark extended on a north-west to south-east axis a short way south-east of Enclosure B21 for a distance of approximately 50 m. A second cropmark set at right-angles to the first, formed perhaps the southern corner of an enclosure or large field. The second ditch aligned north-east to south-west was traced for approximately 30 m. Adjoining the junction of the two cropmarks to the south-west, was a hypocausted building (Area C). It is tentatively suggested that the cropmarks formed the south-west and south-east sides of an enclosure linked to Enclosure B21, Ditch B165 and the row of post-pits.

The hypocausted building (Area C) (Fig. 54)

Frank Jenkins

Area C contained the lower portion of a small heated Roman building, comprising a main hypocausted room, a stoke-

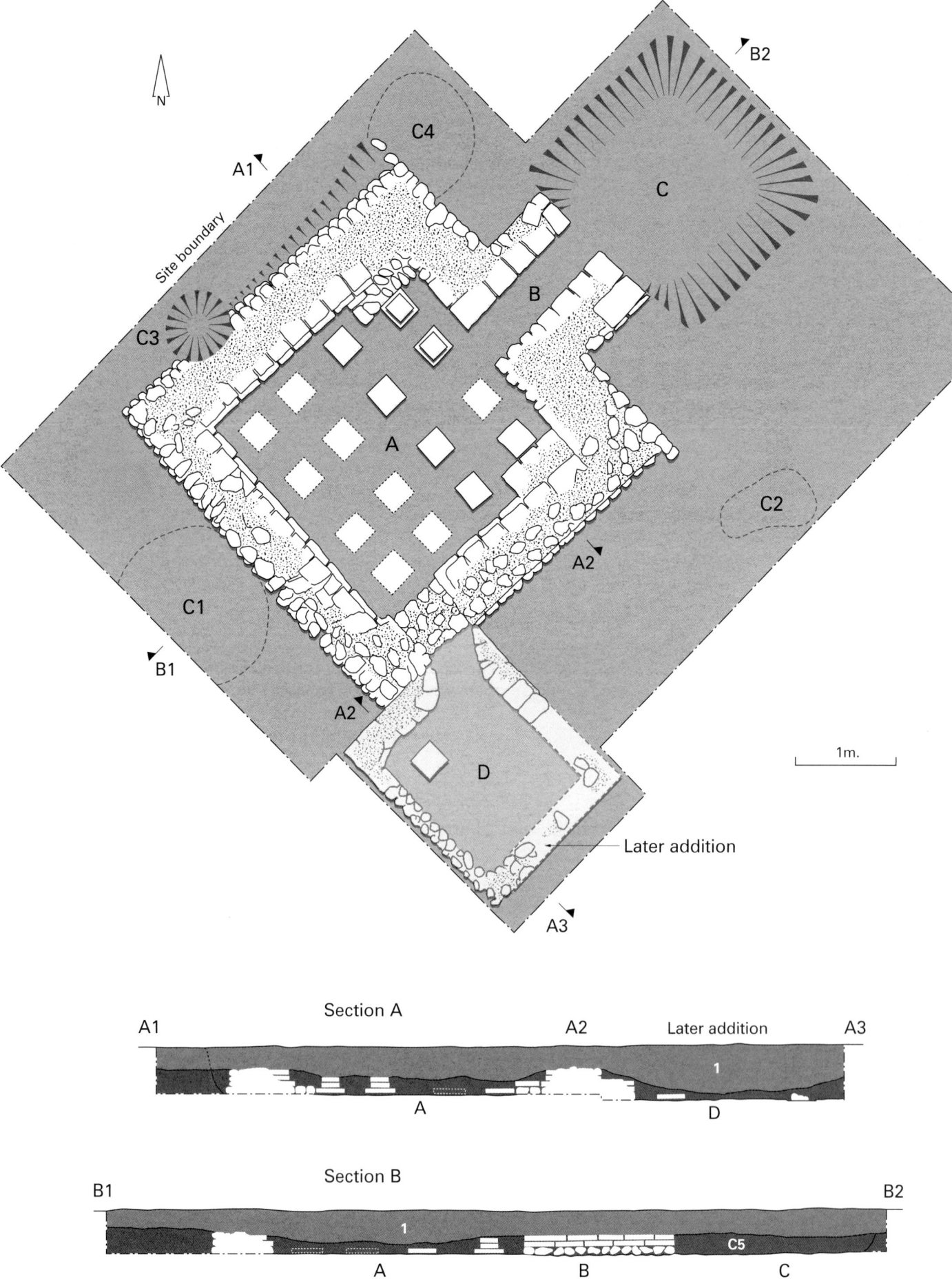

Fig. 54. Period 5B. Area C hypocaust structure.

hole and a small hypocausted room attached to the main structure.

The main room (A) (Fig. 54, Pl. XI)

The larger hypocausted room, connected to the flue of the furnace, was built in a construction pit cut from the original ground surface down into natural gravel. On the north-west side, the pit had been excavated wider than necessary and the space between its cut edge and the north-west wall had been filled with small flat water-rolled stones probably from the coast.

The hypocaust measured 2.44 m. (north-east to south-west) by 2.51 m. The surviving wall height was on average 0.25 m. Each wall consisted of courses of water-rolled flints bonded with white mortar, faced internally with regularly-laid courses of red tiles. The footing consisted of a further course of water-rolled flint and was wider than the wall, with a 0.05 m. offset on either side. The lowest course of the facing tiles was similarly offset. The offset formed by these and the footing rose approximately 0.13 m. from the bottom of the hypocaust.

The lower floor of the hypocaust was of *opus signinum*. The floor of the heated room above was originally supported on tile *pilae*. The lower part of two *pilae* remained, consisting of two tiles 0.19 m. square, stacked above a third basal tile 0.28 m. square, the whole standing on a pad of mortar laid on the underfloor. The basal tiles of five *pilae* remained *in situ*. In addition, square pads of mortar on the underfloor indicated where a further nine *pilae* had stood. The total of sixteen *pilae* stood in four rows of four, aligned with the axis of the flue, but slightly skew in relation to the structure's walls. In each corner of the hypocaust at its north-east end, the lower part of a rectangular plinth was recorded consisting of flints laid in courses, bonded with white mortar. Each plinth measured 0.69 by 0.31 m. In the space between the plinths stood one of the rows of *pilae*. As these and the two plinths were set close to the inner mouth of the furnace flue, it is likely that they had carried the weight of a concrete bath, installed in the heated room above. Support for this suggestion was provided by fragments of white concrete present in debris that had fallen into the hypocaust. Each piece retained a quarter-round convex moulding possibly from such a bath. Debris from within the hypocaust also included pieces of painted wall plaster and fragments of box-flue tiles, derived from vertical flues in the walls of the heated room. In addition, a fragment of a voussoir box-flue indicated that the building originally had a barrel-vaulted roof or sub roof.

The furnace (B)

A furnace, 0.76 m. long and aligned north-east to south-west was connected to a flue 0.61 m. long through the north-east wall of the hypocaust. Between the side walls of the furnace was a channel 0.40 m. wide. The wall on the south-east side was 0.60 m. wide; the other was only 0.40 m. wide. As recorded, the walls forming the sides of the furnace consisted of water-rolled flints, overlaid by a course of tiles. The sides of the flue were similarly constructed. The base of the furnace was of fire reddened natural gravel, covered with a layer of ashes.

The stoke-hole (C)

The furnace was stoked from an external pit, cut roughly square and measuring 2.30 m. north-west to south-east by 2 m. Only the lower part of the pit remained, cut into the natural gravel, its base covered with a layer of compacted ashes. A fourth-century coin was found lying on the hard surface of the ashes.

The small hypocaust (D) (Pl. XII)

A small rectangular structure was recorded abutting the southern corner of the main structure. The room, measuring internally 1.50 m. (north-west to south-east) by 1.30 m., was defined to the north-east and north-west by walls approximately 0.30 m. wide. The south-west wall was 0.18 m. wide. Much of the eastern corner of the structure had been quarried long before later plough damage, but wall widths were generally 0.30 m. The surviving walls were of similar construction to those of the main hypocaust. This and the presence of a straight joint between the walls of both buildings suggest that the smaller room was added shortly after completion of the main structure.

A short angled flue passed through the wall of Structure D built up against the exterior face of hypocaust A's south-east wall, surviving as a shallow 0.59 m. wide slot in the top of that wall. The base of this slot was at a slightly higher level than the under floor of the main hypocaust (A).

The floor of the small heated room was of natural gravel covered with a thin layer of soot. Lying on the floor was a single tile 0.05 m. thick and approximately 0.28 m. square. The tile rested on clean gravel and presumably represented the base of a *pila*, its position indicating an original arrangement of perhaps four such *pilae*. No other clean square patches of gravel were recorded, presumably because after the other *pilae* were removed the soot had eventually been trampled over where they were originally positioned.

The finds

The bulk of the pottery was recovered from debris on the floor of the main hypocaust (A) (thirty-eight sherds), the loam backfill of the stoke-pit (C5) (141 sherds) and from unstratified rubble associated with the plough-damaged structure (D) (eighty-two sherds). All of the material was residual and included a high proportion of 'Belgic' grog-

Pl. XI. Period 5. Area C. Hypocaust structure, looking south-west. Scale 2 m.

tempered sherds and Roman pottery of later first- and second-century date.

The backfill of the stoke-pit (C5) included seven sherds of Central Gaulish samian ware dated c. A.D. 125–55, including a stamped vessel (No. 584, p. 244).

The plough soil provided one mortaria sherd (Fig. 142, No. 595), dating from the later second century, together with one possible Late Roman coarse sandy ware sherd.

Evidence for later occupation

In Area A the extensive field system appears to have gone into disuse by the early to mid second century. The latest dated material from Area A was recovered from a rubbish pit (A274) dated by ceramics to the mid to late second century, found cutting a field boundary ditch (A267).

In Area B use of the B21 enclosure, attendant field ditches and palisade of post-pits may not, on recovered ceramic dating evidence, extend occupation much beyond the early-to-mid third century.

In Area C, debris filling the hypocausted building contained only first- and second-century finds, save for the fourth-century coin found amongst carbon on the stoke-pit floor, together with the skeleton of a small dog (p. 281). As the coin may have been dropped either during a last firing of the hypocaust or perhaps more likely, during an episode of robbing, occupation of the building or re-use of constituent materials may be assumed to have continued into the fourth century.

Overall, it appears likely that occupation of this part of the hilltop probably ceased by the mid third century. That occupation probably continued nearby is suggested by a few surface finds of post mid third-century date and the fourth-century coin recovered from the hypocausted building.

Discussion

From the later first century A.D. and into the second century, there is a marked increase in the quantities of samian and Canterbury coarsewares being used and discarded, the latter represented by surprisingly large quantities of kitchen wares, lid-seated flanged-rim cooking-jars and bowls being the dominant types. These trends may indicate an increase in population and general wealth, and on Areas B and C, a period of domestic and agricultural expansion and reorganisation.

Pl. XII. Period 5. Area C. Extension to hypocaust structure, looking north-west. Scale 2 m.

Clear evidence for expansion is indicated by the construction of a small hypocausted building a short distance south of the main enclosure. That the building was a bath-house and not a corn-drier is confirmed by the presence of several pieces of painted plaster and quarter-round floor mouldings in *opus signinum*. Unfortunately excavation was confined to this structure, so that any potential relationship with adjacent buildings can only be inferred. Occupation in the area is confirmed by the presence of rubbish pits, some underlying the hypocaust others perhaps contemporary with it.

Also contemporary with the heated building was the formation of a new boundary following the line of the western side of the former B1 enclosure. The new boundary ditch was accompanied by a substantial 'palisade' which may have continued to Enclosure B21.

Worn pot sherds including Southern and Central Gaulish samian recovered from the Area A field ditches indicate that the crops may have been regularly manured throughout the later first and second centuries. However, no Eastern Gaulish samian was recovered and no third- or fourth-century finewares suggesting perhaps that the fields were no longer being used for arable farming by the mid third century. This does not rule out the possibility that the area was used for pasture after this time.

With the exception of coin evidence from the stoke-pit of the hypocausted building, no features in Areas A and B provided evidence post-dating the second half of the third century A.D. For the pottery there is a distinct fall-off following a peak in the late first to mid second century, suggesting a steady decline in occupation culminating with an apparent cessation early in the second half of the third century A.D.

The presence of a few Late Roman finewares from unstratified contexts shows that some form of occupation continued in the vicinity as late as *c.* A.D. 325 or 350. Arguably the latest dated find, a fourth-century coin found lying on the hard surface of ashes filling the hypocaust's stoke hole, also supports the view that some sort of occupation continued into the fourth century. There is little to suggest that occupation may have continued into the second half of the fourth century. The skeleton of a dog, found amongst the *pilae,* may perhaps represent the onset of decay, disuse and abandonment.

PART 3: THE POTTERY

Peter Couldrey, Marion Green, Nigel Macpherson-Grant[8] and Isobel Thompson

The Late Bronze Age/Early Iron Age pottery (Figs 57–100)

Peter Couldrey

Introduction

This report was completed in 1987 and, apart from a few minor alterations, no attempt has been made to bring the discussion up-to-date.

A total number of 9561 sherds, weighing about 60.5 kg., was recovered from features belonging to Periods 2 and 3 dating between *c.* 900 and 400 B.C. This is the largest collection of pottery so far recovered from this period in east Kent and the purpose of this report is to present the ceramic evidence both in terms of the information it can throw on the site and as a body of data for future reference.

In preparing this report, all the 'pre-Belgic' pottery was examined. Within any deposit sherds sharing the same wall thickness, fabric, surface treatment and colours were regarded as belonging to a single vessel. For each of these 'vessels' a record was made of the number of non-fitting sherds, the fabric, wall thickness, surface treatment, colour and weight. In addition, details of the diameter and the percentage of the surviving circumference were recorded for all rims, bases and recognisable shoulders. These details are held in the excavation archive. For the purposes of this report most of the quantification is based on a count of non-fitting sherds.

All rims, bases, decorated sherds and recognisable shoulders were drawn in outline and these full-size drawings were used when constructing the typological classification described below.

Most of the pottery is flint-tempered and, with few exceptions, no attempt was made to fit wall sherds from different features. Very rarely, where sherds shared distinctive traits and an attempt was made to fit them, were joins found. There was not time available for a more thorough attempt to find joins and it is likely that more exist.

This report describes the fabric groups, forms, styles of decoration and categories of surface treatment, followed by a discussion of the chronology, technology and continental influence.

Fabrics

Each sherd was examined and the main inclusions of the fabric identified by eye, supplemented by the use of a hand-lens. In the descriptions which follow the term 'inclusion' is used to describe both naturally occurring and manually added components of the fabric. For each sherd the length and quantity of the main inclusions were recorded. The quantity however was not measured, but identified by eye. The terms used and a broad indication of their meaning, are as follows: 'sparse' (<1 per sq. cm.); 'moderate' (1–4 per sq. cm.); 'common' (5–8 per sq. cm.); 'abundant' (>8 per sq. cm.). The groups listed below were then defined on the basis of type of inclusions.

The distribution of fabrics in contexts dated to Periods 2 and 3, calculated as a percentage of the total number of sherds per period, is shown in Table 1. In practice, most of

---

8. This original report on the Late Iron Age flint-tempered pottery was written by Nigel Macpherson-Grant and is retained in the archive. It included an important review of evidence from several sites in east Kent which were unpublished at the time. Since then the pottery from some of these sites has been discussed elsewhere and an updated discussion of the evidence from east Kent has appeared (Macpherson-Grant 1991, 44–8; Pollard 1995). This shorter report (pp. 176–89) includes many of the points made by Nigel, but refers out to published evidence where possible.

Fabrics	Period 2	Period 3A	Period 3B
1	71	73	70
2	15	10	8
3	3	9	8
4	2	1	4
5			
6	1		1
7			1
8			1
9			
10			
11	1	4	1
12	1		1
13	1	1	1
14	1		1
15	1		
16			1
17			1
18	1		1
19			
20			
21	1		1
22			
23			1
24			
25			
26			1
27			
28			
29		1	
30	1	1	1
31			1
32			
33			
34			
35			1
36			
37			
Total	100	100	106

Table 1. Distribution of fabrics in Periods 2 and 3, shown as a percentage of number of sherds per period.

the sherds (98 per cent) are flint-tempered (Fabrics 1–21) and the boundaries between sub-groups are not precise; but they do serve to reflect the variation present in the assemblage.

Fabric groups

A. Flint

Fabrics in this group are commonly found throughout Periods 2 and 3, when they represent up to 93 per cent of the total (*see* Table 1). The size of the flint inclusions varies from 5 mm. to 7 mm. and their density from sparse to abundant. Additional inclusions of grog and chalk (Fabrics 6–10) were rarely found, except in Period 3B and in the fill of Enclosure ditch B70 where they are probably intrusive.

1. Flint
2. Flint with iron oxide
3. Flint with organic inclusions
4. Flint with organic inclusions and iron oxide
5. Flint with organic inclusions, iron oxide and chalk
6. Flint and grog
7. Flint and grog with iron oxide
8. Flint and grog with organic inclusions
9. Flint and grog with organic inclusions and iron oxide
10. Flint and chalk

B. Flint in Sandy Matrix

The fabrics in this group are noticeably more sandy than those in Group A, probably because the flint inclusions are sparse or sparse-to-moderate. They are found in Periods 2 and 3 but never account for more than 4 per cent, and usually represent less than 1 per cent of the total.

11. Flint in sandy matrix
12. Flint in sandy matrix with iron oxide
13. Flint in sandy matrix with organic inclusions
14. Flint in sandy matrix with organic inclusions and iron oxide
15. Flint in sandy matrix with grog

C. Flint in Quartz Sandy Matrix

These fabrics are distinguished from those in Group B by the greater abundance of quartz grains, often up to 1.5 mm. in size. Sparse-to-moderate inclusions of glauconite are visible, up to 0.3 mm. in size, in Fabrics 19 and 20.

16. Flint in quartz sandy matrix.
17. Flint in quartz sandy matrix with iron oxide
18. Flint in quartz sandy matrix with organic inclusions
19. Flint in quartz sandy matrix with glauconite
20. Flint in quartz sandy matrix with glauconite and organic inclusions

D. Flint in Glauconitic Sandy Matrix

The only fabric in this group has sparse inclusions of flint up to 0.5 mm. in size and the matrix contains abundant grains of glauconite up to 0.2 mm. in size. This fabric is rarely found in the Late Bronze Age/Early Iron Age in east Kent, but its use for vessel Form 39, No. 192, confirms a Period 2 date (*see* pp. 118–20, below).

21. Flint in glauconitic sandy matrix

E. Quartz Sandy

This group consists of sandy fabrics with common to abundant inclusions of quartz. It is distinguished from the previous groups by the absence of flint inclusions. Sherds in these fabrics are rare on the site and are found in Period 3B contexts and in the Enclosure ditch B70 where they are probably intrusive.

22. Quartz sandy matrix
23. Quartz sandy matrix with iron oxide
24. Quartz sandy matrix with organic inclusions
25. Quartz sandy matrix with glauconite

F. Sandy Matrix with Sparse Quartz Grains

These fabrics are rare, and only two sherds of Fabric 26 are known from Period 3B. Sherds in Fabrics 27 and 28 are from later deposits or unstratified contexts.

26. Sandy matrix
27. Sandy matrix with iron oxide
28. Sandy matrix with organic inclusions

G. Glauconitic Sandy Matrix

This fabric is characterised by abundant inclusions of glauconite grains up to 0.2 mm. in size. It is represented by one sherd, weighing 4 g., from Pit B144, and apparently belongs to Period 3A.

29. Glauconitic sandy matrix

H. Grog

This group is characterised by abundant inclusions of grog. It is common during Periods 4 and 5, and appears as an intrusive element in Periods 2 and 3.

30. Grog
31. Grog with iron oxide
32. Grog with organic inclusions
33. Grog with shell inclusions
34. Grog in sandy matrix
35. Grog with flint inclusions
36. Grog with iron oxide and flint inclusions
37. Grog with flint and organic inclusions

Forms

Only seventeen vessels were found with complete or wholly reconstructable profiles, and as a result, the following typology is based mainly on fragmentary rims and bases. When classifying small rim sherds of irregular hand-made vessels, it is rarely possible to identify the complete forms from which they are derived or the functions they served. Indeed, it is often impossible to determine even whether a bowl or a jar is represented. The main criterion used in this classification is shape, supplemented by wall thickness and surface treatment. Each form identified is then subdivided according to diameter.

Many of these forms merge together and this is particularly apparent with vessels with plain convex profiles. These plain forms are treated first and are subdivided according to shape and surface treatment. Forms 1–7 have plain rounded rims and generally smooth surfaces, whereas Forms 8–17 have flattened and expanded rims with coarser surfaces. These are followed by more complex profiles with open forms preceding closed forms. Associated with each description is an illustrated example which is intended to clarify the classification as well as demonstrate areas of similarity between forms.

Plain convex forms

Vessels with a plain rounded rim and generally smooth surfaces:

F1

Globular vessel with a sharply inturned plain rim and wall thickness of 7–10 mm.:
    a) Diameter 16 cm.: 393 (B114)
    b) Diameter 24 cm.: 402 (B271)

F2

Globular vessel with a sharply inturned plain rim and wall thickness of 5–6.5 mm.:
    a) Diameter 18–21 cm.: 46, 65 (B70)
    b) Diameter 26 cm.: 383 (B154)

F3

Globular vessel with a less sharply inturned rim, and with wall thickness of 10–14 mm.:
    a) Diameter 24–26 cm.: 287 (B12)

F4

Bowl with a slightly inturned rim and a wall thickness of 4–7 mm.:
    a) Diameter 10–12 cm.: 96 (B70), 203 (A180)
    b) Diameter 20–22 cm.: 11, 66 (B70), 277 (A118)
    c) Diameter 24–26 cm.: 44, 95 (B70)

F5

Open hemispherical bowl with wall 4–5 mm. thick and plain rim:
    a) Diameter 15 cm.: 236 (B317)
    b) Diameter 18–20 cm.: 43 (B70), 235 (B317)

F6

Open hemispherical bowl with a plain rim, with wall thickness of 5–6 mm.
    a) Diameter 12–16 cm.: 10, 45, 80 (B70)
    b) Diameter 19 cm.: 494 (B267)
    c) Diameter 22–28 cm.: 42, 134–5 (B70)

F7

Open bowl with smooth surfaces and wall thickness of 8–10 mm.:
    a) Diameter 31 cm.: 237 (B317)

F8

Globular vessel with a sharply inturned rim, with a flattened and expanded rim and wall thickness 8–10 mm.:
    a) Diameter 36 cm.: 476 (B266)
    b) Diameter unknown: 335 (B26), 459 (B248)

F9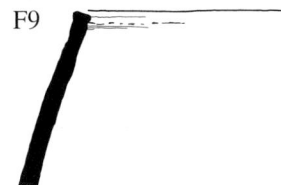

Closed form with straight inturned neck and flat-topped rim, with wall thickness of 8–11 mm.:
    a) Diameter 22–26 cm.: 290 (B12), 409 (B124)
    b) Diameter 34 cm.: 429 (B214)

F10

Globular vessel with a slightly inturned, plain rim and wall thickness of 7–9 mm.:
    a) Diameter 18 cm.: 301 (B244)
    b) Diameter 23–25 cm.: 288 (B12), 406 (B124)

F11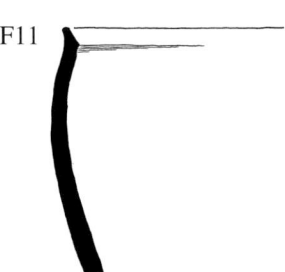

Globular vessel with a short everted rim with internal bevel and wall thickness of 12–18 mm.:
    a) Diameter 30 cm.: 206 (A19)

F12

Convex profiles with inturned flat-topped expanded rims, with wall thickness of 7–10 mm, and roughened external surface:
    a) Diameter 16 cm.: 400 (B271)
    b) Diameter 22–26 cm.: 452 (B245), 483 (B266)
    c) Diameter 30 cm.: 473 (B266)
    d) Diameter unknown: 408 (B124)

F13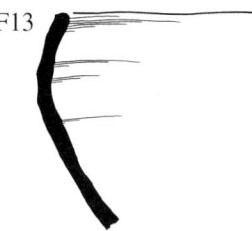

Bowl with rounded shoulder, convex neck and an inturned rim, with wall thickness of 7–9 mm.:
    a) Diameter 25 cm.: 474 (B266)
    b) Diameter 32–38 cm.: 133 (B70)
    c) Diameter unknown: 475 (B266)

F14

Bowl or jar with a very slight or absent shoulder, a continuous convex profile, a flat or expanded rim and wall thickness greater than 8 mm.:
    a) Diameter 20–26 cm.: 220 (A163), 397–8 (B114)
    b) Diameter 28–30 cm.: 371 (B196), 412 (B124)

F15. Open hemispherical bowl with a thickened or expanded rim and wall thickness of 8–10 mm.: example from Pit complex B15, not illustrated.

F16

Open hemispherical bowl with wall thickness of 7–8 mm.:
    a) Diameter 13–20 cm.: 67 (B70) and example from Pit complex B15, not illustrated.

F17

Probable trough with straight sides. These vessels appear to have been associated with salt processing. Several rim fragments were found in Pit B215. All were fired orange throughout and had a wall thickness of 7–10 mm. One has been illustrated:
    a) 375 (B215): extant length 28 cm.

Open forms

F18

Bowl with straight flaring wall and wall thickness of 7–9 mm.:
    a) Diameter 16–18 cm.: 302 (B244), 355 (B200A)
    b) Diameter 22–28 cm.: 89 (B70), 337 (B325), 396 (B114)

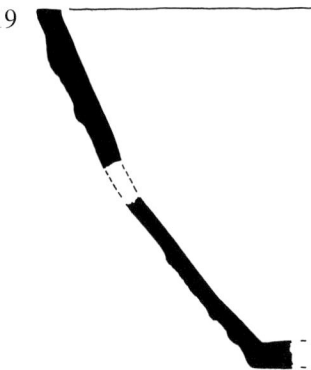
F19

Bowl with straight flaring wall, similar to Form 18, but with heavy rusticated surface treatment and wall thickness of 8–13 mm.:
    a) Diameter 41 cm: 293 (B12)

F20

Small cup or bowl with straight flaring wall and wall thickness of 7–12 mm.:
    a) Diameter 9 cm.: 488 (B266)

F21

Small cup or bowl with straight flaring wall, highly burnished surfaces and an expanded flat-topped rim and wall thickness of 6 mm.:
    a) Diameter c. 13 cm.: 361 (B226), 423 (B147)

F22

Tall jar or vase with straight side and expanded rim (more upright than Form 19). Wall thickness 6 mm.:
    a) Diameter 21.5 cm.: 197 (A5)

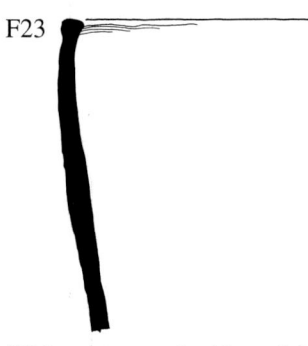

F23

Wide open vessel with straight side and expanded rim, with wall thickness of 9–12 mm.:
   a) Diameter 38 cm.: 170 (A152)

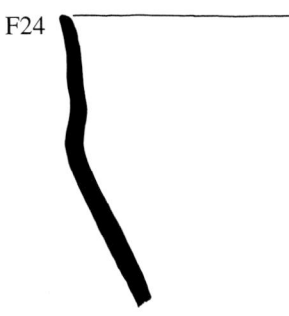

F24

Bowl with flaring body, rounded shoulder, a vertical neck and wall thickness of 8–10 mm.:
   a) Diameter 32 cm.: 416 (B124)

F25

Flaring bowl with a slack shoulder, a slight concave neck and wall thickness 6–10 mm.:
   a) Diameter 16–19 cm.: 69 (B70), 444 (B247)
   b) Diameter 28–34 cm.: 353 (B200A), 370 (B196)
   c) Diameter 42 cm.: 354 (B200A), 372 (B197)

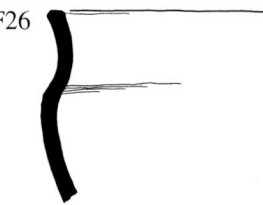

F26

Bowl with a concave neck and everted rim, with wall thickness of 5–7 mm. The diameter of the rim is less than or equal to that of the shoulder:
   a) Diameter 28 cm.: 123 (B70)
   b) Diameter 33 cm.: 122 (B70)
   c) Diameter 42 cm.: 78 (B70)

F27

Bowl with a rounded shoulder, a slight concave neck and an everted rim, with wall thickness of 7–10 mm.:
   a) Diameter 14–16 cm.: 132 (B70)

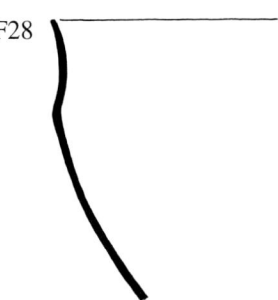

F28

Fine shouldered bowl with concave neck and gently everted rim and wall thickness of 3–5 mm.:
   a) Diameter 15–16 cm.: 193 (A5), 200 (A50), 216 (Area A unstratified)
   b) Diameter 26 cm : 1 (B70)

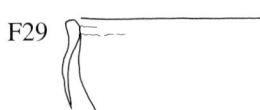

F29

Bowl with a higher shoulder than Form 27 and a short everted rim, with wall thickness of 11 mm.:
   a) Diameter 25 cm.: 319 (B49)

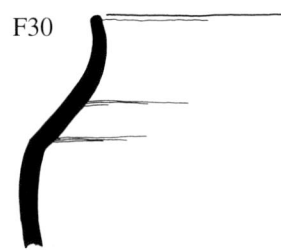

F30

Jar with a slightly everted rim on a sharply concave neck and high almost angular shoulder:
   a) Diameter 18.5 mm.: 53 (B70)

F31

Bowl with a sharply concave neck, irregular everted rim and wall thickness of 9 mm.:
   a) Diameter 31 cm.: 121 (B70)

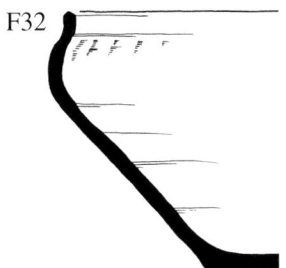

F32

Bowl with rounded shoulder, an inturned concave neck, short upright rim and wall thickness of 7–8 mm.:
    a) Diameter 24–26 cm.: 461, 468 (B266)

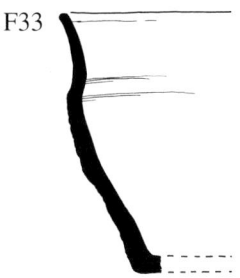

F33

Bowl with an everted rim, concave neck, and heavy rustication beneath the shoulder. The wall thickness is 8–10 mm.:
    a) Diameter 20 cm.: 456 (B245)

F34

Bipartite bowl with a carinated shoulder and wall thickness of 5–10 mm.:
    a) Diameter 13–20 cm.: 384 (B166), 386 (B114), 431 (B119), 462 (B266).
    b) Diameter 23–26 cm.: 299 (B244), 399 (B271)

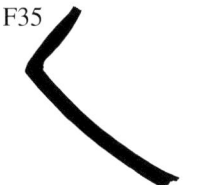

F35

A carinated vessel. Its rim is missing but it appears to have had a pedestal base, which distinguishes it from Form 34. The wall thickness is 7–8 mm.:
    a) Rim diameter unknown: 368 (B196)

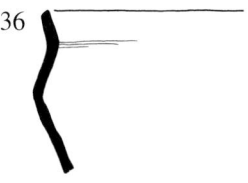

F36

A tripartite jar with an everted, almost flaring, rim and wall thickness of 5–8 mm.:
    a) Diameter 21–23 cm.: 152 (A24), 259 (B80)

F37

A tripartite bowl with carinated shoulder and wall thickness of 4–8 mm.:
    a) Diameter 15 cm.: 378 (B314)
    b) Diameter 20 cm.: 347 (B188)

F38

Fine cup with angular profile and wall thickness of 4 mm.:
    a) Diameter 10 cm.: 317 (B68).

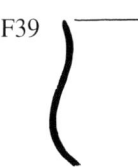

F39

Fine cup or bowl with s-profile and wall thickness of 3–4 mm.:
    a) Diameter 8–9 cm.: 172 (A2), 192 (A5), 255 (B80)
    b) Diameter 12–14 cm.: 4 (B70), 184 (A4)
    c) Diameter unknown: 141 (A24)

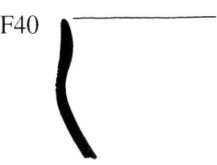

F40

Fine bowl with an upright, internally thickened neck and wall thickness of 4–6 mm.:
    a) Diameter 18–21 cm.: 212 (A187), 252 (B79), 297 (B244), 322 (unstrat)
    b) Diameter 28 cm.: 312 (B131)
    c) Diameter unknown: 278 (B144), 298 (B244)

F41

Fine cup or bowl with a straight slightly inturned neck and wall thickness of 4–6 mm.:
   a) Diameter 9 cm.: 173 (A2)
   b) Diameter 16 cm.: 140 (A24)

F42

Fine bowl with slack shoulder, a flaring everted rim and wall thickness of 4–5 mm.:
   a) Diameter 22 cm.: 100 (B70)

F43

Small bipartite cup or bowl with carinated shoulder and wall thickness of 4–5 mm.:
   a) Diameter 6–9 cm.: 12, 97 (B70)

F44

Straight sided vessel with wiped or smooth surfaces with wall thickness of 6–10 mm.:
   a) Diameter 14–15 cm.: 455 (B245)
   b) Diameter 20 cm.: 425 (B195)

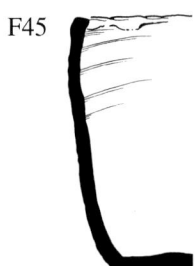
F45

Straight sided vessel, similar to Form 44, but with rough surfaces and with wall thickness of 7 mm.:
   a) Diameter 14 cm.: 202 (A180)

F46

An open vessel with a gentle convex profile and a plain rim with a slight internal bevel. The wall thickness is 4–5 mm.:
   a) Diameter 20.5 cm.: 225 (A208)

Closed forms

F47

Slack shouldered jar with a slightly concave neck and plain thickened rim and wall thickness of 6–8 mm.:
   a) Diameter 13–14 cm.: 331 (B16)

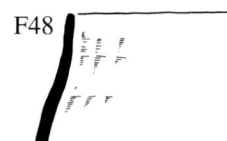
F48

Slack shouldered jar with a gently inturned neck, a plain rim and wall thickness of 5–7 mm.:
   a) Diameter 14 cm.: 143 (A24)
   b) Diameter 18–19 cm.: 145 (A24), 222 (A100)

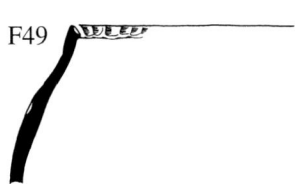
F49

Globular vessel with a slight concave neck, an inturned almost vertical rim and wall thickness of 6–9 mm.:
   a) Diameter 26 cm.: 101 (B70)

F50

Globular vessel with a more pronounced neck than Form 45, but with a similar inturned, almost vertical rim and wall thickness of 6–9 mm.:
   a) Diameter 20–23 cm.: 438 (B172)

F51

Jar with an inturned, almost straight neck, externally expanded flat-topped rim, and wall thickness of 7–11 mm.:
   a) Diameter 23–26 cm.: 443 (B247), 449 (B146), 470 (B266)
   b) Diameter 36 cm.: 369 (B196)
   c) Diameter 43 cm.: 451 (B245)

F52

Jar with rounded shoulder, an inturned, slightly concave neck and externally expanded rim. It has a rusticated surface and wall thickness of 10–15 mm.:
 a) Diameter 23–28 cm.: 346 (B189)
 b) Diameter 38–40 cm.: 373 (B215), 388 (B114)

F53

A globular jar with a short out-turned rim and one or more internal bevels. The wall thickness is 5–7 mm.:
 a) Diameter 18 cm.: 230 (B317)
 b) Diameter 26–28 cm.: 33 (B70), 268 (Area B, unstratified)

F54

A vessel with an inturned smooth concave neck rising to an everted rim with a pronounced internal bevel. The wall thickness is 8–9 mm.:
 a) Diameter 40 cm.: 169 (A181)

F55

Jar with rounded shoulder, concave neck and sharply everted rim and finger-tip decoration on the rim and shoulder. The wall thickness is 7–10 mm.:
 a) Diameter 22.5 cm.: 116 (B70)
 b) Diameter 33–39 cm.: 19, 114 (B70)

F56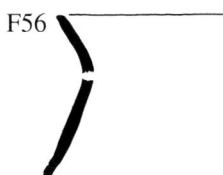

Jar with rounded shoulder, concave neck and plain sharply everted rim, with wall thickness of 5–6 mm.:
 a) Diameter 21 cm.: 142 (A24)

F57

Jar with a concave neck rising in a smooth curve to a plain gently everted rim. The wall thickness is 6–8 mm.:
 a) Diameter 24 cm.: 130 (B70)
 b) Diameter 30–34 cm.: 199 (A8), 309 (B131)
 c) Diameter 38 cm.: 147 (A24)
 d) Diameter 48 cm.: 6, 128 (B70)

F58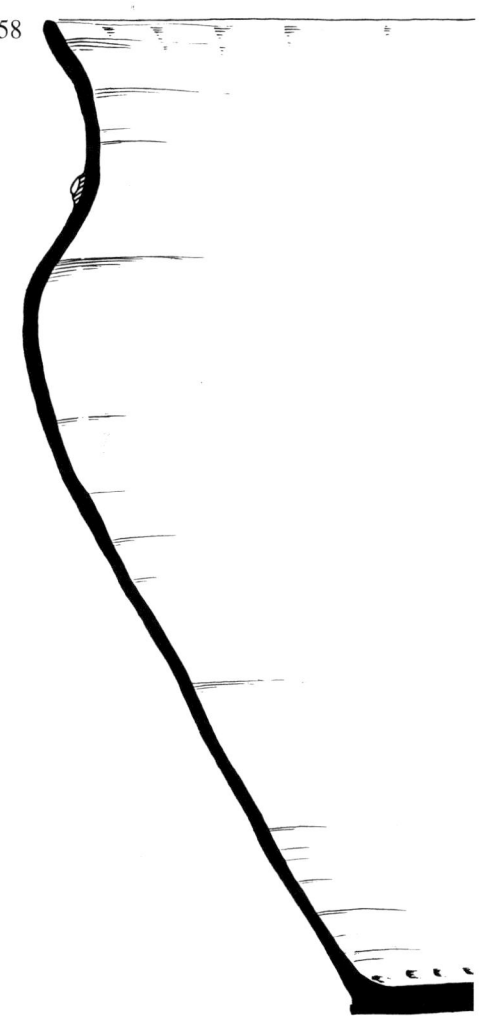

Jar with a concave neck rising in a smooth curve to a plain everted rim, as for Form 57, but decorated with a neck cordon with finger-tip impressions. The wall thickness is 6–8 mm.:
 a) Diameter 38 cm.: 149 (A24)
 b) Diameter 48 cm.: 296 (B12)

F59

Jar with inturned concave neck, rising to an inturned or slightly everted rim. The neck is decorated with a cordon with finger-tip impressions. The wall thickness is 6–8 mm.:
   a) Diameter 34–35 cm.: 180 (A3), 226 (Site A unstratified)
   b) Diameter 38–43 cm.: 272 (B92)

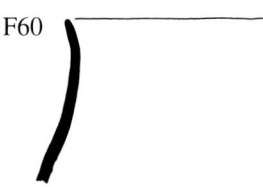

F60

Shouldered jar with inturned concave neck and a slightly everted rim. The wall thickness is 6–9 mm.:
   a) Diameter 18–22 cm.: 175 (A2), 181 (A3)
   b) Diameter 28–38 cm.: 188 (A4), 238–9 (B317)
   c) Diameter 43–48 cm.: 224 (A130)

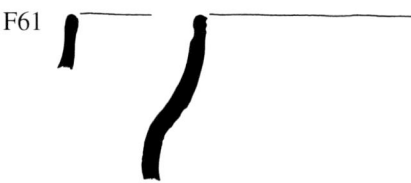

F61

Shouldered jar with inturned concave neck. It is distinguished from Form 60 by having an inturned or upright rim. The wall thickness is 6–10 mm.:
   a) Diameter 21–26 cm.: 363 (B203), 381 (B133), 404 (B124), 454 (B245)
   b) Diameter 31–37 cm.: 49–50 (B70), 411 (B124)
   c) Diameter 42 cm.: 223 (A129)

F62

Jar with a high shoulder and short concave neck. The wall thickness is 8 mm.:
   a) Diameter 16–19 cm.: 9, 115 (B70)

F63

Globular jar with an almost vertical neck. The wall thickness is 6–7 mm.:
   a) Diameter 13–16 cm.: 124 (B70)

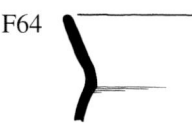

F64

Jar with everted or flaring rim and constricted neck. The wall thickness is 5–8 mm.:
   a) Diameter 14–19 cm.: 495 (B38), 437 (B172)

F65

Globular vessel with short everted rim. The wall thickness is 6–10 mm.:
   a) Diameter 28 cm.: 63 (B70)

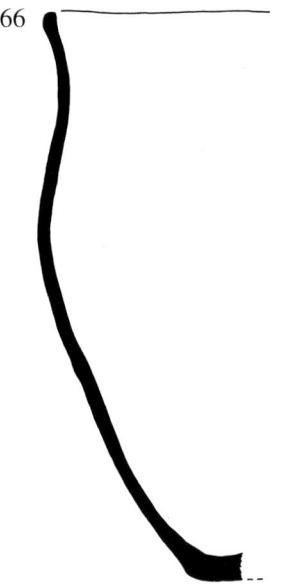

F66

S-profiled jar with slack shoulder and wall thickness of 5–7 mm.:
   a) Diameter 20–27 cm.: 213 (A187), 307 (B131), 315 (B131)

Miscellaneous forms

F67

Large jar with applied cordon and a wall thickness of 18 mm.:
   a) Diameter unknown: 428 (B214)

F68

Large jar with an upright, flat-topped rim with internal thickening. The wall thickness is 8 mm.:
    a) Diameter 30 cm.: 414 (B124)

F69

Vessel with slightly out-turned rim with a flat top and internal and external expansions. This style appears to be related to Form 21 but the surviving rim fragment suggests that the vessel is either very large or rectangular. The wall thickness is 9–10 mm.:
    a) Diameter unknown: 382 (B133)

F70

Rectangular vessel with flat base. The wall thickness is 10 mm.:
    a) 447 (B128)

F71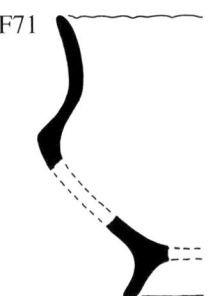

A bowl with a slightly everted rim, angular shoulder and pedestal base. The wall thickness is 7–8 mm.:
    a) Diameter 16.5 cm.: 380 (B133)

F72

A bowl or cup with flaring rim and an angular shoulder. The wall thickness is 5 mm.:
    a) Diameter of shoulder c. 12 cm.: 92 (B70)

F73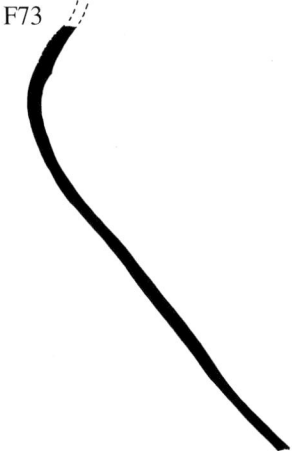

Shouldered jar or bowl with light horizontal grooves above the shoulder. The wall thickness is 5–7 mm.:
    a) Rim diameter unknown: 210 (A153)

F74

A rim with a vertical projection, interpreted here as providing a crenellated appearance, on the basis of the limited available evidence. It is equally possible that it is a base.
    a) Diameter uncertain: 496 (B40)

F75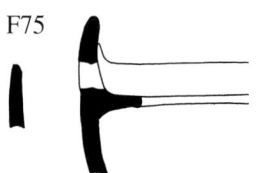

A lug-handled vessel with internal ledge. The wall thickness is 9 mm.
    a) Diameter c. 19.5 cm.: 91 (B70)

Rim types

In most cases, vessels were represented solely by fragmentary rim sherds. Many of these are too small to be identified clearly, or too common to be associated with a specific form. Some, however, share certain consistent features and have been grouped together as defined below:

R1. Flaring rim with wall thickness of 3–4 mm.:
    a) Diameter 11 cm.: 217 (Area A unstratified)
    b) Diameter 14–16 cm.: 3 (B70), 218 (Area A unstratified), 275 (A118)

R2. Flaring everted rim, most are more out-turned than R1, with wall thickness of 5–8 mm.:
- a) Diameter 17 cm.: 168 (A145), 387 (B114)
- b) Diameter 20–26 cm.: 37, 129 (B70), 148 (A24), 176 (A2), 182 (A3), 245 (B317)
- c) Diameter 32–34 cm.: 201 (A155)

R3. Straight flaring rim with wall thickness 5–8 mm.:
- a) Diameter 18 cm.: 435 (B126)
- b) Diameter 22–26 cm.: 35 (B70), 256, 261 (B80), 283 (B12)
- c) Diameter 32–36 cm.: 119 (B70)

R4. Straight flaring rim with low internal bevel and wall thickness of 6–8 mm.:
- a) Diameter 16–20 cm.: 351 (B200)
- b) Diameter unknown: 280 (B144)

R5. Straight flaring rim with internal bevel and wall thickness of 5–6 mm.:
- a) Diameter 16–17.5 cm.: 233 (B317), 34 (B70)
- b) Diameter 21–24 cm.: 38, 94 (B70)

R6. Tall, gently everted rim with smooth or burnished surfaces and wall thickness of 4–6 mm.:
Diameter 14 cm.: 334 (B26), 436 (B132)

R7. Gently everted rim with wall thickness of 6–8 mm.:
- a) Diameter 23–26 cm.: 25, 77 (B70), 316 (B131)
- b) Diameter 30 cm.: 126 (B70)

Base types

Most of the bases are flat. Selected types are defined for purposes of discussion and others remain unclassified.

B1. Flat base, untreated with calcined flints adhering, suggesting that the vessel had been placed on a bed of these grits during manufacture.

B2. Flat base, untreated, generally rough, occasionally with voids suggesting that the vessel had been placed on grass or straw during manufacture.

B3. Flat base, wiped.

B4. Flat base, smooth or burnished.

B5. Pedestal base with smooth or burnished surfaces.

B6. Omphalos base.

Decoration types

Decoration is classified here according to its type and position on the vessel. When mentioned in the text these types are referred to as D1–D43. The association of these types of decoration and the forms outlined above is shown in Table 2.

Rim decoration

D1. Cut grooves
- a) Straight across rim: 120 (B70)
- b) On exterior of rim: 119 (B70)

D2. Broad finger-impressed grooves straight across the rim, forming a wavy profile:
- a) 138 (A24), 229 (B317), 380 (B133)

D3. Regular diagonal grooves forming a 'cable' design:
- a) 7, 21 (B70), 148 (A24), 197 (A5), 279 (B144), 290 (B12)

D4. Finger-tip impressions. This form of decoration is subdivided according to its position on the rim:
- a) On the top: 24, 132 (B70), 144 (A24), 223 (A129), 268 (B97), 301 (B244), 390 (B114), 433 (B119), 444 (B247), 470 (B266)
- b) On the exterior: 53, 56, 58, 61, 73 (B70), 270 (B97)
- c) On the interior: 220 (A163)
- d) On the interior and exterior: 22 (B70)
- e) On the top and exterior: 23 (B70), 383 (B154)

D5. Finger-nail impressions on top:
- a) 51, 57, 81 (B70)

D6. Cable design on top and finger-tip impressions on the interior:
- a) 316 (B131)

D7. Painted vertical lines on the inside:
- a) 131 (B70)

D8. Three light horizontal grooves around the outside:
- a) 235 (B317)

Neck decoration

D9. Plain neck cordon:
- a) 188 (A4), 196 (A5), 207 (A47)

D10. Finger-tip impressions on neck cordon:
- a) 88, 106, 107 (B70), 149 (A24), 177 (A2), 226 (Area A unstratified), 272 (B92), 296 (B12)

Form	1	2	3	4	6	8	9	10	11	12	13	18	19	20	26	27	28	29	32	37	38	40	Total
F2				1																			1
F5							1																1
F9			1																				1
F10				1							1												2
F12																1							1
F14				1												1							2
F16				1						1													2
F22			1																				1
F24										1													1
F25				1																			1
F27				1																			1
F30				1																			1
F34													1										1
F35																					1		1
F38																1							1
F39																3	1						4
F40																6							6
F41																2							2
F49																		1					1
F51				1																			1
F53				1														1		1			3
F55														1				2					3
F56																1							1
F58								2															2
F59								2											1				3
F60							1											1					2
F61				1											1			1					3
F71		1																					1
F73																1							1
R1																							0
R2			1																				1
R3	1																						1
R7				1																			1
Total	1	1	3	10	1	1	1	4	1	1	1	1	1	2	1	14	1	5	1	1	1	1	54

Table 2. Association of form and decoration in Periods 2 and 3.

D11. Finger-tip impressions on neck:
  a) 67, 115 (B70)

D12. Two rows of finger-tip impressions:
  a) 416 (B124)

D13. Finger-nail impressions on neck:
  a) 288 (B12)

D14. Two groups of light horizontal grooves:
  a) 215 (Area A unstratified)

D15. Stab marks above broad shallow grooves:
  example from B269, *not illus.*

D16. Single horizontal groove:
  a) 139 (A24).

D17. Single broad horizontal groove:
  example from B139, *not illus.*

D18. At least two light diagonal grooves:
  a) 399 (B271)

Rim and neck decoration

D19. Finger-tip impressions on rim and neck cordon:
  a) 19 (B70)

Shoulder decoration

D20. Finger-tip impressions:
  a) 109–111 (B70), 171 (A152), 360 (B226), 367 (B207), 412 (B124), 472–3 (B266)

D21. Finger-nail impressions:
  a) 41 (B70)

D22. Finger-tip impressions on cordon:
  a) 108 (B70)

D23. Triangular impressions:
  a) 112 (B70)

D24. Diagonal grooves across a horizontal cordon:
  a) 87 (B70)

D25. Deep almost vertical cuts:
  a) 71 (B70)

D26. Single horizontal groove:
  a) 411 (B124)

D27. Group of fine horizontal grooves:
  a) 4, 34 (B70), 140–42 (A24), 172–3 (A2), 183 (A4), 210 (A153), 212 (A187), 232 (B317), 252 (B79), 278 (B144), 281 (B12), 297–8 (B244), 312 (B131), 317 (B68), 322 (B269, unstratified)

D28. Group of fine horizontal grooves above groups of three or four diagonal grooves:
  a) 192 (A5)

Rim and shoulder

D29. Finger-tip decoration:
  a) 101, 114, 116, 118 (B70), 175 (A2), 404 (B124)

Wall decoration

This category includes those forms of decoration which are found on the walls of vessels as well as those which do not obviously belong to a rim or a shoulder.

D30. Single light curvilinear groove:
  a) Examples from B133 and B164, *not illus.*

D31. Groups of fine horizontal grooves:
  a) Five grooves: 403 (B124)
  b) At least three grooves: 2 (B70), 227 (B317)
  c) At least two grooves: 321 (B270)

D32. Fine 's-shaped' and horizontal grooves:
  a) 230 (B317)

D33. Painted bands from an unknown design:
  a) 497 (B99, unstratified)

D34. Irregular vertical grooves:
  examples from B70 and B128, *not illus.*

D35. Group of light horizontal grooves between 3 and 6 mm. apart:
  examples from B70, B139 and B317, *not illus.*

D36. Combed patterns with narrow grooves:
  a) 352 (B200A)

Composite groups

D37. Two light horizontal grooves on the shoulder and a cordon with finger-tip impressions on the neck:
  a) 180 (A3)

D38. Horizontal grooved zigzag pattern bounded by groups of horizontal grooves:
  a) 33 (B70)

D39. A horizontal band of diagonal impressions bounded above by one broad and one narrow groove and below by narrow grooves:
  a) 189 (A191)

D40. Linear design applied with an inlaid clay slip: a horizontal band containing alternate metopes filled with a diagonal cross or saltire:
  a) 368 (B196)

D41. A painted area from an unknown design:
  a) 498 (unstratified)

Internal surface

D42. Broad horizontal grooves or rilling. This example may belong to the inside of a wide flaring bowl, similar to '*assiettes tronconiques*' on the Continent. However, the sherd is extremely worn and its angle is uncertain:
  a) 385 (B114)

These specific types of decoration have been grouped together into fourteen styles summarised in Table 3.

Surface treatment

Both surfaces of each sherd were recorded in detail, and these details summarised in the ten categories (ST1–10) defined below. The distinction between surface treatment and decoration is sometimes blurred. Here surface treatment is used to describe the overall surface of a sherd. In some

Style code	Description	Decoration types
A	Finger-tip or nail impressions	Types 4, 5, 11-13, 20-22, 29
B	Rim decoration other than A	Types 1-3, 6
C	Applied cordon	Types 9, 10, 19
D	Light narrow horizontal grooves	Types 8, 14, 27, 28, 31, 32, 35
E	Triangular stabbed decoration	Type 23
F	Narrow linear grooves	Types 16, 26
G	Curvilinear grooves	Type 30
H	Miscellaneous linear design	Types 17, 18, 24
I	Zigzag	Type 38
J	Composite groups	Types 15, 37, 39
K	Irregular vertical grooves	Type 34
L	Vertical cuts on shoulder	Type 25
M	Painted design	Types 7, 33, 40, 41
N	Combed designs	Type 36

Table 3. Styles of decoration in Periods 2 and 3.

instances the differential use of surface treatment may produce a decorative effect, such as a zone of burnishing above the shoulder contrasted with heavy rustication beneath (e.g. Nos 454 and 456, Pl. XV). The styles of decoration are defined above and refer to deliberate ornamentation of the surface, which may be added to any of the types of surface treatment shown in Table 4.

Code	Description
ST1	Painted or slipped
ST2	Polished or highly burnished
ST3	Burnished or very smooth
ST4	Smooth
ST5	Wiped smooth
ST6	Wiped or roughly slurried
ST7	Heavily wiped or light rustication
ST8	Rusticated
ST9	Combed
ST10	Heavily wiped with twig, grass or straw

Table 4. Classification of surface treatment in Periods 2 and 3.

Chronology

The main evidence for the chronology of Periods 2 and 3 is derived from the internal stratigraphy and pottery. The metalworking debris offers only a general indication and there are no 'absolute' dates. The relative sequence outlined here is based on a manual seriation of the pottery forms (Table 5) and is supported by the few stratigraphical relationships found on the site. With the exception of Ditch B70, which is treated separately, there is no record of pottery being recovered from specific layers within a feature. In some cases however, a distinction was made between sherds recovered from the surface of a fill and those found securely within it. Where this is the case, only the sherds certain to belong to the fill are regarded as being from sealed contexts and have been used in Table 5.

For the purposes of establishing a chronology, the size of the sample is small; only thirteen features contained more than three classifiable forms, and only seventeen forms are represented by more than three examples. Furthermore, the differences between forms are often based on details and in some cases, such as the distinction between Forms 60 and 61, any chronological significance suggested at Highstead may be fortuitous. Nevertheless, typological comparison of these forms demonstrates that the broad chronological progression indicated in Table 5 is consistent with that found elsewhere.

There are problems with the pottery from two features: Pit B12 and the Enclosure ditch B70. The latter is considered separately below. Pit B12 was small, just 0.46 m. in diameter and 0.36 m. deep, large enough to hold the storage jar, 296, set upright into the ground. The excavation notebook, which normally refers to pottery when present in a feature, has no mention of any other sherds being recovered from this pit. Nevertheless, bags containing eighty-nine other sherds, weighing 1.8 kg. were marked, as well as the individual sherds within them, 'B12'. These appear to represent a legitimate group from the fill of a single feature, but their volume makes it unlikely that they were also in the pit which held the storage jar without this being mentioned in the site notebook. In Table 5, the storage jar, Form 58, is shown in parentheses, associated with the other recognisable forms attributed to Pit B12, though there is some doubt about this association.

This discussion of chronology uses the broad groups indicated in Table 5 and typological parallels of the individual forms from other sites. These are used to identify Periods 2, 3A and 3B and establish their dates. The pottery from B70 is then compared with that from Periods 2 and 3 and elsewhere, and used to propose that the construction of the enclosure ditch should be placed in Period 2. This is followed by proposed dates for pottery forms not included in Table 5.

Wherever possible, parallels have been selected from recently published excavations. They are not exhaustive, but are intended to provide a broad chronological framework for Periods 2 and 3 at Highstead. Many of the forms are more similar to those on the Continent than they are to examples from Britain, and where appropriate, reference is made to continental chronologies (Table 6). The location of sites mentioned in the text is shown in Fig. 55.

Form	Feature	Period 2														Period 3A								
		A50	A5	A4	A130	A3	B92	A145	A155	A2	B317	A24	A8	A100	B80	A187	B79	B131	B144	B12	B244	B126	B214	B325	B166	B119
F28		1	1																							
F22			1																							
F39			1	1						1		1			1											
F60				1	1	1				1	2															
F59						1	1																			
R2					1			1	1	1	1	1				1										
F41										1	1															
F5											2															
F7											1															
F53											1															
R5											1															
F56												1														
F57												1	1					1								
F36												1			1											
F58												1								(1)						
F48												2	1													
R3															2					1		1				
F40														1		1		1	1		2					
F66															1			2								
R7																		1								
R4																			1							
F3																				1						
F19																				1						
F9																				1				1		
F10																				1	1					
F18																					1			1		
F34																					1				1	1
F25																										
F24																										
F61																										
F14																										
F12																										
F69																										
F1																										
F52																										
F13																										
F20																										
F32																										
F8																										
F51																										
F33																										
F44																										
Total		1	3	2	1	3	1	1	1	4	8	9	1	1	4	3	1	5	2	6	5	1	1	1	1	1

Table 5. Seriation of forms in features of Periods 2 and 3.

Table 5 (*continued*). Seriation of forms in features of Periods 2 and 3.

Form	Period 3B																		B70 level 1	B70 level 2	B70 level 3	B70 level 4	B70 level 5	B70 unknown level	Total
	B200A	B197	B124	A129	B203	A163	B133	B271	B114	B215	B266	B196	B248	B26	B247	B146	B245	B195							
F28																			1						3
F22																									1
F39																				1					6
F60																									6
F59																									2
R2																						1		1	9
F41																									2
F5																						1			3
F7																									1
F53																						1			2
R5																						2		1	4
F56																									1
F57																				1				2	6
F36																									2
F58																									2
F48																									3
R3																						1		1	6
F40																									6
F66																									3
R7																					1		1	1	4
R4	1																								2
F3																									1
F19																									1
F9			1																						3
F10			1																						3
F18	1					1																	1		5
F34							1	1	1																6
F25	2	1							1					1											5
F24			1																						1
F61			2	1	1		1									1						2			8
F14			1		1			2	1																5
F12			1					1			2				1										5
F69							1																		1
F1								1	1																2
F52									1	1															2
F13											2													1	3
F20											1														1
F32											2														2
F8											1	1	1												3
F51											1	1				1	1	1							5
F33															1										1
F44															1	1									2
Total	4	1	7	1	1	1	2	3	6	1	10	3	1	1	2	1	5	1	1	2	1	8	2	7	139

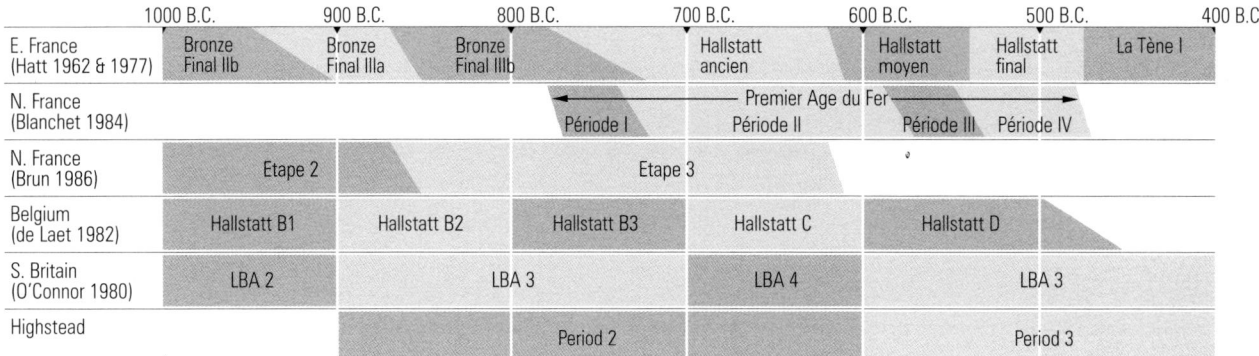

Table 6. Continental chronologies.

Period 2

The pottery recovered from Period 2 includes six bowl forms (5, 7, 28 and 39–41) and ten jar forms (22, 36, 48, 53, 56–60 and 66). The most closely dated vessels are the fineware bowls. Form 28, with a thin wall, clearly defined shoulder and slightly everted rim, is found in two pits within Enclosure A24. A broadly similar example is known from Hallstatt (Ha) B2/B3 contexts at Saint-Georges (Hesbaye), Belgium (Destexhe 1987, pl. 100, form 268).

Open bowls with a slightly inturned rim, Form 4, are found from the Bronze final (Bf) II to late Hallstatt contexts. For example, they are dated to Bf II at Remilly-Aillicourt, 'La Bonne Fache II' (Ardennes) (Blanchet 1984, 331, fig. 186, 2 and 6); to Ha B at Roitzheim, Euskirchen (Desittere 1968, fig. 23, 1); and from Ha B to Ha final at Oleye and Lamine (Destexhe 1987, pl. 43, no. 16, 28 and pl. 89, no. 88–89).

Open hemispherical bowls with plain rims, Form 5, are well known from Late Bronze Age/Early Iron Age assemblages in the Thames valley, e.g. at Aldermaston, Berkshire (Bradley *et al.* 1980, fig. 11, 7; 12, 19A; 13, 30F; 14, 58F; 15, 93F), Petters Sports Field, Egham, Surrey (O'Connell 1986, fig. 41, 1) and Ivinghoe Beacon, Buckinghamshire (Cotton and Frere 1968, fig. 17, 39, 40 and 44); and more locally at Minnis Bay, Birchington (Worsfold 1943, fig. 6, 3) and Mill Hill, Deal (Champion 1980, fig. 6, 10–12). They are also found on the Continent, where they occur from the Bronze final e.g. at Nijon, 'La Mottote' (Haute-Marne) (Lepage 1984, figs 23–4), to Early La Tène, as at Pont-sur-Yonne (Yonne) (Prampart 1981, fig. 6, nos 50–55). Examples similar to Form 5, but with burnished and haematite-coated surfaces, were found at Bridge, Site 5 (Macpherson-Grant 1980a, fig. 11, 59 and 66) and dated to between 1000–800 B.C. (Cunliffe 1980, 177). One vessel from Highstead, 235, has thin walls and light grooves around the rim (D8). Examples with horizontal grooved decoration are common from Ha B contexts in Desittere's (1968) Neuwiedbekken and Zuidwestelijke Loesszone groups, where the light horizontal grooves usually form part of more elaborate designs. Vessel 235 however is more closely paralleled in Bf III contexts, during the ninth and early eighth centuries B.C. at Catenoy, 'Le Camp César' (Oise) (Blanchet and Talon 1987, 198, fig. 9, 9 and 11). In Britain a similar example is known from the floor of hut II at Staple Howe (Brewster 1963, fig. 54, 4, 1).

Fineware cups and bowls, Forms 39–41, are closely related. They are all well made with thin walls, smooth or burnished surfaces and have light horizontal grooves around the shoulder (D27). Form 41, with a plain, slightly inturned rim is broadly similar to bowls from Belgium, e.g. at Donk (van Impe 1980, pl. XV, 3) and Verlaine, 'Blanc Bois' (Hesbaye) (Destexhe 1987, pl. 111, form 362), where it is dated to Ha C/D. Form 40, with an upright neck, closely resembles an isolated vessel from Court St Etienne (Mariën 1958, fig. 30, 31) where Mariën accepted that it may be as early as Ha B, but preferred to regard it as Ha D. At Highstead this form continues in use into Period 3, and is important when considering the transition between these periods.

Jar forms are generally not so distinctive or so closely paralleled as the fineware bowls. The tripartite jar, Form 36, is found at Petters Sports Field (O'Connell 1986, fig. 46, 56) where it is dated to the seventh or sixth century B.C., but absent from the ninth-century assemblage at Runnymede Bridge (Longley 1980). This form evidently had a long life: a vessel similar to the Highstead form, from Site 8 at Bridge (Macpherson-Grant 1980a, fig. 17, 95) was tentatively assigned the period between 500 and 350 B.C. (Cunliffe 1980, 179).

The thin walled bipartite jar, with a pronounced, almost carinated shoulder, Form 48, is similar to an example from Queen Mary's Hospital, Carshalton (Adkins and Needham 1985, fig. 10, 317) and dated to between the tenth and eighth centuries B.C.

Vessels with a short everted rim and pronounced internal bevel, Form 53, are common in Late Bronze Age groups and are known from Bf IIIa, e.g. at Fort-Harrouard (Mohen

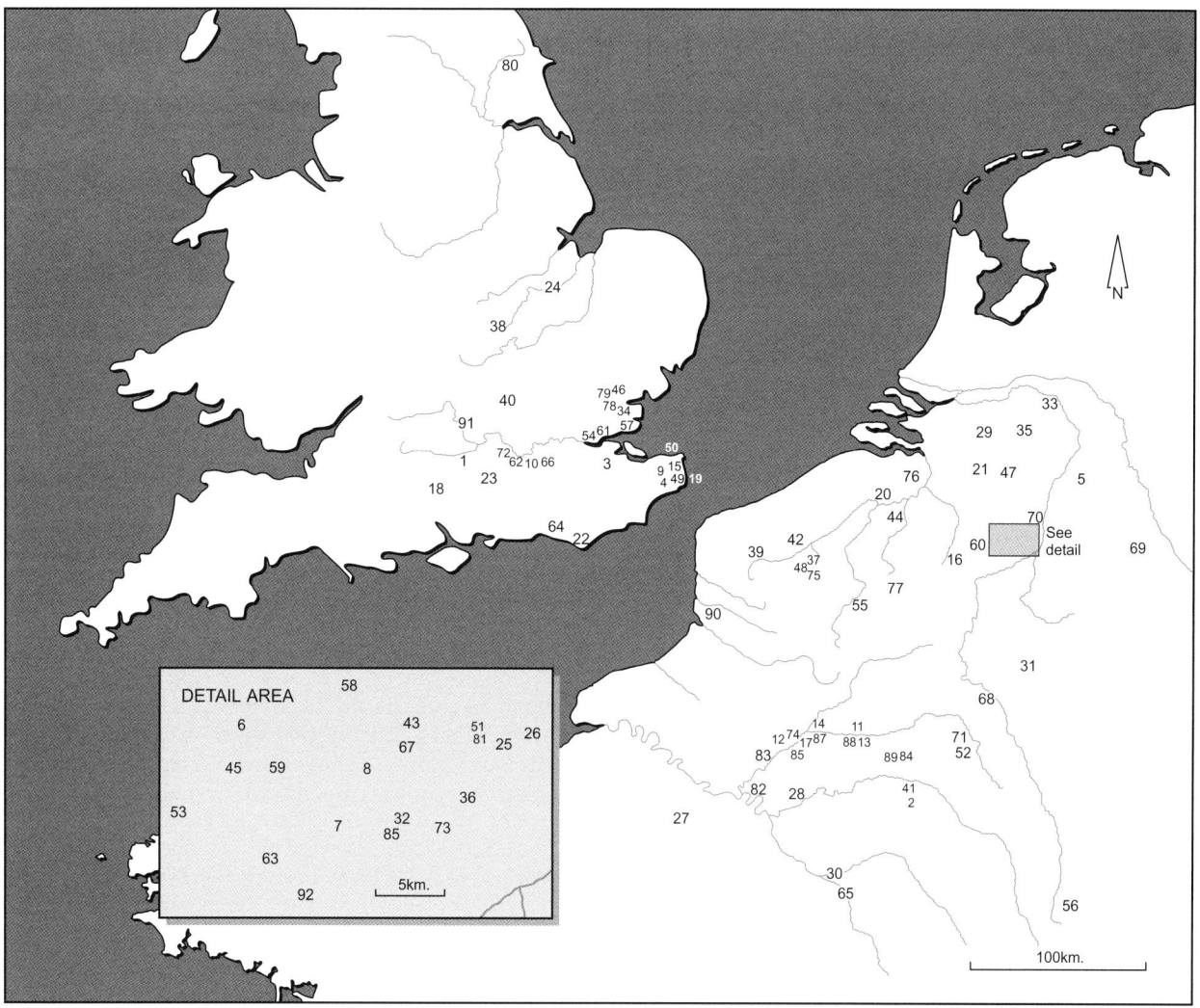

Fig. 55. Sites mentioned in the text. 1: Aldermaston; 2: Aulnay-aux-Planches; 3: Aylesford; 4: Barham; 5: Birgelen; 6: Boelhe; 7: Borlez; 8: Bovenister; 9: Bridge; 10: Brooklands, Weybridge; 11: Bucy-le-Long; 12: Catenoy; 13: Chassemy; 14: Choisy-au-Bac; 15: Cliffsend, Ramsgate; 16: Court St Etienne; 17: La Croix-Saint-Ouen; 18: Danebury; 19: Deal; 20: Destlebergen; 21: Donk; 22: Eastbourne; 23: Farnham; 24: Fengate; 25: Fexhe; 26: Fooz; 27: Fort-Harrouard; 28: Fresnes-sur-Marne; 29: Goirle; 30: Gravon; 31: Hampiré; 32: Haneffe; 33: Haps; 34: Heybridge Basin; 35: Hooidonksche Akkers; 36: Horion; 37: Houplin-Ancoisne; 38: Hunsbury; 39: Inghem; 40: Ivinghoe Beacon; 41: Les Jogasses; 42: Kemmelberg; 43: Lamine; 44: Lede; 45: Lens St Servais; 46: Lofts Farm; 47: Lommel-Kattenbosch; 48: Loos; 49: Mill Hill, Deal; 50: Minnis Bay, Birchington; 51: Momalle; 52: Mont Troté: 53: Moxhe; 54: Mucking; 55: Neuville-sur-Escaut; 56: Nijon, 'La Mottote'; 57: North Shoebury; 58: Oleye; 59: Omal Ste Marie; 60: Orp-le-Grand; 61: Orsett; 62: Petters Sports Field, Egham; 63: Pitet; 64: Plumpton Plain; 65: Pont-sur-Yonne; 66: Queen Mary's Hospital, Carshalton; 67: Remicourt; 68: Remilly-Aillicourt; 69: Roitzheim; 70: Rosmeer; 71: Les Rouliers; 72: Runnymede Bridge: 73: Saint-Georges; 74: Saint Sauveur; 75: Seclin; 76: Sint-Gilles-Waas; 77: Spiennes; 78: Springfield; 79: Springfield Lyons; 80: Staple Howe; 81: Streel; 82: Taverny; 83: Thiverny; 84: Tinqueux; 85: Verberie; 86: Verlaine; 87: Vieux Moulin; 88: Villeneuve-Saint-Germain; 89: Vrigny; 90: Vron; 91: Wallingford; 92: Warnant.

and Bailloud 1987, pl. 15, 5; pl. 21, 8; and pl. 21, 25) and Catenoy, 'Le Camp César' (Blanchet 1984, fig. 187, 15 and 18), and from Bf IIIb at Verberie 'Le Buisson-Campin' (Oise) (Blanchet 1984, fig. 191, 21). They were also recovered from Heybridge Basin, Essex dated to the tenth to ninth centuries B.C. (Brown and Adkins 1988, fig. 11, 9) and Bridge, site 5 (Macpherson-Grant 1980a, fig. 10, 56; fig. 11, 61, 63; fig. 12, 75) placed between 1000–800 B.C.

Jars decorated with applied cordons around the neck, Forms 58 and 59 (D9–D10), are common in Late Bronze Age/Early Iron Age assemblages in Britain and on the Continent (Burgess 1987, fig. 4). In Britain examples are known from the tenth- to eighth-century B.C. assemblages at Carshalton (Adkins and Needham 1985, fig. 4, 7–8), Runnymede Bridge (Longley 1980, fig.36, 402), Mucking, South Rings (Jones and Bond 1980, fig. 3, 13–15) and Springfield Lyons (Brown 1987, fig. 9, 8) and from the seventh- to sixth-century group at Petters Sports Field (O'Connell 1986, fig. 53, 194; fig. 55, 246). On the Continent they fall within Bf III and Blanchet's *Premier Age du Fer* (Blanchet 1984, e.g. fig. 191, 18–19 and fig. 227, 7).

Shouldered jars, similar to Forms 60 and 61 are not closely datable. At Highstead, those with a slightly everted rim, Form 60, are apparently found exclusively in Period 2, while those with an upright or inturned rim, Form 61, continue into Period 3.

Jars with an s-shaped profile, comparable with Highstead Form 66, are not common, though examples have been found in Ha C contexts in Belgium, at Goirle, North Brabant (Desittere 1968, fig. 49, 5) and France at La Croix-Saint-Ouen, 'Le Prieuré' (Freidin 1982, fig. 21, 5; Blanchet 1984, fig. 231, 5).

The tall vase, Form 22, is reminiscent of the *situlae* from Eastbourne (Hodson 1962, fig. 2, 8–11) and broadly similar to an example from Choisy au Bac, Phase II (Friedin 1982, fig. 17, 6), though this is too simple a shape to be closely dated.

Having outlined the forms, it is worth examining the styles of decoration prevalent during Period 2. Decoration of the rims, Styles A–B, is well known from Late Bronze Age/Early Iron Age assemblages in Britain and on the Continent. They are found throughout Periods 2 and 3.

Similarly, the use of neck cordons, Style C, both plain (D9) and with finger-tip impressions (D10), is common and has been included in the discussion of the large jar, Forms 58 and 59. This evidently continued in use as a decoration, though not necessarily on jars, into the early La Tène period, e.g. in France, at Chassemy, Aisne (Rowlett *et al.* 1969). One example, 207, is not associated with a storage jar, and may be on a bowl, though its form is unclear.

The use of light horizontal grooves (Style D) is also part of the standard repertoire of Late Bronze Age/Early Iron Age decoration. They are often associated with more complex designs, e.g. in the middle Thames valley (Bradley *et al.* 1980, fig. 35, 39, 41–6), but in Kent and Essex they more frequently appear as the only decoration on a vessel. They are usually found on fineware cups and bowls (Highstead Forms 38–41) and are known, for example, at Mucking, South Rings (Jones and Bond 1980, fig. 3, nos 3, 6 and 9), North Shoebury, Essex (Brown 1985, fig. 17, 13) and Mill Hill, Deal (Champion 1980, fig. 6, 8–9). The chronology of these cup and bowl forms has been discussed above. However, this decoration is also found on two jars: 142 (Form 56) and 210 (Form 73). Vessel 210 is closely paralleled in Ha B–C contexts in Belgium, e.g. at Court St Etienne (Mariën 1958, fig. 26, 24 and fig. 27) and Saint-Georges (Destexhe 1987, pl. 39, 44). At Verrall's Sandpit, Aylesford, Kent, a coarser version of the same style was used on a more upright jar, which contained a bronze hoard of LBA3 date (O'Connor 1980, 384, and fig. 58B, 5).

The use of two bands of horizontal grooves, D14, is found at Mucking (Jones and Bond 1980, fig. 3, nos 6 and 9), and North Shoebury (Brown 1985, fig. 17, nos 12 and 26, fig. 18, no. 38). At Highstead the only example, 215, is apparently from a jar, though the angle of the sherd is uncertain. Across the Channel, such pairs of bands are found in Ha B/C contexts at Taverny, 'Le Camp de César' (Freidin 1982, fig. 32, 5–7), Nijon, 'La Mottote' (Lepage 1984, fig. 22, 2; fig. 27, 15, 35) and Borlez, in Hesbaye (Destexhe 1987, pl. 91, 130). On their own though, they cannot be used as precise chronological indicators, since they are also known from early La Tène assemblages, as at Hampiré (Cahen-Delhaye 1974, fig. 16, 8), Kemmelberg (van Doorselaer *et al.* 1987, e.g. fig. 42 196–200) and Mont Troté (Rozoy 1986, pl. 12, T32, 8).

The small cup, 192, has groups of diagonal grooves beneath fine horizontal grooves (D28). One worn wall sherd, 227, possibly with three diagonal grooves, (though illustrated as horizontal) may have been decorated in the same way. A similar design occurs on a bowl from Aylesford, which Barrett (1980, fig. 6, 10) includes in his post-Deverel-Rimbury (PDR) 'decorated assemblages'. On the Continent such groups of diagonal grooves are found in Bronze final contexts at Vieux Moulin, 'Saint-Pierre en Chastre' (Oise) (Blanchet 1984, fig. 151, 1) though on a goblet form not found at Highstead. They also appear on a bowl from Gravon (Seine-et-Marne) (Brun 1986, pl. 12, 5), though again the form is not exactly paralleled at Highstead. At Court-St-Etienne a fineware bowl, similar to our Form 40 and dated to Ha D (Mariën 1958, fig. 30, 31) is decorated with light horizontal grooves on the shoulder and short diagonal grooves spaced regularly around the vessel. While not an exact parallel, it is very close to the forms and styles of decoration found at Highstead.

The association of horizontal and overlapping curvilinear grooves (D32) is found on one vessel, 230. A broadly similar design, in which the wave pattern and horizontal grooves are separate, is known from Runnymede Bridge (Longley 1980, fig. 35, 371) where it occurs on the inside of the rim of a jar.

Closed forms						
	Surface treatment (see table 4)					
Wall thickness (mm)	3	4	5	6	7	8
13			♦			
12						
11				■		
10	■		♦			
9		♦		■■	■	
8				♦♦♦	■	
7				♦♦■■■	■■	■■
6	●	●	■	♦♦■■●		
5			■	●		
4		●●				

Open forms						
	Surface treatment (see table 4)					
Wall thickness (mm)	3	4	5	6	7	8
11					■	
10					■	
9		●				
8		■		■		
7				●	●●	
6			●			
5						
4		●●				

Key: ● Period 2   ♦ Period 3A   ■ Period 3B

Table 7. Relationship between surface treatment and average wall thickness of plain convex forms during Periods 2 and 3: closed and open forms.

This style is also found at Birgelen (Desittere 1968, fig. 28, 5) and Court St Etienne (Mariën 1958, fig. 17, 15) where it is dated to Ha B/C. At Choisy-au-Bac an imported vessel with this decoration is thought to have been influenced by 'pseudo-phocéene' pottery of the sixth century (Blanchet 1984, 399–400, fig. 226, 1).

Period 3

There is no sudden break in the ceramic styles found during Period 2 and the start of Period 3. Rather, there is a gradual transition during which a new range of vessels makes its appearance, with a wider variety of surface treatment and decoration. Period 3 is divided into two phases: 3A, in which many of the forms from Period 2 continue to be used, and 3B by which time Period 2 styles have largely fallen out of use.

Period 3A

Vessels first recognised during Period 3A include open bowls and dishes, Forms 18, 19 and 34, and closed jars, Forms 3, 9 and 10. Vessels with plain convex profiles continue to be used. The new ones tend to have thicker walls and coarser surfaces than the earlier forms (Table 7) and this development matches that found on the Continent: Form 3 is found in Early Iron Age contexts in Belgium, e.g. at Rosmeer (Roosens and Lux 1969, pl. VII–IX) and it has been dated to Ha D at Lamine, Hesbaye (Destexhe, 1987, forms 183–96). In the Low Countries the same basic form continues with rougher surfaces. Vessels similar to Forms 9 and 10 are found with rusticated (*eclabousée*) surfaces in La Tène I contexts at Momalle, Horion 'Distrigaz', Moxhe and Lamine (Hesbaye) (Destexhe 1987, forms 187–92) and several examples are known from Haps (Verwers 1972, abb. 52 and 60). However, these forms are not precise chronological indicators and the same general type appears in La Tène III contexts e.g. at Bovenister (Destexhe 1987, pl. 95, form 200).

Flaring bowls with plain rims, Form 18, are broadly similar to late Hallstatt and early La Tène forms from the Low Countries, e.g. at Haps (Verwers 1972) and Fooz, Fosse 2 (Destexhe 1987, pl. 91, form 121), and France, e.g. Vrigny (Marne) (Chossenot *et al.* 1981, fig. 9, T12a) and Fresnes-sur-Marne (Bulard *et al.* 1983, fig. 10, 7 and fig. 12, 10).

	Decoration Style												Total number of decorated sherds	Decorated sherds as % of total sherds within period
	A	B	C	D	E	F	G	H	I	J	K	L	M	N		
Period 3B	60			7		4	4	4		4		4	13	28	1.0
Period 3A	25	25	6	38								6		16	5.0
Period 2	33	10	11	31	5		1	3	5					63	2.2

Table 8. Percentage distribution of styles of decoration during Periods 2 and 3.

They evidently derived from the '*assiettes tronconiques*' of Ha B–D period (*see* for example, Brun 1986, pl. 26, 2.2; 29, 4; 31, 5.2). Related to this form is the wide flaring dish with straight sides and rusticated surface treatment, 293, Form 19. These bowls, sometimes with a slight curve in the profile just below the rim, are well known in the Low Countries where they are dated from Ha C to La Tène I. For example, they are found at Destlebergen (de Laet *et al.* 1987, 102–3, fig. 35, t71.2) dated to Ha C, at Sint-Gillis-Waas, East Flanders (Desittere 1968, fig. 88, 4) dated to Ha C/D, and at Streel, Hesbaye (Destexhe 1987, 152, 4) where they are dated to Ha D. In France the form has been found in La Tène 1 contexts at Houplin-Ancoisne (Lemain-Delerive 1984, fig. 5, 35).

Carinated bipartite bowls with short everted or bead rims (Form 34) are known from sixth- or seventh-century assemblages at Petters Sports Field, Surrey (O'Connell 1986, fig. 49, 121–4), the early land surface at Brooklands, Weybridge (Hamworth and Tomalin 1977, fig. 17, 84) and Orsett, Essex (Barrett 1978). On the Continent they are also known from early La Tène assemblages, e.g. at Spiennes, Camp-à-Cayoux, hutte A (Mariën 1961, fig. 50, nos 56–7 and 62), Remicourt (Destexhe 1987, pl. 98, 231) and Kemmelberg (van Doorselaer *et al.* 1987, fig. 1–4) though these are often shallower than the Highstead examples.

A notable feature of Period 3 is the use of rusticated (*eclabousée*) surface treatment. This occurs sporadically in Ha B groups in the Low Countries, where it apparently derived from earlier urnfield pottery in Germany (Desittere 1967 and 1968). In the lower Rhine it becomes more common when associated with 'Harpstedt' urns in Ha C/D (de Laet 1982, 577) and it rapidly becomes employed on other forms of pottery. Indeed its presence is often used to distinguish Ha D from earlier assemblages. By the early La Tène period its distribution spread to north-east France, where it has been recognised at Vron (Somme) (Gosselin, *et al.* 1984, 36–7, fig. 12, 1–2), Neuville-sur-Escaut (Nord) (Hantute 1984, fig. 12, Q7 and QE14), Houplin-Ancoisne and Loos (Leman-Delerive 1984, fig. 5, 35 and fig. 9, 16–23) and Mont Troté (Rozoy 1987, vol. I, 221, fig. 180). In the Low Countries it continues in use throughout the Iron Age. No certain 'Harpstedt' urns are discernible at Highstead, but the use of rusticated surface treatment becomes a standard feature throughout Period 3.

While only sixteen decorated sherds are attributable to Period 3A it is evident that the main styles of decoration are the same as those found during Period 2 (Table 8): finger-tip and finger-nail impressions and impressed decoration on the rim together account for 50 per cent of the decorated sherds. There was one sherd with an applied cordon and groups of light horizontal grooves (Style D: Table 3) represent 38 per cent. The dates of these styles have been discussed above (p. 120) and they evidently continued in use into Hallstatt D.

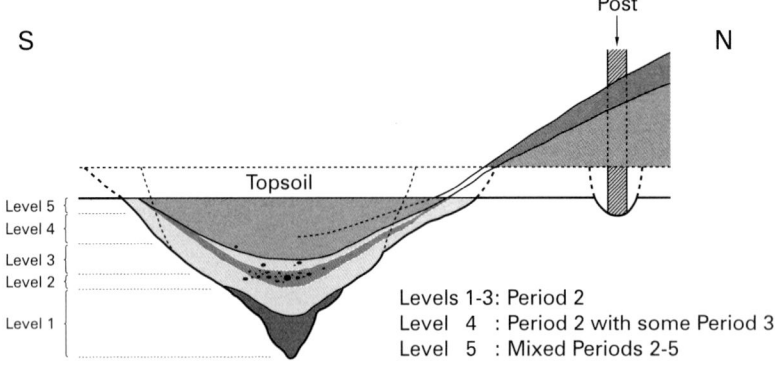

Fig. 56. Enclosure B70. Pottery distribution in ditch fill (*see* Figs 57–66).

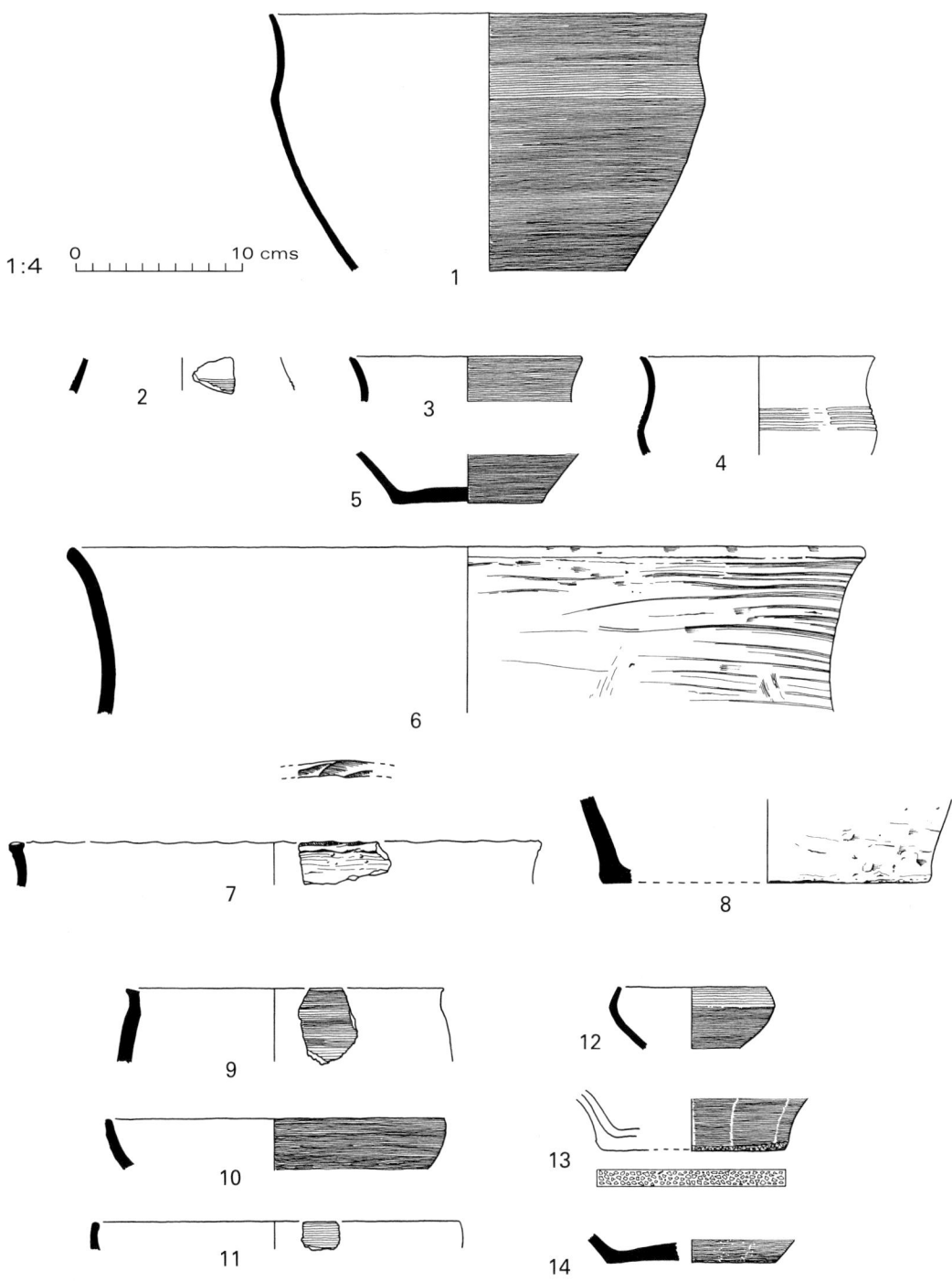

Fig. 57. Pottery from Ditch B70. No. 1, level 1; Nos 2–8, level 2; Nos 9–14, level 3. Scale 1:4.

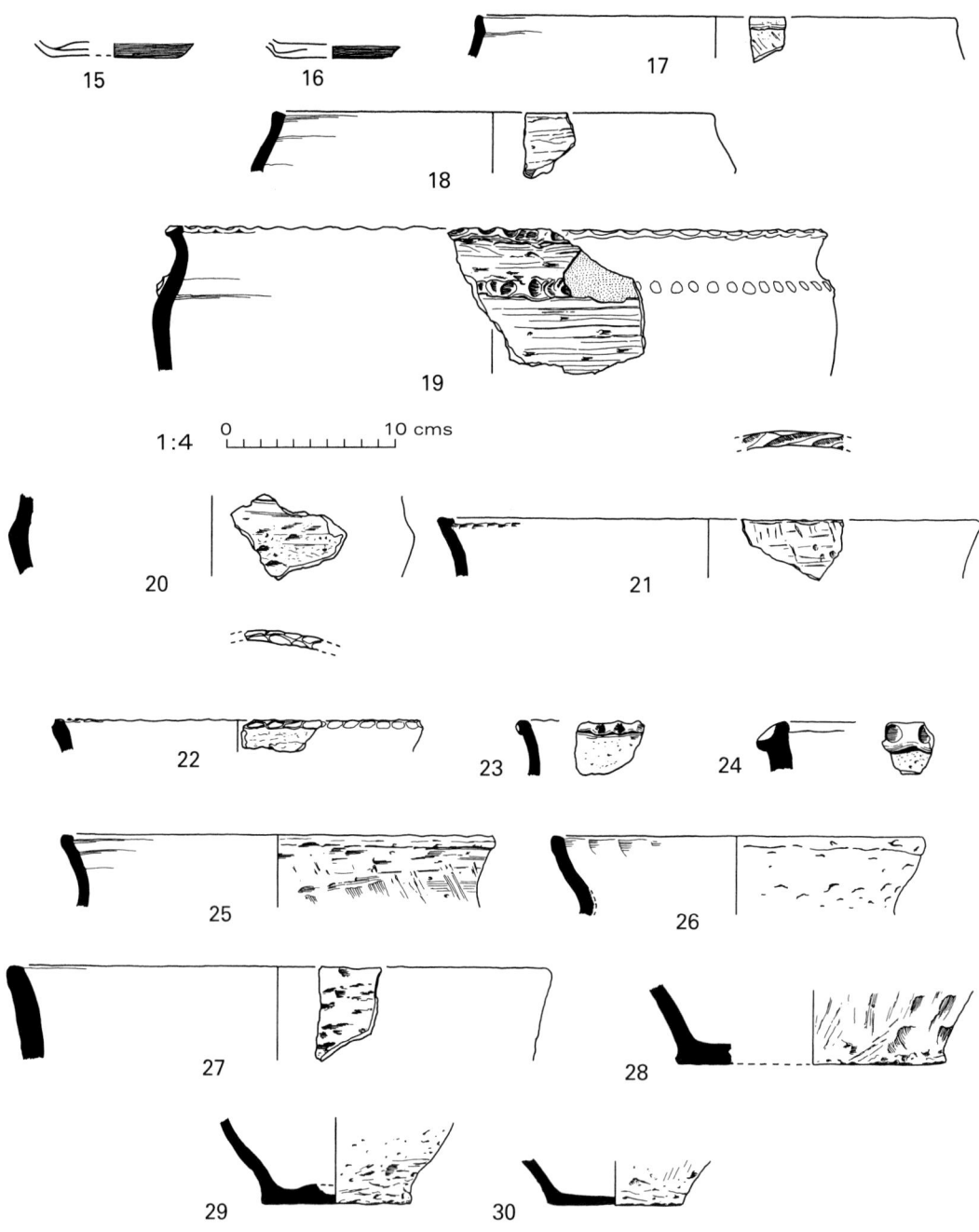

Fig. 58. Pottery from Ditch B70. Nos 15–30, level 3. Scale 1:4.

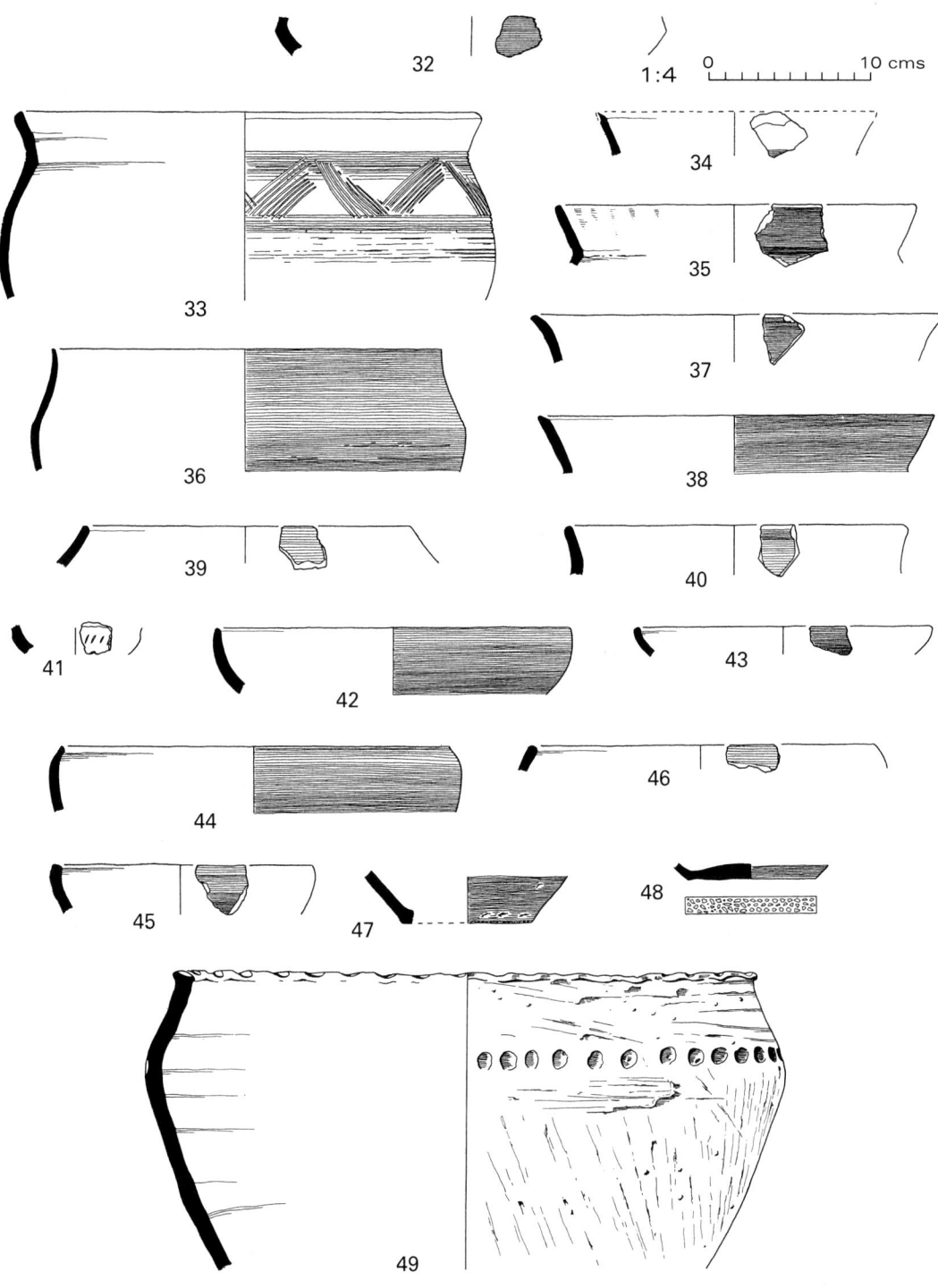

Fig. 59. Pottery from Ditch B70. Nos 32–49, level 4 (No. 32, red-finished). Scale 1:4.

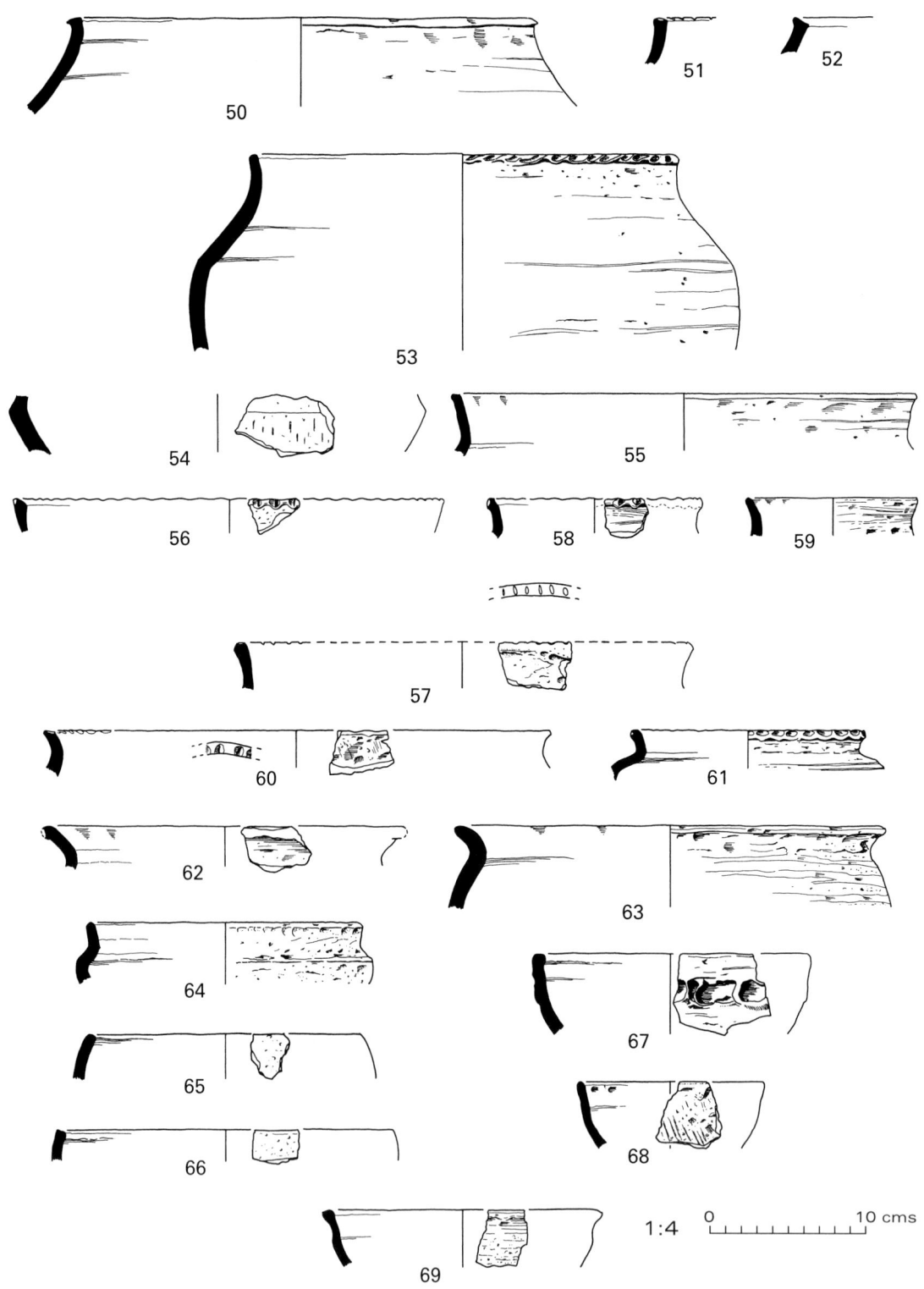

Fig. 60. Pottery from Ditch B70. Nos 50–69, level 4. Scale 1:4.

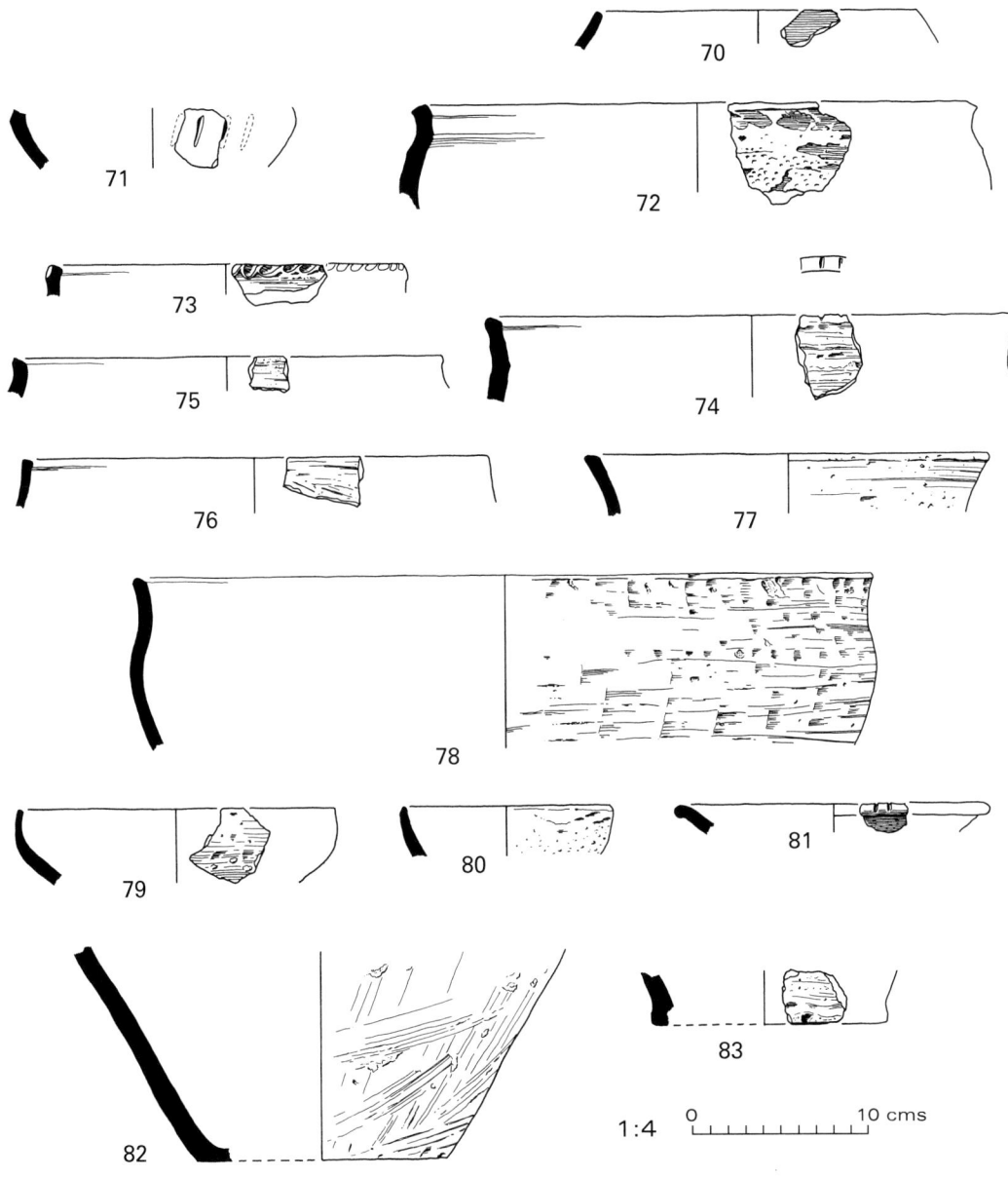

Fig. 61. Pottery from Ditch B70. Nos 70–83, level 5. Scale 1:4.

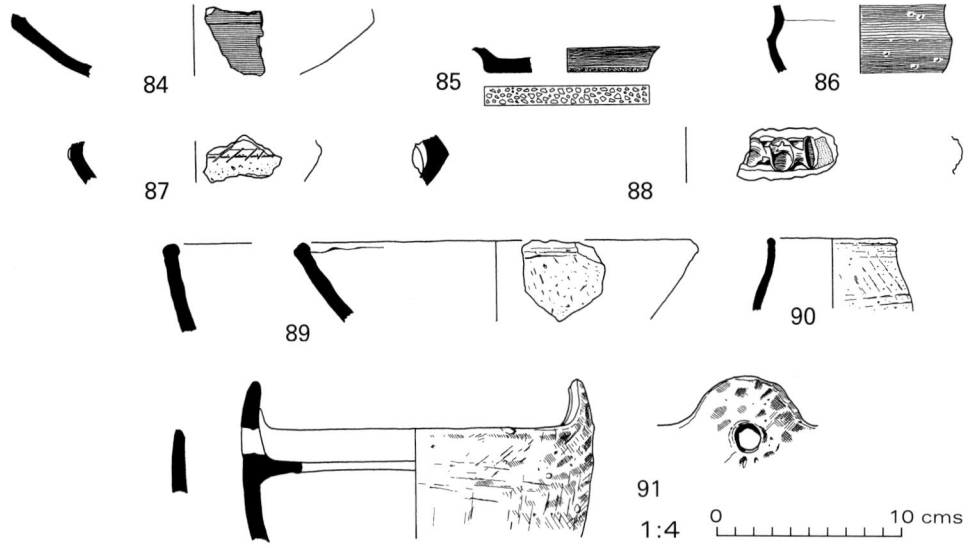

Fig. 62. Pottery from Ditch B70. Nos 84–91, level 5 (No. 84, red-finished). Scale 1:4.

Period 3B

Many of the vessel forms from this period are either too simple to be of much chronological value or are not closely paralleled. Bowl Form 14, with a convex profile and flat-topped rim, is found at Haps (Verwers 1972, abb. 53) and Horion 'Distrigaz' (Destexhe 1987, pl. 92, form 156) where it is dated to La Tène I; but it is also reminiscent of examples dated to Ha B from Saint Georges (Destexhe 1987, pl. 92, form 160).

Form 13, a bowl with a plain convex profile and a rough surface, is comparable with late Hallstatt and early La Tène examples from Haps, Noord Brabant (Verwers 1972, abb. 52), Fooz and Streel (Destexhe 1987, pl. 89 forms 94 and 98).

Form 24, a probable bowl with upright neck and plain rim, is broadly similar to examples dated to periode 1 of Blanchet's (1984) Premier Age du Fer at Choisy au Bac (Talon 1987, fig. 10, 10), late Hallstatt and early La Tène at Haps (Verwers 1972, abb. 26, 224) and to Ha D at Destelbergen (de Laet 1986, fig. 30, t8,2).

More closely dated however, is the carinated vessel, 368, with burnished surfaces and a zone of painted decoration beneath the shoulder. Although the profile is incomplete, it appears to have had a pedestal or foot-ring base and a vertical or out-turned rim. The decoration consists of bands of red coating alternating with black burnished surfaces and, just below the shoulder, a row of crosses within metopes, apparently created with slip laid within grooves. These may originally have been pink in colour, though they are now light brown (Munsell no. 2.5YR4/2) on a red haematite-coated background (*see* Appendix 1) The form may be compared with vessels dated to La Tène I, e.g. at Mont Troté, (Ardennes) (Rozoy 1987, pl 13, 32.3; pl. 15, 36.1; pl. 41, 102.1 and 102.5; pl. 43, 106.2 and pl. 44, 107.2), Tinqueux (Marne) (Flouest and Stead 1981, fig. 4, T5d and fig. 10 T21b and 22b) and Kemmelberg (van Doorselaer *et al.* 1987, fig. 39, fig. 180–83). The decorative motif is well represented on late Hallstatt pottery, e.g. at Thiverny (Oise) (Durvin and Brunaux 1983, 14) and early La Tène examples are known from the Marne valley and the Ardennes, where it is most commonly found on round-bodied forms, e.g. Mont Troté and Les Rouliers (Rozoy 1987, Vol. 1, 150, table 29). It does however appear on carinated forms at Pernant (Lobjois 1969), and further north at Kemmelberg (van Doorselaer *et al.* 1987, fig. 45, 224–6, fig. 50, 261 and fig. 85, 479) and Houplin-Ancoisne (Leman-Delerive 1984, fig. 4, 22). Usually however, this decoration is lightly grooved rather than painted.

The use of barbotine-painted decoration is known in the Paris basin from Hallstatt D, though its use on Vixian forms is more common south of the Seine (Freidin 1982, 146–8). Similar painted designs are also found during La Tène 1b at Mont Troté, where an ovoid vessel has a white motif based on crosses on a red background (Rozoy 1987, MT 107) and in the Belgian Ardennes where they occur as lozenges and pendant triangles (Cahen-Delhaye 1983, fig. 5). The position of the decoration on the Highstead example however, beneath the shoulder rather than above, is unusual and is generally restricted to vessels with high shoulders as at Bucy-le-Long,

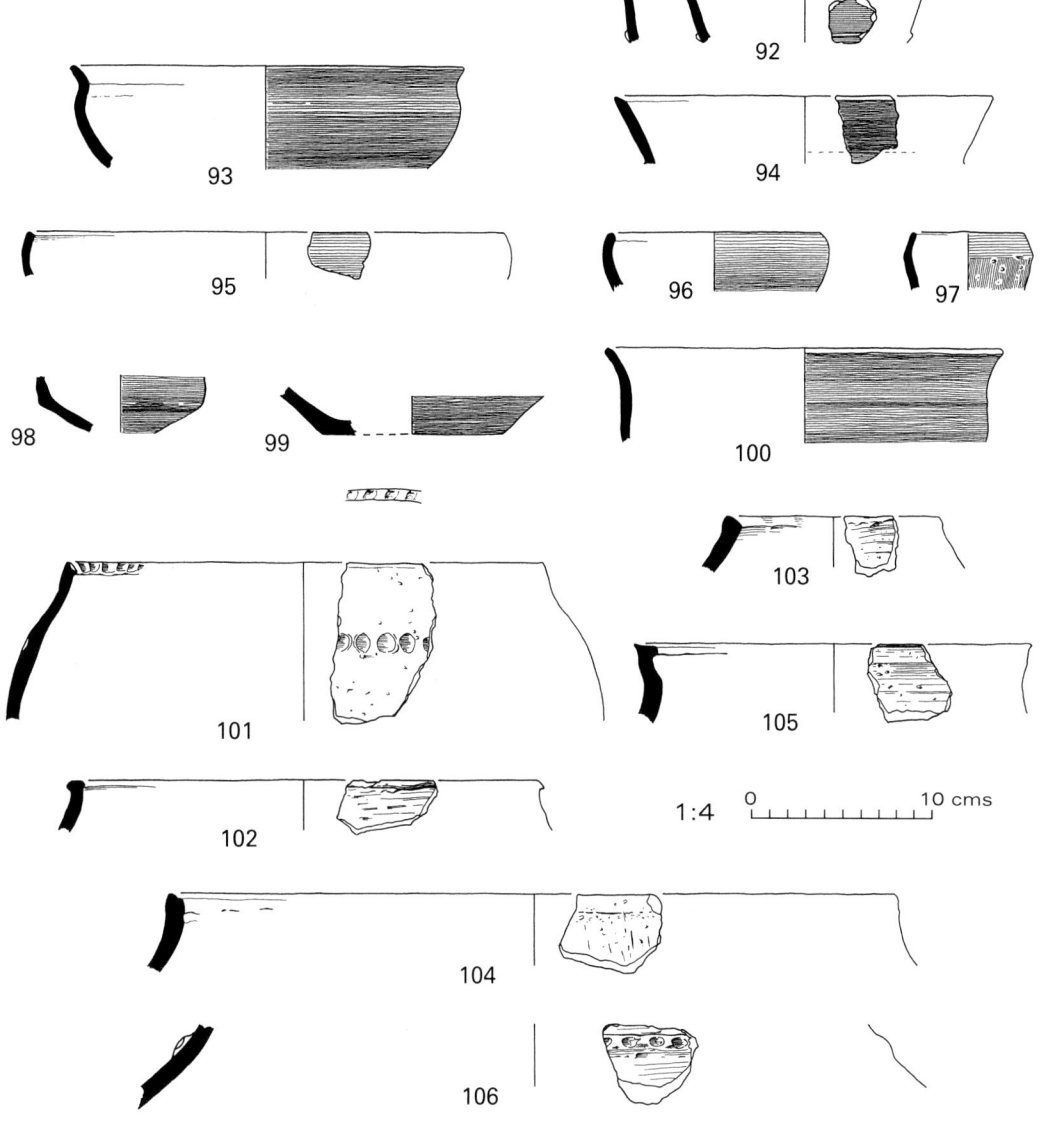

Fig. 63. Pottery from Ditch B70. Nos 92–106, unknown depths (No. 92, red-finished). Scale 1:4.

Aisne (Lobjois *et al.* 1974, fig. 6.1) and Kemmelberg (van Doorselaer 1987, fig. 49, 258). While no identical vessel can be found, the shape, style and method of application of the decoration on this example from Highstead are all paralleled during the late Hallstatt and La Tène I periods.

A comparable painted design, though more coarsely applied, was found on an 'onion' pot from Bridge (Macpherson-Grant 1980a, fig. 4.8) and dated to *c*. 500–350 B.C. (Cunliffe 1980); while concentric lozenges, like those from the Belgian Ardennes (Cahen-Delhaye 1983, fig. 4, 2) were painted on an onion pot from Eastbourne (Hodson 1962, fig. 1, 1 and pl. XXI, 1).

Period 3B sees other changes in decoration (Table 8). There is a marked decline in the use of bands of light horizontal grooves (Style D). Finger-tip and finger-nail impressions continue, now accounting for 60 per cent of the decorated sherds recovered. Alongside this, there is a restricted use of linear grooved styles. One sherd, No. 411 (D26), has a single horizontal groove on the shoulder and another, No. 399 (D18), has at least two light diagonal grooves, apparently unrelated to Period 2 styles. One vessel (not illustrated) from Pit B128 is decorated with a design consisting of irregular, almost vertical, deep grooves. On the Continent a similar technique is found on early La Tène

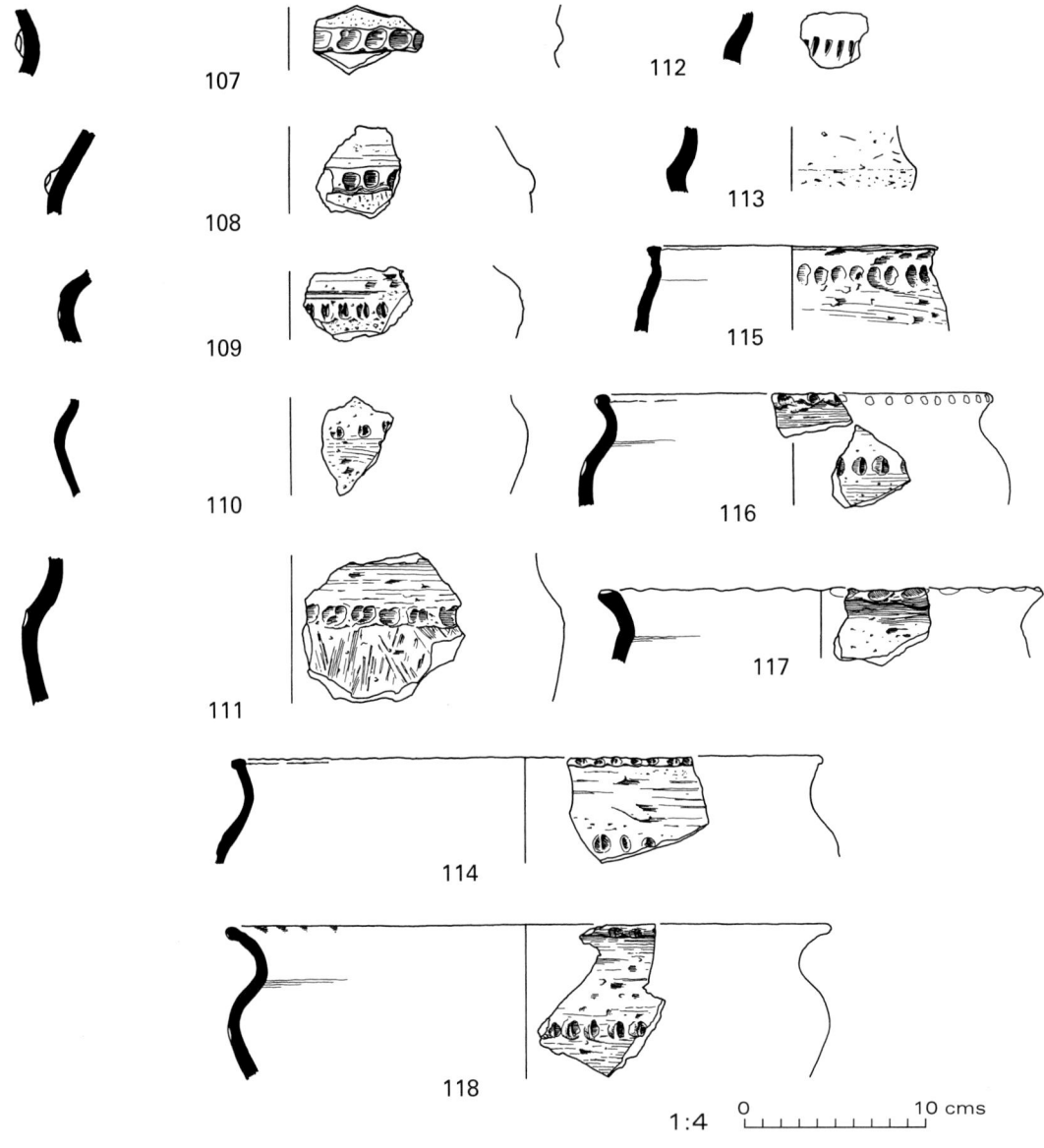

Fig. 64. Pottery from Ditch B70. Nos 107–18, unknown depths. Scale 1:4.

vessels in the Low Countries, e.g. at Haps (Verwers 1972, abb. 68–70 and 75, no. 439) and Tierceau, Orp-le-Grand (Cahen-Delhaye 1973a, fig. 9, 3) and this evidently continued in use into the Late Iron Age by which time it had acquired a more regular appearance, as at Bovenister (Destexhe 1987, pl. 115, 409–10).

Three sherds (No. 352, and examples from B124 and B132) were found with combed decoration. The overall pattern however, remains unclear. Combing of the whole surface is well known from the late Iron Age and is found at Highstead in Period 4 contexts. There is a chance that these sherds are intrusive. On the Continent however, combed decoration is known from the Early Iron Age, as at Warnant (Ha D) and Haneffe (LT 1) in Hesbaye (Destexhe 1987, pl. 50, 9–11, pl. 71, F2, 10–11) and it is not necessary to relegate these examples from Highstead to a late date.

Absolute dates

This rapid survey of continental parallels of forms and decoration now enables the chronology of these periods to be considered in terms of conventional dates.

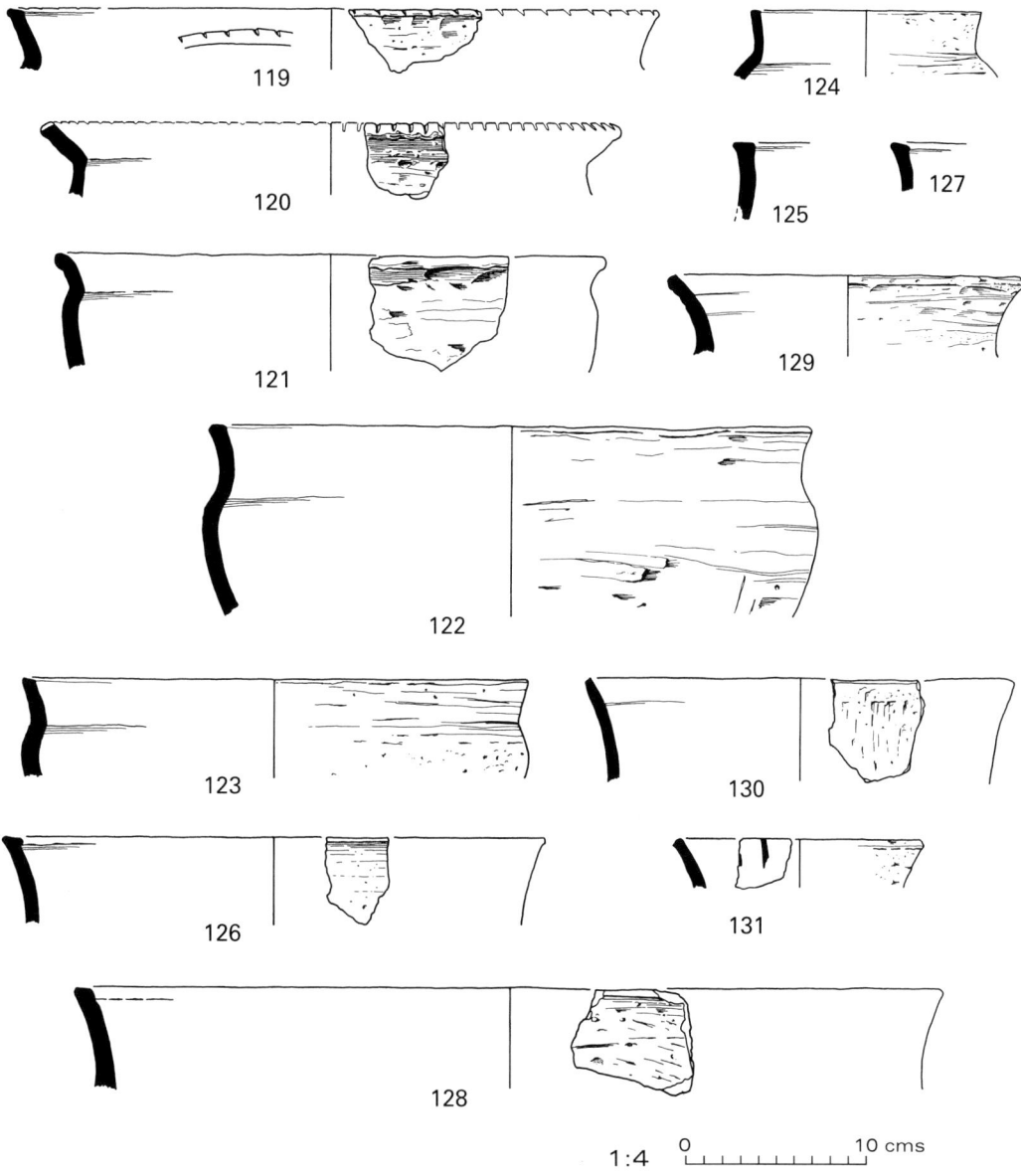

Fig. 65. Pottery from Ditch B70. Nos 119–31, unknown depths. Scale 1:4.

The evidence from Period 2 suggests that it falls within Hallstatt B to C, with the emphasis on Hallstatt C. Thus it may be placed broadly within the ninth to seventh centuries B.C. The beginning of Period 3 sees the continued use of fineware bowls, Form 40, and the arrival of rusticated surface treatment. This may conveniently be placed at the start of Hallstatt D, about 600 B.C. As we have seen, parallels for Period 3B have been cited from late Hallstatt and La Tène I assemblages, and although some of the forms evidently continued until La Tène III, no certain La Tène II forms have been recognised. It is significant that, with two possible exceptions, the form most representative of the Middle Iron Age (La Tène II) in Kent, a vessel with everted rim and foot-ring base, is absent from Period 3 deposits. The first exception is a fragmentary rim (Fig. 88, No. 356) in a flint-tempered fabric from one of the post-holes associated with Structure B200 (pp. 145–9 below). The date of this structure is uncertain; it falls either late within Period 3B or early in Period 4, dependent largely on the date of this sherd. The second exception is an everted rim in grog and

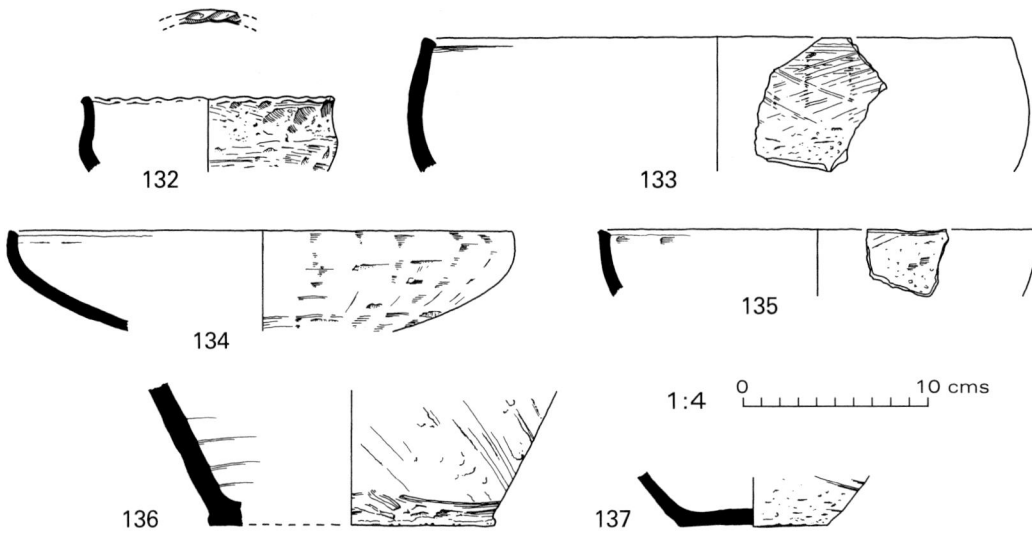

Fig. 66. Pottery from Ditch B70. Nos 132–7, unknown depths. Scale 1:4.

flint-tempered fabric from Pit B245 (Fig. 101, No. 5), which also contained a second sherd of grog-tempered 'Belgic' pottery. Both these sherds are regarded as intrusive. Dating the end of Period 3 is more problematical. It is certainly over by c. 350 B.C. However, the small number of early La Tène decorated vessels at Highstead compared with the greater numbers that have been found at other sites in east Kent, may be due to a chronological variation and it is likely that the end of Period 3B coincides with the end of La Tène Ia at about 400 B.C.

Enclosure B70

Enclosure ditch B70 is considered separately here because, with the exception of reference to one 'black' layer and the 'bottom silt', sherds were recorded by depth from the surface within their excavated segment, rather than by context. Scale drawings of the sections (Fig. 17) demonstrate that there were distinct layers within the fill and that, except near the terminals, a broadly similar stratigraphical succession appears throughout the excavated segments. It is clear that the filling of the ditch did not occur as a single event.

For the purpose of this discussion, the fill is divided into five levels (Fig. 56): Level 1 comprises the identified primary fill and everything below -1.20 m., down to a depth as great as -2.10 m.; Level 2 from -1.20 m. to -1 m.; Level 3 from -1 m. to -0.60 m.; Level 4 from -0.60 m. to -0.20 m.; and Level 5 consists of material recovered from above -0.20 m., which includes intrusive 'Belgic' and Roman sherds. While most sherds can be attributed to one or more of these levels, the depths of some were not recorded. Examining the distribution of pottery from these artificial horizontal levels ignores the irregular profiles of the layers and any disturbance that may have occurred. They are clearly unreliable as a basis for a firm chronology but do provide an indication of a trend.

From the bottom silt were recovered thirty sherds, from one vessel, with a flat base 9 cm. in diameter and wall thickness of 5–6 mm. From the remainder of Level 1 were just ten sherds, representing possibly two vessels, one with wall thickness of 5–6 mm. (No. 1, Form 28) and another with a wall just 2–4 mm. thick.

Level 2 produced twenty-five sherds. Their wall thickness and surface treatment show that they represent a range of vessels from fineware cups or bowls with walls 3–4 mm. thick, to larger vessels, possibly used for cooking or storage, with walls up to 8 mm. thick. One sherd has a rusticated surface and is regarded as being intrusive.

Twenty-one of the vessels from the ditch are of forms already identified in Periods 2 and 3 (Table 5). The bulk of the fill, up to and including Level 4, contained twelve vessels of these forms of which nine (75 per cent) belong to Period 2, the largest concentration being recovered from Level 4 itself. This indicates that the ditch was substantially filled during Period 2, with Period 3 forms appearing in Level 5 and as a minority element in Level 4.

Other evidence for chronology may be sought from the forms which do not appear in Table 5.

One example of the plain convex closed Form 2, 65, was found in Level 4. This is paralleled in Bronze final IIIa contexts on the Continent, e.g. at Catenoy (Blanchet and Talon 1987, fig. 12, 1 and 3). It is also similar to the hook rim jars of Barrett's (1980) plain ware assemblages, though

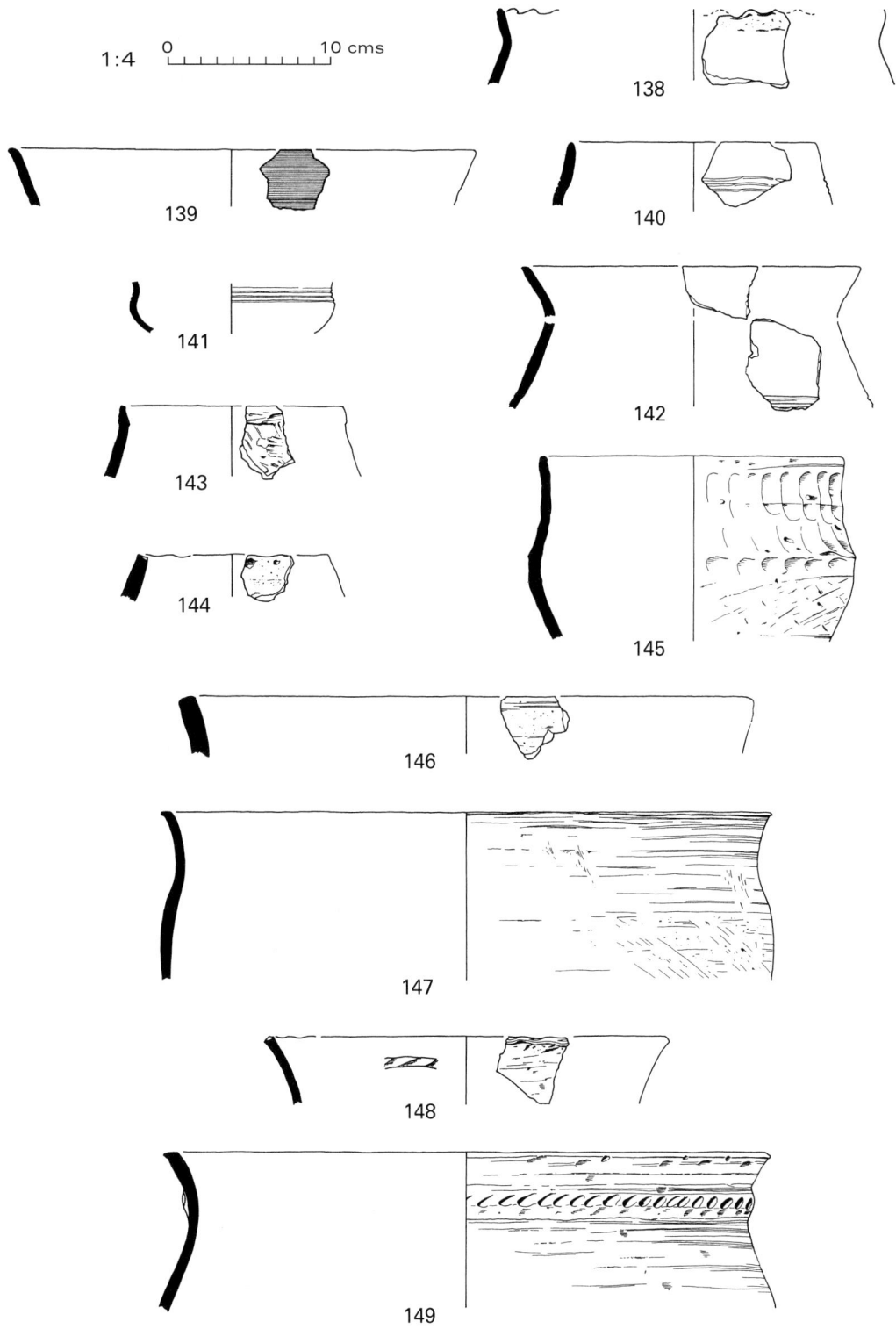

Fig. 67. Period 2 pottery from Enclosure A24. Nos 138–49 (No. 139, red-finished). Scale 1:4.

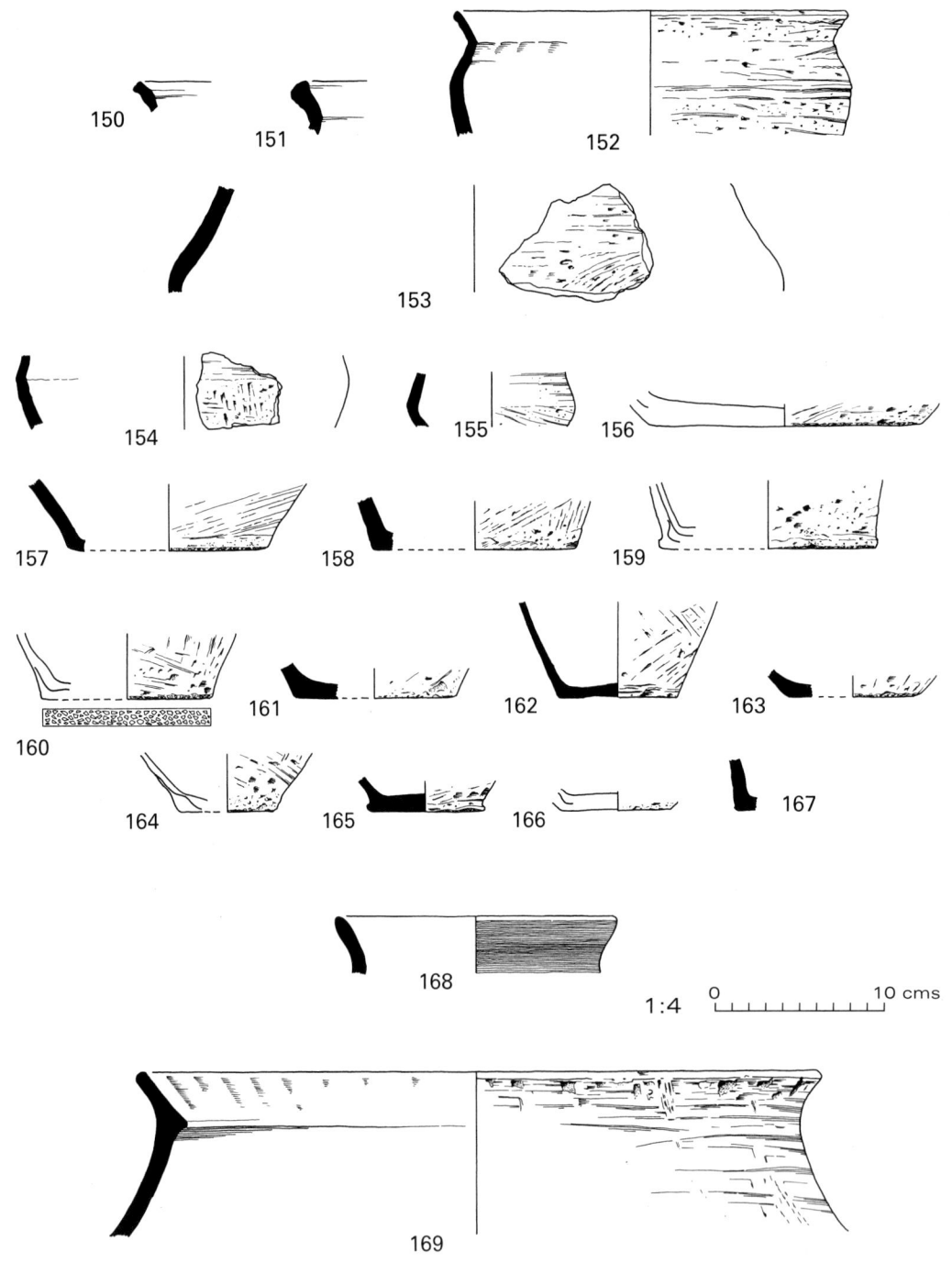

Fig. 68. Period 2 pottery. Nos 150–67, Enclosure A24; No. 168, Post-pit A145; No. 169, Pit A18. Scale 1:4.

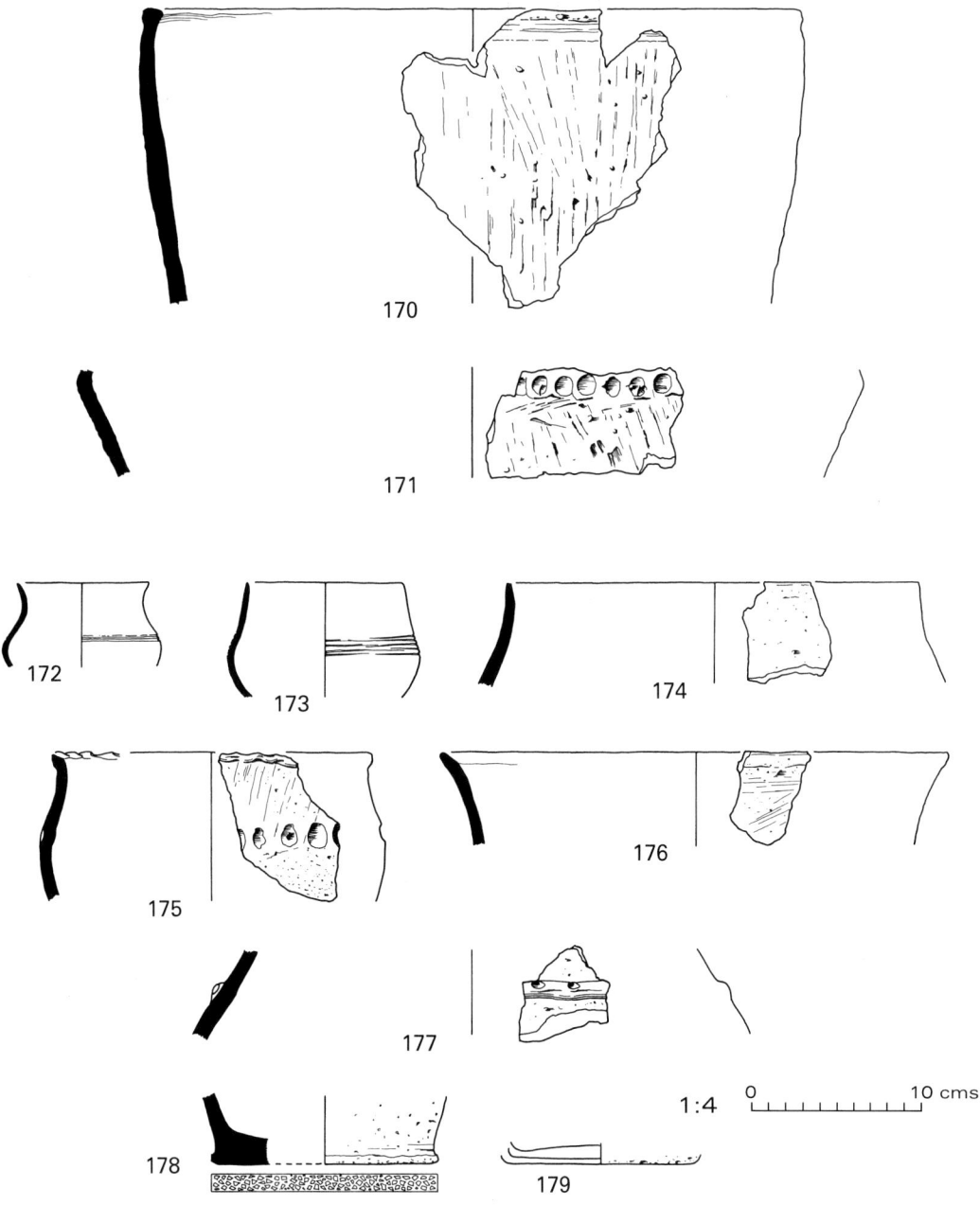

Fig. 69. Period 2 pottery. Nos 170–71, Pit A152; Nos 172–9, Pit A2. Scale 1:4.

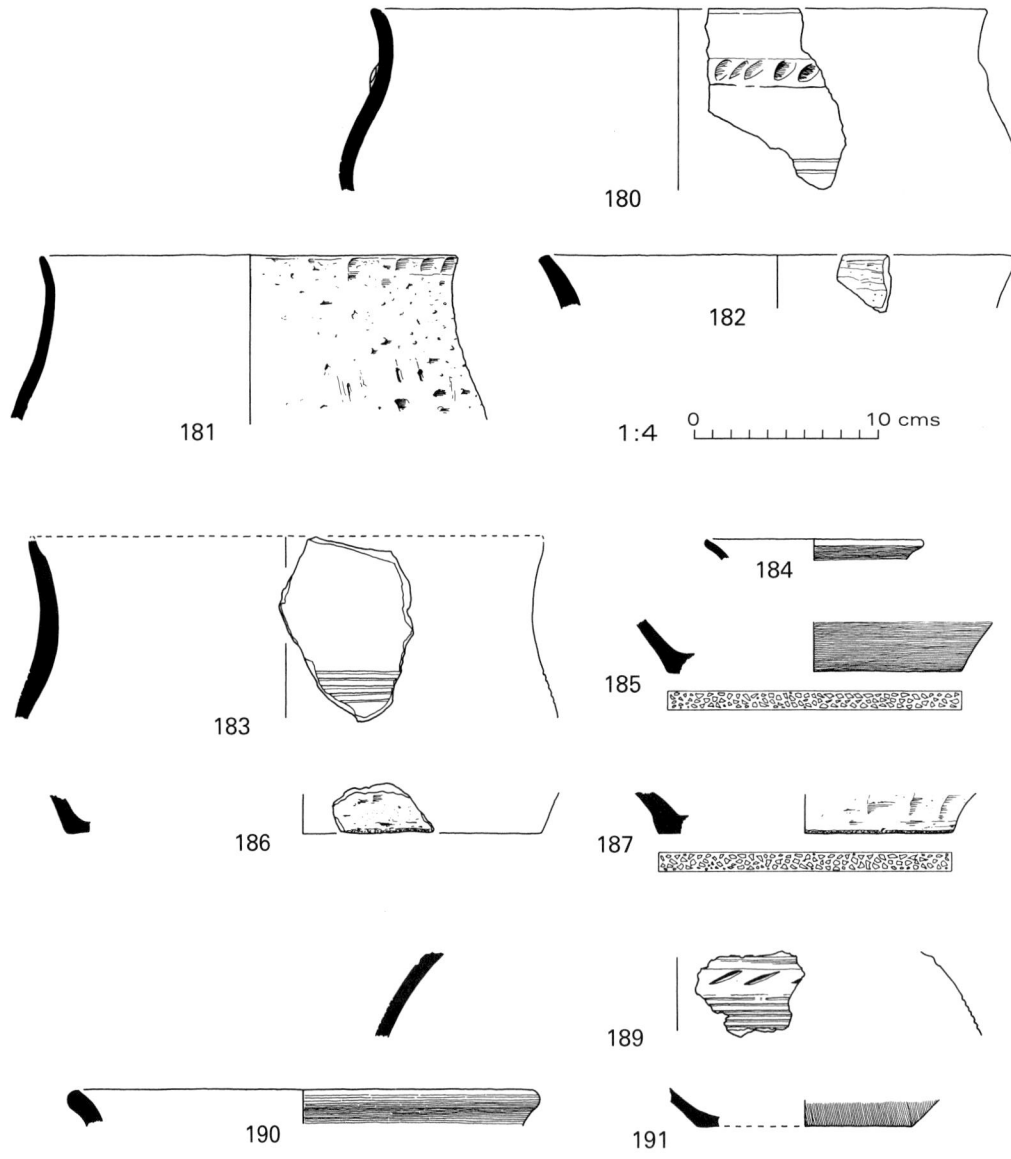

Fig. 70. Period 2 pottery. Nos 180–82, Pit A3; Nos 183–7, Pit A4; Nos 189–91, Gully A191. Scale 1:4.

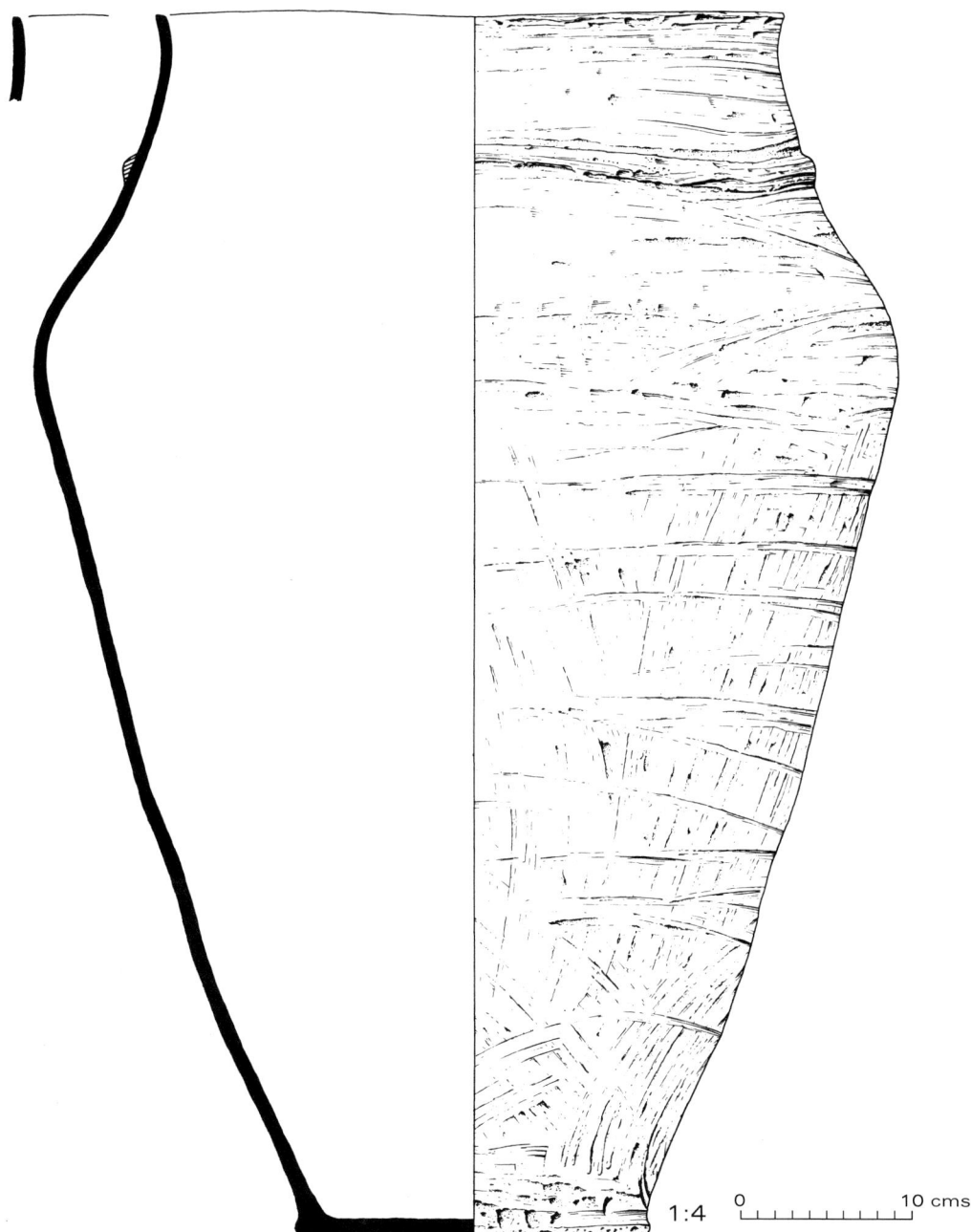

Fig. 71. Period 2 pottery. No. 188, Pit A4. Scale 1:4.

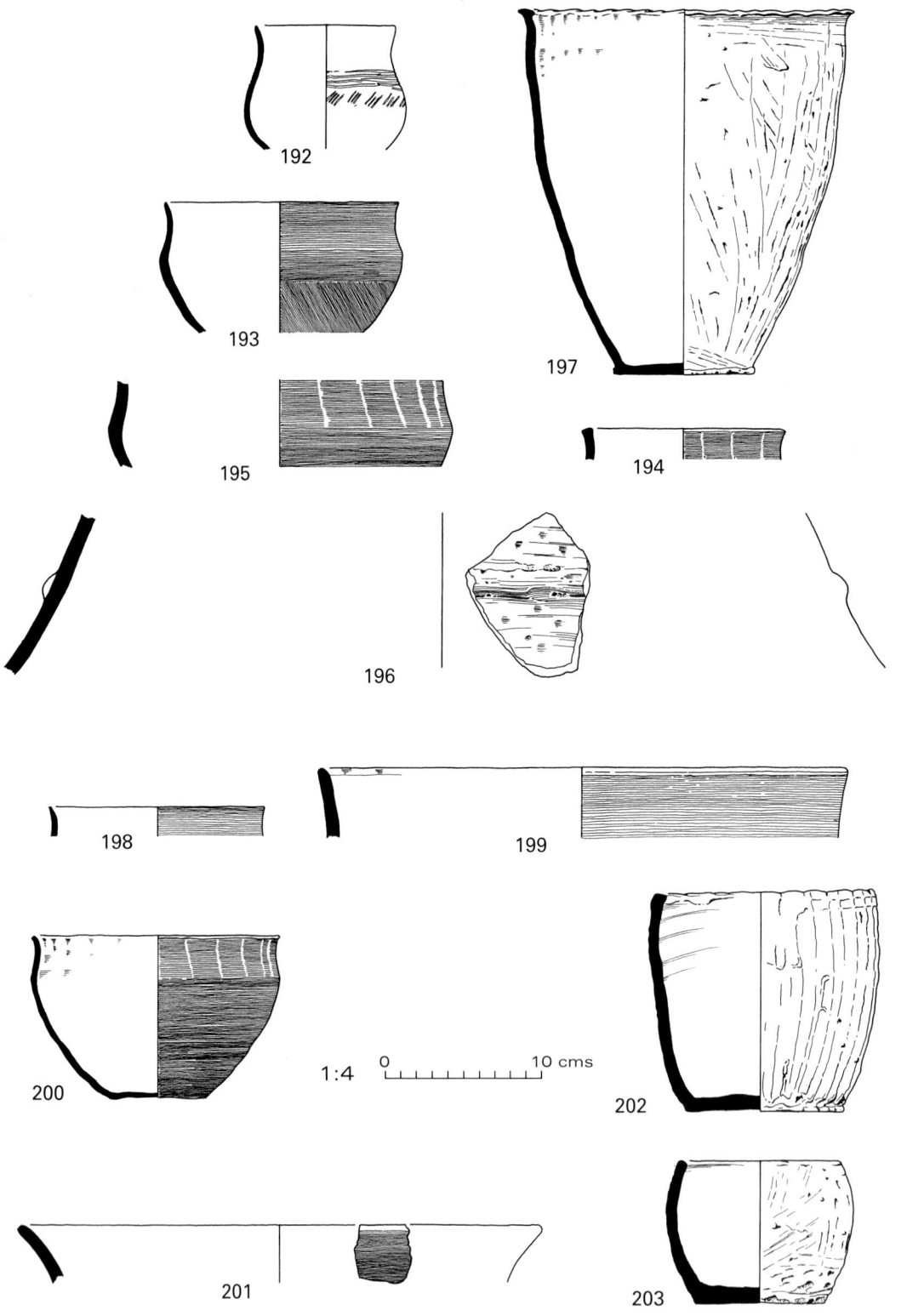

Fig. 72. Period 2 pottery. Nos 192–7, Pit A5; Nos 198–9, Pit A8; No. 200, Pit A50; No. 201, Pit A155; Nos 202–3, Pit A180. Scale 1:4.

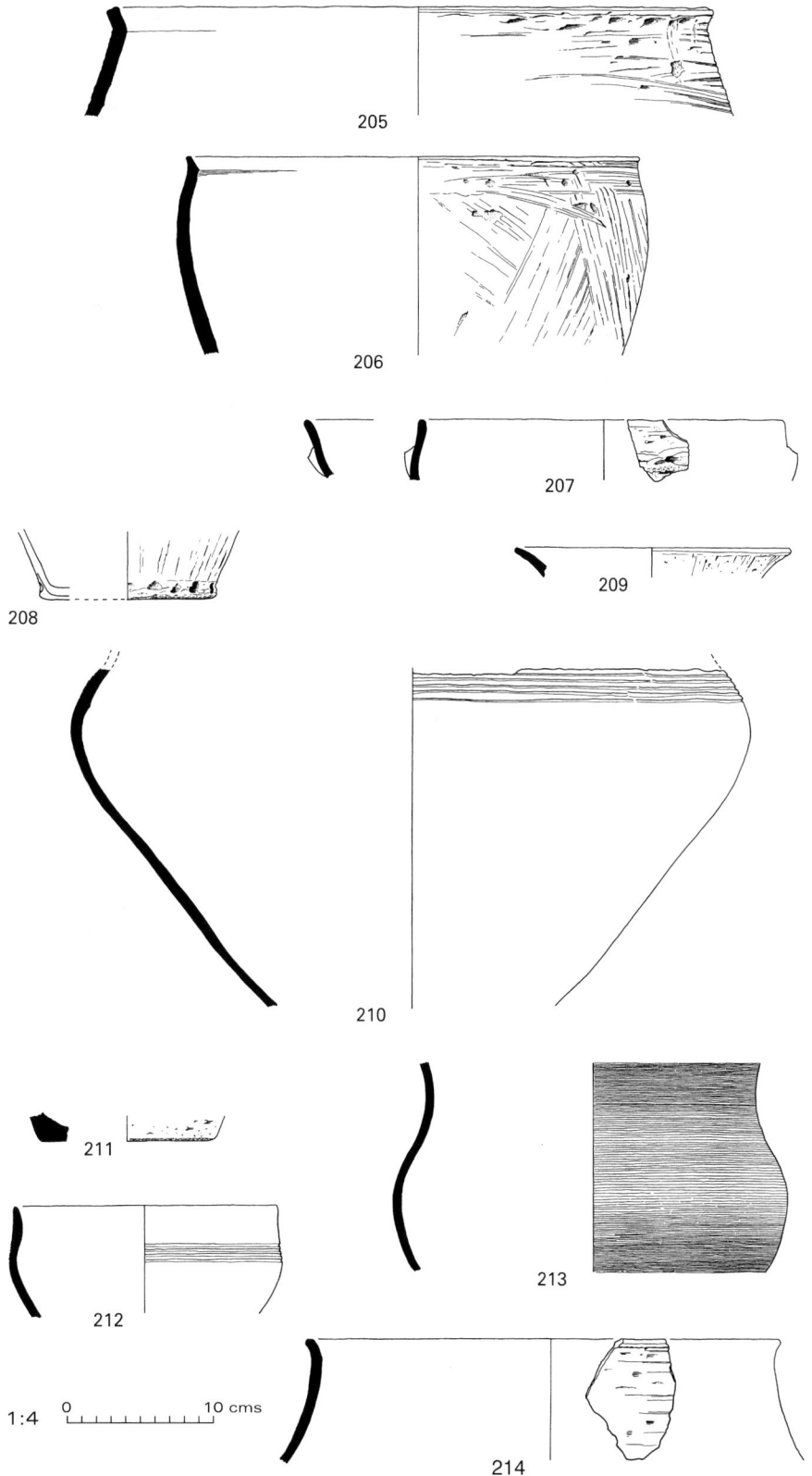

Fig. 73. Period 2 pottery. No. 205, Pit A227; No. 206, Post-pit A19; Nos 207–8, Pit A47; Nos 209–10, Pit A153; No. 211, Pit A179; Nos 212–14, Pit A187. Scale 1:4.

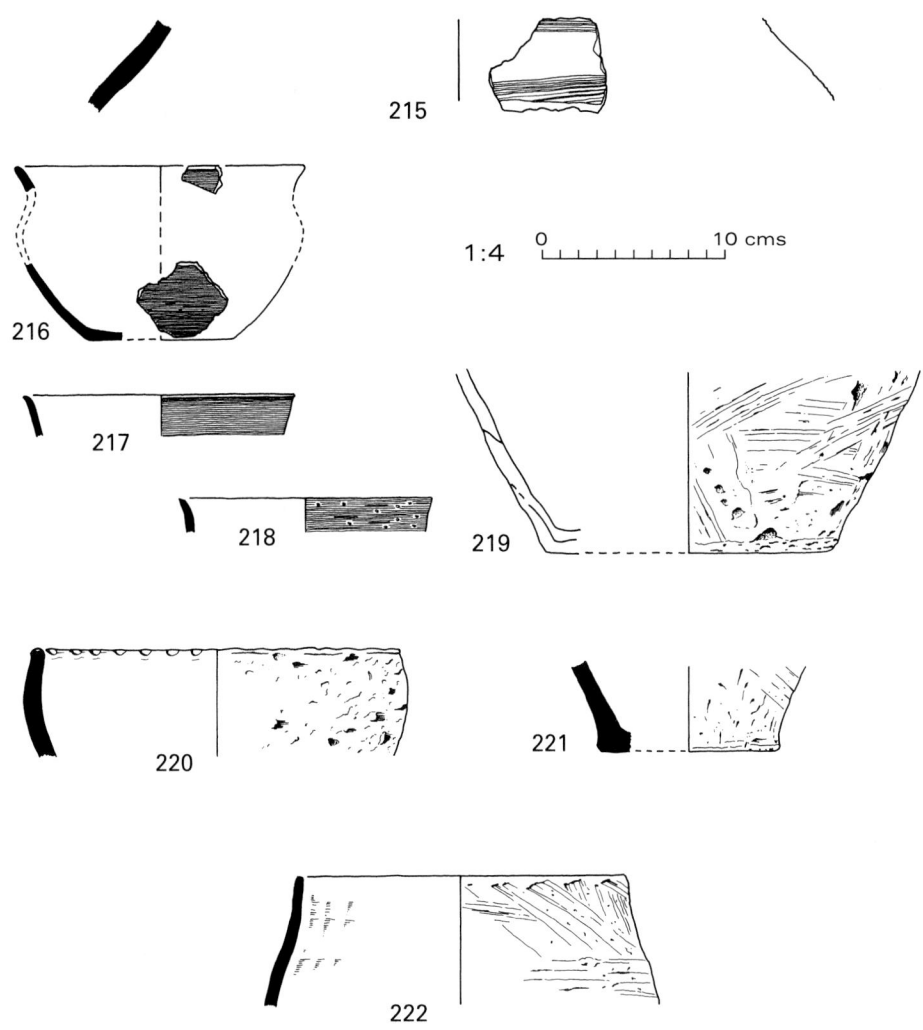

Fig. 74. Period 2 pottery. Nos 215–19, Post-pit A158; No. 220, Post-pit A163; No. 221, Post-hole A143; No. 222, Pit A100. Scale 1:4.

using profile shape of the rim alone is not sufficient to provide a close date. Within the range of plain convex jars there is a general tendency for Period 2 forms to have thinner walls and finer surfaces than those of Period 3 (Table 7).

The fine open bowl, Form 6, occurs twice within Level 4 (Nos 42 and 45). As with the closed forms, plain open bowls are found throughout Periods 2 and 3. The same propensity for finer vessels in the earlier period, although generally true, is not so evident with bowls (Table 7), and may not be a reliable indication of chronology. If accepted however, it does tend to suggest that bowl No. 67, Form 16, with heavy finger-tip decoration may belong to Period 3 rather than 2. It is broadly similar to an example from Destlebergen (de Laet *et al.* 1986, fig. 30, t1.2), dated to Ha C/D.

The open bowl, No. 100, with a gently everted rim, Form 42 (from an unknown depth), has been found in PDR assemblages, such as Aldermaston (Bradley *et al.* 1980, 233, fig. 11, type 1), Farnham (Elsdon 1982, fig 7, 39) and Runnymede Bridge (Longley 1980, fig. 26, 164 and 167). On the Continent bowls with similar external profiles often have internal bevels, e.g. at Fort-Harrouard (Mohen and Bailloud 1987, pl. 59, 24; pl. 70, 6).

Plain biconical bowls, Form 43, Nos 12 (Level 1) and 97 (from an unknown depth), are also known from Late Bronze Age assemblages, such as Runnymede Bridge (Longley 1980, fig. 43, type 4a), Petters Sports Field (O'Connell 1986, fig. 48, 98–101) and Minnis Bay (Worsfold 1943, fig. 6, 4). Evidence from Runnymede Bridge and Petters Sports

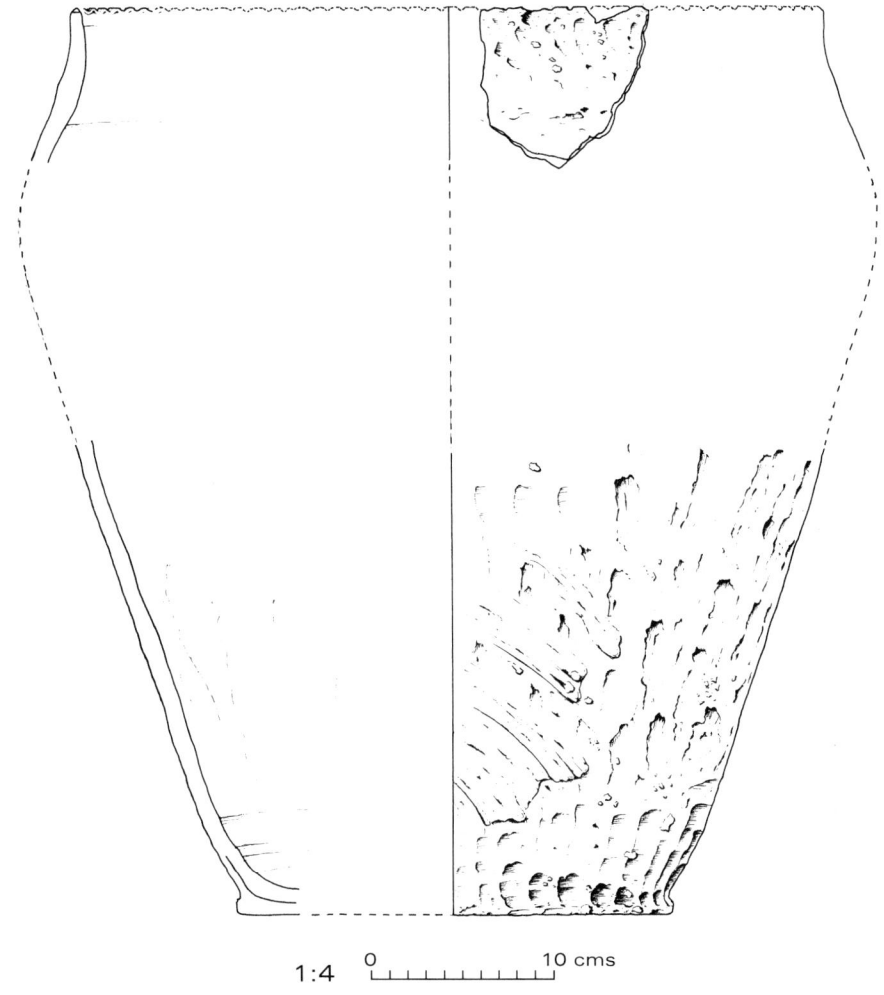

Fig. 75. Period 2 pottery. No. 223, Pit A129. Scale 1:4.

Field suggests that examples such as these, with plain rims, preceded those with bead rims (Longley 1980; O'Connell 1986).

Handled vessels with an internal ledge, similar to No. 91 (Level 5), Form 75, are known from other Late Bronze Age/Early Iron Age sites in Britain and on the Continent, but they are rarely closely datable. Examples have been found at Hunsbury, Northants (Fell 1936, fig. 7, L6 and fig. 8, L5), Fengate (Hawkes and Fell 1943, fig. 10, misc 5), Danebury (Cunliffe 1984, 307, fig. 6.78, 560) and Wallingford dated to the ninth or eighth centuries B.C. (Thomas et al. 1986, fig. 4, 26). Rare examples are also known from France, e.g. from the Aisne and Charente valleys (Brun 1986, pl. 63, 12; Gomez 1984, fig. 2, 1), where the latter has been dated to Ha. ancien. The vessels quoted here differ widely in detail; they may have served different functions and been in use over a long period.

One example of Form 72, No. 92, (from an unknown depth), has a narrow horizontal groove just above the shoulder and shows signs of having been coated with haematite. It is similar to Jogassian forms of the sixth or early fifth century. However, the sherd is small and worn and its angle is unclear. Its date must remain uncertain. Other forms from Ditch B70 are not closely datable.

Some of these forms are clearly of an early date contemporary with Period 2. An early date is also supported by the decoration; there were just seventeen decorated sherds from Levels 1–4 (<1 per cent of the total), but the range of

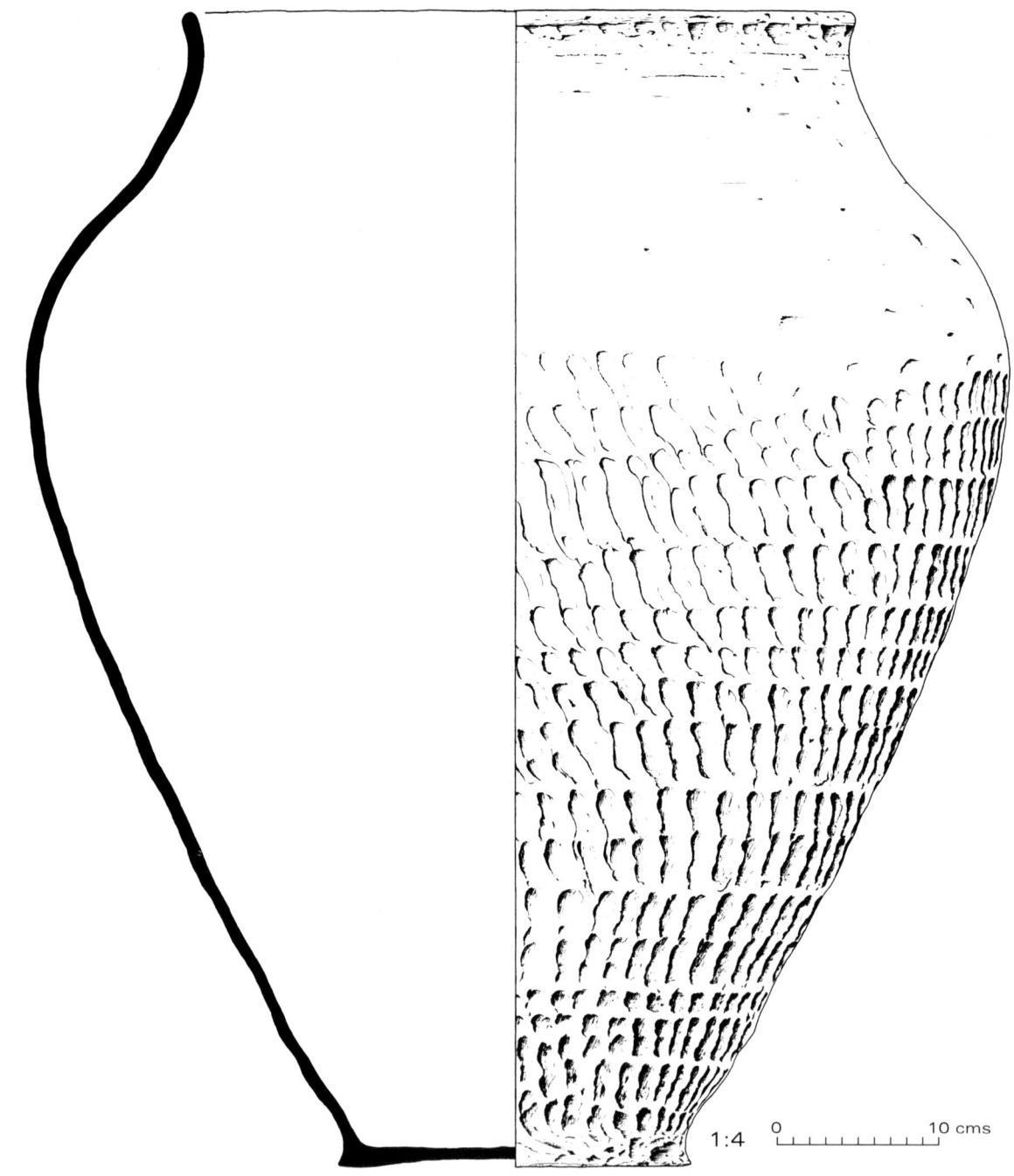

Fig. 76. Period 2 pottery. No. 224, Pit A130. Scale 1:4.

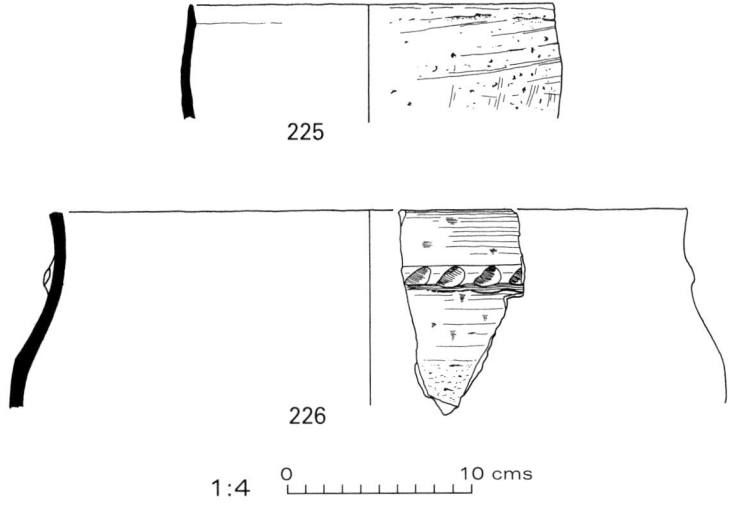

Fig. 77. Period 2 pottery. No. 225, natural hollow A208; No. 226, unstratified, Area A. Scale 1:4.

styles is similar to that recovered from Period 2 (Table 8: Styles A–D and I).

The chronology of most of these styles has been commented on above. Style I, a zone of zigzags running between two bands of horizontal grooves, was found on one vessel, 33, and is paralleled in Late Bronze Age assemblages, e.g. at North Shoebury (Brown 1985, fig. 18, 39) and Plumpton Plain, Site B (Hawkes 1935, fig. 12, f). As noted by Hawkes, the same style occurs at Fort-Harrouard in Bf IIb–IIIa contexts (Mohen and Bailloud 1987, pl. 20, 11–12; pl. 23, 3; pl. 24, 7). An early example from Tombe Z2 at Aulnay-aux-Planches, dated by Chertier to his CU I, c. 1200–1000 B.C. (Chertier 1976, fig. 31, 1) has recently been reconsidered by Brun and placed in his Etape 2, contemporary with Bf IIb–IIIa (Brun 1986, 32).

Other decorated sherds were recovered either from the top of the fill, Level 5, or from unknown depths and account for a very small percentage of the total. Stabbed decoration, similar to Style E, 112, is known from Bronze final contexts, e.g. at Catenoy, 'Le Camp César' (Oise) (Blanchet and Talon 1987, fig. 12, 2 and 6), and from Ha B/C contexts at Lens St Servais 'de Puydt' and Pitet (Hesbaye) (Destexhe 1987, pl. 40, 10–11 and 15, and pl. 103, 323). However, this style is found sporadically throughout the Iron Age, as at Moxhe and Haneffe 'Jointy' (Destexhe 1987, pl. 117, 454–5).

A small sherd from a shoulder, 87, is decorated with a horizontal line, possibly on a cordon, crossed by short diagonal grooves (D24). A similar design, with short vertical lines, is known from Runnymede Bridge (Longley 1980, fig. 22, 63) and from phase I at Choisy-au-Bac (Talon 1987, fig. 11, 10).

From this study of the pottery in the Enclosure ditch B70, it is clear that just sixty-five sherds entered it while it filled to a depth of about 1.10 m. (Levels 1 and 2). The fills within these levels comprised sandy silt, at the bottom, followed by gravel interleaved with sand. This fill could have been rapid from the weathering of the sides of the ditch. It remained open, receiving Period 2 debris in Levels 3 and 4, until it was substantially filled early during Period 3. Certainly Period 2 pits immediately outside the ditch, including B79, B80 and B317, contained rubbish, including metalworking debris, which was contemporary with material that was being discarded into Levels 3 and 4, when the ditch had filled to half its depth. On the strength of this evidence it is argued that the fill of the B70 enclosure ditch belongs to Period 2, possibly early within the period. It certainly formed a key element on the landscape throughout Period 2 and into Period 3.

Settlement pattern during Periods 2 and 3

The chronological progression indicated in Table 5 has provided a broad guide to phasing, but it is not suitable for detailed sequencing of individual features which have few recognizable forms. There is clearly some overlap caused by the variable lifespan of forms; and the picture may be further blurred by residual or intrusive material. Nevertheless, using these features as a basis for examining the changing pattern of settlement, a coherent view does emerge.

Period 2 saw the construction of Enclosure ditch B70 and, presumably, the palisade and entrance post-pits, and Enclosure A24 together with its internal features: A2–A5, A8, A50, A155 and A187; and A100 and A130 outside. Pit

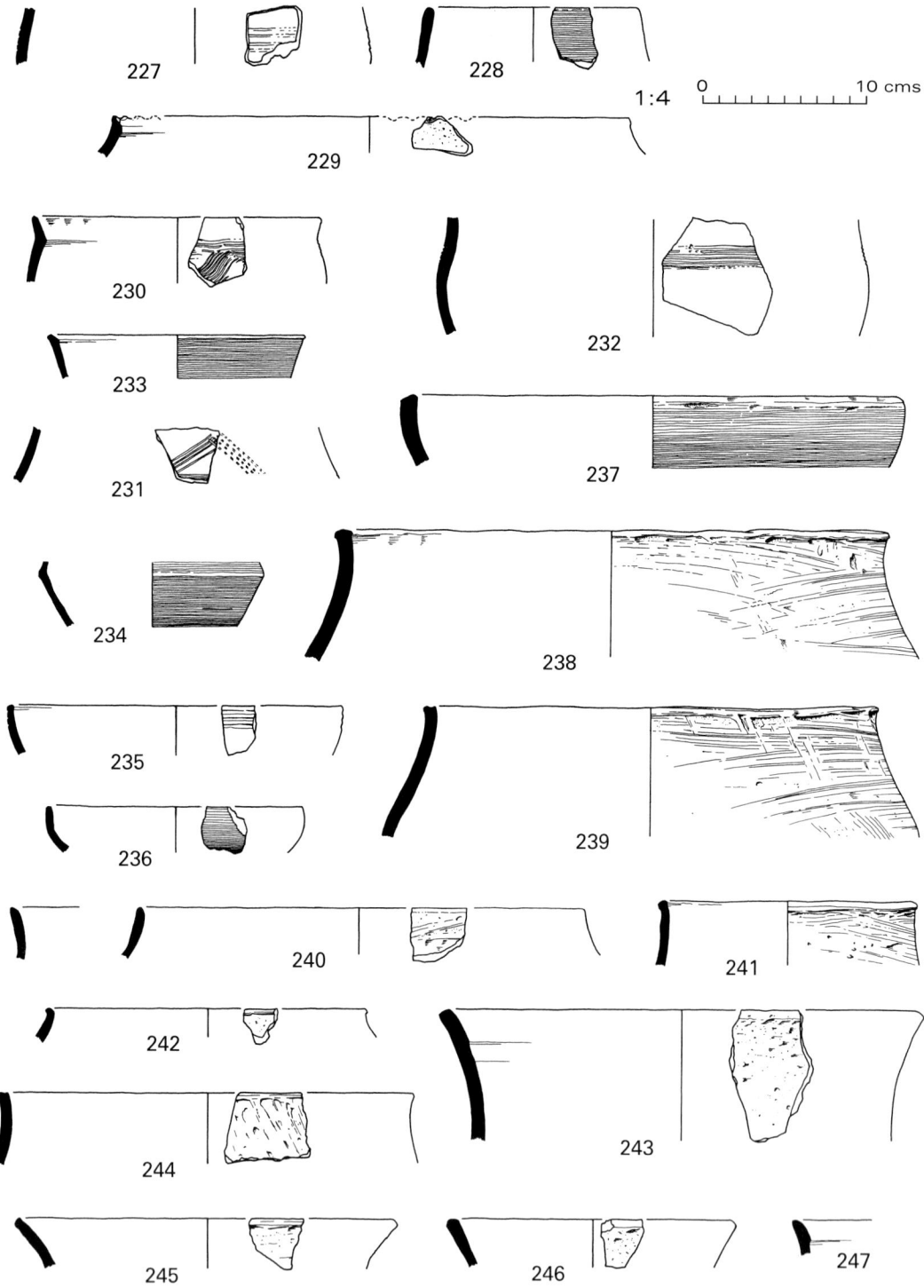

Fig. 78. Period 2 pottery. Nos 227–47, Pit B317. Scale 1:4.

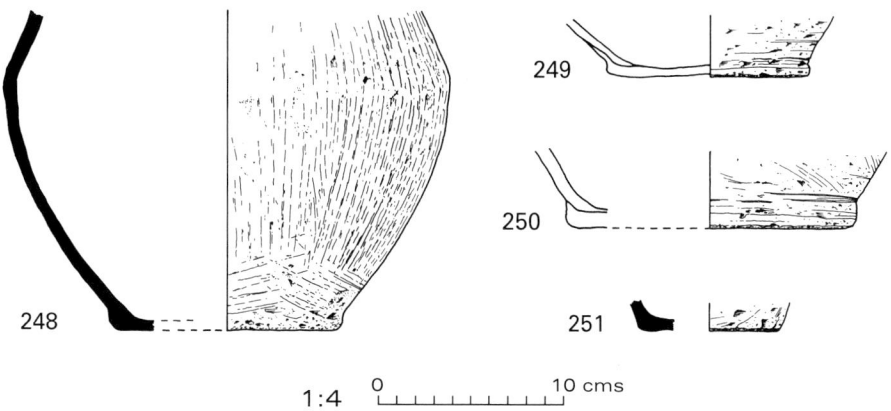

Fig. 79. Period 2 pottery. Nos 248–51, Pit B317. Scale 1:4.

A129, outside Enclosure A24, may also belong perhaps late within this period. Its association with Period 3 features in Table 5 is caused by the appearance of a single vessel of Form 61, which might have been in use earlier than suggested in Table 5. This period also sees activity outside Enclosure B70, represented by the fill of pits B79, B80 and B317.

Period 3 witnessed the spread of open settlement over a wide area, and the use of huts with ring-ditches. Detailed subdivision of these periods is possible using topographical evidence and, in some cases, stratigraphy, and this is described above (pp. 62–5). The ceramic evidence alone is not sufficiently precise to contribute to detailed phasing within this broad framework.

Chronology of Structure B200

While the broad divisions outlined above form a general guide to the main chronology of the site, a note on Structure B200 is appropriate because an understanding of the ceramic evidence is necessary when considering its date.

The structure consists of over ninety small post-holes, forming a double row of posts in a subrectangular plan, with an apparent entrance facing south-east. Details of its construction are discussed above (pp 47–9). One post-hole from the structure was dug into the fill of Hearth B219. Inside the structure, though not in direct stratigraphical association with it, were several pits (Figs 33 and 34).

The earliest feature, Hearth B219 (Fig. 34), whose fill was cut by Post-hole B488, produced fourteen flint-tempered body sherds, one with a lightly rusticated surface and one with a rough, partially combed surface. While the evidence is slight, this is likely to fall within Period 3B.

Pottery was recovered from four of the internal pits: B200A and B200B, B226 and B174. Pit B200A was cut by Pit B200B, but at the time of excavation the fills were not distinguished. The resulting collection of twenty-nine sherds from both pits includes nine rusticated sherds, five rims (Fig. 88, Nos 350–51 and 353–55) and a combed sherd, illustrated with the grooves running vertically (Fig. 88, No. 352), though its angle is uncertain and the grooves could also be interpreted as horizontal. While the combed sherd could belong to the Late Iron Age, this and the other sherds from the group can all be accommodated within Period 3B.

Pit B226, which cut into the fill of Pit B227, contained eleven sherds of flint-tempered pottery, including two possible rusticated sherds and two rims (Fig. 88, 360–1), one with finger-tip impressions around the shoulder. These clearly fall within Period 3B.

Pit B174 contained just two sherds, both illustrated (Fig. 88, Nos 348–9). Neither is closely datable. The base (No. 349) has four perforations and is in a heavily flint-tempered fabric. No. 348, a globular jar with everted rim whose form and small diameter distinguish it from the jars found in the fourth to first centuries B.C. A late Period 3B date is likely.

In addition, there are thirty-two flint-tempered sherds which almost certainly came from the post-holes forming Structure B200. These sherds were amalgamated to form a single collection and there is no longer any means of identifying which post-hole held which sherds. Twenty-six of these were undiagnostic body sherds, one with a lightly rusticated surface, and there were one base (Fig. 88, 359), one shoulder (Fig. 88, 357) and three possible rims of which two are illustrated (Fig. 88, 356 and 358). Shown as a rim, No. 358, was extremely worn, with uncertain angle and diameter. It might even have been a base. As illustrated however, its form, an expanded inturned rim, could be placed late in Period 3B or early in Period 4. No. 356 was slightly worn but is clearly a fragmentary everted rim. Treated in isolation, this everted

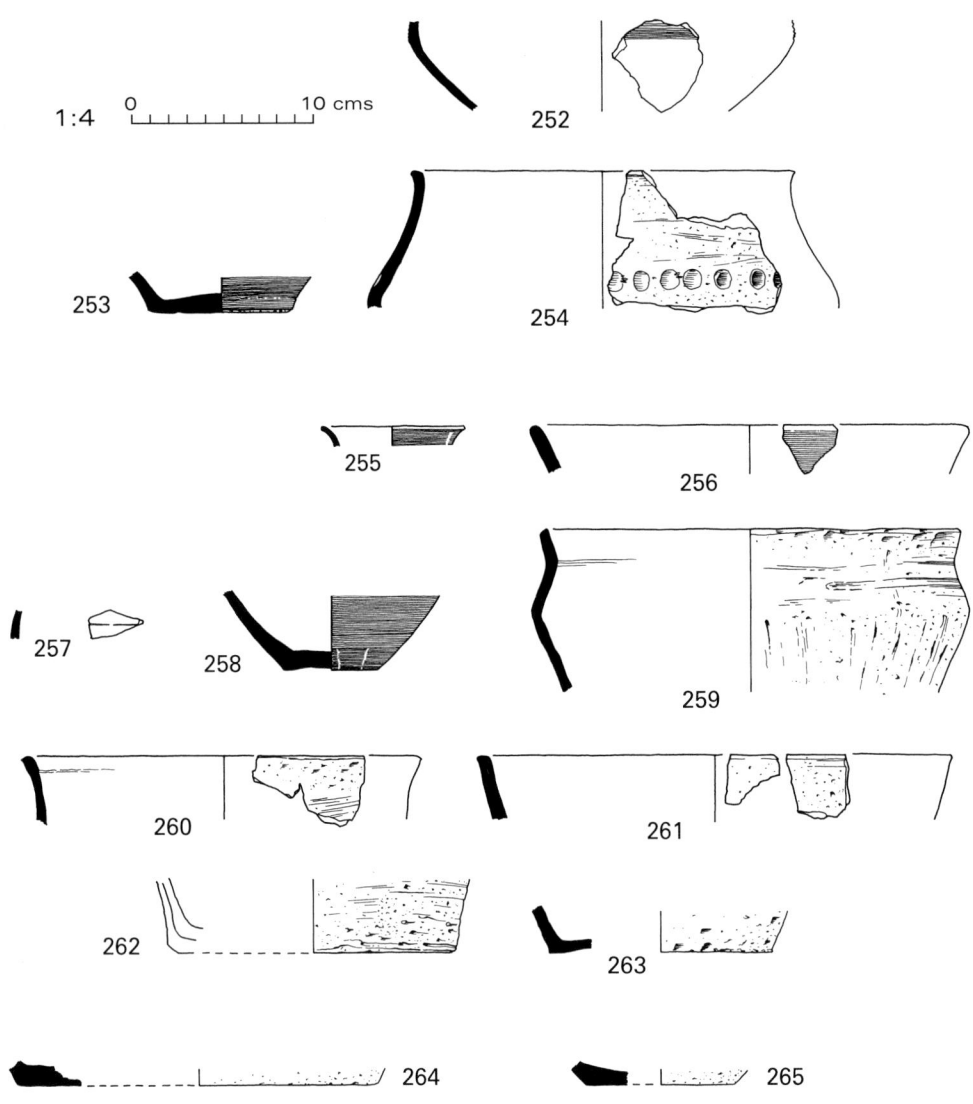

Fig. 80. Period 2 pottery. Nos 252–4, Pit B79; Nos 255–63, Pit B80; Nos 264–5, Pit B81. Scale 1:4.

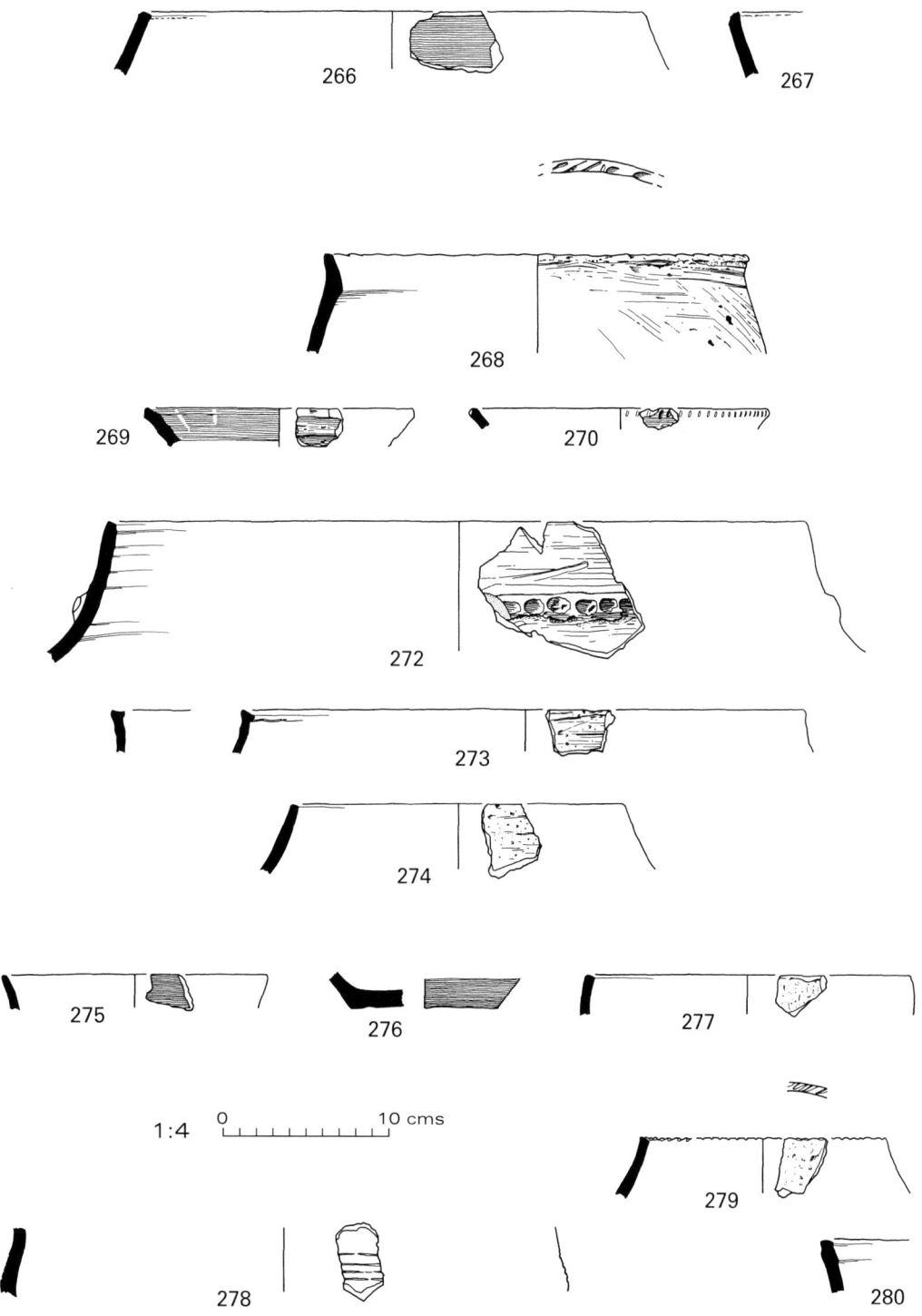

Fig. 81. Period 2 pottery. Nos 266–7, Pit B84; Nos 268–70, Pit 97; Nos 272–4, Pit B92. Period 3A pottery. Nos 275–7, Enclosure A118; Nos 278–80, Enclosure B144. Scale 1:4.

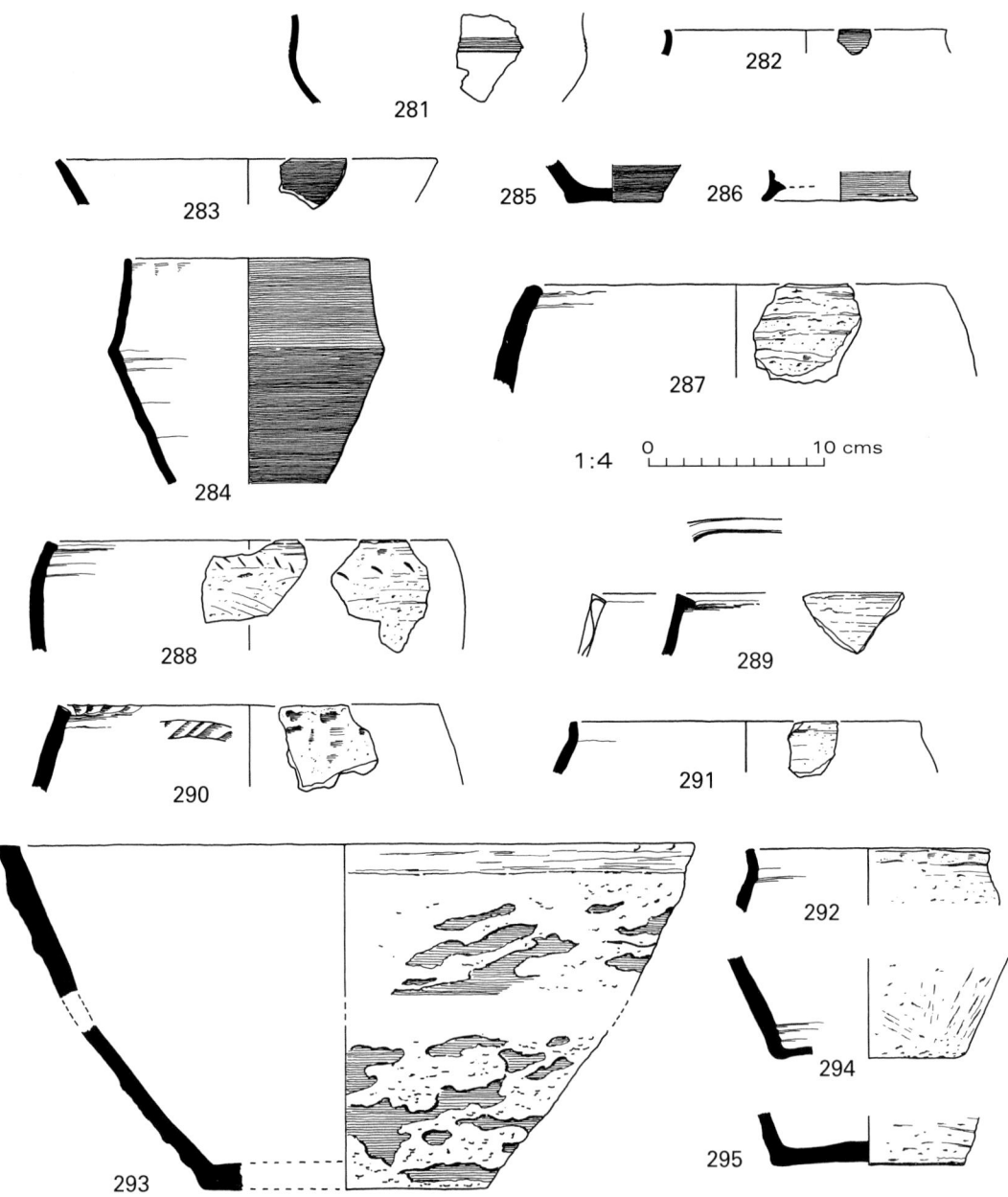

Fig. 82. Period 3A pottery. Nos 281–95, Pit B12. Scale 1:4.

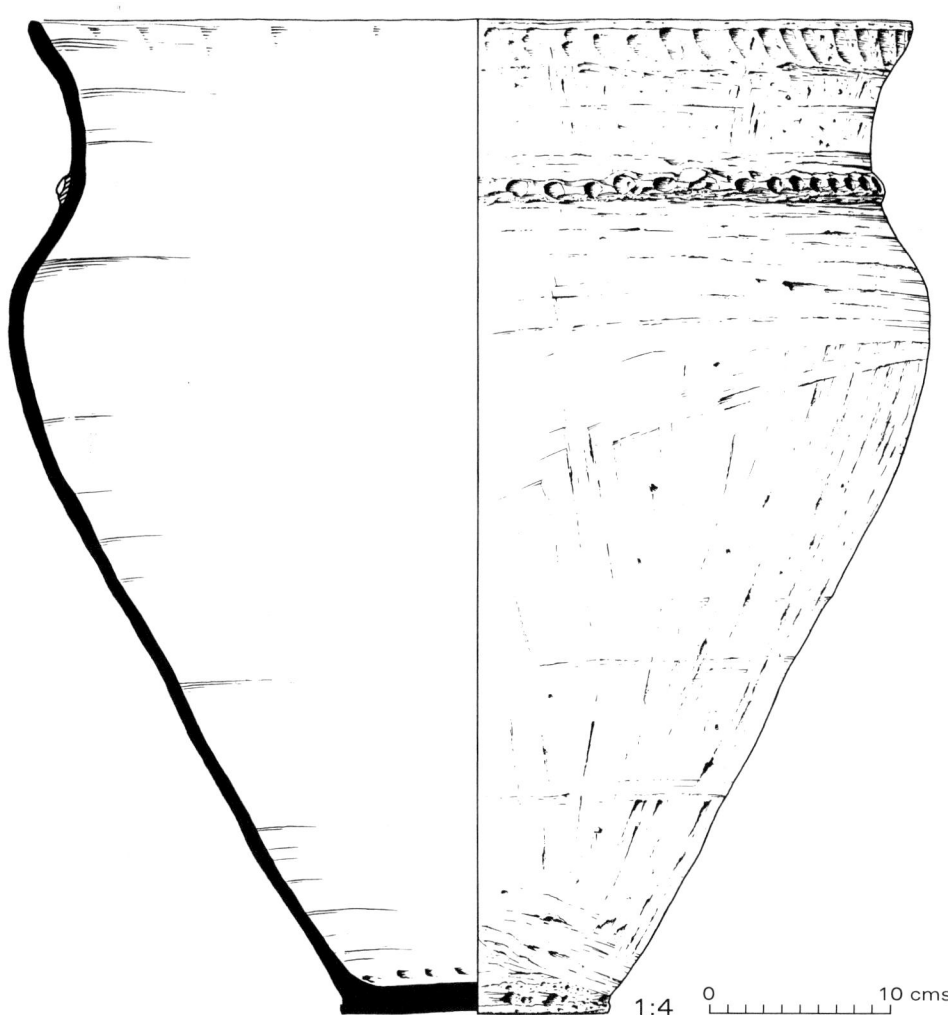

Fig. 83. Period 3A pottery. No. 296, Pit B12. Scale 1:4.

rim could be dated between the fourth and first centuries B.C., late in Period 3B or early in Period 4. Alternatively, it could be intrusive having derived from the nearby Period 4 or 5 activity (Ditch B14, assigned to Period 5A, passed close to the outside of the entrance of the structure).

Dating the structure is problematic. One sherd from one of its post-holes is clearly of the type associated with everted-rim and foot-ring jars; one other rim could be contemporary with it. The remaining sherds are undiagnostic. The internal pits may have preceded the structure, in which case their position appears to have been respected by its walls, or they may be contemporary. All the pottery from these pits can be accommodated within Period 3B. Thus the ceramic evidence suggests that the structure B200 could date to any time between the fourth and mid first centuries B.C. The absence of any pure grog-tempered pottery or 'Belgic' forms suggests that it certainly precedes the second half of the first century B.C.

Chronology of vessels not included in the seriation

It now remains to examine the chronology of those vessel forms which, through accident of burial, do not appear in the seriation in Table 5. Some of these may be dated by reference to typological parallels.

Form 11, an open bowl with a short everted rim and internal bevel, No. 206, from Pit A19, is paralleled in Late Bronze Age contexts as at Heybridge Basin, Essex (Brown

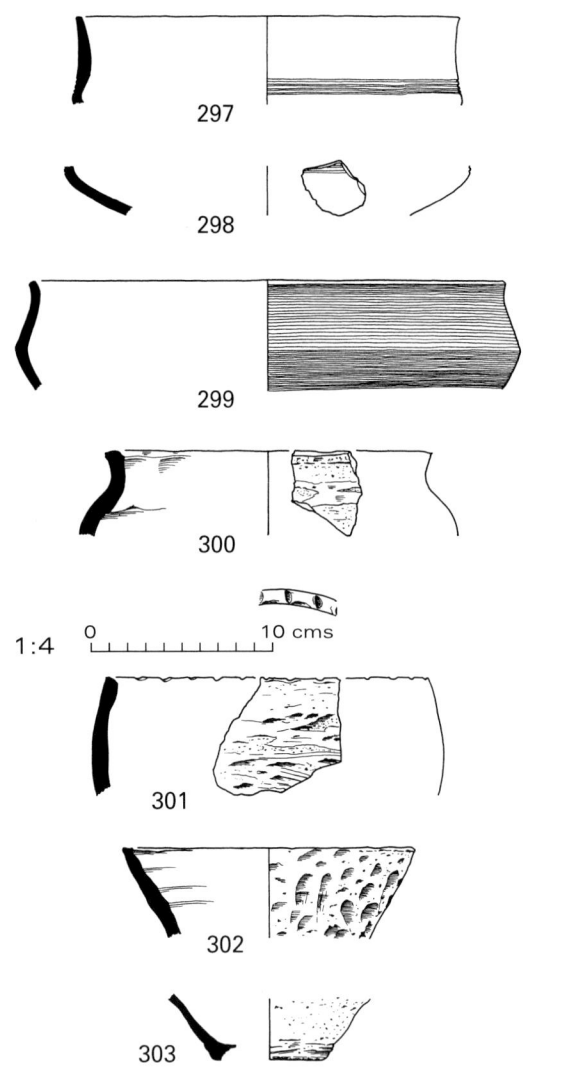

Fig. 84. Period 3A pottery. Nos 297–303, Pit B244. Scale 1:4.

of Form 11, a Period 2 date is supported by the position of Pit A181 within Enclosure A24.

The thin-walled tripartite cup, No. 317, Form 38, with its light horizontal grooved decoration, is broadly similar to Forms 39–41, shown above to fall within Periods 2–3A. This particular example is not closely paralleled, but a plain version of the same form is found in the Ha B assemblage at Pitet (Hesbaye) (Destexhe 1987, pl. 98, 240), suggesting that a Period 2 or 3A date would be appropriate here.

Similarly, a Period 2 date may be assigned to Form 73, 210. This vessel has already been mentioned when discussing light horizontal grooved decoration, but its form is also paralleled in contemporary deposits, as at Court St Etienne (Mariën 1958, fig. 26, 24), Donk (van Impe 1980, pl. X, 7) and Saint Georges (Destexhe 1987, pl. 39, 44) where it is dated to Ha B2/B3.

The small bowl with a flat-topped expanded rim, Form 21, 423, is reminiscent of late Ha forms, as at Les Rouliers (Rozoy 1986, pl. 119, RO93, 3 and 4). But it is closer to early La Tène forms, e.g. at Chassemy (Rowlett et al. 1969, fig. 29,11), though most of these have plain rims, as at Villeneuve-Saint-Germain (Aisne) (Debord 1981, fig. 10, 78E07, 008) and Tinqueux (Marne) (Flouest and Stead 1981, fig. 10, T21a).

The pedestalled vessel, Form 71, 380, with finger-tip impressions on the rim, is closely parallelled by a vessel from an early La Tène burial at Juseret, Bercheux-la-Hutte, in the Belgian Ardennes (de Laet 1982, fig. 292).

The tripartite bowl with carinated shoulder, Form 37, 347 and 378, is not closely dated, but examples are known from early La Tène contexts, as at Kemmelberg (van Doorselaer et al. 1987, fig. 40, 186–8) and Vrigny (Marne) (Chossenot et al. 1981, fig. 9, T15, C). No. 347 is incomplete and it is possible that it had a wide flaring rim, reminiscent of Jogassian forms (Favret 1936, fig. 43, 106).

Jars with flaring rims and constricted neck, similar to Form 64, 342 and 437, are not closely datable, though a broadly similar example is known from the upper fill of the well at Lofts Farm, Essex, dated to between the eighth and fifth centuries B.C. (Brown 1988, fig. 16, 62).

Form 74, with a vertical projection on the rim is not closely paralleled. The reconstruction shown here, 496, suggests that it may have had a crenellated appearance. However, such an interpretation is uncertain. A bowl from La Tène I contexts at Lamine does have a single projection (Destexhe 1987, pl. 91, 123), but with a more gentle slope than this example from Highstead. Occasionally vessels with deep finger-tip impressions, which produce grooves across the rim, have been described as crenellated (e.g. Cahen-Delhaye 1973a, fig. 10, 32) but these are not as deep as this example. Perhaps the closest parallels are to be found among the continental scalloped-rim vessels ('*lapenschalen*', '*coups a bord ourlé*' or '*en parasol*'). These generally have undulating rims, as the name suggests; but some examples have more clearly defined projections, as at Hooidonksche

and Adkins 1988, fig. 11, 9) where a similar bowl from well F267, is dated from the tenth to ninth centuries B.C. Examples are also known from Bf IIIa groups at Fort-Harrouard (Mohen and Bailloud 1987, pl. 12, 4) and Bf IIIb at Verberie, 'Le Buisson-Campin' (Oise) and Saint-Sauveur 'La Prévôtée' (Oise) (Blanchet 1984, fig. 191, 21 and fig. 192, 8). These dates, together with the position of Pit A19 within Enclosure A24, would support its attribution to Period 2.

The large jar with incurving concave neck and heavily accentuated internal bevel, similar to No. 169, Form 54, from Pit A181, occurs at Court St Etienne, where examples have been dated to Ha B (Mariën 1958, fig. 29, 51). As in the case

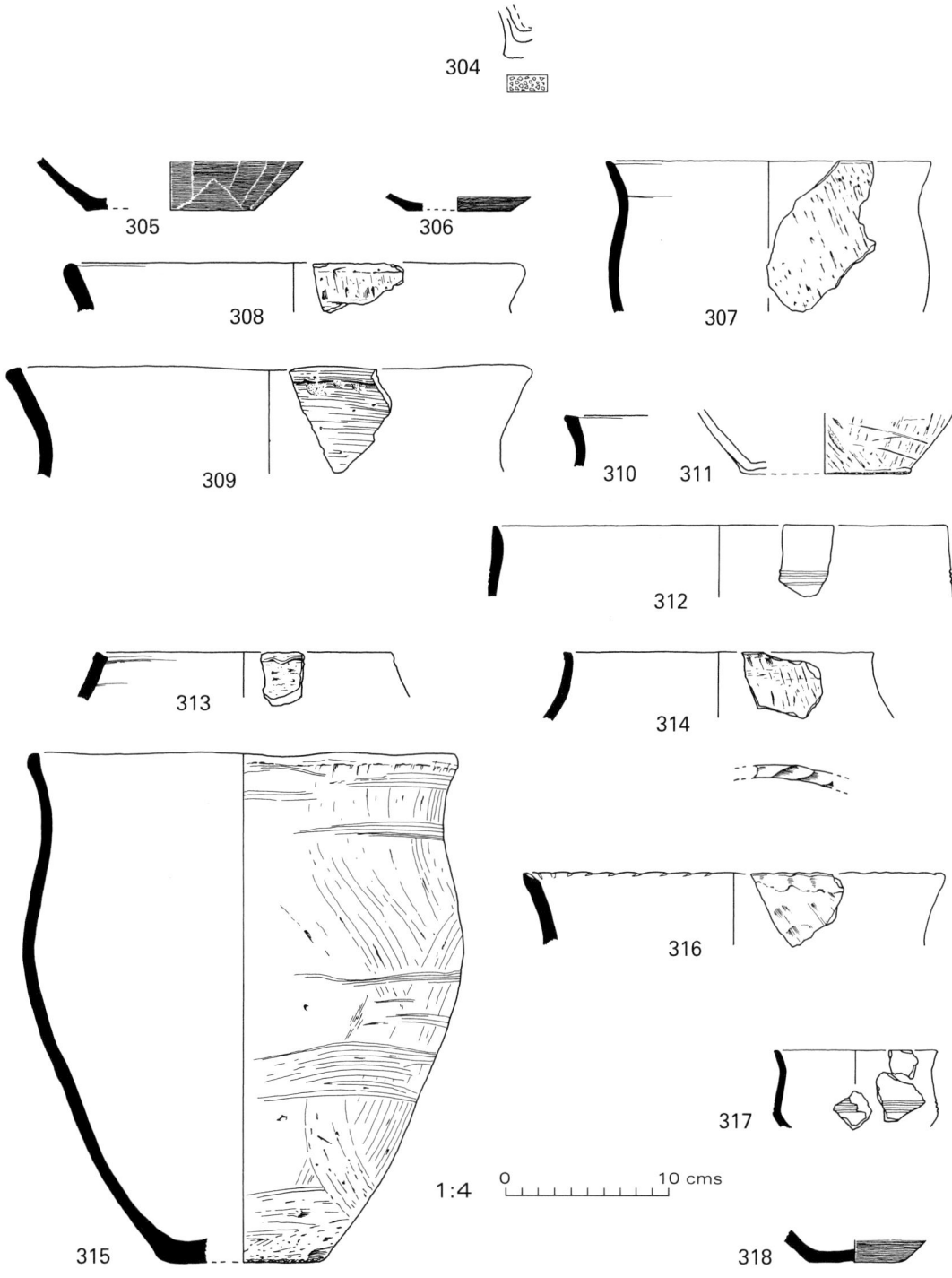

Fig. 85. Period 3A pottery. No. 304, Pit B71; Nos 305–11, context 101, Pit B131; Nos 312–16, context 131, Pit B131; Nos 317–18, Post-hole B68. Scale 1:4.

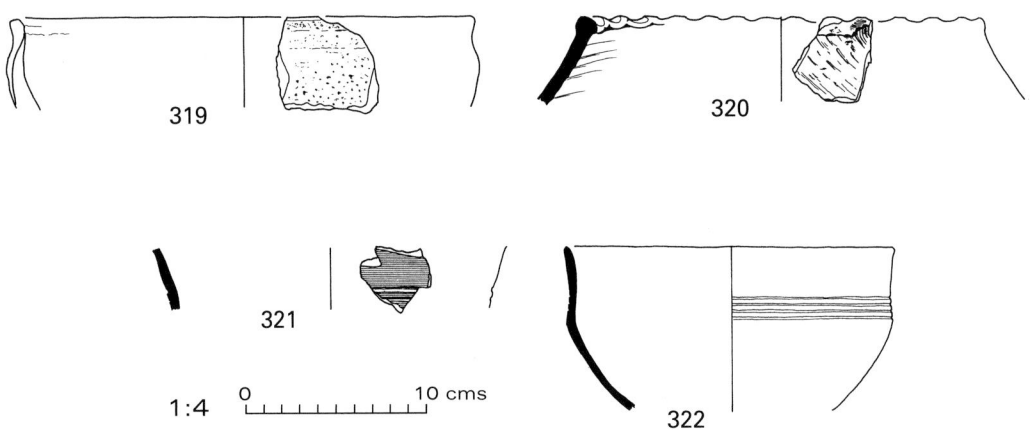

Fig. 86. Period 3A pottery. No. 319, Post-hole B49; No. 320, Post-hole B36; No. 321 (red-finished), Pit B270; No. 322, unstratified. Scale 1:4.

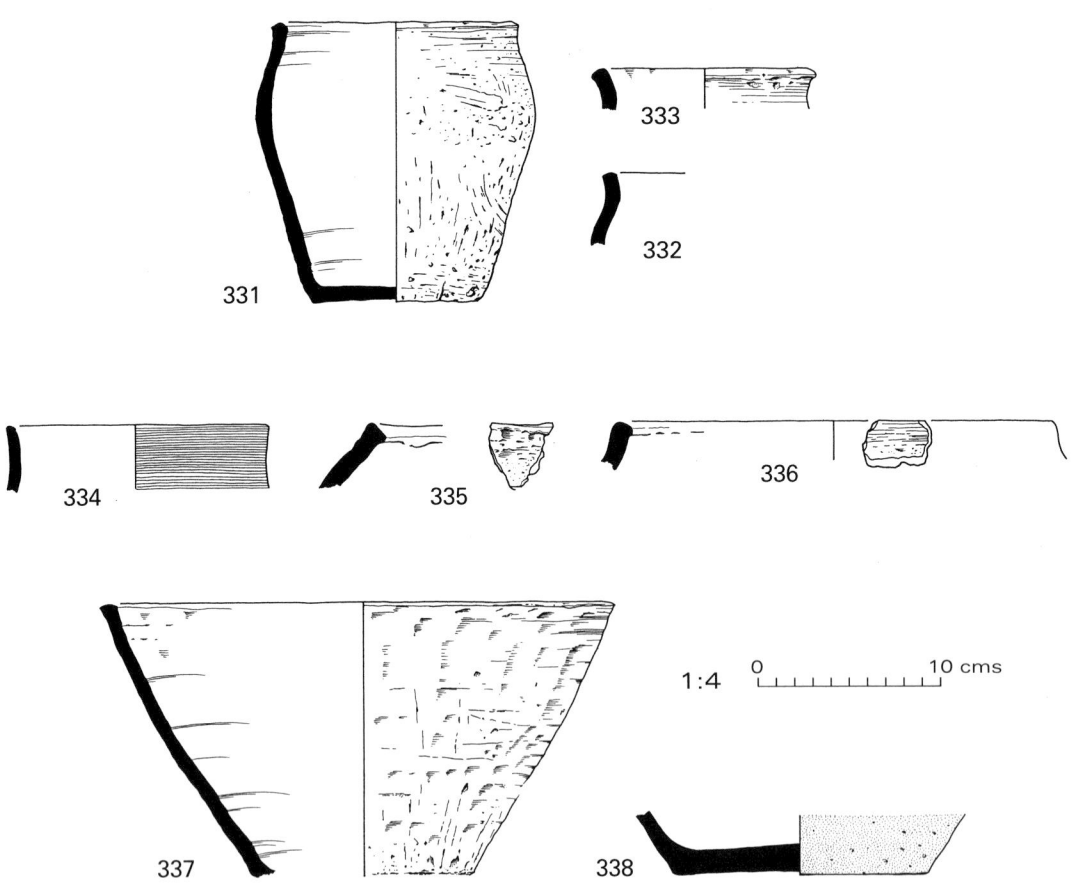

Fig. 87. Period 3B pottery. Nos 331–3, Gully B16; Nos 334–6, Gully B26; Nos 337–8, Gully B325. Scale 1:4.

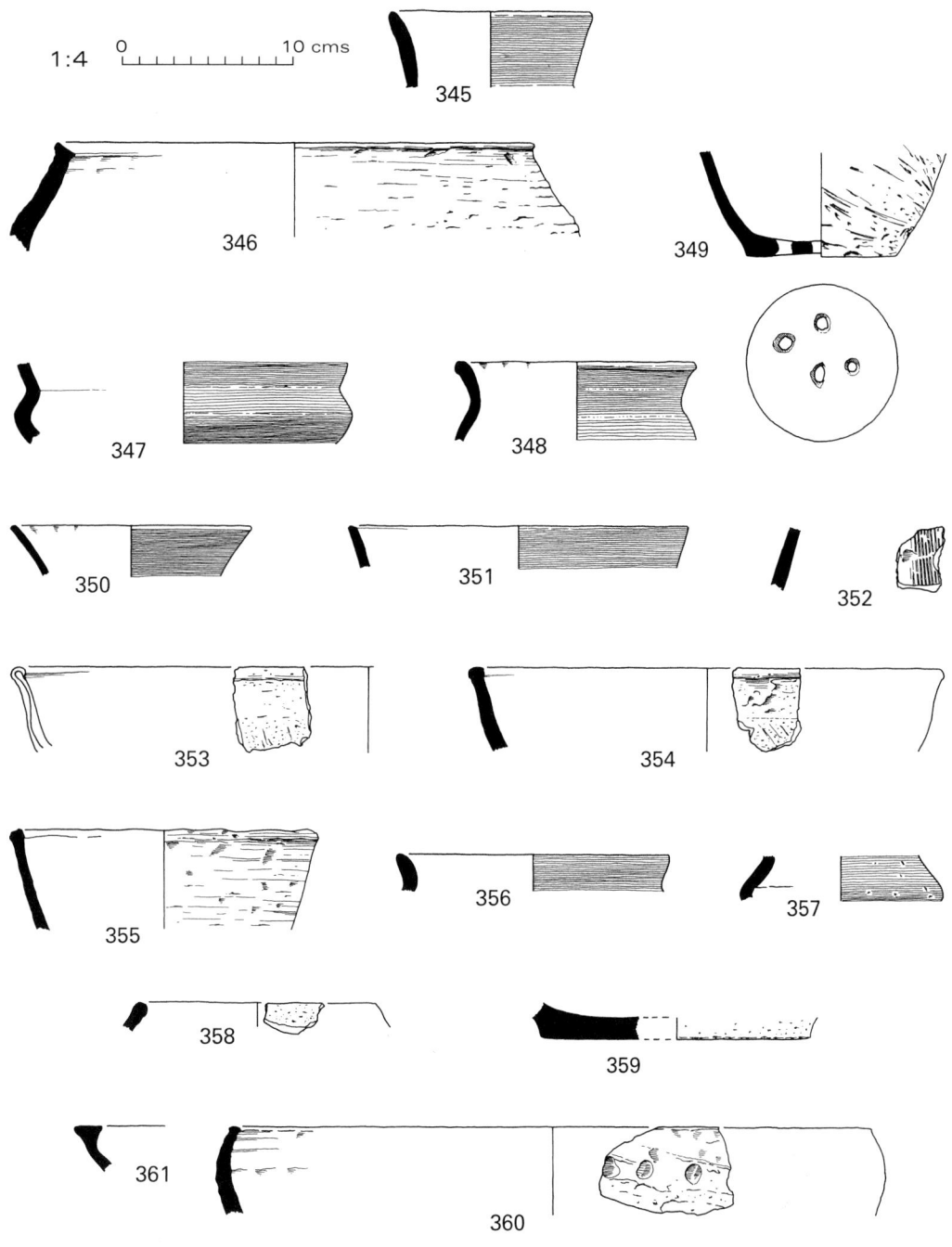

Fig. 88. Period 3B pottery. Nos 345–6, Pit B189; No. 347, Hearth B188; Nos 348–9, Pit B174; Nos 350–55, Pit group B200A; Nos 356–59 post-holes forming Structure B200; Nos 360–61, Pit B226. Scale 1:4.

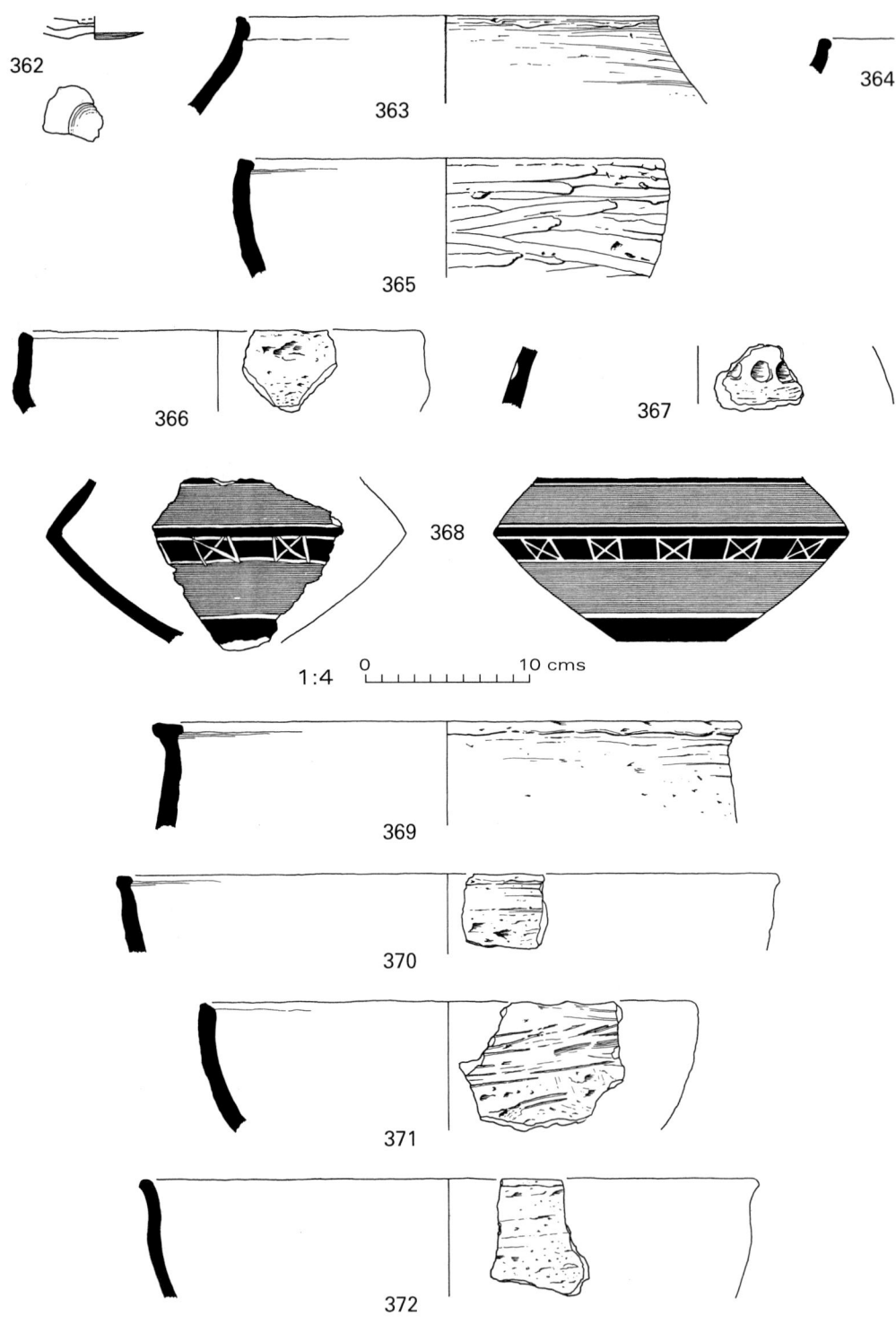

Fig. 89. Period 3B pottery. No. 362, Pit B177; Nos 363–5, Pit B203; Nos 366–7, Hearth B207; Nos 368–71, Post-pit B196 (No. 368, polychrome-decorated with idealised reconstruction); No. 372, Post-pit B197. Scale 1:4.

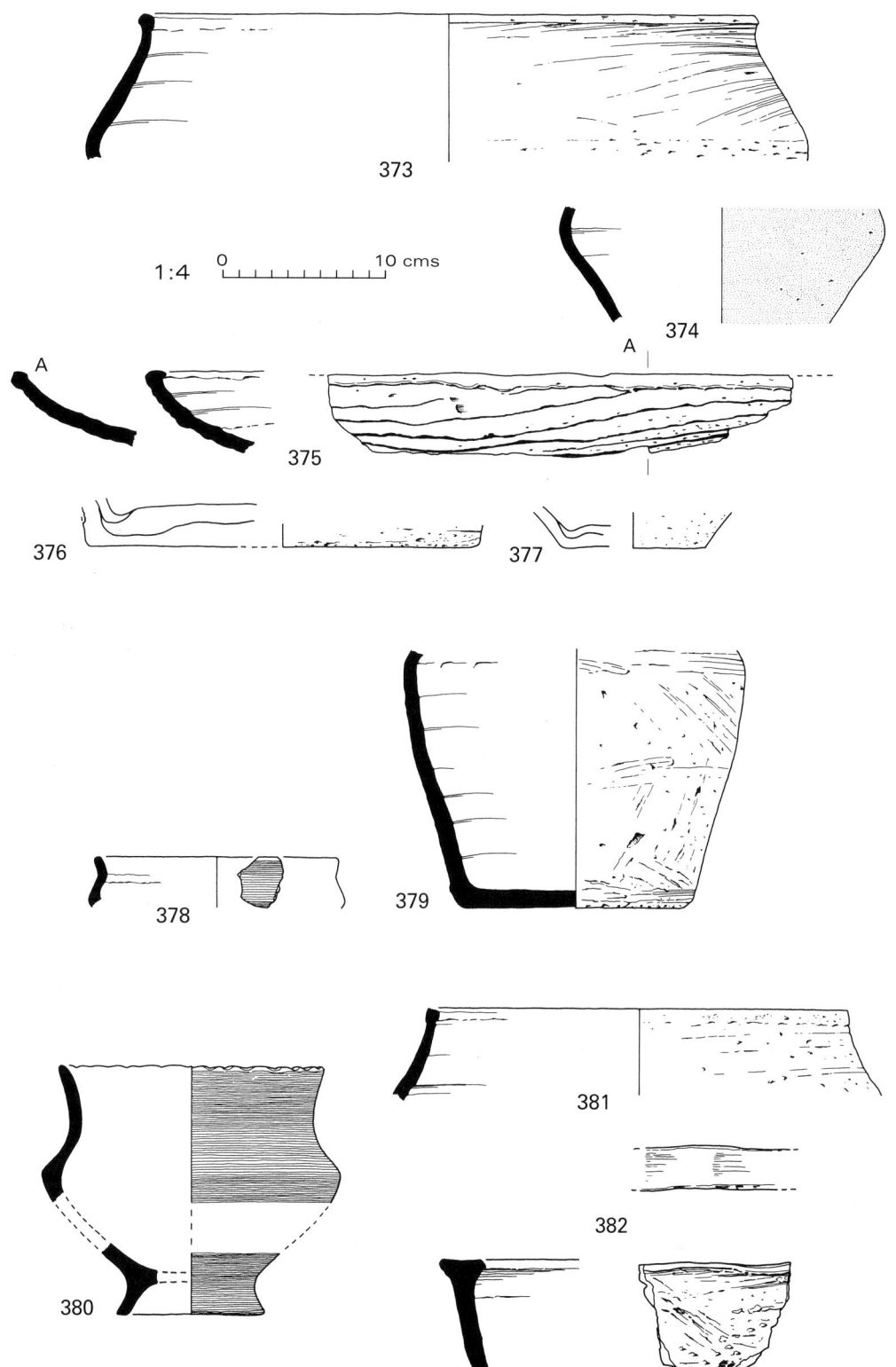

Fig. 90. Period 3B pottery. Nos 373–7, Pit B215; Nos 378–9, Pit B314; Nos 380–82, Pit B133. Scale 1:4.

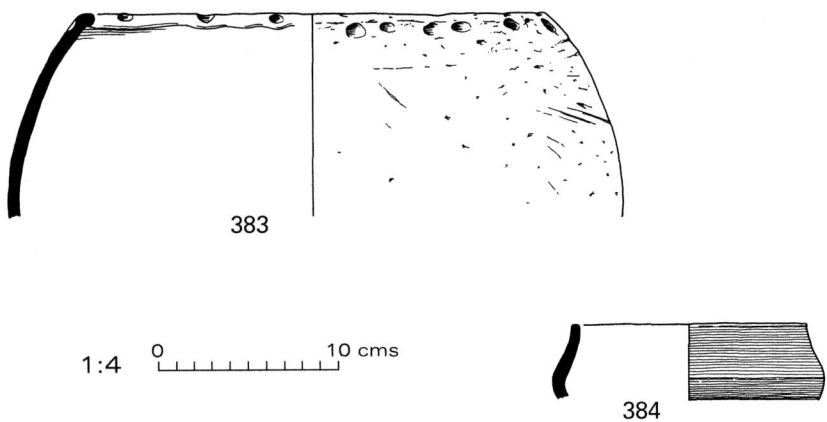

Fig. 91. Period 3B pottery. No. 383, Pit B154; No. 384, Pit B166. Scale 1:4.

Akkers (van den Broeke 1980, fig. 15, B17). A Period 3 date would accommodate these examples, which are known from late Hallstatt and early La Tène periods. An alternative interpretation is that it is from a base; a bowl from an inhumation at Chamesson, 'Bouchot-Bouchard' had multiple feet, consisting of projections similar to those on No. 343 (Brun 1986, pl. 61,2). This was associated with an iron Hallstatt sword and attributed to Brun's Etape 3 (Ha B2–C) (Brun 1986, pl. 68).

Shallow troughs of possibly hemispherical sections, No. 375, Form 17, are similar to vessels which were apparently used for the transport of marine salt at Hooidonksche Akkers (van den Broeke 1980, fig. 25, 2–4). These examples from Highstead were all found in the fill of Pit B215 (*see* pp. 268–9, below). They were extremely fragmentary and one or more vessels may be represented. From Pit B128, sherds of a base from a rectangular vessel, Form 70, which has been shown by chemical analysis to have contained salt, may belong to the same vessel as 375.

Most of the remaining styles of decoration are not sufficiently distinctive to be dated closely; but there is one exception: Sherd 189, from Gully A191 is decorated with horizontal grooves and oval stab impressions (D39) broadly similar to an example from the Ha B/C urnfield at Donk (van Impe 1980b, pl. X, 1). This, together with its position within Enclosure A24, would support a Period 2 date.

The dates outlined here are based on conventional calendar dates ascribed to the continental chronological periods, using typological comparisons. This is partly due to the obvious continental affinities of the material, but also to the current problems in using radiocarbon dates from some of the appropriate British sites (Tite *et al.* 1987). While more radiocarbon dates are becoming available from excavations of settlement sites on the Continent, it is still too early for a thorough review of pottery chronologies. Much of the continental material used in this discussion is itself dated on the basis of typology, and few of the examples cited are associated with metalwork on which the original chronologies are based. While variation in the archaeological record is not solely dependant on chronology, this approach has provided an initial framework; but clearly there is a need to establish an independent chronological sequence for the Late Bronze Age/Early Iron Age in east Kent.

Technology

In Period 3B there is some evidence for local manufacture. The excavation notebook records that a large portion of the fill of Pit B133 (p. 54 and Fig. 36, layer 1) contained 'vast quantities' of unfired clay, much of it with 'white grits which occur in the Iron Age pottery'. These unfired clay lumps no longer survive, but it is likely that they represented raw material, already mixed with flint temper, ready for making pots. At the bottom of the pit was a layer of clay (Fig. 36, layer 2). It is possible that this formed the base of an area used for foot kneading (Rye 1981, 19) or trampling, an action undertaken to eliminate air pockets and ensure a homogeneous distribution of moisture and inclusions in tempered clay. While this often occurs above ground, it is also carried out in pits (Rice 1987, 119). The excavation notebook however, makes no reference to flint grits being included within the clay layer at the bottom, so such an interpretation must remain inconclusive. The clay may have been in place awaiting the arrival of suitable tempering agents before being mixed.

In addition to the unfired clay lumps, the fill also contained 287 sherds of pottery of which twenty were at least

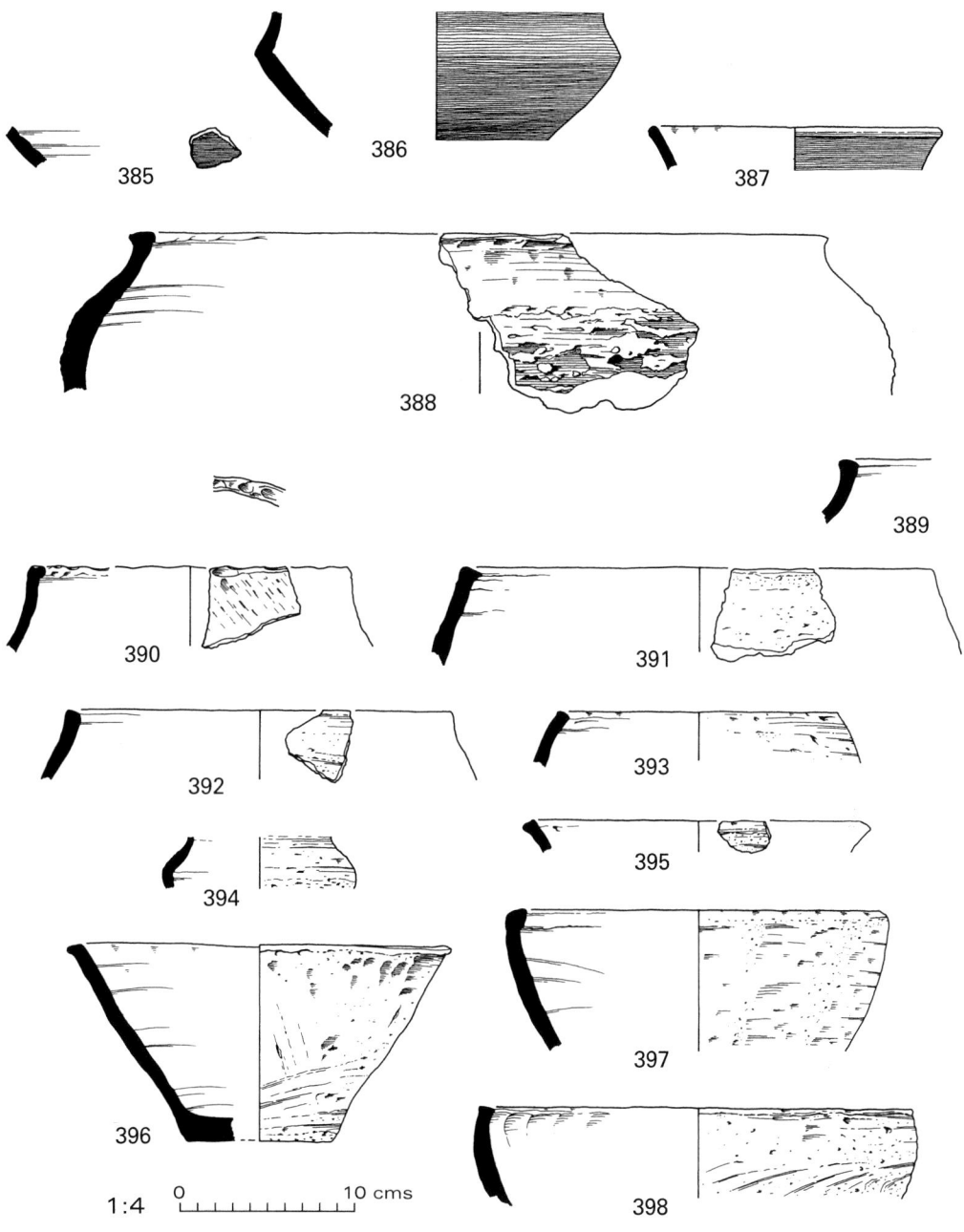

Fig. 92. Period 3B pottery. Nos 385–98, Pit B114. Scale 1:4.

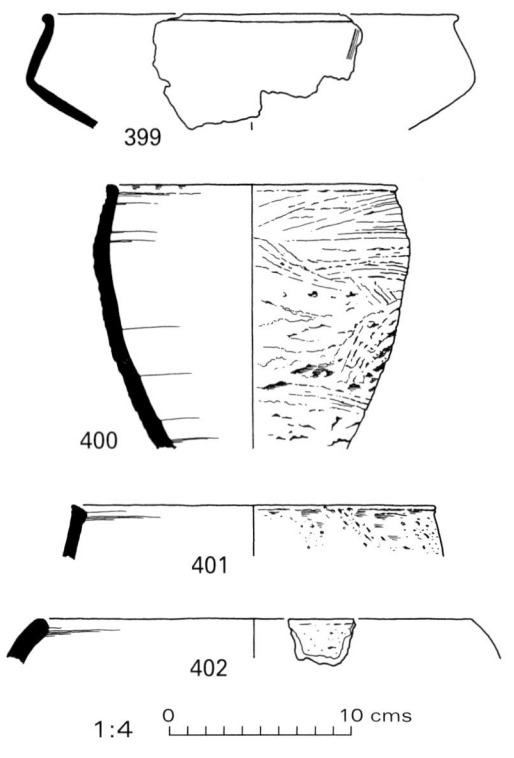

Fig. 93. Period 3B pottery. Nos 399–402, Pit B271. Scale 1:4.

partially covered with a cream layer on either the interior or exterior and, in three examples, across the fractured core. This was similar to that found on sherds in Pit B215 (pp. 268–9) and likely to have been the result of salt processing. The fill also contained a rim possibly from a salt evaporation pan (Fig. 90, No. 382). Two sherds show signs of having been burnt or refired, being coloured light grey to orange, though they need not have been wasters. The remaining sherds, including ninety-three with moderate to heavy rustication, were like any others found on the site and provide the main dating evidence. The pottery appears to have been found throughout the fill, interspersed among the lumps of unfired clay, suggesting that it and the clay had been discarded in the pit rather than stored awaiting use. Whatever the function of the pit, the unfired clay lumps provide almost certain evidence for the manufacture of pottery on the site.

Few vessels revealed clear signs of their method of manufacture. In this section the slight evidence which does exist is reviewed, showing the range of techniques recognised from Periods 2 and 3.

Pinching or hand-moulding from a single lump of clay is most suited to small pots, and one likely example, No. 488, is known from Period 3. It is also possible to employ this method for fineware bowls within the size range of Forms 38–41 (Berensohn 1974, 24–35), but the evidence from Highstead suggests that this was not used. For example, Form 38 with angular profiles, or Form 40 with regular horizontal variations in the wall thickness, would be difficult to construct using this technique. Its use for larger vessels is not easily recognised, and is indeed less likely than coiling or slab building (Berensohn 1974, 55–63).

For other vessels, construction began with a flat base which was slab built. These have been classified in four categories (Types B1–B4, p. 112). Many of these have flint grits protruding beneath them (Type B1, Pl. XIII). This trait has been noticed in Late Bronze Age deposits, e.g. at Mucking, (Jones and Bond 1980, 477), Farnham Green (Elsdon 1982, 129), Runnymede Bridge (Longley 1980, 65), Ivinghoe Beacon and Brooklands, Weybridge (Hamworth and Tomalin 1977, 24, no. 23). Its distribution at Highstead suggests that it was used throughout Periods 2 and 3 (Period 2: 35 per cent; Period 3A: 15 per cent and Period 3B: 30 per cent); though the figures for the distribution of this type of base may be exaggerated since they are easily recognised, while small worn fragments of other flat bases may have been classified as wall sherds.

Most of the flat bases were wiped (Type B3) (Period 2: 43 per cent; Period 3A: 47 per cent and Period 3B: 28 per cent), except when they had been placed on a bed of calcined flint grits.

Pl. XIII. Period 2 pottery. Abundant flint grits adhering beneath a flat base.

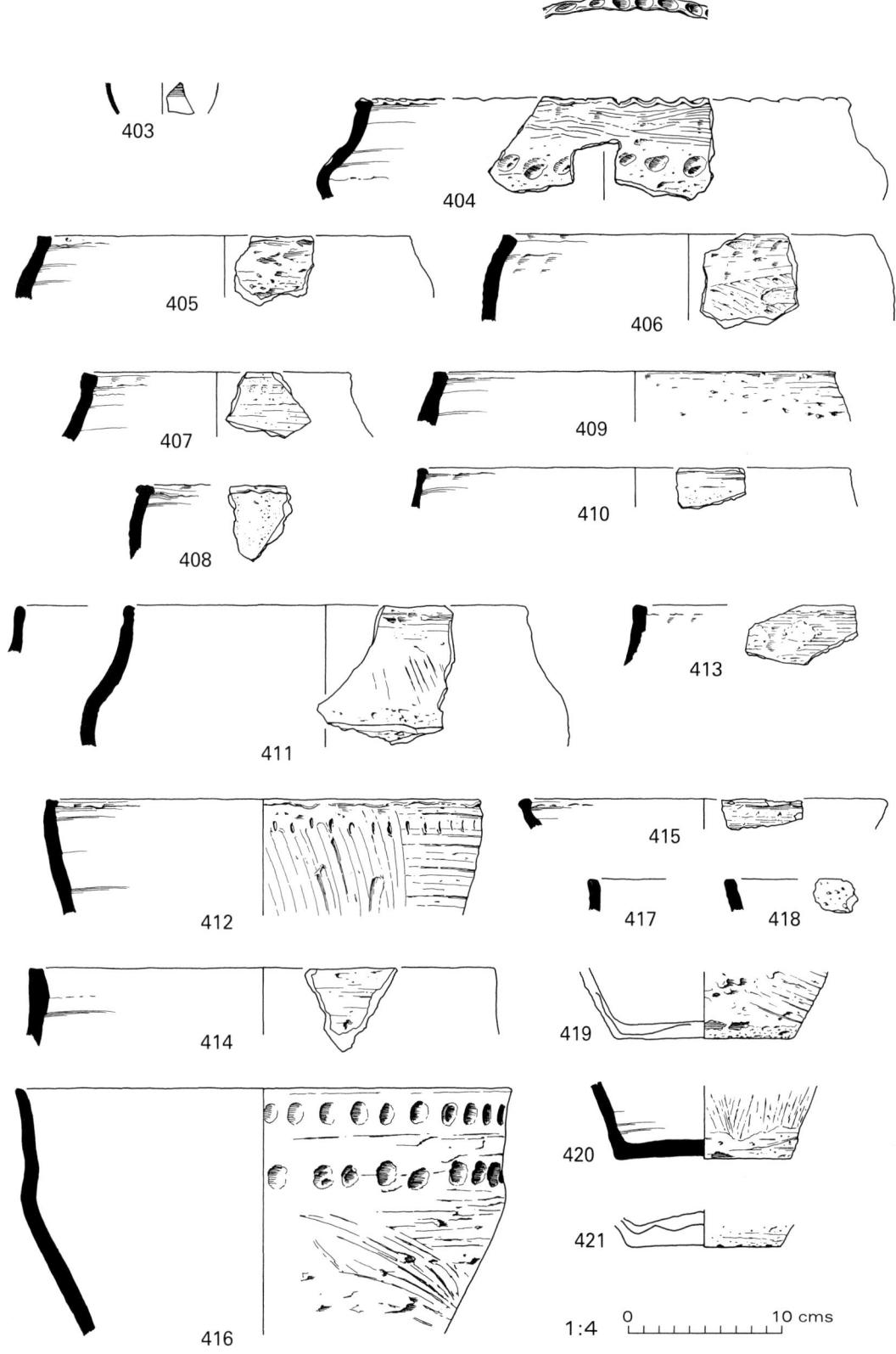

Fig. 94. Period 3B pottery. Nos 403–21, Pit B124. Scale 1:4.

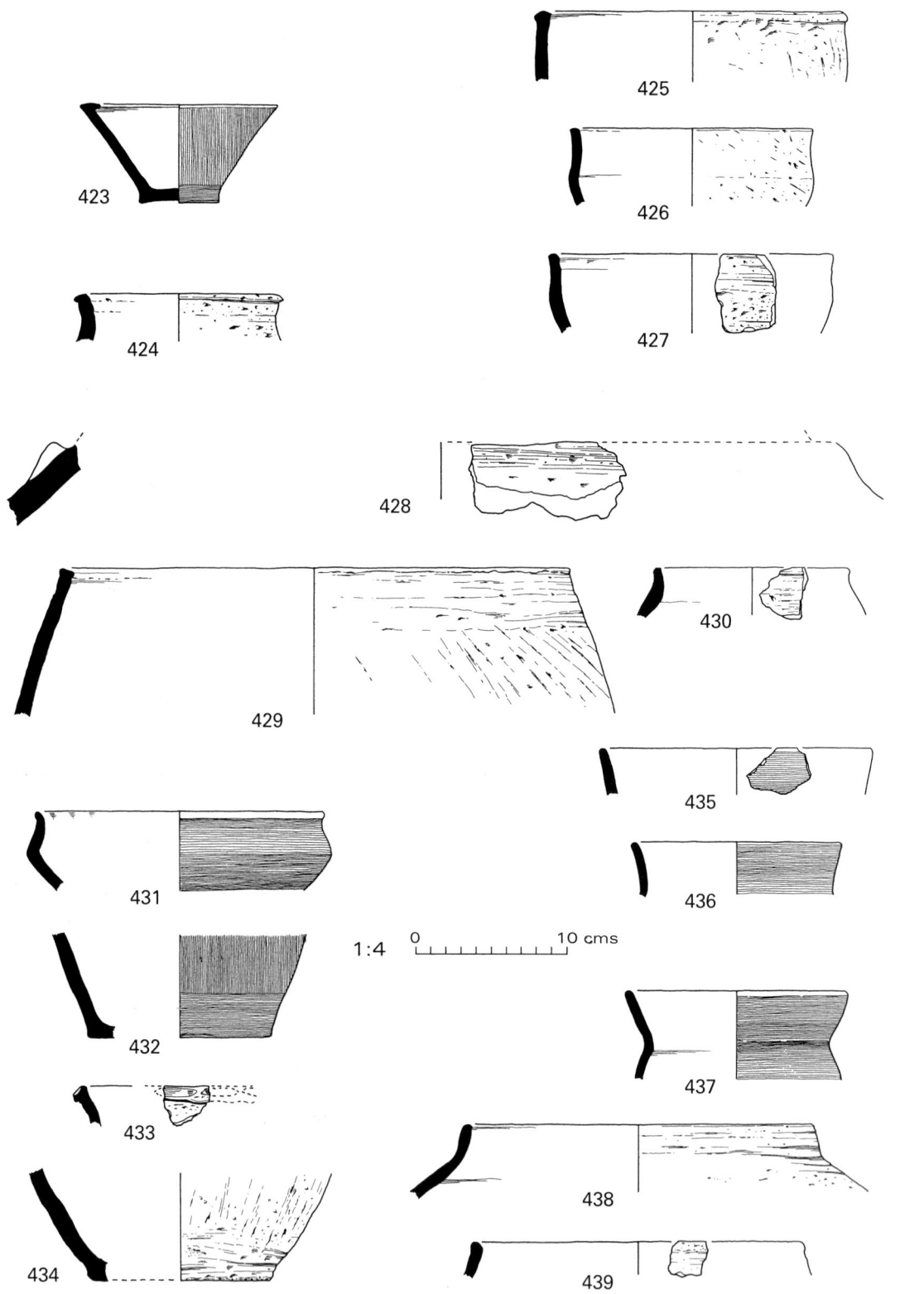

Fig. 95. Period 3B pottery. No. 423, Pit B147; No. 424, Pit B168; Nos 425–7, Pit B195; Nos 428–30, Pit B214; Nos 431–4, Pit B119; No. 435, Pit B126; No. 436, Hearth B132; Nos 437–9, Pit B172. Scale 1:4.

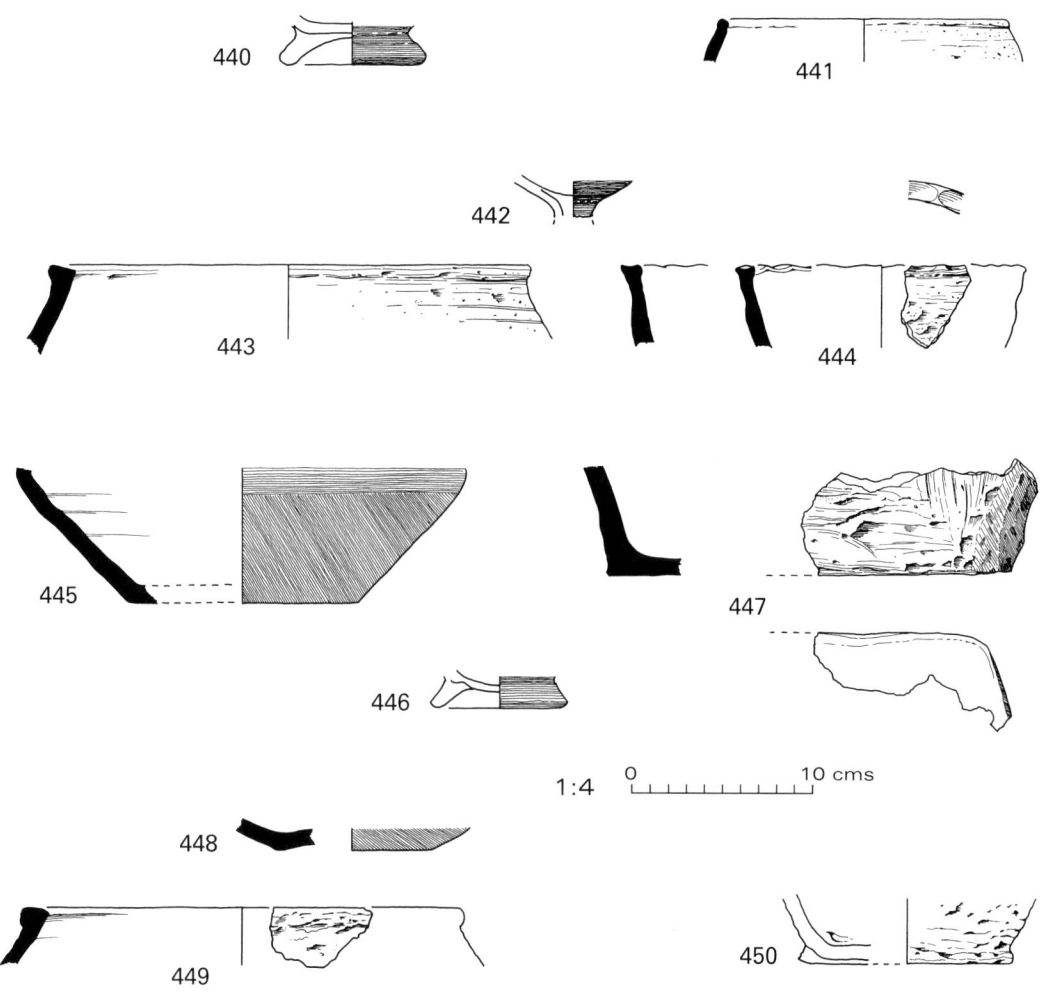

Fig. 96. Period 3B pottery. No. 440, Hearth B180; No. 441, Hearth B228; Nos 442–4, Pit B247; Nos 445–7, Pit B128; Nos 448–9, Pit B146; No. 450, Pit B218. Scale 1:4.

The walls of the pots were then built on these slab bases. Sometimes, e.g. 178, the wall was constructed leaving the edge of the base protruding, and on other examples an additional coil was added to the exterior of the base, perhaps to strengthen the join, producing the same effect. Some examples, such as 490 show the wall built eccentrically over the base. Exceptionally a few vessels show that additional coils were added to the inside of the wall to strengthen the join.

Many sherds have single edges which show signs of having broken along the line of an original join. Sometimes a pair of parallel edges shows this characteristic. While these could reflect the use of slab construction, they are probably more likely to represent coil building, and this, in the absence of evidence to the contrary, appears to have been the preferred method of manufacture for most of the vessels from Periods 2 and 3.

Apart from the bases, clear evidence of slab building, although sometimes cited as common in Late Bronze Age/Early Iron Age cermics, is rare at Highstead. One storage jar, however, from Period 2, 188, has surface marks which reveal details of its construction: horizontal tiers of slabs, with their edges pressed together, were arranged with staggered vertical joins. The surface was then wiped. The resulting pattern, still visible on the surface, closely resembles Rye's illustration (1981, fig. 55e) of that associated with slab construction. Other examples are not so readily identified.

Slab building was used however for the construction of the walls and bases of the rectangular vessel 447.

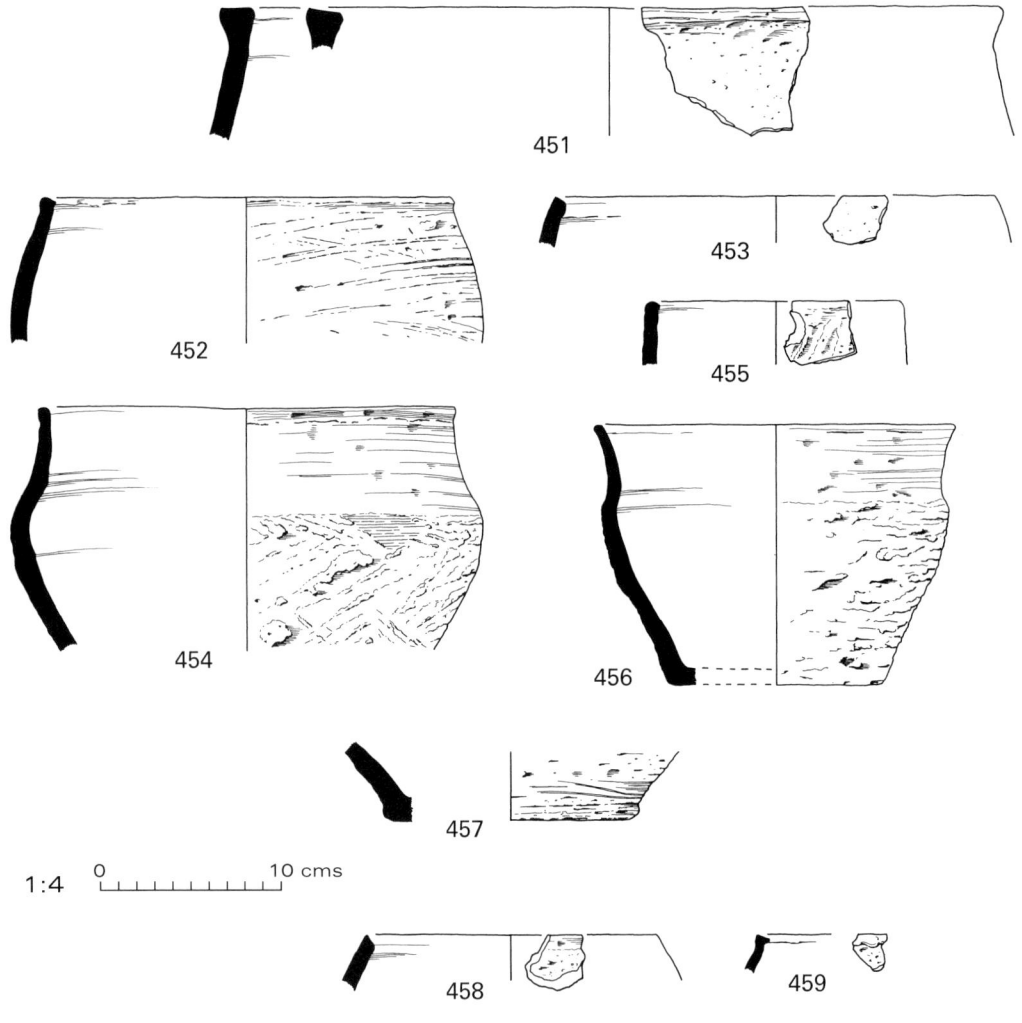

Fig. 97. Period 3B pottery. Nos 451–7, Pit B245; Nos 458–9, Pit B248. Scale 1:4.

Occasional use of the potter's wheel is known on the Continent from late Hallstatt times (Wells 1980, 58), but although it is possible that some of the fineware bowls were constructed in this way, no positive evidence for this survives at Highstead. The use of flint-tempered fabrics, while occasionally employed for wheel-turned vessels in the Late Iron Age (Thompson 1982, 13), is likely to have hindered its adoption here.

While coils or slabs were being added to the walls, their surfaces were wiped or smoothed to strengthen and hide the joins. After their initial formation, the walls would begin to dry out, a process which had to be controlled to prevent cracking. Additional surface treatment was then applied at different stages of the drying.

A classification of the range of surface treatment has been described above and Table 9 shows its distribution during Periods 2 and 3. These broad categories cover a wide range of techniques. Rare examples (e.g. 202) have vertical or diagonal drawing marks where walls have been pulled upwards as part of the formation process (cf. Rye 1981, fig. 57b). As the clay became drier, scraping the surface with a hard sharp implement would produce flint drag marks, a trait sometimes found on larger jars (cf. Rye 1981, fig. 71 and 72).

At the leather hard stage the heavy slip or slurry used for rustication would have been applied. This rustication can have a variety of forms, from a wet slurry with lumps of clay and flint (Pl. XIV) to a harsher, drier application

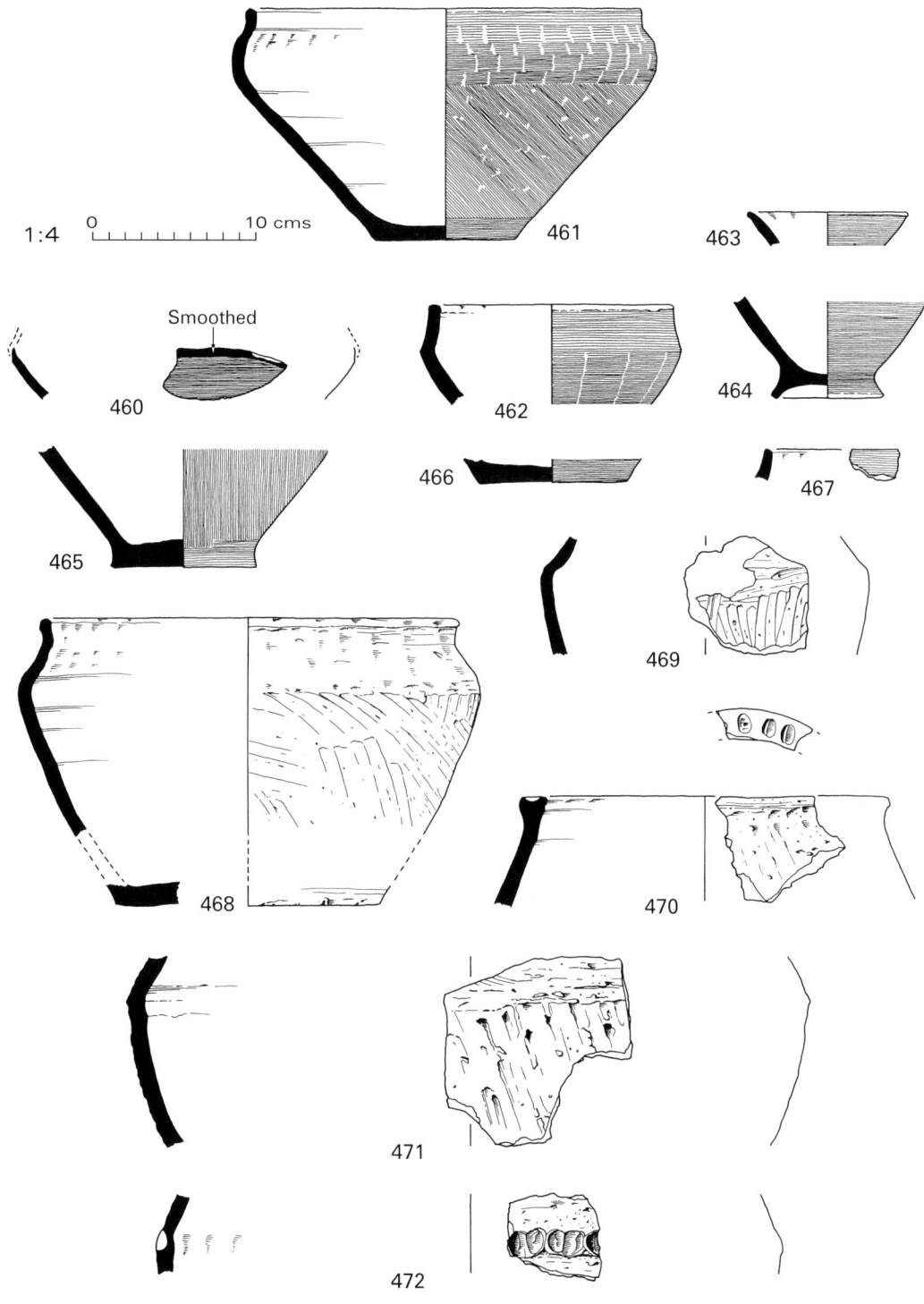

Fig. 98. Period 3B pottery. Nos 460–72, Pit B266. Scale 1:4.

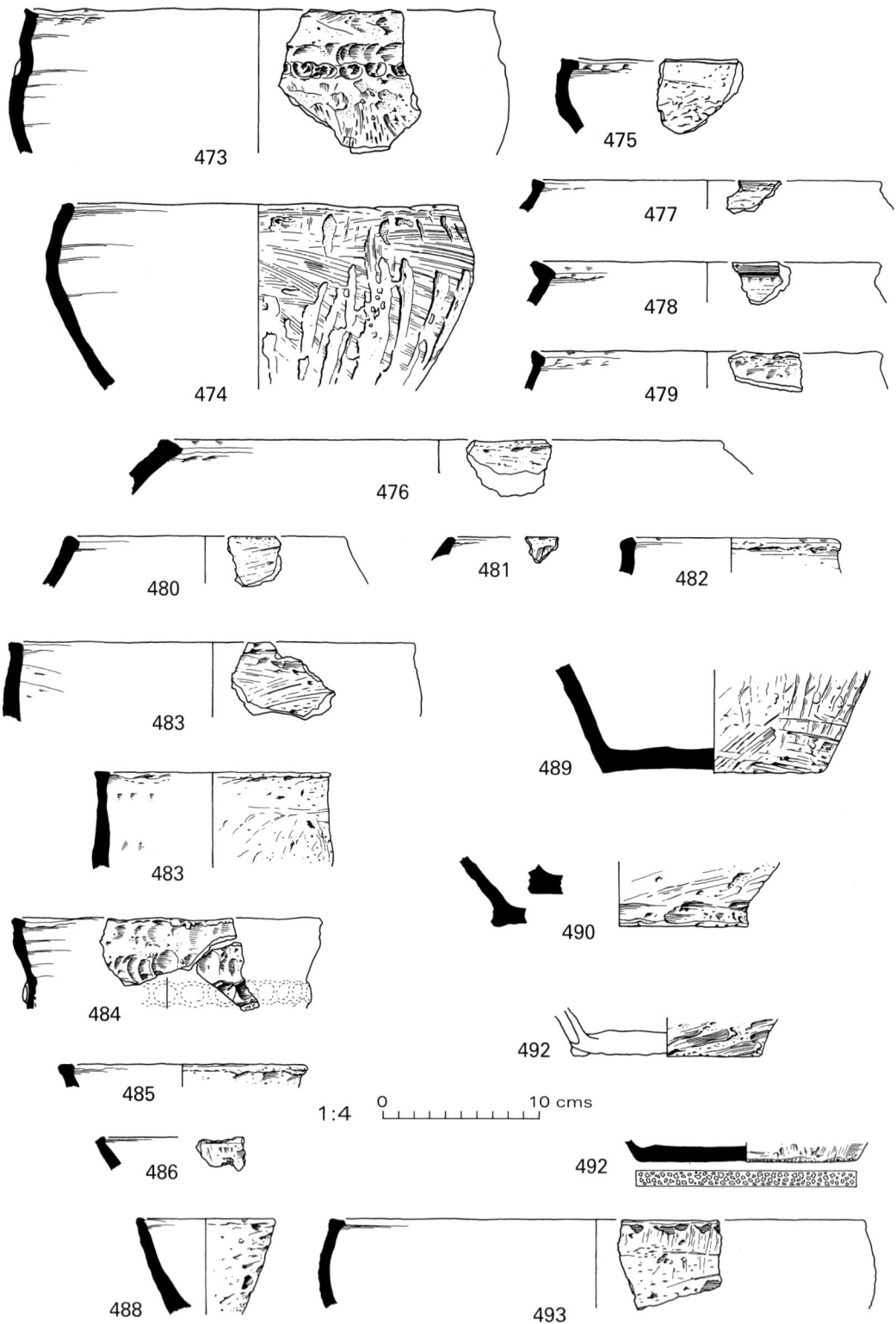

Fig. 99. Period 3B pottery. Nos 473–93, Pit B266. Scale 1:4.

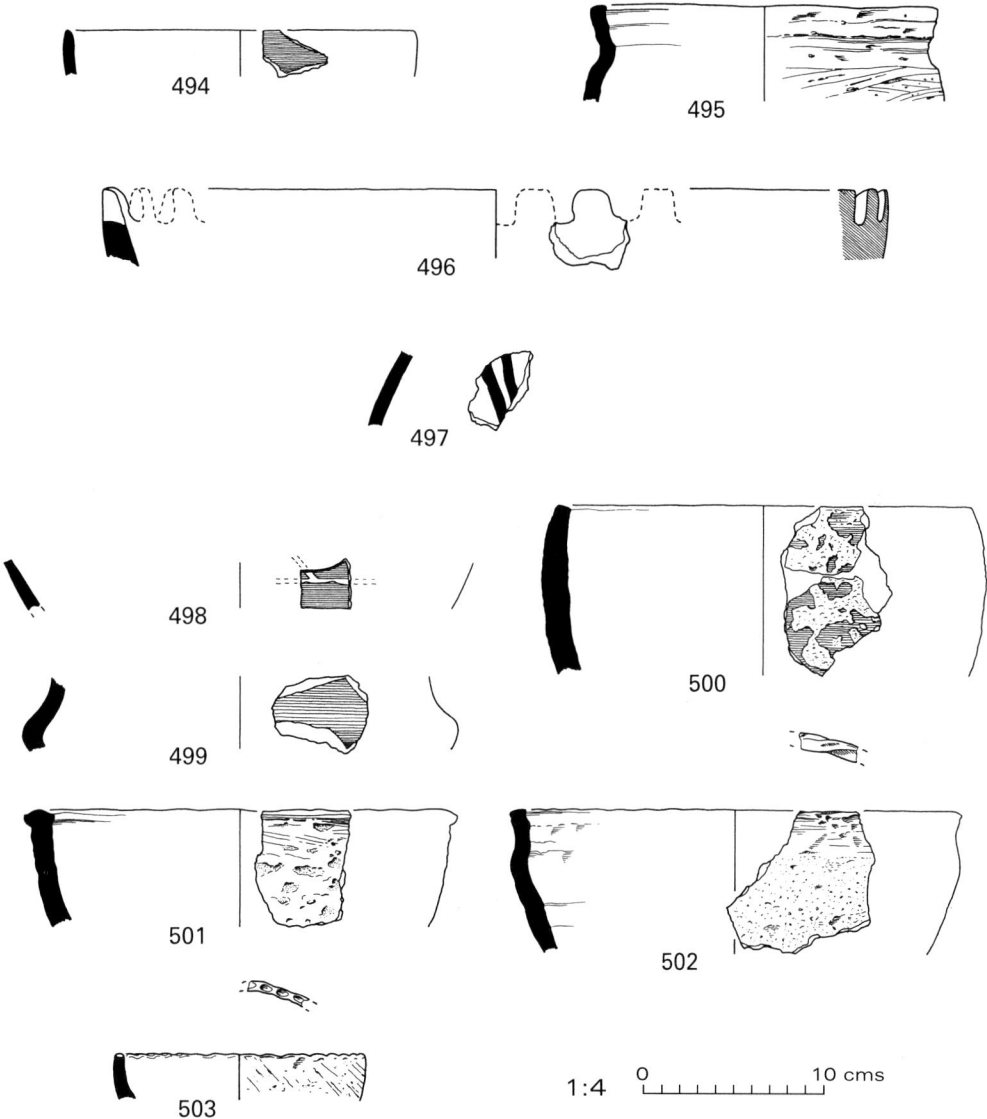

Fig. 100. Period 3B and unstratified pottery. No. 494, Pit B267; No. 495, Post-hole B38; No. 496, Post-hole B40; No. 497, ?painted design, unstratified; Nos 498–503 residual in Pit complex B15 (No. 498, red-finished with painted design). Scale 1:4.

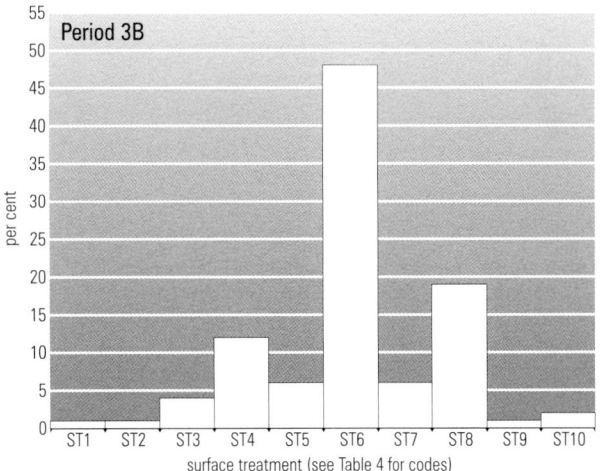

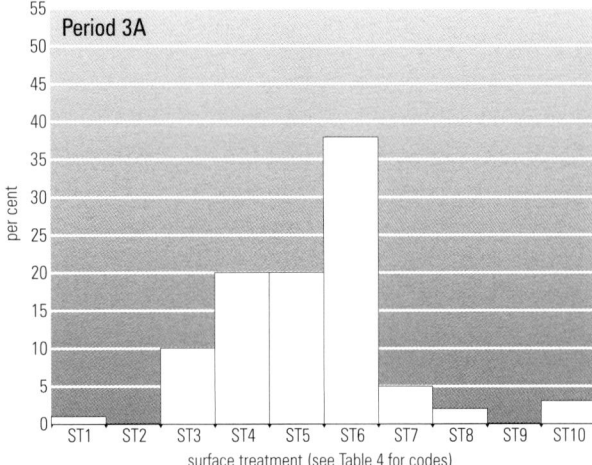

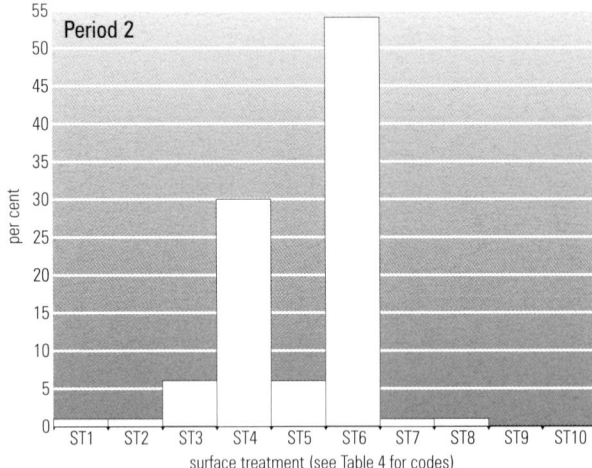

Table 9. Distribution of types of surface treatment during Periods 2 and 3.

which produces an almost pebble-dashed effect (Pl. XV) or a mixture of the two. In some cases the fabric of the clay used for rustication differed from that of the main body of the pot, e.g. that on 400, which contains noticeably more iron oxide than the main body.

Also at the leather hard stage, cordons would have been applied (one example has been placed onto grooves possibly to increase adhesion, Pl. XVI). Burnishing and polishing would have been carried out and a fine slip or paint applied at this stage or later. Laboratory examination shows that the haematite coating on vessel 368 was applied by burnishing (*see* pp. 301–2) and this would have required a hard surface. The painted design was added after the burnishing.

Some vessels received a variety of treatments at different points on the surface. Most noticeably, Forms 33 and 61 were burnished above the shoulder and rusticated beneath (Pl. XV). Both of these processes would have been carried out while the clay was leather hard.

When the wall was strong enough, the pot could be turned over and the base wiped, smoothed or burnished (B3–B4) and a pedestal added. There is one example of a pedestal base from Pit B12, 286, attributed to Period 3A, though this may be intrusive. Four of the remaining examples are from Period 3B features: B128, B133, B180 and B266. One from B138, attributed to Period 4A, may be residual.

The evidence also shows that decoration was applied at different stages of drying. Finger-tip decoration was often applied while the clay was still plastic. This displaced the clay and produced raised edges, e.g. on the rims and shoulders of 113, 117 and 389. The clay may have been in a soft leather-hard stage for some shallower examples. Grooved and stabbed designs without raised edges, would have been cut while the clay was leather hard, as would the small triangular decoration (D23) (Rye 1981, 66).

There is no evidence for any surface treatment being applied after the pots had been fired.

The percentage distribution of surface treatment throughout Periods 2 and 3 is shown in Table 9. From this it is evident that there was a tendency for pottery to become coarser during Period 3, particularly with the widespread adoption of rustication (Type ST8). At the same time there is a corresponding increase in the thickness of walls. This is apparent from vessels with plain convex profiles (Table 7), but is also found when examining all the sherds from this period (Table 10). Taken together these trends create a general impression of decline in the standards of pottery manufacture. Although there are obvious examples of fine vessels during Period 3B, such as 368, the thin walls of Period 2 and the use of flint temper less than 0.5 mm. in size rarely appear during Period 3B.

The initial impression though, that the quality of the pottery had fallen, that it was manufactured with less care and more hurriedly, is not supported by closer study. By examining the methods of application of decoration and

Pl. XIV. Period 3B pottery. Rusticated surface.

The evidence of fabrics suggests that most of the vessels could have been manufactured locally. Head Brickearth is found within 2 km. from the site, both to the south-east towards Chislet and to the north-west at Broomfield. Particle-size analysis has shown that clay grades make up between 9–30 per cent of this brickearth, and that they contain iron oxides and quartz with some glauconite (Smart *et al.* 1966, 213–6). This would probably have provided suitable clay, after preparation, to form the matrix for most of the fabrics, with the exception of Fabrics 21 and 29, which had a heavily glauconitic sandy matrix. While fragments of flint are sometimes present in the brickearth, it appears that this source was rarely used. The evidence from the pottery is that calcined grey flint was predominant and that this was deliberately added as temper. Its source may have been the Upper Chalk, which is found about 1 km. to the south-east (Holmes 1981, 24–5; Smart *et al.* 1966, 142–62).

Two fabrics (21 and 29) have a glauconitic sandy matrix, and Fabric 21 has sparse inclusions of apparently calcined flint up to 0.50 mm. in length. These fabrics are represented

surface treatment, it is possible to gain a broad, if rather simplistic, understanding of the number of stages required in the manufacture of this pottery. It is evident that although the walls had become thicker and the surfaces coarser, vessels made during Period 3B required just as many stages of manufacture as those of the earlier periods. The effort required to produce a rusticated surface was not insignificant. Potters were still capable of producing spectacular finewares with burnished and painted surfaces. The roughening of the surfaces on the coarser wares was a deliberate change in style and this pottery was not apparently produced more hurriedly or with less care than the earlier material.

Continental influence

It will be evident from the parallels cited in the discussion of chronology that much of the pottery shares traits with continental material. Positive evidence for actual imports however, is slight. When looking for likely imports, it is convenient to consider three groups of vessels: those whose fabrics demonstrate that they could not have been manufactured locally; high quality finewares, which may have been made by specialist, rather than local, potters; and those whose manufacturing technique required unusual skill, possibly reflecting external influence.

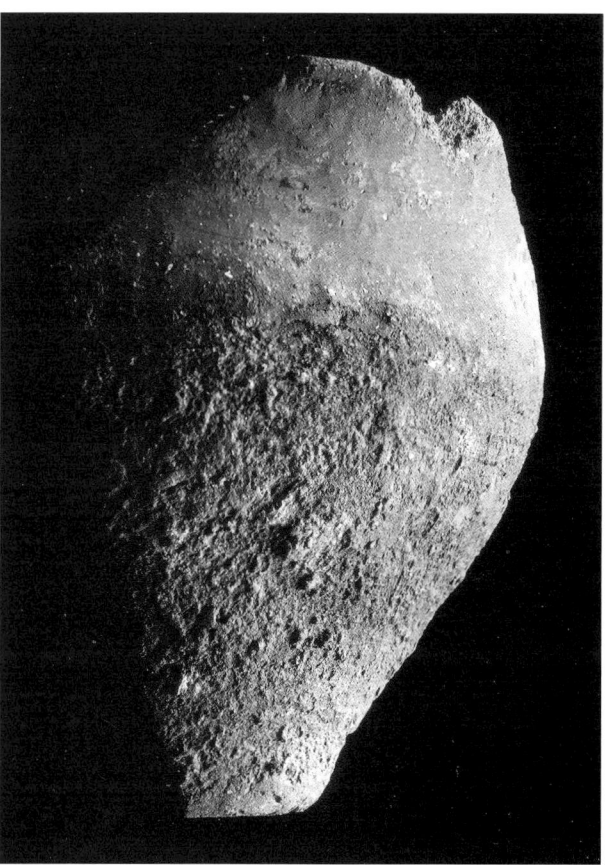

Pl. XV. Period 3B pottery. Bowl no. 456, with burnished surface above the shoulder and rustication beneath.

Pl. XVI. Period 2 pottery. Detail of cordon applied to storage jar (No. 188).

by only five sherds. Glauconite occurs sporadically in the brickearth, but not in a sufficient quantity for use as the source for these fabrics. A more likely local source of this is the Bullhead Bed, a sub-division of the Thanet Beds, which outcrops to the south and east of Highstead. This includes sub-rounded quartz grains and rounded grains of glauconite (Smart *et al*. 1966, 176–8 and 182–8). However, clays containing the appropriate quantity and size of grains have still to be located, and it is possible that vessels in these fabrics were not made locally. Such fabrics are known from the upper Medway valley, around Maidstone, where they become more common during the Middle and Late Iron Age (Thompson 1982, 7, map 2, Greensand fabric).

The small cup, 192 (Pl. XVII), in addition to being made from fine glauconitic sandy clay (Fabric 21), has thin walls (3–4 mm. thick) and neatly executed decoration. It clearly represents the work of an accomplished craftsman. Fragments of vessels with similar decoration have been found at other sites in Kent, as at Aylesford near Maidstone (Barrett 1980, fig. 6.10), though not in the same fabric, and it is possible that they were manufactured at one location and 'traded'. A more detailed analysis of morphology and fabric, and comparison with vessels from other sites, is required to demonstrate this. Other interpretations are still possible: they may represent the work of itinerant potters, or of local potters with selective access to the finer clay. It is probably misleading to regard those who made the cooking and storage vessels of coarser fabrics as less competent than those who made the fineware bowls. Each vessel was made according to its requirements and a very fine-grained fabric would not have been suitable for cooking-pots.

The use of an unusual and specialised technique, is to be found in the use of inlaid decoration on vessel 368. This was evidently made by a highly skilled potter, who was familiar with the method used on the Continent. The flint-tempered fabric of this pot however (Fabric 8), suggests that it was probably of local manufacture.

It appears then that all of the vessels could have been made locally and that probably none were imported from the Continent. Nevertheless, it is clear that the pottery reveals familiarity with the styles and techniques found across the Channel and some degree of contact is evident. The continental parallels cited above have been primarily aimed at establishing a chronology and no attempt has been made to provide a detailed survey of all related types. However, the evidence established does allow some preliminary observations to be made.

Some of the forms from Period 2 occur widely throughout southern and eastern England and France, maintaining a tradition that existed certainly as early as the Early Bronze

Pl. XVII, Period 2 pottery. Late Bronze Age/Early Iron Age cup (No. 192).

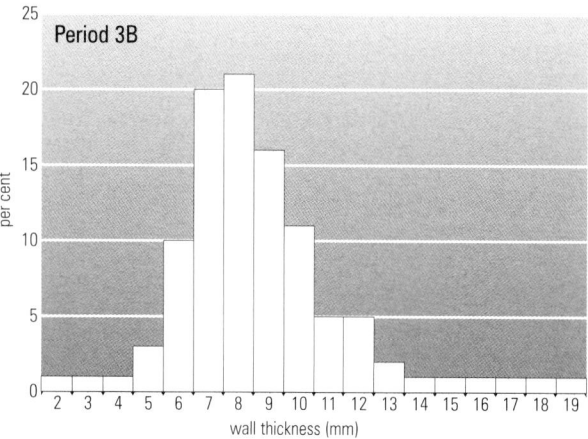
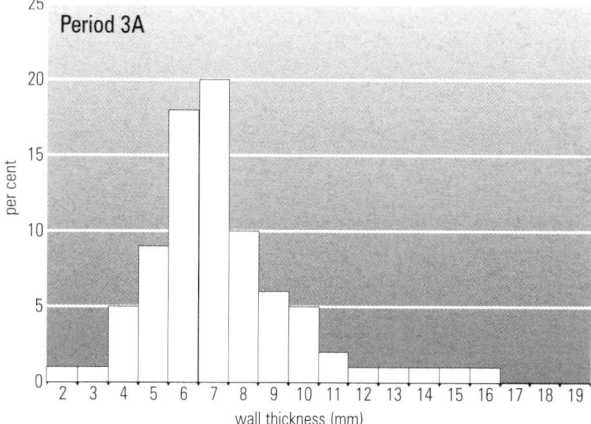
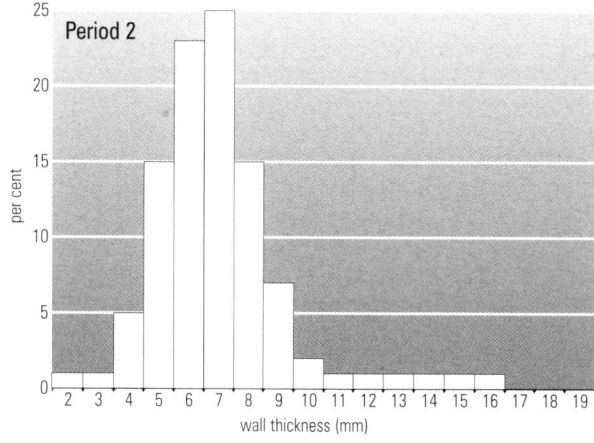

Table 10. Distribution of wall thickness during Periods 2 and 3.

Age. As an example, the distribution of jars broadly similar to Form 58, with neck cordons decorated with finger-tip impressions, extends from north-eastern France, through western France and into northern Spain (Burgess 1987, fig. 4).

Other forms and decoration exhibit a more restricted distribution: In particular the bowls and jars with light horizontal grooved decoration (Forms 40, 41, 56 and 73) occur in Belgium and north-eastern France, though those with perhaps the closest similarities are found in Court-St-Etienne and sites in Hesbaye, an area corresponding to Desitterre's Central- and South-Belgian group (Desittere 1968, 136, Kaart 2). In Britain their distribution also extends up the lower Thames valley.

Although Period 3A witnesses a shift of location from enclosed to an open settlement, the pottery does not reflect any sudden stylistic change. Instead, we see a continuation of the existing forms and the adoption of rusticated (*éclaboussée*) surface treatment. This need represent no more than a maintenance of the same level of contact with the Continent, but because it involves surface treatment, and is recognizable from small wall sherds rather than only identifiable forms, it is more easily distinguished than earlier traits and perhaps creates a superficial impression of stronger continental influence. In practice, the number of forms closely paralleled on the Continent is small. A feature of the rusticated vessels, shared by Highstead and the material from the Lower Rhine, is the variety of plain convex profiles. These were common, but varied in detail and the forms were evidently less clearly defined than in earlier periods. Nevertheless, if the Ha D date is accepted for the arrival of rustication at Highstead, current evidence suggests that the source of this tradition was Belgium, rather than north-east France, where such surface treatment is not found until early La Tène.

In addition to vessels with rusticated surfaces, others have been paralleled with forms across the Channel. Many are found in Belgium, or southern Netherlands and some in France. In particular, Form 35, with inlaid painted designs, has traits closely paralleled in the Marne region. However, fineware vessels with 'Marnian' traits are known from the Low Countries (cf. de Laet 1982, fig. 273) and some may have been imported. As a rule decorated examples are found in Belgium and the southern Netherlands rather than further north. Thus the presence of 'Marnian' style pottery at Highstead need not imply direct contact with the Marnian zone, where other aspects of the archaeological record exhibit strong regional variation (Duval 1984), but with people further north..

However, comparison of pottery from sites on either side of the Channel is distorted in two ways. Firstly, there are differences in the contexts: while most of the Highstead pottery is fragmentary and evidently represents domestic refuse, much of the continental evidence is from cemeteries with deliberate burial of complete vessels representing a restricted, more formal, range of ceramics. Secondly, little is known about the settlement of north-east France, particularly from the departments bordering the Channel: Pas-de-Calais, Somme and Seine-Maritime. Excavations at Inghem, (Pas-de-Calais) (Leman 1982) may provide some information for the Late Bronze Age/Early Iron Age, but most of the evidence for activity during this period is confined to bronze hoards often recovered by accident (Blanchet 1984, 221–374). From the early La Tène period, recent excavations have provided evidence of settlements (Lemain-Delerive 1984) and these have produced material comparable with that from Highstead and other sites in east Kent.

Since this report was first written the picture has changed with a considerable increase in the number of excavated and published sites in north-eastern France, producing new evidence of cross-Channel contact from the Early Bronze Age to early La Tène Iron Age (e.g. Blancquaert and Bostyn 1998; Hurtrelle *et al.* 1990; Desfossés *et al.* 2000; Bourgeois and Talon 2005). The broad pattern of the use of rustication has not changed (it is still not found in France until the early La Tène period), but more detailed stylistic links are now evident between northern France and east Kent.

In conclusion, it has been argued that some degree of continental contact may be recognised throughout Periods 2 and 3, but it is evident that the range of forms and decoration shared across the Channel represents just a subset of the ceramic repertoire current at the time. While this may reflect differing contexts, it appears that there was no wholesale borrowing or imposition of ceramic tradition, nor is there a single location to propose as a source of contact, migration or invasion. Rather, the evidence from Highstead suggests that the Channel was no barrier; each community was aware of the ceramic traditions and fashions of its neighbours, but chose to borrow or imitate those traits, forms and styles of decoration it found suitable.

Catalogue of illustrated vessels from Periods 2 and 3

This catalogue provides a summary description of the illustrated vessels, showing the context, fabric code, form and decoration as defined in the text. The internal and external surfaces and core are described by colour, followed by a surface treatment code, as defined in Table 4 (0 denotes original surface has worn away). The following codes are used for colour: bk, black; br, brown; d, dark; gr, grey; l, light; or, orange; rd, red; yel, yellow.

Pot No.	Context	Fabric	Form	Decor	Interior	Exterior	Core	Pot No.	Context	Fabric	Form	Decor	Interior	Exterior	Core
1	B70	1	F28		dgr.5	dgr.4	dgr	46	B70	2	F2		lgr/br.4	dgr.4	lgr
2	B70	1		D31	dgr.4	dgr.4	gr/dgr	47	B70	1			dgr.4	dgr.5	dgr
3	B70	1	R1		dgr/br.4	dgr.4	dgr	48	B70	1	B1		dgr.5	dgr.4	dgr
4	B70	2	F39	D27	dgr.4	dgr/br.4	dgr	49	B70	1	F61		dgr.6	dgr.6	dgr
5	B70	2			gr/br.3	dgr.4	dgr	50	B70	1	F61		orbr.6	orbr.6	lgr
6	B70	1	F57		gr.5	gr.5	gr	51	B70	1		D5	dor/br.6	dor/br.5	dor/br
7	B70	1		D3	dgr.6	dgr.6	dgr	52	B70	1			gr/br.6	gr.5	dgr
8	B70	1			gr/br.4	gr/br.5	dgr	53	B70	1	F30	D4	lbr/gr.5	lbr/gr.5	lbr/gr
9	B70	4	F62		bk.4	or/br.4	dgr	54	B70	1			br.5	dgr/br.5	gr
10	B70	2	F6		br/dgr.4	br/dgr.4	dgr	55	B70	1			dgr.5	dgr.6	bk
11	B70	1	F4		gr.5	lgr/gr.4	gr	56	B70	1		D4	gr.6	gr/br.6	dgr
12	B70	1	F43		bk.4	bk.4	gr	57	B70	1		D5	dorbr.6	dorbr.6	dorbr.6
13	B70	1	B1		dgr.6	dgr.6	dgr	58	B70	1		D4	gr.6	gr.6	dgr
14	B70	1			br/gr.4	dgr.4	dgr	59	B70	1			dgr.6	dgr/br.5	dgr
15	B70	1			dgr.5	dgr.5	dgr	60	B70	1			dgr.4	dgr/orbr.4	dgr
16	B70	2			dbr.6	lbr/dgr.5	lgr/yelbr	61	B70	1		D4	dgr.6	dgr.6	dgr
17	B70	1			dgr/br.6	gr.5	dgr	62	B70	1			gr.6	dgr.6	dgr
18	B70	1			dgr.5	gr5	dgr	63	B70	2	F65		br.5	gr.5	gr
19	B70	1	F55	D19	dgr/br.6	dgr.6	dgr	64	B70	11			dgr.5	dgr.5	dgr
20	B70	1			gr/br.5	gr.6	gr	65	B70	1	F2		gr.5	dgr.5	dgr
21	B70	1		D3	dgr/lgr.6	gr/br.6	lgr	66	B70	1	F4		dgr.5	dgr/dbr.5	dgr
22	B70	3		D4	dgr/br.6	br.0	dgr	67	B70	1	F16	D11	gr/br.5	gr/br.6	gr
23	B70	1		D4	bk.5	gr.6	dgr	68	B70	1			or.6	or.6	or
24	B70	1		D4	dgr.4	dgr/orbr.4	dgr	69	B70	1	F25		gr/br.6	br/dgr.6	gr
25	B70	1	R7		gr/br.6	gr/br.6	gr	70	B70	1			dgr.5	dgr.5	dgr
26	B70	1			dgr.5	gr/dbr.5	dgr	71	B70	1		D25	dgr.5	dgr/dbr.5	dgr
27	B70	1			gr/br.5	gr.6	dgr	72	B70	1			bk.5	dgr.8	dgr
28	B70	1			dgr.6	br.6	gr	73	B70	1		D4	dgr.4	dgr.5	dgr
29	B70	1			dgr.6	dgr.6	dgr	74	B70	1			dgr.6	dgr.6	dgr
30	B70	2			yel/gr.6	lgr/br.6	yel/br	75	B70	1			gr/br.5	dgr.5	dgr
31	not used							76	B70	1			gr.6	dgr.5	dgr
32	B70	1			dgr/br.5	drd.1	dgr	77	B70	4	R7		or/br.5	or/br.5	gr
33	B70	1	F53	D38	gr/br.4	dgr.3	dgr	78	B70	2	F26		bk.5	br/bk.3	dgr/bk
34	B70	1	R5	D27	dgr.3	dgr.3	gr	79	B70	1			dgr.5	dgr/dbr.5	dgr
35	B70	1	R3		dgr.4	dgr.3	dgr	80	B70	2	F6		gr.5	dgr/gr.5	dgr
36	B70	1			gr.3	gr.3	gr	81	B70	1		D5	gr/br.5	gr.6	dgr
37	B70	1	R2		gr.4	gr.3	dgr	82	B70	1			lbr/gr.5	lbr/gr.5	lbr/gr
38	B70	1	R5		dgr.3	dgr.3	gr	83	B70	1			dgr.6	dgr/br.5	dgr
39	B70	1			dgr.4	dgr/br.3	dgr	84	B70	1			br.4	rd/br.1	dgr
40	B70	1			gr/br.4	gr/br.4	dgr	85	B70	2	B1		dgr.3	dgr.5	gr
41	B70	1		D21	dgr.5	dgr/gr.5	dgr	86	B70	1			dgr.4	dgr.3	dgr
42	B70	8	F6		dgr/brgr.4	dgr/brgr.5	dgr	87	B70	11		D24	dgr.4	gr/dgr.6	dgr
43	B70	1	F5		gr/dgr.5	dgr/4	dbr	88	B70	1		D10	dgr.5	dgr.5	dgr
44	B70	1	F4		br.3	br.3	bk	89	B70	3	F18		dgr.6	gr/dgr.6	dgr
45	B70	1	F6		dgr.6	dgr.6	lgr	90	B70	1			br.6	dbr/gr.5	gr

Pot No.	Context	Fabric	Form	Decor	Interior	Exterior	Core	Pot No.	Context	Fabric	Form	Decor	Interior	Exterior	Core
91	B70	1	F75		dgr.5	dgr.4	dgr	144	A24	1		D4	gr.4	gr.5	dgr
92	B70	2	F72		dgr	drd.1	dgr	145	A24	2	F48		dgr/dbr.6	dgr/br/orbr.6	gr/dgr
93	B70	11			dgr.3	dgr.3	dgr	146	A24	1			gr/br.6	gr/br.6	dgr/br
94	B70	1	R5		dgr.4	dgr.3	gr	147	A24	2	F57		dgr/br.5	dgr/dbr.4/5	lgr
95	B70	1	F4		gr/br.5	gr/br.5	gr	148	A24	2	R2	D3	gr/br.6	gr/br.6	gr/br
96	B70	4	F4		dgr/br5	gr/br.6	gr	149	A24	2	F58	D10	br.4	br.4	lgr
97	B70	4	F43		dgr.3	dgr/lbr.4	dgr	150	A24	1			dgr.4	br/gr.5	gr
98	B70	1			dgr.5	dgr.3	dgr	151	A24	2			gr/rdbr.6	or/br.6	gr/or
99	B70	1			dgr.6	or/br.5	gr	152	A24	2	F36		dgr/br.6	dgr.6	dgr
100	B70	1	F42		dgr.4	lbr.4	gr/br	153	A24	1			dgr.6	gr.6	gr/br
101	B70	2	F49	D29	br.0	br.0	dgr	154	A24	13			gr.6	dgr.4	dgr
102	B70	1			dgr.5	gr.6	lgr	155	A24	1			gr.0	lrd.0	gr
103	B70	1			dgr/br.6	gr.6	dgr	156	A24	1			lbr.5	lbr.5	gr/lbr
104	B70	1			dgr.5	gr.6	dgr	157	A24	1			gr/lbr.6	gr/lbr.5	dgr
105	B70	1			dgr.6	dgr.6	gr	158	A24	1			dgr.6	gr/br.6	dgr
106	B70	1		D10	gr/br.5	br.5	gr	159	A24	2			lbr.5	lgr/dbr.0	lgr
107	B70	13		D10	dgr.4	lbr.4	lgr	160	A24	1	B1		dgr.6	gr/br.6	dgr
108	B70	1		D22	gr/br.5	gr.6	gr	161	A24	6			dgr.5	gr.0	rd/orbr
109	B70	2		D20	br.6	gr.6	gr	162	A24	2			lgr.5/0	dgr/br.6	dgr
110	B70	4		D20	lgr.6	br/gr.6	gr	163	A24	2			dgr.4	dgr.5	dgr
111	B70	4		D20	lgr.6	br/gr.6	gr/br	164	A24	1			dgr.6	dgr.5	dgr
112	B70	1		D23	dgr/br.4	dgr/br.4/3	gr	165	A24	2			gr.5	dgr.6	gr
113	B70	1			dgr.5	dgr.5	dgr	166	A24	1			dgr.6	dgr/dbr.6	dgr
114	B70	1	F55	D29	dgr.5	dgr.5	gr	167	A24	1			gr.6	gr/br.6	gr
115	B70	1	F62	D11	dgr.6	dgr.6	dgr	168	A145	1	R2		dgr.4	dgr.3	dgr
116	B70	2	F55	D29	dgr/grbr.5	dgr.5	gr	169	A181	1	F54		dgr.3	dgr.4	gr/br
117	B70	1			gr.6	gr.5	gr	170	A152	16	F23		dgr.6	dgr/dbr.6	dgr/br
118	B70	1		D29	gr.6	gr.6	gr	171	A152	1		D20	gr.6	gr.6	gr
119	B70	1	R3	D1	lbr.5	lbr.5	gr	172	A2	1	F39	D27	dgr/bk.3	dgr.3	dgr
120	B70	2		D1	gr.6	dgr.6	gr/dgr	173	A2	1	F41	D27	br/dgr.3	br/dgr.3	dgr
121	B70	4	F31		lgr/br.6	dgr/br.5/6	dgr	174	A2	1			lbr.6	lbr.4	gr
122	B70	1	F26		dbr/gr/bk.5	dbr/gr/bk.5	dgr/bk	175	A2	2	F60	D29	br/dgr.6	orbr.6	dgr
123	B70	1	F26		gr.6	gr.6	gr	176	A2	1	R2		br.6	gr.6	dgr
124	B70	3	F63		dgr.5	dgr.6	bk	177	A2	1		D10	dgr.0	or/br.5	lbr
125	B70	1			dgr.5	dgr.5	gr	178	A2	2	B1		or.6	or.6	or/dbr
126	B70	1	R7		or.6	or.6	dgr	179	A2	1			gr.6	br/5	or/br
127	B70	1			dgr.5	dgr.6	gr	180	A3	2	F59	D37	dgr.0	gr/0	dgr
128	B70	2	F57		dgr.5	dgr/lgr.3	dgr	181	A3	2	F60		orbr/dgr.6	orbr/dgr.6	dgr
129	B70	2	R2		dgr.6	dgr.6	lgr	182	A3	1	R2		dgr/5	dgr/3	dgr
130	B70	2	F57		gr.6	gr.6	gr	183	A4	2		D27	dgr/br.3	dbr/gr.3	dgr/br
131	B70	1		D7	gr/dgr/6	dgr/dbr.6	lgr	184	A4	1	F39		dgr.3	dgr.3	dgr
132	B70	1	F27	D4	bk.5	bk.5	bk	185	A4	2	B1		dgr.4	lyelbr.4	gr
133	B70	1	F13		bk.5	bk/br.5	bk	186	A4	2			dgr.2	dgr/grbr.2	dgr
134	B70	2	F6		bk.5	dgr.3/5	bk	187	A4	1	B1		dgr.2	lbr/gr.2	dgr
135	B70	1	F6		dgr.4	gr/dgr.3	gr	188	A4	1	F60	D9	dgr.5	br.3	lgr
136	B70	1			gr/br.4	gr/br.5	dgr	189	A191	2		D39	dgr.4	dgr/br.4	dgr
137	B70	1			dgr.5	dgr/br.5	lgr	190	A191	1			dgr.3	dgr.3	dgr
138	A24	1		D2	0	or/br.0	lgr	191	A191	2			lgr/br.4	lgr/br.4	lgr/br
139	A24	3		D16	dgr.4	drd.1	dgr	192	A5	21	F39	D28	dgr.3	dbr/gr.4/3	dgr
140	A24	1	F41	D27	dgr.3	dgr.3	gr	193	A5	1	F28		dgr/br.3	dgr/br.3	dgr/br
141	A24	4	F39	D27	dgr.3	dgr.3	dgr	194	A5	1			dgr.5/0	dgr.3	dgr
142	A24	3	F56	D27	gr/dgr.4/2	dgr.4/2	gr/dgr	195	A5	14			dgr.3	dgr.3	br/gr
143	A24	1	F48		dbr.6	dgr.6	gr/br	196	A5	2		D9	lbr/gr.6	lbr/dgr.3	lbr/gr

Pot No.	Context	Fabric	Form	Decor	Interior	Exterior	Core
197	A5	1	F22	D3	br/dgr.5	br/dgr.5	br/dgr
198	A8	2			br.3	br/gr.3/0	lgr/orbr
199	A8	2	F57		dgr.4	dgr/grbr.4/2	dgr
200	A50	1	F28		gr.6	dgr.5/6	dgr
201	A155	1	R2		dgr.4	dgr.6	dgr
202	A180	1	F45		dgr.6	dgr.6	dgr
203	A180	1	F4		dgr.7	br.6	dgr
204	not used						
205	A227	3			gr/br.5	gr.6	gr/br
206	A19	2	F11		rdbr/dgr.5	rdbr/dgr.4/3	gr/grbr
207	A47	2		D9	gr/br.5	gr/br/5	gr
208	A47	1			dgr.5	dgr.5	dgr
209	A153	1			dgr.4	dgr.5	dgr
210	A153	2	F73	D27	dgr.6	dbr.3/4	dgr
211	A179	11			dgr.5	dgr.5	dgr
212	A187	2	F40	D27	dgr.3	dgr.3	gr
213	A187	2	F66		dgr.4	br.4	dgr
214	A187	2			dgr(lbr).4	dgr(lbr).3	dgr
215	A u/s	2		D14	dgr.4	br/dgr.4	dgr
216	A u/s	2	F28		gr/br.3	gr/br.3	gr
217	A u/s	2	R1		dgr.3	dgr.3	lgr
218	A u/s	2	R1		dgr.3	dgr.3	gr
219	A u/s	2			dgr/br.5	dbr/gr.6	dgr
220	A163	1	F14	D4	dgr.5	dgr.7	dgr
221	A143	3			br/gr.6	br/gr.6	br/gr
222	A100	1	F48		br.6	br/dgr.6	dgr
223	A129	1	F61	D4	or/br/dgr.6	or/br/dgr.6	or/br/dgr
224	A130	1	F60		br/dgr.6	lor/br.6	dgr
225	A208	1	F46		dgr/br.5	dgr.6	dgr
226	A u/s	1	F59	D10	gr/br.5	dgr/br.4	dgr
227	B317	2		D31	lgr.4/0	gr/or.0	gr
228	B317	1			lgr/orbr.0	gr(or).0	lgr
229	B317	1		D2	dgr.6	0	lgr
230	B317	1	F53	D32	dgr.4/2	dgr.4/2	dgr
231	B317	2			dgr.5	gr/dgr.4	gr
232	B317	2		D27	bk/dgr.4/0	gr.4/5	gr
233	B317	1	R5		dgr.6	dgr.6	dgr
234	B317	15			gr.3	gr/dgr.4	dgr
235	B317	1	F5	D8	dgr.4	dgr/bk.4/2	dgr
236	B317	1	F5		gr.5	dgr(br).4/0	gr
237	B317	2	F7		lorbr.4	gr/br.4	gr/br
238	B317	2	F60		gr/dgr.5	gr/dgr/br.4	gr/br
239	B317	2	F60		dbr/dgr.6	dgr/grbr.5	br
240	B317	1			orbr/lbr.5	br.4	or/dgr
241	B317	1			br/dgr.5	br.4	gr
242	B317	1			dgr.4	dorbr.4	gr/br
243	B317	1			dgr.0	br/bk.0	lgr
244	B317	1			dgr.6	gr/br.6	gr
245	B317	1	R2		br(orbr).4/2	gr/br.3	dgr
246	B317	2			dgr.4	dgr/br.4	dgr
247	B317	2			or.4/0	or.4/0	or
248	B317	2			dgr.5	gr(or/rd).5	dgr
249	B317	1			lgr/br.6	lgr/orbr.6	lgr
250	B317	1			bk.4	br/dgr.4	dgr
251	B317	1			dgr.6	dgr.5	dgr
252	B79	2	F40	D27	dgr/gr.3/2	dgr.4	dgr
253	B79	1			dgr.3	dgr/br.5	dgr
254	B79	2			dgr.6	dgr/orbr.0	gr/dgr
255	B80	2	F39		dgr.3	dgr.2	dgr
256	B80	1	R3		dgr.4	lgr/br.3	gr
257	B80	1			0	gr.5	gr
258	B80	1			gr/4	gr.3	gr
259	B80	1	F36		gr/br.5	gr.6	gr/br
260	B80	1			dbr.6	dgr.6	gr
261	B80	1	R3		dgr.5	lgr/br.5	lgr
262	B80	2			dgr.6	dgr/br.6	dgr
263	B80	1			br.6	gr/dgr.6	dgr
264	B81	1			dgr/br.5	dgr/br.5	dgr/br
265	B81	2			dgr.5	dgr/br.6	dgr
266	B84	1			dgr.4	dgr.3	dgr
267	B84	1			dgr.3	dgr.3	dgr
268	B u/s	1	F53	D4	gr/br.5	gr/br.5	gr
269	B u/s	1			dgr.3	dgr.4	dgr
270	B u/s	1		D4	dgr.4	dgr.4	dgr
271	not used						
272	B92	1	F59	D10	br.5	gr.5	dgr
273	B92	1			gr.6	br.6	dgr/br
274	B92	2			gr.6	gr/br.6	lgr/lbr
275	A118	2	R1		dgr.3	lgr/orbr.3	gr/lgr
276	A118	2			dgr.5	dgr.5	lgr
277	A118	1	F4		dgr.6	dgr.6	lgr/dbr
278	B144	1	F40	D27	br.0	gr/or.0	lgr
279	B144	2		D3	lor/br.5	dgr.5	lgr
280	B144	1	R4		dgr.6	dgr/br.6	dgr
281	B12	1		D27	gr.3	gr/br.3	dgr
282	B12	1			dgr/lbr.5	lbr.4	gr/dgr
283	B12	1	R3		dgr.4	dgr.4	dgr
284	B12	3			dgr.3	dgr.3	dgr
285	B12	1			gr/dgr.4	dgr/gr.3	gr/dgr
286	B12	1	B5		dgr.4	dgr.3	dgr
287	B12	2	F3		dgr.6	dgr/lbr.5	gr/dgr
288	B12	1	F10	D13	gr.3	dgr/br.6	gr
289	B12	1			gr/br.5	gr.5	dgr
290	B12	1	F9	D3	dgr.6/0	dgr.6/0	dgr/br
291	B12	1			dgr/gr.5	gr.5	gr/gr
292	B12	2			lgr.6	lgr/br.6	dgr
293	B12	1	F19		dgr.3	br/gr.8	dgr
294	B12	3			gr.3	gr/dgr.6	gr/dgr
295	B12	1			gr/br.5	gr.5	dgr
296	B12	1	F58	D10	bk.5	br/dgr.4	dgr
297	B244	1	F40	D27	dgr.4	gr/dgr.4	dgr
298	B244	1	F40	D27	dgr.4	gr/dgr.3	gr/dgr
299	B244	2	F34		dbr/dgr.3	dbr/dgr.4	dgr
300	B244	1			dgr.6	dgr.6	dgr
301	B244	11	F10	D4	dgr.5	dgr.5	dgr
302	B244	1	F18		dgr.6	dgr.6	dgr

Pot No.	Context	Fabric	Form	Decor	Interior	Exterior	Core
303	B244	1			dgr.6	dgr.6	dgr
304	B71	1	B1		orbr.6	br.6	dgr
305	B131	1			dgr.4/2	dgr.4/2	dgr/br
306	B131	1			br/gr.3	br/gr.3	br/gr
307	B131	3	F66		dbr/gr.6	lgr/gr.6	dgr
308	B131	2			or/br.6	or/br.6	or/br
309	B131	1	F57		gr.5	dgr.5	dgr
310	B131	1			lbr.3	lbr.3	lbr
311	B131	1			dgr/br.5	dgr/br.10	dgr/br
312	B131	1	F40	D27	dgr/gr.3	dgr/gr.3	gr
313	B131	2			gr/lbr.6	dgr.6/0	gr
314	B131	2			gr/lbr.6	dgr.6	gr
315	B131	1	F66		dgr/br.6	dgr.6	dgr/br
316	B131	2	R7	D6	lbr.6	br.6	dgr/gr
317	B68	1	F38	D27	lor/br.5	dgr.4	dgr
318	B68	1			dgr.6	dgr.5	dgr
319	B49	1	F29		gr/5	dgr/6	dgr
320	B36	1			dgr/dbr.6	dgr.6	dgr
321	B270	2		D31	dgr/br.5	dgr/br.6/7	dgr/br
322	B u/s	1	F40	D27	dgr.3	dgr.4/0	lgr
323 - 330	not used						
331	B16	2	F47		dgr.6	dgr.6	dgr
332	B16	3			lgr.4	lgr/br.5	gr/lgr
333	B16	1			gr.6	dgr.5	dgr
334	B26	1	R6		or/br.4	or/dgr.3	dgr/lbr
335	B26	1	F8		dgr.4	dgr.6	dgr
336	B26	3			dgr/grbr.6	dgr/.4	dgr
337	B325	2	F18		dgr.2	dgr/br.4	dgr
338	B325	1			gr.4	br/dgr.5	gr
339 - 344	not used						
345	B189	2			lgr.4/0	lgr.4/0	lgr
346	B189	1	F52		gr/br.6	gr/dgr.7	dgr
347	B188	1	F37		dgr.5	gr.6	dgr
348	B174	1			dgr.4	dgr.3	gr
349	B174	1	B1		dgr.6	gr.6	gr
350	B200A	1			gr.4	dgr.4	gr/dgr
351	B200A	1	R4		lgr.4	lgr.4	gr
352	B200A	2		D36	or/br.6	or/br.9	or/br
353	B200A	3	F25		dgr.6	dgr/orbr.6	dgr
354	B200A	1	F25		dgr.6/3	dgr/br.3	dgr
355	B200A	3	F18		dgr.6	dgr.6	dgr
356	B200	1			dgr.4/0	dgr.4/0	dgr
357	B200	13			dgr.5	dgr.5	dgr
358	B200	1			dgr.0	dgr.0	yel/br
359	B200	1			or/br.6	gr/lgr.6	gr/lgr
360	B226	2		D20	br.6	dgr/br.6	dgr/br
361	B226	1	F21		dgr.0	dgr/rdbr.0	lgr
362	B177	1	B6		lbr.4	lbr.4	lbr
363	B203	1	F61		gr/br.6	gr/br.5	dgr/br
364	B203	11			dgr.4	dgr.5	dgr
365	B203	1			br/gr.6	dgr/grbr.6	dgr
366	B207	1			rd/br.6	dgr/rd/br.6	dgr
367	B207	1		D20	dgr.3	br.6	dgr/br
368	B196	4	F35	D40	dgr.3	dgr/rd.1/2	br/gr
369	B196	9	F51		dgr.3	br/grbr.6	dgr
370	B196	3	F25		lbr.6	gr/br.6	dgr
371	B196	2	F14		or.6	or.6	dgr
372	B197	1	F25		orbr/dgr.6	lgr.6	lgr/gr
373	B215	2	F52		dgr/orbr.4&7	lbr.4	lgr/grbr
374	B215	11			or.4	or.4	or
375	B215	1	F17		or/br.7	or/br.7	or/br
376	B215	1			or/br.4	or/br.4	or/br
377	B215	11			or.5	or.4	or
378	B314	2	F37		dgr.5	br/dbr.4/5	dgr
379	B314	1			dgr.6	gr/dbr.6	dgr
380	B133	17	F71, B5	D2	lor/rd.0	lor/rd.0	lor/rd
381	B133	1	F61		gr/br.5	gr/br.6	gr
382	B133	2	F69		lgr/or.5	lgr/or.7	lgr/or
383	B154	2	F2	D4	gr/dgr.0	dgr/lyelbr.0	dgr
384	B166	2	F34		gr/br.4	gr/br.4	dgr
385	B114	1		D42	gr.4	dgr.4	gr/br
386	B114	11	F34		lor/br.4	dgr/ltbr.2	lgr
387	B114	1	R2		dgr.4	dgr/lgr.4	dgr/lgr
388	B114	2	F52		dgr.5	dgr.5	drdbr
389	B114	1			dgr.6	dbr/dgr(or).6	dgr
390	B114	1		D4	dgr.6	dbr/dgr.6	dgr
391	B114	1			dgr/gr.6	lgr.6	lgr/dgr
392	B114	1			dgr.6	lgr/lbr.6	gr
393	B114	3	F1		dgr.6	gr/dgr/orbr.4	gr
394	B114	1			gr.5	gr/br.6	dgr
395	B114	1			gr.6	gr.6	gr
396	B114	2	F18		br/gr.5	gr/br.3	dgr
397	B114	2	F14		gr/lbr.3	dgr.4	dgr
398	B114	1	F14		gr.5	gr/yelbr.4/6	gr/dgr
399	B271	1	F34	D18	dgr.3	dgr.4	gr/dgr
400	B271	2	F12		gr/br.5	gr/br.6/8	gr/br
401	B271	1			gr.6	gr.6	gr
402	B271	1	F1		dgr.4	br/gr.5	gr
403	B124	1		D31	gr/dgr.4	gr/dgr.4	dgr
404	B124	1	F61	D29	gr.3	dgr.3	gr
405	B124	1			br/gr.6	br/gr.3/6	br/dgr
406	B124	1	F10		gr.3	gr/dgr.3/7	gr
407	B124	1			dgr/br.6	dgr.6	dgr
408	B124	1	F12		dgr.6	lgr/br.6	dgr
409	B124	1	F9		dgr.3	dgr.6	dgr
410	B124	1			br/dgr.6	lgr.6	lgr
411	B124	1	F61	D26	lbr/dgr.3	gr/lbr.5	dgr
412	B124	1	F14	D20	br/dgr.5	br/dgr.6	orbr/dgr
413	B124	1			gr/br.6	gr/br.6	gr
414	B124	2	F68		lbr.6	br.4	gr
415	B124	1			dgr.4	dgr.5	br/dgr
416	B124	2	F24	D12	dgr.3	dbr/gr.6/10	gr
417	B124	1			br/gr.3/0	br/gr.3/0	gr
418	B124	1			gr/br.6	gr.5	dgr

Pot No.	Context	Fabric	Form	Decor	Interior	Exterior	Core
419	B124	1			gr/or/br.5	or/br.5	rd/orbr
420	B124	1			br.3	br.4	dgr
421	B124	2			gr/br.4	gr/br.4	gr
422	not used						
423	B147	1	F21		dgr/br.3	dgr/br.2	dgr
424	B168	3			gr.6	or/br.6	dgr
425	B195	4	F44		dgr.3	dgr.5	dgr
426	B195	3			dgr.3	br.4	dgr
427	B195	11			yelbr.4	yelbr.4/6	yelbr
428	B214	1	F67		br/dgr.6	dgr.6	dgr
429	B214	4	F9		or/br.6	lbr.5	lbr/dgr
430	B214	1			dbr.6	dgr/br.6/0	dgr
431	B119	3	F34		dgr.4	dgr.4	dgr
432	B119	3			dgr.5	dgr.5	dgr
433	B119	3		D4	gr/br.6	dgr.5	dgr
434	B119	3			dgr.5	dgr.5	dgr
435	B126	12	R3		dgr.3	dgr/br.3	gr
436	B132	1	R6		dgr.4	dgr.3	dgr
437	B172	3	F64		gr.4	gr.4	dgr
438	B172	2	F50		gr.6	lbr.6	dgr
439	B172	2			gr/dgr.4	gr/dgr.5	gr
440	B180	1	B5		dgr.3	gr/br.3	dgr
441	B228	1			br.4	orbr.6	gr/orbr
442	B247	1			gr.4	gr.3	dgr
443	B247	1	F51		gr.5	or/br.5	dgr
444	B247	1	F25	D4	dgr.6	dgr.6	dgr
445	B128	1			dgr.3	dgr.3	dgr
446	B128	2	B5		dgr/br.4	dgr/br.4	dgr
447	B128	1	F70		or.6	or.6	or
448	B146	1	B6		dgr.3	dgr.3	dgr
449	B146	1	F51		gr/br.6	gr/br/7	dgr
450	B218	1			dgr.6	brgr/dgr.6	dgr
451	B245	3	F51		lbr/gr.6	lbr/orbr/gr.6	gr/br
452	B245	1	F12		dgr.6	gr/dgr.6/10	dgr
453	B245	1			or/br.6	or/br.6	gr
454	B245	4	F61		dgr.3	dgr/br.2/8	dgr/br
455	B245	1	F44		dgr.6	br/gr.3/6	dgr
456	B245	1	F33		rd/br.4	dgr.8	dgr/dbr
457	B245	7			dgr.6	dgr/br.10	gr
458	B248	1			dgr.6	dgr.6	lgr
459	B248	1	F8		br.6	or/br.6	gr
460	B266	3			br.6	br.6	bk/br
461	B266	1	F32		gr/dgr/br.3	gr/dgr.4	gr/dgr
462	B266	1	F34		dgr.3	dgr.3	dgr
463	B266	1			bk.4	bk.4	bk
464	B266	1	B5		gr/orbr.3/0	gr/br.3/0	orbr/dgr
465	B266	1			lbr.4	lbr.3/4	dgr/lbr
466	B266	3			dgr.6	dgr/gr.5	dgr
467	B266	1			gr.4	gr.4	gr
468	B266	1	F32		grbr/dgr.5/3	bk/dgr/br.3/6	dgr
469	B266	4			br/orbr.6	gr(orbr).6	gr
470	B266	1	F51	D4	rdbr.5	rdbr/bkgr.4	dgr/bk
471	B266	1			br.6	gr/br.6	dgr
472	B266	1		D20	dgr/br.5	dgr/dbr.6	br
473	B266	1	F12	D20	bk/orlgr.6	bk/grbr/br.4/6	lgr/br
474	B266	4	F13		dgr/gr.6	dgr.7	dgr/gr
475	B266	1	F13		gr/dgr.6	gr/dgr.6	bk
476	B266	1	F8		orbr.6	gr.6	bk
477	B266	3			dgr.5	dgr.5	dgr
478	B266	3			dgr/gr.4	dgr/gr.5	dgr
479	B266	3			dgr.5	dgr.5	dgr
480	B266	3			drdbr.6	br.6	dgr
481	B266	3			dgr/gr.4	dgr.0	grbr/bk
482	B266	3			dgr/gr.4	gr/br.4	dgr
483	B266	1	F12		dgr.7	dgr/grbr.7	dgr
484	B266	1			dgr/bk.6	dgr/bk.6	dgr/bk
485	B266	1			dgr.6	dgr.6	gr
486	B266	2			gr/dgr.6	lbr.6	gr
487	B266	3			dgr/gr.4	dgr/gr.5	dgr/gr
488	B266	3	F20		gr/lbr.6	gr/lbr.6	gr/lbr
489	B266	2			dgr/br.3	br.6	drdbr/gr
490	B266	1			gr/br.6	dgr.6	dgr
491	B266	2			dgr.6	gr/br.6	dgr/br
492	B266	3	B1		dgr.6	dgr/br.5	dgr
493	B266	1			br.6	bk/br.8	bk/br
494	B267	2	F6		gr.4	gr.4	dgr
495	B38	2	F64		dgr.6	dgr.6	dgr
496	B40	1	F74		gr/br.5	Part/br.5	dgr
497	B u/s	1		D33	gr.3	gr.3	gr
498	B15	1		D41	dgr.3	dor/br/dgr.1/3	dgr
499	B15	1			dgr.3	dgr.3	dgr
500	B15	4			br.6	br.8	dgr
501	B15	1	F15		dgr.6	dbr/gr.6	dgr
502	B15	1		D3	lbr.3	dgr/orbr.6	dgr
503	B15	3	F16	D4	lgr/gr.3	br.5	dgr

The Late Iron Age pottery (Figs 101–24)

Peter Couldrey and Isobel Thompson

Late Iron Age pottery was found in Period 4 contexts and as an intrusive element in features of Periods 2–3. A few scraps were recovered from Period 5 deposits, but were clearly residual. This report concentrates on the material from Period 4. Study of the features allocated to Period 4 and 5 is helped by stratigraphical evidence which was largely missing from Periods 2–3. Unfortunately the profusion of intercutting features also presents an increased incidence of residual and intrusive sherds. Most of the pottery from Period 4 is characterised by Late Iron Age material comprising both grog-tempered 'Belgic' sherds and flint-tempered forms. The final phase, Period 4D, is post-conquest and, as well as standard Romano-British pottery, witnesses the use of a fine sandy fabric for 'Belgic' forms.

This section reports on the Late Iron Age flint-tempered material from Area B with the exception of Pit complex B15, which contained a considerable quantity of pottery from the Early Iron Age to Roman period. The large quantity of Roman pottery is responsible for its allocation to Period 4D–5A, but it has been omitted from discussion here because of the mixed nature of the assemblage. Only a small quantity was recovered from Area A. A report on the grog-tempered 'Belgic' pottery by Isobel Thompson appears below (pp. 189–214); the fine sandy ware is discussed by Marion Green with the Roman pottery (pp. 217–21). Table 13 combines information to show the distribution of the main forms, and Table 15 the main fabric groups throughout Period 4 features.

The detailed chronology of the development of Late Iron Age pottery in east Kent still requires clarification. It is evident that there was a long-established tradition of flint tempering and that this continued into the Late Iron Age and appeared alongside grog-tempered 'Belgic' vessels. The excavations at Highstead have provided examples of some of the forms in circulation, but cannot supply the much needed absolute dates.

The method of study adopted here is to define the main 'flint-tempered' forms and examine their association with each other and with 'Belgic' pottery, identifying their distribution throughout periods 4A–4D. Reference is made to the forms described by Isobel Thompson in her corpus (Thompson 1982), though inevitably, fragmentary rims from Highstead cannot always be attributed to a form defined on the basis of a complete profile.

The fabric codes employed here are the same as those defined for Periods 2–3 (*see* pp. 102–3), with the following additions:

Fabric 38: Grog with chalk: This fabric is primarily grog-tempered with the addition of sparse quantities of chalk up to 2 mm. in size (*see* p. 191).

Fabric 39: Shell: This fabric is vesicular with voids representing moderate inclusions of shell which have leached out.

Fabric 40: Fine sandy, as described by Marion Green (p. 217).

Fabric 41: Other including Romano-British.

The distribution of fabrics throughout Period 4 features is shown in Table 14. In the discussion which follows the term 'flint-tempered' is used to refer to all fabrics whose main inclusion is flint, as opposed to 'grog-tempered' which refers to those fabrics whose main inclusion is grog, i.e. Fabrics 30–38.

Flint-tempered pottery from Period 4

Peter Couldrey

Forms

Most of the recognisable forms appear to be jars. No complete profiles survived and the differences distinguished here are based on minor variations in rim profile. Some examples, such as Form 1, are similar to those from Periods 2–3 and they may be residual. They are included here to present the complete range of likely Late Iron Age forms found in Period 4 features.

F1: Plain inturned rim: 56 (A274)
F2: Inturned bead rim: 1 (B12), 39 (A255) (Thompson C1-2?)
F3: Plain inturned internally-thickened rim with flat top (club rim): 36 (B4), 48 (B164), 54 (B13) (Thompson C3)
F4: Inturned rim with slight signs of a lid-seating groove, and internal and external projections: 47 (B164) (Thompson C5-1/D3-2)
F5: Plain short upright rim on inturned concave neck: 26 (B4/B7), 30 (B7) (Thompson C4)
F6: Plain upright rim: 2 (B124), 4 (B264), 28 (B7)
F7: Plain upright rim on globular jar, offset at base of neck: 27 (B7)
F8: Thickened upright rim on globular jar. The rim and inner lip have been finished with a distinctive horizontal facetted burnish: 15 (B139), 18 (B262)
F9: Upright rim with internal thickening. The rim displays light horizontal facetting: 35 (B4), 50 (B164)
F10: Thickened bead rim. The inner surface of the rim displays light horizontal facetting: 21 (A228), 40 (B143)
F11: Short everted rim on globular jar: 6 (A139), 8 (B144), 20 (A228)
F12: Short everted rim on rounded jar with angled shoulder: 31 (B7)
F13: Everted rim on globular jar: 32 (B4), 34 (B4)

The association of forms and fabrics is shown in Table 11.

Decoration

Six main decorative styles have been identified and are listed below:

1: Rough combing or furrowing
   a) Horizontal beneath shoulder: 31.
   b) Rough horizontal combing beneath neck, diagonal below: 1
   c) Panels of diagonal combing below neck: 2
   d) Rough arcade pattern: 36, 37, 39, 48, 54, 56
   e) Horizontal above vertical combing: 43.
2: Horizontal groove around base of neck: 22, 26, 27
3: Light linear grooved decoration: 11, 12
4: Light curvilinear groove: 51
5: Broad low cordon and grooves: 7
6: Cordons and grooves producing a light rippled effect on the surface: 16, 30, 38

The association of the forms and decoration is shown in Table 12.

The nature of the assemblage

The distribution of pottery forms during Period 4 is shown in Table 13. The start of Period 4 occurs after there has been no archaeological trace of activity on the site for almost 300 years. Prior to this almost all the pottery used had been flint-tempered and a large quantity (c. 9500 sherds) was recovered from features of periods 2 and 3. Many sherds from the earlier

Fabric / Form	1	3	4	13	14	33	35	Total
1							1	1
2		1					1	2
3	1						2	3
4	1							1
5					1		1	2
6	2			1				3
7	1							1
8	2							2
9	1						1	2
10	1	1						2
11	3							3
12							1	1
13	2							2
14		1						1
15	1							1
16	3					1		4
17				1				1
18							2	2
19	1						1	2
20	1			1				2
21			1					1
22	1							1
23							1	1
24							1	1
25							1	1
Total	21	3	1	3	1	1	13	43

Table 11. Association of flint-tempered forms and fabric during Period 4.

F14: Thick short everted rim, with internal horizontal facetting, on globular jar: 17 (B191) (Thompson B5-4)
F15: Heavily everted rim on rounded jar: 7 (A260)
F16: Everted rims with straight, bevelled, internal face: 5 (B245), 24 (B1/B9), 25 (B1/B4), 37 (B4), 61 (B23)
F17: Everted bead rim: 23 (B4/B9)
F18: Short everted rim on neck, offset with cordon: 16 (B141), 38 (A255)
F19: plain everted rim: 41 (B1), 45 (B164)
F20: S-shaped jar/bowl: 9 (B18), 51 (B164)
F21: Jar with corrugated shoulder: 10 (B139)
F22: Plain open hemispherical bowl: 46 (B164)
F23: Flaring bowl: 43 (B1)
F24: Plain flaring lid: 44 (B1) (Thompson L6)
F25: Pedestal base: 42 (B1) (Thompson A4)

Decoration / Form	1a	1b	1c	1d	1e	2	4	5	6	Total
1				1						1
3		1		1						2
4				3						3
5						1			1	2
6			1							1
7							1			1
12	1									1
15								1		1
16				1						1
18									1	1
20					1					1
23				1						1
Total	1	1	1	6	1	2	1	1	2	16

Table 12. Association of form and decoration during Period 4.

occupation are likely to have been incorporated into Period 4 and later features, derived from casual loss, refuse middens which had long since been eroded away, and points where the earlier features were cut by Late Iron Age ditches and pits. This continued use of flint-tempered fabrics makes the task of identifying residual sherds hazardous.

Out of a total of 558 flint-tempered sherds found in Period 4 features, two (<0.5 per cent) had traces of red surface coating and are probably residual. Their proportion of the total is slightly less than found in Periods 2–3 (< 1 per cent, *see* Table 9). Forty-eight examples (9 per cent) had rusticated surfaces, smaller than the corresponding proportion (18 per cent) found during Period 3B (Table 9). The date of the demise of rustication remains uncertain. It is rarely found associated with 'Belgic' pottery. These from Period 4 features at Highstead may well be residual.

While it may be difficult to identify residual body sherds, very few Period 2–3 forms have been found in Period 4 features. Instead, Late Iron Age forms are clearly recognisable and provide the main dating evidence for the early phases.

Dating

Dating evidence is based on the internal stratigraphy, which has been used to define features attributed to Periods 4A–4D, and typological comparison with ceramics from other sites in east Kent. Table 13 shows the distribution of Late Iron Age and 'Belgic' forms throughout Period 4 features. The forms have been subdivided into five main fabric groups: 'flint-tempered' (Fabrics 1–16), Dressel 1B, grog-tempered (Fabrics 30–38), Fine Sandy Ware and other Roman fabrics. As can be seen, the sample of recognisable forms from periods 4A and 4B is small.

The earliest features, from Period 4A, produced five recognisable 'flint-tempered' forms: 8, 14, 18, 20 and 21. Form 20, a smooth s-profiled bowl (9 and 51) is broadly similar to the everted rim/foot-ring vessels found during *c.* 350–100/50 B.C. in west and east Kent. The light curvilinear decoration on 51 is found on examples which are likely to date late within that period, though they precede the appearance of grog-tempered pottery (Couldrey 1984, fig. 16.41; Piercy-Fox 1969, p.191, fig. 5.11). This example has smooth surfaces and a wall thickness of *c.* 5–5.5 mm. Examples of the form are known closer to Highstead, from the water-hole at Bigbury (Thompson 1983, fig.10, 76 and 78; fig.11, 81). This water-hole also produced vessels similar to the other forms current during Period 4A: Form 8, the globular jar with thickened upright rim (Thompson 1983, fig.10, 38); form 14, (Thompson 1983, fig.11, 71) and form 21, 10, the corrugated jar (Thompson 1983, fig.11, 73 in flint-tempered fabric, and fig. 12, 90 and 91, both grog-tempered).

The existence of some of these forms at Barham Downs (Macpherson-Grant 1991, 45; Macpherson-Grant 1980a, fig.17, 93–4) in contexts which contained no grog-tempered vessels may be taken as evidence for their chronological precedence. Once established however, some of these forms continued in use into the first century A.D.: see for example, the Canterbury Marlowe excavations (Pollard 1995). Several other sites have these flint-tempered forms occurring alongside grog-tempered vessels. This evidence has been discussed by Nigel Macpherson-Grant (1991).

The evidence from the Bigbury water-hole is valuable in providing a sealed context associated with independent dates. The water-hole contained a wider range of forms than that from Period 4A at Highstead, but significantly included flint-tempered forms and early grog-tempered pieces. Two radiocarbon dates from the layer of ash, the lowest pottery-bearing context, were combined to give dates of 160–140 or 120–50 cal B.C. (Clark and Thompson 1989, 303). An archaeomagnetic date from the silt at the top of the water-hole filling (Clark 1983) has been recalibrated to 245–150 B.C. at the 68 per cent confidence level, and 300–90 B.C. at 95 per cent confidence (Clark and Thompson 1989, 304). While these dates do allow some flexibility in the interpretation of the date of the fill of the water-hole, they do suggest that the use of grog tempering in east Kent can be placed as early as *c.* 120–100 B.C. Drawing conclusions from the evidence of just one feature is risky: firstly, there was earlier settlement at Bigbury, which may have provided a source of contamination within the fill. Secondly, the handle of a Dressel 1 amphora was found in the spoil heap and while the excavator was convinced that 'there is almost no doubt that it came from the water-hole filling' (Thompson 1983, 256 and fig. 12, 105), its precise form (1a or 1b) is unknown and it cannot strictly be relied upon in a discussion of the chronology of the fill. A larger number of dated associations would be useful.

Some support for a second-century date for the introduction of grog tempering can be found in northern France. Firstly, the development of grog-tempered straight-sided and globular vessels with thickened rims and combed decoration is found alongside shell tempering, possibly as early as the mid second century B.C. (Blancquaert *et al.* 1998, 133); though secure independent dating evidence is lacking. Secondly, although its original form is uncertain, the corrugated shoulder from Highstead (No. 10) is very similar to shoulders found on bottles ('bouteilles'), e.g. at La Calotterie, dated to the second half of the second century B.C. (Blancquaert 2000, 395), using parallels with a typological scheme proposed for Acy-Romance (Ardennes) (Lambot 1996).

In addition to the flint-tempered examples, some grog-tempered sherds were found in Period 4A features. Ditch B17 produced one example of a grog-tempered form C1-2, dated to early or mid first century B.C. Ditch B141 however, produced eight forms (Table 13, including Nos 16 and 64–69) including *terra nigra* and *terra rubra* copies as well as an imitation Hofheim flagon, and a G1-12 plate dated to the first half of the first century A.D. This group is regarded as intrusive, being derived either from the Period 4C occupation in the same area, or from the Period 4D/5A Enclosure ditch B164, which cut it.

A broad date of c. 120–50 B.C. may be proposed for the pottery from Period 4A, which was followed by Period 4B apparently without a break, though it could have started as late as 100 B.C.

Period 4B

The main evidence for the date of Period 4B is provided by a sherd of Dressel 1B amphora, dating to c. 60–10 B.C. (Table 23, below), from Pit B262. Apart from that, just one flint-tempered form (Form 17, No. 23) was recognised which might be related to Period 4B. It was recovered from the intersection of Ditches B4 and B9, the former allocated to Period 4C. This particular example, with a gently concave neck, is not closely datable. The only other recognisable forms comprise a grog-tempered 'T-shaped' rim (No. 73) and a worn fragment, possibly from a Cam. 165 jug. Taken together, however, these amount to a very small sample and could include intrusive sherds. Period 4B is placed between c. 50–25 B.C., the date of the end of this period being governed by the evidence for Period 4C.

Period 4C

A larger number of recognisable forms (almost certainly all jars) is available from Period 4C features. By contrast, in this period, grog-tempered sherds are in the majority, accounting for 14.6 kg. from the fills of Ditches B4 and B7 (Table 14), and they provide the main dating evidence. Flint-tempered forms included globular jars with everted rims and thickened upright rims, sometimes with a single groove beneath the neck (Nos 26 and 27). Three decorated examples (Nos 30, 31 and 36) are in grog-and-flint-tempered fabric (Fabric 35).

No. 28, the plain globular jar with an upright rim (Form 6) is an early form, found at Barham Downs (Macpherson-Grant 1980a, fig. 17, 90) but apparently absent from later assemblages such as Marlowe Period 1 (Pollard 1995; Thompson and Green 1995).

Plain globular jars with everted rims, form 13 (Nos 32 and 34), are found in the water-hole at Bigbury (Thompson 1983, fig. 12, 88 and 98) and Canterbury, Castle Street-Stour Street (Macpherson-Grant 1991, 46), but are rare after the first century B.C. By then large storage jars with similar rims or more heavily everted rims (such as No. 7, though this was intrusive in a Period 2 feature) are more frequently associated with grooves, cordons and burnished decoration.

The jar form 12 (No. 31), shares its generally globular profile and short everted rim with form 11; but its angled shoulder and combed decoration has more in common with Thompson's C4 jars which occur in Marlowe Period 1 (e.g. Pollard 1995, fig. 269, 10) but are frequently post-conquest. Form 9, a globular jar with upright, internally thickened, rim (Nos 35, 50) is clearly similar to early forms from Barham Downs, Lord of the Manor in Thanet, and Canterbury (Macpherson-Grant 1991, 46) but continues to the end of the first century B.C. (Thompson C1-2).

Jars with short plain upright rims on inturned convex necks, form 5 (Nos 26 and 30), are similar to examples from post-conquest contexts in east Kent (Thompson C4), but are also found in Marlowe Period 1 (Pollard 1995, fig. 269, 10 and 275,108). These examples tend to be in hard grog-tempered fabric, while No. 30 from Ditch B7 is in the softer grog-and-flint-tempered fabric, supporting a first-century B.C. date. Form 3, with plain inturned, internally thickened rims (Nos 36 and 48), are a well known 'Belgic' type (Thompson C3), recognised to start in the first century B.C. Period 4C also saw the appearance of form 7 (No. 27), similar to form 6, except it has the junction between neck and shoulder accentuated by a groove.

Dating this period, using the larger sample of grog-tempered forms, produced an initial range of between the first century B.C. and mid first century A.D. (with the exception of Ditch B2 which contained predominantly post-conquest material, *see* p. 197). Allowing for Period 4B features stratified between Periods 4A and 4C, a start date of c. 25 B.C. might be more appropriate for Period 4C and would accommodate the ceramic evidence.

Of the Period 4C features, Ditch B4 contained the largest group of grog-tempered pottery, with thirty-three examples of recognisable forms (Table 13). While some of these could start as early as the first century B.C., all occur within the first half of the first century A.D. The same date accommodates the grog-tempered forms recovered from Ditch B7. Ditch B2 however, was recut for much of its length by field boundary B525 and produced grog-tempered forms, all falling within the range of those from Ditch B4. B2 also included sherds in romanised fabrics and some clear mid second-century pottery. It is assumed that this later pottery is intrusive, being derived from the recut field boundary.

Period 4D

Several flint and flint-and-grog-tempered forms were recovered from Period 4D contexts, which spanned c. A.D. 50–75, dated by grog-tempered and Roman pottery. Examples of forms 3 and 9 continued from Period 4C. New forms include a probable lid, form 24 (No. 44), a pedestal base, form 25 (No. 42) and bowls, forms 22 and 23. The plain hemispherical bowl (No. 46) is a common form in the Early and Middle Iron Age (periods 2 and 3) and this example may be residual. In Late Iron Age contexts they tend to have some demarcation just beneath the rim, as at Barham Downs, where one is associated with Period 4A forms (Macpherson-Grant 1980a, fig. 17, 86) or a more formal bead rim, as at

Period Feature	4a B139	4a B141	4a B18	4a B191	4a B17	4b B262	4b B3	4b B10	4b/c B9/B4	4c B7	4c B4/B7	4c B4	4c B34	4c B2	4c/d B1/B4	4c/d? B143	4d B5	4d B25	4d B22/23	4d B164	4d B1	Total
Flint-tempered forms (Fabrics 1-29)																						
21	1																					1
8	1				1																	2
18		1																				1
20			1																	1		2
14				1																		1
17									1													1
6										1												1
7										1												1
12										1												1
5										1	1											2
13										1		2										3
9												1								1		2
3												1								1		2
16															2							2
10																1						1
4																				1		1
19																				1	1	2
22																				1		1
23																				1		1
24																				1		1
25																				1		1
Dressel 1b						1						2										3
Grog-tempered forms (Fabrics 30-38)																						
E1	1																					1
TN copy	1																					1
TR copy	1																					1
G6	1																			1		2
G1-12	1																					1
B2-1	1									1		4										6
C4	1											3								2		6
C1-2				1																1		2
?Cam 165						1																1
T-shaped rim							1															1
C3										1		5						1				7
B2-3										1												1
E3-1										1			1							2		4
B1-1												1	2									3
B3												2										2
B3-7												1										1
C2-3												2	1									3
C6-1												6	1						1	1		9
C7-1												4	2									6
D2-4												1										1
E2-2												1										1
E3-2												1										1
G5-6												1										1
L6												1										1
C8-1																	1	1		1		3
G1-6																		1		4		5
A1																				1		1
C7-3																				1		1
E1-2																				1		1
G1-7																				2		2
G1-11																				1		1
L1																				2		2
L8																				1		1

Period	4a	4a	4a	4a	4a	4b	4b	4b	4b/c	4c	4c	4c	4c	4c	4c/d	4c/d?	4d	4d	4d	4d	4d	Total
Feature	B139	B141	B18	B191	B17	B262	B3	B10	B9/B4	B7	B4/B7	B4	B34	B2	B1/B4	B143	B5	B25	B22/23	B164	B1	
Fine Sandy Ware (Fabric 40)																						
C1-2																				6	1	7
C1-4																				1		1
D3-4																				1		1
B2-4																				2		2
B1-1/B1-2																				1		1
B1-6																				4		4
G5-1																				4		4
C4																				3	1	4
D2-4																				1		1
D3-1																				1		1
S1																				1		1
L6																				1		1
G1-6																					1	1
Romano-British forms (Fabric 41)																				20	53	73
Total	2	8	1	1	1	2	1	1	1	9	1	39	1	6	2	1	1	3	1	72	61	215

Table 13. Distribution of forms from Area B in Period 4. Figures for Romano-British forms are minimum values.

Bigbury where a decorated example was recovered from the water-hole (Thompson 1983, fig.11, 74a). More occurrences are known in grog-tempered fabric, though also with a bead rim (Thompson D3-1/G2-2; Pollard 1995, fig. 269, 18).

The flaring bowl, form 23 (No. 43) could also be residual, again occurring at Barham Downs (Macpherson-Grant 1980a, fig.17, 91), but is not common in 'Belgic' contexts. In this instance the combed decoration and flint-and-grog-tempered fabric supports its attribution to Period 4. The possible plain lid, form 24 (No. 44) in flint-and-grog-tempered fabric, could belong to Thompson's types L2 or L6, occurring in pre- and post-conquest contexts (Pollard 1995, form 37). The pedestal base, form 25 (No. 42), also in flint-and-grog-tempered fabric, is known from first century B.C. and A.D. contexts (Thompson A4).

Other forms, such as the globular jars with short everted rim, 20 (form 11), with thickened bead rim, 21 (form 10), and with simple bead rim, 39 (Form 2), are similar to globular jars from earlier in Period 4. The remaining vessel types are less precisely defined: plain everted rims (Form 19) could belong to a variety of forms (No. 41 is in a hard fabric and is wheel thrown); as could the short everted rims with a straight, bevelled, internal face (form 16). Finally, the inturned, lightly recessed rim, form 4 (No. 47) is a common form in the first centuries B.C. and post conquest (e.g. Couldrey 1984, 45, form 2) and is clearly related to 'T-shaped' grog-tempered forms.

This period also saw the first appearance of Fine Sandy Ware (Table 14) in Ditch B164. This fabric is used for 'Belgic' forms and is dated to c. A.D. 50–70, though it may have started just before the conquest (see p. 217). Ditch B164 was first dug in Period 4D, but remained in use into and possibly throughout Period 5A. The key dating evidence for Period 4D is provided by the Fine Sandy Ware, supplemented by examples of grog-tempered and Romano-British pottery and is placed between A.D. 50–75 (p. 214).

Discussion of the flint-tempered pottery

In spite of the problems caused by intrusive and residual pottery, a credible picture of changing ceramic traditions can be identified during Period 4. After a phase of abandonment, Period 4 sees the arrival of new pottery forms and decoration in flint-tempered fabrics. These are followed by the use of grog temper which rapidly becomes the dominant fabric and is employed in a much wider, more standardised range of forms. Many of the globular forms, with inturned bead or thickened rims, begin in flint temper and continue in grog-tempered fabric. The smaller jar with everted rim (Form 20) in flint-tempered fabric, is replaced by a varied range of more specialised forms in grog temper.

Evidence from elsewhere in Kent shows that, at a time when the excavated area of Highstead was deserted, between c. 400–125 B.C., these everted rim jars, sometimes decorated with light curvilinear grooves (No. 51) and often highly burnished, represented probably the finest pottery in use. They represent an insular development, popular in Kent, but largely unknown across the Channel, a situation reflected in other aspects of material culture at the time.

| Fabric | Flint | | | | | | | | | | Grog | | | | Shell | FSW | Other | Total |
	1	2	3	4	5	11	12	13	14	16	30	33	35	38	39	40	41	Sherds
Period 4A																		
B8	2	1																3
B17	3		1	1							10							15
B18							1				3						2	6
B20	1																	1
B137	6	2																8
B138	2																	2
B139	25	2	1	1		3		1			6		4				4	47
B141	4	19	1								47		1	2			5	79
B142	1	1				1												3
B160	1																2	3
B167	3	2	1			1												7
B191	1		1	1														3
Period 4A Total	49	27	5	3	0	5	0	2	0	0	66	0	5	2	0	0	13	177
Period 4A %	27.68	15.25	2.82	1.69	0.00	2.82	0.00	1.13	0.00	0.00	37.29	0.00	2.82	1.13	0.00	0.00	7.34	100
Period 4B																		
B3	1										6							7
B9	13	3	1	1														18
B10											1							1
B33																	6	6
B262	1												1					2
Period 4B Total	15	3	1	1	0	0	0	0	0	0	7	0	1	0	0	0	6	34
Period 4B %	50.00	8.82	2.94	2.94	0.00	0.00	0.00	0.00	0.00	0.00	20.59	0.00	2.94	0.00	0.00	0.00	17.65	100
Period 4C																		
B2		2									157						14	173
B4	74	13	11	4	2	6	2	4	1		442	1	12	2			4	578
B7	6		10				2				84		5		1			108
B32	1																	1
B34	1		1								2							4
B143	9	3	3			1												16
Period 4C Total	91	18	25	4	2	7	4	4	1	0	685	1	17	2	1	0	18	880
Period 4C %	10.34	2.05	2.84	0.45	0.23	0.80	0.45	0.45	0.11	0.00	77.84	0.11	1.93	0.23	0.11	0.00	2.05	100
Period 4D																		
B5											3						1	4
B25			1	1				1			20						53	76
B1	43	26	35	13		4	1	4	2	2	390		5			7	342	874
B164	94	31	13	5		6			1		419		5	1		413	298	1285
Period 4D Total	137	57	49	19	0	10	1	4	3	2	832	0	10	1	0	420	694	2239
Period 4D %	6.12	2.55	2.19	0.85	0.00	0.45	0.04	0.18	0.13	0.09	37.16	0.00	0.45	0.04	0.00	18.76	31.00	100
Period 4 Total	292	105	80	27	2	22	5	10	4	2	1590	1	33	5	1	420	731	3330
Period 4 %	8.77	3.15	2.40	0.81	0.06	0.66	0.15	0.30	0.12	0.06	47.75	0.03	0.99	0.15	0.03	12.61	21.95	100

Table 14. Distribution of fabrics using the number of sherds from Area B during Period 4. Figures for fabrics 40 (Fine Sandy Ware) and 41 (other Roman) in Ditch B1 and Ditch B164 are approximate.

By the beginning of Period 4, communication across the Channel, evident during periods 2–3, is noticeable again. The everted rim jar had largely fallen out of use and the new forms, together with the adoption of grog tempering, are once again found on the Continent. Thus the ceramic evidence suggests that settlement at Highstead, in a commanding position overlooking the Wantsum, was inextricably linked to close continental relations: thriving when there were strong cross-Channel ties.

Catalogue of illustrated vessels

Intrusive in Periods 2 and 3 (Fig. 101)

1. A globular bead-rimmed jar with comb decoration in flint and organic tempered fabric. The surface has irregular internal finger-smoothing and the exterior has light combing with vertical strokes followed by horizontal and diagonal combing. (Fabric 3, Form 2, Pit B12, Period 3A).
   The bulk of the pottery from Pit B12 has been placed in Period 3A (*see* pp. 37, 115). It also contained a single Roman sherd, which is regarded as intrusive. The decoration and form of this vessel is very typical of local 'Belgic' pottery (Thompson type C1-2).

2. A globular jar with a plain upright rim in flint-tempered fabric. It is apparently decorated with spaced diagonal grooving, though the surface between the panels of grooves is worn. The interior is burnished and the exterior has been wiped. (Fabric 1, Form 6, Pit B124, Period 3B).
   In addition to the bulk of Period 3B pottery, Pit B124 contained two sherds tempered with flint-and-grog and two purely grog-tempered sherds which are regarded as intrusive. It is close to the ditch of Enclosure B3, attributed to Period 4B. This form is similar to 'Belgic' examples (cf. Thompson C2-1) and the use of diagonal combing is common, though rarely in separate panels, as on this example.

4. A flint-tempered jar with plain upright rim. The surfaces have been wiped and there is light burnishing on the top of the rim. (Fabric 13, Form 6, Post-pit B264, Period 3B).
   Pit B264 has been attributed to Period 3B and this rim may be intrusive from Period 4A activity in Building B262.

5. A shouldered jar or bowl in flint-and-grog tempered fabric. The flint is sparse. The shoulder is slightly angular rather than rounded. The exterior is burnished and the interior appears to have been smoothed, though it is now worn. (Fabric 35, Form 16, Pit B245, Period 3B).
   Pit B245 is securely placed in Period 3B. The form of this vessel is unusual for Period 3B, being closer to the everted rim/foot-ring jars of *c.* 300–100 B.C.; and its fabric, a mixture of grog and flint, more acceptable in a Period 4 context. It is regarded as intrusive from Period 4 activity.

6. A globular jar with a short everted rim in flint-tempered fabric. The exterior has been wiped and the interior burnished. (Fabric 1, Form 11, Post-hole A139, Period 2)
   Post-hole A139 has been placed in Period 2, near the eastern end of A24's southern ditch segment. The terminal portion of the Period 4D Ditch A229 cut the earlier ditch at this point and this sherd is almost certainly derived from the Period 4D activity.

7. Large flint-tempered jar with an everted rim and a fine quality burnished finish. The upper shoulder is decorated with two broad horizontal grooves. (Fabric 1, Form 15, Enclosure A260, Period 2).
   A260 has been placed in Period 2 (*see* p. 32); but this sherd is undoubtedly similar to 'Belgic' grog-tempered vessels (cf. Thompson C6-1), of a form, common in east Kent, which may have begun late in the first century B.C., but is more usually found in early first century A.D. contexts e.g. Faversham (Philp 1968, fig. 23, 168; 24, 211 and Thompson 1982, 262, no. 21) and Canterbury (Thompson 1995, fig. 275, 103). The flint-tempered fabric of this example from Highstead may indicate an early date, but supporting evidence is lacking.

8. A thick everted rim from a flint-tempered jar. The whole of the exterior and top of the interior, down to just beneath the bottom of the rim, have been burnished. (Fabric 1, Form 11, Top of fill of B144, Period 3A).
   Ditch B144 has been attributed to Period 3A, but this globular jar with a thickened slightly everted rim is late Iron Age and is regarded as intrusive.

Periods 4 and 5 (Figs 102–7)

9. An s-profiled jar or bowl in a sandy flint-and-organic tempered fabric. It has an even moderate exterior burnish and light internal smoothing, though is now worn. (Fabric 13, Form 20, Ditch B18, Period 4A).

10. A corrugated shoulder with a deep burnished groove in a fabric tempered with flint, organic and iron oxide inclusions. The surfaces are dark grey. The exterior has been burnished horizontally, leaving some of the flint inclusions visible. The interior is worn. (Fabric 4, Form 21, Ditch B139, Period 4A).

11. A flint-tempered sherd decorated with light burnished grooves. The sherd is grey to dark grey throughout. The interior is worn and the exterior smooth with few flint inclusions visible. (Fabric 1, Ditch B139, Period 4A).

12. Flint-tempered sherd decorated with two horizontal incised lines. It has a smooth surfaces, showing a small amount of wear. With its narrow incised lines (*c.* 0.8–1 mm. wide) this sherd has more in common with the decorative styles of Period 3 than with the grooves found on 'Belgic' vessels of the Late Iron Age. This sherd is probably residual. (Fabric 1, Ditch B139, Period 4A).

13. A flint-tempered base, probably from a jar. The exterior has been wiped smooth, with few flints visible and the interior is smooth but worn. (Fabric 1, Ditch B139, Period 4A).

14. Flint tempered base from a jar. Both surfaces have been wiped smooth, with some flint drag on the exterior. (Fabric 1, Ditch B139, Period 4A).

15. Upright thickened bead rim from a flint-tempered jar, with distinctive horizontal facetted burnish to rim and inner lip. Beneath the rim, the surfaces have been roughly wiped. (Fabric 1, Form 8, B139, Period 4A).

16. Small jar in grog-and-flint temper with hard smooth burnished surfaces. There is a cordon and groove running beneath the neck. The flint tempering is sparse. (Fabric 35, Form 18, B141, Period 4A).

17. A globular jar with a thick everted rim, in flint-and-organic tempered fabric. The surfaces have been wiped with some flints visible and signs of rough burnishing on the interior. The rough burnishing on the rim produces a multiple facetted effect. (Fabric 3, Form 14, Pit B191, Period 4A).

18. A small refired worn rim sherd from a flint-tempered jar. The upright thickened rim has traces of horizontal faceting on the exterior. (Fabric 1, Form 8, Pit B262, Period 4B).

20. A short everted rim, probably from a globular jar, in flint-tempered fabric. The surfaces are smooth and the sherd is

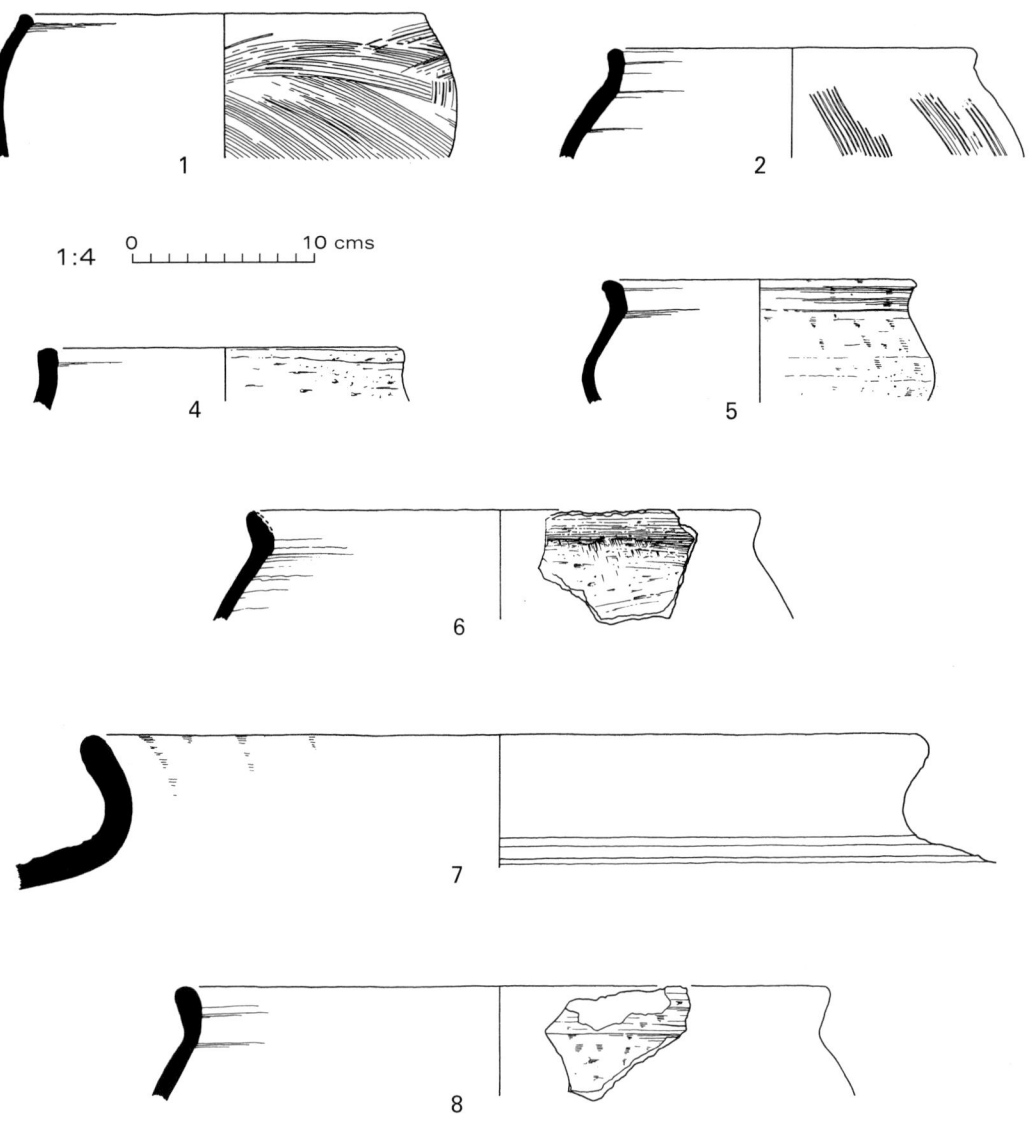

Fig. 101. Late Iron Age pottery from earlier features. No. 1, Pit B12; No. 2, Pit B124; No. 4, Post-pit B264; No. 5, Pit B245; No. 6, Post-pit A139; No. 7, Ditch A260; No. 8, Ditch B144. Scale 1:4.

dark grey throughout. (Fabric 1, Form 11, A228, Period 4D).

21. A thickened bead rim with light horizontal facetting around the inside. The surfaces are grey-brown and have been wiped smooth. The core is dark grey. (Fabric 1, Form 10, A228, Period 4D).

22. The upper shoulder and neck from a flint-tempered vessel with a broad groove running around the neck. The interior is worn and the exterior, also worn, shows signs of having been burnished. (Fabric 1, Intersection of Ditches B4 and B9, Period 4B/4C).

23. An irregular rim from a jar or beaker in a sandy fabric tempered with flint and organic inclusions. The surfaces have been wiped smooth. (Fabric 13, Form 17, Intersection of Ditches B4 and B9, Period 4B/4C).

24. An everted flint-tempered rim probably from a jar. The rim has a deep slightly bevelled interior and slightly beaded inner lip. It has been wiped smooth overall. (Fabric 1, Form 16, Intersection of Ditches B1 and B4, Period 4C/4D).

25. A flint-tempered rim of a similar type to No. 24. The flat topped rim has been smoothed but the overall finish has been wiped. (Fabric 1, Form 16, Intersection of Ditches B1 and B4, Period 4C/4D).

26. A probable inturned rim from a jar of fine flint and iron oxide tempered fabric with organic inclusions. The angle and diameter are uncertain. It has traces of a horizontal groove

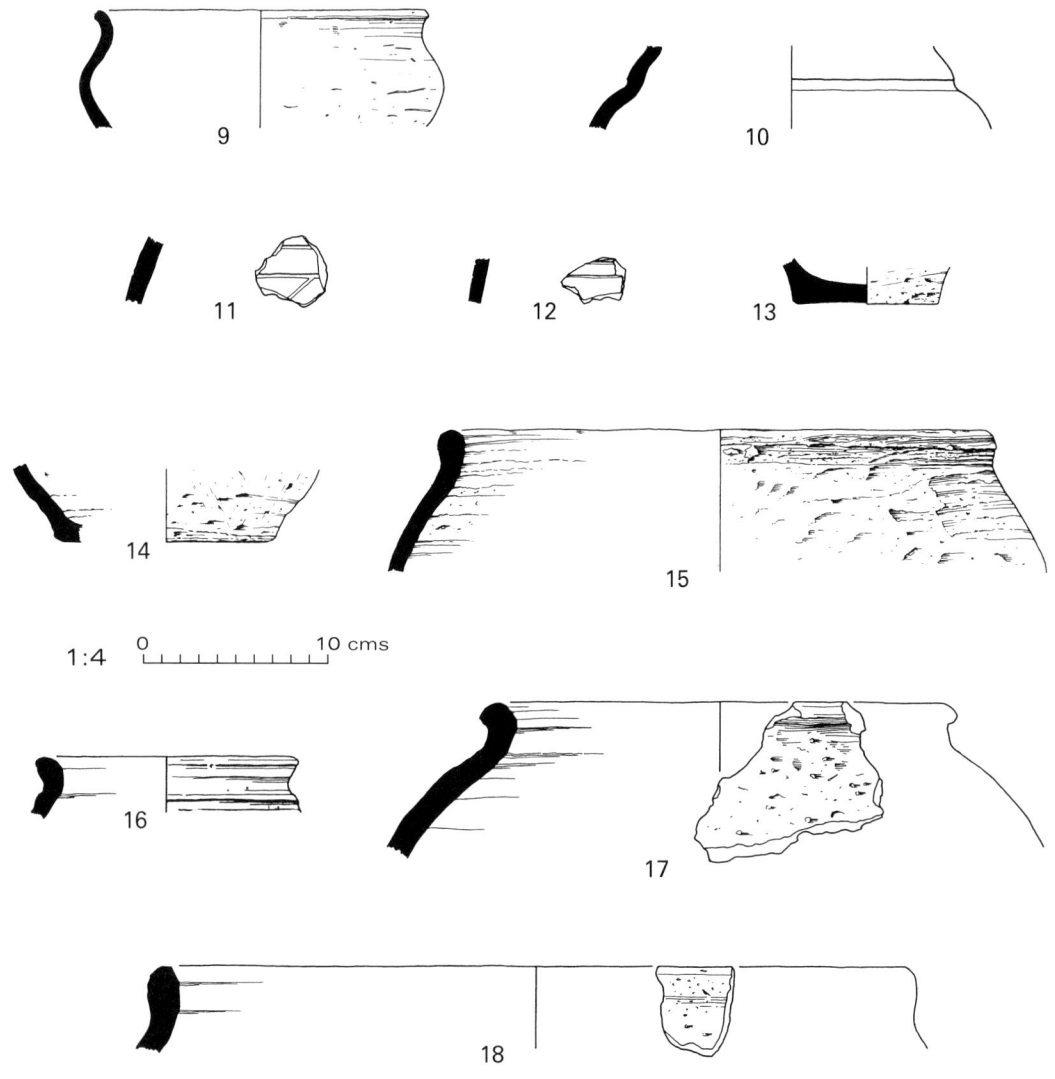

Fig. 102. Late Iron Age pottery from Period 4 features. No. 9, Ditch B18; Nos 10–15, Ditch B139; No. 16, Ditch B141; No. 17, Pit B191; No. 18, Pit B262. Scale 1:4.

around the bottom of the neck. It was evidently burnished overall. (Fabric 14, Form 5, Intersection of Ditches B4 and B7, Period 4C).

27. Small flint-tempered jar with a single broad groove at the junction of shoulder and neck. The surfaces have been wiped smooth and some flint inclusions protrude. (Fabric 1, Form 7, Ditch B7, Period 4C).

28. A globular jar with plain upright rim in flint-tempered fabric. Both surfaces have been wiped, with few flint inclusions protruding. (Fabric 1, Form 6, Ditch B7, Period 4C).

29. Small and worn rim sherd from a flint-and-organic tempered jar. The angle is uncertain: it could be flat-topped or as drawn. (Fabric 3, Ditch B7).

30. A large storage jar of grog-and-flint tempered fabric. The exterior is decorated with broad grooves on either side of a cordon. The interior of the rim shows a facetted finish and both surfaces appear to have been lightly burnished. (Fabric 35, Form 5, Ditch B7, Period 4C).

31. Jar with a slightly everted rim in grog-and-flint tempered fabric, with traces of horizontal combing just beneath the shoulder. The surfaces are smooth, though worn, and both show some signs of having been burnished. (Fabric 35, Form 12, Top of Ditch B7, Period 4C).

32. Large flint-tempered jar with everted rim. The surfaces have been wiped, vertically on the exterior and horizontally around the rim, leaving few flints visible. (Fabric 1, Form 13, Ditch B4, Period 4C).

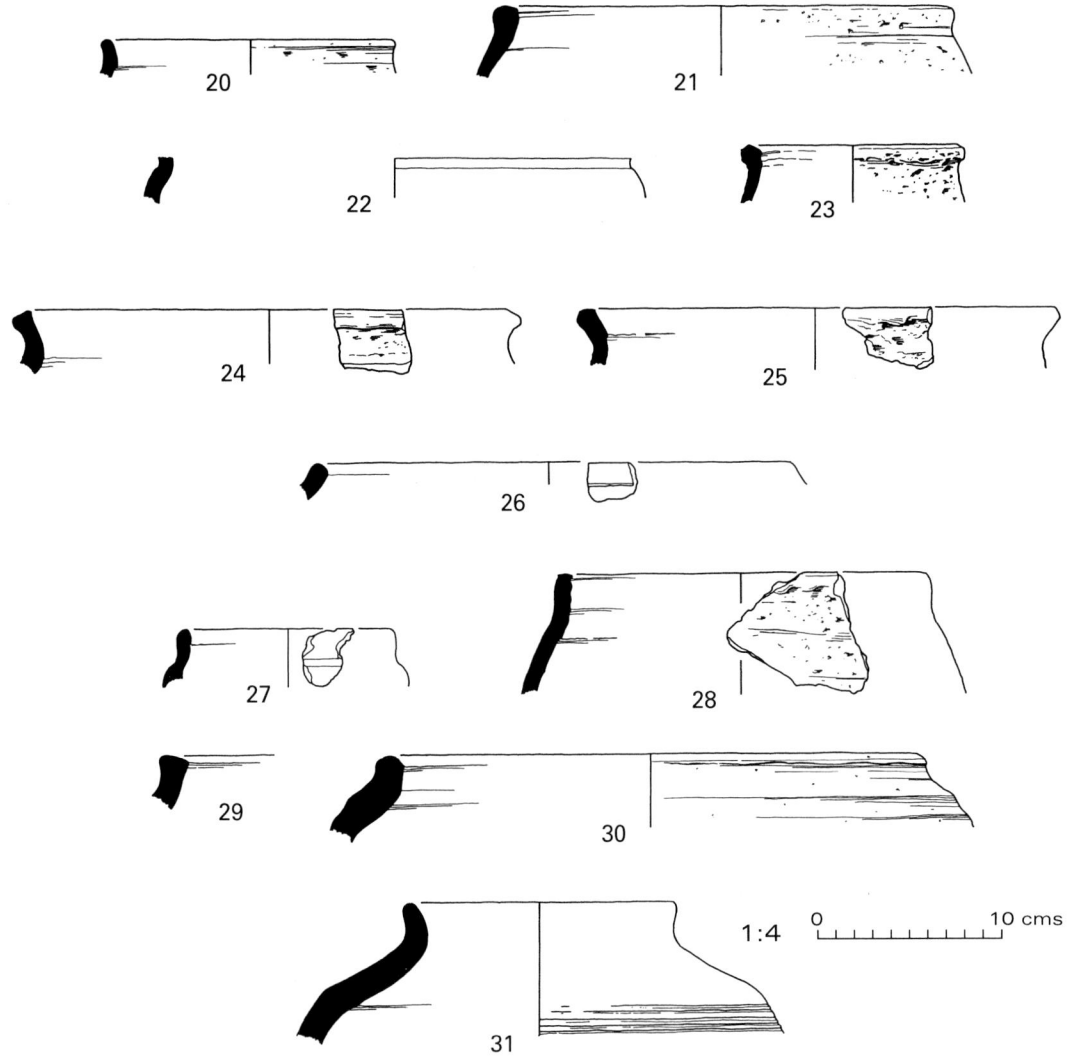

Fig. 103. Late Iron Age pottery from Period 4 features. No. 20, Ditch A229; No. 21, Pit A228; Nos 22–3, intersection of ditches B4 and B9; Nos 24–5, intersection of ditches B1 and B9; No. 26, intersection of ditches B4 and B7; Nos 27–31, Ditch B7. Scale 1:4.

33. A flint-tempered jar with everted, slightly flaring rim. The exterior has been wiped smooth and interior burnished. (Fabric 1, Ditch B4, Period 4C).
34. A jar with thickened everted rim in flint-tempered fabric. The interior is worn, but the exterior shows traces of horizontal burnishing.(Fabric 1, Form 13, Ditch B4, Period 4C).
35. A small jar with thickened upright or slightly everted rim in flint-tempered fabric. The exterior is burnished to produce a shiny black surface. The interior is worn but appears to have been smooth. The interior of the rim shows a light horizontal facetted finish. (Fabric 1, Form 9, Ditch B4, Period 4C).
36. A grog-and-flint tempered jar with inturned, internally-thickened rim. The rim and internal surface have been wiped smooth and there is rough almost horizontal combing beneath the neck. (Fabric 35, Form 3, Top of Ditch B4, Period 4C).
37. A flint-and-grog tempered jar with an everted rim with internal bevel. There is a trace of a single incised line, possibly forming the upper part of combed arcade decoration, on the exterior. (Fabric 35, Form 16, Ditch B4, Period 4C).
38. A slightly thickened everted rim from a grog-and-flint tempered jar. There is a slight cordon on the neck. The interior and rim are worn and the exterior has been burnished. (Fabric 35, Form 18, Pit A255, Period 4D).
39. An inturned bead rim in grog-and-flint tempered fabric with traces of rough arcaded combing. Both surfaces are worn, but appear to have been wiped smooth, with light traces of burnishing beneath the rim on the exterior. (Fabric 35, Form 2, Pit A255, Period 4D).
40. A worn fragment of an upright or slightly everted thickened rim in flint-tempered fabric with organic inclusions. There

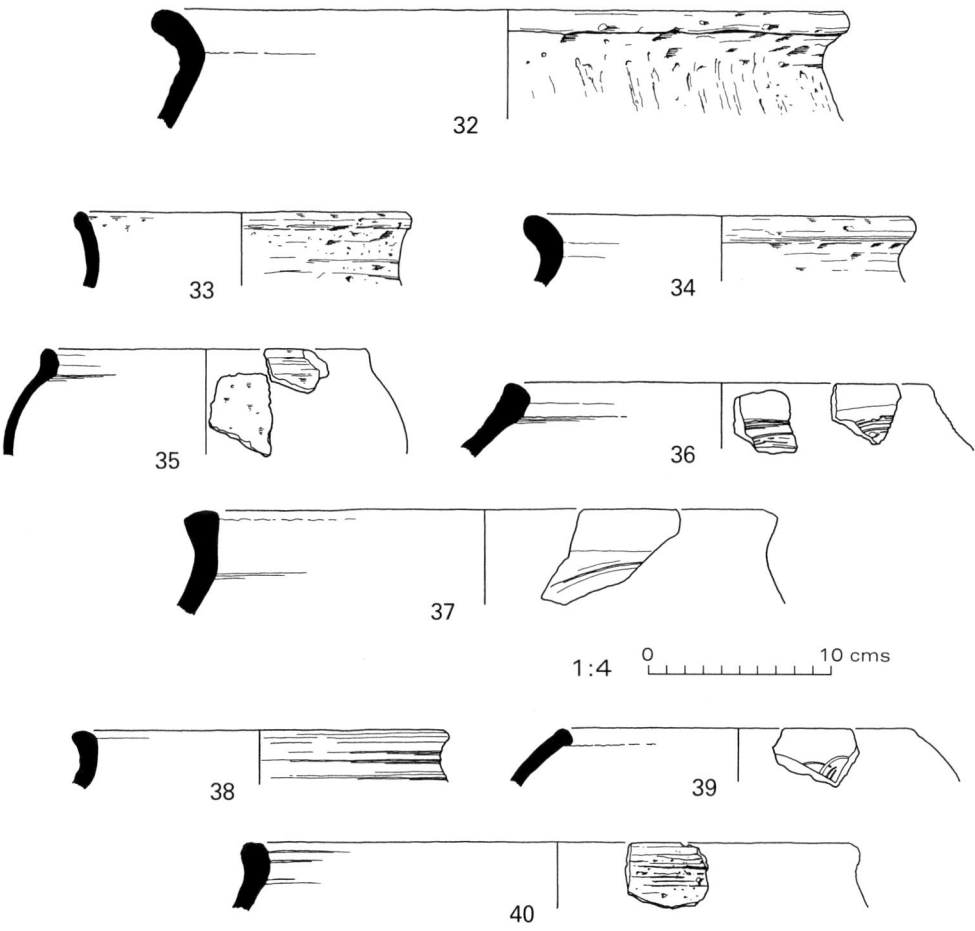

Fig. 104. Late Iron Age pottery from Period 4 features. Nos 32–7, Ditch B4; Nos 38–9, Pit A255; No. 40, Ditch B143. Scale 1:4.

are slight traces of horizontal faceting on the inside of the rim, and rough burnishing on the exterior. (Fabric 3, Form 10, Ditch B143, Period 4C).

41. An everted rim from a hard sandy grog-and-flint tempered jar or bowl. The vessel is wheel thrown and lightly burnished overall. The core is light grey; the surfaces grey and there is a red-brown margin. (Fabric 35, Form 19, Ditch B1, Period 4D–5A).

42. The base of a pedestal jar in grog-and-flint tempered fabric. It is thick, heavy and worn and was evidently burnished overall. (Fabric 35, Form 25, Ditch B1, Period 4D–5A).

43. A flaring bowl in grog-and-flint tempered fabric. It is decorated with vertical and horizontal deep 'combing'. The interior has been wiped and the exterior, above the combing, and rim has been wiped smooth and partially burnished. (Fabric 35, Form 23, Ditch B1, Period 4D–5A).

44. A probable lid in grog-and-flint tempered fabric. Both surfaces have been wiped. (Fabric 35, Form 24, Ditch B1, Period 4D–5A).

45. A plain everted rim from a small jar or bowl in flint-tempered fabric. It has been lightly burnished overall. (Fabric 1, Form 19, Ditch B164, Period 4D–5A).

46. A flint-tempered bowl. The interior has been smoothed and the exterior wiped leaving the surface rough. The rim has been pinched in and wiped smooth. (Fabric 1, Form 22, Ditch B164 Period 4D–5A).

47. A flint-tempered bowl or jar with an inturned lid-seated rim. The lid-seating groove is rather superficial. It has been wiped overall with light burnishing on the exterior. (Fabric 1, Form 4, Ditch B164, Period 4D–5A).

48. An inturned internally-thickened rim in flint-tempered fabric. The exterior is decorated with an arcaded deeply combed motif. (Fabric 1, Form 3, Ditch B164 Period 4D–5A).

49. A small flint-and-grog tempered jar with internally bevelled rim. Both surfaces have been wiped. (Fabric 6, Ditch B164, Period 4D–5A).

50. A storage jar with an upright internally-thickened rim in flint-and-grog tempered fabric. The interior has been wiped and

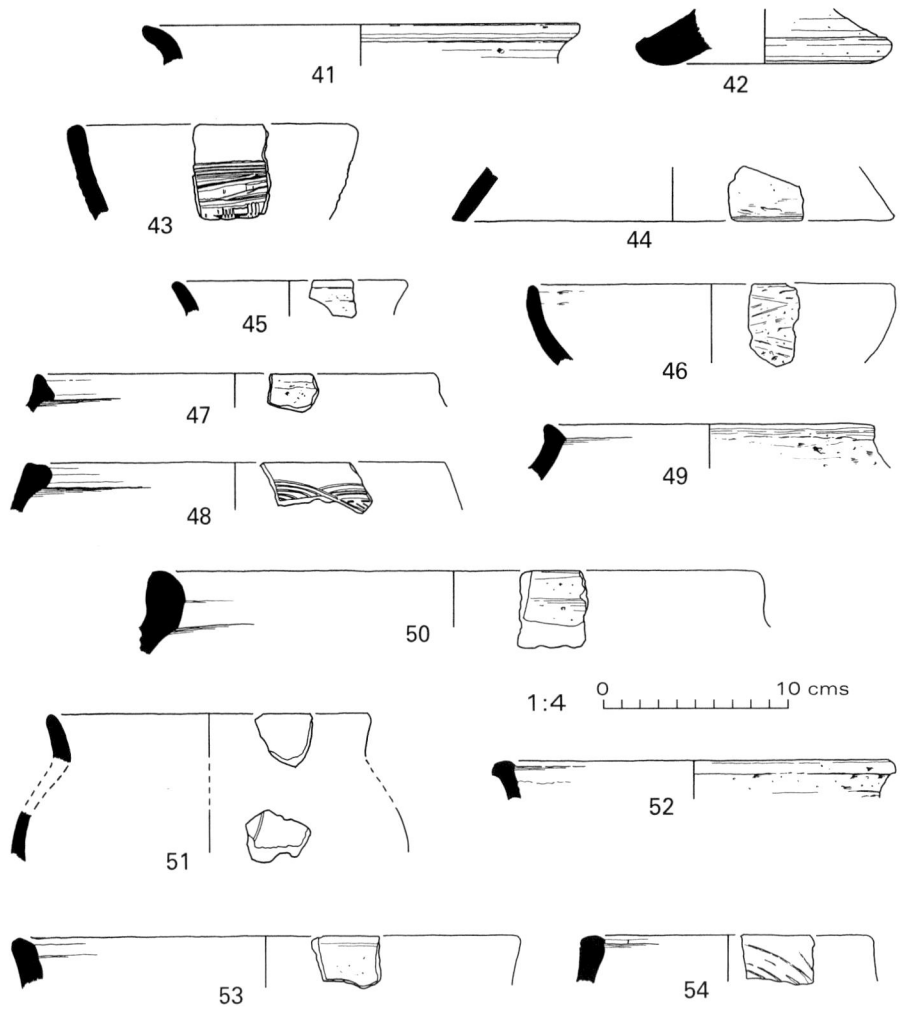

Fig. 105. Late Iron Age pottery from Period 4 and Period 5 features. Nos 41–4, Ditch B1; Nos 45–51, Ditch B164; No. 52, Ditch B187; No. 53, Ditch A254; No. 54, Pit B13. Scale 1:4.

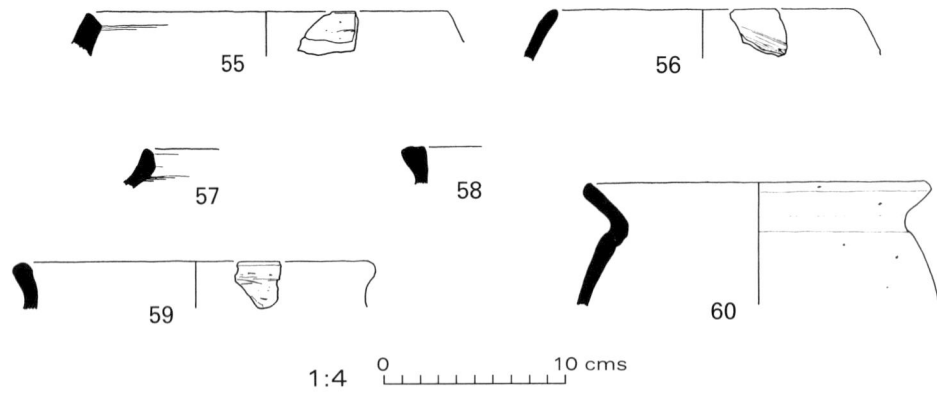

Fig. 106. Late Iron Age pottery from unstratified and Period 5 features. No. 56, Pit A274; No. 57, Pit C1; No. 58, Post-hole B346; No. 59, Post-hole B347; No. 60, unstratified. Scale 1:4.

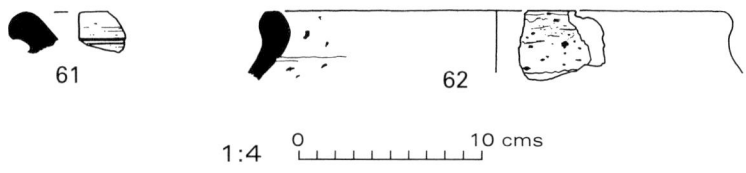

Fig. 107. Late Iron Age grog- and shell-tempered pottery from unstratified and Period 5 features. No. 61, Ditch B23; No. 62, unstratified. Scale 1:4.

the remaining surfaces lightly burnished. There is a lightly facetted finish to the outer rim surface. (Fabric 35, Form 9, Ditch B164, Period 4D–5A).

51. An everted rim jar in flint-tempered fabric. The surfaces are dark grey and have been burnished and the core is grey. The exterior is decorated with a light curvilinear grooves. (Fabric 1, Form 20, Ditch B164, Period 4D–5A).
52. A plain slightly everted rim in a grog-and-flint tempered fabric. The sherd is worn but the surfaces appear to have been wiped or lightly burnished overall. (Fabric 35, Ditch A254, Period 5A).
53. A jar with 'rippled' neck in grog-and-flint tempered fabric. The interior has been wiped, with moderate burnishing on the rim and light rippling and tooling on the neck. (Fabric 35, Unstratified, Area A).
54. A grog-and-flint tempered jar with a plain inturned internally-thickened rim with traces of light diagonal combing on the exterior. (Fabric 35, Form 3, Pit B13, Period 5A).
55. A plain rim in grog-and-flint tempered fabric. The angle and diameter are uncertain. The surfaces are brown and smooth. the core is dark grey. (Fabric 35, Unstratified, Area A).
56. A jar with plain inturned rim in grog-and-flint tempered fabric. There are traces of diagonal comb finishing and the surfaces have been lightly burnished. (Fabric 35, Form 1, Pit A274, Period 5B).
57. A fragmentary rim sherd in flint-tempered fabric. The surfaces are smooth with traces of burnish on the exterior. The surfaces are light brown and the core dark grey. (Fabric 1, Pit C1, Period 5A).
58. A worn rim in flint-tempered fabric. Its angle and diameter are uncertain. The surfaces are smooth and the sherd is grey to dark grey throughout. (Fabric 1, Post-hole B346, Period 5B).
59. A thickened everted rim in grog-and-flint tempered fabric. The angle and diameter are uncertain. The surfaces are smooth and the sherd is dark grey throughout. (Fabric 1, Post-hole B347, Period 5B).
60. An everted rim jar in flint-tempered fabric. The surfaces have been wiped smooth and the exterior shows signs of burnishing. (Fabric 1, Unstratified, Area B).
61. A fragment of a rim from a large grog-and-shell tempered storage jar. The surfaces are orange-brown and have been wiped smooth. The core is dark grey. (Fabric 33, Form 16, Ditch B23, Period 5A).
62. A jar with thickened rounded rim in shell-tempered fabric. The surfaces have been wiped smooth. (Fabric 39, Unstratified. Area C).

Grog-tempered pottery

Isobel Thompson [9]

This assemblage was originally examined in 1987. It consisted of 41.5 kg. of grog-tempered Late Iron Age pottery from Area B, and another 10 kg. from Area A. A catalogue was drawn up, with a brief summary; some minimal quantification was done, but the work proceeded no further until early 2004. In the interval, other assemblages from Late Iron Age and early Roman sites in Kent have become available, providing useful parallels for the Highstead site. Funding constraints have meant that the report presented here is not fully updated. It has however been possible to reconsider the grog-tempered pottery from those features which have been rephased and assigned to Period 4. Other features have not been revisited; the pottery catalogue for these is as it was in 1987.

The forms and parallels of the illustrated vessels and others mentioned in the main text are presented below. This is a small proportion of the complete assemblage.

Fabrics

The date of the appearance of grog-tempered fabrics in east Kent is not resolved (see above and Macpherson-Grant 1992b), but two recently-discovered assemblages have provided useful new information both on the date and on cross-currents in style and fabric in the first century B.C. At Hawkinge, Folkestone (Thompson 2001a) a single large assemblage from a pit comprised a remarkable collection of vessels in four main fabric groups, grog, flint, a distinctive fine sandy, and coarse sandy. In addition, there was a significant minority fabric, grog-and-flint. In stylistic terms the grog-tempered vessels appear to be slightly later than Bigbury, but earlier than the early Canterbury groups. The fine sandy fabric from Hawkinge, apparently made in the Folkestone area, was used for 'saucepan pot' forms, and two decorated vessels are Sussex types. The Hawkinge assemblage represents the Late Iron Age of both east Kent and east Sussex, and although the date of its deposition is uncertain, the vessels ought to represent production covering approximately the period 80–30 B.C. (Thompson 2001a).

---

9. Report revised September 2004.

Fabric Form	Grog	Grog and Flint	Grog and Chalk
A1	Ditch B1, Ditch B4, Ditch B164	Ditch B1	
B1-1	Pit A80, Pit A87, Pit A125, Ditch A229, Pit A274, Ditch B1, Ditch B2 (one flaring, which is late); Pit Complex B15		
B1-6	A184, Area A unstratified, Pit B186,		
B2-1	Pit A255, Pit A274, Ditch B4, Ditch B7, Pit Complex B15, Ditch B141	Ditch B141	Ditch B4
B2-3	Ditch B7		
B2-4	Ditch B1		
B3	Ditch B4		
B3-1	Pit A53, Ditch A127, Ditch B1, Pit B13, Pit Complex B15,		
B3-2	Pit Complex B15		
B3-4	Ditch B1		
B3-6	Pit A125		
B3-7	Ditch B4		
B3-8	Pit Complex B15		
B5-3 or B5-5	Ditch B4, Pit Complex B15		
C1-2	Pit A87, Ditch A229, Pit A274, Pit Complex B15, Ditch B17, Ditch B164, Pit B268		
C1-4	Ditch A229, Pit A274, Ditch B1		
C2-3	Pit A87, Pit A255, Ditch B1, Ditch B4	Area B unstratified	
C3	Ditch A262, Ditch B7, Ditch B3, Pit A126, Ditch B1, Pit A74	Pit A255, Pit A274, Area A unstratified, Pit B13, Ditch B4, Pit B12	
C4	Pit A87, Pit A126, Ditch A229, Pit A274, Ditch B1, Ditch B4, Pit Complex B15, Ditch B141, Ditch B164		
C6-1	Pit A87, Pit A126, Ditch B1, Ditch B4, Ditch B7, Pit B13, Pit Complex B15, Ditch B164	Ditch B139, Area B unstratified	
C7-1	Pit A274, Ditch B1, Ditch B2, Ditch B4, Ditch B7, Pit Complex B15	Area A unstratified, Ditch B7	
C7-3	Ditch B2, Ditch B4, Ditch B164		
C7-4	Area B unstratified		
C8-1	Cremation A119, Ditch B1, Pit B13, Pit Complex B15, Ditch B164		
D1-1	Pit A255, Pit Complex B15	Pit B245, Pit B262	
D2-4	Ditch B4, Ditch B7		
E1-2	Ditch B1, Ditch B7, Ditch B164		
E2-2	Ditch B4		
E2-3	Pit A255, Ditch B4, Ditch B7, Pit Complex B15		
E3-1	Grave A36, Ditch B1,	Ditch B7, Ditch B34, Pit Complex B15, Ditch B164	
E3-2	Ditch B4		
F5	Ditch B1		
G1			Pit Complex B15
G1-1	Ditch B4, Pit Complex B15		
G1-2	Ditch B4		
G1-3	Ditch B7		
G1-4	Pit A255		
G1-6	Pit A87, Pit A122, Ditch A262, Ditch B1, Pit Complex B15, Ditch B164, Pit B268		
G1-7	Ditch B164		
G1-9	Ditch B1		
G1-11	Ditch B1, Pit Complex B15, Ditch B164		
G1-12			Ditch B141
G2-2	Ditch A262		
G2-4	Pit A122		
G3-4	Pit A75		
G5-3	Ditch A123		
G5-5	Pit A87		
G5-6	Ditch A123, Pit A125, Pit A255, Pit Complex B15		
G6	Ditch B1, Pit B13, Ditch B141, Ditch B164		
L1	Ditch B164		
L2	Ditch A229, Pit A255, Ditch B1	C5	
L6	Pit A274, Ditch B4, Pit Complex B15, Ditch B165		
L7	Ditch B165		
L8	Pit Complex B15, Ditch B164		

The assemblage from the Whitfield-Eastry by-pass (Thompson 2001b) was found only a few miles from Hawkinge, and is earlier in character. It contains only a small proportion of grog-tempered vessels, but marks the period when flint tempering was beginning to give way to grog. The Hawkinge assemblage is not particularly similar to Bigbury, but Whitfield has links with both Bigbury and Hawkinge (and like Hawkinge, has links with the Late Iron Age of Sussex) and is apparently earlier than c. 80 B.C. (Thompson 2001b). It might be noted that all the Whitfield grog-tempered forms were to become standard ones (A1, B2-1, C1-2, ?C2-3, C6-1, D2-4 and a carinated cup).

With these two new assemblages, and others (the Deal burials for instance, Parfitt 1995) it is now possible to reassess other sites, which have comparable associations of local Iron Age flint-tempered and grog-tempered vessels (and mixtures of the two). These sites include Aylesford, Borden, and early Canterbury contexts. Residuality, however, is still a problem at Canterbury, as it also is at Highstead.

The Highstead grog-tempered fabric is not as conspicuously hard as that of Canterbury. It has the normal dark grey core with a certain amount of mica apparently naturally present in the clay, and with smoothed or burnished dark grey surfaces. Sherds from large thick storage jars are often red or buff in surface colour.

The term 'Belgic' is still in common use for Late Iron Age grog-tempered pottery with distinctive curving forms. In other parts of south-eastern England the appearance of this ceramic type in itself marks the 'Late Iron Age', but in Kent this does not apply.

The grog-tempered fabric referred to here is generally distinguished by abundant inclusions of grog, but also embraces sandier variations which may show signs of having been wheel-thrown and are referred to as 'Romanised'. Other variations which contain additional inclusions have been identified separately and are described below. The codes used are those employed earlier in this report, particularly in Table 14, with cross-references to the East Kent Fabric series, where appropriate.

Grog-with-flint (Fabric 35; East Kent Fabric B3)

This fabric is a hybrid between the local Late Iron Age flint tempering and the new grog, and is found by the early first century B.C. A range of vessels is represented at Highstead, in forms which are generally early (Table 15).

Grog-with-chalk (Fabric 38; East Kent Fabric B4)

The fabric is the familiar grog, with the addition of small pieces of a white chalky substance which is easily scratched with the fingernail and is unlike shell. It is a largely pre-conquest variant, presumably local (Lyne (2003) considers that it comes from the Folkestone area). Two classifiable forms are represented (Table 16). The only other instances at Highstead were another rim, from B15, and a small sherd with combed surface in B164.

Grog-with-shell (Fabric 33; East Kent Fabric B5?)

Grog-with-shell is found alongside grog on sites throughout south-eastern England, before and after the conquest. It is only ever present in small quantities, although it is likely that it is not always recognised. Forms mainly comprise coarse jars. The east Kent fabric B5 is defined as "Belgic' grog-and-sand tempered ware with occasional shell flecks, an early variant of coarse grog-tempered ware' (Parfitt 2003, 139). No classifiable forms were recovered in this fabric; hence its absence from Table 15. There was one sherd in Ditch B4 (Period 4C); a flat jar base in Pit complex B15 (Period 4D–5A) and a small plain rim sherd in B23 (Period 5A). These may be examples of the later more ubiquitous grog-with-shell rather than the early fabric B5.

Forms

The range of forms at Highstead is considerable. It includes all the early standards as seen at Whitfield (above), together with other coarse jar types and a range of copies of Gallo-Belgic imports. None of them is really unusual, and the range of cordoned jars (B forms) is not particularly extensive. These are summarized in Table 16.

Imitations of imported forms

Plates, butt beakers and jugs comprise the great majority here, as is normal for east Kent, where the range of imported forms is small. The occurrence of other, more unusual cups and bowls, however, marks Highstead out as apparently prosperous for a rural settlement. *Terra rubra* is imitated using a fine-grained fabric (referred to as TR4), often brown rather than grey, with deliberately controlled oxidised surfaces of a pale orange which are smoothed rather than burnished. It is rarely used for plates, since they nearly always copy *terra nigra* forms, but it is normal for the G6 jugs (which, confusingly, are usually copying the shape of the white Hofheim flagons).

Only the plate forms (G1) have much indication of early or late dating. Apart from the oddity included under the heading G1-12 (No. 322, with chalk inclusions, below) the Period 4 features of Area B include only the G1-1 form (Nos 116–7, 191) and its variants G1-2 (No. 118 with convex outer wall) and G1-3 (No. 87 with a bead rim), and these are characteristic of the first half of the first century A.D. and are the standard pre-conquest shape. In the Period 5 features, however, the overwhelmingly predominant form is

Opposite: Table 15. Distribution of grog-tempered forms from areas A and B.

Form	Description	Date range and comments
A1	Pedestal urn with ordinary foot	Standard, from early 1st cent BC, on settlement sites usually represented only by the pedestal
B1-1	Rim of plain everted-rim necked jar	Standard plain form, from later 1st cent BC until after the Roman conquest; a tendency in Kent for upright rims
B1-6	Lid-seated jar	Copy of the imported 'mica-dusted' Cam 162 form, found in large quantities at Skeleton Green and Braughing (Partridge 1981), but rare in Kent
B2-1	Rim of everted-rim jar with rippled shoulder	Standard, often hand-made and typologically early in 1st cent BC contexts
B2-3	Tall jar with rippled shoulder	Variation of a standard form, most common in earlier contexts; can have decoration
B2-4	Round ripple-necked jar	Popular in East Kent from 1st cent BC to post-conquest
B3	Everted rim jar with bulges between cordons on shoulder	Standard wheel-made form, in general later than B2 jars
B3-1	Cordoned jar with diagonal line decoration	Less common in Period 4 features, in which B2 forms are the standard. Strong overhang of some B1 and B3 rims is a late feature also known at Canterbury
B3-2	Jar with a tall narrow cordoned rim	Most common in Herts, but also found in Kent at Canterbury and Richborough. Most date to 1st cent AD.
B3-4	Round cordoned jar with short wide neck	Common in Kent, but not elsewhere. Some parallels are post-conquest
B3-6	Tall jar with wide rim and shoulder cordons	Originates in 1st cent BC. Only one previous example from Kent.
B3-7	Tall jar with wide neck and all-over cordons and/or decoration	Not common, but occurs from later 1st cent BC onwards. Several in Kent, but several are Romanised
B3-8	Tall narrow mouthed cordoned jar	Usually a late form, often post-conquest and when decorated invariably has a lattice design as here
B5-3 or B5-5	Barrel jar with grooves, either tall or globular	The globular form is well-known in Kent, from later 1st cent BC
C1-2	Rim of rounded bead-rim jar	Standard coarse-ware jar form
C1-2/3	Bead-rim jar	
C1-4	Bead rims with prominent internal rim thickening	This variant is more common in Kent than C1-2
C2-3	Plain everted-rim jar, no offset	Not common in grog, and probably derives from earlier Iron Age jars
C3	Plain inturned jar rim usually with internal rim thickening	A hand-made form derived from earlier Iron Age, although it can last into later 1st cent AD. The heavy combed decoration on some is found in Canterbury
C4	Round-shouldered jar with inset below slightly everted or bead rim, often with decoration on shoulder	An East Kent form of the 1st cent AD, often post-conquest, though its appearance in B141 and B4 suggests an earlier emergence.
C6-1	Storage jar, large	Standard, from early 1st cent BC, found on all settlement sites and lasts in grog into 2nd cent AD
C7-1	Rilled jar with everted rim	Not a standard form in Kent; though it is known from Faversham and Canterbury (Bennett et al. 1982, fig. 57,19 & 25)
C7-3	Wide-mouthed rilled jar often with bead rim	Occasional variant, slightly more common in Kent than C7-1
C7-4	Wide-mouthed bowl with some horizontal combing on body	Elsewhere known only at Braughing, Herts, and only one unstratified example here
C8-1	Coarse jar with offset neck and stabbed decoration on shoulder	Although elsewhere this is an early form, deriving from Iron Age jars, here it appears only late in Period 4

G1-6, often well made and varied; this is the standard east Kent plate form and has a very strong post-conquest bias (Thompson 1982, 459).

Form G1-4, copying Cam.4, occurs in grog, large and well made, in Area A: in Period 4 Pit A255 (No. 145) and with some admixture of sand from an unstratified context. These have a Kent parallel in a grog-tempered example from nearby Westbere (Thompson 1982, 453, 858).

The sandy G1-7 could be pre- or post-conquest; the G1-9 (No. 258) is Claudian or later (Thompson 1982, 467).

The G1-11 form constitutes an odd and recognizably local variation: straight wall, wide rim diameter, flat base and a bead rim. That from B1, No. 235, is a rim only; from B164 No. 225 is very wide, thick, black, and hand-made; and No. 194, from B15 has a hole in the wall drilled before firing, and others possibly in the base: this in fact relates it to the S1 form of wide-mouthed bowls with strainer bases, although the base holes in these are much finer (Thompson 1982, 559). Another, of very similar shape and with large holes pierced in the base before firing, came from Pit C5, Area C. There is a similar bead-rimmed G1-11 from Swarling (Thompson 1982, 471, 473), and several from Canterbury (Bennett *et al.* 1982, fig. 58, no. 41; fig. 64, nos 126–7; Frere and Stow 1983, fig. 80, no. 58, two examples). One of those from Canterbury (1982, fig. 64, no. 126) has a slight carination and small foot-ring, making it similar to some examples of the carinated bowl form G2-4 (Thompson 1982, 487), 'native ware copies and variants

Form	Description	Date range and comments
D1-1	Plain bowl with offset neck and often one cordon	Bowl version of standard B1 jars; more common in burials in Kent
D2-4	Round bowl with rippled shoulder	Bowl version of B2 jars, common in Kent, including Whitfield and Hawkinge, and in the Deal burials
E1-2	Carinated wide-mouth bowl with multiple cordons	One of the most common of carinated forms, well known in Kent from later 1st cent BC
E2-2	Squat wide-mouthed cup, rounded profile, cordoned and/or corrugated body	An East Kent form from at least later 1st cent BC; not post-conquest
E2-3	Squat wide-mouthed cup, rounded profile, rippled on shoulder	Another East Kent form, also known in local Iron Age fabrics
E3-1	Plain wide-mouthed everted rim cup, with shoulder cordon	Cup form of standard B1 jars
E3-2	Plain everted rim cup with exaggerated neck above offset	Not common in Kent
F5	Pedestal base	
G1	Plate of uncertain form	Example in grog-and-chalk fabric
G1-1	Straight-walled plate copying Gallo-Belgic form Cam 1	Standard pre-conquest plate form, from late 1st cent BC
G1-2	Similar to G1-1 but copying Cam 2, with bulging wall	Not common; usually pre-conquest
G1-3	G1-1 with bead rim	Usually a Herts form, rare in Kent; here a variant
G1-4	Copy of Gallo-Belgic form Cam 4	Rare in Kent, but known in Canterbury area
G1-6	Copy of Gallo-Belgic forms Cam 7 and 8, compact dish with deep offset vertical wall and internal moulding	Common in East Kent; mostly post-conquest
G1-7	Copy of Gallo-Belgic form Cam 12	Could be pre- or post-conquest
G1-9	Copy of Gallo-Belgic form Cam 14	
G1-11	Native plate with straight wall	An odd, local variation
G1-12	Native plate with slightly moulded wall	Local varieties that do not relate directly to any one imported shape
G2-2	Plain shallow wide-mouthed bowl related to imported bowls	Found in Canterbury; not otherwise known in Kent
G2-4	Wide carinated bowl	The example from Highstead is an oddity, which appears closest to a pair of deep-sided bowls from Kelvedon (Thompson 1982, 487). It does not have the carination and may be loosely related to local plate form G1-11.
G3-4	Globular cup copying Cam 91 and other beakers	Rare form, not previously known in Kent. Post-conquest.
G5-3	Small butt-beaker	
G5-5	Decorated butt-beaker with offset neck	
G5-6	Butt-beaker rim or fragment	Ubiquitous form in 1st cent AD
G6	Jug, copying Cam 161 (or other)	From end of 1st cent BC
L1	High bell-shaped lid with slightly out-turned rim	The example from Highstead is unusual. Lids in general are perhaps more common in Kent than elsewhere - mainly from Highstead and Canterbury
L2	High bell-shaped lid, rim not turned out	Basic native form, also known in local Iron Age fabrics
L6	Plain conical lid	Standard pre- and post-conquest form
L7	Conical lid with slightly inturned rim	A standard native lid form, not very common, but also known from Canterbury
L8	Conical lid with out-turned rim	Usually post-conquest

Opposite and above: Table 16. 'Belgic' forms at Highstead.

of early scarce forms that are Roman and romanising at Sheepen' and their conquest period date seems paralleled in the G1-11 form in Kent.

Area A has some individual specimens of unusual forms not found in Area B. The G2-2 bowl from A262 is not derived from a Gallo-Belgic form, but belongs to a small group vaguely related to continental Iron Age bowls (Thompson 1982, 481); rather similar wide-mouthed bowls of unusual appearance occurred in Area B, designated form C7-4 (below). The G2-4 (No. 273, A122) is an oddity, which in appearance is nearest to a pair of deep, straight-sided bowls from Kelvedon, Essex (Thompson 1982, 487) but does not have the carination which is part of the form's definition, relating to early Roman bowls; it may here be related to the local plate form G1-11, above.

The G3-4 consists of sherds from a globular cup in 'TR4', from Period 5A Pit A75; it is a rare form copying Cam. 91 and other Gallo-Belgic beakers, and not previously known in Kent. The form in general is conquest period (Thompson 1982, 499).

The only remaining form to discuss here is B1-6 of which two occurred in Area A: Pit A184, No. 134, in a possibly romanised fabric, and an unstratified example in 'TR4', not illustrated. These two vessels are unlike the grey B1 everted rim jars with rim grooves noted below; these have the red finish which imitates *terra rubra* and

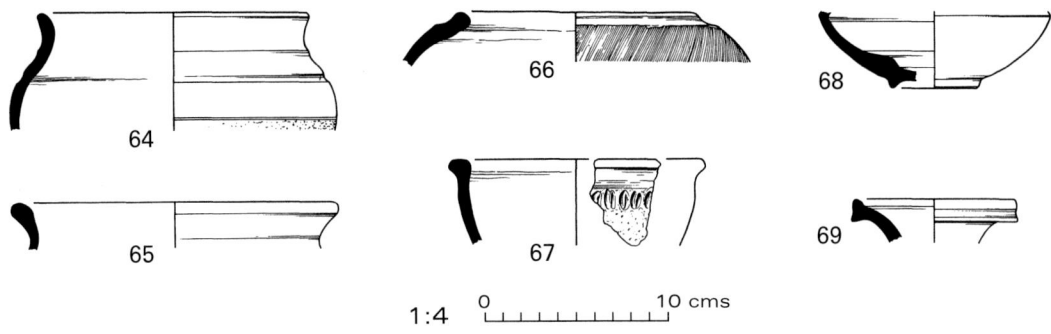

Fig. 108. 'Belgic' grog-tempered pottery from Period 4A. Nos 64–9, Ditch B141. Scale 1:4.

thus qualify as B1-6, a form made in large numbers at Prae Wood, Hertfordshire, there copying, with or without the shoulder cordon, imported mica-dusted 'beer-jars' Cam. 262 (Thompson 1982, 111). It is not improbable that Cam. 262 was also imported to Canterbury, which itself has a B1-6 (Bennett et al. 1982, fig. 62, no. 89, in 'TR4', from later backfill phases of the Area I ditch). The form is otherwise unknown in Kent. Its date in Hertfordshire is from the beginning of the first century A.D. and many of the Prae Wood examples are pre-conquest.

Catalogue of grog-tempered pottery

The following catalogue describes the pottery in order of figure number. These have been grouped according to context within fabric group. In some cases reference is made to 'unstratified' groups. This refers to pottery which has been recovered from the surface of a feature, rather than securely within the fill, but which can be associated with sherds from the fill with a reasonable degree of confidence.

Ditch B141, Period 4A

64. B2-1, dark grey, only slightly rippled neck, irregularly tooled shoulder and neck, well smoothed outer surface. A common standard form in grog, from the early first century B.C. onwards.
65. Jar rim fragment, hand-made, grey, hard, no burnish.
66. C4, hand-made, coarse, hard and lumpy; patchy dark grey-buff, fine diagonal combing, no burnish. This form is very common in east Kent, but not in the first century B.C.
67. Out-turned bowl, hand-made, dark grey, fairly coarse fabric, not hard; tooled neck, incised depressions. This has a parallel in grog from Ebbsfleet (Perkins 1992, fig. 12, no. 85), apparently belonging to c. A.D. 25–50/75, but is also found in local Late Iron Age hand-made wares, from the Dover Spine Main (Macpherson-Grant 1997) in a fine sandy fabric, and the Whitfield-Eastry by-pass, in flint temper; early first century B.C. The decoration on this specimen is unusual and is more reminiscent of the earlier period.
68. Carinated cup base with small foot-ring, dark grey, grey-brown inner surface, smooth unburnished dark grey outer surface.
69. G6 jug rim, imitating a Hofheim flagon; the fine brown fabric with dark grey inner surface and rim, orange underside; neatly made, small but not thin. The commonest form of pre-conquest jug copy, and nearly always in this brown fabric. The earliest appear in the late first century B.C.

See also No. 322, pp. 213–4.

Ditch B17, Period 4A

71. C1-2, hand-made; brown-grey, smoothed, worn. This specimen looks much like local Late Iron Age versions in fabrics other than grog (as at Ebbsfleet, Perkins 1992, fig.10, nos 44, 48); it is not yet a true bead-rim jar.
72. Everted rim, dark grey, burnished outer surface.

Ditch B10, Period 4B

73. T-shaped rim, grey with red below worn dark grey surfaces. This shape is known in local Late Iron Age fabrics: Bigbury 1978 (Thompson 1983, fig.11, no. 63); Whitfield-Eastry by-pass (c. 100–80 B.C.), in Fabric 1, large size; and also large but in grog in the Hawkinge pit group (c. 80–30 B.C.). These are all first century B.C., but there is also a larger version in grog from Canterbury Castle Area 1 ditch (first century A.D. and later: Bennett et al. 1982, fig. 60, no. 69). The form evidently appears in grog over a long period.

Ditch A262, Period 4D

74. Possibly classifiable as C3, small, hand-made, but more like the local Late Iron Age saucepan pots of the first century B.C.; dark grey. There is not enough of this vessel to be sure of its form. A grog-tempered saucepan pot occurred in the Hawkinge pit group.
75. C3, probably hand-made, fine grey-brown, red roughish inner surface and dark grey very smooth outer surface. This specimen does not look like the hard, usually combed, jars

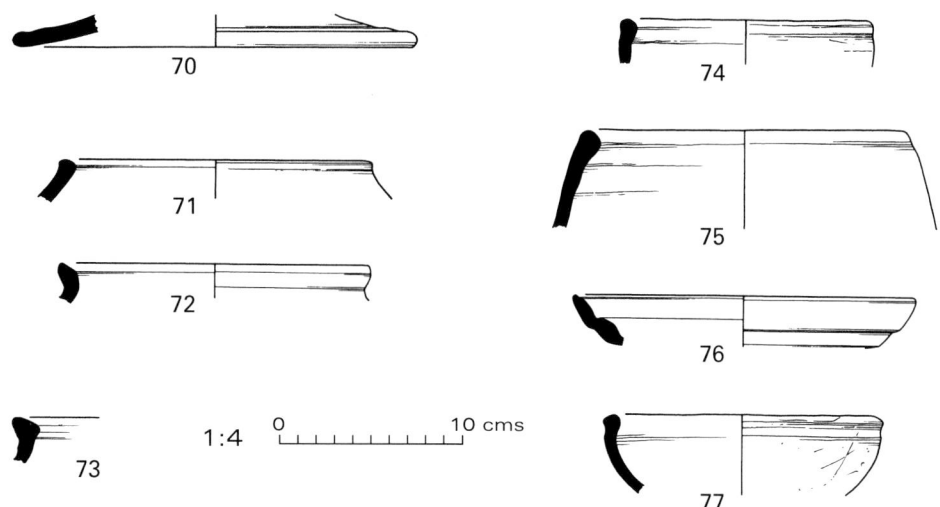

Fig. 109. 'Belgic' grog-tempered pottery from unstratified, Periods 4A–B and 4D features. Nos 71–2, Ditch B17; No. 73, Ditch B10; Nos 74–7, Ditch A262. Scale 1:4.

familiar in Canterbury in the mid first century A.D., and should be pre-conquest and could be first century B.C., although there is a plain burnished one from 49 Burgate Street (Boyle 1990, no. 51, 'A.D. 50-85').

76. G1-6 plate, probably refired; coarse worn pale grey, red-grey surfaces, very worn especially outer surface.
77. G2-2 bowl, wide, rather sandy dark grey; grey-red-buff patchy outer surface, fairly smooth. Three similar bowls came from Whitehall Road, Canterbury (Frere *et al.* 1987, fig. 73, no. 41).

Clearly there is a residual factor here; the import copies are normal Canterbury types of the mid first century A.D. and likely to be post-conquest, but the other two vessels may be much older.

Enclosure B7, Period 4C

78. B2-1, dark grey, shallow ripples, very worn outer surface but once burnished. Cf. Whitehall Road, Canterbury (Frere *et al.* 1987, fig. 76, no. 105); this is Claudian, although it is a standard early form.
79. C3, hand-made, rather crude, dark grey, rough combed decoration. Another, with similar decoration, is known from Margate (Thompson 1982, 235, 237).
80. C6-1 storage jar base, coarse, rather soapy, dark grey-buff, reddish inner surface. This was from the intersection of ditches 7, 8, and 9.
81. B2-3 but rilled (C7-1), brown-grey, dark grey surfaces; burnished rippled neck similar to No. 78 above, shallow incised rilling below, with zig-zag decoration tooled on top. Similar examples (without the extra zig-zag) are known from Whitehall Road, Canterbury, in the primary occupation (Frere *et al.* 1987, fig.74, nos 67–8); early first century A.D.
82. D2-4 shoulder sherd, worn dark grey with paler grey core and inner surface.

83. E1-2 cup rim, good red-brown, dark grey very smooth surfaces, very well made.
84. E2-3 cup rim, dark grey, smooth.
85. E3-1 cup rim, dark grey, burnished.
86. E cup rim, dark grey, smooth.
87. G1-3 plate, dark grey, smoothed. The plate is slightly deeper than in the drawing. This is an unusual form for Kent, but is a variation of the standard pre-conquest plate form.
88. Small flat base, worn dark brown-grey.

This group is pre-conquest. Some pieces are likely to be first century B.C., but the plate dates to the first half of the first century A.D. Overall, the group is similar to early Canterbury assemblages such as those from Whitehall Road (Frere *et al.* 1987, figs 72–6).

Ditch B4, Period 4C

89. A1 pedestal base, thick and solid, grey-brown, dark grey patchy surfaces. *Unstratified.*
90. B1 or B3 jar rim, grey-brown, dark grey surfaces, smoothed. *Unstratified.*
91. B2-1, rather flattened rim, brown-grey, very smooth outer surface.
92. B2-1, dark grey, burnished heavily outer surface, irregular rippling. A very similar example, including the neck finish, is from 49 Burgate, Canterbury (Boyle 1990, no. 13; pre-conquest).
93. B2-1, grey, red surfaces, some smoothing at rim.
94. B3 shoulder, strongly cordoned, good brown-red fabric with dark grey surfaces, tooled outer surface, well made.
95. B3-7 jar, many pieces, fairly thin, well made, brown-grey hard fabric with grey core, smoothed surfaces with faint burnished decoration. There are parallels for the form and decoration from Borough Green, and Heybridge, Essex (Thompson 1982, 167).

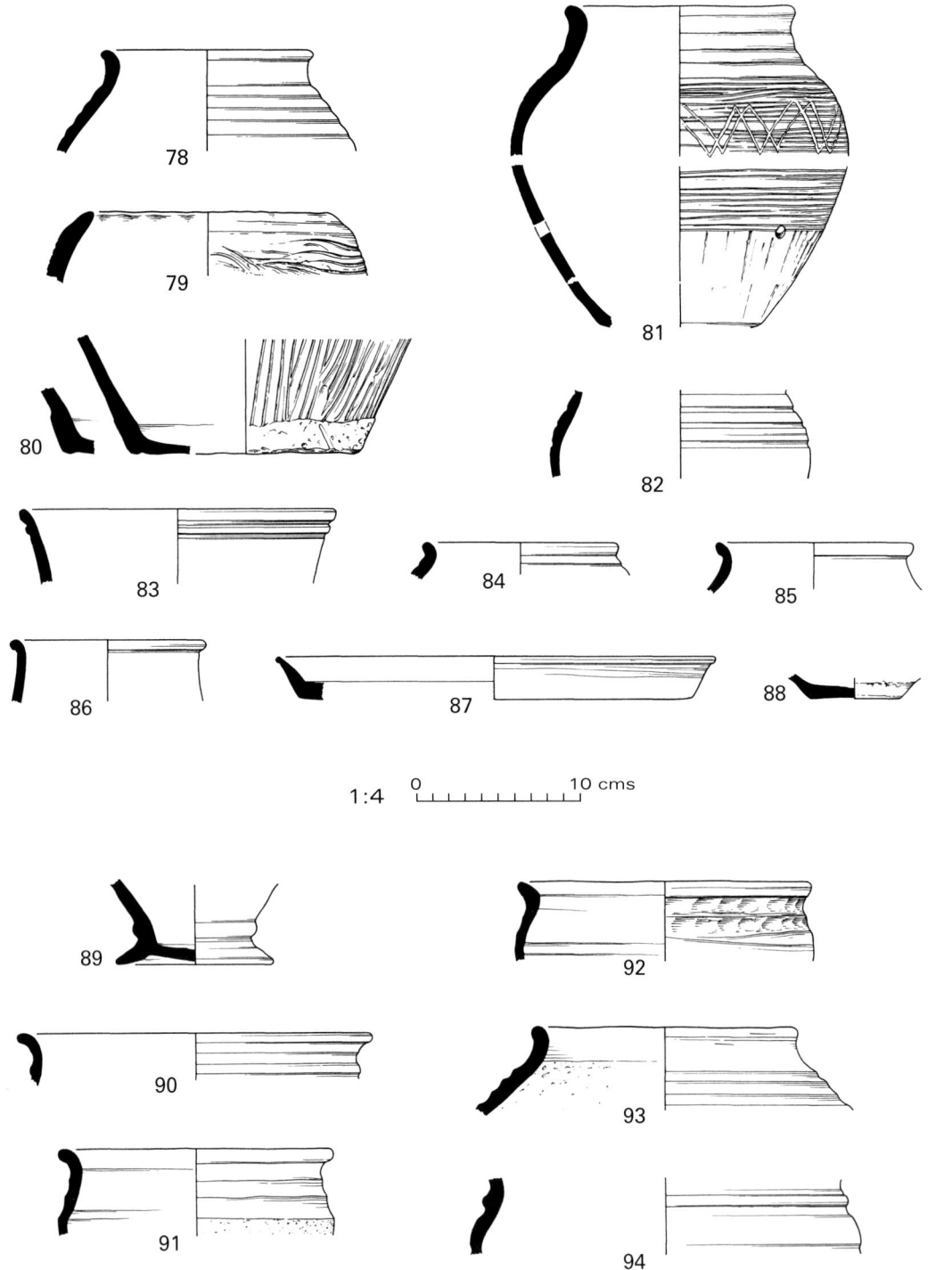

Fig. 110. 'Belgic' grog-tempered pottery from Period 4C features. Nos 78–88, Ditch B7; Nos 89–90, unstratified; Nos 91–4, Ditch B4. Scale 1:4.

96. B5-3 or B5-5 rim, small, brown-grey, burnished outer surface. *Unstratified*.
97. C2-3, hand-made, quite hard, grey, brown surfaces, well burnished outer surface; rather irregular rim, shallow incised decoration. For the distinctive decoration, as Fig. 113, No. 142, there is a parallel at Margate, and another from Minnis Bay, Birchington (Thompson 1982, 235, 237).
98. C2-3, hand-made, coarse thick dark grey, tooled smooth outer surface.
99. C3, hand-made, dark grey, smooth outer surface, rather irregularly shaped.
100. C3, probably wheel-made, upright variety; brown, dark grey surfaces, burnished outer surface; neat, well made. This looks like a 'saucepan pot', which can occur in grog (as at Hawkinge) but is always hand-made. There is not enough of this vessel to be sure. *Unstratified*.
101. C3, hand-made, irregular, coarse; hard patchy brown-grey, shallow combing. For similar vessels see 49 Burgate, Canterbury (Boyle 1990, nos 24–5 and others, pre-conquest).
102. C3, hard, thick and coarse, dark grey, combed.
103. C3, upright variety, good brown-grey, darker surfaces, burnished outer surface and well over rim*; cf . no. 100*.
104. C3, fairly hard, good grey, hand-made, brown-grey surfaces, smoothed on neck and rim, wide shallow rilling and then rough below. *Unstratified*.
105. C4, fairly regular shape, coarse, grey-brown and patchy, possibly somewhat underfired; rough finish, combed outer surface. For similar vessels, including the decoration see Boyle 1990, no. 40 and Thompson 1982, 239. With the decoration this is an east Kent form with many Canterbury examples, often post-conquest.
106. Similar to C4, hand-made, grey, brown surfaces; thick worn burnish on neck, shallow combing, partly horizontal, below.
107. C4, small rim, grey; sharp shoulder, faint vertical wiping.
108. C6-1 sherd, large single piece, well made, grey, buff outer surface, shallow decorative combing.
109. C6-1, primitive shape, thick, hard, dark grey.
110. C7-1, small, fairly thin, dark grey, quite coarse and vesiculated.
111. C7-1, well made, grey, dark grey burnished neck and rim; fine rilling. Several body sherds also.
112. D2-4 bowl sherd, dark grey, heavy burnish on irregular wide cordons. Also a small strongly cordoned sherd possibly from a similar vessel, dark grey, well tooled. Similar vessels are known from Canterbury (see, for example Boyle 1990, no. 6).
113. E2-2 small cup, fairly thin, brown with grey surfaces, burnished outer surface.
114. E2-3 cup, small, dark grey, rather irregular rippling, burnished and tooled outer surface. *Unstratified*.
115. E3-2 cup, coarse thick dark grey, burnished quite roughly on outer surface; hole drilled after firing.
116. G1-1 plate, several pieces, mostly joining, thick with small stubby rim; good grey fabric with black, red, and white inclusions, not hard fired, smooth dark grey surfaces. *Unstratified*.
117. G1-1 plate, dark grey, hard and well fired, good grey fabric, now reddish patches outer surface on rim; smoothed surfaces. *Unstratified*.
118. G1-2 plate, hard smooth grey, well made. *Unstratified*.
119. L6 with slight bead, hand-made, dark grey, ?burnt whitish patch.
120. Everted rim scrap, dark grey with black and red grog particles, dark grey surfaces, heavily burnished outer surface.
121. Odd jar rim, hand-made, irregular, grey-brown. Probably first century B.C. and possibly early.
122. Base, rather coarse, patchy buff-grey, shallow tooled depressions. There is a similar base in the Hawkinge pit. *Unstratified*.
123. Base, hand-made, well made, dark grey, fine burnished lines all over outer surface and underneath.

See also No. 321, p. 213.

This group may have some earlier pieces but in general dates to the first half of the first century A.D., with little (apart from a romanised sherd) which needs to be post-conquest. Even the C4 specimens look early enough to be pre-A.D. 43. The plates are consistent with this. The forms are those common in east Kent at the time, with links in particular with Canterbury, and with Margate and Birchington.

Ditch B34, Period 4C

124. E3-1, dark grey, rather lumpy, very dark outer surface once burnished.

Ditch B2, Period 4C

125. B1-1 jar rim, very perfunctory shaping; grey core, red below dark grey surfaces, smoothed neck and rim. The somewhat upright rim shape is a Kent feature; the plain shaping here may imply a late date.
126. B1-1, late form with strongly overhanging rim, grey, red below darker grey surfaces, no burnish. Probably post-conquest.
127. C7-1 rilled jar, coarse dark grey, patchy brown-grey surfaces, faint fine rilling, quite hard-fired. Rim is grooved. *Unstratified*.
128. C7-3 (C3 with heavy grooves on shoulder), dark grey throughout. *Unstratified*.
129. Strongly everted jar rim, brittle red romanised fabric, with some visible dark grey grog inclusions; lumpy dark grey surfaces, burnished neck and rim.

A post-conquest date must be assigned to the grog-tempered pottery from this ditch; almost all of it could have been made after A.D. 50, and deposited later. It looks distinctly later than the other ditch groups assigned to Period 4C.

Pit A126, Period 4D

130. C3, hand-made, dark grey, tooled and burnished buff-orange neck.

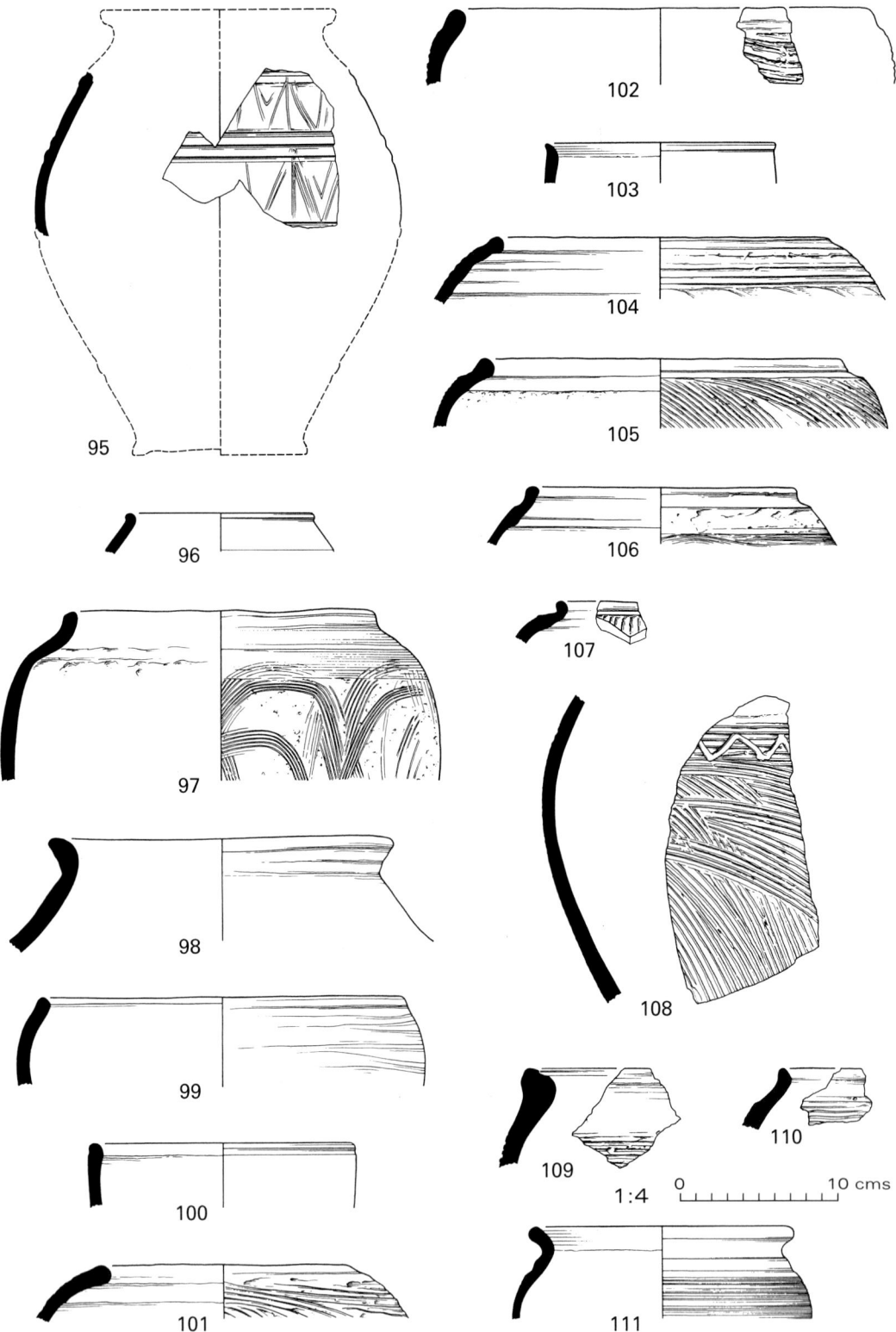

Fig. 111. 'Belgic' grog-tempered pottery from Period 4C. No. 95, Ditch B4; No. 96, unstratified; Nos 97–102, Ditch B4; Nos 103–4, unstratified; Nos 105–11, Ditch B4. Scale 1:4.

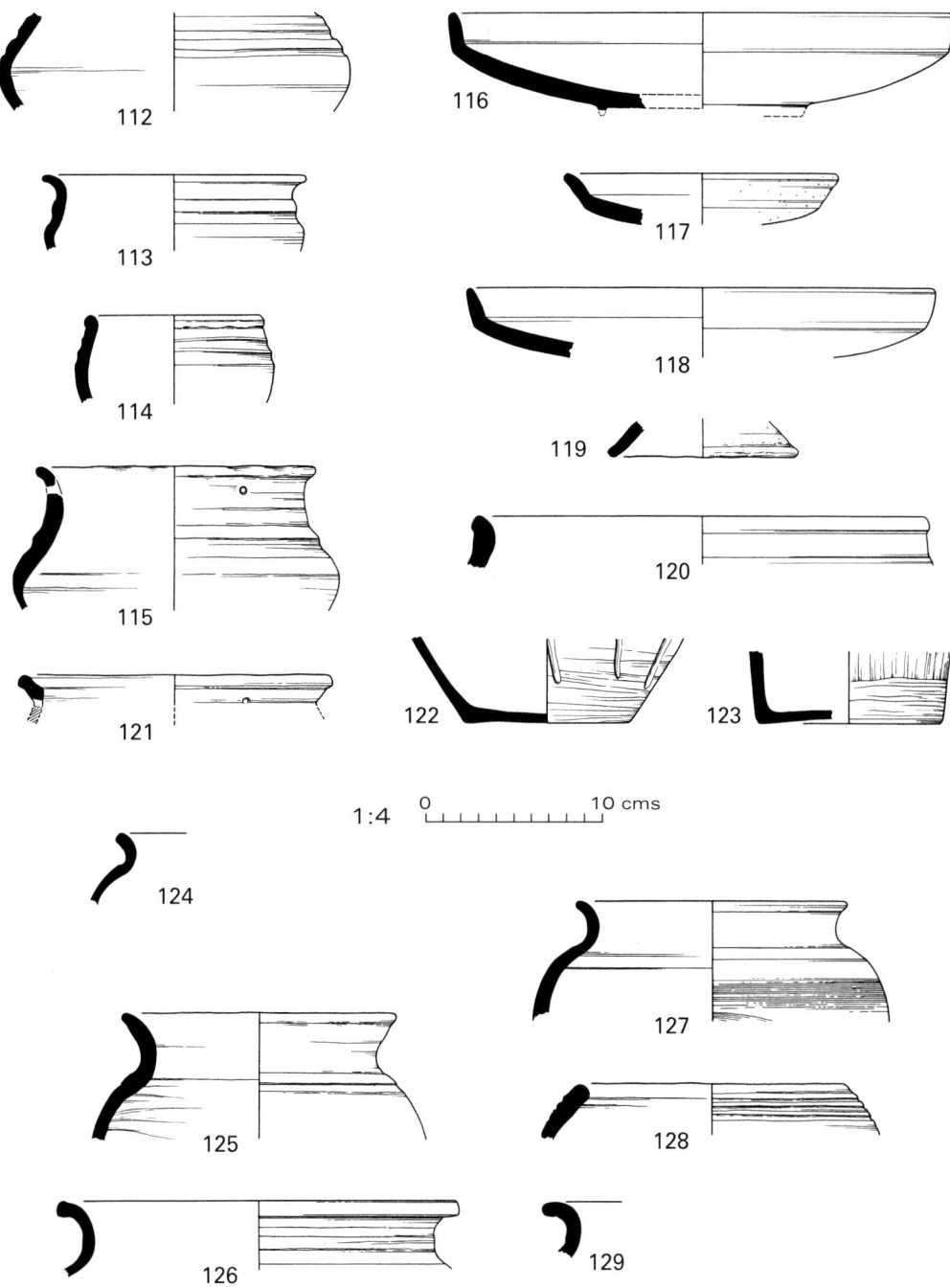

Fig. 112. 'Belgic' grog-tempered pottery from Period 4C features. Nos 112–13, Ditch B4; No. 114, unstratified; No. 115, Ditch B4; Nos 116–18, unstratified; Nos 119–20, Ditch B4; No. 121, unstratified; Nos 122–3, Ditch B4; No. 124, Ditch B34; Nos 125–9, Ditch B2. Scale 1:4.

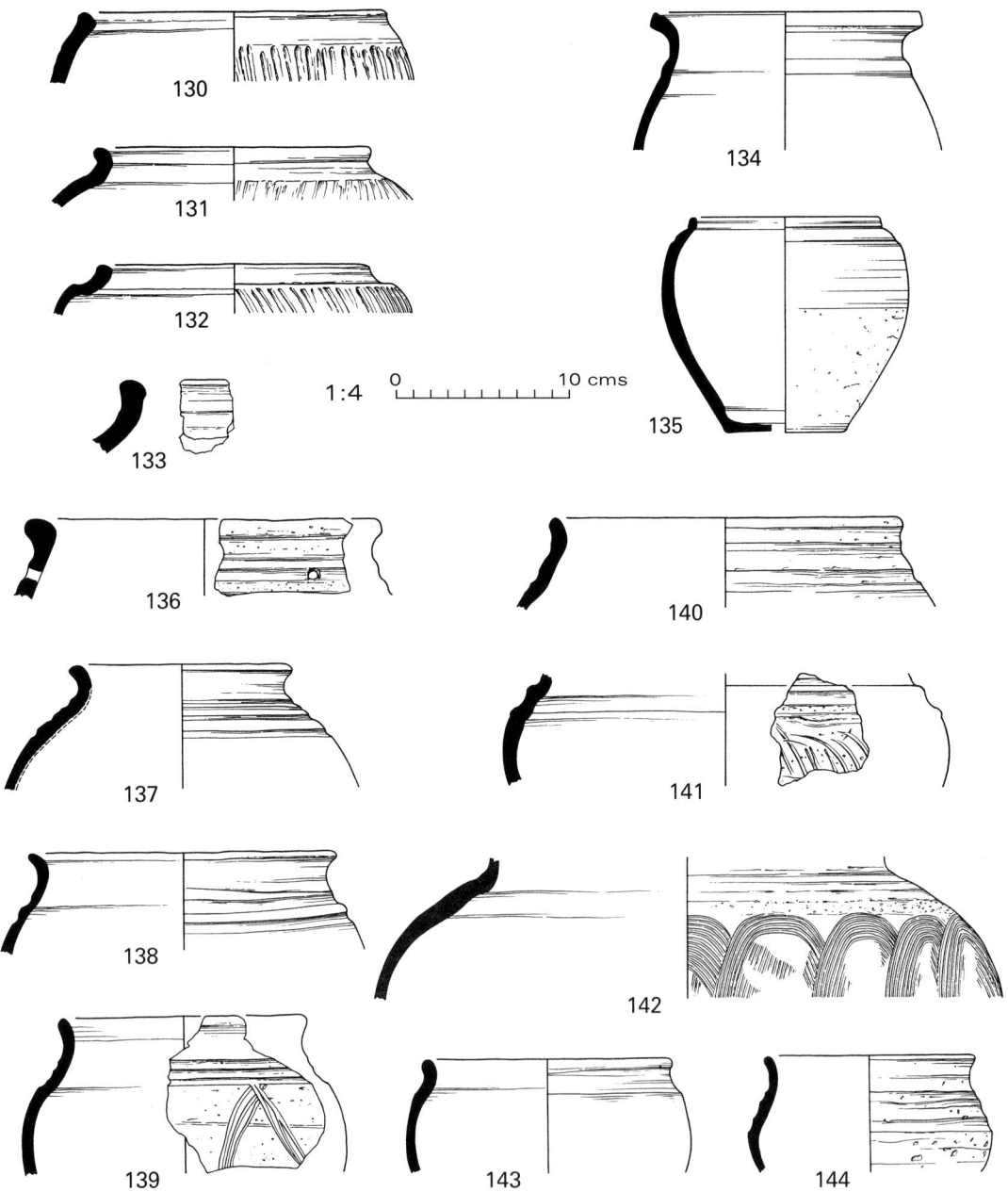

Fig. 113. 'Belgic' grog-tempered pottery from Period 4D features. Nos 130–33, Pit A126; Nos 134–5, Pit A184; Nos 136–44, Pit A255. Scale 1:4.

131. C4, worn and irregular, grey, worn to orange outer surface.
132. C4, hand-made, worn, grey, no burnish.
133. C6-1, hand-made, thick, dark grey, coarse, tooled outer surface.

In form and decoration these are Canterbury types of the mid first century A.D.

Pit A255, Period 4D

136. B2-1, hand-made, thick coarse grey-brown, dark grey worn surfaces, tooled and burnished outer surface; hole drilled after firing.
137. B2-1, fairly thick and coarse, dark grey worn off inner surface, patchy outer surface, smoothed and possibly worn.

Two wide cordons, neatly made; slight irregularity to rim; large narrow-mouthed jar.

138. B2-1, probably hand-made, irregular ripples; thin, dark grey, tooled outer surface.
139. B2-1, good grey-brown fabric, fairly evenly made and fired, shallow ripple neck, burnished decoration below. There are good parallels for both form and decoration, which were common in east Kent: examples are from Whitehall Road, Canterbury (Frere *et al.* 1987, fig. 75, no. 80; fig. 77, no. 128) and the Mill Hill cemetery at Deal (Parfitt 1995, figs 62, 63, 66). Some date to the later first century B.C., others are closer to the conquest.
140. B2-1, one sherd; probably hand-made, dark grey, grey-brown smoothed surfaces; neck tooled.
141. B2 shoulder, thick dark grey-brown, roughly shaped, heavy tooling, almost incised combing.
142. C2-3, large, fairly soft coarse dark grey, patchy brown-grey surfaces; some alteration of colour between two joining sherds; tooled neck; fine combed decoration. For the decoration, see No. 97, with a parallel at Birchington.
143. D1-1 bowl, hand-made, dark grey, irregular burnish on outer surface.
144. E2-3 cup, hand-made, long ripple neck; dark grey, worn to red inner surface, tooled patchy brown-dark grey outer surface; reddish at rim; quite thin; good fabric.
145. G1-4 plate, large, neatly made, dark grey, patchy, burnished inner surface and over rim. This is an unusual form in Kent, but it is found at Canterbury (e.g. Whitehall Road primary occupation of hut, Frere *et al.* 1987, fig. 74, no. 70) where close copies of Gallo-Belgic imported plates might be expected; they are less common in the countryside, and suggest a degree of status. The date is from *c.* 10 B.C. to the Claudian period.
146. G5-6 butt beaker sherd, small, thin; fine brown fabric, red below red-brown very smooth surfaces, fine faint rouletting outer surface beneath burnished base of cordon. This is from a good quality vessel in a version of grog-tempering which deliberately imitated *terra rubra*, and should date to the first half of the first century A.D.
147. L2 lid, large, bell-shaped, neatly made; patchy dark grey-brown.
148. Jar base with small omphalos, coarse and thick, grey with dark grey surfaces.

Nothing in this group needs to be later than the conquest. It looks earlier as a whole than the group from Ditch A229, and does not have the distinctive Canterbury C1 and C4 jars which are often conquest period and later. It does have pre-conquest copies of imported forms.

Ditch A229, Period 4D

149. B1-1 jar rim, fairly small and thin, dark grey, neatly made, heavy burnish on neck, fine diagonal combing on body. Very similar to examples from Canterbury, such as Bennett *et al.* 1982, fig. 57, no. 24, from the Area 1 ditch at Canterbury Castle (pre-A.D. 65).
150. Long jar rim and neck, brown-grey burnished neck, soapy.
151. C1-2 (cf. C7-3), small, lumpy dark grey, coarse fabric, some pale soft lumps.
152. C1-4 (cf. C7-3), fairly large, coarse, grey, worn; fired quite hard; at least partly hand-made; thick bead rim. Nos 151 and 152 are Canterbury types, with the thick rim and heavy combing (Thompson 1982, 217, 225). They can be post-conquest.
153. C4, similar fabric, red patch on neck and rim; faint decoration.
154. L2 lid, small rim, at least partly hand-made; grey-brown, roughly shaped inner surface and roughly smoothed outer surface.

There is nothing here to suggest a date much past the conquest (except perhaps for No. 149, but this is not much).

Ditch B25, Period 4D

155. Plain everted rim, no surviving neck, lumpy dark grey. *Unstratified.*

Pit complex B15, Period 4D–5A (Figs 114–16)

Whilst it is certain that B15 was open to receive rubbish from Period 4D much of its pottery and finds are clearly Roman and this bias is reflected in the strong post-conquest and romanising element in the material detailed below.

156. B1-1 jar, hard, burnished exterior and over rim.
157. B1-1 jar with sharp offset, hard, heavy dark burnish on neck, rough below.
158. B1-1, very shallow cordon.
159. B1-1, small, neatly made, smooth exterior, shallow depressions.
160. B1-1, small, thin, finely made; traces of black deposit (?paint) on inner rim. No surviving external burnish; deep incised decoration.
161. B1-1, quite large, meant as a good pot, but rather irregular rim thickness; strong neat overhang; smoothed.
162. B1-1, hard numerous large grog inclusions; well smoothed, some burnish.
163. B2-1 jar, lumpy fabric.
164. B3-1 jar? with flared rim, brittle fabric, no burnish.
165. B3-1, large, flaring rim, hard fired, much irregular grog, hard surfaces, no burnish. Faint diagonal tooled decoration.
166. B3-2 jar, small, thick, irregular shaping, no burnish.
167. B3-8 large multi-cordoned jar shoulder, smoothed exterior, burnished grooves and lattice decoration.
168. B5 barrel jar form, small, smoothed exterior. Mostly pre A.D 43.
169. C1-2, bead rim jar, probably hand-made, combed.
170. C4 jar, small, quite coarsely made, smooth neck, probably not a lug on combed shoulder.
171. C6-1 storage jar shoulder, quite hard and unfinished; joining piece burnt red all through (post-loss); deep diagonal slashes.
172. C6-1 rim, very large, coarse and heavy, but neatly made; interior surface mostly worn away; stabbed dot decoration above combing.
173. C6-1 rim, also large and heavy, similar to 172, oblong stabbing marks on smoothed surface.

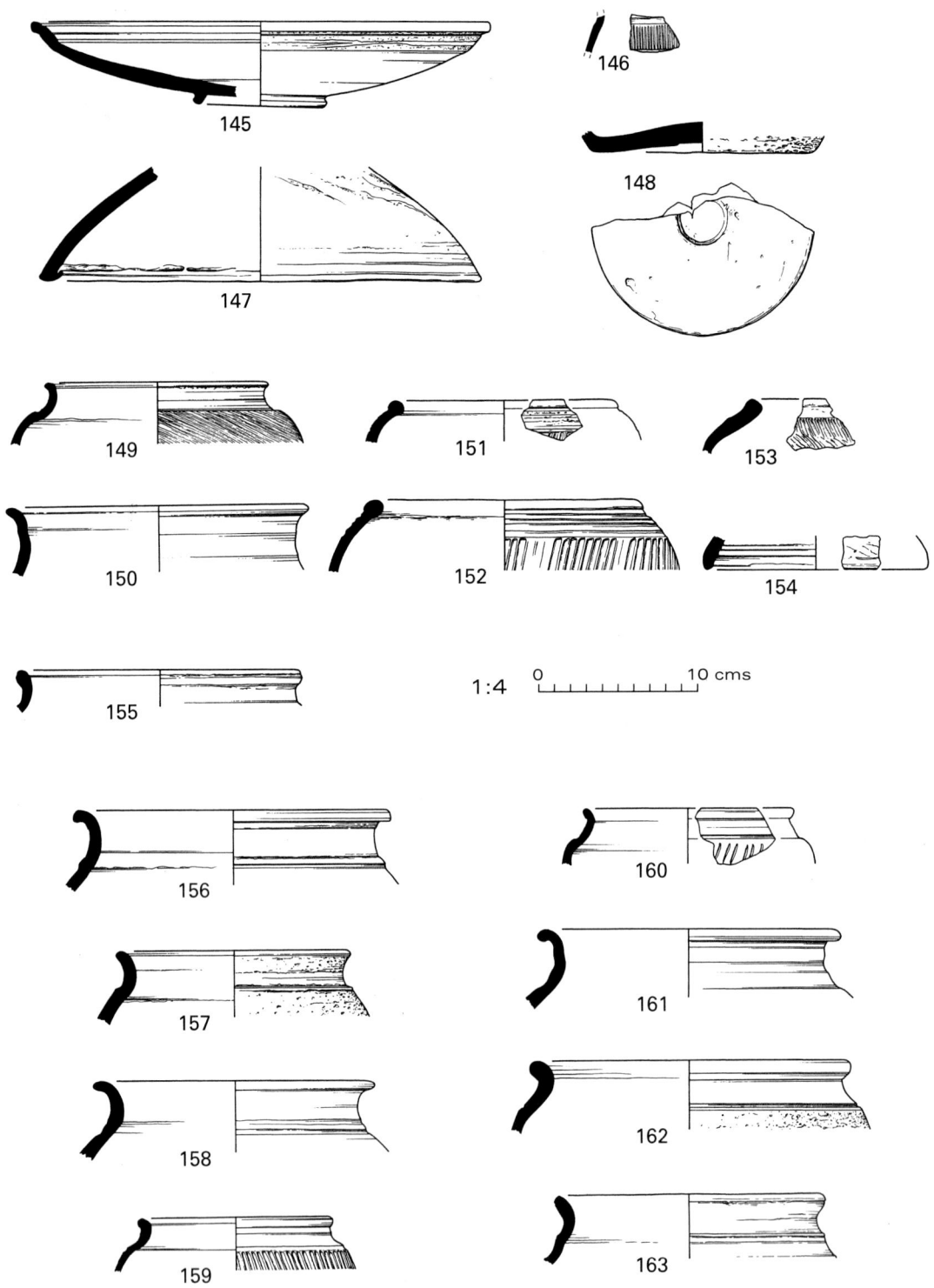

Fig. 114. 'Belgic' grog-tempered pottery from Periods 4D and 4D-5A features. Nos 145–8, Pit A255; Nos 149–54, Ditch A229; No. 155, Ditch B25; Nos 156–63, Pit complex B15. Scale 1:4.

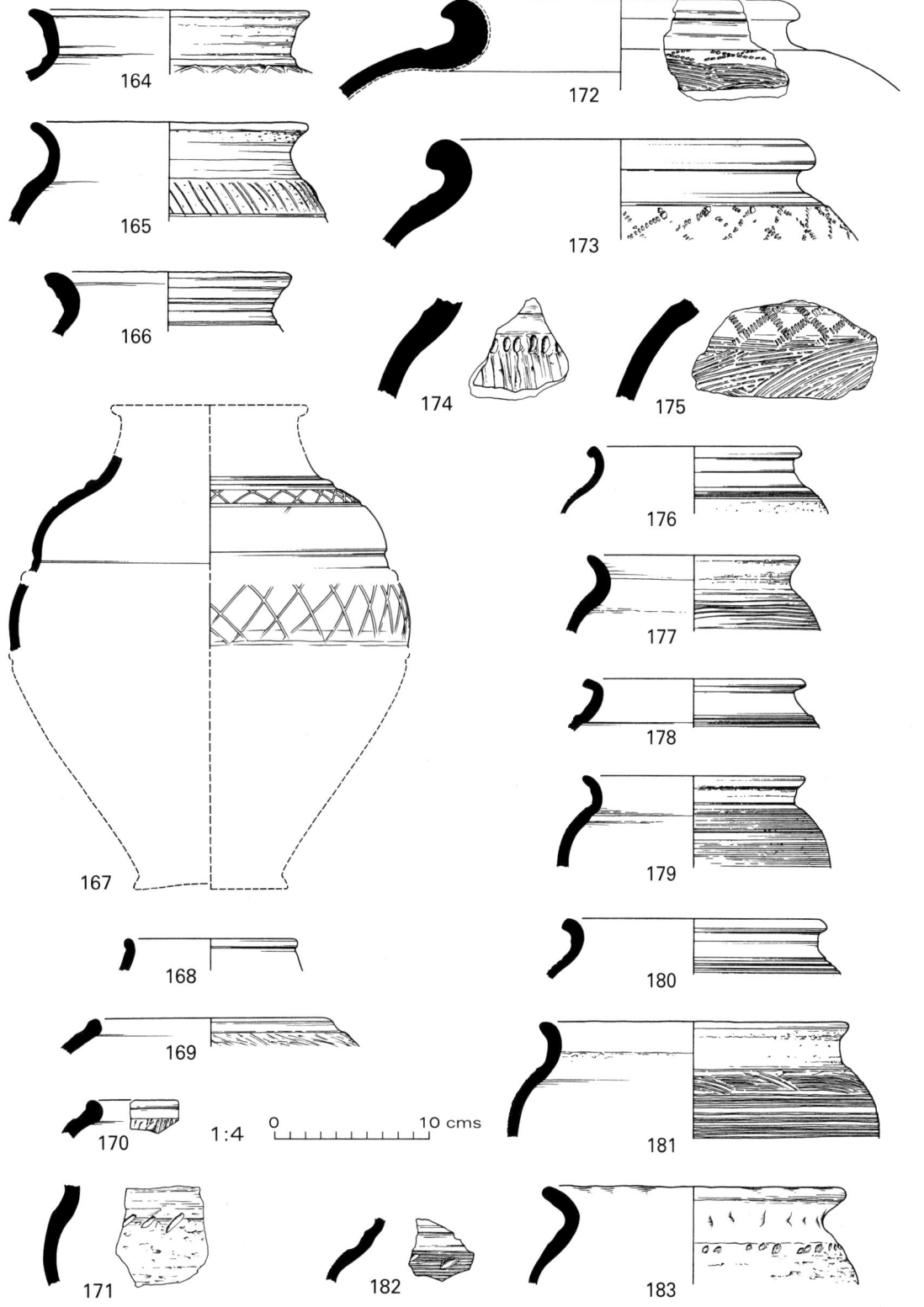

Fig. 115. 'Belgic' grog-tempered pottery from Period 4D–5A features. Nos 164–83, Pit complex B15. Scale 1:4.

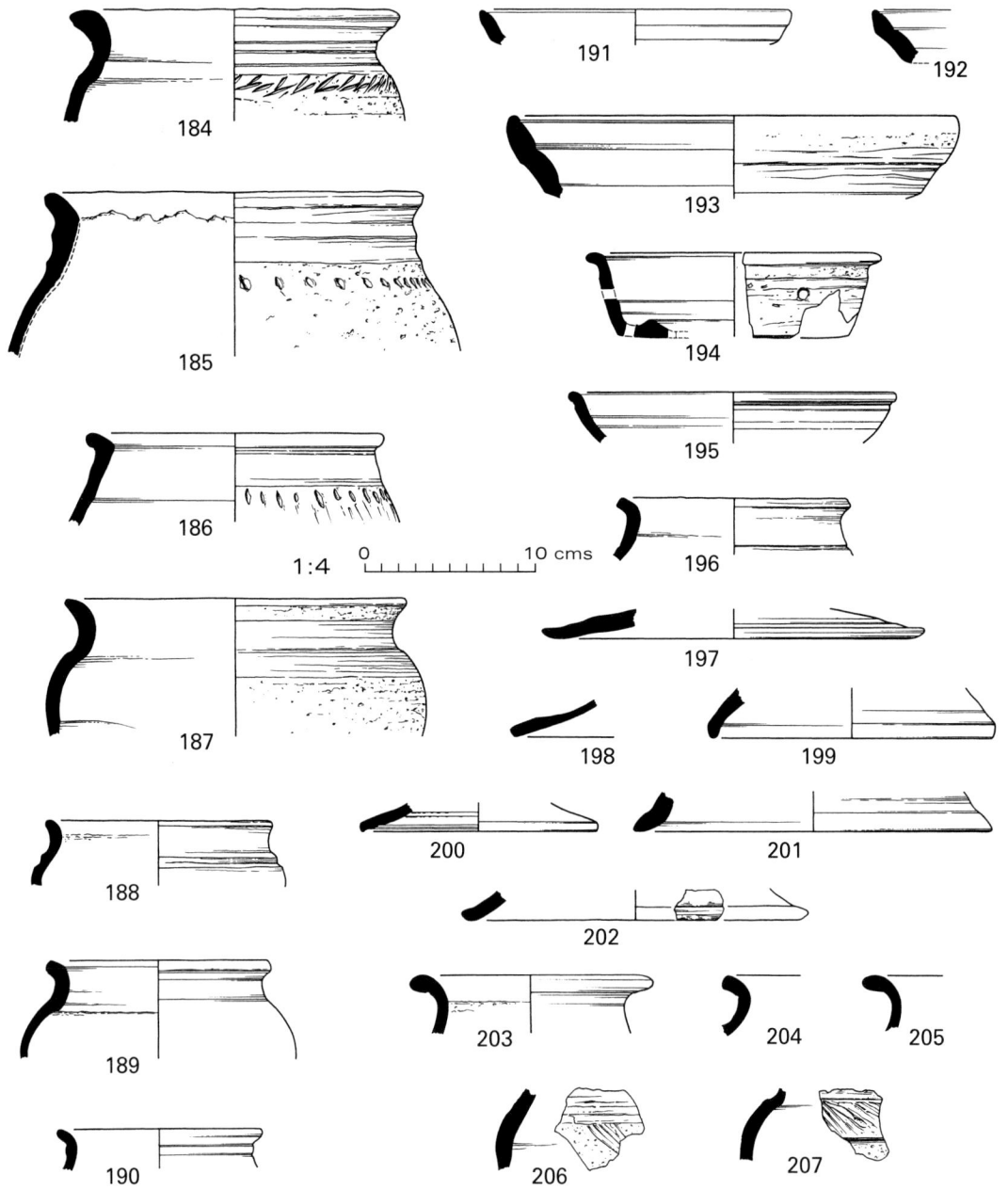

Fig. 116. 'Belgic' grog-tempered pottery from Period 4D–5A features. Nos 184–207, Pit complex B15. Scale 1:4.

174. C6-1 shoulder, rough decoration of large depressions above diagonal combing similar to C8-1.
175. C6-1, essentially as 174, decoration variant.
176. C7-1 jar, thin, hard, burnished neck, narrow rilling.
177. C7-1, not large; coarse, lumpy, tooled on neck, faint shallow rilling.
178. C7-1, romanised, hard pale grey.
179. C7-1, rather lumpy, ?romanised, fine rilling on body, burnish on neck and over rim.
180. C7-1, burnished, neat rim, shallow rilling below offset.
181. C7-1, fairly large, partly hand-made, lumpy, coarse; quite neat rilling, roughly burnished on neck and over rim.
182. C8-1 jar, shoulder, long burnished neck with ripple above large depressions on combing; lumpy fabric.
183. C8-1, with flaring rim, rather irregularly made, ?hand-made, hard lumpy, rather laminated in break; lumpy uneven surfaces; shallow indentations.

184. C8-1, large, at least partly hand-made, slightly gritty. Smoothed neck and rim, rough herringbone incised decoration and faint scoring below.
185. C8-1, large, grainy fabric, irregular external surface, shallow half-hearted stabbed decoration below roughly smoothed neck.
186. C8-1, similar but smaller, well smoothed surfaces, haphazard slashed decoration.
187. D1-1 plain bowl, not very well finished.
188. E2-3 cup, quite small, at least partly hand-made, quite hard, fine temper, no (remaining) burnish.
189. E3-1 cup rim, thick neatly made rim, above thinner body; hard fabric, smoothed exterior but a little irregular.
190. E form cup rim. Good fabric, burnished.
191. (G1-1) plate fragment, small vessel, short, slight groove near rim similar to the post-conquest form G1-9, but this hardly makes a G1-9 offset. Pre A.D. 43, residual.
192. G1-6 plate sherd, fairly hard, smoothed.
193. G1-6 plate, large and thick, numerous inclusions; no burnish.
194. G1-11 local bowl form, fairly hard; one hole, pierced before firing (others?).
195. Imitation *terra nigra* bowl, possibly without grog. Very smooth surfaces.
196. ?G5-6 butt beaker rim, exterior burnished.
197. L6 lid, probably hand-made, rough surfaces.
198. L6 lid, hand-made, rather lumpy, very thin at top.
199. L7 lid, quite well made, smoothed surfaces.
200. L7 lid, some sand, quite well made on wheel, smoothed surfaces.
201. L8 lid, hand-made.
202. L8 lid, smoothed.
203. Strongly everted rim fragment, burnished exterior and over rim.
204. Rim, strongly everted, neatly made, burnished as 203.
205. Rim, thick and large, heavily everted, smooth surfaces, especially over rim.
206. Decorated shoulder sherd, hard and coarse, heavy burnish on neck, tooled decoration.
207. Decorated shoulder sherd, lumpy, slashed.

Exceptions to the normal fabric colour range: 165 (noticeable blue-grey), 188 (pale grey), 196 (red-grey), 180, 204, 207 (red, 204 throughout). Patchy firing colours noted for 157, 177, 183, 184, 188 (reddish) and 201. A relatively high proportion of oxidised/partially oxidised material is present: 168, 172, 174–5, 185–6, 193 (pale red), 161, 166 (red-brown), 160, 180 (pale brown), 165, 197 (brown).

Ditch B164, Period 4D–5A (Fig. 117)

208. A1 pedestal base, not quite flat. Thick, coarse, smoothed; underneath well finished.
209. C1-2 bead rim jar, hand-made, rather coarse gritty grog fabric; smoothed exterior and over rim; thick shoulder and rim, but thinner below.
210. C4 jar, coarse, lumpy.
211. C4, but large and coarse like C6-1 forms.
212. C6-1 storage jar base, with distinct facets; thick, coarse, soft.
213. C7-3 jar, hand-made, rather coarse gritty fabric, smooth rim, fine rilling below.
214. C8-1, neatly made coarse jar, quite thin, brittle fabric, lumpy surfaces; tooled neck, neat decoration incised on lumpy surfaces below.
215. E1-2 cup rim, fairly smooth. Mostly pre A.D. 43, residual.
216. E3-1 cup, long neck. (Intrusive into Period 3A Enclosure ditch B144, derived from either B164 or Period 4C Enclosure ditch B7).
217. E3-1 cup, odd upright neck, burnished neck, some rilling on lower body.
218. G1-7 plate, small and deep; well burnished surfaces, neatly made, smoother inner surface.
219. G1-6, coarser, worn.
220. G1-6, very thick and tall, smoothed interior.
221. G1-6, small, deep, thick, smoothed.
222. G1-6, thick and rather coarse; smoothed, especially interior; exterior worn, some sandy grains, and traces of black deposit.
223. G1-7, top half only, not very well burnished.
224. Plate base, thick fairly coarse; mesh of lines scratched on upper (inner) surface. Worn.
225. G1-11, odd local form, hand-made, large and thick, good fabric, burnished strongly overall, including interior and under base.
226. G6 jug, fairly fine; fine pale red exterior imitating *terra rubra*, well smoothed. Black stain inside lip, dribbled.
227. L1 lid, hand-made, thick, worn, rather soft. Roughly smoothed.
228. Odd L1 lid, thick at rim and very thin at top, lumpy; tooled and slashed decoration.
229. L8 lid; fairly coarse black and red inclusions; better finished on exterior.

Normal dark range of fabric and surface colours, except for 215 (pale brown overall), 220 (overall patchy grey-brown), 214, 219, 227 all have dark grey exteriors, with pale brown or brown interiors, except 227 (pale brown-red underside); 211 ?refired with buff or grey-orange patches.

Ditch B1, Period 4D–5A (Figs 118–19)

Nos 230–7 all from primary ditch fill.
230. A1 pedestal base fragment, once very smooth, now very worn.
231. A1 pedestal base fragment, hard.
232. B3-4 shoulder from cordoned jar, quite thin, originally burnished externally.
233. C6-1 storage jar rim, large sherd, very neatly made; sharp rim, fine waved combing beneath deep wide incised shoulder decoration.
234. F5 small pedestal base, thick and hard.
235. G1-11 plate, smoothed surfaces.
236. G6 jug rim and handle, fairly thick, rather coarsely grained fabric.
237. L2 lid, small, neatly made, smooth surfaces.
238. B1-1 jar rim, with internal ledge, hard, very well made; very smooth internally, exterior burnished pale grey (cf. B1-6, but this is grey).

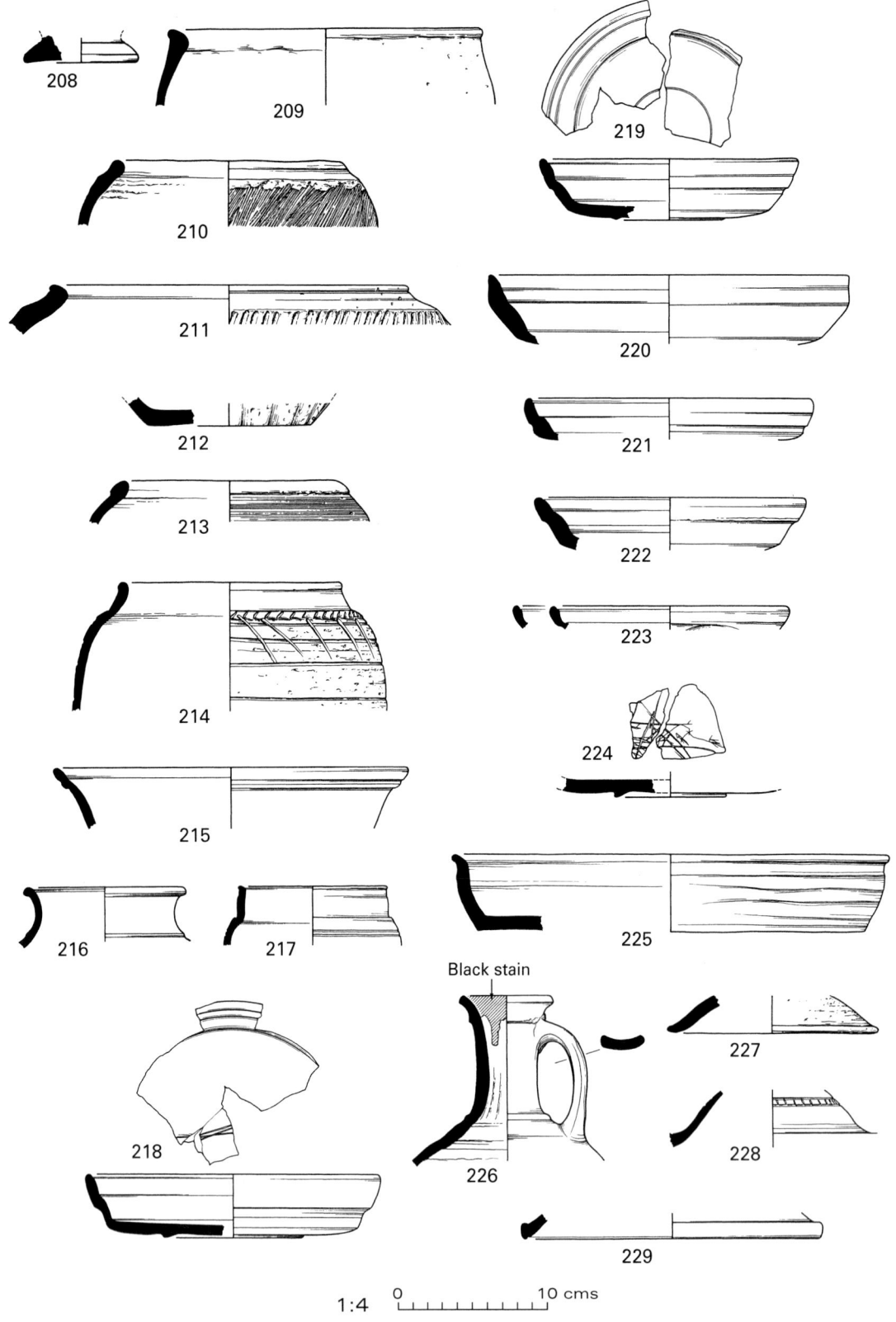

Fig. 117. 'Belgic' grog-tempered pottery from Period 4D–5A features. Nos 208–29, Ditch B164. Scale 1:4.

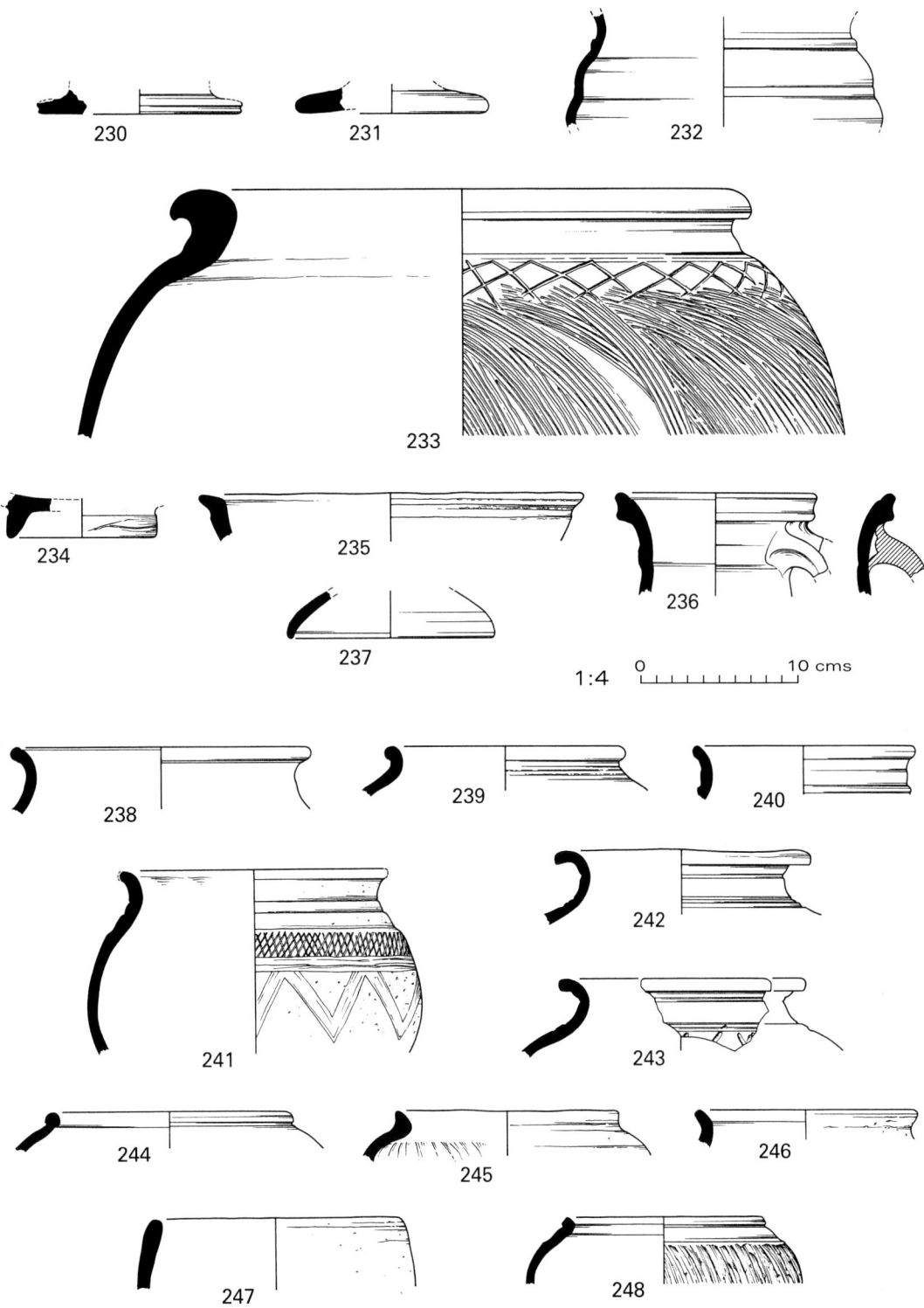

Fig. 118. 'Belgic' grog-tempered pottery from Period 4D–5A features. Nos 230–37, Ditch B1, primary fill; Nos 238–48, Ditch B1, upper fill. Scale 1:4.

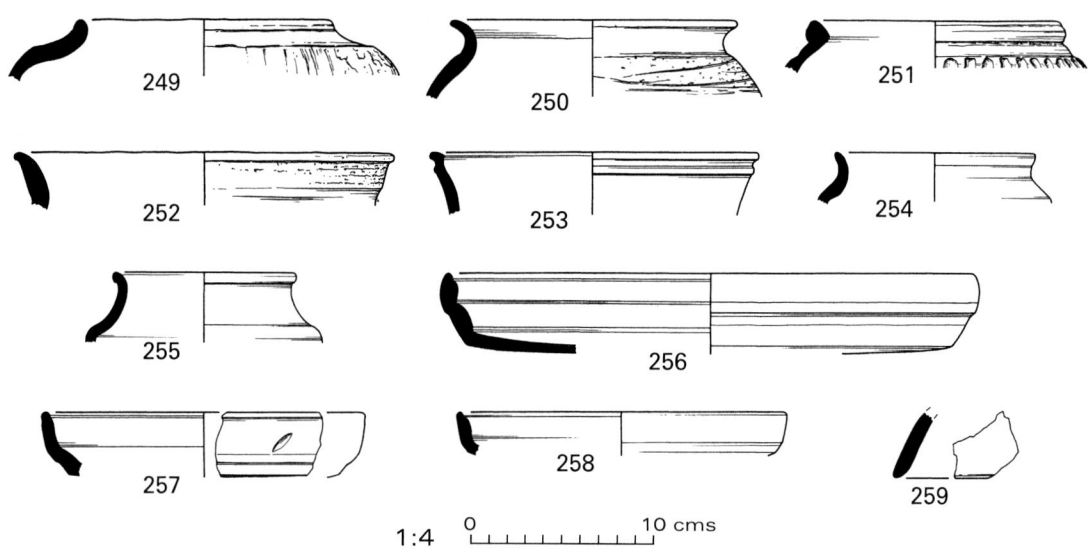

Fig. 119 'Belgic' grog-tempered pottery from Period 4D–5A features. Nos 249–59, Ditch B1. Scale 1:4.

239. B1-1, good jar rim, well smoothed externally.
240. Small jar rim, worn, ?burnt post-loss.
241. B2-4 jar, not burnished; stepped rather than rippled shoulder, faint tooled decoration.
242. B3-1/2, with late strongly everted rim, large grog inclusions, hard fired, sharp edge to rim, smoothed but not burnished.
243. B3-1, neatly made, wide shallow burnished decoration. Hard and apparently post-conquest.
244. C1-4 jar, thickened bead rim, smoothed exterior.
245. C2-3 jar, hand-made, fairly coarse, smoothed lumpy surfaces. Mostly pre A.D. 43, possibly residual.
246. C2-3 rim fragment, hand-made, thick burnished exterior. Comment as 245.
247. C3 jar, upright version, quite thick and coarse, grey and large red inclusions, smoothed surfaces. Pre A.D. 43, residual.
248. C4 jar, quite thin and neat, but coarse fabric; fine incised decoration.
249. C4, thick, coarse, worn exterior.
250. C7-1 jar, thin at rim, fine shallow irregular rilling.
251. C8-1 coarse jar, heavy external burnish.
252. ?E1-2 cup rim, thick and rather coarse, smooth interior, lumpy outer surface.
253. E1-2 cup rim, thin, burnished overall. Mostly pre A.D. 43, possibly residual.
254. E3-1 cup rim, smooth but no burnish.
255. E3-1, thin, neat.
256. G1-6 plate, large and very well made, well smoothed surfaces, three large sherds.
257. G1-6, smoothed surfaces, especially interior.
258. G1-9 plate, smoothed surfaces.
259. L2 lid, small, smooth surfaces.

Exceptions to the general fabric/surface colour range are 244, 252 (buff-grey fabric), 231 (pale grey fabric), 235 (odd pale buff throughout), 232, 233, 259 (red or red-brown fabric, grey/dark grey surfaces), 240 (possibly refired red throughout), and 243, 234, 236 (all with pale red surfaces).

Burial A36, Period 5A (Fig. 120)

260. E3-1 cup, only partly wheel made; softish grey-brown-red with dark grey surfaces, well tooled on neck. Mostly pre A.D. 43.

Cremation A119, Period 5A (Fig. 120)

261. C8-1 jar, now in sherds; coarse, irregular, wide rim; lumpy softish brown, dark grey surfaces with rough burnish on neck and over rim; large red patch on exterior lower half, knobbly surfaces, slashes on shoulder; sooty patches.

Pit A125, Period 5A (Fig. 120)

262. B1-1 jar rim, slightly gritty fabric, burnished exterior and well over rim.
263. B3-6 shoulder, large jar, coarse, hard fired, burnished on shoulder once.
264. G5-6 butt beaker, large and rather coarse; thick softish fabric, once burnished with rough tooled decoration. Not fired hard.
265. G5-6, part of butt beaker, re-used with broken edge deliberately smoothed. Quite thin, well made, but not quite the best fabric. Smooth with sharp details, plain shallow cordon.

Brown fabrics for 264–5, otherwise normal; patchy grey surfaces for 263, rest dark grey.

Unstratified Area A (Fig. 120)

266. C3 jar, thick, reddish surfaces, coarse decoration. Pre A.D. 43, ought to be residual.
267. Grey sherd with burnished decoration.

Pit A53, Period 5A (Fig. 120)

268. B3-1 jar rim, neatly made with long neck, but smallish diameter, smooth surfaces. Grey-brown throughout, patchy externally.

Pit A74, Period 5A (Fig. 120)

269. C3 jar, very small, quite coarse, hand-made, thin at rim, thin rough combing. Smooth dark grey surfaces. Pre A.D. 43 ?residual.

Pit A80, Period 5A (Fig. 120)

270. B1-1 plain jar, hard and brittle with slightly sandy feel; pale red-brown patchy surfaces. Deep wide diagonal incised lines on shoulder, smooth neck.

Pit A96, Period 5A (Fig. 120)

271. Jar rim, wide-mouthed, of B2 or B3 form. Very worn.

Pit A122, Period 5A (Fig. 121)

272. G1-6 plate, quite small, dark grey, worn.
273. G2-4 deep bowl of local variety. Good thick grog, grey; dark grey surfaces, plain but neatly shaped. Two shallow incised lines below shoulder; very neat burnished rim, tooled neck, slightly rougher below.

Pit B268, Period 5A (Fig. 121)

274. C1-2 jar rim fragment, hand-made, smoothed.
275. G1-6 plate, very sharp featured, quite thick, broken along mid joint. Good brown fabric, brown smooth surfaces.

Pit B13, Period 5A (Fig. 121)

276. B3-1 jar, brittle, hard; one hole drilled in neck after firing; smoothed exterior, but uneven and battered. Second cordon just appears at base of sherd.
277. C6-1 storage jar, rim and shoulder; stabbed holes forming pattern over fine rilling, with a white deposit in the small holes.
278. C6-1 shoulder, small stabbing marks forming pattern.
279. C6-1 shoulder, with combing below stabbed pattern.
280. C8-1 jar, small, incised depressions on shoulder.
281. G6 jug neck and rim, narrow, very plain. Smoothed exterior, usual pale red in imitation of *terra rubra*. Not enough remains to show handle.
282. G6 jug rim, rather thick and coarse, handle attachment edge survives. Red.

Most of the above have been burnt, red all through.

Ditch A123, Period 5A (Fig. 121)

283. G5-3, small butt beaker.
284. G5-6, butt beaker rim, small, thin, worn.

Both with grey fabrics, 284 with pale orange-buff surfaces.

Pit A87, Period 5A (Figs 121–2)

285. B1-1 plain jar rim, fairly large diameter, thin. Pale grey grog. No burnish. Worn.
286. C1-2 jar, half rim diameter remaining; smooth interior, coarse patchy exterior. Pattern with straight lines, not curves. Neatly made but looks coarse and worn.
287. C1-2, but cup size, very small. Neatly made, shallow, incised pattern.
288. Plain jar rim, tooled neck, worn.
289. Thick triangular-sectioned everted rim, possibly C2-3.
290. C4 jar, thick, worn inner surface, burnished neck.
291. C4, burnished, sharp rim.
292. C4, hard, neatly made, worn, smoothed neck, faint decoration.
293. C4 with T-shaped rim section, apparently hand-made, very coarse fabric with red and pale buff large grog grains (as well as grey); smooth interior, roughly combed.
294. C6-1, very large storage jar, very dense hard fabric, grog and small grits.
295. Base of probable C6-1.
296. Carinated cup, lower half. Thin, worn.
297. G1-6 plate.
298. Plate base.
299. G5-5 butt beaker, neat shape, large, well made but worn; originally burnished, fine rouletting.
300. Decorated sherd, quite coarse fabric, knobbly surfaces, neat stabbed decoration.

Brown or red-brown fabrics for 287–8, 290, 294; thick red sandwich to dark grey core below red surfaces; 285 with pale yellow-buff surfaces, 286, 293 patchy pale red.

Ditch A127, Period 5A (Fig. 122)

301. B3-1 jar, grey, rough buff-orange surfaces, perhaps with exterior originally tooled, fairly wide-necked.

Pit B186, Period 5A (Fig. 122)

302. Debased B1-6 plate form (one sherd); deep, irregular rim, and partly hand-made. Smoothed surfaces, groove inside rim, black deposit on upper exterior, probably soot from possible use as lid (302A).

Pit A274, Period 5B (Fig. 122)

303. B2-1 rim, neatly made, fairly hard.
304. B1-1 jar, small, quite thick, burnished only on rim top.

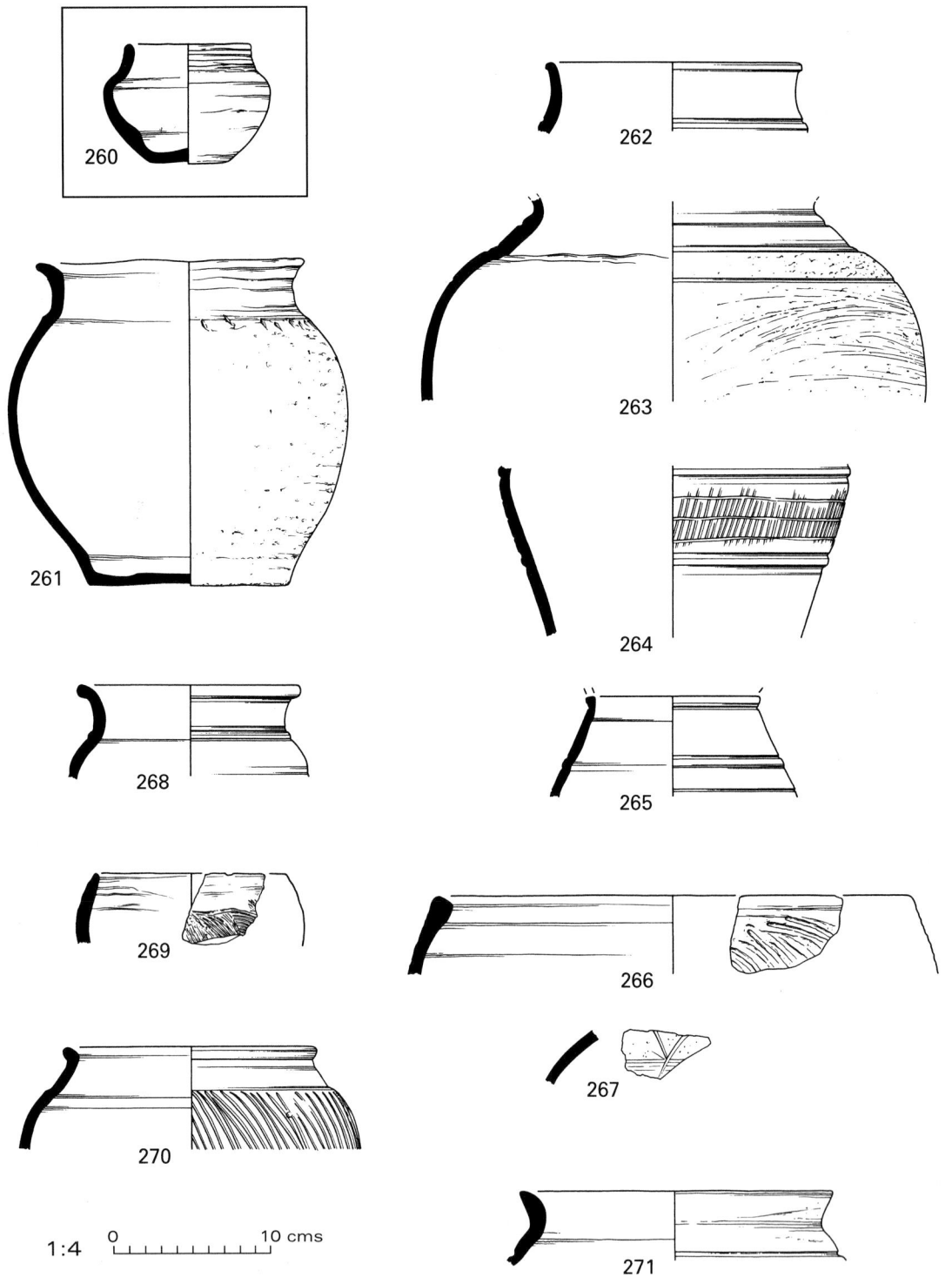

Fig. 120. 'Belgic' grog-tempered pottery from Periods 5A–5B features. No. 260, Inhumation A36; No. 261, Cremation A119; Nos 262–5, Pit A125; Nos 266–7, Area A unstratified; No. 268, Pit A53; No. 269, Pit A74; No. 270, Post-pit A80; No. 271, Pit A96. Scale 1:4.

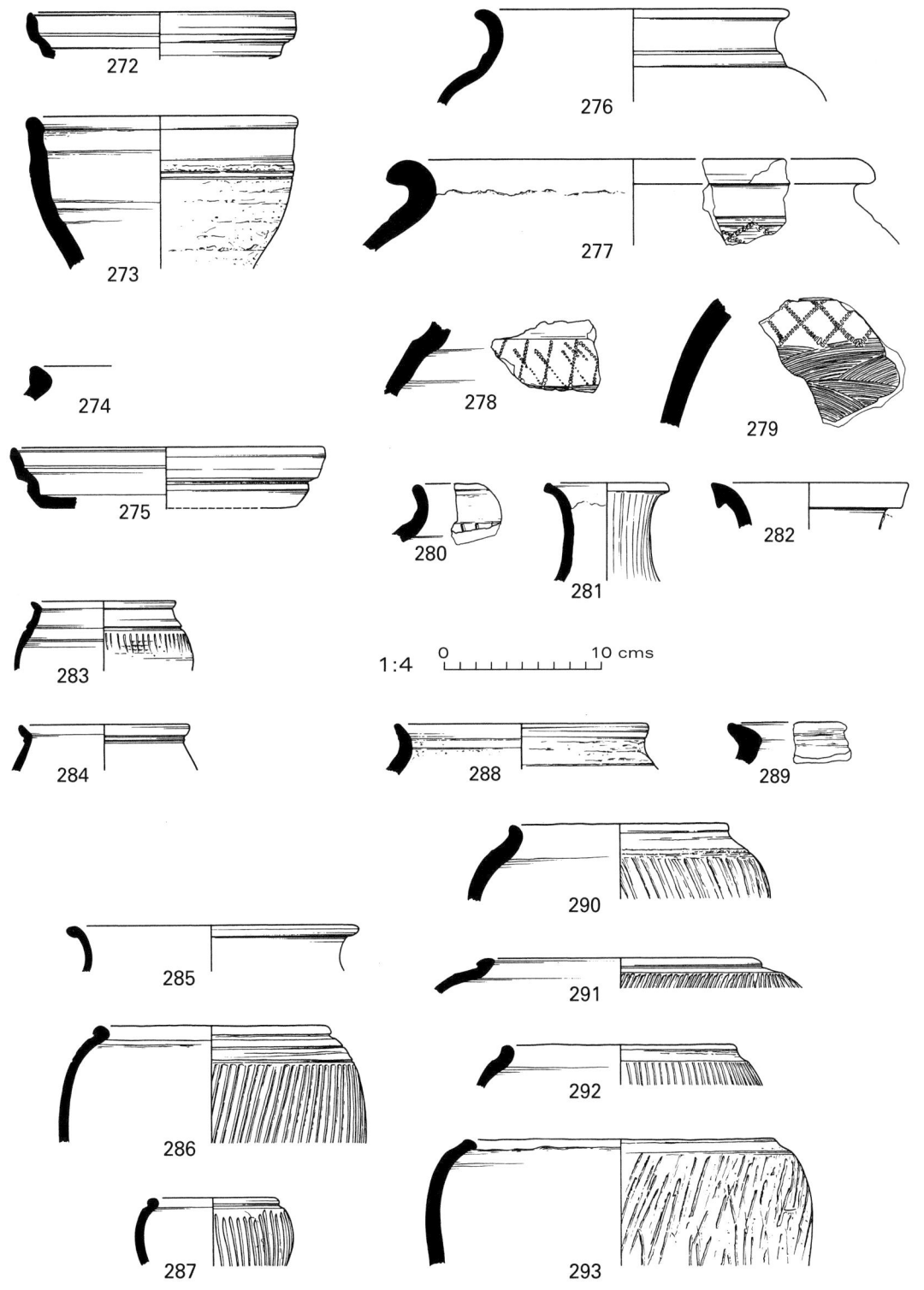

Fig. 121. 'Belgic' grog-tempered pottery from Periods 5A–5B features. Nos 272–3, Pit A122; Nos 274–5, Pit B268; Nos 276–82, Pit B13; Nos 283–4, Ditch A123; Nos 285–93, Pit A87. Scale 1:4.

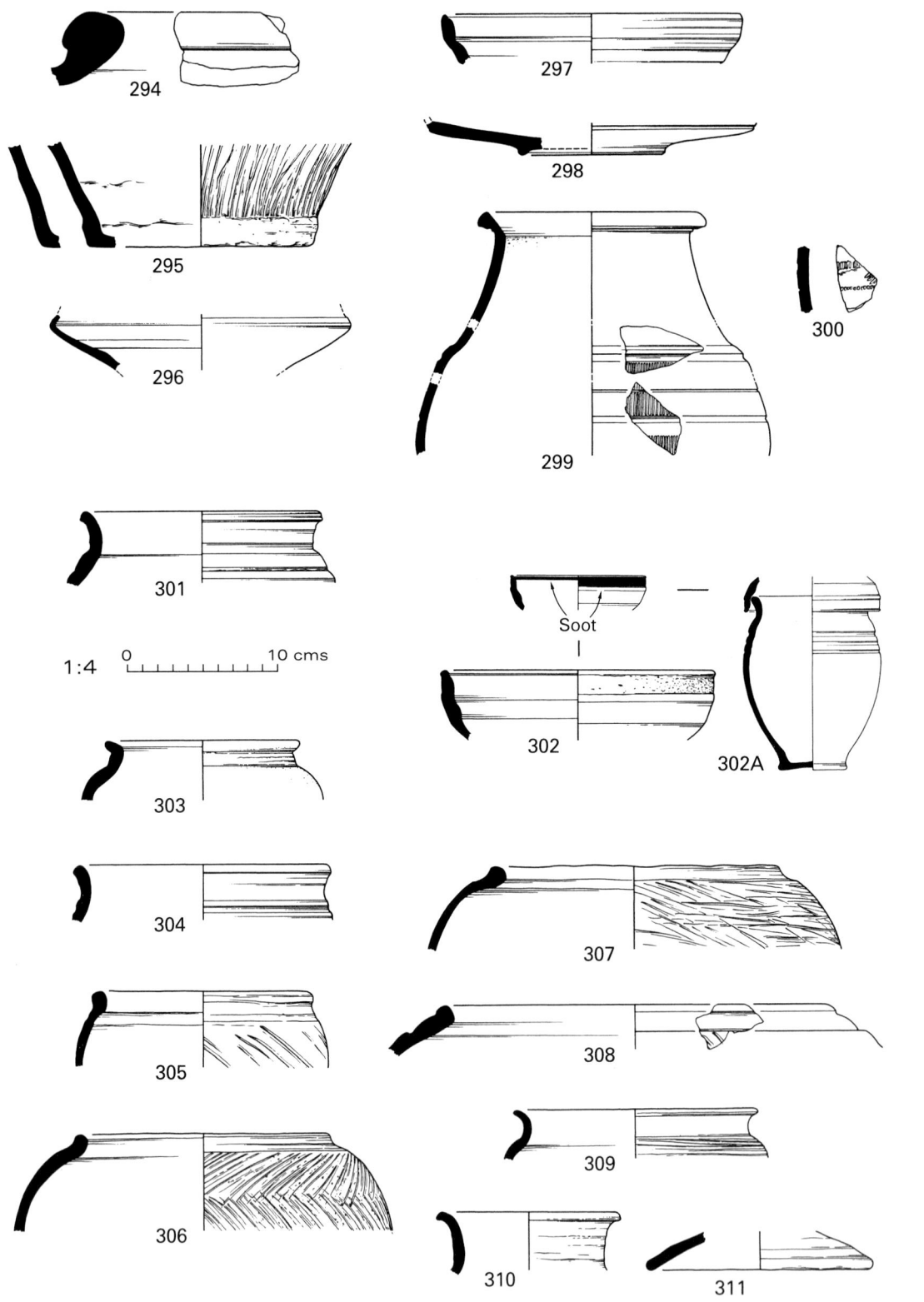

Fig. 122. 'Belgic' grog-tempered pottery from Periods 5A–5B features. Nos 294–300, Pit A87; No. 301, Ditch A127; No. 302, with 302A showing possible reconstruction as a lid, Pit B186; Nos 303–11, Pit A274. Scale 1:4.

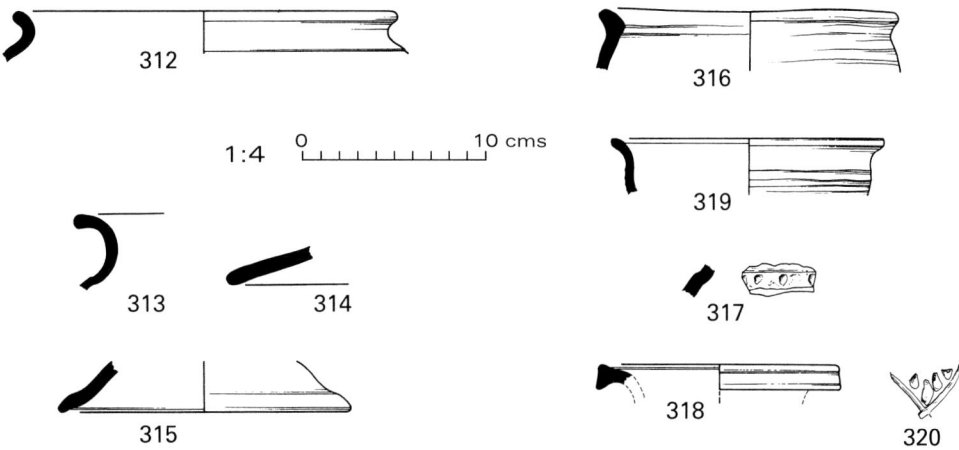

Fig. 123. Period 5B, unstratified or intrusive 'Belgic' grog-tempered pottery. No. 312, Ditch B21; Nos 313–15, Ditch B165; No. 316, Post-pit A150; No. 317, Post-hole A214; No. 318, Post-hole B205; No. 319, unstratified Area B; No. 320, ?potter's mark, unstratified. Scale 1:4.

305. C1-2 jar, hand-made, neatly made, neat deep incised decoration, widely spaced.
306. C1-2, hand-made, burnished neck, fairly neat fine combing below.
307. C1-4 jar, hand-made, irregular, quite thin body. Thick rim, broken at thin point on girth. Fairly hard, fairly fine grog, smoothed neck, roughly scratched marks below.
308. C4 jar, quite thick, smoothed; signs of strong slashing or combing on shoulder.
309. C7-1 small, rilled jar rim, worn, rather soft.
310. Jar rim, fairly coarse, worn surfaces, once smoothed and exterior burnished. Meant to be quite elegant, but not thin.
311. L6 lid, worn, exterior surface almost completely worn away; slightly vesiculated at break, rough exterior originally.

Pale grey-brown fabric for 308, red-brown for 311, patchy grey-buff surfaces for 305–7, 309 red all through, possibly burnt.

Ditch B21, Period 5B (Fig. 123)

312. Everted rim, dark grey, roughly finished.

Ditch B165, Period 5B (Fig. 123)

313. *Romanised* jar rim with strong overhang, hard brittle grey, very smooth surfaces, burnished exterior.
314. L6 lid, lumpy surfaces, especially exterior.
315. L7 lid, coarse, hand-made, worn smoothed surfaces.

Unstratified or intrusive pottery (Fig. 123)

316. C2-3 jar, hand-made, with primitive look, softish brown, dark grey surfaces, heavy burnish on rim and exterior. (Intrusive into Pit A150, Period 2, Enclosure A24).
317. C8-1 shoulder, soapy, dark grey, brown below dark grey surfaces, lumpy but tooled exterior, shallow depressions. (Intrusive into Post-hole A214, Period 2, Enclosure A24).
318. G6 jug rim fragment, red-brown fabric, smooth, pale red exterior, imitating *terra rubra*. (Intrusive into Post-hole B205, Period 3B, Structure B29).
319. C7-4 rilled bowl, small; thin, irregular rim, hard, grey, burnished exterior. (Unstratified, Area B).
320. Unstratified. Potter's mark?

Grog and chalk-filled ware (Fig. 124)

Ditch B4, Enclosure B7, Period 4C

321. Grog-with-chalk: B2-1 (with rilling), two pieces, joining; a fairly hefty jar, thick and hard, dark grey core with plenty of grog; fine-medium and a few large chalk lumps visible in the breaks. Slightly vesiculated dark grey surfaces, tooled outside, and traces of rilling below the shoulder rippling.

Ditch B141, Period 4A

322. Grog-with-chalk: G1-12 plate, three sherds, two joining. Grey grog with a whitish soft substance leaving small holes in the surface, but unlike shell. Dark grey surfaces; not a

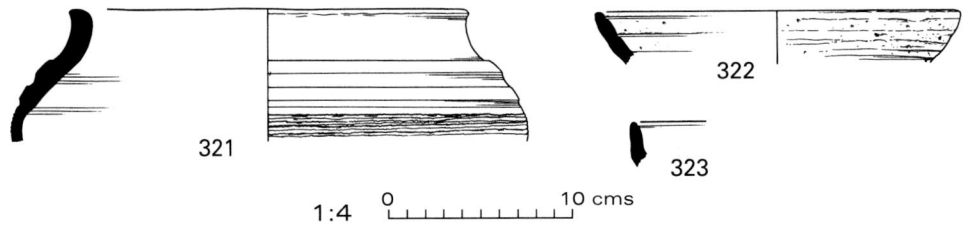

Fig. 124. 'Belgic' grog- and-chalk-tempered pottery from Period 4 features. No. 321, Ditch B4; No. 322, Ditch B141; No. 323, Pit complex B15. Scale 1:4.

large or deep specimen. The form is a catch-all for plates with comparatively deep walls, unrelated to any particular imported type. They are not common, but belong to the first half of the first century A.D. and possibly slightly later.

Pit complex B15, Period 4D–5A

323. G1-type plate fragment. Essentially grogged, with sparse fine chalk inclusions.

The chalk inclusions are very soft to the fingernail and the larger ones must have constituted weak points in the fabric. This fabric-type appears to be an occasional local variant of grog-tempering. Two other sherds are from the Period 5A Ditch B181, and Ditch B164 of the Period 4D–5A Enclosure B1 (*see* p. 221).

The Roman pottery (Figs 125–42)

Marion Green

Summary

The range of ceramics found at the rural site of Highstead broadly reflects that of Canterbury from the pre-Flavian to mid Antonine period, the site being especially notable for its range and quantities of 'Belgic' sandy and Romano-British Canterbury-type sandy wares. Groups were selected for publication from Enclosure B1, Ditch B164 and Pit complex B15. There are also specialist reports on Early Gaulish wares, amphorae, samian wares, Roman and Romano-British finewares and mortaria.

Tables 22, 24, 25, 26 and 28 provide a graphic representation of quantities of specialist wares occurring at Highstead throughout the period of the site's occupation. Any interpretation of the data should take into account the relatively small amount of material recovered; VRE statistics were not considered appropriate. Little occupation material of the later second century onwards was recovered to enable any real comparisons to be made with Canterbury. However, some points can be noted (*see* below).

Full archive catalogues have been compiled for selected groups published herein and for the specialist ware reports.

Codes used in the following reports and tables are as follows: CC: Canterbury Castle (Bennett *et al.* 1982); CBR: Cakebread Robey (Bennett forthcoming); MCP: Marlowe Car Park, MT: Marlowe Theatre (both Blockley *et al.* 1995). This report was written in 1988 before publication of the *National Roman Fabric Reference Collection* (Tomber and Dore 1998). Quantification of material for the selected groups was by sherd count and Vessel Rim Equivalent (VRE).

Period 4D–5A: *c.* A.D. 50–150

Pre-Flavian material (*c.* A.D. 50–70) at Highstead is best represented by the group from Ditch B164 of Enclosure B1. The high proportion in the assemblage of a fine sandy ware fashioned in 'Belgic' style is perhaps most notable (Table 17), matched only by 'Belgic' grogged ware in quantity. These sandy wares have occurred at Canterbury, but infrequently and in very small numbers, the grogged version being the dominant type there in the Early Roman period (Pollard 1995; Macpherson-Grant 1982). It may be that the sandy vessels were produced outside the town, perhaps in a rural location such as Highstead itself. Stylistically certain examples suggest origins in the immediate pre-conquest period.

'Stuppington Lane' and 'North Gaulish' Canterbury-type sandy wares both occur in small amounts throughout the site, with most of the 'North Gaulish' material deriving from Ditch B164. Of the rural sites in Kent studied by Dr Pollard, Highstead was the only one found to have the latter (Reed Avenue type: Pollard 1982). He suggests that Richborough, where the evidence is greater, attracted these products by virtue of its status as a military base. This, together with albeit slight evidence from an early imported fineware in B164 (a fine White Ware flagon, Rigby p. 238) may suggest that Highstead experienced some degree of early military activity.

Ditch B164: Total sherd count: 1,136; Total VRE: 1,384

Fabric	percentage proportion of assemblage	
	VRE	sherd count
Late Iron Age to 'Belgic'		
grog and flint-tempered ware		0.4
grog and chalk-tempered ware		0.1
'Belgic'		
grogged ware	26.7	37.1
fine sandy ware	37.9	36.5
'Belgic' to early Roman		
'Stuppington Lane' coarse sandy ware; local	0.3	0.6
Gallo-Belgic wares: ?TR 1 (C)	0.7	0.1
fine White Ware: Rigby WW1		0.2
Pompeian Red Ware: Peacock Fabric 2 (?later)		0.1
Early Roman: pre Flavian		
'NG' Canterbury-type coarse grey sandy ware	7.4	2.0
coarse orange sandy ware; probably local	3.0	0.7
Samian: South Gaul	1.8	0.4
Lyon Ware		0.1
fine White Ware: Rigby WW2 (one vessel)		5.7
Early Roman or Roman: pre Flavian or Flavian		
Canterbury-type coarse grey sandy ware	1.4	2.9
pink-buff coarse sandy ware; probably local	1.6	2.0
Upchurch-type wares		
fine grey ware	2.0	2.0
fine red ware with slip	4.2	2.2
fine purple-grey with slip	7.2	5.0
fine sandy purple-grey with slip	2.8	0.2
?Central Gaul micaceous fine ware	0.9	0.4
Samian: South Gaul	1.0	0.8
Roman: first to second century		
miscellaneous coarse grey sandy wares		0.1
miscellaneous fine grey sandy wares	0.7	0.1
amphorae: Dressel 20		0.2
fine White Ware: Rigby WW1 (mica-coated)		0.1
White Ware: Rigby WW3		0.1
Samian: Central Gaul	0.4	0.1
Later Roman: late second to third century		
Samian: East Gaul		0.1
?Late Roman: late third to fourth century		
miscellaneous fine wares		0.1

Table 17. Ditch B164, Period 4D: fabric quantification by sherd count and Vessel Rim Equivalent.

Fine oxidised Upchurch-type wares are never common in Canterbury, where the majority of later first- to second-century vessels occur in a fine grey fabric. Ditch B164 produced an elaborate oxidised beaker or jar, unparalleled at Canterbury (No. 369). The majority of the purple-grey sherds represented one vessel (Table 17).

Flavian to mid Antonine period material at Highstead is best represented by the assemblages from Ditch B1 and Pit complex B15 (*see* p. 225).

The fabric range of the two groups compares well with material from Canterbury. The range and quantity of Canterbury-type sandy wares indicates that the rural site was dependent on that centre for the vast majority of its 'kitchen' wares, as was most of east Kent from the mid Flavian to mid second century (Pollard 1982). Most of the albeit small corpus of second-century mortaria were local Kent products (*see* Table 28).

Only a handful of identifiable non-local coarsewares of the later first to early–mid second century were recovered from the entire site (excluding specialist wares); these being one or possibly two early Alice Holt and eight 'Brockley Hill' sherds.

There was little evidence of BB2 at Highstead. Pollard has noted that the ware had no real impact on the Canterbury market until the second half of the second century. Certainly it is during this period that activity at Highstead appears to decline with occupation perhaps shifting to an area as yet unexcavated. Of the BB2 that was in use, it is the writer's impression that much of this, again, may well have been of local, Kent, manufacture.

Types of fine tableware found at the site generally reflect those in use at Canterbury, with Southern and Central Gaulish samian being predominant with smaller quantities of other imports (*see* Tables 25 and 26). Most of the small corpus of amphorae was of Dressel 20 type from Southern Spain, this being typical of the period in Canterbury (Table 24).

Period 5B: *c.* A.D. 150–250+

There was very little ceramic evidence attributable to this period. Wares of the later second to mid third century typically found at Canterbury (for example BB2 and a hard-fired grey sandy ware) are very few in number at Highstead. However, it is possible that some of the Upchurch-type fine grey wares may belong to this period.

Most noticeable is the perhaps complete absence of Native Coarse Ware. The few possible body sherds could equally well be 'Belgic' products. Although Native Coarse Ware only represents a small proportion of assemblages at Canterbury (for example less than 5 per cent on the Marlowe sites: Pollard 1995, 705) it continued to fulfill the need for large storage jars from the mid to late second century, through to at least the end of the third. The type is commonly found on cremation burial sites outside the town, often functioning as the funerary urn. Pollard has observed that Native Coarse Ware is found throughout north-east Kent, where its distribution parallels that of Canterbury sandy wares of the Flavian to Early Hadrianic period. He also notes that if the ware was not actually produced at Canterbury, this pattern does suggest a 'natural trade/exchange zone' (Pollard 1982). It seems likely then, given the presence and quantities of Canterbury-type sandy wares at Highstead, that the community would have utilized Native Coarse Ware. Its absence in the excavation area should perhaps therefore be viewed as another indication of a shift in occupation in the later second century.

Examples of colour-coat finewares of the mid second to mid third century such as Moselkeramik and Central Gaulish 'Rhenish' ware are very rare at Highstead, but these are never very common in Canterbury. Similarly there is very little East Gaulish samian at the site.

Later Roman ceramics at Highstead

No late Roman features were detected at the site, although slight ceramic evidence suggests that some activity took place outside the excavated area. Pit complex B15 appears to have continued in use receiving refuse up to the end of the third century or even into the fourth, with all eight late Roman grogged sherds from the site and most of the fifteen Oxfordshire fineware sherds being recovered from this feature. Only two sherds of Nene Valley-type colour coats were found and no evidence of other fourth-century imported pottery, for example Portchester 'D', Mayen ware or other exotic continental types.

Pottery from Ditch B164 (Figs 125–9)

Marion Green

The ditch is considered to have been cut around the mid first century A.D., contemporary with and at right angles to Ditch B1, the two forming the early Roman Enclosure B1. Both cut through earlier prehistoric features on the site. As a result it was decided that detail for flint-tempered pottery from both ditches should be omitted from Tables 17 and 20 where the range and relative quantities of pottery types recovered is otherwise presented.

The bulk of the B164 ditch assemblage is considered to be pre-Flavian (*c.* A.D. 50–70) with some evidence for extending into the early Flavian period. Dating evidence is provided by South Gaulish samian (pp. 242–4), other early finewares (p. 233), 'North Gaulish' style Canterbury-type sandy wares (Pollard 1982; Pollard 1995, 597, Green 1995, 633) and other early local types, the forms of 'Belgic' grogged ware occurring (p. 205, Tables 15 and 16), and the high percentage of 'Belgic' fine sandy wares, some of which exhibit characteristics suggesting pre-conquest production.

There is relatively little typically Flavian and later material, Canterbury-type sandy wares, samian and rough-cast colour coats, for example.

It appears that sometime towards the end of the first century, Ditch B1 became the preferred dumping ground (rather than B164) with B1 remaining open until perhaps the late second century.

The particular interest of the Ditch B164 group is two-fold. Firstly the 'Belgic' style fine sandy vessels (Figs 125–7) represent the most comprehensive single group of the ware to be examined to date from Trust excavations and are therefore given special attention. Secondly, there are certain form types in other wares which are either rare or unparalleled in Canterbury. In the following section a full report of the 'Belgic' fine sandy wares is followed by a summary of other material occurring in the group.

Indigenous 'Belgic' fine sandy wares

In his report of early Roman pottery from the first four Marlowe excavations Dr Pollard describes and discusses a group of 'indigenous' sandy wares of 'Belgic' style. He notes that the group does not in fact occur in his Period 1 sample (*c.* 25–70/80), but does appear in other areas of the town (Pollard 1995, 597). These occurrences have on the whole been infrequent and small in quantity. Dr Pollard concludes that either the group is generally rare or that its use was primarily of the Flavian period; he suggests that the fine quality small jars or beakers (cf. Nos 347–9) here are mainly Neronian to Flavian, with some earlier and some later examples occurring (Pollard 1982).

'Belgic' sandy wares did however occur on the fifth Marlowe excavation (Green 1995, fig. 283, nos 238–41) in a pit whose main period of use was considered to be *c.* 50–80. The ware is considerably more common at Highstead, where it represents 36.5 per cent by sherd count of the ditch group under discussion (Table 17), paralleled only by 'Belgic' grogged ware. Given the scarcity of Flavian material it is suggested that here this pottery was in production perhaps in the pre-conquest period, several examples being crude enough to be hand-made, some paralleling earlier 'Belgic' grogged vessels, (*see* below). It may have become more established in the mid first century, finally tailing off in the early Flavian years.

Standards of manufacture vary from the clearly hand-made to the well executed with fine decoration. Most form types can be paralleled by 'Belgic' grogged vessels found in Dr Isobel Thompson's type series (Thompson 1982). Certain jar types with corrugated bodies for example, may be early while the high-shouldered small jars (Thompson Type C4) are likely to be post-conquest. That fairly close parallels do exist between the two types does suggest a certain immediate influence.

The range of fine sandy ware form types as seen in Figs 125–7 is unparalleled from Canterbury and the majority of the illustrated vessels came from the Highstead B164 assemblage. 'Belgic' fine sandy wares occurring in other contexts at Highstead were also examined with a view to supplementing the formal range. Selected examples are included in the figures, with these contexts clearly marked.

Neckless jars

324–331: High shoulder with bead rim: cf. Thompson C1–2.

Examples from Canterbury are rare; one close parallel for Nos 324–5 here occurred at the Canterbury Castle site (Macpherson-Grant 1982, fig. 63, no. 111); the group is not closely dated.

Grogged examples of C1–2 occur mostly in Period 1 on the Marlowe sites, which included some possible pre-conquest/conquest groups.

Three, possibly four, of the Highstead vessels are irregular enough to be hand-made (324, 326, 328 with evidence of internal rim knife trimming and ?330). Surface colours range from clear grey, grey-brown to clear orange, patchy orange/black, indicating some irregularity in firing. A range of decorative techniques is evident: horizontal tooling (324–6); combing (328); simple burnishing, now partially worn (330), and burnished lattice (331). This last vessel is comparatively well executed and is unusual in its triangular bead rim; it could be a bowl form.

332: As above with internal rim thickening: cf. Thompson C1–4.

No parallels were traced in published groups from Canterbury.

Grogged examples appear in Period 2 on the Marlowe sites (*c.* 70/80–100/110), in Period 1 on the Cakebread sites (CB/R I; group dated up to early Flavian) and in the primary ditch and re-cut phases (mostly pre-Flavian) and backfill phase at Canterbury Castle.

The Highstead vessel is fairly regular, possibly a good hand-made example; surfaces are patchy black-brown with shallow horizontal decorative tooling on the exterior.

333: High shoulder with lid-seat rim: cf. Thompson D3–4.

No parallels of this type were traced in either grogged or fine sandy ware.

Lid-seated vessels in Canterbury are very rare in any primarily first-century fabric; the few found are given full parallels here. Two examples have appeared in a sandy ware; one (cf. Thompson D3–2) from a Period 1 group on the Marlowe site (Green 1995, fig 283, no. 239) and another (cf. D3–2) from a Period 2 group in 'Stuppington Lane' ware (Pollard 1995, fig. 277, no. 141). Three examples occur in grogged ware; one (D3–2) in a Period 1 (probably pre-conquest) group on the Marlowe site (Pollard 1995 fig. 268, no. 3), another (D3–2) in a Period 1 (up to early Flavian) group on Cakebread Robey I (Green forthcoming b, no. 34) and a third from a Period 2 group on the Marlowe site (Pollard 1995 fig. 280, no. 190).

The Highstead vessel feels hand-made with an irregular rim interior, but is well executed overall. Surfaces are reduced with a good burnish on the lid-seat exterior and on the cordons. The style of decoration, (burnished chevron and lattice) is by far the most elaborate of the entire group.

Necked jars

334–7: Corrugated body and everted rim: cf. Thompson B2–1, B2–3 and B2–4.

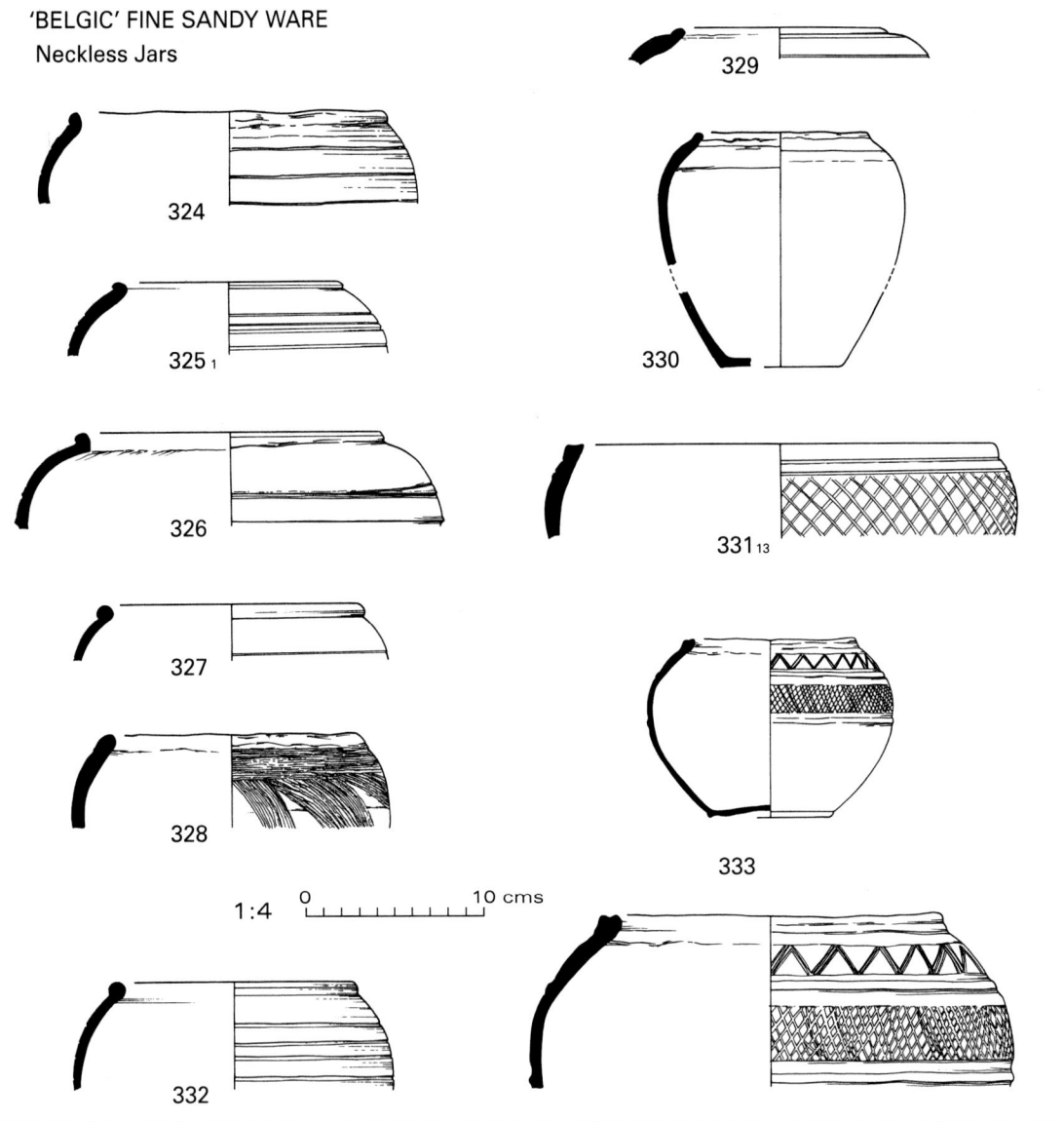

Fig. 125. 'Belgic'/Early Roman pottery from Ditch B164 and supplementary contexts. Scale 1:4.

No parallels were traced. Examples of grogged corrugated jars occur in Period 1 groups at the Marlowe and Cakebread sites and in the Canterbury Castle Area I ditch. Thompson notes that hand-made examples of B2–1 and especially B2–3 occur in grogged ware and that hand-made versions of B2–1 are 'typologically early'. The Highstead sandy jars 334–5 and probably 336, are essentially hand-made. Type B2–4 was a form apparently popular in Kent, sometimes in a greensand fabric (Thompson 1982) and this is perhaps the closest parallel for 334–5 here; however, caution should be taken in attempting to draw too close a parallel between these grogged and sandy vessels; collectively the date range for grogged B types paralleled here spans the first century B.C. to post-conquest.

Of the Highstead vessels, 334 has black surfaces and is burnished externally down to the girth and over inner lip, the rim being quite irregular. 335 has pale grey surfaces. The squared rim is irregular with finger nail incisions where it was formed; sherds probably of the same vessel (lower body) exhibit finger drag marks and the base is crude and simple. 336 has black surfaces burnished down to the girth (as 334); a small cordon sits below a rim with a slight recess. 337 is included in this group as its general appearance is similar and the complete vessel may have

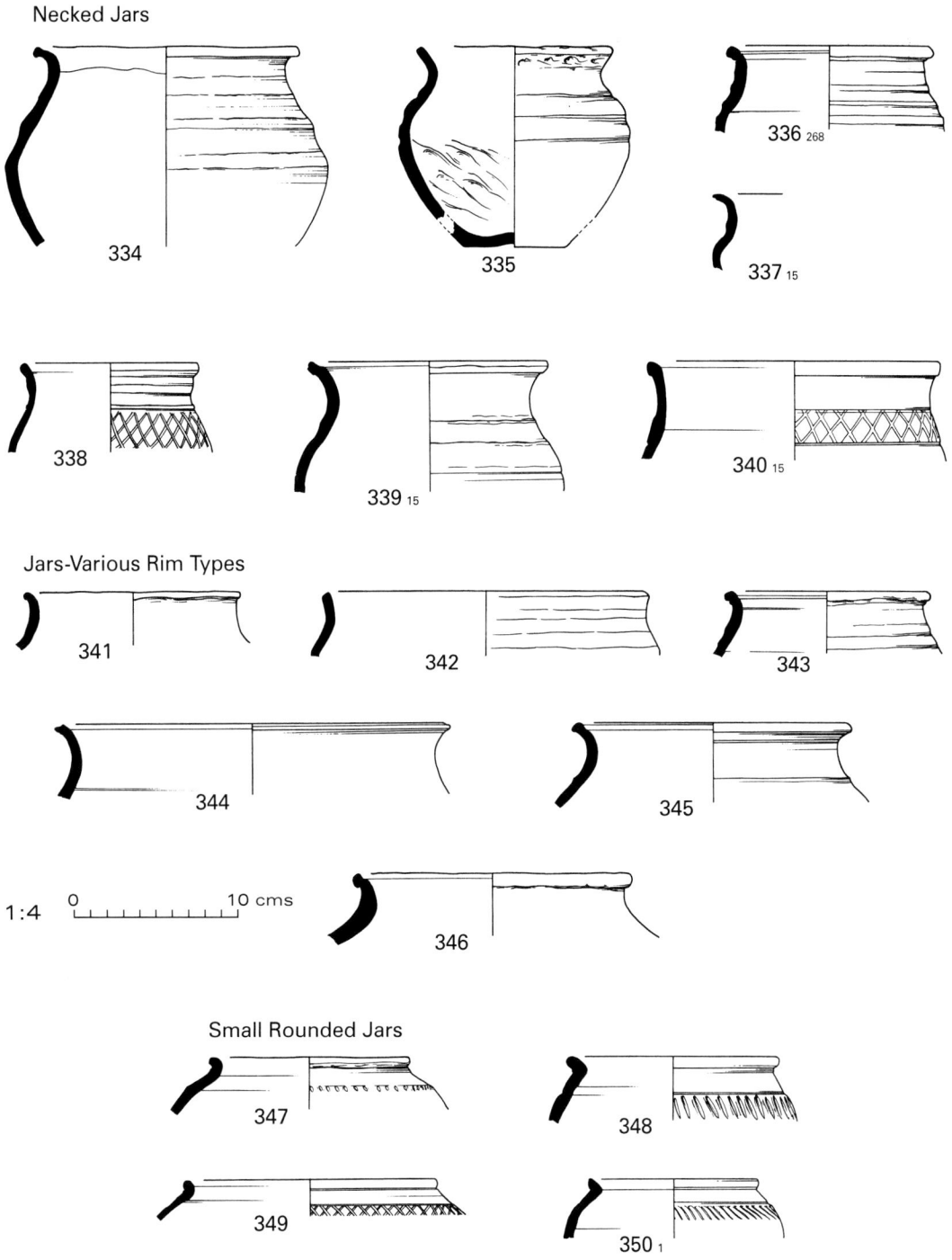

Fig. 126. 'Belgic'/Early Roman pottery from Ditch B164 and supplementary contexts. Scale 1:4.

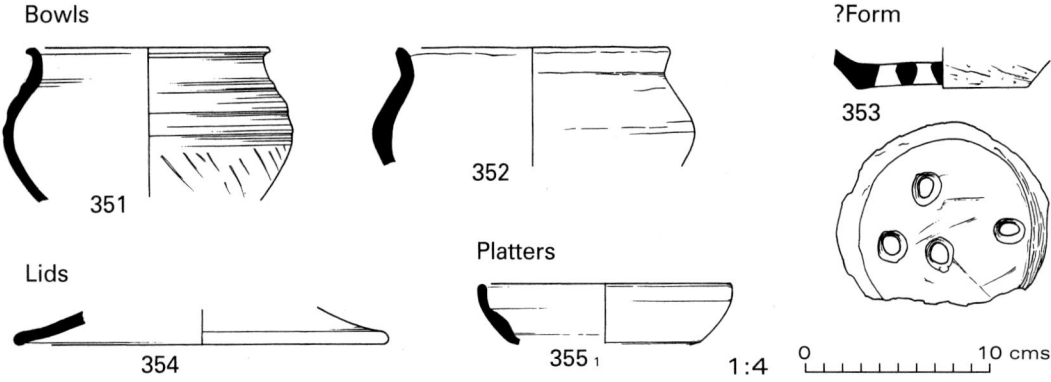

Fig. 127. 'Belgic'/Early Roman pottery from Ditch B164 and supplementary contexts. Scale 1:4.

been of this type. Surfaces are black, the exterior perhaps originally burnished overall.

338: Rounded body and everted rim: cf. Thompson B1–1/B1–2.

No parallels were traced. Examples in grogged ware from Canterbury are few and occur in Period 2 on the Marlowe site. 338 was possibly made on a slow wheel or turntable, having a better finish overall than many of the other vessels; the pale brown exterior surface displays burnished lattice decoration, the burnish now being generally quite worn.

339: Rounded body and recessed rim: cf. Thompson B types.

General parallels in grogged ware only can be made with vessels from Period 1 on the Marlowe sites but none have the rim recess. 339 here has reduced surfaces with external neck burnish.

340: Rounded body and bead rim: cf. Thompson B types.

General parallels only in grogged ware. Mid-brown exterior, orange interior, with worn external body burnish and lattice decoration on shoulder.

341–6: Rims only

341 has a small, crude bead rim; surfaces are orange. 342 is irregular enough to be hand-made; dull burnished black exterior. 343–6 form a loose group of recessed rims; some comparison could be made with Thompson B1–6 in grogged ware (lid-seated jars copying imported types). 343, a butt beaker copy, cf. Thompson G5–1 types; black surfaces; burnished exterior and inner rim which has a slight recess; irregular double bead rim; slight rippling on neck. 344 has dark grey surfaces with very dull burnish on neck exterior and inner rim. 345 has grey surfaces probably originally burnished on exterior and inner rim; slight rim recess and slight ripple on neck; irregular external finishing facets. 346 has an unusually thick section; surfaces are grey; irregular bead rim with slight recess.

Small rounded jars

347–350: High shoulder, inset neck and bead or everted rim: cf. Thompson C4

Though examples from Canterbury are relatively few, they are more frequent than any other form type discussed so far. Of the published material, examples appear in: the Period 1 pit group on the Marlowe Theatre site dated c. 50–80, with some earlier material (Green 1995, fig. 283, no. 241) with neat 'slash' style shoulder decoration (cf. 348, 350 here); the ditch at Canterbury Castle, primary and re-cut phases, essentially pre-Flavian, but with a Flavian element (CC fig. 56, no. 10 with 'finger nail' impressed decoration); as above, backfill, not closely dated (CC figs 64–5, nos 132, 133 with 'slash' style shoulder decoration); the Period II road ditch fills at the castle, the group noted by Pollard as representing mid–late first and late first- to early second-century wares at Canterbury (CC fig. 73, no. 230 again with 'slash' style decoration).

It is probably safe to place this particular type later in the form sequence at Highstead. The grogged ware version (Thompson C4) has a post-conquest bias, the form being very popular in Canterbury and east Kent and rare elsewhere (Thompson 1995, 627).

The Highstead vessels and Canterbury examples quoted here are all of a high standard, well-executed and clearly superior in finish to any of the other 'Belgic' sandy types. This may also indicate a later date of production. Although the sample is still small, it is worth noting that with the exception of 347 and 349 from Highstead and no. 10. from Canterbury Castle (*see* above), all others exhibit the same decorative style, a shoulder band of very neat 'slash' style rouletting or regular combing of some kind. The 'finger nail' pattern (as no. 10 above at the castle) tends to be less regular and is perhaps more widely used on grogged versions (CC fig. 56, nos 11 and 12 for example).

Of the Highstead vessels, 347 has grey-brown surfaces and simple stabbing around the shoulder. 348 has pale grey surfaces with 'slash' style decoration. 349 has grey-brown surfaces with burnished lattice shoulder decoration. 350 has pale grey surfaces and fine 'slash' style decoration.

Bowls

351: Corrugated body, necked with flattened everted rim: cf. Thompson D2–4.

No parallels were traced. A grogged example occurs in a Period 2 group on the Marlowe site.

The Highstead vessel is reduced, burnished black on the exterior down to the girth and on inner rim; the burnish is good and the vessel is essentially hand-made, as the corrugated jars above; lower body has been wiped.

352: Rounded plain body with everted rim: cf. Thompson D3–1.

This vessel is clearly hand-made and no close parallels have been found in grogged or fine sandy ware.

Surfaces are grey-brown; overall construction is quite irregular.

353: ?Form: pierced base.

Grogged ware strainers in Thompson's type series (Thompson S1) have many close-set perforations. The holes in the Highstead base, pierced from the underside, are large; perhaps a function other than the straining of foodstuffs is involved here. The sherd is from a fairly large vessel with pale brown exterior and grey interior.

Strainers are infrequent finds in Canterbury, but sherds have appeared in second- to third-century Native Coarse Ware and Upchurch-type fine grey ware.

Lids

354: Simple tip: cf. Thompson L6.

No other sandy types were traced. Lids in grogged ware are relatively rare in Canterbury, one example occurs on the Marlowe site in a Period 1 group (?pre-conquest/conquest).

354 here is quite well made with brown-black surfaces and blackened inner rim.

Platters

355: With internal moulding: cf. Thompson G1–6

Sandy platters of any type are rare, but G1–6, a post-conquest form is quite common at Canterbury in grogged ware.

355 has reduced, smooth surfaces.

Other wares (Figs 128–9)

The samian (p. 244), early Gaulish and other finewares (Tables 21 and 22), amphorae (pp. 237–42), 'Belgic' coarsewares (p. 205) are reported separately. Full archive catalogues for the remaining material from B164 have been compiled. Fabric descriptions can be found in Pollard 1995. A summary of the illustrated pottery is presented here by fabric group.

'Stuppington Lane' ware

356–7: See Macpherson-Grant 1980b, Pollard 1982 and Pollard 1995, 595 for fabric description and discussion of this local ware.

356 here has a very short neck and weakly defined shoulder; 357 is illustrated as a bowl form, but may be a lid, unknown in either case at the kiln site.

Pre-Flavian Canterbury-type grey sandy ware

358–364: The pre-Flavian industry and the 'North Gaul' ('NG') style have been discussed at some length by Pollard (1982; 1995). The fabric of these early types and later Flavian-Antonine products is the same. Of the local sandy sherds in B164 the majority of those with identifiable form were of 'NG' type while only two worn fragments (*not illus.*) were assigned to the later industry; remaining bodysherds which make up the majority of the Canterbury-type grey sandy ware in the table are undiagnostic and could belong to either phase.

358–9 are probably from round-bodied jars unknown as yet from a kiln site, but considered to belong to this early phase (cf. Pollard 1982, no. 49; Green 1995, fig. 284, nos 242–6). 360 is a similar type. A parallel for the high-shouldered jar (361) is found at the pre-Flavian kiln site at St Stephen's (SS Area II, Jenkins 1956, no. 15) though the latter has a larger rim. 362 is a type which may have originated in the earlier phase and continued into the Flavian and later industry. It appears on the Cakebread I site in Period 1 (Green forthcoming b, no. 32), at Canterbury Castle (CC fig. 75, nos 282, 284–5) and at Richborough in pits dated to the third quarter of the first century (reference in Pollard 1982). It has no kiln site attribution as yet, but is apparently closely paralleled in North Gaul (Pollard 1995, 598). 363 is probably from a carinated bowl (cf. 364) and can be found at the SS Area II site (no. 14) and at Reed Avenue, Canterbury (unpublished). A three-rib flagon handle (*not illus.*) is also likely to be from an early vessel, cf. example from SS Area II, no. 1; the handle (and body sherds of the same vessel) bear traces of a cream slip and several are blistered and fragmented.

Pink-buff sandy ware, probably local

365–6: Two identifiable forms can again be paralleled at the SS Area II site, (365–6 here, SS Area II nos 26 and 1 respectively). The Highstead carinated jar (365) is a large vessel and a type that appears very rarely in Canterbury; one example was traced from the Canterbury Castle Area I ditch backfill (CC

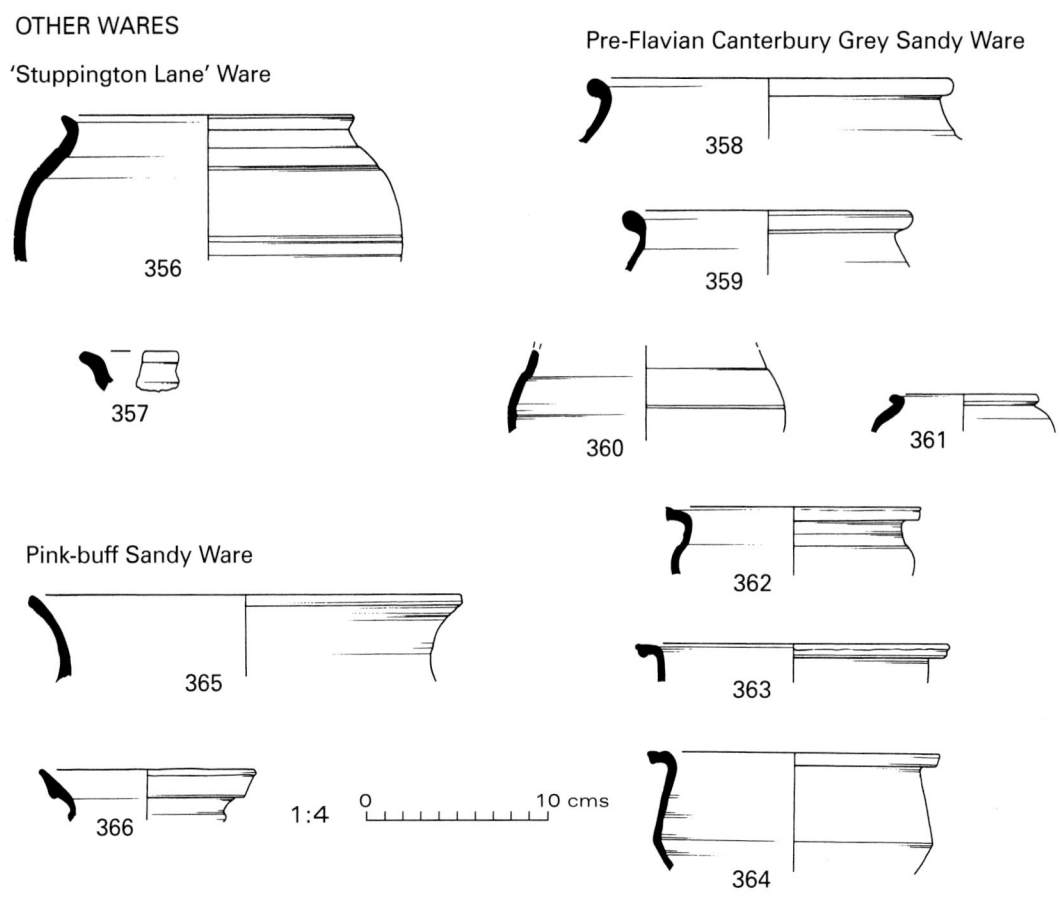

Fig. 128. Early Roman pottery from Ditch B164. Scale 1:4.

fig. 66, no. 177) unfortunately not closely dated. Examples of collar-rim flagons, as 366 here, are again rare, but also occur in 'Belgic' grogged and fine white ware at Canterbury. Pink-buff wares from Canterbury sites have been largely associated with later, Flavian-Antonine, flagon forms.

Orange sandy ware, ?local

367: This carinated beaker or jar has a finer sandy fabric, with a weak, worn cream slip, and is well executed overall. It forms a close parallel with a vessel from the SS Area II site (no. 25 in a grey coarser ware) and the Canterbury Castle vessel cited above. Again this form in this fabric would be unusual in the town; no examples occurred in the Period 1 (A.D. 25–70/80) sample from the Marlowe sites. Bi-conical and carinated vessels are more familiar in Upchurch-type fine grey ware. Orange, red and pink-buff wares in fabrics resembling Canterbury grey ware are all likely to be local products, the only difference being in the firing conditions.

Upchurch-type wares

368–371: The term 'Upchurch' ware is used at Canterbury to describe a fine grey ware occurring in the late first century, continuing to at least the third, and appearing in a wide range of forms during this time. In addition, there occurs consistently a small range of fabrics comparable to the latter in quality, which appear to differ only in colour. On grounds of this fabric similarity they are grouped together under this heading (*see also* B1 and B15, pp. 227–31).

Upchurch-type fine grey ware

368: The majority of the sherds were rims or body sherds of carinated beakers or jars. The only near complete example of a beaker or small jar came from Site A and was the sole vessel from an early Romano-British grave (Fig. 129, No. 374, Grave A119A). The type could be dated broadly later first to early second century at Canterbury. The high-

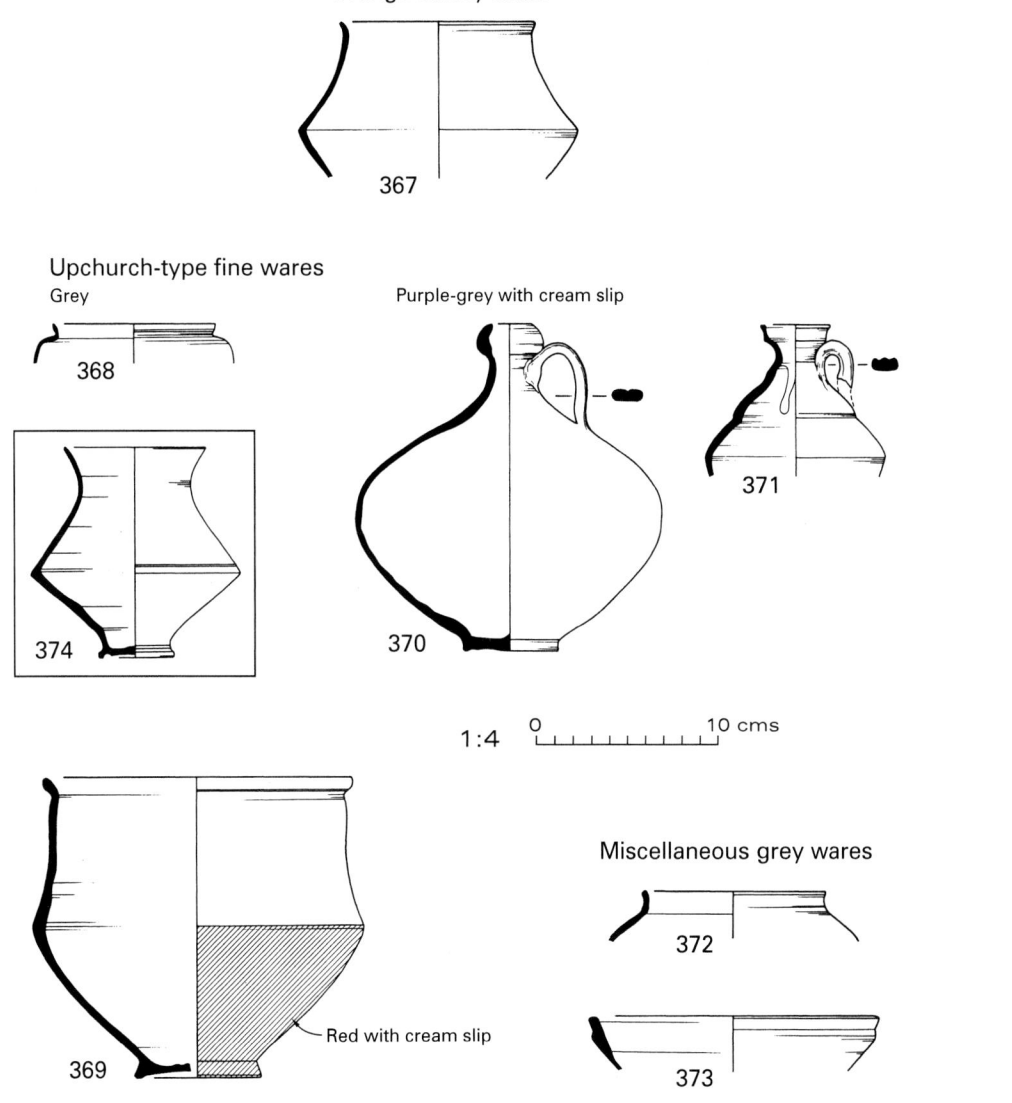

Fig. 129. Early Roman pottery from Ditch B164 and Grave A119A (No. 374, *inset*). Scale 1:4.

shouldered beaker or jar illustrated here (368), from B164 is finely executed. Similar vessels appeared in the Canterbury Castle ditch backfill (CC fig. 66, nos 156–8).

Fine red ware with cream slip

369: The large beaker or jar illustrated here is quite exceptional and unparalleled at Canterbury. The fabric has moderate–abundant fine mica content; the exterior of the vessel was originally either red-slipped or burnished above the carination, while the lower body was cream-slipped. The surface is now worn, but the original bold colour contrast was doubtless very striking. The form can be compared with Thompson's plain carinated cups (Type E1–4, sometimes red surfaced) in 'Belgic' grogged ware, apparently popular in the first half of the first century A.D. but also occurring after the conquest (Thompson 1982). There is also some similarity to Thompson G2–4 (wide carinated bowls), occurring both in pre- and post-conquest periods.

Fine purple-grey wares with cream slip

This ware is perhaps exclusively confined to flagon types; certainly this is the indication from Canterbury material.
370–1 here appear superficially the same, but the latter is a slightly sandy fabric, whereas the former is comparable to the fine grey wares above. 370 is well executed with a slip that is generally worn. No parallels for this flagon were

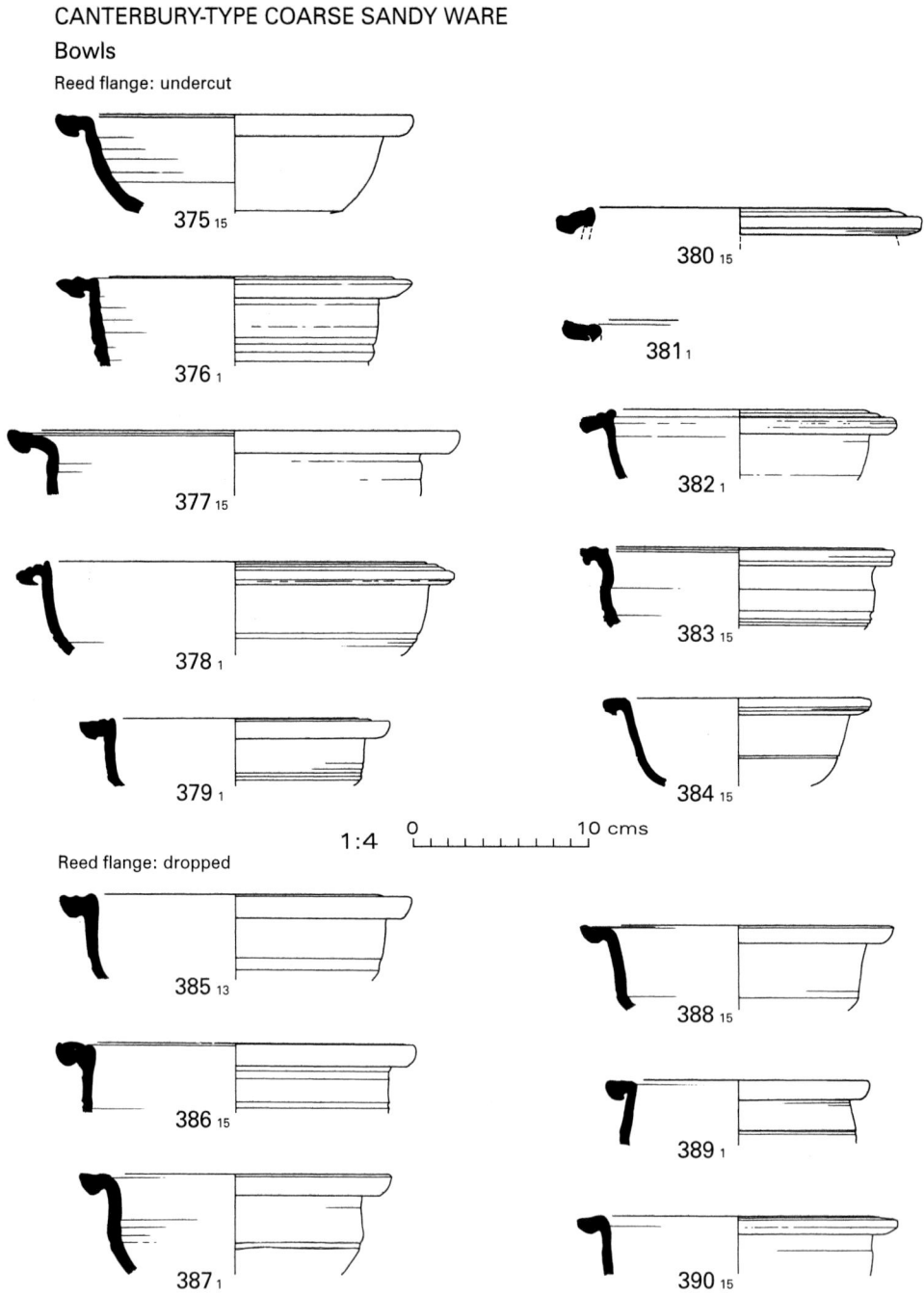

Fig. 130. Roman pottery from Ditch B1, Pit complex B15 and supplementary contexts. Scale 1:4.

found in published groups from Canterbury. The cream slip of 371 has survived well; a flagon from Canterbury Castle in slipped purple-grey ware has a similar cup rim, but this is the only comparison (Area I ditch backfill, fig. 66, no. 176); otherwise no parallels were found.

Miscellaneous grey wares

372–3: 372 a beaker or small jar, has a fine sandy fabric with pink-brown interior and grey-black exterior, burnished with close-set horizontal bands; inner lip also burnished. The fabric of 373, a dish or platter, is reduced and coarsely sandy.

Pottery from Ditch B1 and Pit complex B15

(Figs 130–37)

Marion Green

The bulk of the material from both of these contexts can be assigned to the Flavian to mid Antonine period, *c.* A.D. 75–150/70. The tail-off point may be slightly earlier based on the relatively small amount of BB2 found compared to the mass of local Canterbury sandy wares.

The small quantity of mid to late second- to third-century sherds recovered from Ditch B1 is probably the product of a later recut. Pit complex B15 is thought to have remained open until the end of Period 5A (*c.* A.D. 150).

The range and relative quantities of pottery types recovered from these two large assemblages are presented in Table 20; full ware analyses for each group have been catalogued. The policy of omitting detailed pre-Late Iron Age residual wares from B164 statistics (p. 216) also applies to B1 and B15 as both features cut earlier contexts.

The types of pottery occurring in B1 and B15 are broadly similar; that there is simply more material in the latter is the one significant difference.

The impressive group of Canterbury-type sandy wares warranted special emphasis. Figs 130–35 illustrate the complete formal range from B1 and B15 combined, supplemented by selected examples from other contexts at the site (contexts clearly marked in the figures). Table 19 illustrates the quantified formal range as represented by B1 and B15 only.

In the following report a discussion of the Canterbury-type sandy wares from the site is followed by a summary of the other material examined in each of the two study groups (Figs 136–7).

Canterbury-type sandy wares (Figs 130–35; Tables 18–19)

In his thesis on Roman pottery in Kent, Dr Pollard devotes a chapter to discussion of the sandy coarseware industry at Canterbury and in its environs, beginning as is presently understood in the pre-Flavian period, peaking in the later first to early second century and continuing at least to the close of the Antonine era (Pollard 1982).

It is primarily the mid Flavian to Antonine phase of production that is represented at Highstead, where the two features under discussion here have jointly produced the most comprehensive range of forms to be published to date.

Published groups from Canterbury sites include:

Simon Langton Yard: pit 4 (well), c. A.D. 130–60 (Wilson 1995, 689). In terms of range, this is the best of the published groups noted here. Forms include reed flange bowls, lid-seat flange dishes and lid-seat neckless jars.

Cakebread Robey IV: 'shrine', occupation levels, c. A.D. 125–65 (Green forthcoming a). Not illustrated, but statistics published. Forms include reed flange bowls, lid-seat flange bowls, lids, bead and flange dishes and lid-seat neckless jars.

Canterbury Castle Area II: timber building, Phase I floor, early to mid second century (Macpherson-Grant 1982, fig. 78). The group is not quantified but forms include reed flange bowls, lid with pulley-style and snub nose rims and lid-seat neckless jars.

East of Marlowe Theatre CXVI E14: road, c. A.D. 130–170 (Wilson 1995, 686). Forms include reed flange bowls and lid-seat neckless jars.

Of the material recovered from the extensive Marlowe excavations, only limited quantities of local sandy ware were examined, the second-century phase there warranting only minimal ceramic analysis. Attention was devoted rather to earlier occupation and the activities of the later Roman period.

It is apparent from Table 18 that few direct parallels can be drawn between individual Highstead vessels and types from published Canterbury kiln site assemblages. There is a scarcity of identifiable pre-Flavian types, although some early products do occur at the site (Fig. 128, Nos 358–64, Ditch B164).

More general parallels can be made by grouping together certain forms into broader categories; all styles of reed flange bowls or all lid-seat neckless jars for example. We then have larger numbers that could span the entire Flavian-Antonine period of production.

There are few instances of types considered to have been introduced in the Antonine period, for example, new flagon forms (Pollard 1982). On the evidence of Canterbury-type sandy wares in isolation, this suggests that the corpus may not be later than *c.* A.D. 150; absence or paucity of other, later second-century wares (p. 216) would appear to support this.

The range at Highstead: a summary

Reed flange bowls and lid-seat neckless jars respectively appear to be the most popular vessel types, based on B1 and B15 data (Table 19). Subjective assessment indicates that these

Form type		Kiln site parallels	Comments on Highstead vessels
Bowls			
375-402	reed flange	cf. WG I, nos 9-11, DJ nos 22-26 379: WG I, no. 11 388: SS I, no. 8 401: DJ, no. 23 402: WG I, no. 10	375, 377: shallow reeding 383: unusual (short) flange 384: no reeding, overall style very similar 388, 390: vestigial reeding 386: rounded reeding 401: unusually small flange
403-11	lid-seat flange	cf. RAV (one unpublished example)	
not illus	simple flange		?early industry; fragment only
412-3	other flange bowls		
414		inturned rim	unusual form, notches along rim top
Dishes			
415-20	lid-seated flange	415-7, 419: cf. WG I, no. 13 418: cf. WG I, no. 14	417 smoothed surfaces 418 ?lid-seat 420 'pulley' style rim
421-5	bead and flange		421-2 ?lid-seated; lid types with recessed undertip would be suitable (e.g. 433, 450) 423 may be essentially lid-seated 425 unusual form; small bead and stubby flange
not illus	simple inturned rim		?local: cf. Pompeian Red Ware dishes
Lids			
426-8	grips only		
429-437	triangular tip	cf. WG I, no. 8, NL no. 16; especially 437	
438-444	folded back lip		438 double fold-back 439-40 tip folded back and tooled to give top groove
445	cordoned		
446-7	'pulley' rim		
448	snub nose		
449-50	blunt tip		449 ?early industry 450 clear differential firing effect on underside probably due to kiln stacking
not illus	bead rim		
Jars: neckless			
451-70	lid-seat flange	453-4, 457, cf. DJ no. 27 456, 459 WG I no. 7 464 NL no. 9 470 DJ no. 28	few close parallels; more general ones could be made
471-5	reeded flange		472 jar/bowl form; 475 ?necked
476-9	bevel rim	477 cf. WG I no. 7	more general parallels could be made with WG I no. 7; possibly designed to take a lid 479 warped rim
Jars: necked			
480-3	everted rim		483 cf. Pollard 1982, no. 52, possibly pre-Flavian
484-493	roll rim	484 cf. DJ nos 33-35 485-6 cf. NL nos 4, 6 respectively	484 harder fired than the typical ware 493 ?lid-seated; 'kick' to rim tip
494-6	hook rim		496 ?necked
497-500	lid-seated	497 cf. NL nos 2, 5	
501-3			501-2 could take a lid 502 roughly tooled, erratic shallow notches grouped on inner rim edge
504-6	triangular everted rim		505 ?lid-seated 506 probably lid-seated, slight 'pulley' rim
507-8	small jars with everted rim		'Belgic' affinities: similar forms occur in grogged ware; 508 cf. Thompson 1982, C2-2
509			?large jar
Flagons			
510	angle-everted rim	cf. DJ no. 54, not an exact parallel	
511	cupped ring-neck /conical neck	cf. WG III no. 18; SS I no. 2; SS II no. 6 (conical type)	
512	pulley-rim	cf. WG I no. 5	
513	horizontal flange neck	cf. WG I no. 4	
514	plain flange rim	cf. DJ no. 49	evidence of handle attachment

Codes: RAV: Reed Avenue: pre-Flavian (unpublished); SS II: St Stephen's Area II: pre-Flavian (Jenkins 1956); NL: North Lane: Flavian-Trajanic (Macpherson-Grant 1978); WG I: Whitehall Gardens Area I: Flavian-Hadrianic (Jenkins 1960); SS I: St Stephen's Area I: Flavian-Antonine (Jenkins 1956); DJ: Dane John: Antonine (Kirkman 1940); WG III: Whitehall Gardens Area III: Antonine (Jenkins 1960)

are also the types most in demand at Canterbury. Highstead has a wider range of reed flange bowls than the published kiln site material illustrates. Most examples fall into three broad styles: the 'undercut' flange (e.g. 375, 377, 380); the 'dropped' flange (e.g. 386, 388, 390) and the 'upturned' flange (e.g. 391–3). Some examples have very shallow or vestigial reeding or, as 384, none at all; in this case, the overall style confines it to this group. Diameters range from *c.* 13–26 cm., with most vessels around 20–22 cm.

Although the term 'lid-seat' is confined here to clearly concave flange types, several other forms may also take a lid; for example, the reed flange (e.g. 471–2, 474, unusual for this jar type) or bevel rim (e.g. 476–9) neckless jars or the reed flange bowls. Neckless jars here, 451–70, have a complete diameter range of *c.* 12–22 cm. with most around 15–17 cm., making this form the most standardized in terms of size.

Diameters of lids do not appear to respect any particular vessel type and vary from 14–25 cm. The wide range of styles here has very few kiln site parallels and few in published groups.

Necked jars constitute a fairly miscellaneous collection with roll rims of various styles being the most frequent; again some jars were possibly designed to take a lid.

Other forms occurring and notes pertinent to particular vessels are detailed in Table 18.

In conclusion, it is apparent that many of the forms found at Highstead have no parallels in the published kiln site material, particularly the necked jars and lids. A review of the kiln site assemblages excavated to date would be welcome, as would the opportunity to explore new sites, ideally an industrial complex.

Other wares (Figs 136–7)

Table 20 (p. 236) presents the full range and quantification of wares recovered.

Upchurch-type wares

Upchurch-type fine grey ware

515–26, 539–61: A variety of forms was recorded from both contexts, the general range being comparable to the 'shrine' material on Cakebread Robey IV (Green forthcoming a). Long-necked jars and segmental bowls were the most popular types, the latter especially occurring in early to mid second-century groups in the town (*see* below); unusual vessels include the fragment of a girth type beaker (561), presumably earlier than the bulk of the corpus and the deep bowl (522) perhaps third century or even later. Few examples from Highstead have retained their burnish, where one would expect to see it on vessels recovered at Canterbury; this was also very noticeable among the BB2 wares (*see* below).

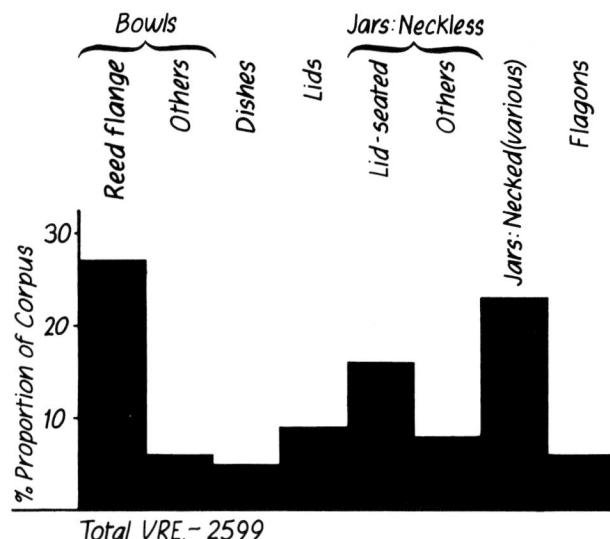

Table 19. Canterbury-type coarse sandy ware. Summary of forms occurring at Highstead as represented by Ditch B1 and Pit complex B15. Quantification by Vessel Rim Equivalent.

515–17, 539–46: Jars
No complete profiles, but body sherds and many rims with long sweeping necks, suggest carinated forms, with fewer rounded jars; cf. examples of carinated and rounded jars from the Roman road east of the Marlowe Theatre dated *c.* 130–70 (Wilson 1995, 686), a pit in the St George's Street apsed building dated *c.* 130–60 (Wilson 1983, fig. 81, nos 75,78) and the single carinated jar with neck cordon from a cremation at St Augustine's College, dated mid Flavian to early Hadrianic (Pollard 1981, fig. 6, no. 1). 546 here, a lid-seated vessel, is a familiar form occurring in Canterbury-type sandy ware.

518–9, 526, 547–50, 561: Beakers
Globular beaker/small jar (547): The form also occurs in 'Belgic' grogged and fine sandy wares (e.g. 347–50), with decorated shoulder. 'Poppyhead' type (526, 548–9): cf. 549, rouletted example, with vessel from the Marlowe sites dated Flavian to ?mid second century (Pollard 1995, fig. 281, no. 195 from oven, R5, MIII). Girth type (561): cf. Cam. 84. Wall-sided type (550): worn compass-scribed decoration, cf. ?residual late first- to second-century example from the Marlowe sites (Pollard 1995, fig. 316, no. 517). Butt beaker type (518): cf. example from Canterbury Castle Area 1 ditch backfill, not closely dated (Macpherson-Grant 1982, fig. 66, no. 169). ?Ovoid type (519): cf. ?residual late second- to third-century example from the Marlowe sites (Pollard 1995, fig. 319, 570).

Opposite: Table 18. Comparison of Canterbury-type sandy wares at Highstead (B1, B15) with kiln site assemblages from the town.

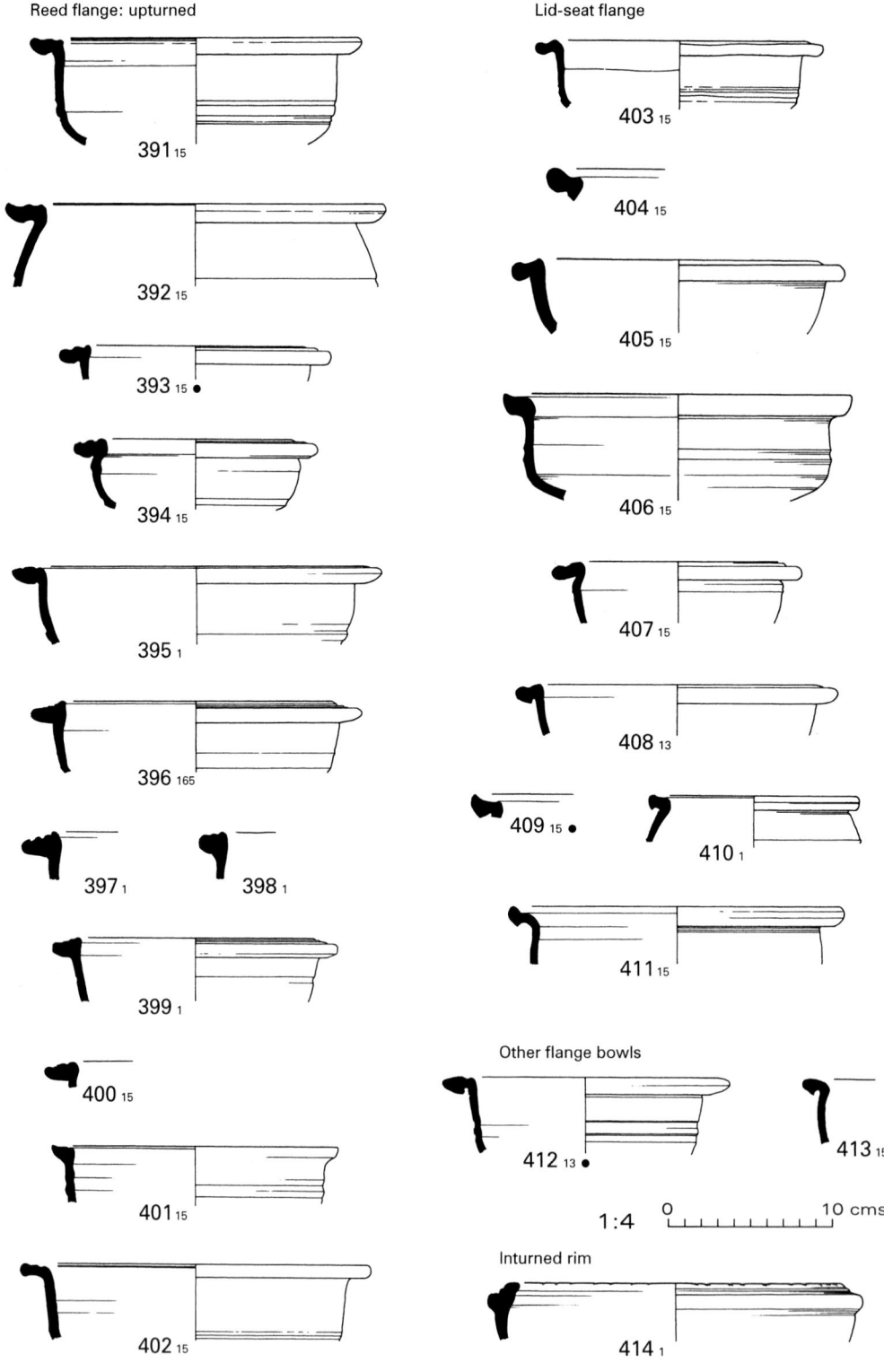

Fig. 131. Roman pottery from Ditch B1, Pit complex B15 and supplementary contexts (● = oxidised). Scale 1:4.

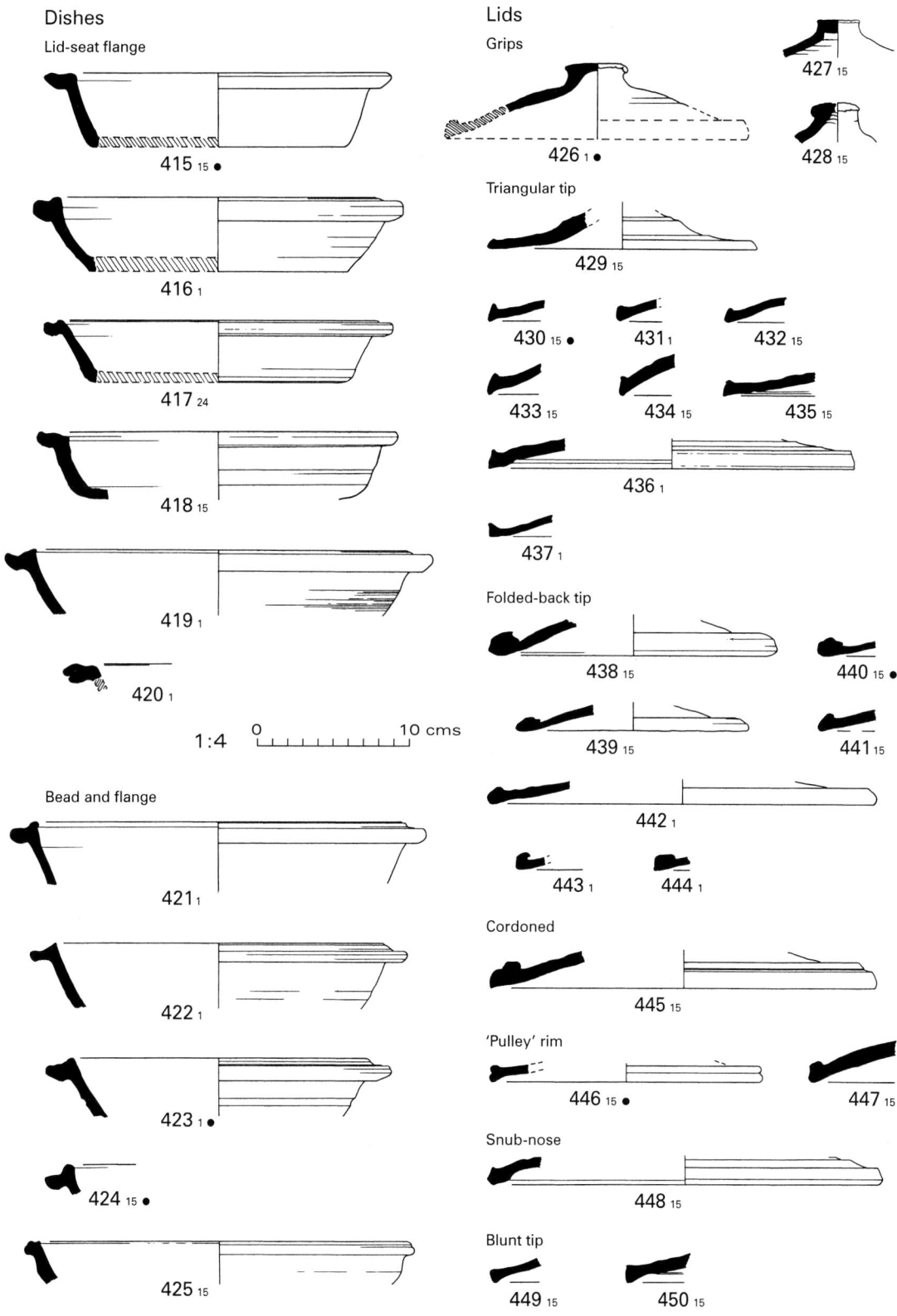

Fig. 132. Roman pottery from Ditch B1, Pit complex B15 and supplementary contexts (● = oxidised). Scale 1:4.

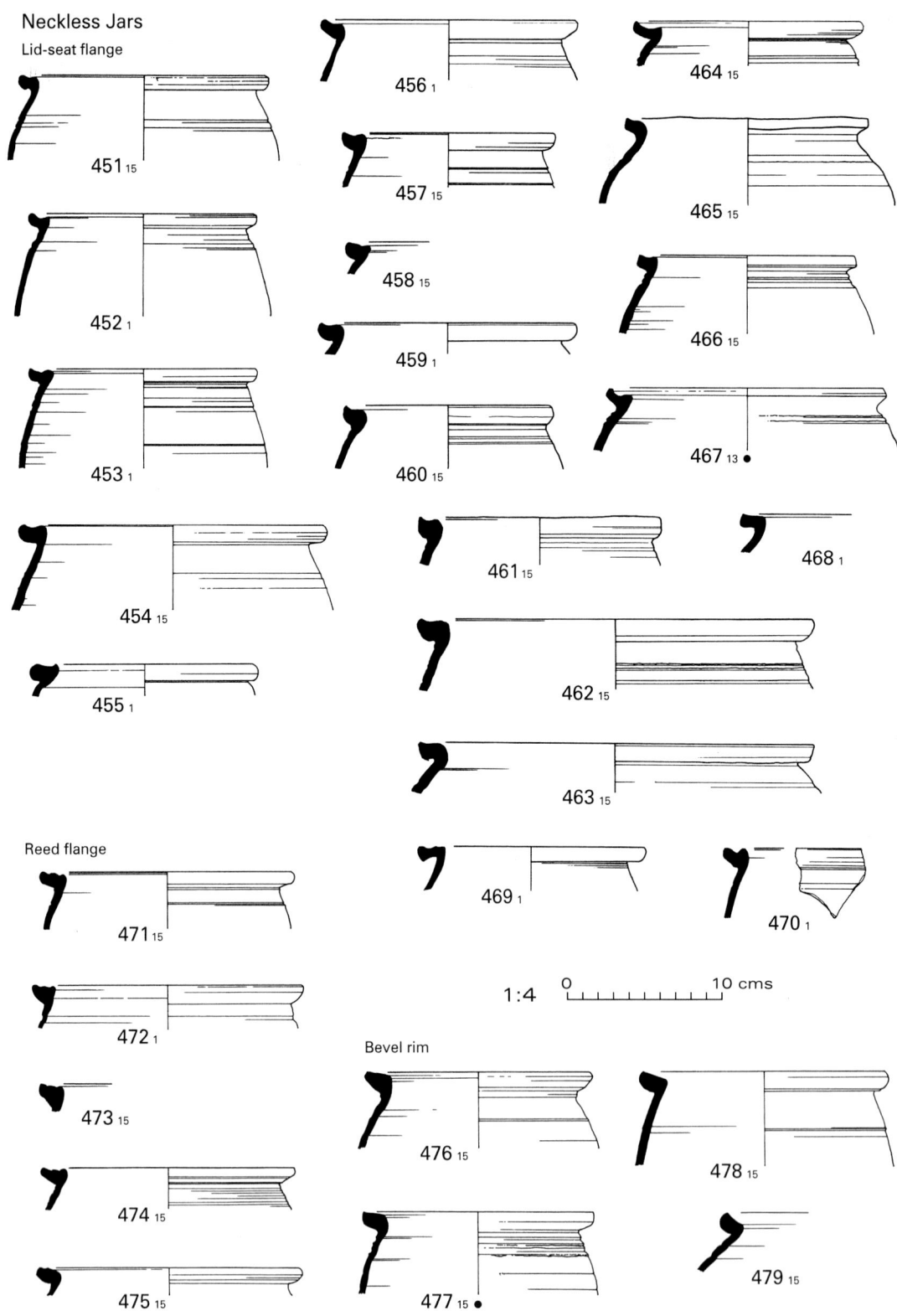

Fig. 133. Roman pottery from Ditch B1, Pit complex B15 and supplementary contexts (● = oxidised). Scale 1:4.

520–1, 523, 551–60: Segmental bowls
A range of everted rim, bead rim and flanged types was present; 520 and 553 here may be deeper vessels. Segmental bowls of various types from Canterbury occur at Canterbury Castle Area II, pit, probably Vespasianic-Trajanic (Macpherson-Grant 1982, fig. 77, dating by Pollard); Canterbury Castle Area I, ditch backfill, not closely dated (Macpherson-Grant 1982, fig. 66); St George's Street apsed building, pit 4, c. A.D. 110–30 (Wilson 1983, fig. 81); St George's Street apsed building, pit, c. A.D. 130–60 (Wilson 1983, fig. 81); Cakebread Robey IV 'shrine', occupation levels, c. A.D. 125–65 (Green forthcoming a); site east of the Marlowe Theatre, road, c. A.D. 130–70 (Wilson 1995, 686); Simon Langton Yard, pit 4 (well), c. A.D. 130–60 (Wilson 1995, 689).

522, 524: Round bodied bowls
524 here with rouletted rim/neck, cf. plain bowl from a context on the Marlowe sites dated to the late fourth century, but including pottery of the late third onwards (Pollard 1995, fig. 317, 542); cf. also Oxfordshire colour-coat form C74/75 (Young 1977, figs 61–2). 522 here, flange only, may be from a deep bowl.

525: Flasks
No close parallels in the Canterbury material, but other flasks appear to occur from the late second century onwards. Examples occur from: a pit on Marlowe IV dating to the late second to third century (vessel not published); a late second- to third-century cremation group at Cranmer House (Pollard 1987, no. 27D, small vessel); late fourth-century loam level on Marlowe III (Pollard 1995, fig. 316, 511); early to mid fifth-century decay levels on Marlowe IIB (Pollard 1995, fig. 317, no. 528); mid fourth- to mid fifth-century 'dark earth' levels on Marlowe I with residual late second-century to third-century pottery (Pollard 1995, fig. 319, no. 572).

Upchurch-type fine oxidised ware

527, 562: Rim fragments were recovered from a few jars and segmental bowls. 562 here can be paralleled by a bowl with rounded wall from the Marlowe sites, group dated late second to mid third century (Pollard 1995, fig. 309, no. 381). Several other sherds were also present from wall-sided vessels including a few with compass-scribed decoration. A parallel for the cup with low carination (527) can be found in 'Belgic' grogged ware (cf. Thompson Type E1-4); the fabric has a fine sand content and appears superficially very similar to the prolific Upchurch-type fine grey wares.

Upchurch-type fine buff ware

563–5: Again examples were few and included a small group of necked jars (cf. examples from Canterbury Castle Area I ditch, fig. 66, nos 155–58, with 563 here) segmental bowls of various types (564 here has a squared bead rim) and beakers including a wall-sided vessel (565 with faint traces of external cream slip), a compass-scribed example (cf. 550 in fine grey ware, ?same vessel) and sherds with bands of narrow vertical combing, cf. Cam. 84 girth beakers.

Mica-coated White Ware

528: Collar rim flagon in fairly fine grain pale cream fabric with sparse to moderate small red inclusions (?Rigby WW3); worn gold-orange micaceous external slip; body sherd has evidence of a bifid handle. The quality of this flagon suggests an import.

Mica-coated oxidised sandy ware ?local

529: A similar dish with inturned rim described as orange sandy ware with buff exterior occurred at the Canterbury Castle Area II timber building; the group is not closely dated (Macpherson-Grant 1982, fig. 79, no. 367). The fabric of the Highstead vessel contains a number of red-brown inclusions and is generally coarser than Rigby's Mica Coated Red Ware (Rigby 1995, 643); the gold overall micaceous slip is worn, particularly on the interior.

Alice Holt ware

566–7: 566, fragment of an oxidised bead rim neckless jar; late first to early second century (Paul Tyers, pers. comm.). 567, jar with internal rilling below a bead rim (?Alice Holt).

Black-burnished ware: BB1 and BB1 type

530–1, 568: For a full discussion of both BB1 and BB2 in Kent see Pollard 1982 and 1995; he notes that BB1 reached Kent during the Hadrianic period in very small numbers, being rapidly overtaken by BB2. The pie-dish (530) exhibits burnished lattice decoration, cf. Gillam Type 307, and the wall/base sherd from a jar (531, BB1 type) shows evidence of acute lattice burnish almost down to the base. The everted rim jar (568, BB1 type) is an unusual find and no parallels were found from Canterbury; the form is simple with only a slight bead to the rim and acute lattice burnish.

Black-burnished ware: BB2

532–7: It appears that BB2 does not make any real impact on the Canterbury market until the latter half of the second century, when trade there in local sandy wares is on the decline (Pollard 1982). If we can apply this theory to the rural site at Highstead, then the small percentage of BB2 is significant in assessing a date ceiling for the main period of occupation there. Although no total site quantification has been made for the Roman pottery at Highstead, initial examination of all the material indicated that there was relatively little BB2

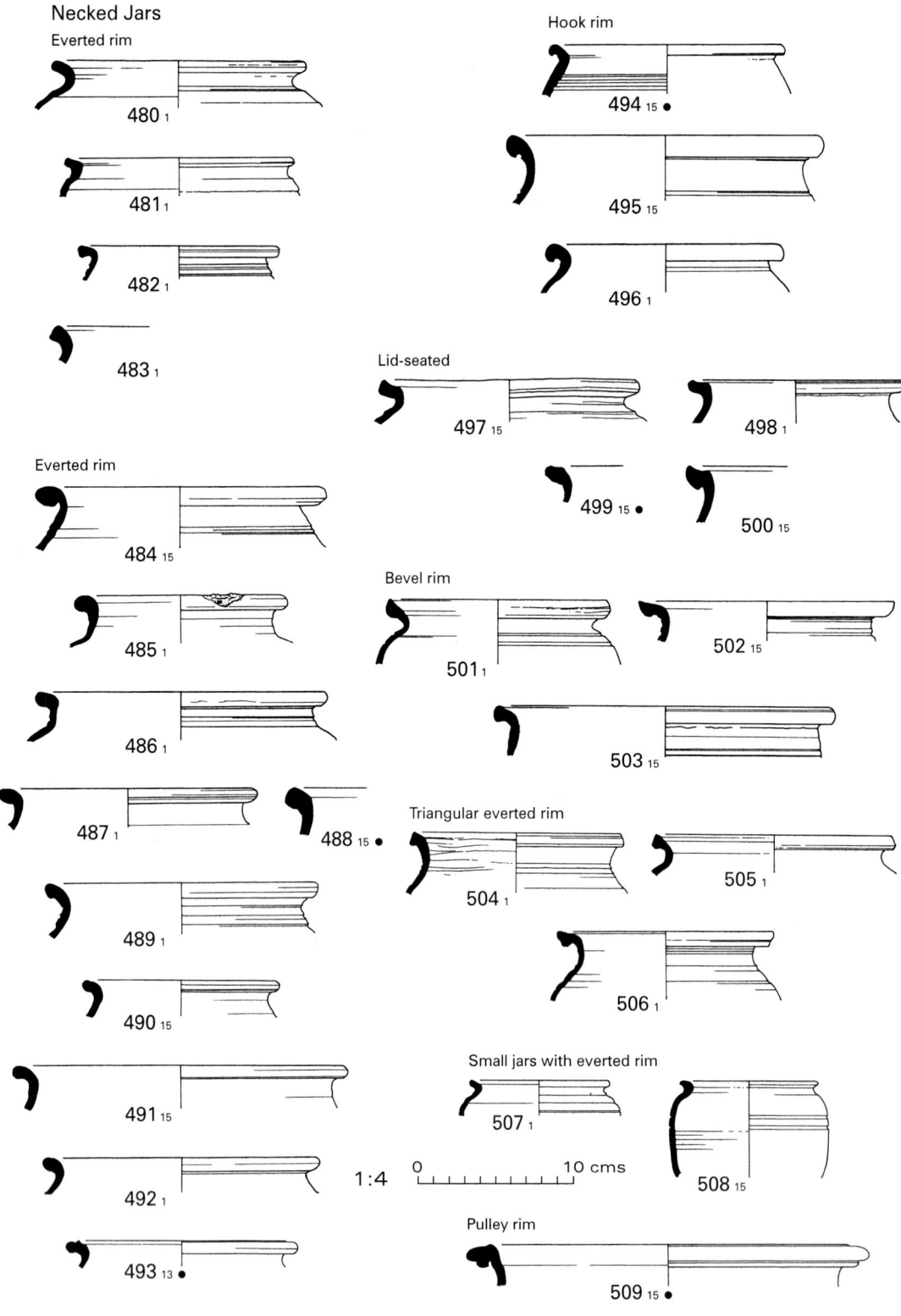

Fig. 134. Roman pottery from Ditch B1, Pit complex B15 and supplementary contexts (● = oxidised = oxidised). Scale 1:4.

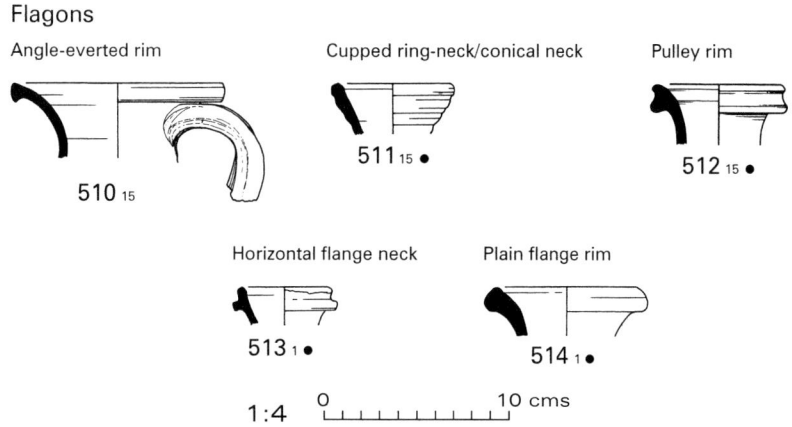

Fig. 135. Roman pottery from Ditch B1, Pit complex B15 and supplementary contexts (• = oxidised). Scale 1:4.

present, while quantities of Canterbury sandy ware were much greater.

Most examples from B1 and B15 were of pie-dishes with various rim types. Nearly all were decorated, characteristic of the Hadrianic–mid Antonine period at Canterbury, either with burnished lattice design or in one case burnished hatching. Very few dog-dishes were present, two plain and one decorated example.

While many Highstead examples of BB2 appear to share characteristics of both Colchester and Kent products as defined by Williams (1977) and Pollard (1995), the author would suggest that they show more traits of the Kent industries (dark grey or black dull surfaces, irregular wall thickness, rounded profiles), including some possible east Kent products.

Decorated pie-dish: Gillam Type 222 (Nos 532, 534): Typical Hadrianic–mid Antonine form at Canterbury. 532 with rounded profile and worn burnish; possible east Kent product (cf. Pollard 1990, 174, fig. 58, no. 7). Many of the vessels now exhibit very eroded burnish making assessment of possible sources based on this factor difficult. 534 here is a tall example with even wall thickness, well executed lattice burnishing (though worn now) and a fairly fine fracture. ?Colchester/(Kent) product.

Plain pie-dish: Gillam Type 225 (No. 533): Very few examples; typical of the late Antonine–mid third century at Canterbury. This example has a finer fracture than 'east Kent' types, but does have some characteristics of the latter; wall thickening near the base and rounded profile with no real chamfer, black overall with no real burnish surviving. Probable Kent (?east Kent) product.

Decorated dog-dish (No. 535): cf. Gillam and Mann 1970, fig. 2, no. 19. Typical of the Hadrianic–mid Antonine period at Canterbury. Pink external surface with worn burnish decoration; fine sandy fracture; inturned rim tip.

Plain dog-dish: Gillam Type 234 (Nos 536–7): Pollard notes that some plain dog-dishes occur in the Hadrianic–mid Antonine period, but it is more typical of the late second–mid third century and later at Canterbury. 536, small example with fairly fine fracture; even thickness. 537, larger example, more rounded profile, fine fracture. ?Kent product.

Miscellaneous fine grey sandy wares

538 and **569–571**: 538, flange rim segmental bowl; source unknown. 569, jar with slightly hooked roll rim and good finish. 570, lid-seated jar. 571, probably hemispherical bowl with warped depressed flange.

Miscellaneous fine black sandy ware

572: A single example of stamped coarseware was recovered from the site; flat platter/bowl base with illiterate/damaged central stamp enclosed by a bordered band of pseudo-rouletting.

The Early Gaulish and other imported finewares (Fig. 138)

Valery Rigby[10] *and Marion Green*

The report by Valery Rigby is presented as Table 21, while Table 22 condenses the data. It is apparent that there is very little material attributable to the post-conquest period, later examples of *terra nigra* for example or white ware butt beakers. The corpus is very small totalling one hundred sherds with seventy-four of these belonging to one vessel (note dating for this flagon below). For an overview of the more extensive corpus recovered at Canterbury see Rigby (1995, 640–70)

---

10. Report submitted 1989.

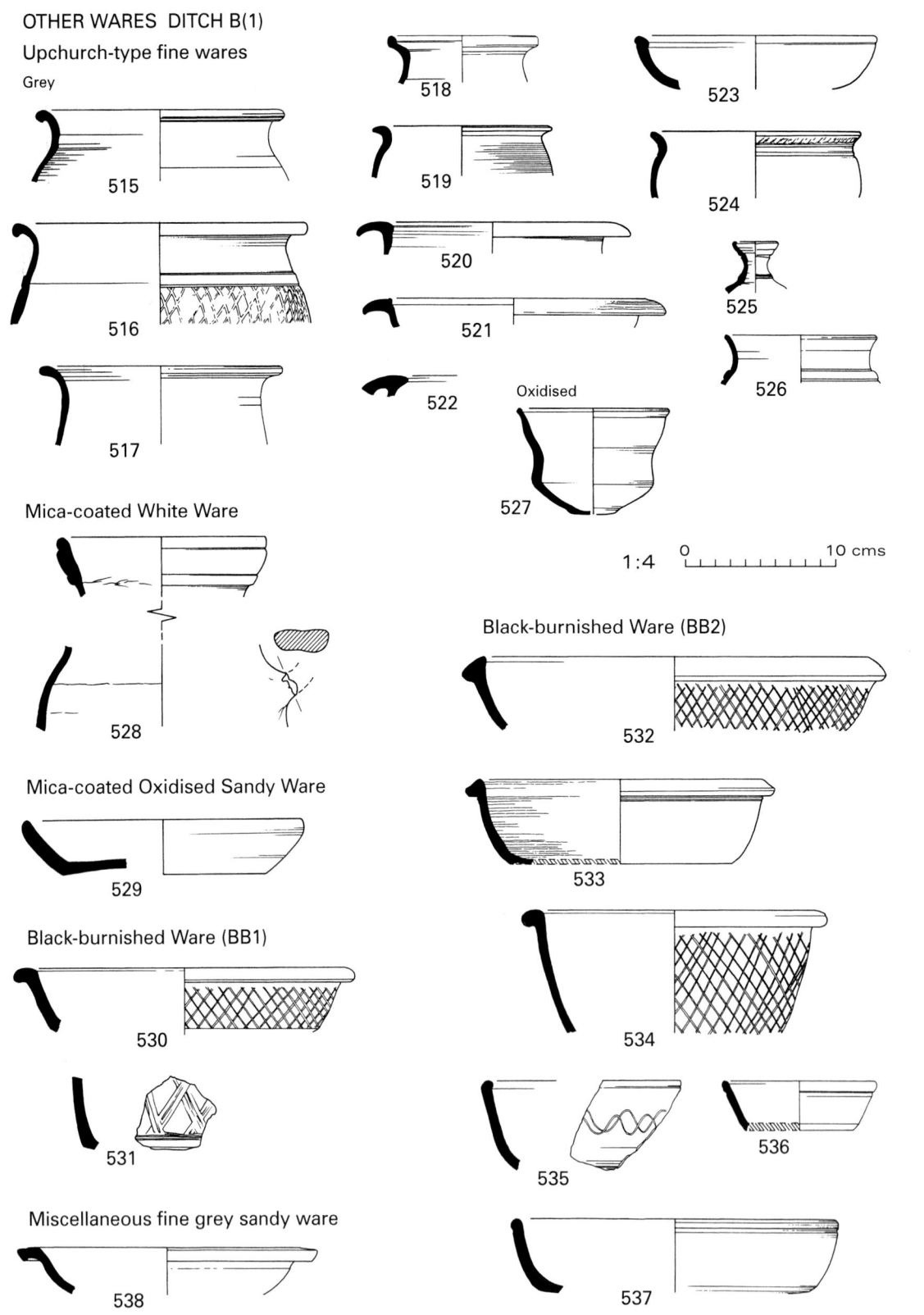

Fig. 136. Roman pottery from Ditch B1. Scale 1:4.

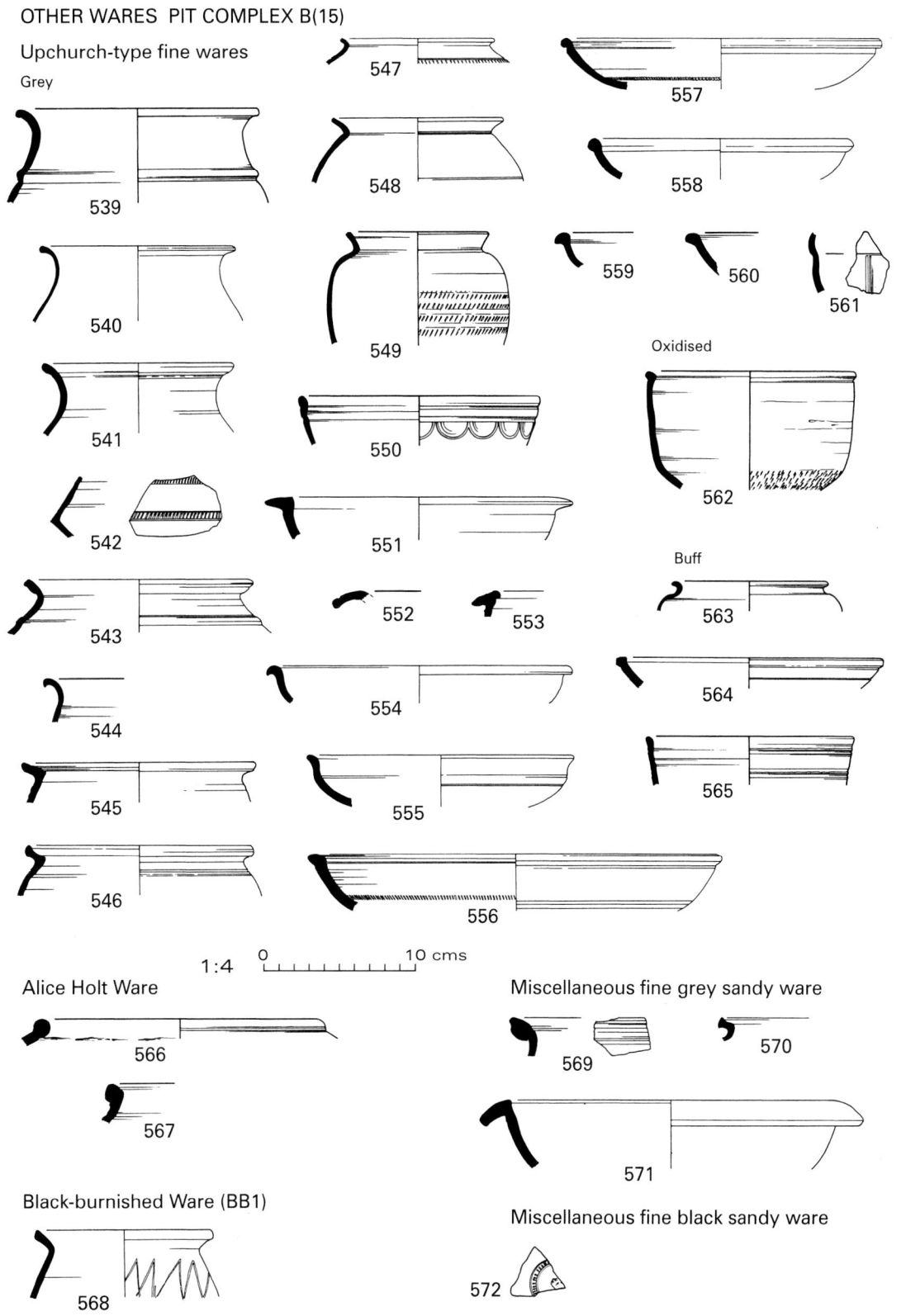

Fig. 137. Roman pottery from Pit complex B15. Scale 1:4.

Enclosure ditch B1: Total sherd count: 744; Total VRE: 2,554
Pit complex B15: Total sherd count: 1,519; Total VRE: 4,292

Fabric	Percentage proportion of assemblage			
	Enclosure ditch B1		Pit complex B15	
	VRE	sherd count	VRE	sherd count
Late Iron Age to 'Belgic'				
grog and flint-tempered ware				
grog and chalk-tempered ware				
'Belgic'				
grogged ware	17.6	53.0	25.3	57.1
fine sandy ware	1.3	0.9	0.9	1.4
coarse sandy ware			0.2	0.4
'chaff'-tempered ware			0.4	0.2
'Belgic' to early Roman				
'Stuppington Lane' coarse sandy ware; local		0.2		0.1
Gallo-Belgic wares:				
TR 1(A)		0.2		
TR 1(C)	0.3	0.3		
Early Roman: pre Flavian				
Lyon Ware				0.1
mica-coated White Ware (WW): ?early/later	0.4	0.3		
mortaria (Hartley fab. 1B)			0.3	0.1
Samian: South Gaul, pre Flavian/Flavian		0.4		0.3
Roman: Flavian to Antonine				
Samian: South Gaul	8.3	7.4	5.5	4.1
Canterbury-type coarse sandy ware (oxidised and reduced)	39.8	15.3	37.1	16.9
white-cream coarse sandy ware: probably local				0.2
white-cream fine sandy ware: ?local				0.3
other white-cream ware				0.1
Upchurch-type wares:				
fine grey ware	16.1	5.4	17.8	6.9
fine oxidised ware	1.2	0.8	1.6	1.8
fine oxidised ware with slip				0.4
fine buff ware		0.3	2.9	1.7
Alice Holt ware			0.2	0.1
Verulamium 'Brockley Hill' ware				0.1
black-burnished wares:				
BB1	0.3	0.3	0.3	0.1
BB2	5.0	2.5	0.9	0.5
mica-coated orange coarse sandy ware	1.3	0.5		
miscellaneous fine grey sandy ware	0.7	0.2	0.8	0.3
miscellaneous fine black sandy ware				0.1
miscellaneous black fine grained ware		0.2		
amphorae:				
Dressel 20		0.9	0.6	0.8
Pelichet 46		0.9		
Pelichet 47	0.9	0.2		0.4
?source		0.2		
mortaria:				
Hartley fab. 1B				0.1
Hartley fab. 1D				0.1
Hartley fab 2A		0.2	0.4	0.1
Hartley fab 2B		0.2		
Hartley fab. 2E		0.2		
Colchester/?North Gaul colour-coat ware	0.4	0.5	0.3	0.1
Lower Rhineland fab. 1	0.5	0.8		0.4
Rigby White Ware III		0.4		
Samian:				
Central Gaul	4.0	6.1	2.3	2.2
Southern Gaul	0.4	0.5		
miscellaneous fine wares			0.2	0.1
Later Roman: mid/late second to third century				
miscellaneous coarse grey sandy ware	0.8	0.3	0.9	0.2
Samian: Eastern Gaul		0.3	0.1	0.2
Central Gaulish 'Rhenish' colour-coat ware	0.6	0.2		
probable Rigby White Ware IV		0.2		
Late Roman: late third to fourth century				
grogged ware (probably late Romano-British)			0.8	0.5
mortaria: Hartley fab. 3				0.1
Oxfordshire colour-coat ware			0.4	0.8
Oxfordshire 'parchment' ware				0.1

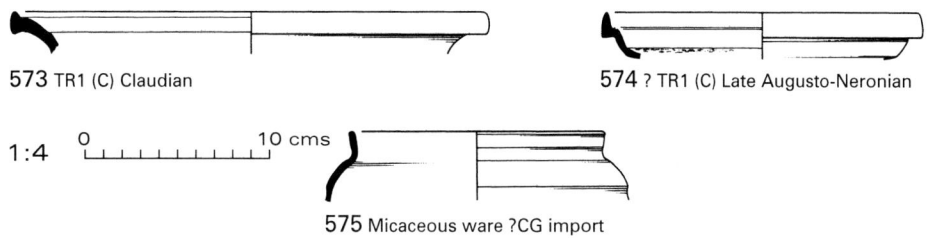

Fig. 138. Early Gaulish finewares. Scale 1:4.

where two vessels from Highstead, together with selected examples from other non-Marlowe sites, are illustrated.

The amphorae (Fig. 139)

Introduction

Marion Green

The range of types at Highstead is rather limited compared with Canterbury, but as is the case in the town, Dressel 20 is dominant. Although the complete corpus of material is small, two stamps were found, one from a Dressel 1B amphora and the other from a Dressel 20. Date ranges presented in Table 24 indicate the entire period of use for each type, as it is presently understood. Paul Arthur's report below suggests more specific dating pertinent to Highstead.

The amphorae

Paul Arthur [11]

Amphorae types recovered from the excavations at Highstead are presented in Table 23.

The six Italian Dressel 1, wine amphora, sherds form a numerical 10 per cent of the total number of amphora sherds discovered at Highstead. Characterised by their volcanic inclusions in the fabric they probably belong to form Dressel 1B, produced between about 60–10 B.C. and are clearly to be associated with the pre-Roman activity at the site. A stub fragment (intrusive in Pit B266, p. 62) bears an eroded and broken stamp .A(...) which is not identifiable (Fig. 139, No. 576). Two further fragments of Dressel 1B were recovered from the same context.

Two Dressel 1B sherds from a pre-conquest deposit (Enclosure ditch B4) are in a reddish-brown fabric with a greenish white slip (Fig. 139, No. 577). Dr Lea Jones kindly thin-sectioned one of the sherds, and reports: 'The main constituent of this piece is angular and sub-angular quartz 0.04–0.01 mm. A fair number of the quartz grains are polycrystalline and rounded. Occasionally there are grains of round to sub-angular orthoclase feldspar, *c.* 0.02 mm. in diameter, one of which shows perthitic intergrowths of plagioclase feldspar. Less frequent inclusions comprise haematite nodules up to 1 mm. in diameter, and fine textured red sandstone fragments (*c.* 0.03 mm. diameter). The matrix is reddish-brown, faintly anisotropic and contains silt-sized particles of fine quartz scattered evenly throughout. There are also sparse spicules of fine muscovite mica. The clay for this vessel was apparently derived from a sedimentary background'. Even though this vessel is of Dressel 1B form, its petrology, with an absence of volcanic inclusions, does not confirm an Italian origin. Though there are large areas of sedimentary deposits throughout Italy, a possible Spanish origin may not be ruled out. It is worth bearing in mind that Dressel 1 amphorae appear to have been produced on occasion in southern Spain (Beltran Lloris 1977, 107–8), whilst Dressel 1-Pascual 1 amphorae from Catalonia, though with a different fabric and rim form to the Highstead vessel, are now attested in pre-conquest contexts in Britain, at Cleavel Point and Hengistbury Head (Williams 1981).

The relatively high number of Dressel 1Bs at Highstead may perhaps be related to a 'gateway port' predating the Roman town of *Durovernum Cantiacorum*, where abundant examples are now coming to light (Arthur 1986).

Twelve fragments of a southern Spanish fish sauce amphora with rim form attributable to Pelichet 46 were recovered from the same pre-conquest context (Enclosure ditch B4). However, this material is considered to be almost certainly intrusive. Pelichet 46 is not generally recognised as having been produced much earlier than Flavian times.

Most of the other vessels came from post-conquest contexts and were probably all imported to the site during the first hundred years or so of Roman occupation. Three types are represented (bar one unidentified body sherd), the southern Spanish Dressel 20 oil amphora, the Pelichet 46 or similar fish sauce amphora and the southern Gaulish Pelichet 47, which is generally believed to have contained wine. These vessels are standard early Imperial imports to Britain. Of note nonetheless, is a Dressel 20 handle from

---

11. Report submitted 1989.

Opposite: Table 20. Enclosure ditch B1 and Pit complex B15, Period 5A. Fabric quantification by sherd count and Vessel Rim Equivalent.

Feature and period	Fabric and form	Source/comments	Dating
Area A			
A255 pit, 4D	CG import Mica TN platter CAM 11	Very worn	Late Augusto-Tiberian
A229 ditch, 4D	Flagon wares (White Wares) WW 1, Cam. 136 or small CAM 161 WW 1, sherd only	Single-handled version of CAM. 161 or small CAM. 161 or single-handled CAM. 136.	Tiberio-Neronian
A246/249 ditch intersections, 4D	GB imports TR 1 (A), Platter: CAM. 51	Very worn. Vesle/Marne area	Late Augustan
A122 pit, 5A	Flagon wares WW 1, sherd only		Pre-Flavian
A14 ditch, 5A	Probable EG wares Beaker: HOL. 26	Micaceous soft fine-grain red ware. Probable import.	Mid to late first century
A274 pit, 5B	CG imports Mica TN, platter GB imports TR 3, Butt beakers CAM. 112	Burnt. ?Residual Apricot matrix; cream slip. Notched scroll rouletting	Late Augusto-Tiberian ?Late Augustan
Unstratified	GB imports TR 3 beaker	Orange ware	Tiberio-Claudian
Unstratified	GB imports TN, Platter: CAM. 13	Worn	Tiberio-(Claudian)
Unstratified	Possible NG imports (White Wares) 1B, Butt beaker: CAM. 113	Typical fabric; cordon and cornice. ?Picardy	Pre-Claudian
Area B			
Post-pit B138, 4A	Flagon wares WW 2, Three-rib strap handle and sherds. Same vessel as B164 below (MJG).		
Enclosure ditch B1, 4D-5A	GB imports TR 1 (A), Pedestal cup: probably CAM. 76 TR 1 (C), Platter: CAM. 5 TR 1 (C), Platter: CAM. 5 Fig. 168, 573,	Worn Orange with darker slip	Tiberio-Claudian Tiberio-(Claudian) Claudian
Enclosure ditch B1, ditch B164, 4D-5A	GB imports ?TR 1 (C),Platter CAM. 7/8 Fig. 168, 574 Flagon wares WW 1, closed form; ?flagon WW 1, sherds WW2, flagon WW 3, sherd Miscellaneous fine wares Necked jar Fig. 168, 575	Heavily burnt Mica 'gilt' coating. CG Import This form has 'military' associations. Same vessel as B138 above ?Import or 'local' Micaceous orange-buff ware; burnished with trace of external red slip. ?Import (CG)	Late Augusto-Neronian First to second century Probably A.D. 50-70 but WW 2 likely to have overall range of Tiberio-Neronian Late first to second century Mid to late first century
Enclosure B1, B366 palisade post-hole, 5B	Possible NG imports II A, Butt beaker: CAM. 113	Cordon and cornice rim. Typical early rim form of CAM. Version, but atypical fabric. Fine-grain white with pure clay matrix. ?Picardy. Residual	Pre-Claudian

References in the table are as follows: HOL. (Holwerda 1941); CAM. = Camulodunum (Hawkes and Hull 1947): GB, CG, NG, EG = Gallo-Belgic, Central, North, East Gaul. Fabric descriptions for the Gallo-Belgic wares can be found in Rigby 1981, and for the remainder, Rigby 1995.

Table 21. Early Gaulish and other imported wares.

Opposite: Table 22. Early Gaulish and other imports. Areas A and B.

Early Gaulish and other imports. Highstead A and B.

Source	Fabric	Sherd count	Years AD
?Central and East Gaul	Misc. Fine wares	5	30–80
	?Rigby WW3 Mica Slip	2	Not Dated
	Rigby WW3	1	80–200
Flagon wares: Imported/local	Rigby WW2	74	40–250 (One vessel)
	Rigby WW1 Mica Slip	1	0–200
	Rigby WW1	5 (1, 2)	Also 2 not dated
Possibly North Gaul (Picardy?)	Rigby IIA	1	
	Rigby IB	1	
Gallia-Belgica	TN	1	
	TR 3	2	?
	TR 1(C)	3 ?1 (1, 1)	
	TR 1(A)	2	
Central Gaul	Mica TN	2	
	Total	100	

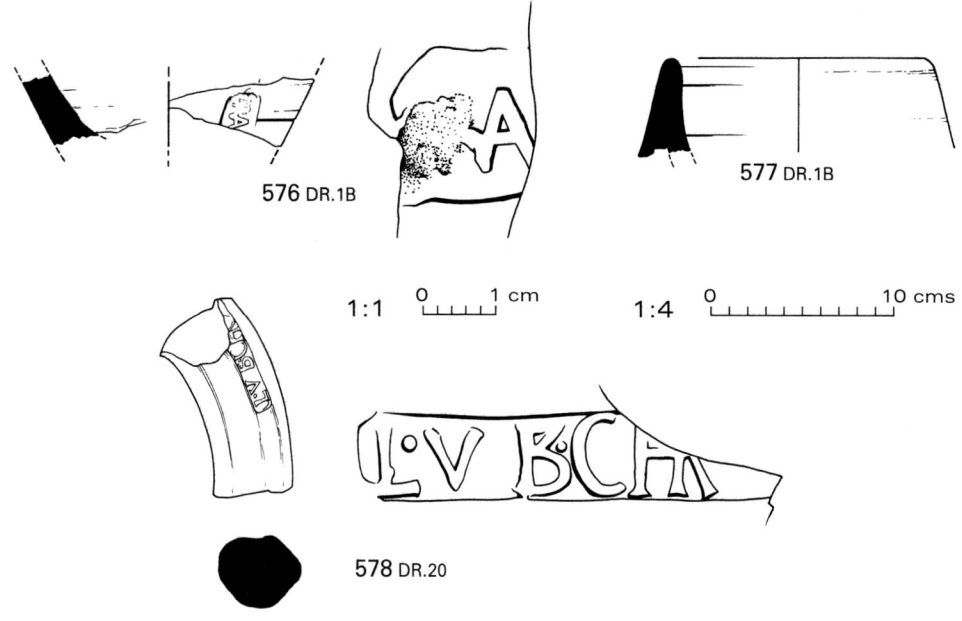

Fig. 139. Roman amphorae (scale 1:4) and stamps (scale: 1:1).

Area A	Period	Dressel 1B	Dressel 20	Pelichet 46	Pelichet 47	Southern Gaul	?Source
A267, ditch	5A		1				
A55, ditch	5A		1				
A276, ditch	5A		1				
A274, pit	5B		1				
A(u/s)			1				
Area B							
B16 house gully	3B		1				
B266, pit	3B	3					
B4, enclosure ditch	4C	2		12			
B25, ditch	4D			1			
B262, pit	4B	1					
B236, ditch	5A				1		
B15, pit complex	4D-5A		12		6		
B13, pit	5A	1	1				
B1, enclosure ditch	4D-5A		7	7	1		1
B164, ditch	4D-5A		2				
B355, palisade post-hole	5B	1	1				
Area C							
C5, pit	5A		3			1	

Table 23. Amphorae quantified by sherd count.

Amphorae. Highstead A,B,C.

Source	Sherd count	Years B.C. / A.D. date range
? Source	1	Not Dated
S. Gaul	1	Not Dated
S. Gaul (Pel. 47)	8	c. 50–300 AD
S. Spain (Pel. 46)	20	c. 60–110 AD (One vessel)
S. Spain (DR. 20)	28	c. 50–300 AD
	3	Stamp c. 80–150 AD
Italy/S. Spain (DR. 1B)	8	c. 50 BC – AD 0
Total	69	

Table 24. Amphorae. Areas A, B and C.

Period 4B Pit complex B15 bearing the stamp L.VIB. CHR(OM) (Fig. 139, No. 578), which Callender suggests dates from the end of the first to the beginning of the second century A.D. (Callender 1965, no. 981). A further Dressel 20 handle appears to bear 'chisel' marks near its basal end, perhaps indicating a deliberate attempt at its removal from the body of the vessel.

Four amphora sherds were recovered from the Area C hypocaust stoke-pit C5, which appears datable to the second century A.D. They comprise three fragments of Dressel 20 and one sherd of a southern Gaulish vessel.

The samian [12]

Summary

Maggy Taylor

A relatively small amount of samian was recovered from Highstead, a possible maximum of 220 vessels. The material indicates continuous use of the ware from the mid first century (as illustrated by the earliest vessel with a Claudian date) to the early third century, and reflects the general distribution pattern for this part of Kent. There is a peak in the Flavian period, with sixty-six vessels and a later one in the Antonine with nineteen (Table 25).

The earliest material, a decorated Dragendorff 29 from Southern Gaul in the style of the Claudio-Neronian pottery Bassus, and twelve pre-Flavian plain vessels, comes from Ditch B1 and Pit complex B15, both of Period 4D–5A date. There are also decorated bowls by the Flavian potter Crucuro; from the Germanus workshop; a 'probable' Meddillus and the Flavian-Trajanic potter Biragillus. Of particular interest is the presence of a late Montans bowl by the Malcio-Chresimus group dated *c.* A.D. 110–40.

The Trajanic potters of Les Martres-de-Veyre are represented, with work by Drusus I, Igocatus, Medetus-Ranto and Donnaucus. From Lezoux are three bowls by the Cinnamus workshop and the Sacer-Cinnamus group.

Products from Eastern Gaul are few, one bowl from Rheinzabern and one from Blickweiler. Vessels from Blickweiler are scarce in Britain, but have previously also been found in small quantities elsewhere in east Kent, including Canterbury (Bird 1995, 774–5; The Archaeology of Canterbury III, forthcoming).

The collection contains an unusually high proportion of the barbotine-leaf decorated forms Dragendorff 35 and 36 and Curle 11 (20 per cent of the corpus). Several vessels appear to have been used as mortars. The entire slip has been worn away in the interior of these vessels and small pits ground out of the surface. The preference was for the small cups Dragendorff 27 and 35. The inside of the foot-ring of a Dragendorff 38 had also been used in this way.

A catalogue of the decorated samian is published here and the four potters' stamps illustrated. The plain samian catalogue is held with the site archive.

The decorated samian (Fig. 140)

Joanna Bird and Maggy Taylor [13]

Enclosure ditch B2: Period 4C (see p. 75)

Dr. 29, SG, scroll in upper frieze with part of a large rosette-shaped flower with pointed petals; a similar one was used by Meddillus (Knorr 1919, 55K). *c.* A.D. 70–85.

Dr. 37, CG. Has links with the potters Donnaucus and Sacer. The ovolo and leaf-tip ornament are on S&S pl. 83.9, the wreath on pl. 43, 499, the crane, pl. 47.549. Both potters used pigmies, but have not previously been recorded as using this one O 696 a. *c.* A.D. 130–50.

Pit complex B15: Period 4D–5A

Dr. 37, SG, a fragment of lower wall with panels of saltire-like leaf arrangements, bead-row borders and figure, possibly Diana, four-fronded leaf and the wavy line borders with rosette terminals, used by Crucuro of La Graufesenque, similar bowl (Knorr 1952, 20A), basal wreath probably s-gadroons. *c.* A.D. 75–90.

Dr. 29, SG, scroll in upper frieze, acorn and spurred leaf, as used by Bassus (Knorr 1952, 7c) also found at Richborough (Bushe-Fox 1932, pl. XIII, no. 9). *c.* A.D. 50–65.

Dr. 37, SG, basal band of s-gadroons used by several potters. Flavian.

579. Dr. 37, SG, (two sherds) with trident-tongued ovolo. Motifs such as the festoon and spiral and the general style are all typical late SG (e.g. H. pl. 88), lion, is a smaller version of one used by Severus (Knorr 1952, 834), the timpanist (H. 19 pl. 84), the Bacchus and leopard are small variants of (H. 19 pl. 70), the slip unusually smooth, silky and orange-toned for this date. *c.* A.D. 80–110.

Dr. 37, CG, by Drusus/X3 of Les Martres-de-Veyre; the leafed festoon, beaded cup, astragalus and acanthus motif are all variously on S&S pl. 11, nos 135, 137, 139. The figure is not certainly identifiable. *c.* A.D. 100–125.

Dr. 37, SG, panels divided by wavy line borders, containing the saltire with four-lobed leaf and Diana and hound used by Crucuro of La Graufesenque. For a similar bowl, see Knorr, 52, taf. 20, A. *c.* A.D. 75–90.

Dr. 37, CG, Medetus-Ranto/X8 and X9 used this beaded circle with central star (S&S fig. 9, 12), this and the wavy

---

12. All of the reports on the samian were first submitted in 1989.
13. Abbreviations in the catalogue are as follows: CW2: Transactions of the Cumberland and Westmoreland Antiquarian and Archaeological Society; Dr.: Dragendorff; H.: Hermet 1934; LRF: Ludowici *et al.* 1963; O: Oswald 1936–7; S&S: Stanfield and Simpson 1958.

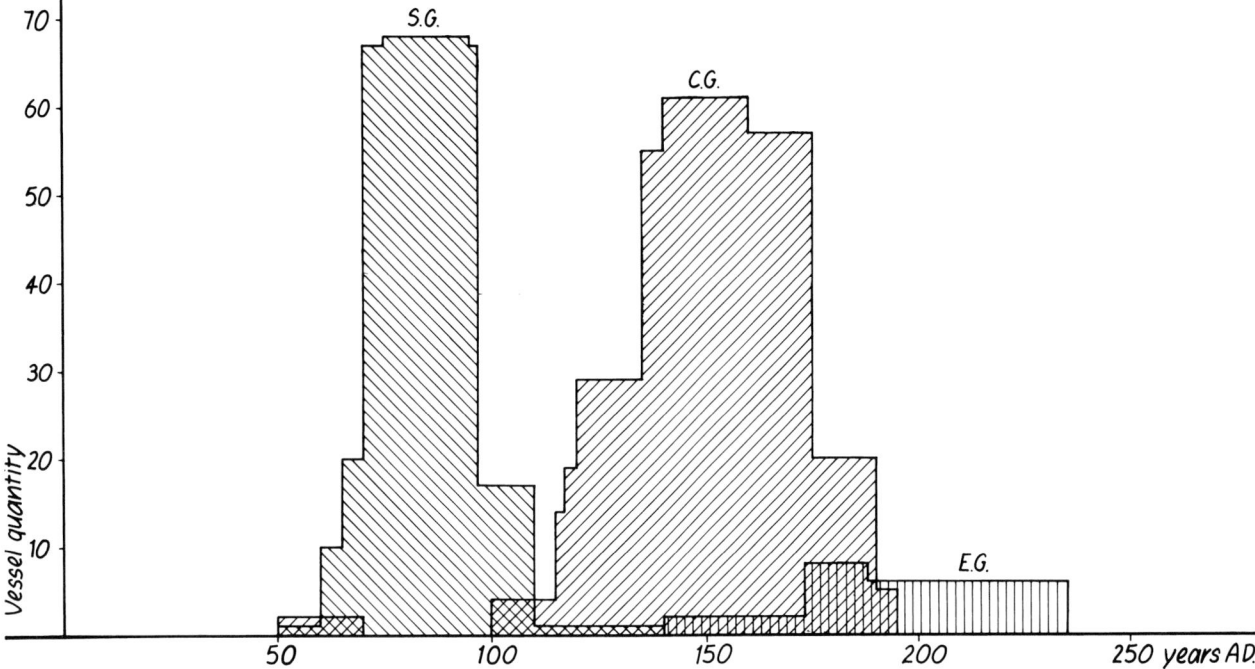

Table 25. Samian. Form quantity and date range.

line border with rosette terminals are on S&S pl. 29.344. *c.* A.D. 100–125.

Ditch B236: Period 5A

Dr. 37, CG (five sherds) by Igocatus/X4 of Les Martres-de-Veyre. S&S pl. 17 has the ovolo, leaf cross ornament and wavy line border (215), the large figure and rosette terminal (221, the timpanist is on pl. 19. 235. This vessel was smudged in removal from the mould. It was broken and mended in antiquity with lead rivets; one is still in place. The slip of the interior has been removed in use. *c.* A.D. 100–125.

Enclosure ditch B1: Period 4D–5A

580. Dr. 37, CG, either Martialis ii or Attianus ii of Lezoux. Martialis used the erotic group (O.H.) on bowls from Lezoux and Mancetter. The Lezoux bowl also has the trifid (?Rogers 1974, G113) and possibly the astragalus. Attianus used the trifid on a stamped bowl from Vechten (S&S pl. 87.25), the leaf cross (Rogers 1974, L3 or L4) on a stamped bowl from York and the tree (Rogers 1974, N7). This is slightly more likely to be by Martialis than Attianus. *c.* A.D. 125–45. (B.M.D.)

Dr. 37, CG, (two sherds) by Cinnamus of Lezoux, the same arrangement with geese facing right, large leaf in a festoon and tendril binding was found at Ovilava (Karnitsch 1959, taf. 72.3), the leaf, scroll and astragalus are on S&S pl. 162.58. *c.* A.D. 150–75.

Dr. 37, EG, ovolo used at Rheinzabern by several potters (LRF E2) but very rarely with a border and never one like this. Same ovolo used at Blickweiler with big beads, as here (Knorr and Sprater 1927, taf. 15–16 including bowls of Cambo), fabric likely to be Blickweiler. Figure not identifiable. Antonine probably.

Dr. 37, CG, by Donnaucus/X13 of Les Martres-de-Veyre, the ovolo with rosette tongue is on S&S pl. 46.547, the grass tuft (pl. 45.525), the bead-row and lion (pl. 47.555 and 558) and the snake on rocks (pl. 49.584). A bowl from the same mould was found at London in the Regis House group (unpublished). *c.* A.D. 100–125.

Pit A274: Period 5B

Dr. 37, SG, ovolo with damaged three-pronged tongue, shallow panel with hare above one with spiral (not attributable). Flavian.

Dr. 37, SG (two sherds) ovolo with four-pronged tongue, probably one used by Biragillus (K19, taf. 16.16); he also used the same poppy heads and wavy line borders, the winged victory is 0 805 B. *c.* A.D. 80–100.

Ditch B165: Period 5B

Dr. 37, SG, Montans, ovolo and wavy line as Simpson 1976, fig. 5, 15, by the Malcio-Chresimus group, other motifs not identifiable. *c.* A.D. 110–40.

Unstratified

Dr. 37, CG (seven sherds) Sacer-Cinnamus group, the huntsman and bear are on Karnitsch 1959, taf. 77, 2 and 2A and S&S pl. 163.72 and pl. 82.5, the panthers (S&S pl. 82, 2 and pl. 84.16), the stag (S&S pl. 85.9 and pl. 163.66) ovolo blurred, close to Sacer, Attianus series or Cinnamus 6. Very abraded sherds. *c.* A.D. 130–60. Area A u/s.

Dr. 37, CG (two sherds), double banded medallion and astragalus of Cinnamus (cf. S&S pl. 160.40) ovolo possible Cinnamus 2. Sherds badly abraded and burnt. *c.* A.D. 150–75. Area A u/s.

Dr. 29, probably SG, panel of arrowheads in upper frieze, no rouletting above decoration. Fabric suggests pre-Flavian date. Intrusive in Period 3B Pit B195.

Dr. 37, EG, Rheinzabern, lion or panther and possibly a boar neither identifiable, probably a third smaller animal beneath. Later second century to mid third century. Area B u/s

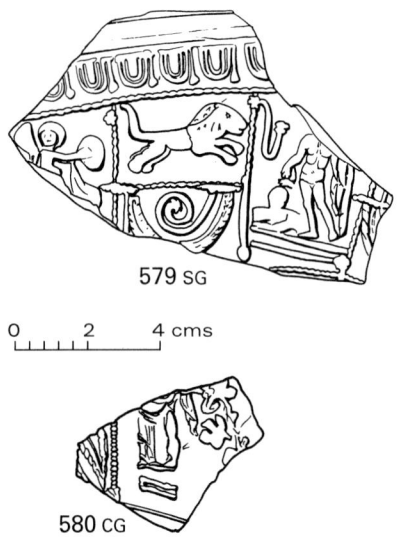

Fig. 140. Decorated samian. Scale 1:2.

The stamped samian

Brenda Dickinson

581 CG

Annius ii, 2a, 33 // Lezoux (a). A stamp noted in Period IIc at *Verulamium* (*c.* A.D. 140–150). One of his others is in a late Hadrianic context on Hadrian's Wall (CW2 XXX (1930), 186, no. 6). *c.* A.D. 130–50. Enclosure ditch B164, Period 4D–5A.

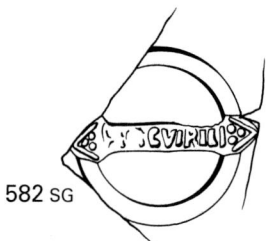

582 SG

L. Cosius Virilis 12c 33 OFLCVIRILI. This stamp is known from La Graufesenque (Vernhet 1976, fig. 4.10) and the main site at Corbridge. It is not particularly closely dated but stamps from many of his other dies at Domitianic foundations and his use of form 29 give a range of *c.* A.D. 70–100. Enclosure ditch B1, Period 4D–5A.

583 CG

Not identified. CG probably. Pit complex B15, Period 4D–5A.

584 CG

Not identified. Eight petalled rosette on wall-sided bowl CG. Hypocaust stoke-pit, C5, Period 5B.

Graffiti

Maggy Taylor

585 CG

Incomplete three letter graffito, incised onto Dr. 37, CG. Hadrianic-Antonine. Enclosure ditch B1, Period 4D–5A.

The Roman and Romano-British finewares

Marion Green

Archive reports have been compiled for all material and a summary only is presented here. As with other specialist wares (samian excepted) the corpus is small, but again reflects the types occurring in the city. From Table 26 it is apparent that of the datable material, the majority was of the type likely to have been in use during the later first and second centuries. Evidence of types occurring in the later Roman period is scarce; one sherd of Central Gaulish 'Rhenish' ware, although this is never very common at Canterbury. Some of the Rigby wares (probably all pentice beakers) may be attributable to the later second to third centuries or later. In Table 26, they are placed only broadly in the chronological sequence, as are other undated wares. The two major types to be found in later third- and fourth-century Canterbury (Oxfordshire and Nene Valley Type colour-coats) also appear at Highstead, indicating some limited late Roman activity.

Fabric descriptions for Rigby White Wares can be found in Rigby (1995, 651–3); for the remaining wares, see Greene 1979 (Lyon ware); Peacock 1977 (Pompeian Red Ware); Anderson 1980 (Lower Rhineland Fabric 1, Colchester and North Gaul colour-coats); Young 1977 (Oxfordshire finewares) and Perrin 1980 (Nene Valley colour-coats).

The mortaria [14]

Introduction

Marion Green

Table 27 describes all of the mortaria recovered from Highstead; Table 28 condenses the data and illustrates concentrations of ware sources (predominantly Kent) and their main period of use. The corpus of material, although small, generally reflects the range of fabric types found at Canterbury; the two sherds of Oxfordshire mortaria reflect the apparent scarcity of late Roman activity at the site (*see* p. 216). Certain fabric group re-assessments have been made by Kay Hartley in the light of the Highstead material. A revision of Fabric group 2 (Hartley 1982) is included below with a note on the possible occurrence of later Roman Much Hadham vessels. For descriptions of other fabrics represented at Highstead, see Hartley 1982.

The mortaria (Figs 141–2)

Kay Hartley

Fabrics 2A–2E (revised)

It is difficult to assess the significance of fabric differences in this range of iron bearing clays and they have been differentiated primarily according to the texture, the colour being considered only if the difference is very distinctive (*see* below). More than one of them could have been produced at one workshop while similar fabrics could be produced at different workshops which had similar clay and trituration material available. These fabrics are common in mortaria in Kent.

However, at least some of these fabrics appear identical with those produced at Much Hadham in Hertfordshire and perhaps elsewhere in that area and perhaps in Essex. There is no evidence to show that Much Hadham ever produced many mortaria; what there is indicates a very small production in the second century and a rather more extensive one in the late third and fourth centuries. The rim-profiles associated with second-century mortaria in Kent which are in Fabrics 2A–E point to local production, but some or all of those in Fabrics 2A–E dated later than the mid third century may well come from Much Hadham or allied sources. A comprehensive study of the fabrics is necessary but there does remain the very real possibility that similar clays were being used at workshops which are so far apart.

Fabric 2A

A fairly coarse orange-brown fabric (Munsell 2.5YR6/8–5YR7/8) sometimes with a thin drab core or a thicker sandwich core of pale grey between pale brown layers. The surface often has a rough grainy texture quite similar to the coarser mortarium fabrics produced in the *Verulamium* region; this could be the result of weathering and some which are a little smoother may indicate the unweathered surface. Frequent inclusions of sub-angular, fairly ill-sorted (up to 2 mm.) quartz with some flint and red-brown fragments. Trituration grit (little surviving) consists of opaque flint with red-brown and very occasional grey (?shale) fragments. Some have a self-coloured surface or surface slip and others a cream slip.

Fabric 2B

Hard, slightly micaceous fabric; colour variable from orange-brown to pale brown (Munsell 2.5YR6/8-7.5YR6/6) often with a thick core varying from pale grey to drab pale brown. Fairly frequent inclusions but not as coarse as Fabric 2A; sub-angular, fairly well-sorted quartz, some flint and black fragments. Trituration grit mainly of opaque flint with some quartz, red-brown and black fragments.

Fabric 2C

Hard, slightly micaceous, fine-textured, orange-brown fabric (Munsell 2.5YR5/8) with a well defined, dark grey core, which may be marked with a streak of pale brown at its edges. No inclusions visible at x10 magnification. Trituration grit mainly of opaque flint, translucent and opaque quartz with some red-brown fragments.

---

14. Report submitted 1989.

Roman & Romano-British Finewares. Highstead A,B,C.

Source	Sherd count	Years AD (50–400)
Misc. Finewares unidentified	4	Not Dated
Nene Valley type cc	2	c. 200–400
Oxon 'Parchment'	1	c. 240–400
Oxon cc	14	c. 240–400
Rigby IV (?NG)	1	Not Dated
Rigby III (?NG)	3	Not Dated
Rigby IIC (?NG)	1	Not Dated
CG 'Rhenish' cc	1	c. 150–230
?Source Mica coated sandy ware	4	Not Dated
Colchester/NG cc	27	c. 90–250
L. Rhine Fab 1/ Nene Valley cc.	1	c. 60–250
L. Rhine Fab 1	16 +?3	c. 90–200
Pompeian Red Ware Fab 2	1	c. 50–130 ?
Lyon	2	c. 50–70
Total	81	

Table 26. Roman and Romano-British finewares. Areas A, B and C.

Feature and period	Fabric	Source	Comments	Dating
Area A				
A263 ditch, 4D	2A	Kent	Flange and spout. Stamp. Vessel as 249 below. Intrusive. Fig. 141, No. 586	A.D. 120-60
A103 ditch, 4D	2B	probably Kent	Flange. Intrusive	A.D. 110-70
A249 ditch, 4D	2A	Kent	Body sherd. Same vessel as A263, above. Intrusive	A.D. 120-60
A245 ditch, 5A	1A	import, probably Gaul	Burnt flange and spout. Probably related to Bushe-Fox 1913, fig. 19, form 26-30	c. A.D. 100-50
	-	probably Colchester	Spout	c. A.D. 140-80
A u/s	1B	Colchester	Flange. Stamp. Fig. 141, No. 587	A.D. 160-200
	1B	Colchester	Flange. Stamp. Fig. 141, No. 588	A.D. 130-70
	1B	Kent	Flange; cream-brown variant. Fig. 141, No. 589	c. A.D. 160-200
	1	Origin unknown	Rim	second century
	2B	Kent	Flange. Joins sherd from B25. Fig. 141, No. 590	probably A.D. 150-200
Area B				
B51 post-hole, 3A	1B	Colchester, Kent or import	Body sherd, well worn. *Intrusive*	
B2 enclosure ditch, 4C	1D	Kent, probably Canterbury	Flange. Type as B15 below	probably A.D. 130-70
	1D	Kent	Flange. ?Same vessel as 594 from B165	A.D. 120-70
	2B	Kent	Flange. Fig. 141, No. 591	A.D. 120-70
B25 ditch, 4D	-	-	Flange with distal bead. Joins u/s sherd from Area A	
	2B	Colchester, Kent or import	Body sherd. *Intrusive*	first or second century
B262 pit, 4B	8	Verulamium region	Fragmentary rim. Intrusive	probably A.D. 90-130
B15 pit complex, 4D-5A	1B	Probably Colchester, possibly Kent	Body sherd	Second century, possibly later
	1D	Kent	Spout. Type as B2 above	A.D. 120-70
	1	Import, probably Rhenish	Perhaps Eifel area where general type is common. See Hawkes and Hull 1947, fig. 53, no. 31 for closest parallel; Niblett 1985, Types 26-30; Frere 1972, fig. 102, no. 93; Frere 1984, 293. Fig. 141, No. 592	A.D. 40-60 in Britain
	2A	Kent	Flange. Fig. 142, No. 593	c. A.D. 110-60
	3	Oxfordshire	Body sherd. Probably not common in Kent before A.D. 170	c. A.D. 100-400
B1 enclosure ditch, 4D-5A	2A	Probably Kent	Body sherd	late first or second century
	2B	Probably Kent	Burnt body sherd	probaby second century
	2E	Probably Kent	Body sherd	late first or second century
B165, ditch, 5B	1D	Kent	Flange. ?Same vessel as B2 above. Fig. 142, No. 594	A.D. 120-70.
Area C				
Hypocaust rubble, 5B	2B	Kent	Flange	Probably A.D. 130-70
C u/s	3	Oxfordshire	Burnt body sherd. Probably not common in Kent before A.D. 170	A.D. 100-400

Table 27. Mortaria.

Fabric 2D

Hard, fine-textured fabric, varying in colour from almost chocolate brown at surface with thick orange-brown core (Munsell 7.5YR4/4–2.5YR5/8) to pinkish-brown at the surface with a thick, slightly purplish-pink core (Munsell 5YR7/6–2.5YR6.4). Few inclusions visible at x10 magnification; tiny quartz and red-brown fragments with occasional larger white chalk fragments. Trituration grit consists of quartz, flint and an amount of red-brown fragments and black fragments (?iron slag).

Fabric 2E

Fine, but grainy, fabric, orange-brown (Munsell 2.5YR5/8) with tiny quartz inclusions barely visible at x10 magnification. Trituration grit (little surviving) of opaque flint. Traces of cream slip on some examples.

The stamped mortaria (Fig. 141)

586. A mortarium in Fabric 2A, diameter *c.* 30 cm., with fragmentary stamps to each side of the spout. These stamps can be attributed to Valentinus whose products have been found at the following sites: Caerleon, Canterbury (3), Corbridge, Dorking, Dover (2), Highstead, London (6), Slayhills, Upchurch and Wroxeter. His rim-forms indicate activity within the period A.D. 110–60. Both the fabrics and the distribution of his work suggest that he had two workshops; the earlier one, probably active before A.D. 120, was in the *Verulamium* region, the later one in Kent. The range of rim-forms in the different fabrics indicates that

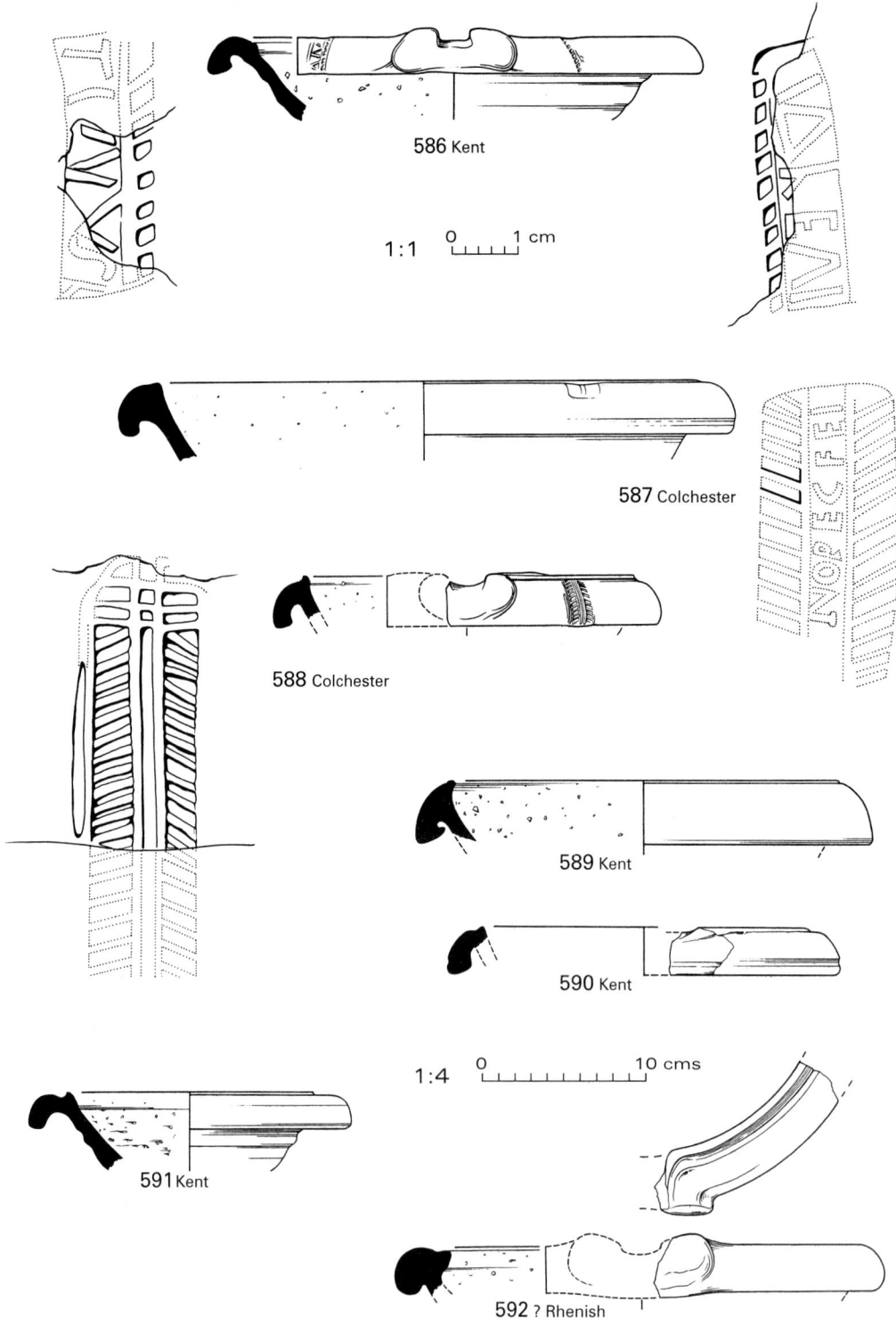

Fig. 141. Mortaria (scale 1:4) and stamps (scale 1:1).

Mortaria. Highstead A, B, C.

Source	Sherd count	Date range (Years AD)
? Source Fab 1	1	c. 100–200
Oxfordshire Fab 3	2	c. 100–400
Colchester/Kent/ import Fab 2B	1	c. 50–200
Fab 1B	1	Not dated
Colchester/(Kent) Fab 1B	1	c. 100–225
Colchester others	3	Same vessel, c. 130–180
Fab 1B	2	Same vessel, c. 150–200
	1	c. 130–170
Kent probable Canterbury Fab 1D	2	Same vessel, c. 110–160
Probable Kent Fab 2E	1	c. 80–200
Fab 2B	1	c. 80–200
	1	c. 90–150
Fab 2A	1	c. 70–200
Kent Fab 2B	2	Same vessel, c. 140–200
	1	c. 120–170
	2	Same vessel, c. 120–200
Fab 2A	2	Same vessel, c. 120–180
	2	Same vessel, c. 120–180
Fab 1E	1	c. 150–200
Fab 1D	3	c. 120–180
Verulamium region Fab 8	1	c. 70–110
Import: prob. Gaul Fab 1A	2	Same vessel, c. 100–170
Import: prob. Rhineland Fab 1	1	c. 60–80
Total	35	

Table 28. Mortaria. Areas A, B and C.

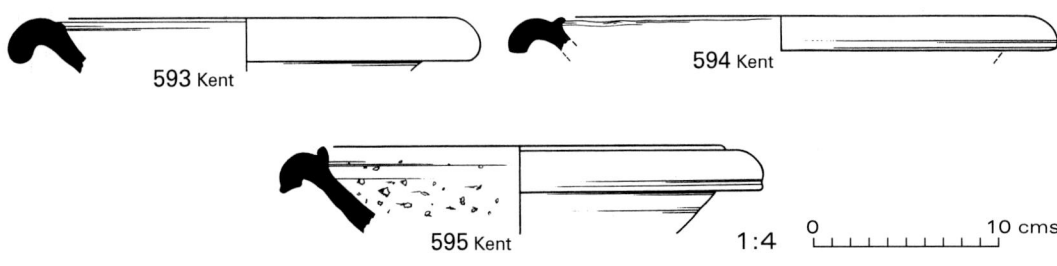

Fig. 142. Mortaria. Scale 1:4.

his Kent activity was within the period A.D. 120–60. Ditch A263, Period 4D.

587. A weathered mortarium in Fabric 1B, diameter c. 36 cm., made in the Colchester kilns (Hull 1963, fig. 67, no. 1). The stamp is too abraded for normal identification, but the dimensions of stamp and borders and the two diagonal bars surviving in the top border fit only one stamp-type of one of the Colchester potters, Cunopectus. His activity can be attributed to A.D. 160–200. (A u/s).

588. A mortarium in Fabric 1B, diameter 24 cm., made at Colchester. The stamp is from the most commonly used of the Colchester herringbone dies (Hull 1963, fig. 60, no. 30). More than forty mortaria with this stamp are known from sites in south-eastern and north-eastern England; and twenty-nine from sites in Scotland (MacIvor et al. 1981, 261–64 for discussion and details of distribution in Scotland; also Thomas 1988). Stamps from the same die are so common on sites of Antonine foundation in Scotland that A.D. 140–65 must cover the period of its *floruit*. Stamps from the same die are also recorded from South Shields (2), and stamps from other herringbone dies which are probably contemporary are known from Benwell and Birdoswald, all sites on Hadrian's Wall; a stamp has also been found in the destruction deposit at Corbridge which is known to contain residual material. The die's use should fall sometime within the period A.D. 130–70. (A u/s).

PART 4: OTHER FINDS

Flints (Figs 143–7)

Elizabeth Healey [15]

Some 257 chipped stone artefacts were retained from the excavations in areas A and B and from surface collections. The material is catalogued according to these groupings, but in view of the possibility that not all the material was retained together with the uncertainty of integrity of the groups, the artefacts will be treated as a single entity (the detailed supposed breakdown is deposited with the archive). The artefacts are in reasonably fresh condition but some have suffered post-depositional damage. The composition of the assemblages is as follows:

	Area A A	Area B B	General surface G	Probably surface
Cores	1	6	9	1
Flakes	6	61	61	37
Retouched pieces	1	17	42	15
Totals	8	84	112	53

Table 29. Composition of the flint assemblage.

Raw materials

All the artefacts are made of flint of reasonable flaking quality. One piece of chert was also recovered. Cortex varies from soft chalky white to thin hard and grey or even black; there is sometimes an orange-yellow band beneath the cortex. The flints range in colour from black or dark grey to pale grey, sometimes with a brownish tinge. Many of the artefacts have been stained orange and some pieces are patinated. The difference in colouration and cortex type suggests that different types of flint were used, though all could have been found relatively locally. The flint used for the ground-and-polished axe is of superior quality and may have been imported from further afield.

I am grateful to Nigel Macpherson-Grant for the following observations: 'The impression at the time of excavation was that the gravel of the terrace on which the sites are located was mainly small pebbles and contained very little nodular material and was therefore unsuitable as a source of raw material. Some of the flint may be naturally derived from the brickearth, especially that with the orange band beneath the cortex, but some may have come from flint-bearing chalk somewhat further afield.'

Reduction strategies

Because of the nature of the assemblage, the extended area it was found in and the chronological range of diagnostic types (*see* below) it is likely that more than one reduction strategy is represented, although it has not been possible to disentangle them in the present collection. The majority of the flakes (75 per cent) are less than 50 mm. in length and quite squat (92 per cent fall into the width to length ratio of under 2:5). Striking platform remnants are usually plain and two are cortical (47 per cent), 19 per cent are linear and a further 17 per cent faceted or dihedral. The rest are splintered or shattered. The flakes from Area B have a higher proportion with cortex on them and are more likely to terminate in a hinge fracture than the flakes from the other groups. Interestingly the pieces with more blade-like dimensions come from the surface collection (G). A small number of flakes, mainly from the Harbour collection (pp. xix, 15), tend to be wide and to have a higher incidence of faceted striking platform remnants; they also have multi-

---

15. Reported completed 1987, revised 2004.

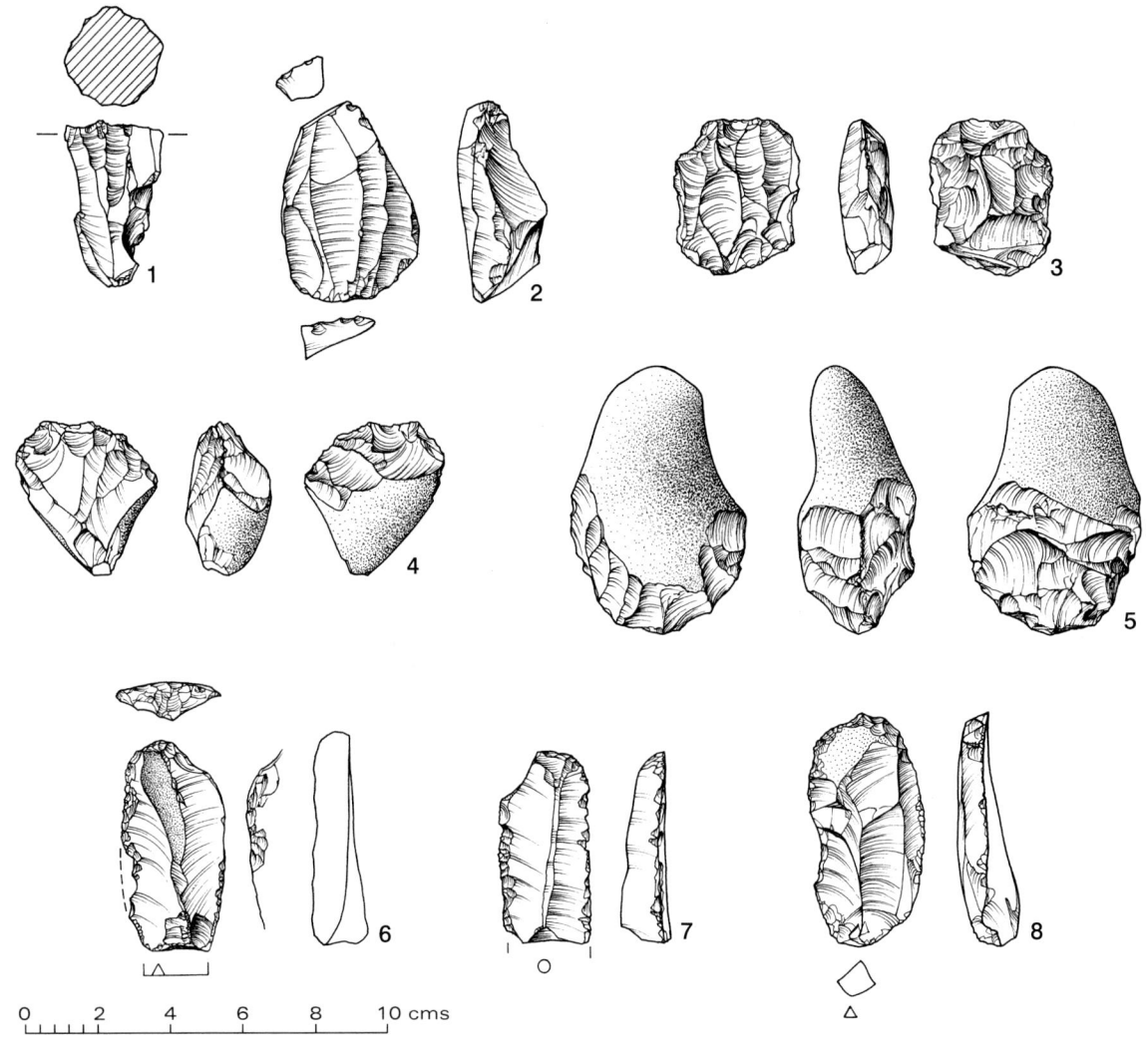

Fig. 143. Cores (Nos 1–3), choppers (Nos 4 and 5) and scrapers (Nos 6–8). Scale 1:2.

directional scarring on the dorsal surface and a markedly concave curvature when viewed in profile and give the impression of resulting from shaping a bifacial object or similar (cf. Newcomer 1971).

Cores also show differentiation in type by area – unidirectional cores with more blade-like scars were only found in the group designated G and may correspond to the elongated flakes also from that group. The other cores are bi-directional or globular, the flatter ones tending to be sub-discoidal; two have keeled edges.

Choppers (4–5)

In addition to the cores two cortex covered nodules have bi-directional flaking on their edges forming a convex shape and are slightly battered; they fall into the category generally described as choppers or chopping tools though they do grade into the keeled core category.

Hammerstones (48–49)

Three almost spherical stones with abraded areas on them were recovered; such objects are generally termed hammerstones though their purpose is far from certain. Their use in flint working is questionable as flint hammerstones tend to shatter easily, but other suggestions for their use include the dressing of the surface of a quern or for pounding of grit or burnt flint for pottery temper (Clark *et al.* 1960, 225). One (49) has been shaped by flaking, or is possibly a re-used core (cf. Saville 1981, 5) with abrasion around its circumference, another

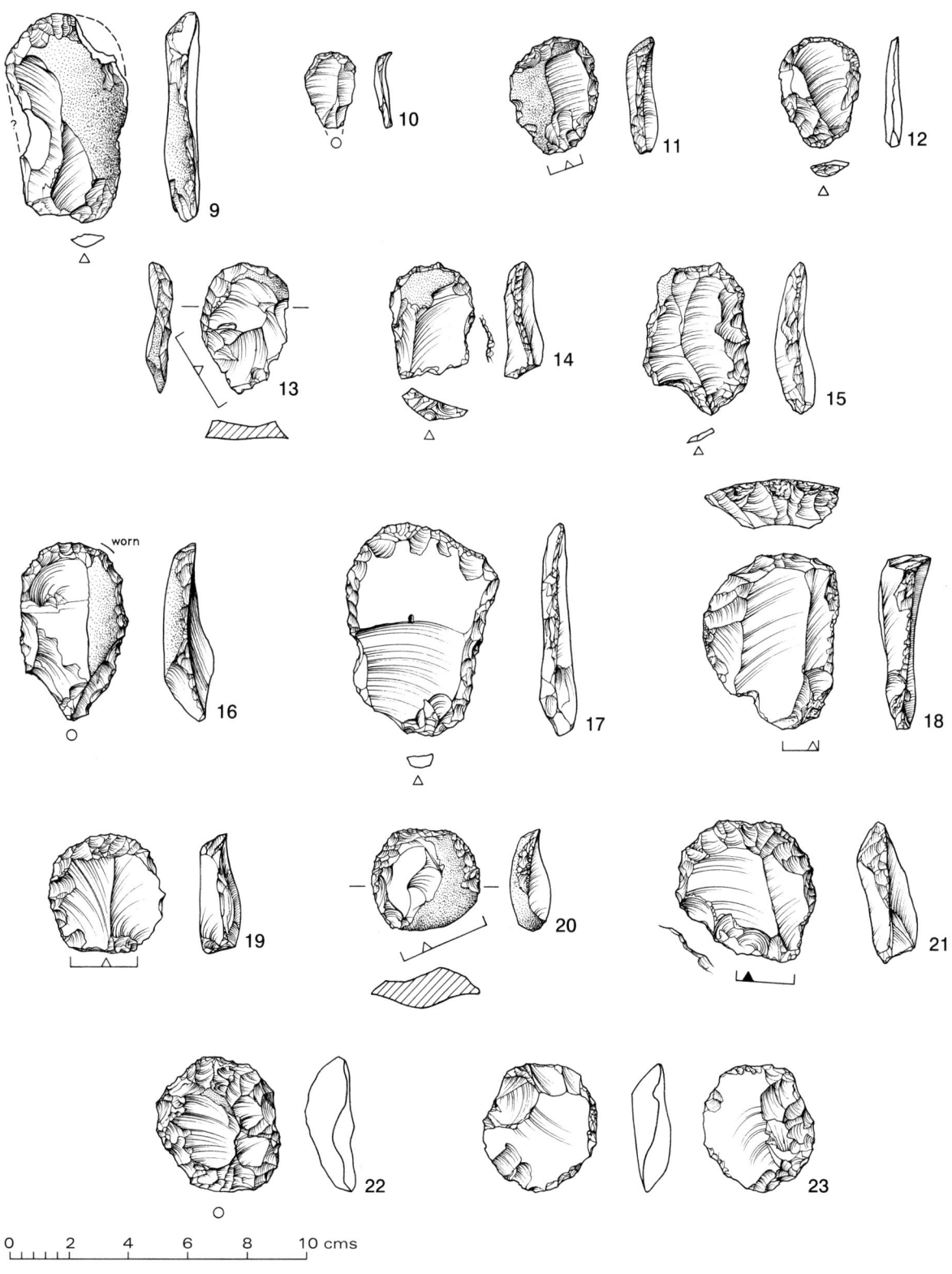

Fig. 144. Scrapers. Scale 1:2.

(48) has a flat surface with ring cracks or incipient cones of percussion all over it and the third is abraded all over.

Retouched pieces

These are grouped according to conventional categories to facilitate comparison with other sites, but it should be noted that the terms do not necessarily have any functional connotation.

The retouched pieces comprise:

> Scrapers: 20
> Edge retouch: 71 (?marginal retouch?)
> Piercers: 6
> Axes: 5
> Fabricator: 1
> Arrowheads: 2 (1 leaf-shaped and 1 oblique)
> Bifacially retouched points: 3
> Knife: 1
> Serrated blade: 1
> Microlith: 1?

Scrapers (6–23)

This is the most common type of retouched artefact, although, based on the extent of the retouched edge, there are a number of sub-categories within the group.

> End scrapers: 3 (6–8)
> Extended end: 7 (9–15)
> End-and-side: 10 (16–23)

The scraper-edge generally has a rounded contour and is at an abrupt or semi-abrupt angle to the ventral face; the retouch rarely extends beyond the thickness of the flake. Apart from the three end scrapers on elongated flakes the blanks are squat mirroring the flake population though the blanks tend to be slightly longer and thicker.

Edge retouch (24–25, 42–47) (?marginal retouch)

The seventy-one artefacts in this category have retouch on their ends or lateral edges which does not alter the original shape of the flake. Some of this retouch may have been caused by post-depositional agencies, but amongst the more certain pieces (the criteria for distinguishing deliberate retouch is the shape of the edge and the regularity and extent of retouch (Moss 1983)), there are five pieces with marginal retouch (43–45) two of which are abrupt; a blade-like piece with retouch across the distal end (42), and a tanged flake. Five flakes have retouch in concave areas one of which has additional edge retouch (24 and 25) and may be purposeful; however, notching is one of the more common products of trampling (Odell 2004, 66f). It is not clear whether the two triangular-shaped pieces (38 and 39) with retouch around the perimeter should be included here or whether they are more akin to the bifacially retouched points (*see* below)

Piercers (26–28)

This category is defined by a point delineated by retouch. There are two sub-forms. In four instances (as 26) minimal but abrupt retouch has been applied to a flake with a naturally pointed shape; on one of these the retouch continues along the side of the flake. There are three other examples (28) with more pronounced elongated and more heavily retouched points.

Axes (29–31)

There are three core tools which have been flaked to a quadrangular section, the cutting edge of one (30) is formed by a transverse blow. One bifacially flaked fragment (not illustrated) is likely to be the fragment of an axe.

The other axe (31) is a fragment of a reworked ground and polished axe of pale grey flint. Although the original form is not reconstructable it clearly came from towards the butt end of a largish axe with flattened sides. It was well finished with all the shaping scars fully ground out. It is not clear whether it was reworked as a source of good quality raw material or whether reworking carried some other connotation.

Fabricator (32)

This rod-like piece is flaked on all surfaces with a lozenge-shaped cross section. One side has been worn smooth presumably by use. It is more similar to the category of Neolithic/Bronze Age fabricators rather than the Mesolithic type discussed by Saville (1977, 4).

Arrowheads (33–34)

One of the arrowheads (33) is a small bifacially flaked leaf-shaped arrowhead of Green's type 4B (Green 1984, 21 tables 1 and 3). The other (34) is a transverse arrowhead of his oblique type.

Bifacially flaked leaf-shaped points (35–37)

The two complete bifacially flaked leaf-shaped points are relatively small measuring 50 and 42 mm. in length respectively. The fragment (37) appears to come from a much larger example. It is not clear whether the two triangular objects (38 and 39) should be included in this category or whether they are marginally retouched pieces which fortuitously resemble laurel-leaves.

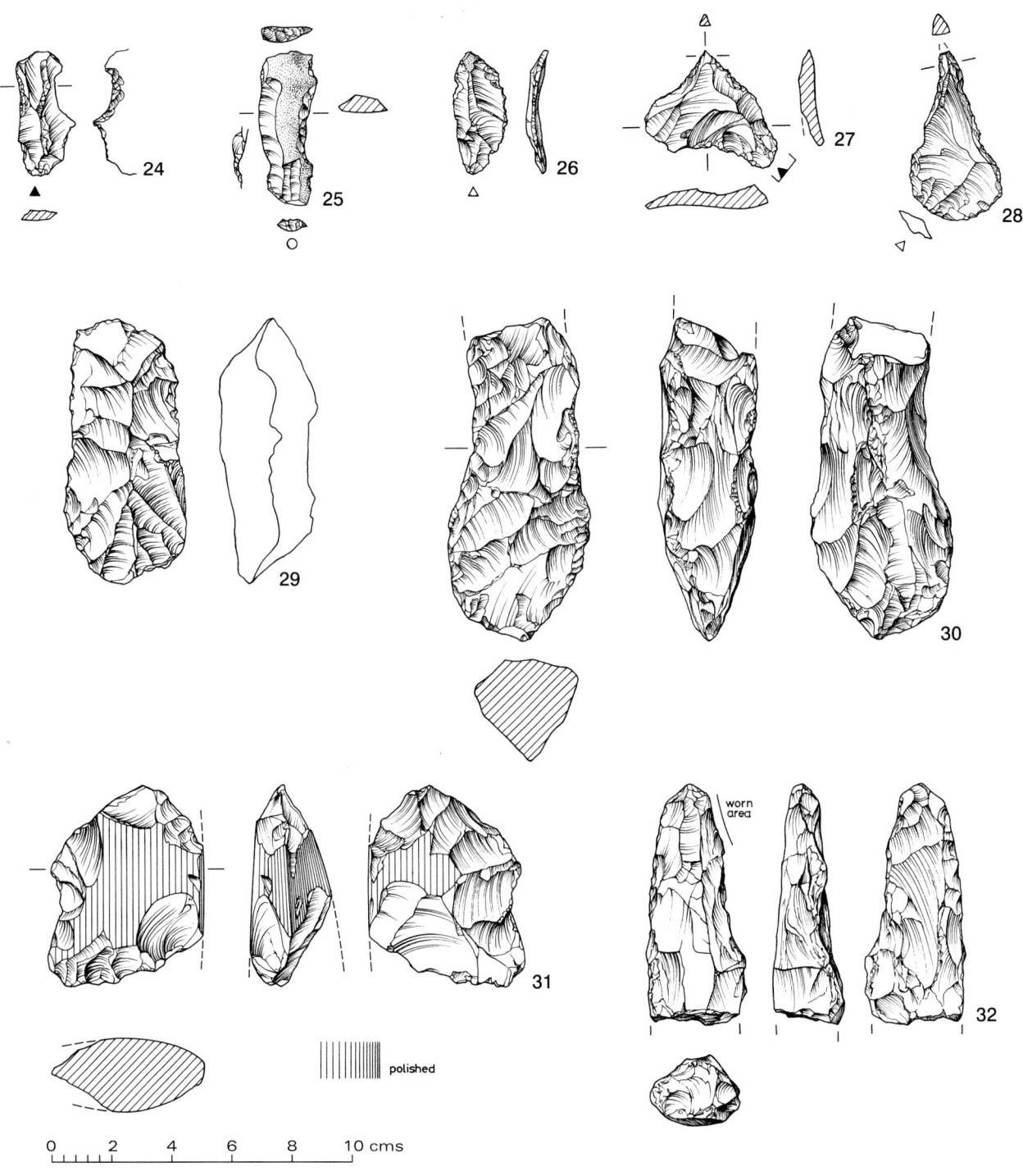

Fig. 145. Flints with marginal retouch (Nos 24 and 25), piercers (Nos 26–28, axes (Nos 29-31) and a fabricator (No. 32). Scale 1:2.

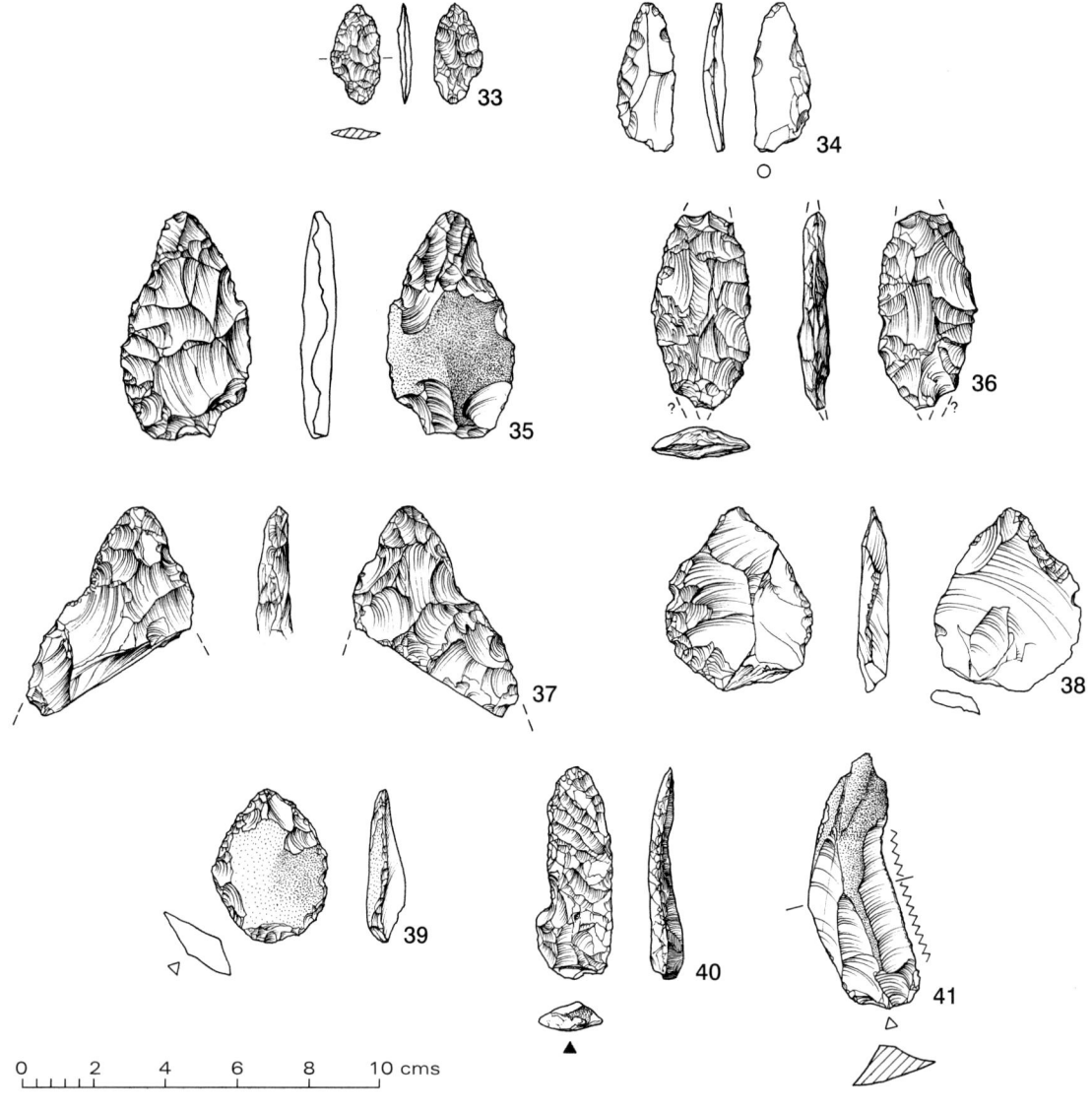

Fig. 146. Arrowheads (Nos 33 and 34), leaf-shaped points (Nos 35–7 and ?Nos 38–9), knife (No. 40) and blade (No. 41). Scale 1:2.

Knife (40)

The knife is an example of a classic plano-convex knife (Clark 1932) with typical fine, sub-parallel (?pressure) retouch on its dorsal surface. The proximal end has been broken and it is somewhat damaged along the left edge; there is some chipping on its ventral face too.

Serrated blade (41)

This blade-like piece has regular, minute denticulations along one lateral margin together with a narrow band of gloss.

Microlith

A fragment of a possible microlith was recovered, but it is too fragmentary to categorise further.

Discussion

The more chronologically diagnostic tools such as the arrowheads and the axes suggest the assemblage originated from the different cultural horizons, the disturbance being caused by the later occupation of the site.

Mesolithic activity is attested by the core-axe sharpened with a transverse blow and a fragment of a microlith

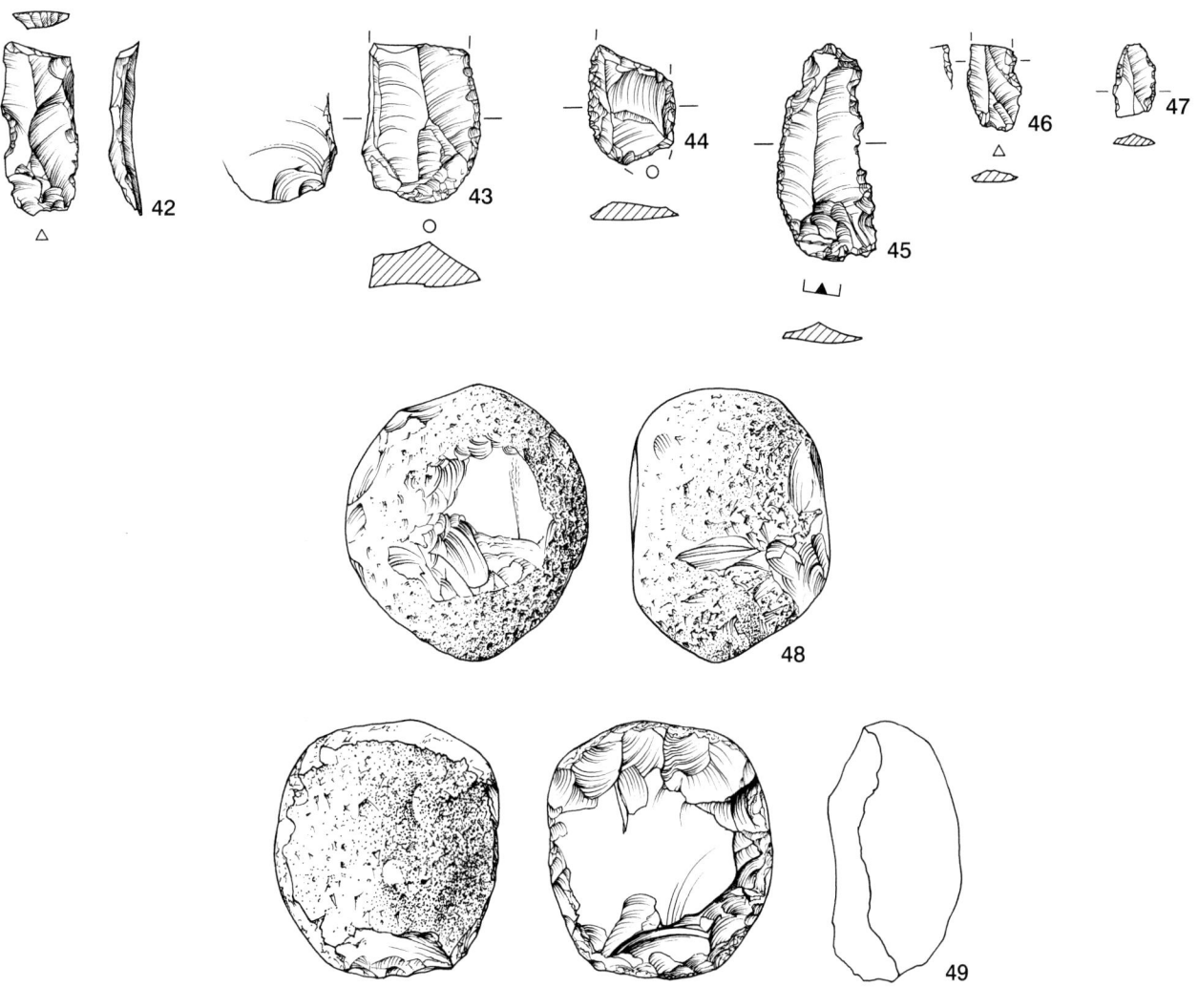

Fig. 147. Flints with marginal retouch (Nos 42–7) and hammerstones (Nos 48 and 49). Scale 1:2.

recovered in Area B. In the original catalogue microliths are recorded but no others were present in the collection seen by the author. It is also possible that the blade-like core and the objects made on more elongated blanks belong to this horizon but see also below.

The leaf-shaped arrowhead and the bifacially worked leaf-shaped pieces (laurel leaves) suggest an earlier Neolithic presence as possibly does the ground and polished axe, although it should be noted that the form of the arrowhead is common and its currency seems to extend from the fourth to the second millennium (Green 1984). Earlier Neolithic artefacts are notoriously difficult to separate out of a mixed assemblage, but it is possible that the blade-like aspect to some of technological features could belong to this period (Healy 1984; Pitts 1978; Pitts and Jacobi 1979, 172–3).

Later Neolithic activity rests on the oblique arrowhead which is typical of Grooved Ware assemblages and has a restricted date range (Green 1984), though it is possible that the lozenge-shaped fabricator could belong to this period of activity (Smith 1965). Choppers and chopping tools are also features of late Neolithic sites such as Arreton Down and Durrington Walls (Alexander and Ozanne 1960, F38; Wainwright and Longworth 1971, 158 and F8).

The plano-convex knife is of a form which is often attributed to the Early Bronze Age (Clark 1932, 158–62; 1933, 271), but is also found in Neolithic contexts (Healey and Robertson-Mackay 1983, 20).

It is interesting to note that a certain amount of flint was found in the ditches of the Period 2 enclosures B70 and A24 (Peter Couldrey, pers. comm.). What appears to be contemporary flint working is known elsewhere in the ditches of enclosures such as Mucking North Ring (Healey 1988) and Springfield (Healey in preparation) and later Bronze Age/Early Iron Age flintworking is now relatively well attested (Humphrey and Young 1999; 2003). Unfortunately in the case of Highstead the stratigraphic information is insufficient to ascertain whether this was also the situation.

The area is rich in Mesolithic and Neolithic material and the wide range of dates is not surprising (Jacobi 1982; Clarke 1982). Wymer, for example lists a considerable quantity of Mesolithic material from the immediate area as well as further afield (Wymer 1988, especially 151, 158 and 169).

Interpretation of culturally mixed lithic scatters is complicated (and is becoming a research topic in its own right see English Heritage 2002; Lisk *et al.* 1998) yet it should not be surprising to find lithic artefacts spread over most of the landscape as human activity is spacially continuous (Foley 1981). However, identification of the different activities represented when the material is disturbed is beyond the scope of this paper (*see* Gardiner 2004).

Evidence for metalworking

Mould fragments (Figs 148–50)

Stuart Needham

The Period 2 pit B80 produced a considerable quantity of fired clay. A group of clay mould fragments for the manufacture of copper alloy pins was isolated from amongst this material. The following report details and discusses the surviving mould fragments (some better pieces were stolen from site during the excavation, see Nos 36–42).

Technology

All of the identifiable clay mould fragments from pit group B80 seem to belong to two-piece moulds for the casting of copper alloy pins. The larger of the two mould pieces, Type I, would in complete form have embodied a matrix for the whole of the shank as well as the underside of the pin's head. The second mould piece is a small cap bearing the impression of the upper surface of the head, Type II. Precise registration of these two components was achieved by means of matching bulb and notch devices situated on the horizontal contact faces encircling the pin heads. Evidence for these registration devices survives on at least four mould units (B–E), probably on a fifth (F), and may be presumed though not proven for the unbroken unit (A). In three cases only a single bulb and notch appears to have existed, while in the fourth (B) two are present on the contact face separated by about one third of the perimeter. Notches are consistently cut into the edges of Type I mould pieces, and are generally narrow and deep. The corresponding bulbs on the Type II pieces on the other hand tend to be low rounded domes which, in their present form at least, do not fill notches, and may well never have done, especially if formed by pressing the damp clay of Type II pieces gently against earlier made notched Type I pieces.

The use of this form of two-piece mould implies formation around a pattern, the separable cap allowing its withdrawal, in contrast to the production of an investment mould (single piece) in the *cire perdue* process. On re-assembling the two mould pieces the head ends were enveloped in a thin wrap of clay to secure them.

The matrices in mould units B, C and D have similar dimensions and could easily have been formed successively around a single pattern. The abraded remnant of F could also match their dimensions. Minor differences in dimensions which exist (in the order of tenths of millimetres) could be accounted for by differential shrinkage of the clay in drying or by the abrasion of matrix surfaces. The pin cast in unit E would however have had a larger head and thus presumably derives from a distinct pattern.

Where matrix surfaces are dirt-free, they appear smooth; this could not be the result of subsequent surface finish in view of their inaccessibility for the most part and must derive from the pattern. The material of the patterns cannot be determined, but copper alloy pins themselves could easily have been used, or alternatively bone or polished wooden patterns with a similar smooth finish.

As the head end of the mould unit was sealed in the process of assembly, the melt would have been introduced from the tips of pins. Clearly this gate would need to be sufficiently wide to allow the melt to fill the cavity as quickly as possible. Consequently the opening is likely to remain the diameter of the shank with the point created only in post-cast working. This procedure was followed for similar pin moulds from Fort-Harrouard, Eure-et-Loir, France (Mohen 1973, 43).

If the tip of a model was left projecting a little beyond this gate in the mould formation process, this would facilitate withdrawal by pushing it up from the tip. Pin patterns of this particular form with flat heads might otherwise be difficult to withdraw cleanly. It would not for example be possible to have an appendage on the head of the pattern as this would spoil the matrix of the cap-piece.

Casting was evidently done in multiple. Fragment No. 17 retains the gate ends of two moulds set side-by-side while fragments Nos 1 and 15 each have a wedge of clay attached to the head end. In the former case this can be shown to have bound together units A (fragment No. 1) and D (fragment No. 10) with the aid of another linking fillet No. 22. Another pair of joined tube fragments apparently bore evidence of at least two further mould units in a fan formation (No. 42).

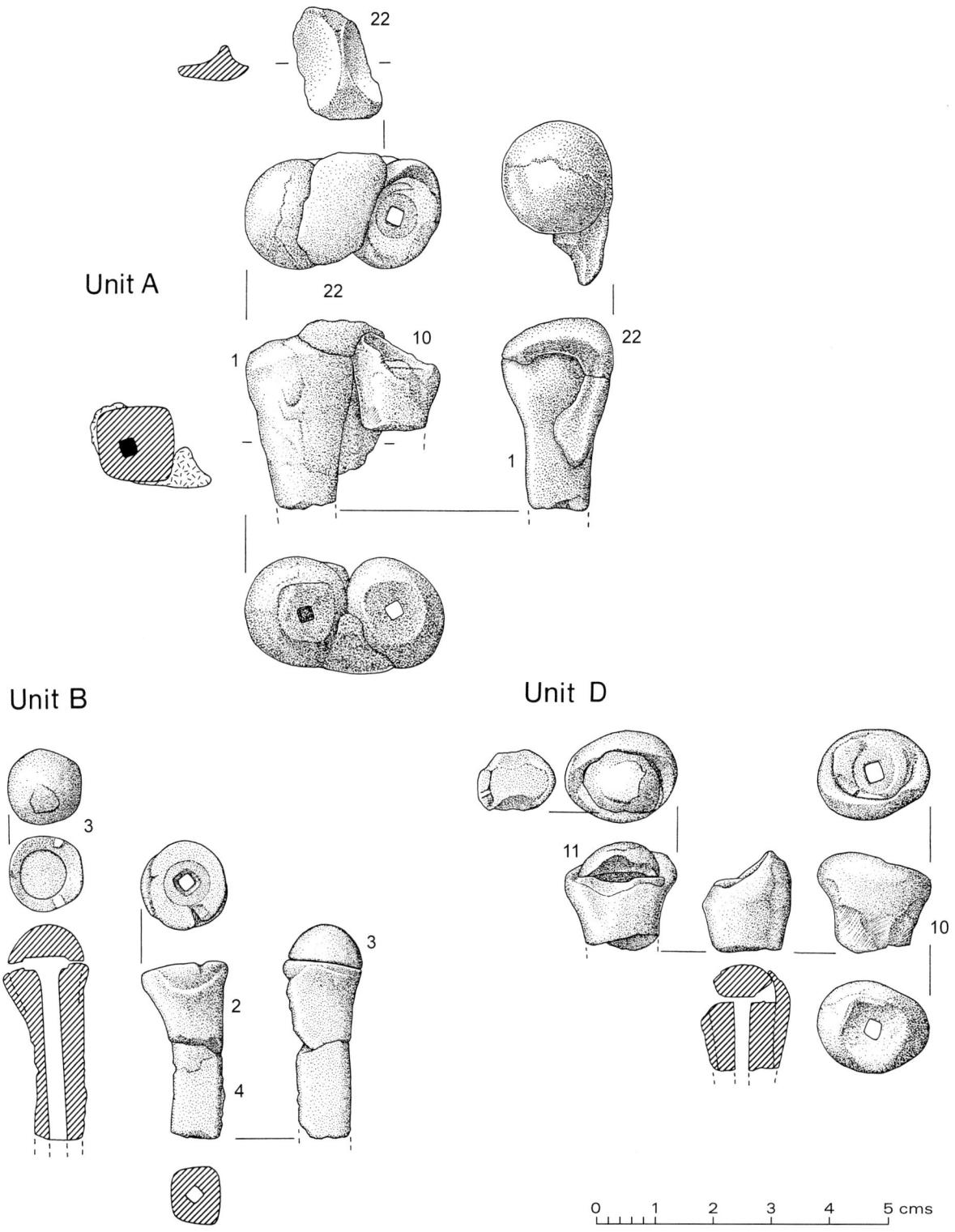

Fig. 148. Pin mould fragments belonging to mould units A, B and D. Units A and D belong to the same mould bank. Scale 1:1.

Other likely fragments of joining fillets are present in the assemblage, notably fragment No. 21. The bulbous lower end of mould units around the pin head and the close setting of their gate ends would give rise to a fan-shaped arrangement or a block-grouping known elsewhere for multiple pin casting (e.g. Fort-Harrouard: Mohen 1973, 43). These may be taken to be a logical arrangement given the general shape of pin moulds.

The two gate ends surviving in fragment No. 17 have been held together by a wrap of clay fully extant along one side and partially surviving around either end. This might have originally enclosed just the two moulds, but if accommodating more these seem likely to have formed a rectangular block in plan rather than continuing in a linear fan. The gate wrap projects above the mould ends, tapers to a thin rounded crest and originally would have enclosed a small conical or pyramidal basin to serve as a reservoir for the melt.

A finger print had become impressed into the enveloping clay wrap of fragment No. 10, just towards the underside of the pin's head, and a complementary print was taken on the inner surface of a linking fillet which survives, that attached to No. 1.

Removal of castings would necessitate breaking open the enveloping wrap around the head of the pin, and may also have led to reduction of the shank portion of the mould into short lengths of the order retrieved in excavation. One unbroken head end (No. 1) has clearly not had a casting removed, and radiography suggests that there is no partial casting preserved within its cavity. It had however been banked up with at least one other mould unit, C (No. 10), in preparation for casting, and as the latter has its head broken open, it seems likely that this at least had yielded a successful casting. The failure of Unit A to fill up could have been due to a blockage higher up the matrix (that is towards the tip of the pin), or to premature freezing of the melt in that particular matrix. As the fanned or block arrangement of moulds was evidently designed to link a number of inlets to a single reservoir the moulds should have filled simultaneously and the failure cannot therefore be put down to the melt running out, or solidifying, before Unit A was reached.

Apart from the finishing of the tip, already detailed, there would have been a small amount of trimming to do around the edge of the pin's head where a casting flash projecting horizontally might have formed at the valve junction.

Miscellaneous mould fragments (Fig. 150)

Two of the larger fragments among the remainder merit comment, as they seem to belong to moulds other than for pins.

Fragment No. 31 has a relatively thick broken inner edge which could have accommodated a recess for a midrib, but no certain downturning of the matrix face survives to support this. The short stretch of matrix edge extant is approximately straight. The piece is most likely to belong to a mould for a thin blade either for a sword, rapier or knife or, if associated with a midrib, for a spearhead.

The strongly curved inner face on fragment No. 33 could derive from the socket or midrib of a spearhead, or similar tubular casting, or alternatively from the angle of the body of an axe-like tool.

Mould units for pins in the later Bronze Age

The casting of pins using the form of mould assembly recovered at Highstead was not previously in evidence from Britain, but two sites in neighbouring lands have yielded strikingly similar casting debris belonging to this period. At Fort-Harrouard, Eure, northern France, a large quantity of clay mould fragments was discovered in association with hearths interpreted as metalworking fires (Philippe 1927, 33–46). Amongst this body of material are a number of pieces from pin moulds, two-piece, with one long valve accommodating the length of the shank, and one small cap-piece covering the head (Philippe 1935, 26–7, fig. 7; Mohen 1973, 42–3, fig. 6). These two components had been bound together with a thin slip of clay prior to casting, and there is circumstantial evidence for the multiple banking of individual pin units in blocks or fanned linear arrangement. This takes the form of two mould stem sections, one circular, the other a concave-square, which would be complementary in such grouping. This pattern of complementary stem surfaces may not have been so accentuated on the Highstead moulds to judge from the few lengths of stem extant, but otherwise the technology involved seems to have been closely comparable on the two sites. This link is further strengthened by the fact that the production of disc-headed pins was common to both sets of equipment (Mohen's *épingle a petite tête cylindrique*: 1973, 43). Diameters of the heads and shanks (7–8 mm. and 3.5 mm. approx.) of Fort-Harrouard pin matrices are closely comparable to the equivalent Highstead dimensions. The Fort-Harrouard shanks would appear to have been consistently round-sectioned in contrast to the unusual square Highstead examples, but otherwise there should have been little to distinguish the two sets of pins cast.

In quite another direction, an equally important assemblage of copper alloy casting debris has been recovered in more recent excavations at Rathgall, Co. Wicklow, Ireland (Raftery 1971; Raftery 1976, 345–6). A metalworking area (workshop) has been recognised on the site comprising hearths, structures and attendant spreads of the clay casting debris. It lies immediately outside a small ditched enclosure surrounding a substantial circular building. The casting of a variety of copper alloy implement types is attested by the mould material, but a number of pin moulds have gone un-noted in the interim accounts and I am indebted to Barry Raftery for information about them. The Rathgall moulds repeat the association seen at Highstead and Fort-Harrouard between mould design and the morphology of the cast pins,

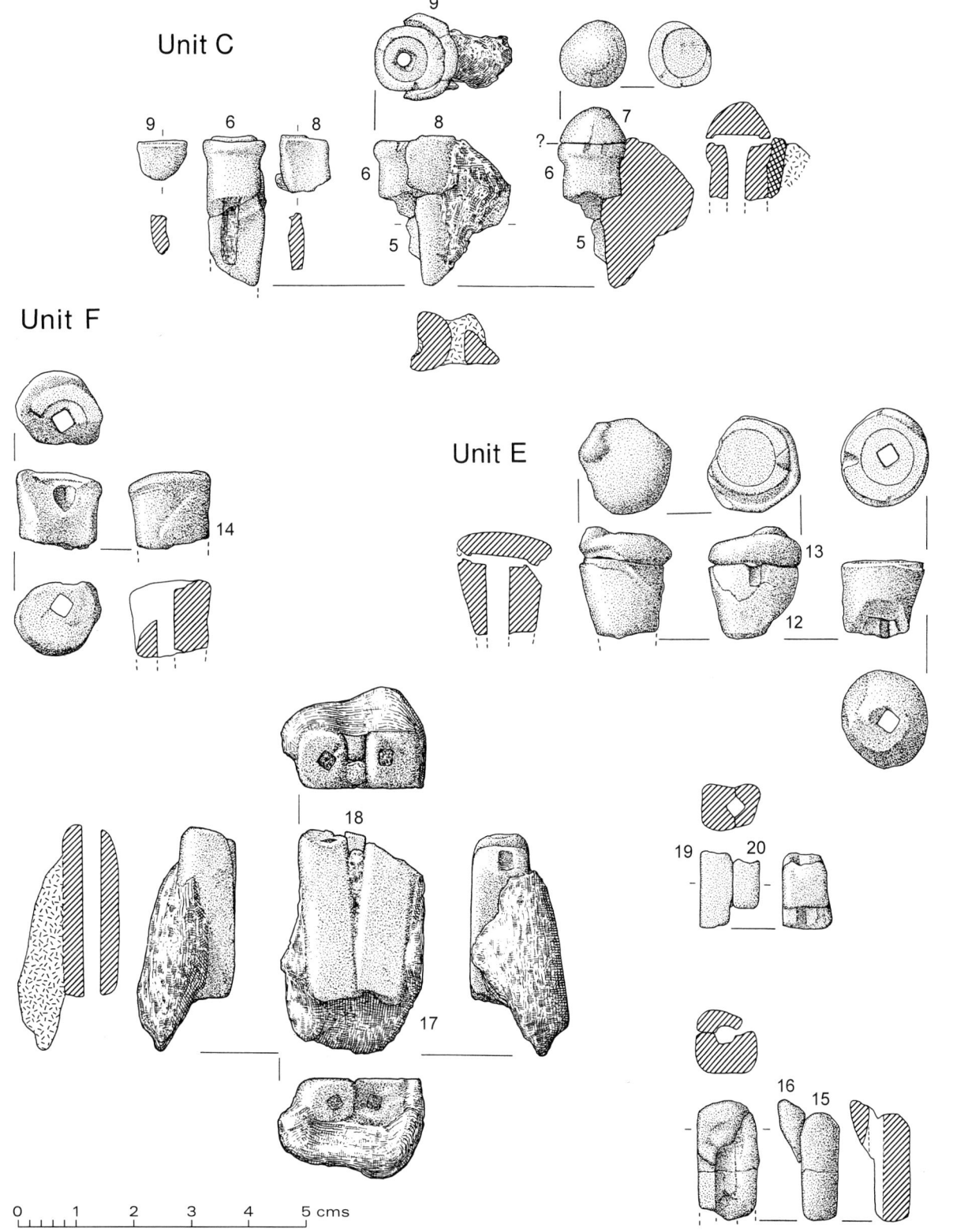

Fig. 149. Pin mould fragments belonging to mould units C, E and F and unattributed stem fragments. Scale 1:1.

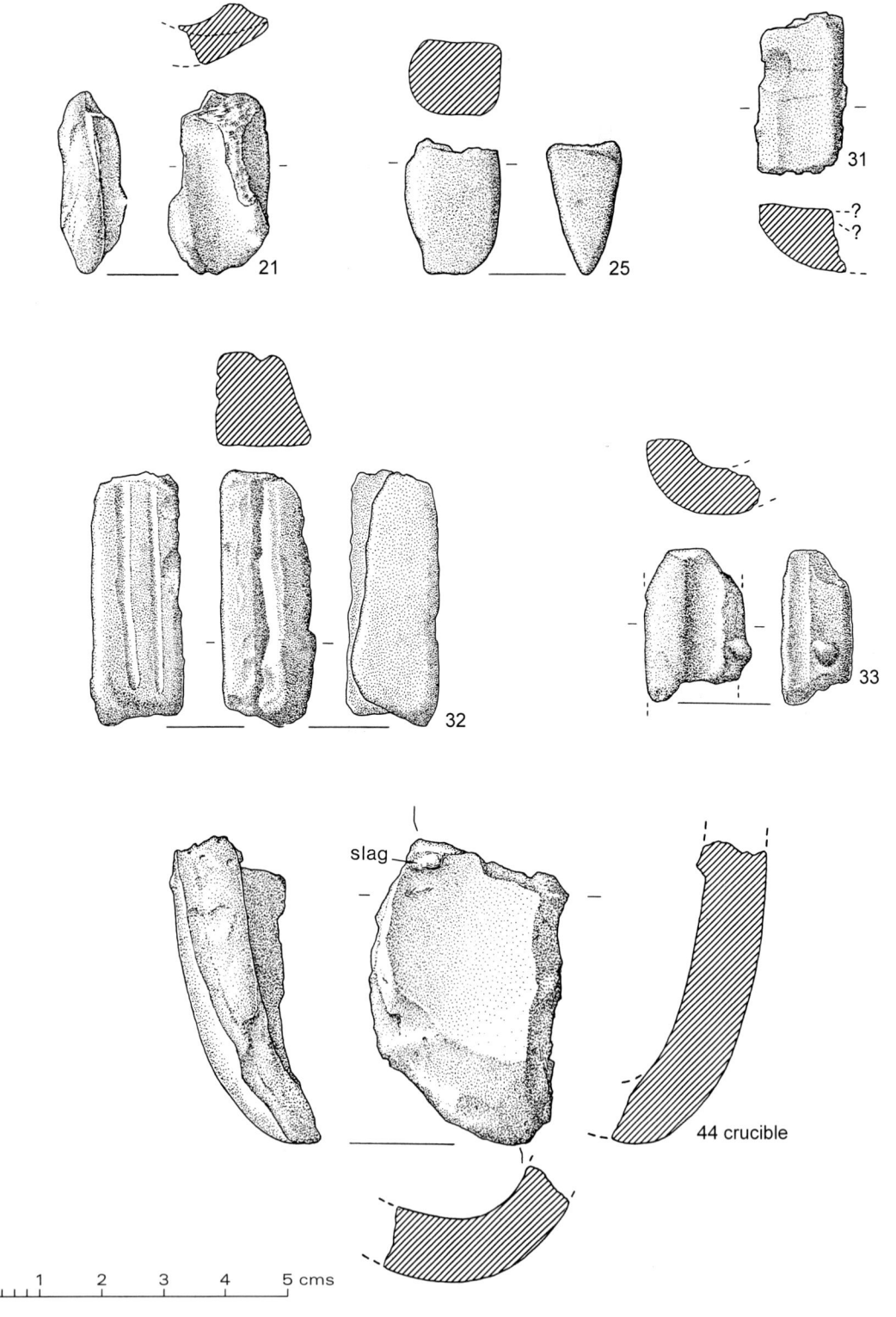

Fig. 150. Miscellaneous clay refractory fragments and crucible (No. 44). Scale 1:1.

which are again disc-headed. Shank sections would have been round.

Insecurely dated, but possibly referable to the Late Bronze Age, is a group of unpublished clay mould fragments from Aylesford, Kent (British Museum registration 1888 10–24 35), which include pin moulds and others of indeterminate types. They were acquired with material from the Belgic cemetery type-site, the implication being that they came from the same gravel pit although they have escaped notice in the literature (Evans 1890; Birchall 1965). Evidence for a pre-'Belgic' settlement on the site may be adduced from non-funerary pits containing charcoal and broken pottery and sherds of 'earlier' pottery (Evans 1890, 319–20, 324–5), examples of which surviving in the British Museum may be attributed to Late Bronze/Early Iron Age traditions (Barrett 1980).

The Aylesford moulds would apparently again have produced simple disc-headed pins similar to the Highstead examples. However, despite the proximity of the two sites, a totally different mould assembly was used at Aylesford. A bivalve mould system meant that the pin matrix was split longitudinally between the two valves which would have led to casting flashes along the shank. Depending on the extent of post-cast working, Aylesford products might have differed in fine typological detail from those made at Highstead.

Pin typology and dating (Fig. 151)

From the mould units best preserved at Highstead it is evident that the cast products would have been simple disc-headed pins of a consistent form. Both top and underside of the heads would have been quite flat and the edges are also flat with crisp angles giving the whole head a coin-like form. The shanks would have had a crisp square cross-section, often however with an increasing tendency for bowed sides towards the head end. Although the shank expanded a little at this end it still met the head in a fairly crisp angle.

The Highstead products were obviously extremely simple disc-headed pins, a form which one would be reluctant to date when devoid of context. However, the close comparisons drawn with moulds from Late Bronze Age settlements at Rathgall and Fort-Harrouard make it worthwhile considering related Bronze Age pins. Although over fifty pins with disc or nail heads are known in Britain, the series presents a variety of forms in detail. A good proportion have the addition of specific features such as flanged rims, dished tops, central pimples and concentric mouldings, rendering them more diagnostic. Despite the simple Highstead form, no pin replicates all of its features. In particular, square-sectioned shanks are extremely rare on any British prehistoric pins. One example is that from Walney North End Site I, Cumbria (Barnes and Jackson 1978, 200, fig. I.6). The head is of conical rather than disc form and attribution of the pin to the Late Bronze Age relies on the circumstantial evidence of a second pin found previously at the same spot.

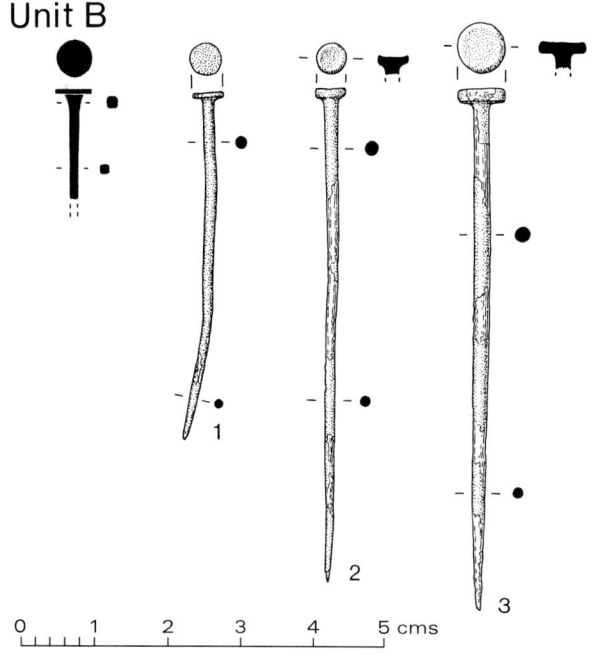

Fig. 151. Form of pins as would be cast in Highstead Unit B, with comparable nail-headed bronze pins. 1: plain head, Lakenheath, Suffolk (BM reg. 1882, 2–4,3); 2: flanged head, 'South Wiltshire' (BM reg. 1855, 5–3,3); 3: Haslingfield, Cambridgeshire (WG 2016). Scale 1:1.

Disc heads which most closely match the size and shape of the Highstead matrices are found on British pins from for example Lakenheath, Suffolk (British Museum registration 1882 2–4 3), Staple Howe, North Yorkshire (Brewster 1963, 114, fig. 63.1) and Heathery Burn, Co. Durham (Britton 1968, GB 55, no. 101). The last two may be dated by their associations to the early first millennium B.C. These and more particularly the occurrence of very similar mould assemblies for casting such pins on Late Bronze Age sites at Rathgall and Fort-Harrouard allow the Highstead moulds to be dated to that phase.

Postscript: Since this text was first submitted the Fort-Harrouard pin moulds have been published again in Mohen and Bailloud (1987, 131–2, fig. 74).

Catalogue

Pin mould components:
Type I: mould piece for shank and underside of pin head
Type Ia: fragment with underside of head
Type Ib: shank fragment, middle part
Type Ic: shank fragment, probable or certain ingate (i.e. tip end)
Type II: cap piece for top of pin head

Abbreviations: EW (enveloping wrap); LF (linking fillets of clay, binding mould units to one another); LFG (linking fillets incorporating gate); RD (registration device).

Dimensions (all in millimetres): L (length); W (width); B (breadth); T (thickness); dh (diameter of head); max. dim. (maximum dimension); dst (diameter of shank at top); dsb (diameter of shank at break); DH (maximum depth of head matrix, below contact face (in either Type Ia or II mould piece)).

Colours are described by means of the Munsell System.

Mould fragments from Pit B80 (Figs 148–50)

1. Type Ia and II; EW intact; LF attached on one side around underside of bulb; RD unknown; top of EW a shallow cone, a little irregular; carination separates from convex profile underside which narrows to subsquare stem section; faint fingerprint impressed in LF, probably taken from that on 10.
Mould unit A, joins 22 which links to unit D (No. 10). Mould: L 29, dh 18.5–19; dsb 10. Matrix: dsb 2.5. Colour: 10YR9/4; buff.

2. Type Ia; some EW extant; RD, two deep v-notches on perimeter separated by approx. 100°; contact face appears very slightly out-sloped; stem section rounded with shank matrix off-centre.
Mould unit B, joins 4 and almost certainly matches 3. Mould: L 15, dh 14–14.5. Matrix: dh 7.5; DH 0.5; dst 4.2; dsb 2.7. Colour: 10YR9/4; buff.

3. Type II; small fragment EW attached; contact face tends to be very slightly insloped; RD two low knobs set on perimeter separated by approx. 100°; cap of hemispherical form.
Mould unit B, almost certainly complementary valve to No. 2. Mould: d cap 12.5–13; D cap 6.5. Matrix: dh 7.8; DH 1.0. Colour: 10YR9/4; buff.

4. Type Ib; sub-square stem section; matrix aligned diagonally and off-centrally placed.
Mould unit B, joins No. 2, break dirty and presumably ancient. Mould: L 16; d stem 9.5–9.7. Matrix: dsb (upper) 2.7; dsb (lower) 2.4. Colour: 10YR9/4; buff.

5–6 & 8–9. Type Ia; four joining fragments with fragmentary EW, LF and some soil attached; break between 5 and 6 dirty; RD a single v-notch in perimeter of rather irregular contact face; constriction of mould below head irregular, part with pronounced dent; subsquare stem section half missing for much of extant length; EW fragments (8, 9) retain small ledge moulding along inner edge representing impression of valve junction where cap edge had protruded beyond the Type I valve.
Mould unit C. Mould: L 25; dh 11.3–12.5; d stem at 5/6 junction 9.5–11.3. Matrix: dh 7.2–7.7; dst 4.0; dsb at 5/6 junction *c*. 3. Colour: 10YR8/4; buff

7. Type II; crudely hemispherical cap, abraded on one side with loss of contact face; matrix not perfectly circular, some tendency for flattened sides; very low bump is possible RD. Possibly complementary to No. 5, etc., but extant diameter does not seem large enough to create ledge impression on fragments 8 and 9, neither are dh measurements compatible. Mould: d cap 11.7; D cap 6. Matrix: dh 7.8 (or less)–8.3; DH 0.7. Colour: 10YR9/4; buff.

10. Type Ia; much EW extant including part of flange lapping cap piece and which bears carination around outside; RD, very narrow deep v-notch in contact face; latter abraded on one side with loss of matrix edge; fingerprint preserved in outer surface of EW beneath bulb; tending to squared section at lower break.
Mould unit D, complementary to No. 11; seats against LF No. 22 linking it to unit A (No. 1). Mould: L 11 + 4 (EW flange); dh (including EW) 19.5. Matrix: dh 7.5; dst 3.7; dsb 2.6. Colour: 10YR8/4; buff.

11. Type II; thin crust of EW on top; near hemispherical cap; short stretch of contact face only bordering matrix edge slightly overhung; very low bump is probably RD, this supported by matching it up with notch on No. 10 which makes the EW attached to the two fragments almost join up.
Mould unit D, complementary to No. 10. Mould: D cap 13; D cap 6. Matrix: dh ?7.5; DH 1.0. Colour: 10YR8/4; buff.

12. Type Ia; EW survives around most of exterior; contact face of variable width tending to slight concavity and gently insloped; interrupted by relatively broad v-notch into perimeter; matrix head forms neat circle.
Mould unit E, complementary to No. 13. Mould: L 13; dh 16.5 (including EW). Matrix: dh 9.5; DH 0.8; dst 4.0; dsb 2.8. Colour: 10R7/10–5YR7/8; orange.

13. Type II; EW virtually intact over whole cap, retains ledge moulding on one side formed due to valve sides not being flush at their junction; cap evidently flat and disc-like; contact face tending to convex; good v-shaped bump for RD; matrix circular.
Mould unit E; complementary to No. 12. Mould: d cap (including EW) 17; D cap 5. Matrix: dh 9.5; DH 1.0. Colour: 7.5YR7/6–5YR7/10–2.5YR7/10; orange.

14. Type Ia; fragment of EW; abraded with much of one side lost; approx. half of matrix head extant; RD deep and narrow v-notch into contact face.
Mould unit F. Mould: L 12.5; dh 15. Matrix: dh *c*. 7.5; DH 0.5 (+); dst *c*. 3.5; dsb 2.7. Colour: 10YR5/1–7.5YR8/4; grey.

15–16. Type Ib; two probably joining fragments (fresh break) forming virtually complete subsquare cross-section at one end; matrix section skewed in relation to mould and a little off-centre. Not certainly attributable to any mould unit defined above.
Mould: L 20.5; d stem 10–11. Matrix: ds 2.7. Colour: 10YR9/4; buff.

17. Type Ic; two stems of subsquare section converging to meet at one end where enclosed on three sides by LF; latter survives standing proud on long side with wedge-shaped long section, almost certainly forming part of gate; one of matrix sections markedly skew to that of mould.
Two mould units represented; not certainly any defined above, but possibly one belonging to unit E on the grounds of colour.
Mould 1: L 29; db 9–10; d gate 7–8. Mould 2: L 26; db 10; d gate *c*. 8. Matrix 1: dsb 2.8; ds gate *c*. 2.8. Matrix 2: dsb *c*. 2.8; ds gate *c*. 2.8. Gate wall: D 9; thickness at base 7. Colour: 10R7/10–10YR8/6–10YR8/4; red-yellow.

18. Tiny fragment of LF joining No. 17. Colour: 5YR7/8; orange.
19–20. Type Ib; two joining fragments making complete cross-section subsquare with some concavity of sides possibly original; matrix section diagonal relative to that of mould and a little off-centre.
Mould unit uncertain, likely to belong with Nos 12–13 or 17 on basis of colour.
Mould: L 12.7; d stem 9–10.5. Matrix: dsb 2.8. Colour: 10R7/8–10YR7/6; red-yellow.
21. Strip of LF with longitudinal ridge between two concave surfaces representing the impression of mould stems; double layering evident at one break. Max. dim. 28.5. Colour: 2.5Y9/2–10YR8/4; buff.
22. Strip of LF wedging between the tops of two mould unit heads. Joins LF attached to No. 1, break ancient, linking mould units A and D (Nos 1 and 10). Max. dim. 22.5. Colour: 10YR9–8/4; buff.
23. Small strip of LF with curved surface and slight angle probably representing underside of mould unit head. Max. dim. 15.5. Colour: 10YR8/4; buff. *Not illus.*
24. Tiny curved fragment of probable EW, with small ridge probably the impression of a valve junction. May belong to mould unit C. Max. dim. 9. Colour: 10YR9/4; buff. *Not illus.*
25. A wedge-shaped lump of clay with a subrectangular cross-section thinning to a rounded chisel-end; the thick end appears to be broken; fabric a little vesicular; with this shape the fragment could plausibly represent the end of a core for a socketed tool, or otherwise belong to a gate. L 21.5; max. W 15.5; max. B 12.0. Colour; 10YR9/4–8/2; pale buff to grey.
26. Possible inner valve fragment with thin wedge-shaped section, one face flat, the other convex. Max. dim. 18; max.T 6.0. Colour: 2.5Y8.5/2, 5Y5/1; dark grey, pale buff. *Not illus.*
27–28. Two joining fragments almost certainly belonging to No. 26, but not joining it. Max. dim. 21.5; max.T 5.3 (excluding attached soil). Colour: 2.5Y8.5/2, 5Y5/1; dark grey, pale buff. *Not illus.*
29. Amorphous abraded lump of slightly vesicular fabric with one ?grog inclusion; possibly core or crucible fragment. Max. dim. 17.5. Colour: 10YR9/1–4; buff. *Not illus.*
30. Strip of fired clay with wedge-shaped long section, possibly LF. Max. dim. 15.5. Colour: 10YR8/4; buff. *Not illus.*
31. An edge fragment of an inner valve from a bivalve mould; in cross-section the matrix face is flat with indications of a slight step close to its edge defining a contact face; the outer face is convex.
Mould: L 25; max.W 14.5; max.T 11.5. Colour: 10YR5/1–8/4; dark grey to buff.
32. A bar of fired clay with one flat, presumably outer, face; a grey coloured strip along the inner side should be fragmentary inner valve; a slightly variable cross-section incorporates small steps or grooves along two corners, though not matching; it is not clear which surface, if any, is the matrix.
Mould: L 39.5; max.W 15.5; max. B 15.5. Colour: 5YR5/1–2.5R7/8 (7.5R7/8); dark grey to pink to orange.
33. Probable inner valve fragment; curved cross-section of approximately constant thickness; the inner face is strongly concave and presumably matrix, but has no distinguishing features; one edge possibly a contact face.
Mould: L 24; max.W 18.5; max.T 8. Colour: 7.5R7/8–10R7/1; pink to grey.
34. Probable inner valve fragment, one face with slight moulding, but form not identifiable; all edges appear broken. Max. dim. 16; max.T 8.5. Colour: 5YR7/10–10YR9/4–5Y7/1; buff to light grey. *Not illus.*
35. Small fragment with crumbly structure, one edge like simple rim, either EW or rim sherd of coarse pottery. W 20.5; max. T 10. Colour: 5YR8/6; buff. *Not illus.*

Stolen mould fragments from Pit B80 (Not illus.)

The theft of a number of better fragments has precluded their detailed study. The following entries are based on site notes.

36. Type I & II; 'squared off round profile; belled at one end; a 'cap' fits the bottom'.
Mould: L 32; ds 7. Colour: red.
37. Types I & II; 'round section; belled bottom, the cap in place, but fractured; square bore free of material; signs of another jointing'.
Mould: L37; ds 11. Colour: yellow merging to red.
38. Type Ib; 'double; ends gone but start of belling present'.
Mould: L35; ds 9 & 6. Colour: red/yellow.
39. Type Ia & II; 'fragment of belled end; the cap fell off on excavation'.
Mould: L 18; ds 9. Colour: yellow with traces of blackening (?firing).
40. 'As No. 39'.
Mould: L 17; ds 8.
41. 'As No. 38'.
Mould: L 19; ds 8.
42. 'Double with traces of a third on one side and definite traces of a fourth on the other side; square bore'.
Mould: L17.5; ds 8. Colour: reddened yellow.

Possible polishing stone

Nigel Macpherson-Grant

Of particular note here is the stone object No. 43 also from the Period 2 Pit B80 (Fig. 152). Now broken, it was originally shaped, smoothed and provided with a drilled hour-glass shaped hole. One side has been rubbed flat, but not polished. According to R.W. Sanderson the stone is a

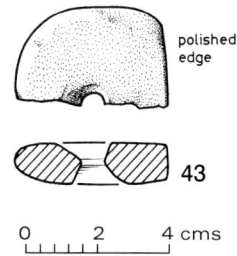

Fig. 152. Perforated stone polisher from Pit B80. Scale 1:2.

'dark, fine-grained sub-greywacke, not of Kentish origin'. Dr Needham has suggested that having been found in association with the pin-moulds, it may have been used as a finishing or polishing stone.

The scientific examination of vitrified material and other debris possibly associated with metallurgy

Paul Craddock and Ian Freestone

The majority of the fragments examined (Table 30) were labelled 'dross' by the excavators. The pieces were all examined visually, and some pieces were analysed qualitatively by non-dispersive x-ray fluorescence. Most of the material was very bloated, highly vitrified calcareous clay. It had been heated by a wood fire and parts were highly glazed due to the fluxing power of the potassium in the wood ash. Several pot sherds had also been inadvertently ash-glazed. All of this suggests high temperatures of the order of 1000–1200°C, but not specifically metallurgy. However association with a crucible fragment stained with copper (*see* below) and a few pieces of fayalite slag derived from iron smelting does suggest metallurgy was being practised, both copper alloy casting and iron smelting. The vitrified clay does not seem to be slagged and so is probably part of the hearth or furnace in which the crucibles of copper or bronze were placed. Similar pieces have appeared on other sites, notably at the Iron Age site of Catswater, Fengate (Pryor 1984) also in association with fragments of slag and crucibles. The vitrified clay at Fengate was also highly calcareous although a considerable distance from chalk deposits.

The crucible (Fig. 150)

Stuart Needham

Amongst a large number of refired ceramics, mainly pottery sherds, from the Period 3B pit B214, was a single sherd which can be positively identified as crucible.

44. Body sherd with strong curvature and reasonably constant thickness; one corner seems to include part of an obtuse apex, probably a base; a sandy, slightly vesicular, fabric with occasional larger quartz grains (up to 1 mm.); core grey (10YR5/1) giving way to a thin whitish crust on the inside, the surface of which is discoloured to purple-grey (10R6/2), and also retains a small dark purple blob of slag, which contains traces of copper (determined by x-ray fluorescence analysis); exterior with thicker white band, partially glossy and green-tinged from vitrification (7.5Y9–8/2). Max. dim. 51.5 mm. Thickness: 8.5–11.5 mm.

	Period	Excavator's description
Area A		
A5, pit	2	copper dross
A24, ditch	2	copper dross
A24B, ditch	2	copper dross and vitrified pottery
A147, post pit	2	copper dross and vitrified pottery
A181, pit	2	copper dross
A227, pit	2	copper dross
Area B		
B41, hearth	2	copper dross
B70, ditch	2	copper dross
B152C, pit	2	copper dross
B317, pit	2	copper dross
B144, ditch	3A	copper dross
B26, gully	3B	iron slag
B31, hearth	3B	metalworking debris
B133, pit	3B	metalworking waste
B147, pit	3B	copper dross and vitrified pottery
B155, hearth	3B	copper dross
B195, pit	3B	iron slag
B200, post-pit	3B	iron slag
B215, pit	3B	iron slag
B141, ditch	4A	iron dross

Table 30. Contexts containing material possibly associated with metalworking.

The sherd is strongly curved in cross-section, the curvature increasing towards one break and possibly indicating a rounded corner. The long-section is more gently curved for the most part, but the outer surface turns inward abruptly close to one end. The corresponding turn on the inner face has not survived, but this end seems most satisfactorily viewed as the base of a subconical vessel with the long axis of the sherd representing its profile. The cross-section would then suggest a subtriangular shape in plan, and a vessel similar to the Dark Age example from Lough Faughan Crannog (Tylecote 1962, 132, fig. 31.9) may be envisaged. As no rim survives on the Highstead sherd its size and capacity are impossible to assess, but a fairly small vessel seems likely and would be appropriate to the casting of ornaments which is attested on the site. However, the crucible sherd comes from feature B214 of Iron Age date. It could therefore either indicate bronze casting in the Iron Age or be residual from Bronze Age metallurgical activity. Subtriangular shaped crucibles, as yet unknown for the Bronze Age, are a recognised feature of Iron Age metalworking occurring for example in the notable Gussage All Saints assemblage (Spratling 1979, 132, fig. 99), and in view of its context the later date must be preferred for the Highstead fragment.

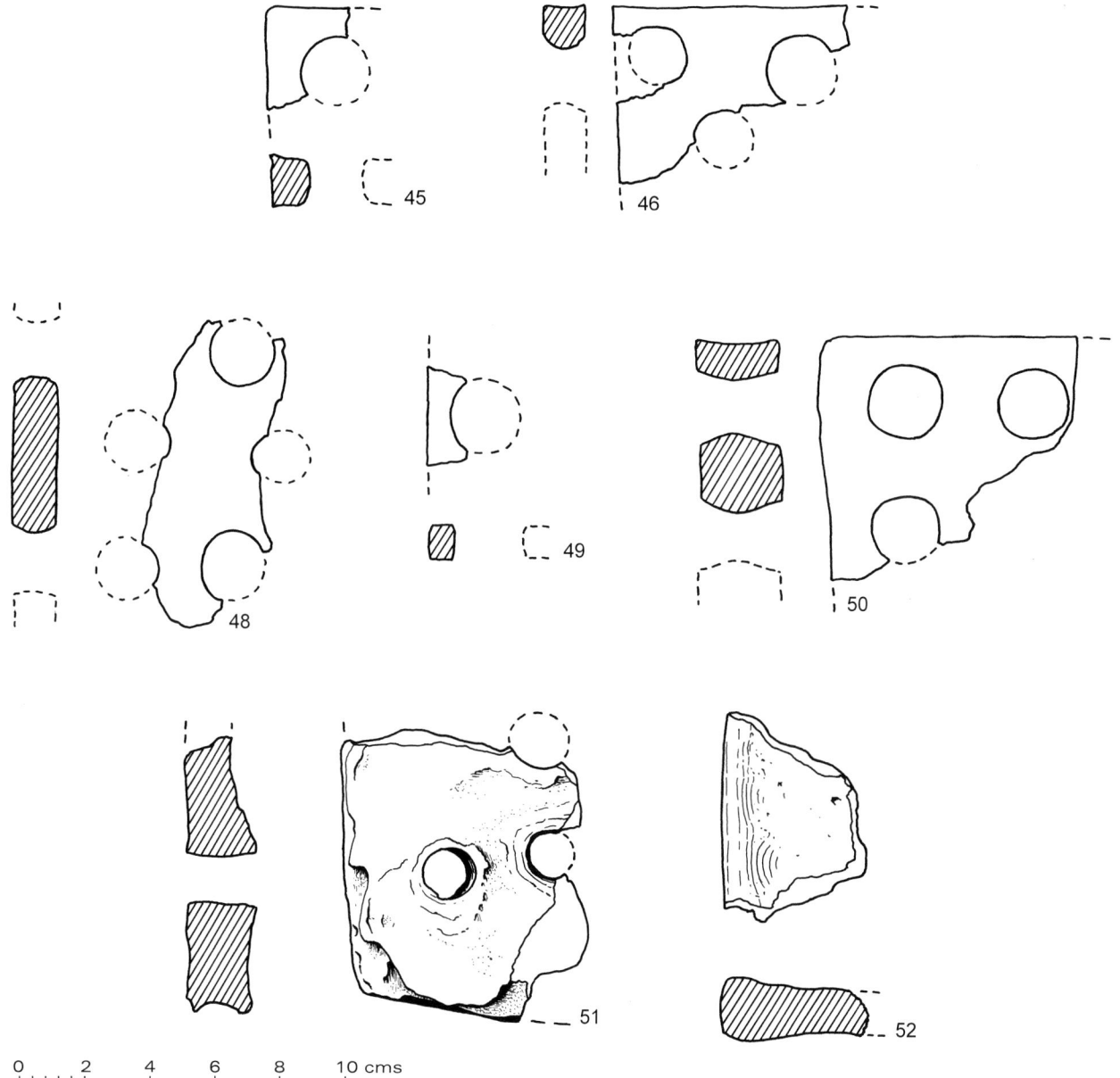

Fig. 153. Perforated pottery slabs. Scale 1:2.

Perforated pottery slabs (Fig. 153)

Nigel Macpherson-Grant [16]

Sixteen fragments of these functionally enigmatic objects were recovered, all from Area B and all confined to Period 2–3B features and layers within and adjacent to Enclosure B70. Of this total, three only survive, the others being stolen at the same time as some of the clay mould fragments. Fortunately seven of these were recorded almost immediately in 1977 (the outline drawings used here). From the surviving information these originally probably square or rectangular slabs fall into two groups: (1) simple perforated slabs and (2) a ?flanged and perforated example.

---

16. Written in 1994.

Simple perforated slabs

45. Corner fragment, 12 mm. thick, flattened edge face; diam. hole: *c.* 13 mm. Pit B79. Period 2. (Lost)
46. Three conjoining corner and side fragments. Max. extant length: 81 mm.; 13 mm. thick. Slightly grooved edge face. Three irregularly spaced holes, with varying diam. 11 mm., 13 mm. Pit B80. Period 2 (Lost).
47. (*Not illus.*) Corner fragment, 10 mm. thick. Flattened edge face. Ditch B70. Period 2. (Lost).
48. Fragment, 14 mm. thick. Traces of five fairly irregularly spaced holes: average diam. 20 mm. Ditch B70. Period 2. (Lost).
49. Side fragment, 11 mm. thick. Flattened edge face. Approx. hole diam. *c.* 14 mm. Ditch B70. Period 2. (Lost).
50. Two conjoining corner fragments, 25 mm. thick. Slightly concave edge face. Three evenly spaced holes: diam. 21 mm. Ditch B70. Period 2. (Lost).
51. Corner fragment. Heavy, fairly hard. Medium-fine moderate flint temper. Thin black core, pale orange lining, buff surfaces. Laminar structure, 20 mm. thick. Three close set but irregularly arranged holes, average diam. 17 mm. One edge with deep formative groove, one slightly grooved then flat. Worn fractures. Post-hole B40. Period 3B.
52. Side fragment, no surviving holes but probably slab. Fairly hard, fairly coarse, moderate flint-temper, oxidised. Irregularly shaped: 20 mm. thick at edge, body 15 mm. Rounded edge face. Pit B74. Period 2.
53. (*Not illus.*) Body fragment, 11 mm. thick. Two surviving holes, average diam. 20 mm. Worn. Pit B131. Period 3A.

?Flanged and perforated slab

54. Only representative of this type. Body fragment. Thick, hard, coarse, with abundant moderate flint temper. Black core, thin orange lining beneath partially oxidised buff-pink/grey surfaces. One surface smoothed, one apparently rough and untreated. Average thickness 28 mm. Traces of four vertical holes, fairly evenly spaced, diam. 23 mm. One horizontally grooved and flat face for approx. half o.a. depth, is difficult to interpret. Slab may have been flanged, the flange also pierced vertically. Pit B317. Period 2. *Not illus.*

Six other fragments (now lost and undrawn) were also recorded, one each from the Period 2 Hearth B41 and Pit B317, two from the enclosure ditch B70 and two more from the Period 3A Pit B131.

Discussion

The distribution of these objects shows quite clearly that for Highstead, their first chronological appearance is in Period 2 and they appear to be associated with metalworking.

Further west, similar slabs also occur from Late Bronze Age or Late Bronze Age/Early Iron Age transition settlements, e.g. Carshalton (Adkins and Needham 1985, 34–36, figs 12–13), Runnymede Bridge (Needham and Longley 1980, 411, fig. 4.2) and Mucking (Jones and Bond 1980, 475) and a number of other sites in the Thames valley area (Champion 1980, 237–8, figs 8–9). The thickness variations amongst the Highstead slabs are consistent with the general range represented by the material from these sites. The probable finishing groove on No. 51 matches closely items from Yiewsley, Middlesex (Champion 1980, fig. 8) and Queen Mary's Hospital, Carshalton, Surrey (Adkins and Needham 1985, fig. 13, 385, 388, 390). With specific reference to this latter site, the apparently irregular hole patterning of Highstead slab No. 48 is very similar to Carshalton 381 and 394. Equally the albeit simple manufacturing bi-products of these slabs (thickened sides and slightly raised edges to some holes) are paralleled at this site. That elsewhere they should often occur from settlements producing evidence of bronze-smithing is possibly no more than a conjunction of characteristic cultural components. However, it is worth noting that amongst the debris dumped into the Section E portion of B70's ditch, the only ingredients were highly vitrified pottery, burnt clay lumps, perforated slabs, charcoal and very little pottery, i.e. this dump was essentially light 'industrial' rather than obviously domestic.

Evidence for salt production

Examination and analysis of fired clay from Pit B215

Mike Heyworth [17]

Fragments of fired clay thought to be associated with production of salt, were examined and analysed. The white surface on the clay contained higher levels of calcium and strontium and is likely to have been caused by iron depletion and enhancement of the soluble salts due to its use in salt production.

Five samples of fired clay were submitted for examination. The sherds came from an Iron Age pit (B215, Period 3B) and were all red oxidised fired fabrics with white deposits on the inside surface. It was suggested that the sherds came from rectangular shallow vessels that may be associated with the production of salt.

The white surface of two sherds was scraped to remove the adhering soil and then analysed by energy dispersive x-

---

17. Report written in 1989.

ray fluorescence (XRF). The clay fabric was also analysed for comparison. The XRF analysis of both the white surface and the clay detected the following elements: potassium, calcium, titanium, manganese, iron, zinc, strontium and zirconium. The relative signal strengths were not however the same, the main differences being that calcium and strontium gave somewhat stronger signals from the white surface.

Matson (1971, 66) describes how a white skin, which can look like an applied slip, could form on fired, iron-containing clay wetted with a saline solution. This is due to the migration of soluble salts to the surface as the clay dries. The salts react with the iron present producing ferric chloride which volatises readily at about 800°C and so is lost. The net result of this process is iron depletion and a corresponding loss of colour together with enhancement of the cationic elements of the soluble salts at the surface of the clay body.

The white surface layer on the ceramic fragments was on the inside of the vessel. In this case the supply of moisture and soluble salts in the clay would have been continually replenished and the mechanism described by Matson would have proceeded almost continuously. This explanation is supported by the analytical results which show the enhanced levels of soluble salts, particularly calcium and strontium, in the white surface layer.

The white surface layer is not a deliberately added slip as there are a number of inclusions in the clay fabric which are also partly within the surface layer. Under the circumstances it seems likely that the white surface layer is caused by iron depletion and an enhancement of the soluble salts on the surface due to the use of the ceramic in the salt making process.

Later prehistoric briquetage from north-east Kent (Figs 90 and 96)

Nigel Macpherson-Grant [18]

The previous section described the analysis of sherds associated with, or derived from pot 375 from the Period 3B pit B215 (*see* p. 52). Michael Heyworth's conclusion is sensibly cautious in the absence of any other clear evidence from the site for the production of salt in bulk. However, as outlined below, 375 has other broad ceramic parallels from the region and, more specifically, has the typically oxidised red-orange/buff-pink surfaces patchily tinged with mauve/purplish zones associated with recognised briquetage types of varying date, e.g. Middle Bronze Age (Brean Down, Somerset: Foster 1990), Early Roman (Cliffe, Kent: Miles 1968), so that a degree of on-site salt production at Highstead is beyond reasonable doubt. The recovered sherd evidence is fragmentary, but near-straight rim and wall sherds suggests that 375 represents a brine evaporating pan of rectangular shape with outward curving walls and a flat base (Fig. 90). Exact length and height is uncertain, but in view of the rather weak structure indicated by 375's profile, its height is unlikely to have exceeded 7–8 cm. (*see* p. 156).

The most distinctive feature of 375 is the rather crude, essentially horizontal, rippled finger-fluted finish to its exterior. This type of furrowed finish is very similar to more carefully produced examples from unpublished briquetage assemblages from two Thanet coastal locations: at Minnis Bay and St Mildred's Bay. Neither of these assemblages have been studied in detail, but both contain similar elements: straight rims and (from St Mildred's Bay) angled corner sherds from rectangular vessels with upright walls; exterior wall surfaces often neatly finished with shallow horizontal furrowing; flat bases and more distinctively the use of a knife to trim rims or create open-ended troughs. A single base and wall sherd representing a similar vessel has recently been recorded from a submerged land-surface site at Swalecliffe in association with spreads of burnt flint, a feature also noted at St Mildred's Bay. The Swalecliffe example lacks the external furrowing, but its form suggests that the practical norm was for the production of upright-walled vessels. Pot 375 is either a chronological variant or, since the Thanet sites, at least, indicate salt-production on some scale, the cruder finish of 375 may suggest localised self-sufficiency (within a common tradition) and/or a one-off example whose walls sagged during manufacture.

The aspect of 375 being a chronological/formal variant is emphasised precisely because very little is known about prehistoric salt production in Kent. Highstead itself has produced two other examples that may represent either evaporation pans or post-production containers: 382 (Pit B133) and 447 (Pit B128) Forms 69–70, both again from Period 3B contexts. Overall the material from Highstead, Swalecliffe and the Thanet sites appears to belong to a common tradition, but a large fragment from a crude and heavy subrectangular/ovoid vessel from Hacklinge, near Worth, if indeed briquetage (Parfitt 1983, 290), underlines the likelihood of chronological/localised variants and that the full formal range employed during a particular period(s) has not been recognised. A complete little highly-burnished rectangular vessel from a Mid–Late Iron Age context at Epple Bay, Birchington (unpublished, Powell-Cotton Museum collection) is remarkably similar in size and form to examples described as 'salt-cake moulds' from West Flanders, Belgium (e.g. Raversijde, near Ostende: Thöen 1975, 59, fig. 35c) of second- and third-century Roman date. Available data there indicates that the latter have at least a later Iron Age ancestry.

---

18. Written in 1994.

The Birchington pot suggests that a search for unusual forms amongst conventional later prehistoric assemblages might be rewarding. If combined with a thorough assessment of extant briquetage material and a comprehensive survey of likely inter-tidal zones, the regional picture might be considerably enhanced.

Summarising, the quantity of material from the Thanet sites suggests that production and distribution stemmed from the same shoreline source, with one or more centres providing the needs of the island. Despite the quantities of burnt flint, the evidence from Swalecliffe is less conclusive, but arrangements may have been similar to Thanet's. The Highstead evidence is rather different. Whilst initial evaporation processes almost certainly took place relatively nearby, along the adjacent shore of the former Wantsum Channel, the final extraction of some, if not all, of the community's salt took place inland and uphill, within the settlement itself. The evidence from Hacklinge is less certain; the complex history of the Lydden valley marshes (seaward of Hacklinge itself) is still not understood and if the material mentioned is briquetage, production may have been either inland, as at Highstead, or associated with estuarine production as in Thanet and possibly Swalecliffe. Chronologically, the Highstead material appears to be specifically confined to Period 3B, i.e. *c.* 500–400 B.C. Vessel-finishing parallels indicate that the Thanet evaporating vessels are temporally close to Highstead 375 and the available site/ceramic data suggests an unconfirmed chronological window spanning Highstead Periods 2–3A and early 3B, arguably between *c.* 900–500 B.C. The Swalecliffe evidence is difficult but is unlikely to be radically earlier or later. The pottery from Hacklinge is broadly equivalent to Highstead Period 2, so this might take the known regional production of salt back to *c.* 900 B.C.

Small finds

Objects of copper alloy (Fig. 154)

Martin Henig[19]

1. Ring (?finger) of simple form and circular section (2 mm.). Diameter: 10 mm. In four fragments. Post-pit A6, s.f. no. 1. Period 2. *Not illus.*
2. Knife blade. Very corroded. Surviving length: 53 mm. Enclosure ditch A24, s.f. no. 25. Period 2. *Not illus.*

The knife fragment No. 2 is definitely associated with the occupation of Enclosure A24. Though the bronze ring is unlikely to be intrusive, there is marginally less certainty. Both are very corroded and fragmentary.

Both pieces were submitted to the Ancient Monuments Laboratory for x-ray fluorescence analysis. In correspondence Justine Bayley commented: 'The ring is a heavily leaded bronze and the blade also a leaded bronze, though apparently without quite as much lead. The difference may be a real one, or may be due to the changes in composition brought about by the corrosion, which may have had different effects on the two pieces. The blade also contained a detectable, though minor, amount of silver. These compositions are not unexpected, since leaded bronzes are common during the Late Bronze Age period and Early Iron Age bronzes are essentially a continuation of the same metalworking tradition. As these pieces are so heavily corroded further attempts to quantify the results are not possible'.

3. Pin, the point is lost, but seems to have been reshaped. The head is of pine-cone ornamentation with cross-hatching as on No. 4 below. Length: 49 mm. Cf. Bushe-Fox 1949, pl. XXXIX, no. 143. Pit complex B15, s.f. no. 52. Period 4D–5A.

Toilet instruments

4. Possible probe, with loop, broken, at the head of the hatched moulding. Length: 112 mm. Pit complex B15, s.f. no. 17. Period 4D–5A.
5. Length of wire terminating in rounded ends, possibly used as a probe. Length: 125 mm. Pit complex B15. s.f. no. 30. Period 4D–5A.
6. Tweezers of simple type; there are two engraved lines down each side. Length: 56 mm. Width: 4.5 mm. Pit complex B15, s.f. no. 27. Period 4D–5A.
7. Tweezers, similar to No. 6 above. Length: 47 mm. Width: 5.7 mm. Ditch B23, s.f. no. 268. Period 5A.
8. Unguent spoon or ear-scoop with ring attachment, broken. Ditch B1, s.f. no. 282. Period 4D–5A.

Miscellaneous

9. Needle, most of the eye is missing. Length: 90 mm. Pit complex B15, s.f. no. 47. Period 4D–5A.
   Another needle, with part of the rectangular eye but with the point missing was recovered from the Period 4D–5A ditch B1 (s.f. no. 250). Extant length: 76 mm. *Not illus.*
10. Pointed end of a heavy pin or stylus, of circular section. Length: 57 mm. Ditch B236, s.f. no. 175. Period 5A.
11. Barbed fish hook. Length: 30 mm. Cf. Cunliffe 1971, 118 and fig. 51, nos 149 and 150. Pit complex B15, s.f. no. 48. Period 4D–5A.
12. Small awl of quadrilateral section and round tang. Length: 33 mm. Cf. iron awl, Manning 1985, pl. 16, E21. Pit B268, s.f. no. 208. Period 5A.
13. Two pieces of wire which join, of squared section. Length: 57 mm. Pit complex B15, s.f. no. 45. Period 4D–5A.

---

19. The reports on the copper alloy and iron objects were submitted in 1988.

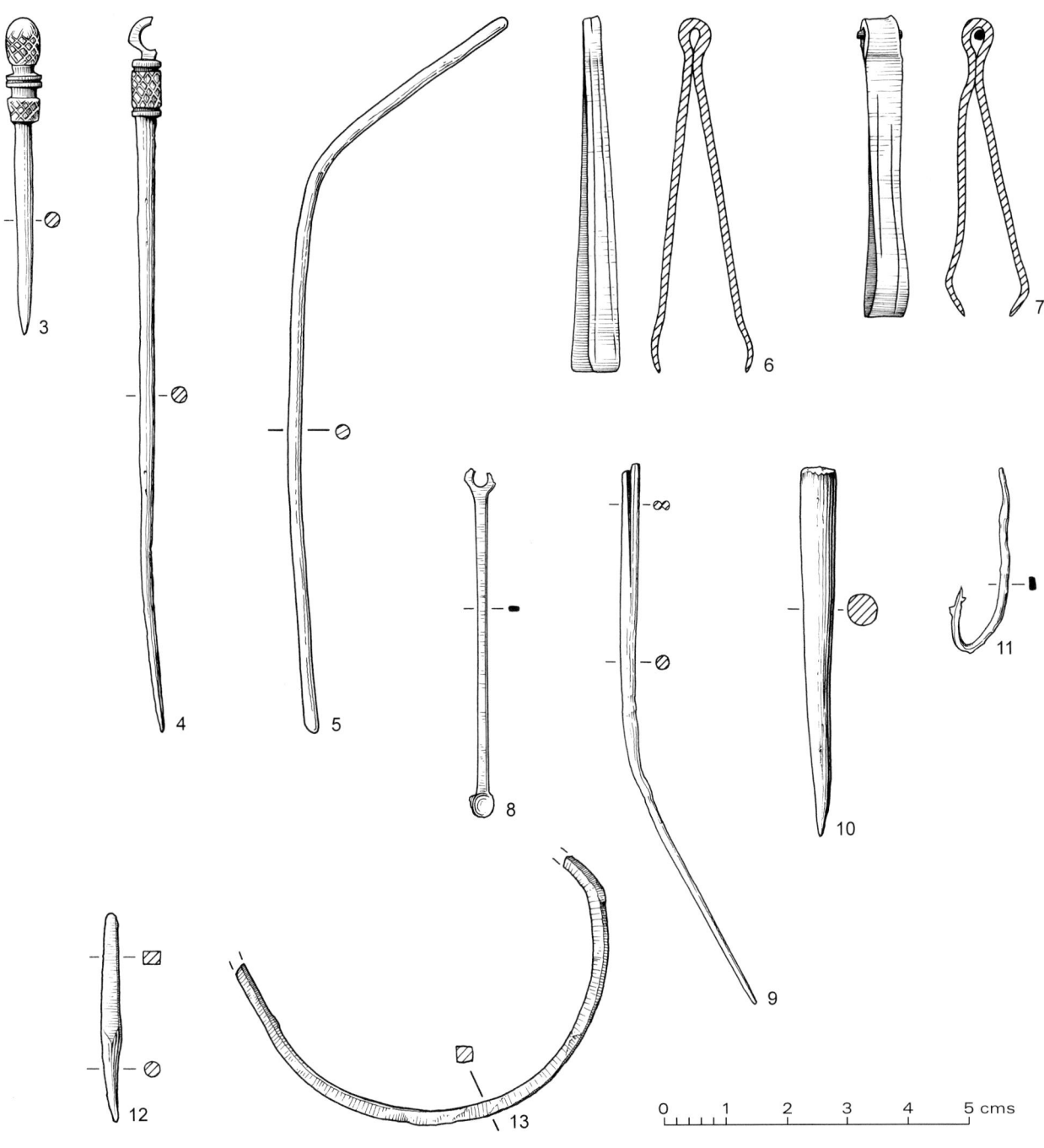

Fig. 154. Objects of copper alloy. Scale 1:1.

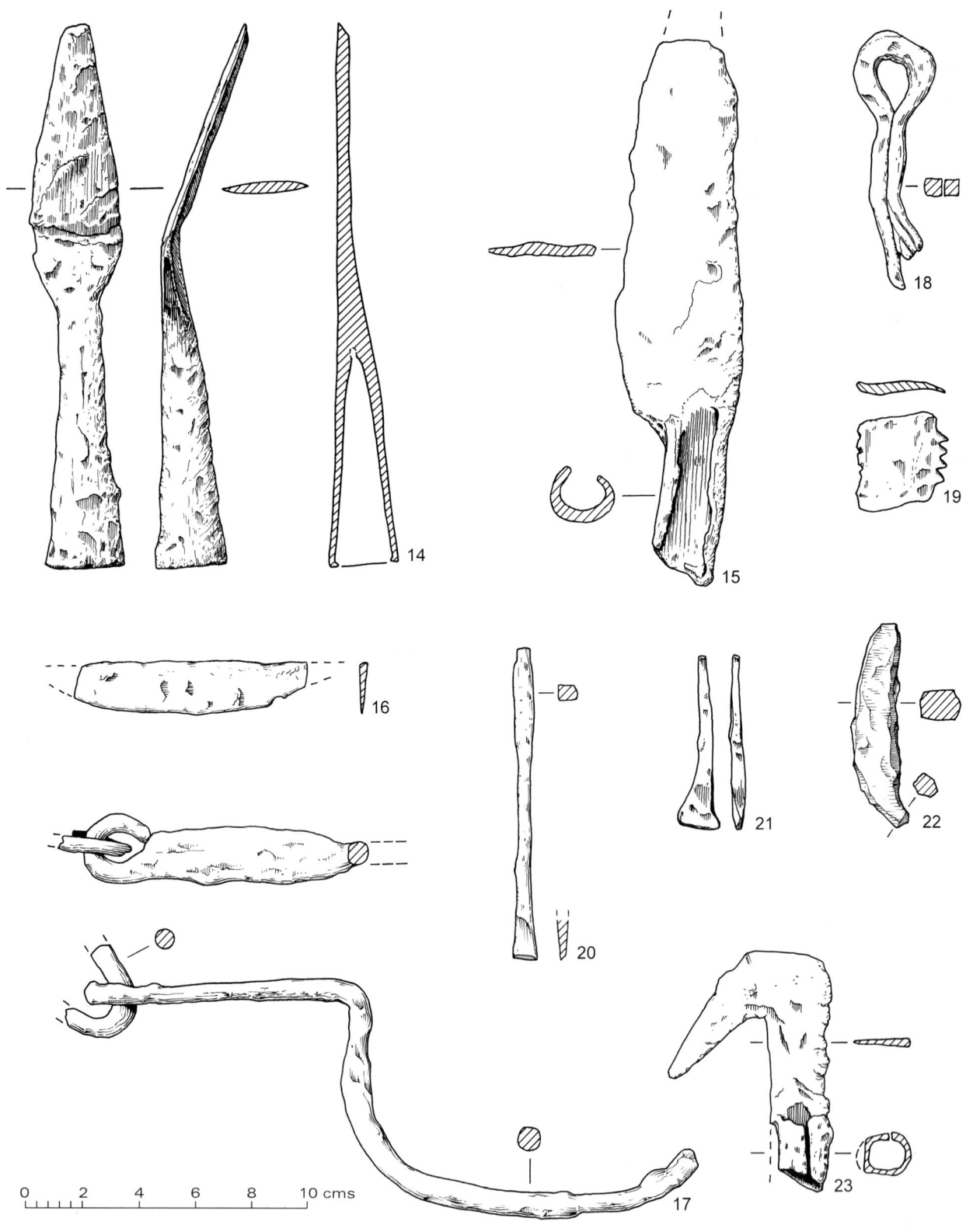

Fig. 155. Objects of iron. Scale 1:2.

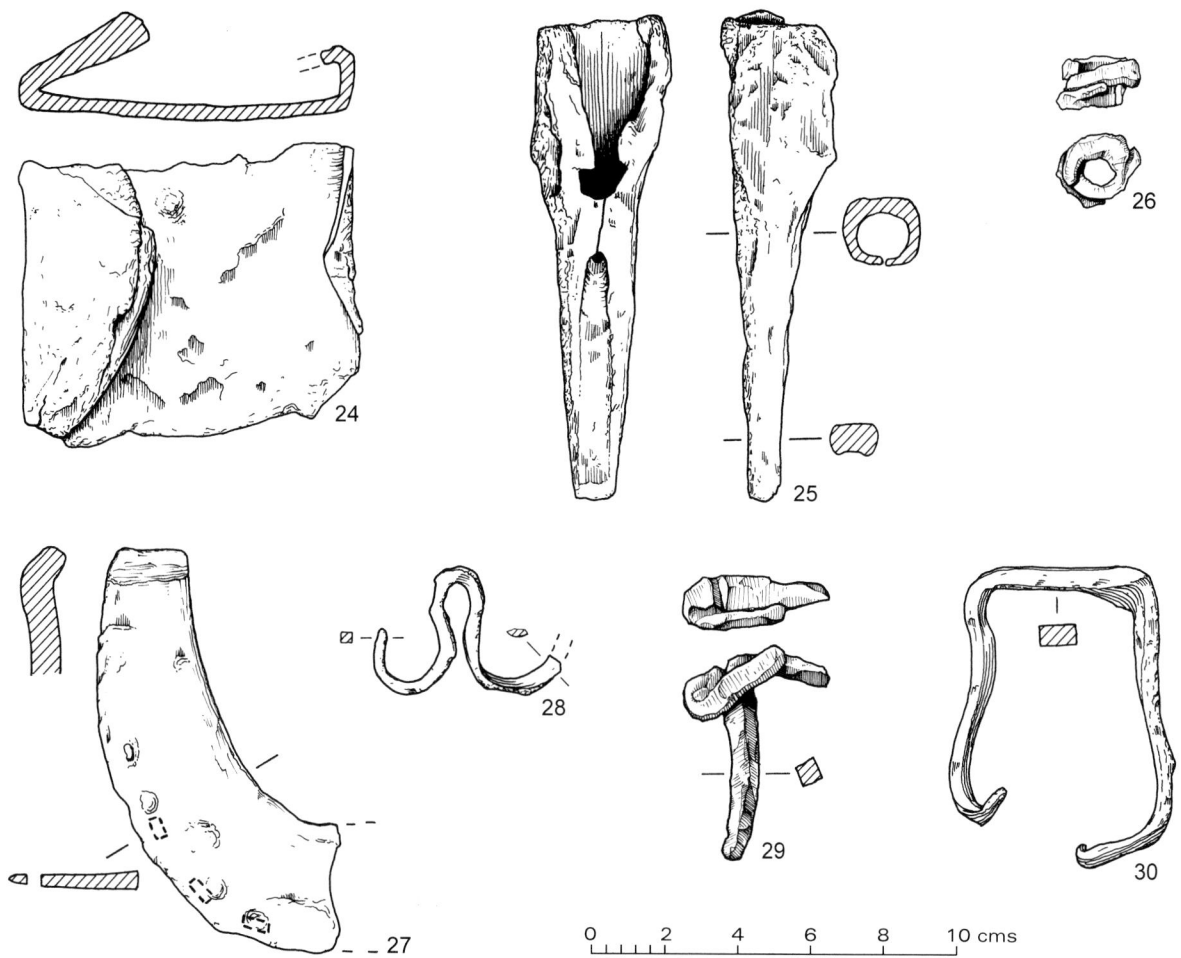

Fig. 156. Objects of iron. Scale 1:2.

Objects of iron (Figs 155–6)

Martin Henig

14. Socketed spearhead, the point is missing and the blade is bent. Length: 185 mm. Cf. Manning 1985, 162–3 and pl. V.78, no. 86, but rivet holes, if any, are not visible. Ditch A24C, s.f. no. 50. Period 2. *Intrusive.*
15. Socketed cleaver, the blade tip is missing. Length: 180 mm. Cf. Manning 1985, 122 and pl. 57, Q.100. Ditch A245 s.f. no. 35. Period 5A.
16. Knife blade, incomplete. Surviving length: 81 mm. Ditch A228, s.f. no. 34. Period 4D.
17. Latch lifter, incomplete. Surviving length: 220 mm. Cf. Manning 1985, 89 and pl. 39, 0.16. Pit complex B15, s.f. no. 22. Period 4D–5A.

    A similar, but fragmented latch lifter was recovered from Period 5A ditch A99 (s.f. no. 26, *not illus.*).

18. Double spike loop. Width: 7 mm. Length: 85 mm. Cf. Manning 1985, 130 and pl. 61, R.42. Ditch B1, s.f. no. 102. Period 4D–5A.

    A fragment of similar loop (s.f. no. 94, width 14 mm.: cf. Manning 1985, 130 and pl. 61, R.44) came from Period 2 hearth/gully/pit feature B152. Intrusive. *Not illus.*
19. Fragment of a saw blade; the teeth are cut in two modules, three teeth per centimetre. Surviving length: 30 mm. Width: 30 mm. Ditch B4, s.f. no. 219 Period 4C.
20. Possible stylus with chisel-like blade. Length: 104 mm. Ditch B2, s.f. no. 261. Period 4C.
21. Tool of rectangular section with tang, possible chisel. Length: 57 mm. Cf. Manning 1985, 24 and pl. 11, B.44. Ditch B2, s.f. no. 257. Period 4C.

    Two similar tools: one fragmentary with a pointed tang: length: 63 mm. (enclosure ditch B156, s.f. no. 228. Period 3B *intrusive*); the other is bent and incomplete: surviving length 45 mm. Ditch B1, s.f. no. 259. Period 4D–5A. *Not illus.*

22. Object with heavy body which terminates in a tang; part of a tool. Length: 67 mm. Pit B13, s.f. no. 35. Period 5A.
23. Socketed hook. Length: 80 mm. Cf. Manning 1985, 56–7 and pl. 24, F.46 and 54, fig. 14, Type II. Pit complex B15, s.f. no. 13. Period 4D–5A.

    Two further hooks were recovered. One with a rivet hole at the socket, length: 100 mm. (Area C Pit 2. Period 5A); the other incomplete, length 75 mm. Pit A274, s.f. no. 62 Pit. Period 5B.
24. Probably a hoe blade fragment. Width: 90 mm. Pit A80, s.f. no. 7. Period 5A.
25. Socketed conical ferrule. Length 125 mm. Cf. Manning 1985, 140–41 and pl. 66, S.57. Enclosure ditch A24, s.f. no. 24. Period 2. Intrusive.
26. Coiled ferrule. Diameter: 15 mm. Cf. Manning 1985, 141 and pl. 67 S.96–9. Ditch B1, s.f. no. 90. Period 4D–5A.
27. Part of a horseshoe with three rivet holes. This is of some importance because of its Roman context. Cf. Manning 1985, 63, footnote 1. Ditch B1, s.f. no. 236. Period 4D–5A.
28. Fine piece of iron work, perhaps part of a link from a cauldron chain. Ditch B1, s.f. no. 152. Period 4D–5A.
29. T-staple. Head width: 65 mm. Length: 55 mm. One arm twisted. Cf. Manning 1985, Nos 161, 162. Pit complex B15, s.f. no. 7. Period 4D–5A.
30. Binding for woodwork. 50 x 75 mm. Cf. Frere and St. Joseph 1974, 88 and fig. 47, no. 97. Pit complex B15, s.f. no. 24. Period 4D–5A.

    Three spring rings (s.f. no. 119: diameter: 20 mm., 25 mm., 45 mm. respectively) with rectangular sections were recovered from the Period 4C ditch B2. *Not illus.*

Roman brooches (Fig. 157)

Don Mackreth [20]

All three brooches are made from a copper alloy.

Colchester

31. The hook is broken and half the eight-coil spring is missing. Each wing has two flutes separated from each other and the end by a narrow groove. The bow is broad, shallow, has a basically flat back and, in profile, a marked bend at the top. It tapers to a rounded foot, with two narrow cross-grooves, and has a narrow central face with two sunken ridges on each side. The catch-plate has traces of walked-scorper decoration across the top. Pit complex B15, s.f. no. 50. Period 4D–5A.

The distribution of the group to which this brooch belongs shows that it is overwhelmingly Kentish, with a few coming from adjacent areas, the furthest flung being singletons from Gloucestershire, Norfolk and Leicestershire. The dating is: Silchester, mid first century with early Flavian pottery (Cotton 1947, 144, fig.7, 10); Colchester, A.D. 54–60 (Niblett 1985, 116, fig.74, 11); Leicester, mid to late first century (Clay and Pollard 1994, 139, fig. 73, 3); Canterbury, two examples, Flavian-Trajanic (Bennett *et al.* 1982, 169, fig. 88.1; Blockley *et al.* 1995, 959, fig. 402.5); Richborough, not later than A.D. 85 (Bushe-Fox 1949, 112, pl. 27, 26); Canterbury, late first to mid/late fourth century (Frere *et al.* 1987, 311, fig. 118, 1); Canterbury, 150–200 (*ibid.*, 185, fig. 65, 7). The style of the brooch and the dating both show that this is a late Colchester which should not really be expected to have survived much beyond, say, A.D. 60–70.

32. In very poor condition, only the start of the spring, the stubs of the wings and the upper bow survive. The wings have no trace of ornament and the bow is plain. Without any diagnostic feature being present, all that can be suggested is that it dates, in use, to before *c.* A.D. 55/60. Pit A274, s.f. no. 58. Period 5B.

Nauheim Derivative

33. The spring has four coils and an internal chord. The pin is missing. The bow is broad and thin and tapers to a pointed foot. The bow above the catch-plate has a pronounced arch in profile and has a line of walked-scorper ornament down the middle. Pit complex B15, s.f. no. 16. Period 4D–5A.

This would have been classified as a Nauheim, had it had a framed catch-plate. However, it is a close successor of that type and is chiefly found in the south-east as defined by the Wash and by central southern England skirting the Midlands. In other words, Dorset, Wiltshire, Oxfordshire and Northamptonshire as well as Lincolnshire are very definitely frontier lands with few specimens.

The dating is: Foxholes Farm, 80–20 B.C. (Partridge 1989, 132, fig. 76, 5); Baldock, A.D. 25–50 (Stead and Rigby 1986, 109, fig. 40, 15); Hod Hill, A.D. 43–50 (B.M. Guide, 16, fig. 8, 2; Richmond 1968, 117–9); Fishbourne, A.D. 43–*c.* 70/75 (Cunliffe 1971, 100, fig.36, 4); Richborough, Claudian (Cunliffe 1968 78 pl. 27, 10); Baldock, A.D. 50–90 (Stead and Rigby 1986, 109, fig. 40, 17); Park Street, before A.D. 75? (O'Neill 1945, 102, fig. 8, 1); Weekley, mid to late first century (Jackson and Dix 1987, M74, fig. 22, 6); Chichester, Flavian (Down 1978, 280, fig. 10.26, 21); Canterbury, A.D. 70/80–100/110 (Blockley *et al.* 1995, 965, fig. 405.34); Fawkham, before A.D. 100 (Philp 1963, 69, fig. 3, 2); Chichester, *c.* A.D. 100 (Down 1978, 280, fig.10.26, 20); Chichester, early second century at latest (*ibid.*, 280,

---

20. First written in 1981, I welcomed the opportunity to revise this report (2004). The cited dating will show just how much things have changed since 1981, and the addition of several thousand more brooches to the corpus has allowed greater refinement in assessing types and subtypes.

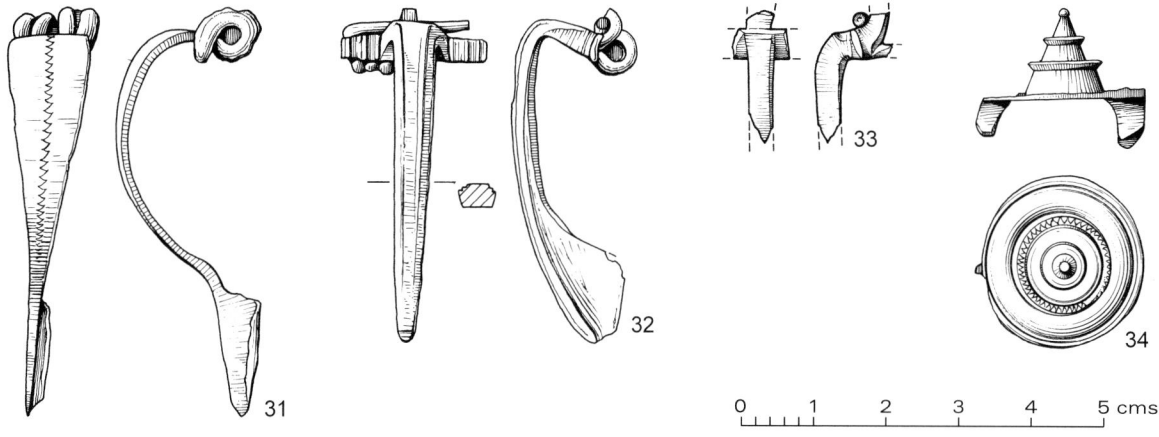

Fig. 157. Copper alloy brooches. Scale 1:1.

fig.10.26, 19); Gadebridge, before A.D. 150? (Neal 1974, 123, fig. 54, 2); Baldock, late third century (Stead and Rigby 1986, 109, fig. 40, 16); Colchester, A.D. 250–300 (Crummy 1983, 7, fig.2,1, 4); Gorhambury, fourth century (Neal *et al.* 1990, 115, fig.121, 5). The basic brooch spans the period from middle/later part of the first century B.C. to sometime in the earlier first century A.D. and none should have been seen in use as late as the early 60s.

Plate

34. The pin was hinged. The form is circular and from the middle rises a steep cone with two ridges and a cap. Around the base is a sunken pulvinated zone and, on the step at the base of the cone, is a line of walked scorper decoration. Ditch B1, s.f. no. 173. Period 4D–5A.

There are two parallels, one from Easton Maudit, Northamptonshire (unpublished) and one from a burial in Winchester, A.D. 70–100 (Biddle 1967, 230, fig. 4, 14).

Roman glass (Fig. 158)

John Shepherd

Area A produced two fragments of glass and Area B twelve fragments. All can be dated to the late first or second century A.D.

35. Fragment from the base of a bowl. Blown. Thick greenish-blue glass. Solid cut-out outsplayed base-ring. Late first or early second century. Ditch A68, s.f. no. 5. Period 5A.
36. Fragment from the rim of a bowl (cf. Charlesworth 1972, 199f., fig. 74, nos 6–10). Blown. Thick dull green glass. Flattened hollow tubular rim. Although this is a long-lived form, the colour of the metal suggests a late first- or second-century date. Pit complex B15, s.f. no. 49. Period 4D–5A.

Of the remainder the following can be dated. None are illustrated.

Late first or early second century: four fragments from the sides of cylindrical bottles (Isings 1957, 67f., Form 51) blown, bluish-green glass (Ditch B1, s.f. no. 168, 169. Period 4D–5A: Pit complex B15, s.f. no. 28. Period 4D–5A).

Late first or second century: fragment from the side of a flask or jar (Isings 1957, 86f., Form 67 or 69f., Form 52), blown thick bluish-green glass (Pit complex B15, s.f. 55. Period 4D–5A); two fragments from the sides of square-sectioned bottles (Isings 1957, 63f., Form 50), mould-blown, dull bluish-green glass with many air bubbles (Pit complex B15, s.f. nos 28 and 51. Period 4D–5A); two fragments from the sides of bottles of indeterminate form, blown, bluish-green glass (Ditch B1, s.f. no. 169 and Pit complex B15, s.f. no. 241, both Period 4D–5A).

Specifically early second century: two fragments from the lower part of a globular jar (Isings 1957, 86f., Form 67) or flask (Isings 1957, 69f., Form 52), blown. Thick bluish-green glass. Pit complex B15, s.f. no. 55. Period 4D–5A.

Fig. 158. Roman glass. Scale 1:2.

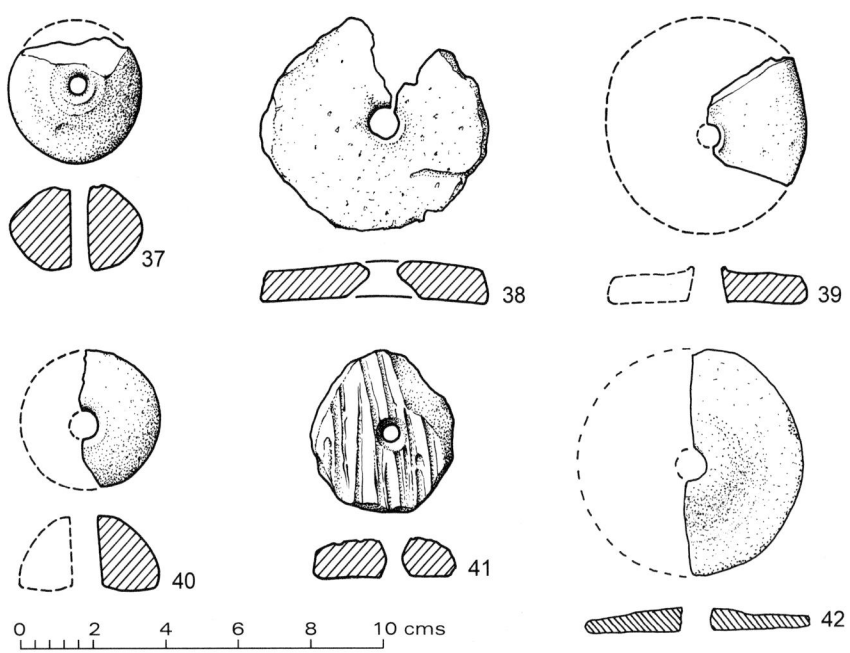

Fig. 159. Fired clay spindlewhorls. Scale 1:2.

Area A also produced one unstratified glass fragment, from the side of a cylindrical bottle (Isings 1957, 67f. Form 51). Blown, thick bluish-green glass. Vertical scratching on exterior surface. Late first or early second century (s.f. no. 65).

Weaving implements (Figs 159–61)

Spindlewhorls and loomweights

Nigel Macpherson-Grant

37. Bi-conical; flint-tempered fabric. Diameter: 40 mm. Central hole: 4–5 mm. Weight: 42 g. Ditch B70, s.f. no. 270. Period 2.
38. Body sherd; flint-tempered fabric. Diameter: 60 mm. Central hole: 8 mm. Existing weight: 30 g. (incomplete). Ditch B70, s.f. no. 278. Period 2.
39. Base sherd; flint-tempered fabric. Incomplete. Central hole: 5 mm. Pit B178, s.f. no. 183. Period 3B.
40. Hemispherical whorl; flint-tempered fabric and blackened from heat. Diameter: 40 mm. Weight: 26 g. Pit complex B15, s.f. no. 12. Period 4D–5A.
41. Pot sherd, 'Belgic' grog-tempered fabric. Diameter approx. 40 mm. Weight: 42 g. Pit B146, s.f. no. 87. Period 3B. Intrusive.
42. Base sherd, of grey grog-tempered Romano British native coarseware, very worn and only half remains. Diameter: 58 mm. Extant weight: 26 g. Pit A87, s.f. no. 13. Period 5A.
43. Base sherd, fine sandy fabric, possibly Roman, mid to late first century. Diameter 58 mm. Weight: 11.7 g. Post-hole A114, s.f. no. 16. Period 5A.
44. Pyramidal fired clay loomweight. Height: 14.5 cm. Base: 110–29 mm. Hole diameter: *c.* 10 mm. Weight: 1.75 kg. Enclosure ditch A24, s.f. no. 70. Period 2.
    Dr Sheila Elsdon has noted (in correspondence) that loomweights of this type are of Late Bronze Age to Early Iron Age in date, and in most southern areas of Britain, probably pre *c.* 500 B.C. After that date, particularly in the south-east, they appear to be replaced by triangular weights.
45. Possibly spherical weight. ?Mark of suspension cord on the inner surface. Enclosure ditch A24, s.f. no. 275. Period 2.
46. Possible weight. Well-fired clay lump with mark on inner surface, perhaps from a suspension cord. Pit B168, s.f. no. 99. Period 3B.

Antler weaving comb

Stephen Greep

47. Undecorated antler weaving comb with a flat section and an oval head. The nine teeth are all lost. Hedges and Hodder Form SL.F (1977, fig. 1, F). Broken. Surviving length: 97 mm. Pit B266, s.f. no. 275. Period 3B.

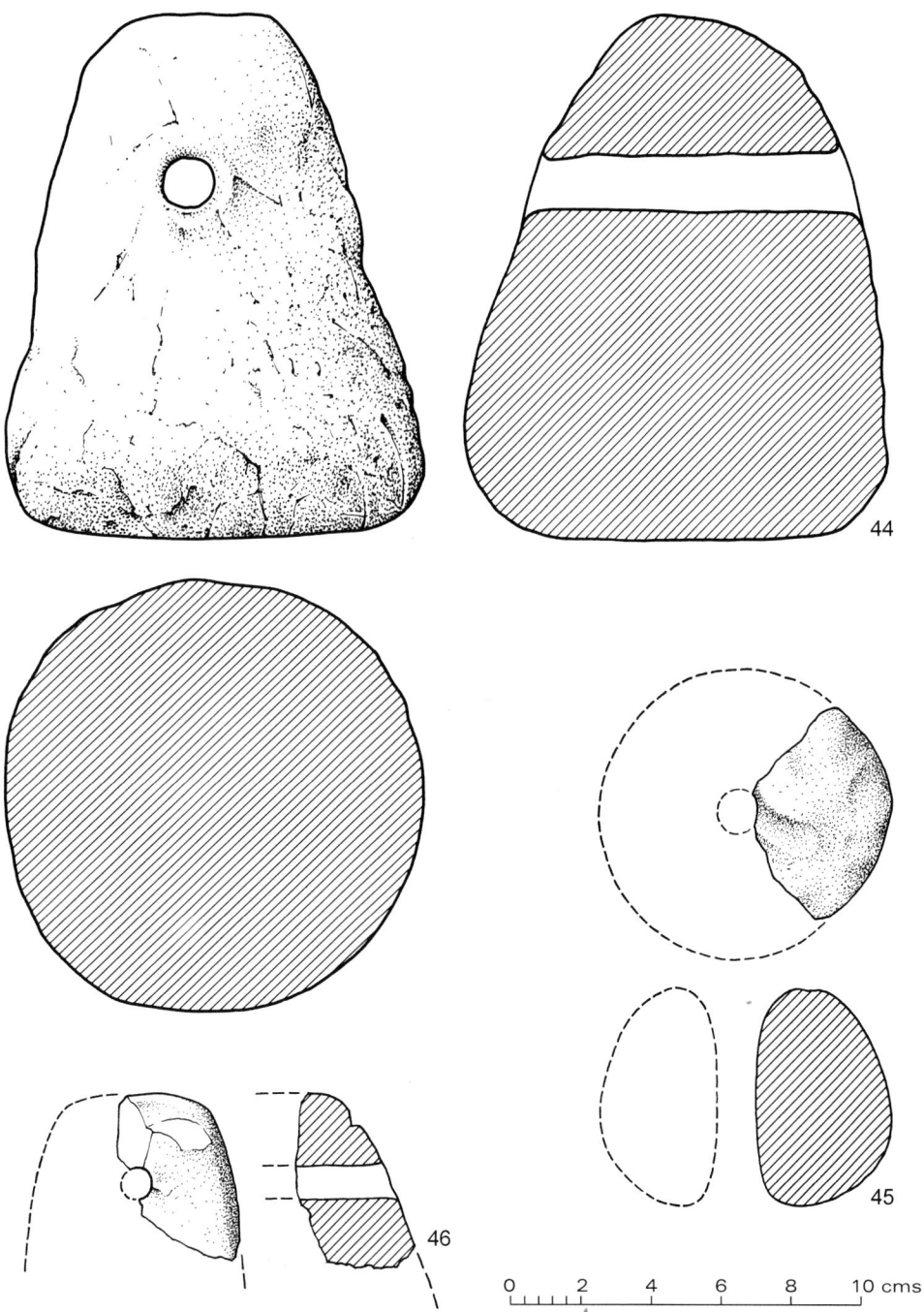

Fig. 160. Loomweights. Scale 1:2.

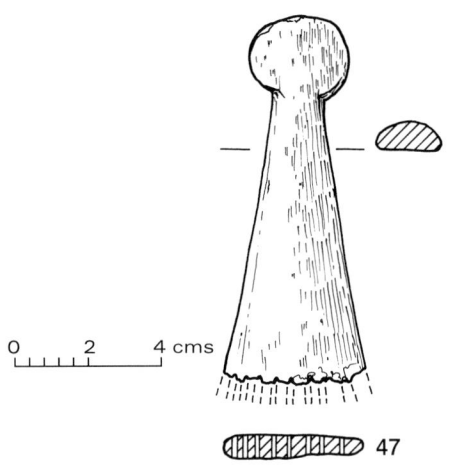

Fig. 161. Antler weaving comb. Scale 1:2.

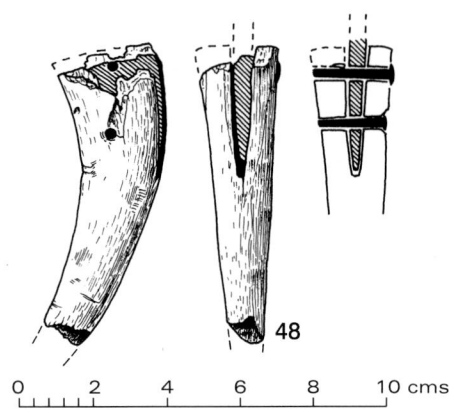

Fig. 162. Antler handle. Scale 1:2.

Object of antler (Fig. 162)

Stephen Greep

48. Handle manufactured from the end of a red deer antler tine, 81.5 mm. long. The surface has been smoothed and a slot cut to receive the tang of an iron implement which remains *in situ* and is held in place by a pair of iron rivets. This slightly unusual method of hafting occurs throughout the Iron Age and Roman periods. Where implements are found in association it is typically used for saws (e.g. Bulleid and Gray 1917, pl. LX and Jacobi 1974, Abb. 12 for Iron Age examples and Curle 1911, pl. LXVIII, 6 for a Roman one, though using an antler beam section rather than a tine), though it is not inconceivable that other implements could also be so hafted. Ditch B4, s.f. no. 271. Period 4C.

Objects of stone (Fig. 163)

Quernstones

Pan Garrard

No complete stones were found, and all appeared to have been discarded as rubbish in pits and ditches after breakage. All are from hand querns. With the exception of the basalt 'pebbles' detailed below, the geological identifications have been made by Martyn Owen of the Geological Museum, London.

49. Part of an upper stone, diameter: 36 cm., hollowed wear on both sides, indicating re-use of the stone until final fracture. Of glauconitic, rather pebbly calcareous sandstone of Lower Greensand, possibly from Folkestone beds. Pit complex B15, s.f. no. 26. Period 4D–5A.
50. Part of a not very worn well-ribbed stone; chisel marks on the outer edge remain from the initial manufacture. Diameter: *c.* 40 cm. Of coarse-grained feldspathic sandstone: Millstone Grit from northern England. Ditch A252, s.f. no. 52. Period 4D.
51. Part of the upper stone of a hand quern, diameter 32 cm. Martyn Owen writes: '... of well-rounded flint pebbles cemented by iron oxide into a conglomerate, probably from the local Tertiary deposits'. For two other unpublished Roman parallels cf. Canterbury Museum Accession no. 8185, upper stone, found in lowest layer Roman street beneath St George's Street by Frank Jenkins in 1951, and Canterbury Museum Accession No. RM 1953/152, lower stone, incorporated into city wall at the Cattle Market (found in 1890). Ditch A245, s.f. no. 37. Period 5A. *Not illus.*

Small shapeless fragments of other quernstones were recovered, chiefly from Area A contexts. All are of Millstone Grit, with the exception of one fragment from the Eifel district in Germany.

Basalt pebbles

Paul Craddock and Ian Freestone

Among the samples examined by the British Museum Research Laboratory were several rounded 'pebbles' of a vesicular basaltic lava. In thin section, subhedral to anhedral phenocrysts of fawn clinopyroxene up to 1 mm. diameter with green pleiochroic cores are set in a groundmass consisting predominantly of fine laths of plagioclase, elongate and equant clinopyroxene and granules of opaque iron-titanium oxide, in a colourless isotropic matrix.

Lava of this type was commonly used for Roman millstones, and these 'pebbles' probably represent re-used fragments from querns. The source of such material is traditionally assigned to Niedermendig (East Eifel,

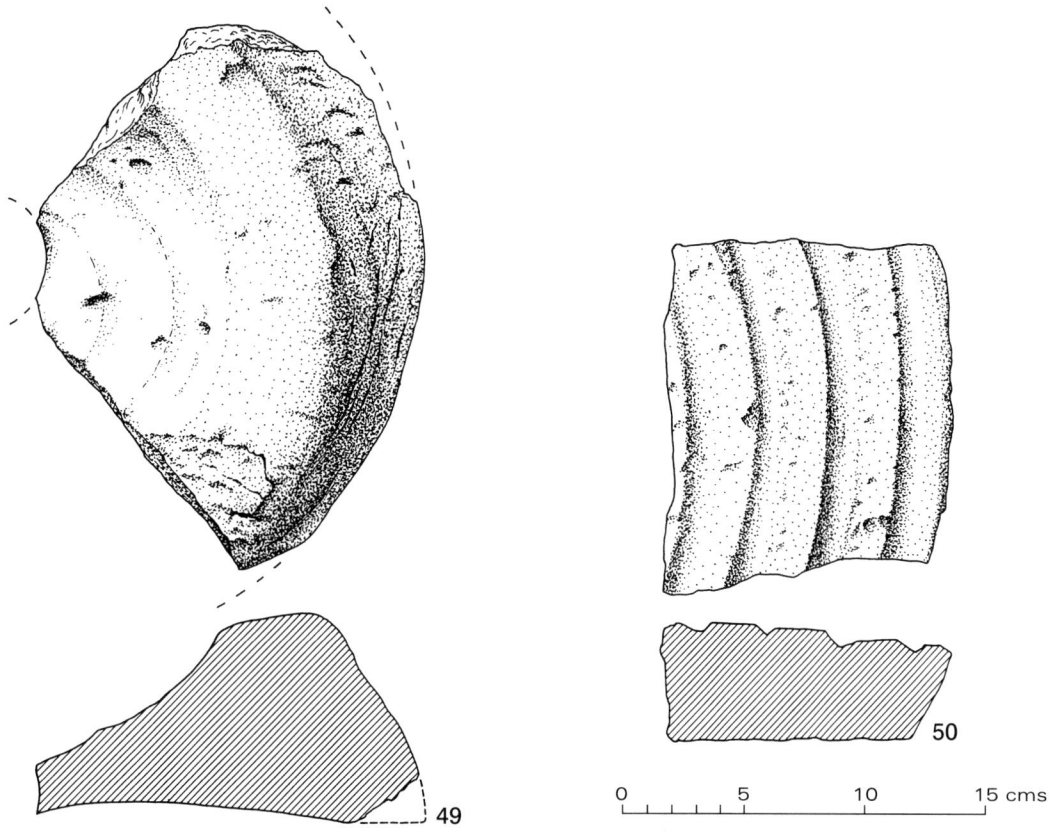

Fig. 163. Quernstones. Scale 1:3.

Germany). However, research carried out at Southampton University (Williams-Thorpe and Thorpe 1988) indicates that the petrography of the Highstead pebbles may also be matched in the Massif Central. Dr Olwen Williams-Thorpe has noted (pers. comm.) that the absence of olivine and the zoning of the pyroxenes tend to favour a Niedermendig origin, but chemical analysis would be required to be certain of this. The evidence to date suggests that the Niedermendig lava was used for hand and water driven rotary millstones, while the French material was used for donkey mills.

The Bones

Human

Only two fragments were recovered, both from the Period 4D–5A Pit complex B15. The following note was kindly supplied by the late Dr Peter Garrard:

Upper two thirds of a right femur, badly eroded over the articular surface of the joint and at the upper end where, posteriorly, the cortex of the bone is partly missing. The upper third of a left radius with some erosion was also present. The bones were of average weight and the clean breaks of both suggest fracture at or after death. Age: fully adult, 20–35 years. Sex: indeterminate.

Mammal and bird bones

Anthony C. King [21]

Given the acidic nature of the Highstead subsoil and a low survival rate for bone, recovered material was grouped into assemblages corresponding with the principal archaeological periods of the excavation. All attributable fragments have been included in the count for each species (Table 31), except for vertebrae and ribs, which have been classed as unidentified to species. Minimum numbers of animals

---

21. This report was submitted in 1988. The author is grateful to Kevin Reilly for providing identifications of the bird bones.

	Period 2	Period 3	Period 4	Period 5	Total
Ox	10	21	88	344	463
Sheep/goat	4	14	29	111	158
Pig		1	6	57	64
Horse	2	4	8	32	46
Dog (includes partially articulated skeleton)				104	104
Roe deer				1	1
Fowl				5	5
Duck				1	1
Wader				1	1
Unidentified	5	48	145	517	714
Total	21	88	276	1069	1557

Table 31. Numbers of identified bones.

Bone	Months	Fused	Unfused	% Unfused
Scapula	7-10	14	0	100
Pelvis	7-10	8	0	100
Humerus dist.	12-18	7	1	93
Radius prox.	12-18	4	0	93
Phalanx I	18	2	0	93
Phalanx II	18	1	0	93
Tibia dist.	24-30	8	3	72
Metac dist.	27-36	11	2	72
Calcaneum	36	6	4	72
Femur prox.	42	3	1	72
Femur dist.	42-48	1	1	67
Tibia prox.	42-48	2	1	67
Humerus prox.	42-48	2	1	67
Radius dist.	42-48	3	1	67

Table 33. Epiphyseal fusion for ox in Period 5.

have been calculated from the most frequently occurring elements of the skeleton of each species (Table 32). The bones from each of the contexts of the excavation have been accumulated into groups corresponding with the site periods for this purpose. As these groups could not be examined in their entirety at the same time, minimum numbers were not calculated on the basis of Chaplin's visual method (1971, 70ff), which has led to results slightly lower than would otherwise have been the case, but in practice this is of no consequence when comparing assemblages.

The state of fusion of epiphyses and tooth wear were noted where relevant, but the small size of the assemblage has meant that there was not enough data for firm conclusions to be drawn. Epiphyseal fusion for ox from Roman levels has been tabulated (Table 33) and trends observable for other species incorporated in the discussion. No measurements or comments on pathology are published here. [22]

Before conclusions can be drawn about the archaeological significance of the assemblage, some account has to be taken of the extent of destruction of the bone by the ancient occupants of the site and by soil processes. Four main destructive processes are involved, namely the butchery of the carcase, cooking practices, the disposal of the remains and subsequent mechanical and chemical attack during burial. It is not proposed here to delineate each individual factor's effect on bone survival, but merely to point out the total effect on the assemblage.

An idea of how much survives can be gained by comparing Table 31 with Table 32, which gives the number of bones per 'minimum animal'. If the whole skeleton survived there would be about 200 bones per animal, depending on the species. Of course, the small size of the assemblage contributes to the low result, but even in the case of Period 5, the number of bones per animal is very low. This may be related to the results of the tooth to bone ratio, which reflect, in all probability, a high degree of destruction of bone by adverse soil conditions. The teeth of adult animals are much harder and denser than the osseous material in a skeleton, and therefore survive better under acidic conditions. So, where the proportion of teeth

	Period 1-2	Period 3A-3B	Period 4A-4D	Period 5A-5F
Ox	1	2	5	14
Sheep/goat	1	2	2	8
Pig		1	1	3
Horse	1	1	1	2
Dog				3
Roe deer				1

Table 32. Minimum number of animals.

		Period 3A-B	Period 4A-D	Period 5A-F
Ox	Bones	10	53	228
	Teeth	11	35	116
	Teeth/bones %	110.0	66.0	50.9
Sheep/goat	Bones	11	13	68
	Teeth	3	16	43
	Teeth/bones %	27.3	123.1	63.2
Pig	Bones	1	4	26
	Teeth	-	4	31
	Teeth/bones %	-	100.0	119.2

Table 34. Bone/teeth ratios.

---

22. At the time of writing it was hoped to produce a report gathering together statistics from a number of Trust sites. This did not prove possible.

is high, as at Highstead, when compared with a mean for nineteen Roman sites given in King 1978 (table 2) it can be concluded that there has been significant destruction of bone. This may have biased the sample differentially in favour of large, dense bones, which would survive the soil conditions better. However, there are smaller more delicate bones in the Highstead assemblage, including some bird bones, which may mean that the known acidic subsoil at the site was not too severe, or else was localised in effect.

The table of fragment numbers (Table 31) shows that the assemblage consists largely of ox bones in all periods. This contrasts with the usual pattern for Iron Age and unromanised sites (King 1985) and may be a result of the bias due to soil conditions mentioned above. Most of the cattle were killed when sub-adult or middle aged, as there were virtually no vertebrae with fused epiphyses (in general under 5 years), yet very few juvenile specimens were found (Table 33). Horse was the other large animal in the assemblage, and it is relevant to note that it is relatively more common than at the nearby contemporary town of Canterbury (King 1982). This seems to have been the case for most rural sites (King 1978, table 4), probably because the horse was used for ranching and transport. The animal species present indicate that a variety of habitats were exploited as food sources. Cattle and sheep were probably grazed in open pasture, while pigs and the roe deer antler show that woodland was also used. The duck and wader bird bones indicate aquatic, probably estuarine zones within the site's food catchment area.

The only chronological trend that may be of significance is the relative increase in the representation of pig in the Roman period. This may be due to increased pork consumption, which has been detected in many other assemblages of the period (King 1985).

There is a trend visible in the overall effect of butchery, cooking and disposal practices. The proportion of bones to teeth increases from the Iron Age to the Roman phases, as a result of a relative increase in the number of lower limb bones (Table 34). The number of bones per 'minimum animal' also increases. This may be due to a tendency in the Roman period to dispose of waste bones (i.e. the lower limb) in the same deposit as other bones.

The direct effect of butchery in the form of cut marks was not often present, and it is not possible to reconstruct the pattern of butchery of the carcase. The number of fragments for each attributable bone indicates that the bones of all species appear to have been broken up to the same extent. However, the actual number of fragments per bone is probably very high when account is taken of the number of unattributable long bone fragments. No horse bones were cut and very few were broken.

Finally, a part of the Roman period assemblage is of interest because it was probably not food refuse. It came from the Area C hypocaust, and consisted of the almost entire skeleton of a small, sub-adult dog and a few sheep/goat and ox bones, one of which appears to have been chewed. Presumably the dog lived (and died) in the hypocaust after its abandonment.

PART 5: DISCUSSION

Timothy Champion

The importance of Highstead

The excavations at Highstead represent one of the most extensive areas of Kent to have been explored archaeologically. At the time of the work in the 1970s there had been no other excavation of comparable extent in the county. In this respect Kent was significantly different from most of the other counties of south-eastern England, where large-scale excavations were well established at a much earlier date and had become an important source of information about the history of human settlement and landscape development. It was not until the archaeological investigations associated with the construction of the Channel Tunnel (Bennett 1988) that similarly large areas were explored; the pace of archaeological investigations picked up considerably after about 1989, but even now, extensive area excavations of this sort have been very few in the county. There have been several important large-scale programmes of excavation in advance of infrastructure developments such as road schemes and, most notably, the Channel Tunnel Rail Link (Booth *et al.* forthcoming), but these projects have involved the examination of a long and relatively narrow transect of the landscape rather than a wider area.

The circumstances of the excavation undoubtedly mean that many questions about the occupation of the area have necessarily to be left unanswered; unfortunately, much of archaeological interest had already been quarried away, some parts of the site were not fully explored, and there are lingering doubts about the details of some of the excavated features. Nevertheless, the Highstead site still presents us with some of the most important archaeological evidence to have been recovered from Kent, for two particular reasons.

First, the area excavated provides one of the very few large glimpses of the settlement history of Kent; it contains a sequence of stratified and intercutting features spanning most of the later prehistoric and Roman periods, in an area large enough for one entire enclosure to be excavated and the spatial relationships of other features to be revealed. The sequence was not complete, however; there was a gap in the Middle Iron Age, and perhaps more surprisingly no features earlier than the Late Bronze Age or later than the Late Roman period were identified. It is, of course, possible that, given the circumstances of excavation, such features were missed or not excavated, since the flint tools show that the area was certainly occupied in the period from the Mesolithic to the Late Neolithic.

Secondly, the stratified sequence of features has allowed a sequence of pottery and other material culture of the Late Bronze Age to Late Roman period to be compiled, albeit with a probable hiatus in the middle of the Iron Age. Though the Roman material was comparatively well known, this was the first opportunity to study stratified assemblages of later prehistoric pottery and, together with subsequent work, has been instrumental in laying the foundations for a secure east Kent ceramic chronology.

Later prehistoric chronology

The delay in publication did not mean that the importance of Highstead went completely unrecognized. The site was well known to archaeologists in Kent and its significance was gradually appreciated more widely. There were occasional references to the enclosures (e.g. Champion 1980, 237), but it was Peter Couldrey's work on the prehistoric pottery that attracted particular attention. The significance of the ceramic assemblages from Periods 2 and 3 was widely known among specialists, and regular references were made to them, for example in the report on the site at Monkton Court Farm, Thanet (Perkins *et al.* 1994), or in discussions of the Early Iron Age pottery of east Kent (Macpherson-Grant 1991; 1992b), or more generally in reviews of the prehistory of

Kent (Champion forthcoming). The importance of this pottery was also recognized at a national scale, when the fourth edition of Cunliffe's standard text book on the Iron Age in Britain added two new ceramic style zones: the 'Highstead 2 group' and the 'Highstead-Dolland's Moor group' were adopted to fill in gaps in the largely unknown prehistory of east Kent (Cunliffe 2005, 94 and 103).

The post-Deverel-Rimbury ceramic sequence in Kent is slowly being established, though there are so far few absolute dates. There are, as yet, no large, well-dated post-Deverel-Rimbury plainware assemblages: the later fills of the Coldharbour Road ditches (Mudd 1994), with radiocarbon dates of 2895±70 BP (OxA-4717), 2880±65 BP (OxA-4719) and 2835±45 BP (Q-3255), the small assemblages from Welling (Couldrey 1988) and Hoo St Werburgh (Moore 2002), and some of the pottery from the ring-ditch enclosure at Mill Hill, Deal (Stebbing 1934; Champion 1980, 233–7 and fig. 6) and sites located in the A2 improvement scheme near Bridge and Barham, south-east of Canterbury (Macpherson-Grant 1980a, especially Sites 1, 5 and 8, Pit 20) may all belong to this phase. Parallels between Highstead Period 2 pottery and Mill Hill and the A2 sites have been noted above in the pottery report, and it seems likely that Period 2 includes forms common in that period, though the bulk of the material seems more typical of the post-Deverel-Rimbury decorated phase, as the discussion of ceramic comparisons and chronology makes clear. Absolute dating of Period 2 is difficult, as there are no radiocarbon dates and a limited number of datable associations. The bronze pins that were being cast at Highstead are not closely datable, and neither is the bronze blade from Enclosure A24, but both should belong in the final stages of Late Bronze Age bronze production, possibly no later than the eighth century B.C.. This helpfully confirms the date of 900–600 B.C. suggested for Period 2 on the grounds of ceramic parallels. Other assemblages from Kent that belong to the post-Deverel-Rimbury decorated phase are still surprisingly rare, but an important collection from Monkton Court Farm, Thanet (Perkins et al. 1994), was loosely associated with three small disturbed hoards of the Ewart Park phase.

The ceramic sequence at Highstead shows an unbroken tradition of production, with Period 3A representing a transition to the next distinctive assemblage, Period 3B. There are still no other published reports of large site assemblages comparable to Period 3B, but the Highstead material has been used to define an 'east Kent rusticated tradition', documented at perhaps as many as thirty sites (Macpherson-Grant 1989). The parallels for this assemblage have been discussed above, but subsequent work in France suggests that the forms, fabrics and decoration are particularly close to those of the pottery excavated at sites found during Channel Tunnel operations there (Blancquaert and Bostyn 1998), raising important questions about the nature of cross-Channel relationships during the Early Iron Age. There are no metalwork associations for this ceramic tradition in Kent, and no radiocarbon dates, and its precise chronology is very uncertain: the general comparison to the north French assemblages, dated there to the Early La Tène period, suggests an approximate range of the fifth to the third century B.C., but both its starting and its finishing date need further research.

The hiatus between Periods 3B and 4 is typical of a wider problem in east Kent (Champion forthcoming), where pottery of the Middle Iron Age is scarcely known except at Bigbury (Thompson 1983). The presence of a very small quantity of comparable forms in Period 4 contexts at Highstead, including s-profile foot-ring bowls and curvilinear decoration, in an otherwise continuous sequence, lends support to the belief that the broad outline of the ceramic sequence is correct and that the break in structural evidence and settlement activity is genuine. The problem, both at Highstead and more widely in east Kent, is to understand the nature of human settlement at this period and why it left so little trace.

The structural sequence of Period 4 is of great importance for our understanding of Late Iron Age chronology. Though pottery of this period has been well known for over a century, the majority of well excavated and well published material from Kent has come from burials. Isobel Thompson's (1982) study of the grog-tempered pottery of south-eastern England showed that the pieces selected for inclusion in burials were not representative of the full range of forms, but also revealed an almost total lack of well excavated domestic assemblages in Kent. The stratigraphic sequence of Periods 4A to 4D at Highstead is therefore an important piece of evidence not only for the range of forms and fabrics in use, but also for the sequence of ceramic change. The earlier part of the sequence does not have any absolute dates or easily datable associations, and there is of course a real possibility of redeposition; nevertheless, the series of assemblages is of great interest. The start date for Period 4C towards the end of the first century B.C. is secure, and the earlier phases seem likely to stretch back for a reasonable period before that. As Peter Couldrey argues, the production of grog-tempered pottery must now most likely be placed well back in the second century, but only the analysis and publication of more well excavated deposits will allow this sequence, and the social and economic changes underlying it, to be fully understood.

Late Bronze Age and earliest Iron Age

The Late Bronze Age phase of the site (Period 2) and the succeeding earliest Iron Age phase (Period 3A) are notable not only for the number of features and the artefactual and industrial evidence they produced, but particularly the number of enclosures, certain or probable, identified within a comparatively small distance of each other. Elsewhere in south-eastern England our evidence consists of isolated enclosures, or in the case of Mucking of two enclosures 1 km. apart. Nowhere else is there evidence of three or more enclosures in such close proximity, and it is unfortunate that the questions raised by this unusual circumstance cannot be answered with any certainty. There is no actual intercutting of enclosures, and no other helpful relationships, so it is impossible to decide on stratigraphic grounds either their relative sequence or which, if any, may have been contemporary. The evidence of artefacts in the middle ditch fills of Enclosure B70 shows that not all the Late Bronze Age activity was of a single phase, and this conclusion is supported by the ceramic sequence. If, as seems likely, the B70 ditch material results from the same phase or episode of activity as the pits in the area outside the enclosure, this may be contemporary with the occupation of some phase of A24 itself, as suggested by the ceramic evidence for a sequence in the occupation of these two enclosures. It also seems likely that the circular enclosure A260 belongs to this phase, though there was only very limited excavation. There are no indications of any sort other than the ceramics to suggest even tentatively a relative date for enclosures A118 and B144, though the little evidence that was recovered suggests that they should be assigned to Period 3A.

In any case, whatever view is taken of the relative sequence of the enclosures, there is an unusual situation to be explained. The enclosures are closely spaced, and cannot be spread over a very long time span either. It is difficult to estimate the life spans of the enclosures: B70 shows no sign of repairs or post replacement, and the absence of observed traces of posts in the post-holes may suggest that it was demolished; A24 was occupied for longer. In the absence of any radiocarbon dates, the only guide to the length of occupation is the pottery, which may all fall within a comparatively short period at the end of the Late Bronze Age. If any of the enclosures are contemporary, it is necessary to explain the social organisation which produced such closely spaced enclosed settlements; if, however, they are all sequential, then the striking difference in shape, form of enclosure and internal layout needs explanation, as well as the comparatively rapid replacement of one enclosure by another. The evidence is important in some way for our understanding of the development of Late Bronze Age settlement, but its true implications may not be understood until we have more information available for comparison.

When attention was first drawn to the existence of enclosures as a distinctive feature of the Late Bronze Age landscape of south-eastern England (Champion 1980; Needham 1992), much emphasis was placed on the characteristically circular plan of the certain examples known at that time, in particular Mucking South Rings (Jones and Bond 1980), Mucking North Ring (Bond 1988) and Mill Hill, Deal (Stebbing 1934). This circular plan has subsequently been confirmed in a reconsideration of the site at Queen Mary's Hospital, Carshalton, Surrey (Adkins and Needham 1985), though this seems to be rather larger than most others, and by new excavations at Springfield Lyons, Essex (Buckley and Hedges 1987) and Hornchurch, Greater London (Guttman and Last 2000). There has also been considerable discussion of possible parallels among sites recorded as cropmarks in air photographs in Essex (Priddy and Buckley 1987, 50–53 and 72; Bond 1988, 53) and more widely in East Anglia (Lawson 1984, 160).

It was also suggested (Champion 1980) that defended enclosures of other shapes might have existed, and the evidence for that assertion needs to be reassessed. The site at Heathrow, excavated in the Second World War, now seems to be a Middle Iron Age enclosure lying on top of a small open settlement of the Late Bronze Age (Grimes and Close-Brooks 1993), but other evidence for rectangular enclosures has been produced: in addition to Highstead B70, there is now also the excavated site of Lofts Farm, Heybridge, Essex (Brown 1988). The irregular enclosure A24 also clearly shows that Late Bronze Age enclosures need not always be of regular geometric plan. This undoubtedly makes the picture of Late Bronze Age settlement more complex. The striking geometric regularity of the circular sites and of the only fully excavated rectangular one at Lofts Farm remains a distinctive feature of the Late Bronze Age, unmatched in domestic settlement plans of other phases, but can no longer be taken as a criterion for distinguishing all enclosures of the period.

Subsequent evcavations in Kent have revealed a wide variety of settlement types in the Late Bronze Age and earliest Iron Age (Champion forthcoming). Unenclosed occupation sites were common, but there was also a wide range of enclosures. No other site comparable to B70 has yet been located, but an oval enclosure very similar to A24 was found in the Ramsgate Harbour approach road excavation (Shand 2001). Much bigger enclosures also existed, such as the subrectangular example at Eddington Farm, Herne Bay (Shand 2002), which may have been comparable to the enigmatic B144. Perhaps the best parallel for Highstead is at Kingsborough Farm, Sheppey (Wessex Archaeology 2002), where excavations have revealed a complex series of Late Bronze Age enclosures, used for both occupation and funerary purposes.

Recent work has also demonstrated that several areas of Kent, especially along the north coast and the Greensand vale, were divided up by field systems constructed in the Middle and Late Bronze Age (Yates 2001; Champion forthcoming). The area excavated at Highstead did not include any features interpreted as field divisions, but the aerial photographic evidence for the wider area around the excavations is of some interest. There is evidence for ditches leading off at right angles from the north-west corner of Enclosure B70, continuing the lines of two of its sides. These have not been investigated and their date is unknown, but the alignment cannot be random. Enclosure B70 may have been the first element in the landscape and may have subsequently served as a focus for the laying out of a system of land division; alternatively, the rectilinear pattern of land division may have been established first, with the enclosure taking its unusual shape from the pre-existing organisation of the landscape.

Enclosure B70

On the basis of the partial excavation and the air photographic evidence, feature B70 was a strongly defended rectangular enclosure, but little information has been recovered concerning its interior. In shape and size it is comparable to the enclosure at Lofts Farm (Brown 1988), though that had two ditches each of rather less substantial proportions. The problems of interpreting the evidence for the precise form of the defences of B70, and in particular the nature of the timber structures, have been discussed above, but in general terms they are similar to Springfield Lyons (Buckley and Hedges 1987). The size of the ditches, the presence of substantial timber revetments (whatever their precise form) and the demarcation of the entrance passage by a double line of timber posts are comparable. The major difference is the location of the timber revetment: at Springfield Lyons the front row of posts is approximately 6 m. inside the inner edge of the ditch, and the timbers are interpreted as the supports for a walkway on the inside of a bank. In the case of B70, however, the gap between ditch and posts is small, and the timbers must represent the front facing of the bank. If the same structures originally extended all round the interior of the ditch as shown on the air photographs, there would have been a massive demand for large structural timbers; unfortunately, we have little evidence for the contemporary environment, and hence cannot tell whether the local gravel terrace would have been able to supply this much wood, or whether it would have had to have been transported from further afield.

It is impossible to say much about the interior of B70 since so little was excavated. It may be noted, however, that the pattern of small pits is well matched on other Late Bronze Age enclosure sites and there seems little reason to doubt that some, at least, of these pits are contemporary with the initial construction and use of the defended enclosure.

One of the most interesting features of B70 was the presence of concentrations of industrial debris and associated artefacts in the ditch fills. It has been argued above that this material was deposited after the defences had begun to collapse, and was derived from industrial activity outside the enclosure itself; the majority of this material is located at or near the top of the first phase of ditch fills. This activity certainly included metalworking, as the presence of the pin moulds shows. There are also quantities of other debris from pyrotechnic processes, such as charcoal, burnt clay and what has been described in this report as copper dross; this may well be a bi-product of metalworking but, as the technical report has shown, an origin in some other fire-using technology cannot be excluded.

It seems reasonable to postulate that all this industrial debris derives from a single phase of activity, and it is thus impossible on stratigraphic grounds to associate the metalworking directly with the primary occupation of B70. The ceramics found with this material would be compatible with a date during the usage of Enclosure A24, though it is impossible to be certain of such an association. But it is also necessary to consider whether there may still be a connection between the industrial activity and Enclosure B70 in the form of the chosen location for an activity area or the deliberate deposition of debris in the ditch. At Springfield Lyons there were no finds of bronze or bronzeworking anywhere in the interior of the site, but two large deposits of bronze casting debris in the terminals of the ditches; these may derive from casting activity carried on outside the enclosure or they may be ritual deposits, perhaps associated with the foundation of the site (Buckley and Hedges 1987, 12). At Petters Sports Field, Egham, Surrey, two hoards of scrap bronze and some other individual bronzes had been deposited at the top of the main filling of a ditch terminal, in a stratigraphic location very similar to that at B70; they may be associated with occupation and activity outside a disused and partially silted up enclosure, but it has also been suggested that their deposition may have been a deliberate marking of a major change in the landscape, immediately prior to the final filling up of the enclosure ditch (O'Connell 1986; Needham 1990). A fragment of a clay mould for casting a bronze ring was found in the ditch at Mill Hill, Deal (Champion 1980, 237 and fig. 5, no. 6), and at another site very near to Highstead, Bogshole Lane (Helm 2003), a small hoard of Late Bronze Age metalwork had been placed in a pit dug into the silted up ditch of an enclosure. These sites show a very clearly structured and meaningful pattern of deposition of material related to metalworking, and there is also evidence for similar treatment of pottery. At Lofts Farm there was a large concentration of pottery and carbonised material, probably derived from a hearth and from some activity such as feasting, deposited in a small section of the outer ditch on the north side of the enclosure; this material was different from the ceramics found elsewhere in the ditches and the interior of the site, and must represent a deliberate deposit at some time after the site had ceased to be occupied (Brown 1988, 269–71).

Though their precise function may now be very difficult to determine, the non-random nature of many Late Bronze Age settlement deposits is becoming increasingly clear. In the present case we are faced with several possibilities: there may be no connection between the industrial activity and the enclosure B70 except spatial coincidence, or there may have been a deliberate association. In the latter case, it is possible that deposits of certain types of material are associated with rituals concerned with the final abandonment of a site and subsequent reorganisation of the landscape, or that abandoned sites were regarded as suitable places for the practice of certain activities or the disposal of certain types of material; if, as the ceramic sequence suggests is possible, the industrial activity outside B70 is contemporary with the occupation of A24, then the choice of a location 300 m. away and next to a disused but still visible enclosure seems unlikely to be mere coincidence.

Enclosure A24

The enclosure A24 was almost totally excavated and represents a further valuable addition to the number of Late Bronze Age enclosures in south-eastern England with complete plans: Mucking South Rings, Mucking North Ring, Springfield Lyons and Lofts Farm are well known, and, as noted above, further sites in Kent, at Ramsgate and on Sheppey, await publication. The bank and ditch structures are very different from those of B70 and closely comparable to those of Mucking North Ring (Bond 1988), in having a comparatively slight ditch and an internal bank with no timber revetment. Many of the known Late Bronze Age enclosures have a continuous ditch and only a single entrance, but the construction of A24 recalls that of Springfield Lyons where the ditch was dug in six segments and there was probably more than one entrance.

The plan of the interior of A24 shows a number of striking characteristics, despite the difficulties of interpretation and the probability of a long occupation with more than one phase of building activity: the concentration of structures at the centre, the presence of a few small pits and no larger ones, large areas of the interior devoid of features, a fence dividing the central structure from the area with no features. These can all be paralleled on other Late Bronze Age sites in the south-east, both individually and as a composite plan.

The central location of what appears to be two phases of the main structure can be well matched at Mucking North Ring period 2 (Bond 1988, fig. 12), Lofts Farm (Brown 1988, fig.8) and Springfield Lyons (Buckley and Hedges 1987, fig. 5). The plans of the individual structures are not particularly easy to reconstruct. They certainly do not conform to one type of well documented Late Bronze Age round-house, characterised by a double ring of post-holes, the inner of which was the main roof support, and with a post diametrically opposite the porch (Guilbert 1982); this is known at Mucking North Ring structure 59 and 152 (Bond 1988, figs 8 and 9) and at Springfield Lyons (Buckley and Hedges 1987, fig. 7). Other types of structure marked by much less distinct, but approximately circular, patterns of post-holes are also known, however, as at Petters Sports Field and Lofts Farm, where the rather oval plan of the post settings for the main building is perhaps the best parallel for the structures in A24.

The interior of A24 contains a number of comparatively shallow pits, seldom more than 0.5 m. in diameter, similar to those known from other Late Bronze Age sites. The strikingly clustered distribution of these pits can also be well matched: Mucking North Ring, Lofts Farm and Springfield Lyons all had concentrations of pits near to the main structures with some areas of the enclosure almost empty. At Mucking North Ring in period 2 a fence was put up dividing the house and pits from an empty area to the south, and a similar scheme has been identified at Lofts Farm, with a fence from the entrance to the house cutting it off from the empty zone to the north. A fence has been recognised in the interior of A24, separating the house and pits from an empty area to the east in a way comparable to the other sites.

The evident similarity of these settlement plans can hardly be coincidence, and this is supported by the pattern of pottery and metalwork deposition recorded from these sites. Of only two bronze objects found in the Late Bronze Age phase, one, the knife blade, had been deposited in the terminal of the ditch of A24 to the right of someone entering what seems to have been the main entrance. This is, of course, precisely the same location as one of the dumps of casting debris at Springfield Lyons. The pottery in A24 is concentrated in the pits near to the main Structure A, and in particular large sherds of finewares; this is a pattern noted at Mucking North Ring (Bond 1988, 34) but not at Lofts Farm (Brown 1988, 271). These patterns of settlement planning, use of space, and of deposition are now recurring themes of the Late Bronze Age sites in the south-east, and point to some important principles of social organisation. Barrett (1989) has suggested that there were significant readjustments of social relationships towards the end of the Bronze Age, in particular focusing on the preparation and serving of food, and these plans may in some way be one physical and spatial manifestation of these changes.

The Late Bronze Age artefacts

Despite the comparatively large area uncovered and the number of structures excavated, the volume of Late Bronze Age material found was small. By far the most plentiful type was pottery, but even so there were few large groups. The pottery has been fully discussed in the specialist report above, and here we need only note that the bulk of the material compares well with collections from other sites which fall into the general category of decorated assemblages, attributed by Barrett (1980) to the later part of the Late Bronze Age; the well finished and often decorated fineware bowls, particularly from the interior of A24, are particularly important.

Objects of bronze were rare, only two being found. The knife blade, as discussed above, may have been a deliberate deposit in the terminal of the ditch of A24, and the bronze ring, found in pieces, may have been old or broken when lost or discarded. Such a pattern seems to be typical of the known Late Bronze Age sites, particularly where extensive excavation gives us confidence in the value of negative evidence; objects of bronze do not seem to have been lost or discarded in any quantity, except for probably ritual deposits, and those objects that were lost are typically small, old or broken. At Springfield Lyons, for instance, no bronze was found (Buckley and Hedges 1987, 5), at Lofts Farm there was a single fragment of a socketed axe blade (Brown 1988, 280), and at Mucking North Ring there were three small fragments, including again a piece of a socketed axe blade (Bond 1988, 21).

The material evidence for industrial activity has also been fully discussed above. The moulds are clear evidence of bronze casting, and the highly vitrified material referred to here as copper dross may also be from metalworking. The considerable quantities of burnt clay and copper dross testify to the extent of pyrotechnic processes on the site. As has already been mentioned, the circular enclosure at Mill Hill, Deal, also produced evidence of bronze casting, in the form of a mould from the ditch fill.

The perforated clay slabs are a type now well known from Late Bronze Age sites in the Thames valley and south-eastern England (Champion 1980, 237–8 and fig. 9; Perkins *et al.* 1994, 311–2) . Other recent finds include Springfield Lyons (Buckley and Hedges 1987, 11), Lofts Farm (Brown 1988, 280), and Mucking North Ring (Bond 1988, 39). These objects are now becoming so frequent on Late Bronze Age sites in the region, but not documented anywhere earlier or later, that they can properly be regarded as a distinctive characteristic of the period. Their function still remains problematic, however; it is even difficult to decide if they are related to some activity or technological process which was only carried out in the Late Bronze Age, or if they are part of a process which was carried out in other ways or with other artefacts in other times. It is remarkable that, despite the growing number of finds, there have been very few large fragments, the slabs having most often been broken into very small pieces. It is clear, nevertheless, that there was considerable variation in the thickness of the slab, and the size and spacing of the holes. There can be far less certainty about the original size of the slabs, but the groove along one side seems to be a common feature; if it was functional, it may have been used to fit two or more slabs together, like tongue-and-groove boards. The slabs appear to have been made of local materials, and do not show any obvious sign of usage. The evidence of association with other artefact types is enigmatic. At Mucking North Ring, a similarity in fabric between the slabs and some items connected with salt production was noted, but no clear association in deposition or spatial distribution was observed in the large excavation outside the enclosure; in the enclosure itself, the majority of slab fragments were found in the ditch fills, with little in the interior, except for one pit which also contained a large quantity of coarseware possibly derived from domestic functions in a nearby house (Bond 1988, 39 and 50). At Highstead, however, the slabs were found associated with the debris of metalworking, particularly in one section of the ditch of Enclosure B70 and the neighbouring pits. This is the clearest pattern of association yet observed, but it still remains uncertain if the slabs had a specifically industrial function, and more careful analysis and interpretation of well excavated sites is needed to pursue this question.

The artefacts associated with weaving are also of types now well known on Late Bronze Age sites in the south-east. The biconical spindlewhorl is typical of the Late Bronze Age (e.g. Mucking North Ring: Bond 1988, fig. 26, 2), as also is the pyramidal loomweight (e.g. Mucking North Ring: Bond 1988, fig. 26, 7–10). The disc-shaped perforated sherds of broken pottery can also be paralleled on Late Bronze Age sites (e.g. Petters Sports Field: O'Connell 1986, fig. 40, 1–5) and these also may be spindlewhorls.

Though the artefact collection from Highstead is not enormous, it is the first modern excavated assemblage from the county and extends our knowledge of the regional Late Bronze Age material culture. As has been described, it has good parallels with other sites in Essex and Surrey, and many of these types are both distinctive and limited to the Late Bronze Age. The characteristic pottery and highly vitrified clay, together with the rarer items such as perforated slabs, loomweights and spindlewhorls, now constitute such a well authenticated and frequently recurring assemblage that they can be confidently used to assign other sites to this period, even on surface evidence alone.

The Late Bronze Age economy

The absence of faunal or botanical remains from the site makes it impossible to discuss the subsistence economy or the environment of the site. The only possible evidence for the production or processing of crops is the single rubbing stone with wear abrasion, perhaps from use on a saddle quern, though its function is far from certain. The presence of livestock is suggested by the spindlewhorls and loomweights. A striking feature of Enclosure A24 is the area devoid of pits or other structures, which for at least part of the life of the site was demarcated by a fence; it is possible that this may have been for penning livestock. There are numerous post-holes in the interiors of B70 and A24 which cannot easily be reconstituted as buildings, though one possible drying rack has been suggested for B70; this structure and others represented by the post-holes may have had a variety of functions in the agricultural economy, but other uses are equally likely.

There is nothing to suggest that the pottery was made from other than local materials, but the raw materials for the bronze casting, as well as the polishing stone and the rubbing stone, must have been acquired from further afield. There are, however, no parallels to the exotic finds from some other sites such as the gold rings from Mucking North Ring (Bond 1988, 21) or the amber bead from Lofts Farm (Brown 1988, 281).

The evidence for industrial activity comes from two locations. It seems highly likely that the vitrified material from the group of features on the north side of the interior of A24 derived from metalworking, and the assemblage in the ditch of B70 and neighbouring pits certainly did originate in bronze casting. If, as has been suggested, this casting episode is contemporary with the occupation of A24, then it was deliberately located at a considerable distance from the main residential area, even though other similar activities were being carried on inside the enclosure. Other Late Bronze Age enclosures have also produced evidence for bronze casting: at Springfield Lyons there were the dumps of casting waste in the ditches, at Petters Sports Field the hoards of scrap bronze, and at Mucking North Ring mould fragments, a crucible fragment and a drop of bronze metal from the casting operation. These finds all suggest a close connection between the enclosures and bronze casting, but the relationship is ambivalent. With the possible exception of A24, it is impossible to show that the metalworking activity took place inside the enclosures, and in some cases it certainly took place outside. We cannot assume that the casting operations and the deposition of the resultant debris were closely linked in space, and the relationship of both practices to enclosures, either in use or disused, needs further investigation.

The location of the Highstead enclosures overlooking what was then the open and navigable channel of the Wantsum is also significant. The coastline around the Wantsum shows a remarkable concentration of Late Bronze Age hoard deposits (Champion 1982, fig. 14), and a clustering of hoards has also been observed near to the enclosure at Springfield Lyons in Essex (Buckley *et al.* 1986). The enclosures may well have played a role in the general pattern of supply and usage of bronze, but it is not clear what role. It may have been an economic one, exercising control over supply, distribution or scrapping and recycling, or it may have been a more complex one associated with the rituals of deposition.

The activities for which we have evidence are somewhat limited and rather mundane, though the quantities of fineware pottery and the bronze casting may be indicative of something more significant. The construction of the enclosures, and especially B70 with its massive timbering, demonstrates the ability to organise labour and materials. Unfortunately, we cannot really place such enclosed settlements in their appropriate social context since we have so little evidence for other contemporary sites. The enclosures have attracted attention by their visibility on air photographs, and our knowledge of other types of site, especially unenclosed settlements, is still inadequate, despite much further archaeological activity since Highstead was excavated.

Early Iron Age

Many of the features of the Early Iron Age phase of occupation can be readily compared to sites elsewhere in southern England, but it is very difficult to find parallels for them in Kent. In fact, Highstead is the one of the first extensive areas of Early Iron Age occupation to be published in the county, and there is little material of any sort for comparison.

The occupation in this phase is an open settlement of a type now being increasingly documented in eastern England, where enclosures are not at all common before the Middle Iron Age; this pattern has been recognised in Essex (Drury 1980; Priddy and Buckley 1987) and the Nene and Ouse valleys (Knight 1984, 210; Pryor 1984, 230–40). Where Early Iron Age sites have been discovered (e.g. in Essex: Drury 1980, fig. 19), they are typically open settlements, with comparatively slight structural traces. It is their very nature that has prevented them being located by air photography or any means of archaeological survey except extensive excavation.

The structures

There are a number of distinct types of structure, including several different traditions for the construction of buildings as well as the pits.

The penannular gullies are the remains of circular structures, though occasionally on some sites they have been interpreted as the surrounds for other activities such as storage of hay or fodder. The gullies were primarily for drainage, rather than structural foundations, and the absence of any recoverable traces of the actual structure inside the gully is not uncommon. Such features are well known elsewhere in southern England, e.g. in the upper Thames valley (Allen *et al.* 1984) and the Nene and Ouse valleys (Knight 1984, 137–43), but examples are difficult to find in Kent. The only close parallel is a site excavated at a site a short distance to the west of Highstead, at Underdown Lane, Eddington (Jarman 2005), where a similar cluster of penannular ditches was found. The most common orientation for the entrance is to the east or south-east, a pattern followed by those at Highstead.

There are two examples, B196 and B329, of the small rectangular structures, usually of four or six posts but occasionally of five, now well known from many Iron Age sites. Their functions may have varied (Ellison and Drewett 1971), but it is now accepted that many were for above-ground storage of grain (Gent 1983). It is again surprising how difficult it is to find published parallels in Kent for such a common Iron Age type; a cluster of post-holes on Barham Downs represents one or more such buildings, possibly one six-post structure with some rebuilding or possibly two with four posts each (Macpherson-Grant 1980, 135 and fig. 3).

On the other hand, the larger rectangular post settings, B29 and B111, represent a building tradition that is much rarer anywhere in England. Rodwell (1978) has suggested that rectangular buildings became common in the final period of the Iron Age in south-eastern England, but there are very few earlier examples. Two buildings with rather irregular plans of post-holes have been reported, at Little Waltham, Essex, from the Middle Iron Age (building R4: Drury 1978, 25 and fig. 19) and from Wollaston, Northamptonshire, probably of Late Bronze Age or Early Iron Age date (Knight 1984, 155). The Highstead structures fall much better into a class of rectangular buildings known in northern France (Villes 1981, figs 20–21) and more widely in western Europe (Audouze and Büchsenschütz 1991, fig. 30b, 21–7) and should surely be related to this cross-Channel tradition rather than to any indigenous practice.

The exotic nature of the small rectangular multi-post structure B200 is even more marked. It has been assigned to this phase on the grounds of location, orientation and the small amount of associated material, but both its plan and its structural technique set it apart from other buildings in England, and again it is necessary to look across the Channel for possible parallels. The method of wall construction using two rows of small posts to retain the main wall fabric is known sporadically from northern France to northern Germany from the Middle Bronze Age onwards (Audouze and Büchsenschütz 1991, 80–82). One of the best known examples is the Early La Tène house from Chassemy, Aisne, France (Boureux et al. 1969). There does not appear to be any exact parallel for the combination of this building technique with the small rectangular plan of B200, though the plan itself would fall within the general range known in northern France (Villes 1981). The distinctive treatment of the single doorway of B200, however, with its double line of posts and single central post, seems to be unique. One interesting structure from northern France of approximately the same size and wall technique is the second phase temple from Gournay-sur-Aronde (Brunaux et al. 1985, fig. 65), but this had a very different treatment of one wall, with a probably open facade rather than a wall with doorway. Despite the uncertainties of its stratigraphic relationships and the lack of parallels in Britain, there seems little doubt on the basis of these examples from across the Channel that B200 represents yet another significant indicator of the degree of continental influence in east Kent in the Iron Age.

The pits of this phase are on average substantially larger than those of the Late Bronze Age, though not as large as those known from sites on different subsoils such as chalk. The suitability of different subsoils for the storage of different commodities may well have affected the functions of the pits and hence the size and shape of pits dug. The evidence for the variety of pit functions has been discussed above. Some were dug in relation to industrial activities such as potting, metalworking and salt-making, and a group of such pits were surrounded by a small gully to form a separately defined activity area, B189. Other pits were more likely to have been for the storage of organic material and food stuffs, especially those lined with an impermeable clay layer. All of these pit types and functions fall within the known range of Iron Age pit usage, especially on gravel subsoils (e.g. Knight 1984, 100–17).

The economy

Because of the poor rate of survival and recovery of organic remains, it is again impossible to say anything about the environment or agricultural economy of the Early Iron Age occupation. The site has also produced a disappointingly poor record of artefacts other than pottery. Nevertheless, some inferences can be drawn about the nature of the activities on the site.

One industry certainly represented is metalworking. Quantities of copper dross were found in contexts of this phase, though it is impossible to be certain that they were not residual from the Late Bronze Age activity. The same is also true of the crucible fragment, though it is of a type more likely to be of Iron Age than of Bronze Age date. The technical report on the dross confirms that some of this may have been derived from iron smelting, and the presence of iron slag also suggests that at least some phases of iron production were being carried out.

Salt production was also being practised, and the use of shallow rectangular vessels agrees with the evidence that exists for salt-making in the first millennium B.C. in south-eastern England, though this so far mostly comes from Essex (Barford 1990). Other evidence for salt production in Kent has now been recognised, as discussed above, and it is clear that this was an important local industry from the Late Bronze Age onwards, though its extent and the precise details of the technology employed remain to be explored.

There is no definite evidence for potting, though pots were probably fired in clamps or bonfires at this time rather than in kilns, but the storage of clay in a pit suggests this as a possibility. The pottery found on the site appears to be of local manufacture, but marks a significant break in the ceramic tradition.

The continental connection

As has been discussed above, the forms, technology and surface finish of much of the pottery, particularly the pots with a 'rusticated' surface, show a close similarity to contemporary ceramic traditions across the Channel, and this tradition can now be recognised as a distinctive and diagnostic feature of Early Iron Age sites in east Kent. This phase of ceramic innovation should also be compared to the evidence discussed above for the similarity in architecture and building techniques of some of the Highstead structures to those across the Channel.

This is a very important addition to our knowledge not only of the cultural sequence of east Kent, but also of the inter-relationship of south-eastern England and the Continent (Champion 1975). The Channel was seldom a barrier to the transmission of ideas and innovations, but the nature of these contacts varies considerably from region to region. The decorated metalwork in eastern England shows one form of cultural adoption with the imitation of continental La Tène styles (Stead 1984), while in east Yorkshire a version of the contemporary La Tène burial tradition was practised (Stead 1979). These items related to prestige or ritual show connections to very widespread European La Tène traditions, but the affiliations of the more utilitarian or domestic items are much more localised. The similarities of pottery discussed above relate the ceramics of east Kent to those of northern France. The distribution of Early Iron Age triangular clay loomweights (Champion 1975, fig. 2) is matched by examples in north-western Europe (Wilhelmi 1977; 1987) and bone combs (Tuohy 1992) are also found on the Continent. The persistent similarities of material culture on either side of the southern North Sea and English Channel throughout later prehistory clearly demonstrate a level of contact and communication that operated at the level of everyday utilitarian items as well as those with obvious prestige or symbolic value.

Clearly there are different types of social process and interaction at work, and we should not explain all such continental contacts in the same manner. The rather sudden introduction of such new techniques of pottery and architecture might be thought to indicate the arrival of a new element in the population, but we really need to know more about the production and use of such material items as pots and living spaces before that conclusion can be accepted. It is perhaps more likely that voyages across the sea were a normal part of social activity, and that social, economic and political networks tied east Kent more closely to their neighbours across the Channel than to those inland.

Late Iron Age and Roman periods

There is a period of several centuries in the Middle Iron Age when evidence for settlement is slight. Then, perhaps in the late second century B.C., the northern part of the area was reoccupied and continued to be the focus of settlement through most of the Roman period. The developing contacts with the Roman world, and finally the conquest by Rome, had significant effects on the economy of the site, particularly visible in the supply of pottery, but the basic function of the site and the organisation of the area around it continued with many minor modifications but largely unchanged in its broad structure. The evidence from these periods is important for the history of regional settlement; comparatively few Late Iron Age occupation sites have been explored in detail, and even in the Roman period, where settlement evidence is much more plentiful, there have been few investigations of landscape organisation and of sites without major buildings.

The enclosures and fields

The northern end of the excavated area persisted as the major location of settlement, with a series of enclosures. Further south still the land was later given over to organized field systems. No actual buildings were located, with the exception of two post-built structures, B159 and B262, both outside the enclosures and probably having an ancillary agricultural role. To judge by the quantities of domestic refuse in the enclosure ditches, the enclosures must have been near to areas of human occupation, and the excavation failed to locate the relevant structures. It is possible that they lay in those parts of the enclosures not examined, or that they were built in a technique which has left no visible traces, perhaps using sole plates rather than earth-fast posts; it is also possible that the enclosures were not actually for occupation, but played some other role in the organisation of the local community. If so, the actual focus of occupation must have been outside the excavated area. At the end of the site's life, the hypocausted bath-house in Area C suggests the close proximity of a house in that location. The only other possible evidence for a structure is the discovery of tile fragments at the southern end of the site, possibly suggesting the existence of a building somewhere in that region.

Elsewhere in Kent, occupation sites of the Late Iron Age are still surprisingly rare. A settlement enclosure has been excavated at Thurnham (Booth *et al.* forthcoming), where an Iron Age site preceded the Roman villa; this consisted of round-house, gullies and four-post structures in a rectangular enclosure. At the Kent International Business Park (Perkins 1998) and on the Whitfield-Eastry by-pass (Parfitt *et al.* 1997) two more rectangular enclosures were excavated, though with less structural evidence. The latter two sites are approximately twice the size of the small enclosure B139. There are no obvious parallels for the polygonal enclosure, B3, though a variety of enclosures and enclosure complexes are now known in Kent. Enclosure complexes are known, for example, at Hillside, Gravesend (Philp and Chenery 1997), Charing Sand Pit (Keller 1990), and Glebelands, Harrietsham (Jarman 2002).

The area to the south of the enclosures developed as one of organised field systems. The first north–south pattern is only patchily recorded, but there is better evidence for the system that soon replaced it on the north-east/south-west axis that structured the usage of the whole region. Though many other areas of south-eastern England show evidence of renewed enclosure activity at this period, evidence for Late Iron Age fields elsewhere in Kent is not common; fragments of rectangular enclosures dating to the Late Iron Age were discovered at Faversham (Philp 1968), which may have been part of a similar system. It is possible, therefore, that the economic and social developments behind the construction of the field systems at Highstead were part of a process affecting a much wider area of England. That process may well have been agricultural intensification, demanding more productive use of available land and a better integration of arable and pastoral activities.

Period 5 at Highstead also produced formal burials, with three inhumations, one of which cut an earlier cremation. The location of a dedicated cemetery area in an organized settlement landscape is known at other sites of this period; burials were located away from the main settlement area within an enclosure in the fields at Owlesbury, Hampshire (Collis 1968), while at Mucking (Jones and Jones 1975, 147) a row of burials was also found placed along the line of a Late Iron Age field boundary. There is a long-lasting tradition of inhumation in east Kent which continued alongside the more common cremation; as at this site, the two rites are sometimes found in the same cemetery. Both forms of burial were used at Mill Hill, Deal (Parfitt 1995), and the poorly recorded cemetery at another site called Highsted, near Sittingbourne (Vale 1987, 368), and for a small group of burials inserted into the ditch of the Neolithic long barrow at Julliberrie's Grave, Chilham (Jessup 1937; 1939).

The economy

The survival of organic material was better from this phase than for the earlier ones, and the animal bones add some information to our inferences from the form of the enclosures. The presence of droveways within the field systems and the regular provision made for access to the enclosures may suggest an important role for livestock in the farming economy, but there is no indication that the site represented anything other than a normal farm for the region. Other activities which may be inferred include textile production and possibly metalworking.

The pottery is a useful indicator of the external contacts of the site, and the changing nature of the economy into which it was integrated. The ceramic assemblages are closely comparable to those from Canterbury, and the site was progressively linked more closely to the town. In the pre-conquest period its access to imported finewares and amphorae was probably due to its proximity to the Iron Age predecessor of the town. After the conquest, Canterbury became the main source of its coarse pottery as large-scale pottery industries and accompanying markets developed.

The development of the landscape

It is unfortunate, though understandable in the circumstances of the excavation, that no environmental evidence was recovered from the site to complement the structural features discovered, and also that no features earlier than the Late Bronze Age were excavated, though the site had clearly been occupied earlier, as shown by the flintwork. As it is, the excavation is the largest sample of the prehistoric landscape of Kent to have been studied in detail, but the information available is restricted. The results are important, however, not just for the history of human occupation in the Highstead region, but for their wider implications for Kent. Considerable effort has been devoted in recent years to the study of the air photographic evidence for east Kent (*see* Edis *et al.* 1989 for a discussion of the problems of classification). The results obtainable from this method can be dramatic, but understanding is limited by the extent to which it is possible to assign reliable functional and chronological interpretations to particular forms of site recognized through aerial photography. There has been no systematic attempt to investigate cropmark sites, and only a restricted number of excavated sites which can serve as a basis for interpretation. In Essex, Priddy and Buckley (1987) have suggested a classification of excavated enclosures in Essex as a first attempt at an interpretation of cropmark enclosure sites there. The excavation evidence from Kent is much less than that from Essex, so the results of the Highstead work are particularly important in this respect.

The earliest features identified were the ring ditches of probable Early Bronze Age barrows surviving as cropmarks. This seems to confirm the general picture from east Kent that, both on the gravels and on the chalk downs, such barrows rarely survive as upstanding monuments (Grinsell 1992). It is unfortunate that the intersection of one such ring ditch with the probable Late Bronze Age Enclosure A118 was not observed and confirmed before being quarried away. If this identification is correct, it strongly suggests that the round barrow was already of slight significance or even totally destroyed by the Late Bronze Age; similar evidence for the very early destruction of Bronze Age barrows has already been suggested from Thanet (Champion 1980, 226).

The agency of such destruction was presumably agriculture in the middle and later parts of the Bronze Age, but such activity has left no positive evidence. No trace was found in the excavated area of a field system of that period. The only possible sign of any such extensive organisation of the landscape was the cropmark evidence for ditches running off at right angles from the northern corners of the Late Bronze Age Enclosure B70, although these were not excavated and the relationship remains obscure. It is possible, however, that the substantial structure of Enclosure B70 was carefully located at what was already a significant node in land divisions, or alternatively that it in turn came to be recognised as such a significant location, either during the Late Bronze Age or at some later stage while it was still visible. In any case, its location would be unlike that of any of the other Late Bronze Age enclosures in the area. Whatever the true chronology of the enclosure and conjoined ditches, the association at Highstead should alert us to the possibility of extensive Bronze Age land divisions. It is interesting to note, therefore, that, despite the recent recognition of Bronze Age enclosures and field systems (Yates 2001), no such features have been identified from aerial photographs rather than excavation. Further examination of the photographic record would be worthwhile, especially for those areas such as the chalk downlands where response to aerial photography is good but recent archaeological investigation has been limited by the scarcity of development sites.

For the Late Bronze Age and the earliest Iron Age, the most obviously relevant conclusions concern the identification of enclosed settlement, though little can said about three of the five enclosures, and the consequent implications for the dating of cropmark enclosures. With the exception of B70, none of the enclosures shows any obvious relationship to any system of land division and the nature of the landscape in which they sat is unknown. Two enclosures of very different shape have been clearly dated to the Late Bronze Age, one roughly rectangular with rounded corners and dimensions between 40 m. and 50 m., the other of irregular subcircular or oval form with a maximum diameter approaching 50 m. This does not mean that all enclosures of such size and shape should belong to the Late Bronze Age, but it does offer a strong basis for inference, especially given the subsequent discovery of a site of similar size, shape and date on the Ramsgate Harbour approach road. Such oval enclosures had not been identified as a significant and recurring type before, and there is no conflicting evidence to suggest an alternative date. It is now impossible, however, to maintain the traditional expectation that the rectangular enclosures should belong to the Late Iron Age or Early Roman period; the Lofts Farm enclosure, for example, was thought before excavation to be of that later date (Brown 1988, 249).

The evidence for the Early Iron Age suggests that settlement was unenclosed. The physical evidence for structures and other features is comparatively slight and it was only the large scale of open-area stripping that allowed the nature of occupation to be recognised. The Period 3B occupation was certainly structured in its use of space, with areas devoted to houses and industrial activities; this may have been constrained by other larger-scale patterns of land use, but, if so, these have not left surviving traces. Though the value of negative evidence is limited until more has been accumulated, the absence of any enclosures than could be dated to the early phase of the Iron Age may well be significant, especially since it conforms to a wider pattern in eastern England. There is little likelihood that occupation of this sort would show up in aerial photography, and it remains unclear what, if any, cropmark sites in the wider landscape should be attributed to the Early Iron Age. If that is borne out in further work, then it may be difficult to locate sites of that date by air photography.

After a hiatus in the Middle Iron Age, during which settlement may have been present in the region but left little trace in the excavation area, a new phase of occupation was initiated in the Late Iron Age which continued until well into the Roman period. This was charcterised by renewed construction of enclosures and field systems with trackways; the pattern of two phases of land division, one in the Middle or Late Bronze Age and one in the Late Iron Age or Early Roman period, is one that is being documented at many other sites in Kent. The main focus for this settlement was a series of enclosures at the north end of the excavation, partially overlying the Late Bronze Age enclosure B70. This relationship may be purely coincidental, or it may be that the topography of the site or even the continued knowledge of the existence of B70 led to this location being favoured for renewed settlement. In any case, the pattern established in the Late Iron Age, with the main residential area at the north and the fields and working areas to the south, was maintained throughout the use of this zone.

The two enclosures, B1 and B3, show that irregular quadrilateral or polygonal features could belong to the later Iron Age or Early Roman period. It is unfortunate that the full extent and plan of the slightly earlier enclosure, B139, could not be determined, but it too looks like an irregular quadrilateral. These were accompanied in the first and second centuries A.D. by the layout of successive field systems. Though the area between Areas A and B was not examined before quarrying, this orientation seems to have been continuous across both sites, suggesting a considerable scale of active landscape management.

Conclusions

Despite the problems of excavation and the uncertainties of interpretation that have been alluded to in this report, the results have been of enormous value for our understanding of the later prehistory of Kent as well as for regions further afield. The evidence for the later part of the Iron Age and the Roman period is predominantly of local or regional interest, but that from the earlier phases will not only have a cumulative effect in promoting our knowledge of hitherto under-researched periods of the archaeology of Kent, but also has a much wider significance.

In the Late Bronze Age, we now have another site with well documented evidence for metalworking, structured deposition, and organised site planning. These Late Bronze Age enclosures are turning out to be some of the most distinctive settlements in British prehistory, as well as some of the most curious, and we need to understand them alongside the more plentiful, but equally structured, deposits of bronze. The Highstead sites are therefore a significant contribution to our knowledge of the Late Bronze Age in south-eastern England.

The most important result from the Early Iron Age is the clear demonstration of the influence of continental traditions in east Kent, as seen in the pottery and the architecture of this phase. This episode will have a profound effect on the way we have to envisage the relationship between south-eastern England and the Continent in the Iron Age.

On the more local level, the value of the results from Highstead will only be fully realised when we have more examples of similarly extensive excavations in east Kent for comparison.

SUMMARY

Excavations carried out between 1975 and 1977 prior to gravel quarrying to the east of Highstead revealed evidence for settlement on the plateau between *c.* 900 and 400 B.C. and again between *c.* 100 B.C. and A.D. 250. In this report the excavated evidence has been supplemented with that from aerial photographs, setting the site firmly within the broader landscape.

Surface collection and chance discoveries have indicated human presence in the area since Palaeolithic times. Worked stone artefacts recovered from the excavated area indicate sporadic occupation from the Mesolithic to late Neolithic (Period 1), though no excavated features can certainly be attributed to this period.

Evidence for settled occupation dates from the Late Bronze Age to Early Iron Age, *c.* 900–600 B.C. (Period 2), when three enclosures were constructed. At the northern end of the site, excavation recovered the causeway and ditch terminals of one (B70) with post-holes representing a substantial revetment and entrance way. Occupation of the interior was attested by pits and post-holes. Contemporary pits were found outside the enclosure, close to the entrance. These features produced pottery and evidence of metalworking including moulds for bronze pins.

A second enclosure was identified from air photographs and a soil stain, while a third (A24) was excavated in its entirety. The latter had four entrance causeways and was occupied over an extended period with evidence for more than one central structure, intercutting pits and hearths, and the blocking of at least one of the entrances. A fence line provided a clear demarcation of activity areas. Artefacts included pottery, metalwork, loomweights and vitrified clay, possibly indicative of metalworking.

The pottery from this period provides the main dating evidence and shows links with other sites in the lower Thames valley and across the Channel in northern France and Belgium.

Between *c.* 600 and 500 B.C. (Period 3A) a fourth enclosure (A118) may have been used and occupation continued within Enclosure B70. Between *c.* 500 and 400 B.C. (Period 3B) activity centred on an open settlement. Circular, square and rectangular buildings were present. One subrectangular structure (B200), unique on the site and possibly of this period, comprised over ninety small post-holes, reflecting continental influence in its architecture. Hearths, gullies and pits associated with domestic settlement and food storage also produced evidence for metalworking, salt processing and pottery production.

Again, dating evidence was provided by the pottery which continued to show continental influence, including attributes which are rarely found outside east Kent, perhaps suggesting stronger continental ties.

After *c.* 400 B.C. the site was abandoned until *c.* 100 B.C. when a series of fields and enclosures was laid out on a new alignment (Periods 4 and 5). These were modified several times and the area remained in use until the mid third century A.D. In the second century A.D. a hypocausted building was constructed but appears to have fallen out of use by *c.* A.D. 250. Stray finds suggest that activity in the area continued into the fourth century, but no features contained material of this date.

Résumé

Les travaux de déblaiement effectués de 1975 à 1977 préalablement à l'exploitation d'une carrière de gravier a mis à jour des traces d'occupation pendant deux périodes allant approximativement de 900 à 400 av. J.-C. et de 100 av. J.-C. jusqu'à 250 apr. J.-C sur le plateau à l'est de Highstead. Ce rapport est complété par la photographie aérienne, qui intègre le site dans l'environnement local.

Des collectes en surface et des trouvailles fortuites prouvent une présence humaine depuis l'époque paléolithique. Des objets en pierre trouvés dans la zone de déblaiement indiquent une occupation sporadique du Mésolithique à la fin du Néolithique (Période 1), bien qu'aucune des traces mises à jour ne puisse être attribuée avec certitude à cette période.

Les traces d'occupation datent de la fin de l'Âge de bronze au début de l'Âge de fer, vers 900–600 av. J.-C. (Période 2), époque à laquelle trois enceintes ont été construites. Dans la section nord du site, le déblaiement a découvert une voie et des fins de tranchées, où (B70) des trous de poteaux indiquent la présence d'un flanquement important et d'une entrée. L'occupation intérieure est attestée par des fonds de cabanes et des trous de poteaux. Des fonds de cabanes contemporains ont été trouvés à l'extérieur de l'enceinte, à proximité de l'entrée. Ils ont produit de la poterie et des traces de travail du métal, incluant des moules pour la fabrication de broches en bronze.

Une deuxième enceinte a été identifiée par la photographie aérienne et par une coloration différente du sol, alors qu'une troisième enceinte (A24) a été déblayée dans sa totalité. Celle-ci contenait quatre voies d'accès et a été occupée pendant une période prolongée. Les traces indiquent la présence de plus d'une structure centrale, se superposant à des fonds de cabanes et des foyers, avec le blocage d'au moins une des entrées. Une ligne de clôture établit une démarcation claire entre les zones d'activité. Les trouvailles témoignent d'activités de poterie et de métallurgie, incluant des contre-poids pour le tissage et de l'argile vitrifiée, indication possible du travail du métal.

La poterie de cette période est la principale source de datation, démontrant des liens avec d'autres sites de la vallée inférieure de la Tamise, ainsi que dans le Nord de la France et en Belgique.

Entre 600 et 500 av. J.-C. (Période 3A) une quatrième enceinte (A118) a pu être utilisée et l'enceinte B70 a continué d'être occupée. La période 500 et 400 av. J.-C. (Période 3B) se caractérise par un habitat sans enceinte. Des constructions circulaires, carrées et rectangulaires sont présentes. Une structure subrectangulaire (B200), unique sur ce site et probablement pour cette période, réunit plus de 90 trous de poteaux, suggérant une influence architecturale continentale. Des foyers, des rigoles et des fonds de cabanes témoignent de la vie domestique et du stockage des aliments. Ils ont produit des traces de travail du métal, de préparation du sel et de fabrication de poterie.

La poterie reste la base principale de la datation et elle continue de présenter une influence continentale, incluant des caractéristiques rarement vues ailleurs que dans la région est du Kent, suggérant peut-être des liens plus forts avec le continent.

À partir de 400 av. J.-C., le site est resté abandonné jusque vers 100 av. J.-C. époque à laquelle plusieurs champs et enceintes ont été créés sur un alignement différent (Périodes 4 et 5). Ils ont été modifiés plusieurs fois et le site est resté occupé jusqu'à la moitié du troisième siècle apr. J.-C. Pendant le deuxième siècle de notre ère, un bâtiment avec hypocauste a été construit, mais il semblerait qu'il ait été abandonné vers 250 apr. J.-C. Des trouvailles hors contexte suggèrent que le site a été utilisé jusqu'au quatrième siècle, mais les traces d'habitat n'ont pas produit de matériel de cette période.

Zusammenfassung

Ausgrabungen östlich von Highstead in den Jahren 1975 bis 1977 und vor den Kiesgrubearbeiten lieferten Zeugnisse einer Besiedlung der Hochebene in den Jahren zwischen ca. 900 und 400 v. Ch. und dann wieder zwischen ca. 100 v. Chr. und 250 n. Chr. In diesem Bericht wurden die Ausgrabungszeugnisse ergänzt durch Luftaufnahmen, welche den Standort klar in der weiteren Landschaft positionieren.

Oberflächenfunde und Zufallsentdeckungen haben auf eine Anwesenheit von Menschen in dem Raum seit der Steinzeit hingewiesen. Steinartefakte aus Ausgrabungsgebieten weisen auf eine sporadische Besiedlung vom Mesolithikum bis zum späten Neolithikum (Periode 1) hin, wenn auch keine Grabungsfunde mit Sicherheit diesem Zeitraum zugeordnet werden können.

Zeugnisse einer Besiedlung reichen vom späten Bronzezeitalter bis zum frühen Eisenzeitalter ca. 900–600 v. Chr. (Periode 2), als drei Einfriedungen errichtet wurden. Am nördlichen Ende des Standorts bargen Ausgrabungen Damm und Grabenenden einer Einfriedung (B70) mit Pfostenlöchern, die eine Futtermauer und einen Eingang von beachtlicher Größe darstellen. Die Bewohnung des Inneren ist durch Gruben und Pfostenlöcher belegt. Grubenanlagen der gleichen Zeit wurden außerhalb der Einfriedung in der Nähe des Eingangs gefunden. Diese Objekte brachten Töpferwaren und Zeugnisse von Metallverarbeitung hervor, einschließlich Formen für Bronzenadeln.

Eine zweite Einfriedung wurde anhand von Luftaufnahmen und einer Bodenverfärbung identifiziert, während eine dritte (A24) in ihrer Gesamtheit offengelegt wurde. Letztere hatte vier Eingangsdämme und wurde über einen ausgedehnten Zeitraum bewohnt, wobei Hinweise auf mehr als eine zentrale Struktur, Verbindungsgruben und Feuerstellen und die Blockierung von zumindest einem der Eingänge vorliegen. Eine Zaunlinie bot eine eindeutige Abgrenzung von Aktivitätsbereichen. Zu den Artefakten zählten Töpferwaren, Metallarbeiten, Webstuhlgewichte und glasierter Ton, der möglicherweise auf Metallverarbeitung hinweist.

Die Töpferwaren aus diesem Zeitraum bieten die wichtigsten Datierungshinweise und zeigen Verbindungen zu anderen Standorten im unteren Themsetal und jenseits des Ärmelkanals in Nordfrankreich und Belgien.

Zwischen ca. 600 und 500 v. Chr. (Periode 3A) wurde möglicherweise eine vierte Einfriedung (A118) genutzt, während Einfriedung B70 weiter bewohnt blieb. Zwischen ca. 500 und 400 v. Chr. (Periode 3B) lag der Schwerpunkt der Aktivitäten bei einer offenen Siedlung. Vorhanden waren runde, quadratische und rechteckige Gebäude. Eine subrectangulare Struktur (B200), die auf dem Standort und möglicherweise für diesen Zeitraum einzigartig ist, bestand aus mehr als neunzig kleinen Pfostenlöchern, worin sich ein kontinentaler Einfluss bei ihrer Architektur reflektiert. Feuerstellen, Abwasserkanäle und Gruben mit häuslicher Besiedlung und Lagerung von Lebensmitteln lieferten auch Hinweise auf Metallbearbeitung, Salzverarbeitung und Herstellung von Keramik.

Auch hier stammen die Datierungshinweise von den Keramikprodukten mit weiterhin kontinentalem Einfluss, darunter Merkmale, die sich selten außerhalb des östlichen Kent finden und vielleicht auf stärkere kontinentale Verbindungen hindeuten.

Nach ca. 400 v. Chr. wurde der Standort bis ca. 100 v. Chr. verlassen, als eine Reihe von Feldern und Einfriedungen nach neuer Ausrichtung angelegt wurden (Perioden 4 und 5). Diese wurden mehrmals modifiziert und das Gebiet blieb bis zur Mitte des dritten Jahrhunderts n. Chr. in Gebrauch. Im zweiten Jahrhundert n. Chr. wurde ein Gebäude mit Hypokaustum errichtet, das jedoch ca. 250 n. Chr. nicht mehr genutzt wurde. Verstreute Funde legen nahe, dass die Aktivität in dem Gebiet bis ins vierte Jahrhundert andauerte. Keines der Objekte enthielt jedoch Material aus diesem Zeitraum.

APPENDIX I

The Beaker pottery

Alex Gibson [23]

The Beaker presence at Highstead is not a great one. Two vessels from the Chislet quarry nearby are included in Clarke's corpus (Nos 393 and 394: Clarke 1970) while a fragment from a third vessel is reported here. The two earlier finds belong to Clarke's European group. They are both rather squat vessels with bell-shaped profiles and low belly carinations, which characterise the group. One vessel (393) has comb-zoned decoration comprising a zone of cross-hatching near the rim (Clarke's motif No. 4), a zone of open lozenge decoration in the neck (Clarke's motif No. 31) and a similarly decorated zone on the belly. Two encircling lines of comb impressions occur near the base of the vessel. The second vessel (394) is decorated all over with encircling lines of comb impressions emphasising the closeness of Clarke's European and All-Over-Combed groups.

The third vessel, found during the 1976 excavations (residual, Pit complex B15, Area B) is represented by a single sherd in a well-made orange-coloured fabric; fine fairly sparse rounded sand inclusions break both surfaces, but lie flush with them and do not detract from the general fineness of the fabric. No other inclusions appear to be present and the sherd averages 8–9 mm. in thickness, with abraded edges. Though the fabric of the sherd would not be out of place within a Beaker assemblage, it is its decoration which provides the only real clue as to its dating. This comprises two (possibly) horizontal rows of small triangular-shaped stabs which suggest a date in the early to mid second millennium (in radiocarbon years B.C.). This decorative motif and technique occur within Beaker and Early Bronze Age assemblages. The latter can be paralleled at Holywell Coombe near Folkestone (Gibson 1998, fig. 6.7, no. 14, 297–8), and on a fingernail-rusticated vessel from Bury St Edmunds (Clarke 1970, No. 1046). Parallels may also be found on vessels from Shoreham (Sussex), Kew (Surrey) and La Varde, Guernsey (Clarke 1970, respectively: Figs 428, 378, 381), and though the present piece is too fragmentary for reconstruction a bulbous vessel of Clarke's East Anglian type may be represented. However, such triangular stabs are also found on Bronze Age pottery, particularly Collared Urns (Longworth 1984, plates 116, 176, 179), although the thickness of this sherd argues against a Bronze Age date.

According to stylistic sequences devised by Clarke (1970), Lanting and van der Waals (1972) and Case (1977), these Beakers lie relatively early in the British sequence (Lanting and van der Waals, step 3; Case's Middle phase), and should date to the start of the British Beaker tradition, perhaps as early as 2500 B.C. Recent radiocarbon chronology, however, has questioned the chronological validity of the stylistic sequences (Kinnes *et al.* 1991). Radiocarbon dates for European style Beakers so far number only one. From Little Pond Ground, a BP date of 3670±80 (HAR-340) was recovered from the associated skeleton calibrating to 2195-2160 or 2145-1945 BC at

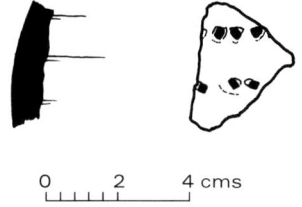

Fig. 164. Beaker sherd from Pit complex B15, Area B. Scale 1:2.

---

23. Report submitted in 1994.

1σ. The East Anglian group is similarly dated by only one radiocarbon date from Cottington Hill (Thanet), Kent where a BP date of 3630±60 (BM-2725) was also obtained from the associated skeleton and calibrates to 2130–2075 or 2045–1930 B.C. at 1σ (Kinnes *et al.* 1991). These single dates are however, statistically too few to allow us to construct a chronology for these early groups, though the fact that they are both from associated human bone does at least verify the association of the date with these vessels. In view of the apparent lateness of the date, it would even be dangerous to use the geographical proximity of the Cottington Hill vessel as a chronological indicator for the East Anglian group in the region (Gibson 1992). One of the major and justifiable criticisms of the British Museum Dating Programme has been that too few vessels have been dated (and from too large a geographical area) to allow for the construction of an internal chronology. More dates are therefore needed from specific regions to try and tie down the nuances of Beaker against dates; this is particularly true of Kent and East Anglia.

The numbers of Beakers and fragments are too few to allow us an insight into exactly what the Beaker presence was at Highstead. The fragment from Pit complex B15 and its degree of abrasion suggest domestic material, but this is by no means unequivocal and the sherd could be little more than residual. The completeness of the two earlier finds might suggest burials, but no record of the circumstances of the finds are known. It is unlikely that so much would survive of either vessel were they from a domestic context (Gibson 1982) unless as part of a much larger assemblage. They may represent burials on the edge of an as yet unlocated settlement. The presence of Neolithic and Iron Age finds from the same general location attest the suitability for settlement of successive phases on this gentle sloping spur.

APPENDIX II

The scientific examination of part of a decorated Iron Age bowl

A.P. Middleton and M.S. Tite

Introduction

The bowl fragment (Fig. 89, No. 368, and p.128) is decorated by narrow (*c.* 1–2 mm.) pale pink bands on a background which is bright red in some areas and purple or brown to black in others. The fabric of the pot has been examined in thin section, using a petrographic microscope. Samples of the various 'paint' colours have been analysed using x-ray diffraction and a sample was also prepared as a polished cross-section for examination in the scanning electron microscope (SEM).

Petrographic examination

The fabric is characterised by common sub-angular flint temper (typically *c.* 0.25–0.75µm); some quartz sand is also present, together with common angular silty quartz. Sparse clay pellets/grog were also observed in the birefringent clay matrix.

X-ray diffraction analysis

The sample from a bright red area gave a diffraction pattern indicating the presence of haematite as a major phase but in none of the other samples was haematite (or any other 'pigment') identified.

SEM examination

Observation of parts of the section corresponding to the bright red areas confirmed the existence of a surface layer rich in iron oxide. This layer was of variable thickness (< 100µm to > 200µm) and contained quartz and clay in addition to particles of iron oxide. In those parts of the section corresponding to the purple-brown colouration there was evidence that the surface zone (*c.* 100µm thick) of the sherd contained a somewhat higher concentration of fine (< 10µm) iron oxide particles than the body clay, though considerably less iron oxide than the bright red areas. The brown areas showed no evidence for the application of any pigmenting material to the surface. The section prepared for examination in the SEM included one of the pink bands and this appeared to coincide with a portion of the surface at which a 'trough' (*c.* 1 mm. wide x 0.3 mm. deep) had been incised and then infilled by a quartz rich slip containing rather sparse particles of iron oxide.

Discussion

The petrographic examination of the fabric of the bowl shows that it is characterised by the use of crushed flint as temper. The fabric is not sufficiently distinctive to be able to assign a provenance to the bowl but it is quite consistent with the use of local materials. Similar flint-tempered fabrics have been observed from other sites in north-east Kent.

The results of the analysis of the various colour finishes indicates that the pigment used was haematite (or ochre): this was apparently applied (probably by burnishing) richly in some areas to produce the bright red finish and rather sparsely in other areas to give the more purple colour. Areas of brown colour were probably achieved by simply burnishing the clay surface. The narrow pink bands may have been produced by the use of a mixture containing a little iron oxide mixed with quartz and clay. Observation in the SEM suggested that this mixture may have been inlaid into grooves incised into the surface of the pot. Examination of the surface of the bowl fragment under a binocular microscope provided some support for this interpretation. No direct evidence was obtained for the nature of the black colourations but this was probably produced in some areas (accidentally) by smoke blackening and in others by deliberate burnishing of carbon black or some similar material into the surface.

ABBREVIATIONS

Antiq. J.	*Antiquaries Journal*
Arch. Cant.	*Archaeologia Cantiana*
Arch. J.	*Archaeological Journal*
B.A.R.	British Archaeological Report
B.J.	*Bonner Jahrbücher*
C.B.A.	Council for British Archaeology
D.O.E.	Department of the Environment
Essex Arch. Hist.	*Essex Archaeology and History*
H.M.S.O.	Her Majesty's Stationery Office
J.A.S.	*Journal of Archaeological Science*
K.A.R.	Kent Archaeological Review
Northants Arch.	*Northamptonshire Archaeology*
P.P.S.	*Proceedings of the Prehistoric Society*
P.S.A.S.	*Proceedings of the Society of Antiquaries of Scotland*
Soc. Ant. Lond. Res. Rep.	Society of Antiquaries of London Research Report
Surrey Arch. Coll.	*Surrey Archaeological Collections*
T.C.W.A.A.S.	*Transactions of the Cumberland and Westmoreland Antiquarian and Archaeological Society*

BIBLIOGRAPHY

Abercrombie, Hon. J. 1912 — *Bronze Age Pottery of Great Britain and Ireland*, Oxford.

Adkins, L. and Needham, S. 1985 — 'New research on a Late Bronze Age enclosure at Queen Mary's Hospital, Carshalton', *Surrey Arch. Coll.* lxxvi, 11–50.

Alexander, J., Ozanne, P.C. and Ozanne, A. 1960 — 'Report on the investigations of a round barrow on Arreton Down, Isle of Wight', *P.P.S.* xxvi, 263–302.

Allen, T., Miles, D. and Palmer, S. 1984 — 'Iron Age buildings in the Upper Thames Valley' in B. Cunliffe and D. Miles (eds), *Aspects of the Iron Age in central southern Britain*, Oxford University Committee for Archaeology Monograph 2, 89–101.

Anderson, A.C. 1980 — *A Guide to Roman Finewares*, Vorda Research Series 1, Highworth.

Arthur, P. 1986 — 'Roman Amphorae from Canterbury', *Britannia* xvii, 237–56.

Audouze, F. and Büchsenschütz, O. 1991 — *Towns, villages and countryside of Celtic Europe*, London.

Barford, P.M. 1990 — 'Appendix 2: Salt production in Essex before the Red Hills' in A.J. Fawn, K.A. Evans, I. McMaster and G.M.R. Davies, *The Red Hills of Essex: salt making in antiquity*, Colchester, 81–4.

Barnes, F. and Jackson, J.G. 1978 — 'Recent finds from Walney North End', *T.C.W.A.A.S.* lxxviii, 199–201.

Barrett, J.C. 1980 — 'The pottery of the Later Bronze Age in Lowland England', *P.P.S.* 46, 297–319.

Barrett, J.C. 1989 — 'Food, metal and gender: questions of social reproduction' in M.L. Sørensen and R. Thomas (eds), *The Bronze Age-Iron Age transition in Europe*, B.A.R. International Series 483, Oxford, 304–20.

Barrett, J. and Bradley, R. (eds) 1980 — *The British Later Bronze Age*, B.A.R. British Series 83, parts i and ii, Oxford.

Beltrán Lloris, M. 1977 — 'Problemas de la morfologia y del concepto historic-geografico, que recubre la nocion tipo' in G. Vallet (ed.), *Méthodes classiques et méthodes formelles dans l'etude des amphores*, Coll. de L'Ecole Française de Rome xxxii, 97–131.

Bennett, P. 1988	'Archaeology and the Channel Tunnel', *Arch. Cant.* cvi, 1–24.
Bennett, P. forthcoming	'Excavations in the Stour Street and Castle Street Areas', The Archaeology of Canterbury VI.
Bennett, P., Frere, S.S. and Stow, S. 1982	*Excavations at Canterbury Castle*, The Archaeology of Canterbury I, Maidstone.
Bennett, P., Macpherson-Grant, N. and Blockley, P. 1980	'Four minor sites excavated by the Canterbury Archaeological Trust, 1978–1979', *Arch. Cant.* xcvi, 267–304.
Berensohn, P. 1974	*Finding One's Way with Clay*, London.
Biddle, M. 1967	'Two Flavian burials from Grange Road, Winchester', *Antiq. J.* xlvii, 224–50.
Birchall, A. 1965	'The Aylesford-Swarling culture: the problem of the Belgae reconsidered', *P.P.S.* xxxi, 241–367.
Bird, J. 1995	'The Italian and Early Samian Ware' in K. Blockley *et al.*, 777–80.
Blanchet, J.C. 1984	'Les premiers métallurgistes en Picardie et dans le Nord de la France', *Mémoire de la Société Préhistorique Française*, 17.
Blanchet, J.C., Bailloud, G., Briard, J., Burgess, C., Gaucher, G., Mohen J.P. and Mordant, C. (eds) 1987	'Les Relations entre le Continent et les Iles Britanniques à l'âge du Bronze', *Revue Archéologique de Picardie et Société Préhistorique Française*.
Blanchet, J.C. and Talon, M. 1987	'L'éperon barré du 'Camp César' à Catenoy (Oise), à l'âge du Bronze final – premiers résultats' in J.C. Blanchet *et al.* (eds), 189–210.
Blancquaert, G. 2000	'La nécropole à incinérations de la zone IV' in 'Les nécropoles de l'âge du fer de La Calotterie' in Y. Desfossés (ed.), 359–427.
Blancquaert, G. and Bostyn, F. 1998	'L'âge du fer à Coquelles et Fréthun (Pas-de-Calais) (Fouilles de Transmanche 1986–1988)', *Revue du Nord* lxxx, 109–37.
Blockley, K., Blockley, M. Blockley, P., Frere, S.S. and Stow, S. 1995	*Excavations in the Marlowe Car Park and Surrounding Areas*, The Archaeology of Canterbury V, Whitstable.
Bond, D. 1988	*Excavation at the North Ring, Mucking, Essex*, East Anglian Archaeology 43, Gressenhall.
Booth, P., Champion, T., Garwood, P., Reynolds, A., Robinson, M. and Munby, J. forthcoming	*The archaeology of Section 1 of the Channel Tunnel Rail Link*, Oxford.
Boureux, M., Rowlett, R.M. and Rowlett, E.S.J. 1969	'A rectangular early La Tène Marnian house at Chassemy (Aisne)', *World Archaeology* 1, 106–35.
Bourgeois, J. and Talon, M. 2005	*L'âge du Bronze du nord de la France dans son contexte européen*, Paris.

Boyle, J. 1990 — 'An excavation at 49 Burgate, Canterbury', *K.A.R.* 100, (May 1990), 1–25.

Bradley R., Lobb, S., Richards, J. and Robinson, M. 1980 — 'Two Late Bronze Age settlements on the Kennet Gravels; excavations at Aldermaston Wharf and Burghfield, Berkshire', *P.P.S.* 46, 217–95.

Brewster, T.C.M. 1963 — *The Excavation of Staple Howe*, The East Riding Archaeological Research Committee, Malton, Yorkshire.

Britton, D. 1968 — *Late Bronze Age finds in the Heathery Burn Cave, Co. Durham, Inventaria Archaeologica*, GB 55, London.

Brown, N. 1985 — 'North Shoebury' in *Essex Arch. Hist.* xvi, 100–102.

Brown, N. 1987 — 'Late Bronze Age Pottery' in D.G. Buckley and J.D. Hedges, 8–11.

Brown, N. 1988 — 'Late Bronze Age enclosure at Lofts Farm, Essex', *P.P.S.* 54, 249–302.

Brown, N. and Adkins, P. 1988 — 'Heybridge Blackwater Sailing Club' in D. Priddy, 243–9.

Brun, P. 1986 — 'La culture des Champs d'Urnes - étude critique dans le Bassin Parisien', *Document d'Archéologie Française*, 4.

Brunaux, J-L., Meniel, P. and Poulin, F. 1985 — *Gournay I. Les fouilles sur le sanctuaire et l'oppidum (1975–1984)*, Amiens.

Buckley, D.G., Brown, N. and Greenwood, P. 1986 — 'Late Bronze Age hoards from the Chelmer Valley, Essex', *Antiq. J.* lxvi, 248–66.

Buckley, D.G. and Hedges, J.D. 1987 — *The Bronze Age and Saxon settlements at Springfield Lyons, Essex: An Interim Report*, Essex County Council Occasional Paper 5, Chelmsford.

Bulard, A., Duhamel, P. and Poulain, T. 1983 — 'Fosses de la Tène ancienne 'Aux Sablons de Fresnes-sur-Marne (Seine-et-Marne)' in 'Les Celtes dans le Nord du Bassin Parisien', *Revue Archéologique de Picardie* 1, 47–65.

Bulleid, A. and Gray, H. St. G. 1917 — *The Glastonbury Lake Village* II, Glastonbury Antiquarian Society.

Burgess. C. 1987 — 'Les rapports entre la France et la Grande-Bretagne pendant l'âge du Bronze: problèmes de poterie et d'habitats' in J.C. Blanchet *et al.* (eds), 307–18.

Bushe-Fox, J.P. 1932 — *Third Report on the Excavations of the Roman Fort at Richborough, Kent*, Soc. Ant. Lond. Res. Rep. x, Oxford.

Bushe-Fox, J.P. 1949 — *Fourth Report on the Excavations of the Roman Fort at Richborough, Kent*, Soc. Ant. Lond. Res. Rep. xvi, Oxford.

Cahen-Delhaye, A. 1973 — *Sondages dans un site d'habitat de l'âge du fer à Orp-le-Grand*, Archaeologia Belgica 151, Brussels.

Cahen-Delhaye, A. 1974 — *Tombelles de La Tène à Hampiré, La Hasse*, Archaeologia Belgica 158, Brussels.

Cahen-Delhaye, A. 1983 — 'Contribution à la chronologie des tombelles Ardennaises (Belgique)', *Helinium* xxiii, 237–56.

Cahen-Delhaye, A., Duval, A., Leman-Delerive, G. and Leman, P. 1984 — *Les Celtes en Belgique et dans le Nord de la France*, Revue du Nord numéro special hors série, Villeneuve-d'Ascq.

Callender, M.H. 1965 — *Roman Amphorae*, Oxford.

Case, H.J. 1977 — 'The Beaker culture in Britain and Ireland' in R. Mercer (ed.), *Beakers in Britain and Europe*, B.A.R. Supplementary Series S26, Oxford, 71–101.

Champion, T.C. 1975 — 'Britain and the European Iron Age', *Archaeologia Atlantica* 1, 127–45.

Champion, T.C. 1980 — 'Settlement and environment in Later Bronze Age Kent' in J. Barrett and R. Bradley (eds), 223–46.

Champion, T.C. 1982 — 'The Bronze Age in Kent' in P.E. Leach (ed.), 31–9.

Champion, T.C. forthcoming — 'Kent from 1500 to 300 B.C.' in C.C. Haselgrove and R.E. Pope (eds), *The earlier Iron Age in Britain and the near continent*, Oxford.

Chaplin, R.E. 1971 — *The Study of Animal Bones from Archaeological Sites*, London.

Charlesworth, D. 1972 — 'The Glass' in S.S. Frere, 196–215.

Chertier, B. 1976 — 'Les nécropoles de la civilisation des champs d'urnes dans la region des Marais de Saint-Gond (Marne)', *VIIIe supplément a Gallia Préhistoire*, Paris.

Chossenot, D., Neiss, R. and Sauget, J.M. 1981 — 'Fouille de sauvetage d'une nécropole de la Tène I à Vrigny (Marne)' in *Mémoires de la Société Archéologique Champenoise* 2, 131–50.

Clark, A.J. 1983 — 'Archaeomagnetic dating at Bigberry' in F.H. Thompson, 275–6.

Clark, A.J. and Thompson F.H. 1989 — 'Revised radiocarbon dates for three hillforts in Kent and Surrey', *Antiq. J.* lix, 303–7.

Clark, J.G.D. 1932 — 'The date of the plano-convex knife in England and Wales', *Antiq. J.* xii, 158–62.

Clark, J.G.D., Higgs, E. and Longworth, I.H. 1960 — 'Excavations at the Neolithic site at Hurst Fen, Mildenhall, Suffolk 1954, 1957 and 1958', *P.P.S.* xxvi, 202–45.

Clarke, A. 1982 — 'The Neolithic of Kent' in P.E. Leach (ed.), 12–24.

Clarke, D.L. 1970 — *The Beaker Pottery of Great Britain and Ireland*, Cambridge University Press.

Clay, P. and Pollard, R. 1994	*Iron Age and Roman Occupation in the West Bridge Area, Leicester, Excavations 1962–1971*, Leicester.
Collis, J.R. 1968	'Excavations at Owlesbury, Hants', *Antiq. J.* xlviii, 18–31.
Cotton, M.A. 1947	'Excavations at Silchester 1938–9', *Archaeologia* 92, 121–67.
Cotton, M.A. and Frere, S.S. 1968	'Ivinghoe Beacon Excavations 1963–65', *Records of Buckinghamshire* xviii, 187–260.
Couldrey, P. 1984	'The Iron Age Pottery' in B. Philp, 38–70.
Couldrey, P. 1988	'Report on the prehistoric pottery from Welling', *K.A.R.* 92, 43–7.
Crummy, N. 1983	*The Roman Small Finds from excavations in Colchester, 1971–9*, Colchester.
Cunliffe, B.W. 1968	*Fifth Report on the Excavations on the Roman Fort at Richborough, Kent*, Soc. Ant. Lond. Res. Rep.xxiii, Oxford.
Cunliffe, B.W. 1971	*Excavations at Fishbourne 1961–1969, Volume II, The Finds*, Soc. Ant. Lond. Res. Rep. xxvii, Leeds.
Cunliffe, B.W. 1980	'Overall discussion of the Iron Age Pottery' in N. Macpherson-Grant 1980a, 174–9.
Cunliffe, B.W. 1984	*Danebury - An Iron Age Hillfort in Hampshire*, C.B.A. Research Report 52, London.
Cunliffe, B.W. 1991	*Iron Age Communities in Britain*, third edition, London.
Cunliffe, B.W. 2005	*Iron Age communities in Britain: an account of England, Scotland and Wales from the seventh century BC to the Roman conquest*, fourth edition, London.
Curle, J. 1911	*A Roman Frontier Post and its People, The Fort of Newstead in the Parish of Melrose*, Glasgow.
Debord, J. 1981	'Un enclos quadrangulaire à remplissage de la Tène Ia, sis à Villeneuve-Saint-Germain (Aisne) (Étude préliminaire)' in *L'Age du Fer en France septentrionale. Mémoires de la Société Archaeologique Champenoise* 2, Châlons-sur-Marne, 107–20.
Desfossés, Y. (ed.) 2000	*Archéologie Préventive en Vallée de Canche - les sites protohistoriques fouillés dans le cadre de le réalisation de l'autoroute A16*, Nord-Ouest Archéologie, 11, Berck-sur-Mer.
Desittere, M. 1967	'Die Grobkeramik der Urnenveldenkultur in Belgien und den Niederlanden und der sogenannte Harpstedter Stil', *Helinium* 7, 260–71.
Desittere, M. 1968	*De Urnenveldenkultur in het gebied Tussen Neder-Rijn en Noordzee* (2 vols) in *Dissertationes Archeologicae Gandenses* xi, Brugge.

Destexhe, G. 1987 — *La Protohistoire en Hesbaye Centrale: Du Bronze final à la romanisation*, Archéologie Hesbignonne 6, Saint-Georges.

Doorselaer, A. van, Putman, R., Vander Gucht, K. and Janssens, F. 1987 — *De Kemmelberg een Keltische bergvesting*, Westvlaamse Archaeolgica Monografieen 3, Kortrijk.

Down. A. 1978 — *Chichester Excavations III*, Chichester.

Dragendorff, H. 1895–6 — 'Classification of Samian Ware Forms, "Terra Sigillata"', *B.J.* xcvi (1895), 18–55 and xcvii (1896), 54–163.

Driver, J., Rady, J. and Sparks, M. 1990 — *Excavations in the Cathedral Precincts, 2. Linacre Garden, 'Meister Omers' and St Gabriel's Chapel,* Archaeology of Canterbury IV, Maidstone.

Drury, P.J. 1980 — 'The early and middle phases of the Iron Age in Essex' in D.G. Buckley (ed.), *Archaeology in Essex to A.D. 1500, 47–54*, C.B.A. Research Report 34, London.

Durvin, P. and Brunaux, J.-L. 1983 — 'Le matérial protohistorique de Thiverny (Oise)' in *Les Celtes dans Le Nord du Bassin Parisien*, Revue Archéologique de Picardie 1, 12–32.

Duval, A. 1984 — 'Regional groups in Western France' in S. Macready and F.H. Thompson, 78–91.

Edis, J., MacLeod, D. and Bewley, R. 1989 — 'An archaeologist's guide to the classification of cropmarks and soilmarks', *Antiquity* lxiii, 112–26.

Ellison, A. and Drewett, P. 1971 — 'Pits and post-holes in the British Early Iron Age: some alternative explanations', *P.P.S.* xxxvii, 183–94.

Elsdon, S.M. 1982 — 'Later Bronze Age Pottery from Farnham: a reappraisal', *Surrey Arch. Coll.* lxxiii, 127–39.

English Heritage 2002 — *Managing Lithic Scatters. Archaeological Guidance for Planning Authorities and Developers*, London.

Evans, A.J. 1890 — 'On a late Celtic urn-field at Aylesford, Kent, and on the Gaulish Illyro-Italic, and classical connexions of the forms of pottery and bronze-work discovered there', *Archaeologia* lii, 315–88.

Favret, Abbé P.M. 1936 — 'Les nécropoles des Jogasses à Chouilly (Marne)', *Préhistoire* v, 24–118.

Fell, C.I. 1936 — 'The Hunsbury Hill-Fort, Northants: a new survey of the material', *Arch. J.* xciii, 57–100.

Flouest, J.-L. and Stead, I. 1981 — 'Fouille de sauvetage à Tinqueux (Marne) 1974' in *Mémoires de la Société Archéologique Champenoise* 2, 151–76.

Foley, R. 1981 — *Off-site archaeology and Human Adaptation in Eastern Africa*, B.A.R. International Series 98, Oxford, Cambridge Monographs in African Archaeology 3.

Foster, J. 1990	'Other Bronze Age artefacts' in M. Bell, *Brean Down excavations 1983–1987*, English Heritage Archaeological Report 15, London, 165–70.
Freidin, N. 1982	*The Early Iron Age in the Paris Basin - Hallstatt C and D*, B.A.R. International Series 131, Oxford.
Frere, S.S. 1972	*Verulamium Excavations* Vol. I, Soc. Ant. Lond. Res. Rep. xxviii, Oxford.
Frere, S.S. 1984	*Verulamium Excavations* Vol. III, Oxford University Committee for Archaeology, Monograph I, Oxford.
Frere, S.S. and St Joseph, J.K. 1974	'The Roman Fortress at Longthorpe' *Britannia* v, 1–129.
Frere, S.S., Stow, S. and Bennett, P. 1982	*Excavations on the Roman and Medieval Defences of Canterbury*, The Archaeology of Canterbury II, Maidstone.
Frere, S.S. and Stow, S. 1983	*Excavations in the St George's Street and Burgate Street Areas*, The Archaeology of Canterbury VII, Maidstone.
Frere, S.S., Bennett, P., Rady, J. and Stow, S. 1987	*Canterbury Excavations: Intra- and Extra-Mural Sites 1949–55 and 1980–84*, The Archaeology of Canterbury VIII, Maidstone.
Gardiner, J. 2004	*Research Frameworks for Holocene Lithics in Britain*, Lithic Studies Society, Oxford.
Gent, H. 1983	'Centralised storage in later prehistoric Britain', *P.P.S.* 49, 243–67.
Gibson A.M. 1992	'The Beaker from Cottington Hill, Ebbsfleet, Ramsgate' Appendix I in D.R.J. Perkins, 269–311.
Gibson, A.M. 1998	'The Neolithic–Early Bronze Age pottery' in R.C. Preece and D.R. Bridgland, *Late Quaternary Environmental change in North-west Europe: Excavations at Holywell Coombe, South-east England*, London, 295–302.
Gillam, J.P. and Mann, J.C. 1970	'The northern British frontier from Antoninus Pius to Caracalla', *Arch. Aeliana* (Ser. 4) xlviii, 1–44.
Gomez, J. 1984	'Du bronze final au l' âge du fer dans le Bassin de la Charente' in C. Mordant and J.P. Thevenot (eds), *Transition Bronze Final Hallstatt Ancien: Colloque, 109e Congres National des Sociétés Savantes*, Dijon, 251–9.
Gosselin, J.-Y., Leman Delerive, G. and Seillier, C. 1984	'Le site protohistorique de Vron (Somme), Silos réutilisés comme sépultures' in A. Cahen-Delhaye *et al.*, 33–40.
Green, H.S. 1984	'Flint arrowheads: typology and interpretation', *Lithics* 5, 19–39.
Green, M.J. 1995	'The Pottery from Pit 683, Marlowe Theatre' in K. Blockley *et al.*, 633–39.

Green, M.J. forthcoming a	'The pottery from the 'shrine' area (CBR IV)' in P. Bennett forthcoming.
Green, M.J. forthcoming b	'The pottery from Hut B1/B2 (CBR I)' in P. Bennett forthcoming.
Greene, K. 1979	*The Pre-Flavian Fine Wares*, Reports on the Excavations at Usk, Vol. I, Cardiff.
Grimes, W.F. and Close-Brooks, J. 1993	'The Excavation of Caesar's Camp, Heathrow, Harmondsworth, Middlesex, 1944', *P.P.S.* 59, 303–60.
Grinsell, L.V. 1992	'The Bronze Age round barrows of Kent', *P.P.S.* 58, 355–84.
Guilbert, G. 1982	'Post-ring symmetry in roundhouses at Moel-y-Gaer and some other sites in prehistoric Britain' in P.J. Drury (ed.), *Structural reconstruction*, B.A.R. British Series 110, Oxford, 67–86.
Guttman, E.B. and Last, J. 2000	'A Late Bronze Age landscape at Hornchurch, Greater London', *P.P.S.* 66, 319–59.
Hamworth, R. and Tomalin, D.J. 1977	*Brooklands, Weybridge: The excavation of an Iron Age and Medieval Site 1964–5 and 1970–71*, Reseach Volume of the Surrey Archaeological Society 4, Guildford.
Hantute, G. 1984	'Le site protohistorique de Neuville-sur-Escaut (Nord)' in A. Cahen-Delhaye *et al.*, 13–24.
Hartley, K. 1982	'The Mortaria' in P. Bennett *et al.*, 150–8.
Haselgrove, C. 2001	'Iron Age Britain in its European setting' in J.R. Collis (ed.), *Society and Settlement in Iron Age Europe, Sheffield*, 37–72.
Hatt, J.J. 1962	'Chronique de Protohistoire VI. Pour une nouvelle chronologie de l'époque hallstattienne. Les trois phases du Premier Age du Fer en Allemagne du Sud et en France de l'Est', *Bulletin de la Société Préhistorique de France* lix, 659–67.
Hatt, J.J. and Roualet, P. 1977	'La chronologie de La Tène en Champagne', *Revue Archéologique de l'Est* xxviii, 7–36.
Hawkes, C.F.C. 1935	'The pottery from the sites of Plumpton Plain', *P.P.S.* i, 39–59.
Hawkes, C.F.C. and Fell, C.I. 1943	'The Early Iron Age settlement at Fengate, Peterborough', *Arch. J.* c, 188–223.
Hawkes, C.F.C. and Hull, M.R. 1947	*Camulodunum*, Soc. Ant. Lond. Res. Rep., xiv, London.
Healey, E. 1988	'The flint industry' in D. Bond, 23–5.
Healey, E. and Robertson-Mackay, R. 1983	'The lithic industries from Staines Causewayed Enclosure and their relationship to other earlier Neolithic industries in Southern Britain', *Lithics* 4, 1–27.

Healy, F. 1984	'Farming and field monuments in the Neolithic in Norfolk' in C. Barringer (ed.), *Aspects of East Anglian Pre-history. 20 years after Rainbird Clarke*, Norwich, 77–140.
Hedges, J. and Buckley, D. 1978	'Excavations at a Neolithic causewayed enclosure, Orsett, Essex, 1975', *P.P.S.* 44, 219–308.
Helm, R. 2003	'Bogshole Lane, Broomfield', *Canterbury's Archaeology 2000–2001*, 23–4.
Hermet, F. 1934	*La Graufesenque (Condatomago)*, Paris.
Hodder, I. and Hedges, J.W. 1977	'Weaving combs: their typology and distribution with some introductory remarks on date and function' in J. Collis (ed.), *The Iron Age in Britain: A Review*, Sheffield, 17–28.
Hodson, F.R. 1962	'Some pottery from Eastbourne, the 'Marnians' and the pre-Roman Iron Age in Southern England', *P.P.S.* xxviii, 140–55.
Holmes, S.C.A. 1981	*Geology of the Country around Faversham*, Memoire of the Geological Survey of Great Britain, London.
Holwerda, J.H. 1941	*Die Belgische Waar in Nijmegen*, Nijmegen.
Hull, M.R. 1963	*The Roman Pottery Kilns of Colchester*, Soc. Ant. Lond. Res. Rep., xxi, Oxford.
Humphrey, J. and Young, R. 1999	'Flint use in later Bronze Age and Iron Age England: still a fiction?', *Lithics* 20, 57–61.
Humphrey, J. and Young, R. 2003	'Flint use in later Bronze Age and Iron Age England? Some criteria for future research' in N. Moloney and M.J. Shott (eds), *Lithic Analysis at the Millennium,* Institute of Archaeology, U.C.L., 79–90.
Hurtrelle, J., Monchy, E., Roger, F., Rossignol, P. and Villes, A. 1990	*Les débuts du second âge du fer dans le Nord de la France*, Les Dossiers de Gauheria 1, Noeux-les-Mines.
van Impe, L. 1980	*Urnenveld uit de Late Bronztijd en de Vroege Ijzertijd te Donk, I*, Archaeologia Belgica 224, Brussels.
Isings, C. 1957	*Roman Glass from Dated Finds*, Groningen.
Jackson, D.A. and Dix, B. 1987	'Late Iron Age and Roman settlement at Weekley, Northants', *Northants Arch.* 21, 41–94.
Jacobi, R.M. 1982	'Later hunters in Kent: Tasmania and the earliest Neolithic' in P.E. Leach (ed.), 12–24.
Jarman, C. 2002	'Glebeland, Marley Road, Harrietsham', *Canterbury's Archaeology 1997–1998*, 16–17.
Jarman, C. 2005	'Underdown Lane, Eddington', *Canterbury's Archaeology 2003–2004*, 14–16.

Jenkins, F. 1956	'A Roman tilery and two pottery kilns at *Durovernum* (Canterbury)', *Antiq. J.* xxxvi, 40–56.
Jenkins, F. 1960	'Two pottery kilns and a tilery of the Roman period at Canterbury (*Durovernum Cantiacorum*)', *Arch. Cant.* lxxiv, 151–61.
Jessup, R.F. 1930	*The Archaeology of Kent*, London.
Jessup, R.F. 1937	'Excavations at Julliberries Grave, Chilham, Kent', *Antiq. J.* xvii, 122–37.
Jessup, R.F. 1939	'Excavations at Julliberries Grave, Chilham, Kent', *Antiq. J.* xix, 260–81.
Jones, M.U. and Bond, D. 1980	'Later Bronze Age settlement at Mucking, Essex' in J. Barrett and R. Bradley (eds), 471–82.
Jones, M.U. and Jones, W.T. 1975	'The crop-mark sites at Mucking, Essex, England' in R. Bruce-Mitford (ed.), *Recent archaeological excavations in Europe*, London, 133–87.
Karnitsch, P. 1959	*Die Reliefsigillata Von Ovilava*, Linz.
Keller, P. 1990	*The excavation of a Late Iron Age and Romano-British site at Charing,* Kent Minor Sites Series 4, Kent Archaeological Rescue Unit, Dover.
King, A.C. 1978	'A comparative survey of bone assemblages from Roman sites in Britain', *Bulletin of the Institute of Archaeology of London* 15, 207–32.
King, A.C. 1982	'The animal bones' in P. Bennett *et al.* 193–205.
King, A.C. 1985	'Animal bones and the dietary identity of military and civilian groups in Roman Britain, Germany and Gaul' in T. Blagg and A.C. King (eds), *Military and Civilian in Roman Britain*, Oxford, 187–217.
Kinnes, I., Gibson, A., Ambers, J., Bowman, S., Leese M. and Boast R. 1991	'Radiocarbon dating and British Beakers: The British Museum Programme', *Scottish Archaeological Review* 8, 35–68.
Kirkman, J.S. 1940	'The Pottery' in 'A Roman pottery kiln at Canterbury', *Arch. Cant.* lii, 118–33.
Knight, D. 1984	*Late Bronze Age and Iron Age settlement in the Nene and Great Ouse basins*, B.A.R. British Series 130, Oxford.
Knorr, R. 1919	*Topfer und Fabriken verzierter Terra-Sigillata des ersten Jahrhunderts*, Stuttgart.
Knorr, R. 1952	*Terra-Sigillata - Gefasse des ersten Jahrhunderts mit Topfernamen*, Stuttgart.

Knorr, R. and Sprater, F. 1927 — *Die westpfalzischen Sigillata-Topferein von Blickweiler und Eschweilerhof*, Speier.

Laet, S.J. de 1982 — *La Belgique d'avant les Romains*, Wetteren.

Laet, S.J. de, Thoen, H. and Bourgeois, J. 1986 — 'Les Fouilles due Seminaire d'Archéologie de la Rijksuniversiteit de Gent à Destlebergen-Eenbeekeinder (1960–1984) et L'Histoire la plus ancienne de la Region de Gent (Gand), Vol. 1 La periode préhistorique' in *Dissertationes Archeologicae Gandenses* xxiii, Brugge.

Lambot, B. 1996 — 'Essai de chronologie du site de La Tène finale d'Acy-Romance (Ardennes)', *Revue Archéologique de Picardie* 3/4, 123–52.

Lanting, J.N. and van der Waals, J.D. 1972 — 'British Beakers as seen from the Continent', *Helinium* 12, 20–46.

Lawson, A.J. 1984 — 'The Bronze Age in East Anglia with particular reference to Norfolk' in C. Baringer (ed.), *Aspects of East Anglian Prehistory*, Norwich, 141–77.

Leach, P.E. (ed.) 1982 — *Archaeology in Kent to A.D. 1500*, C.B.A. Research Report 48, London

Leman, P. 1982 — 'Circonscription du Nord-Pas-de-Calais', *Gallia Prehistoire* xxv (1982–3), 247–8.

Leman-Delerive, G. 1984 — 'Céramique Laténienne domestique de la Région Lilloise (Nord)', *Gallia* xlii, 79–95.

Lepage, L. 1984 — 'Les Age du Fer dans les bassins supérieurs de la Marne, de la Meuse et de l'Aube et le Tumulus de la Mottote à Nijon (Haute-Marne), *Mémoires de la Société Archéologique Champenoise* 3, Chalons-sur-Marne.

Lisk, S., Schofield, J. and Humble, J. 1998 — 'Lithic scatters after PPG16 – local and national perspectives', *Lithics* 19, 24–32.

Lobjois, G. 1969 — 'La nécropole gauloise de Pernant (Aisne)', *Celticum* xviii, 1–284.

Lobjois, G., Debord, J., Langlois, P., Lepere, E., Mathieu, C. and Sinet, R. 1974 — 'Une nécropole de La Tène I à Bucy-Le-Long (Aisne)' in *Cahiers Archéologie de Picardie*, supplément au Bulletin de la Société des Antiquaires de Picardie, Trimestriel 2, 67–96.

Longley, D. 1980 — *Runnymede Bridge 1976: Excavations on the site of a Late Bronze Age Settlement*, Research volume of the Surrey Archaeological Society 6, Guildford.

Longworth, I. 1984 — *The Collared Urns of the Bronze Age*, Cambridge.

Ludowici, W., Ricken, H. and Fischer, C. 1963 — *Die Bilderschusseln der Romischen Topfer von Rheinzabern*, Bonn.

Lyne, M. 2003 — 'Pottery' in K. Parfitt, 138–47.

MacIvor, I., Thomas, M. and Breeze, D.I. 1981   'Excavations on the Antonine Wall Fort of Rough Castle, Stirlingshire, 1957–61', *P.S.A.S.* 110, 230–85.

Macpherson-Grant, N. 1978   'The Pottery' in P. Bennett, 'Excavations at 16–21 North Lane, Canterbury', *Arch. Cant.* xciv, 174–8.

Macpherson-Grant, N. 1980a   'Archaeological work along the A2: 1966–74', *Arch. Cant.* xcvi, 133–83.

Macpherson-Grant, N. 1980b   'Romano-British coarse sandy ware' in P. Bennett *et al.*, 281–9.

Macpherson-Grant, N. 1982   'Part II: The Pottery' in P. Bennett *et al.* 89–168.

Macpherson-Grant, N. 1989   'The pottery from the 1987–89 Channel Tunnel Excavations', *Canterbury's Archaeology 1988–1989*, 60–3.

Macpherson-Grant, N. 1991   'A re-appraisal of prehistoric pottery from Canterbury', *Canterbury's Archaeology 1990–1991*, 38–48.

Macpherson-Grant, N. 1992a   'A review of Late Bronze Age pottery from East Kent', *Canterbury's Archaeology 1991–1992*, 55–63.

Macpherson-Grant, N. 1992b   'Appendix II: The Pottery' in D.R.J. Perkins, 286–301.

Macpherson-Grant, N. 1997   'The Late Iron Age pottery from the Dover Spine Main 1996, context (2)', unpublished report for R.P.S. Clouston project 2905.

Macready S. and Thompson F.H. (eds) 1984   *Cross-Channel trade between Gaul and Britain in the pre-Roman Iron Age*, Society of Antiquaries Occasional Paper (New Series) 4, London.

Manning, W.H. 1985   *Catalogue of Romano-British Iron Tools, Fittings and Weapons in the British Museum*, London.

Mariën, M-E. 1958   *Trouvailles du Champ d'Urnes et des Tombelles Hallstattiennes de Court St Etienne*, Musées Royaux d'Art et d'Histoire Monographie d'Archéologie Nationale 1, Brussels.

Mariën, M-E. 1961   *La Period de la Tène en Belgique, Le Groupe de la Haine*, Musées Royaux d'Art et d'Histoire Monographie d'Archéologie Nationale, 2, Brussels.

Matson, F.R. 1971   'A study of temperatures used in firing ancient Mesopotamian pottery' in R.H. Brill (ed.), *Science and Archaeology*, Cambridge, Mass., 65–79.

Miles, A. 1968   'Romano-British salt-panning hearths at Cliffe', *Arch. Cant.* lxxxiii, 272.

Miles, D. 1984   *Archaeology at Barton Court Farm, Abingdon, Oxon.*, C.B.A. Research Report 50, London.

Mohen, J-P. 1973   'Les moules en terre cuite des bronziers protohistoriques', *Antiquités Nationales* 5, 33–44.

Mohen, J-P. and Bailloud, G. 1987 — *La Vie Quotidienne - Les fouilles du Fort-Harrouard, L'âge du Bronze en France,* Vol. 4, Paris.

Moore, C. 2002 — 'Late Bronze Age, Romano-British and Early/Middle Saxon features at Hoo St Werburgh', *Arch. Cant.* cxxii, 259–74.

Moss, E. 1983 — 'Some comments on edge damage as a factor in functional analysis of stone artefacts', *J.A.S.* x, 231–4.

Mudd, A. 1994 — 'The excavation of a Late Bronze Age site at Coldharbour Road, Gravesend', *Arch. Cant.* cxiv, 363–410.

Neal, D.S. 1974 — *The Excavation of the Roman Villa in Gadebridge Park, Hemel Hempstead, 1963–8,* Soc. Ant. Lond. Res. Rep. xxxi, Leeds.

Neal, D.S., Wardle, A. and Hunn, J. 1990 — *Excavation of the Iron Age, Roman and Medieval settlement at Gorhambury, St. Albans,* English Heritage Archaeological Report 14, London.

Needham, S.P. 1990 — *The Petters Late Bronze Age metalwork: an analytical study of Thames Valley metalworking in its settlement context,* British Museum Occasional Paper 70, London.

Needham, S.P. 1992 — 'The structure of settlement and ritual in the Late Bronze Age of south-east Britain' in C. Mordant and A. Richard (eds), *L'habitat et l'occupation du sol à l'âge du bronze en Europe,* Edition du Comité des Travaux historiques et scientifiques, Paris, 49–69.

Needham, S. and Longley, D. 1980 — 'Runnymede Bridge, Egham: a Late Bronze Age riverside settlement' in J. Barrett and R. Bradley (eds), 397–436.

Newcomer, M.H. 1971 — 'Some quantitative experiments in hand-axe manufacture', *World Archaeology* iii, 85–94.

Niblett, R. 1985 — *Sheepen: an Early Roman Industrial Site at Camulodunum,* C.B.A. Research Report 57, London.

O'Connell, M. 1986 — *Petters Sports Field Egham - Excavation of a Late Bronze Age/Early Iron Age site,* Research Volume of the Surrey Archaeological Society 10, Guildford.

O'Connor, B. 1980 — *Cross Channel Relations in the Later Bronze Age,* B.A.R. International Series 591, Oxford.

Odell, G.H. 2004 — *Lithic Analysis,* New York.

O'Neill, H.E. 1945 — 'The Roman villa at Park Street, near St Albans, Hertfordshire, report on the excavations of 1943–45, *Arch. J.* cii, 21–110.

Oswald, F. 1936 — *Index of Figure-types on Terra Sigillata,* Liverpool.

Parfitt, K. 1983 — 'Reports from local societies', *Arch. Cant.* xcix, 290.

Parfitt, K. 1995 — *Iron Age burials from Mill Hill, Deal,* London.

Parfitt, K. 2003 — 'A Belgic-early Roman site at Great Mongeham, near Deal', *Arch. Cant.* cxxiii, 127–52.

Parfitt, K., Allen, T. and Rady, J. 1997 — 'Whitfield-Eastry By-pass', *Canterbury's Archaeology 1995–1996*, 28–33.

Partridge, C. 1989 — *Foxholes Farm, a Multi-Period Gravel Site*, Hertfordshire Archaeological Trust Monograph, Hertford.

Peacock, D.P.S. 1977 — 'Pompeian Red Ware' in *Pottery and Early Commerce*, London, 147–61.

Perkins, D.R.J. 1992 — 'Archaeological evaluations at Ebbsfleet in the Isle of Thanet', *Arch. Cant.* cx, 269–311.

Perkins, D.R.J. 1998 — 'Kent International Business Park, Manston: excavations and evaluations 1994–97', *Arch. Cant.* xviii, 217–55.

Perkins, D.R.J., Macpherson-Grant, N. and Healey, E. 1994 — 'Monkton Court Farm evaluation, 1992', *Arch. Cant.* xiv, 237–316.

Perrin, R. 1980 — *Roman Pottery from the Nene Valley: A Guide*, Peterborough City Museum Occasional Paper 2, Peterborough.

Phillippe, J. 1927 — *Cinq années de Fouilles au Fort-Harrouard 1921–1925*, Société Normande d'Etudes Préhistoriques, Rouen.

Phillippe, J. 1935 — 'Les fondeurs de bronze au Fort-Harrouard', *L'Anthropologie* 45, 15–31.

Philp, B.J. 1963 — 'The Romano-British farmstead at Eastwood, Fawkham', *Arch. Cant.* lxxviii, 55–73.

Philp, B.J. 1968 — *Excavations at Faversham, 1965*, Kent Archaeological Rescue Unit Monograph Series 1, Crawley.

Philp, B.J. 1984 — The Iron Age farmstead on Farningham Hill' in *Excavations in the Darent Valley*, Kent Archaeological Rescue Unit Monograph Series 4, Dover, 7–71.

Philp, B.J. and Chenery, M. 1997 — *Hillside, Gravesend 1994–95: an outline report on a prehistoric and Romano-British site*, Special Subject Series 11, Kent Archaeological Rescue Unit, Dover.

Piercy-Fox, N. 1969 — 'Caesar's Camp, Keston', *Arch. Cant.* lxxxiv, 185–99.

Pitts, M.W. 1978 — 'Towards and understanding of flint industries in post-glacial England', *Univeristy of London Institute of Archaeology Bulletin* 15, 179–97.

Pitts, M.W. and Jacobi, R.M. 1979 — 'Some aspects of change in flaked stone industries of the Mesolithic and Neolithic of Southern Britain', *J.A.S.* vi, 163–77.

Pollard, R.J. 1981	'Two cremations of the Roman period from St Augustine's College, Canterbury', *Arch. Cant.* xcvii, 318–24.
Pollard, R.J. 1982	*The Roman Pottery of Kent*, Ph.D. thesis, University of Reading.
Pollard, R.J. 1987	'The Pottery' in 'Cranmer House, London Road' in S.S. Frere *et al.*, 284–98.
Pollard, R.J. 1990	'The 'Belgic' and Romano-British Pottery from St Gabriel's Chapel' in J. Driver *et al.*, 170–6.
Pollard, R.J. 1995	'The Pottery: I Belgic and Roman' in K. Blockley *et al.*, 583–814.
Prampart, J-Y. 1981	'Le monument funéraires du bas des Renardières à Pont-sur-Yonne (Yonne) Epoque de la Tène', *Mémoires de la Société Archéologique Champenoise* 2, 263–89.
Priddy, D. 1988	'Work of the Essex County Council Archaeology Section 1983–1984', *Essex Arch. Hist.* xix, 243–9.
Priddy, D. and Buckley, D.G. 1987	'An assessment of excavated enclosures in Essex together with a selection of cropmark sites' in *East Anglian Archaeology* 33, 48–80.
Pryor, F. 1984	*Excavations at Fengate, Peterborough, England: The Fourth Report*, Northamptonshire Archaeological Society, Monograph 2; Royal Ontario Museum Archaeology Monograph 7.
Raftery, B. 1971	'Rathgall, Co. Wicklow: 1970 excavations', *Antiquity* xlv, 296–8.
Raftery, B. 1976	'Rathgall and Irish hillfort problems' in D.W. Harding (ed.), *Hill-forts: later prehistoric earthworks in Britain and Ireland*, London, 339–58.
Rice, P.M. 1987	*Pottery Analysis. A Sourcebook*, Chicago.
Richmond, I. 1968	*Hod Hill, volume two, Excavations carried out between 1951 and 1958 for the Trustees of the British Museum*, London.
Rigby, V. 1981	'The Gallo-Belgic Wares' in C. Partridge, *Skeleton Green: A Late Iron Age and Romano-British Site,* Britannia Monograph Series 2, London, 159–95.
Rigby, V. 1995	'Early Gaulish and Rhenish Imports' in K. Blockley *et al.*, 639–70.
Rodwell, W.J. 1978	'Buildings and settlements in south-east Britain in the late Iron Age' in B. Cunliffe and T. Rowley (eds), *Lowland Iron Age communities in Europe*, B.A.R. International Series 48, Oxford, 25–41.
Rogers, G.B. 1974	*Poteries sigillées de la Gaul Centrale, 1: les motifs non-figurés*, Gallia supplement 28, Paris.
Roosens, G.V. and Lux, H. 1969	*Een nederzetting uit de ijzertijd op de Staberg te Rosmeer*, Archaeologia Belgica 109, Brussels.

Rowlett, R.M., Rowlett, E.S-J. and Boureux, M. 1969	'A rectangular early La Tène Marnian house at Chassemy (Aisne)', *World Archaeology* i, 106–35.
Rozoy, J-G. 1986	*Les Celtes en Champagne - Les Ardennes au second Age du Fer: Le Mont Troté, Les Rouliers*, Vol. II, Mémoires de la Société Archéologique Champenoise, 4.
Rozoy, J-G. 1987	*Les Celtes en Champagne - Les Ardennes au second Age du Fer: Le Mont Troté, Les Rouliers,* Vol I, Mémoires de la Société Archéologique Champenoise, 4.
Rye, O.S. 1981	*Pottery Technology*, Washington.
Saville, A. 1977	'Two Mesolithic implement types', *Northants Arch.* 12, 3–8.
Saville, A. 1981	*Grimes Graves Norfolk: Excavations 1971–72, Vol 2. The Flint Assemblage*, D.O.E. Archaeological Report 11, London.
Shand, G. 2001	'Ramsgate Harbour Approach Road', *Canterbury's Archaeology 1998–1999*, 18–22.
Shand, G. 2002	'Eddington Farm, Herne Bay', *Canterbury's Archaeology 1999–2000*, 18–23.
Simpson, G. 1976	'Decorated *terra sigillata* at Montans', *Britannia* vii, 244–73.
Smart, O., Bisson, G. and Worsamm, B.C. 1966	*Geology of the Country around Canterbury and Folkestone*, Memoire of the Geological Survey of Great Britain, London.
Smith, I.F. 1965	*Windmill Hill and Avebury*, Oxford.
Spratling, M.G. 1979	'The debris of metalworking' in G.J. Wainwright, *Gussage All Saints: An Iron Age Settlement in Dorset*, H.M.S.O., London, 125–49.
Stanfield, A. and Simpson, G. 1958	*Central Gaulish Potters*, Durham.
Stead, I.M. 1979	*The Arras Culture*, York.
Stead, I.M. 1984	'Some notes on imported metalwork in Iron Age Britain' in S. Macready and F.H. Thompson (eds), 43–66.
Stead, I.M. and Rigby, V. 1986	*Baldock, The Excavation of a Roman and Pre-Roman Settlement, 1968–72*, Britannia Monograph Series 7, London.
Stebbing, W.P.D. 1934	'An early Iron Age site at Deal', *Arch. Cant.* xlvi, 207–9.
Swaef, W. de and Bourgeois, J. 1986	*Un habitat du La Tène Ia à Lede (Aalst, Flandre orientale)*, Scolae Archaeologicae 3, Ghent.
Talon, M. 1987	'Les formes céramiques Bronze final et premier Age du Fer de l'habitat de Choisy-au-Bac (Oise)' in J.C. Blanchet *et al.* (eds), 255–74.

Thöen, H. 1975	'Iron Age and Roman salt-making sites on the Belgian Coast' in K.W. de Brisay and K.A. Evans (eds), *Salt, the study of an ancient industry*, Colchester Archaeological Group publication, Colchester, 56–60.
Thomas, G.D. 1988	'Excavations at the Roman civil settlement at Inveresk, 1976–77', *P.S.A.S.* 118, 139–76.
Thomas, R., Robinson, M., Barrett, J.C. and Wilson, B. 1986	'A Late Bronze Age riverside settlement at Wallingford, Oxfordshire', *Arch. J.* cxliii, 174–200.
Thompson, F.H. 1983	'Excavations at Bigberry, near Canterbury, 1978–80', *Antiq. J.* lxiii, 237–78.
Thompson, I. 1982	*Grog-tempered 'Belgic' Pottery of South-eastern England*, B.A.R. British Series 108, Oxford.
Thompson, I. 1995	'The Belgic Pottery of Canterbury' in K. Blockley *et al.*, 625–29.
Thompson, I. 2001a	'Late Iron Age pottery from Hawkinge Airfield, Folkestone, Kent (site code HAF 98)', unpublished report for Archaeology South-East.
Thompson, I. 2001b	'A Late Iron Age ceramic assemblage from Church Whitfield, near Dover, Kent (site code WEB 95/2)', unpublished report for Canterbury Archaeological Trust.
Thompson, I. and Green, M.J. 1995	'The pottery from Hut B3, Marlowe Theatre' in K. Blockley *et al.*, 629–32.
Tite, M.S., Bowman, S.G.E., Ambers, J.C. and Mathews, K.J. 1987	'Preliminary statement on an error in British Museum radiocarbon dates', *Antiquity* lxi, no. 232, 168.
Tomber, R. and Dore, J. 1998	*The National Roman Fabric Reference Collection*, London.
Tuohy, C. 1992	'Long-handled 'weaving-combs' in the Netherlands', *P.P.S.* 58, 385–7.
Tylecote, R.F. 1962	*Metallurgy in Archaeology*, London.
Vale, J. 1987	'Archaeological notes from Kent County Museum Service', *Arch. Cant.* civ, 368–74.
van den Broeke, P.W. 1980	'Bewoningssporen uit de Ijzertijd en Andere Perioden op de Hooidonksche Akkers, Gem. Son en Breugel, Prov. Noord-Brabandt', *Analecta Praehistorica Leidensia* xiii, 6–81.
Vernhet, G. 1976	'Création flavienne de six services de vaisseles à La Graufesenque', *Figlina* i, 13–27.
Verwers, G.J. 1972	*Das Kamp Veld in Haps in Neolithikum, Bronzezeit und Eisenzeit*, Analecta Praehistorica Leidensia v, Leiden.

Villes, A. 1981   'Les bâtiments domestiques Hallstattiens de la Chaussée-sur-Marne et le problème de la maison à l'Age du fer en France septentrionale' in *L'Age du fer en France septentrionale*, Mémoires de la Société Archéologique Champenoise 2, Rheims, 46–97.

Wainwright, G.J. and Longworth, I.H. 1971   *Durrington Walls: Excavations 1966–8*, Soc. Ant. Lond. Res. Rep. xiii, London.

Wells, P.S. 1980   *Culture Contact and Culture Change*, Cambridge.

Wessex Archaeology 2002   *Kingsborough Manor development, Eastchurch, Isle of Sheppey: watching briefs, evaluations and Phase 1, Stage 2 archaeological excavation*, Salisbury.

Wilhelmi, K. 1977   Zur Funktion und Verbreitung dreieckige Tongewichte der Eisenzeit', *Germania* 55, 180–4.

Wilhelmi, K. 1987   'Zur Besiedlungsgenese Englands und des nordwestlichen Kontinent von 1500 vor bis Christi Geburt', *Acta Praehistorica Archaeologica* 19, 71–84.

Williams, D.F. 1977   'The Romano-British black-burnished industry: an essay on characterization by heavy mineral analysis' in D.P.S. Peacock, *Pottery and Early Commerce*, London, 163–215.

Williams, D.F. 1981   'The Roman amphora trade with Late Iron Age Britain' in H. Howard and E.L. Morris (eds), *Production and Distribution: A ceramic viewpoint*, B.A.R. Continental Series 120, Oxford, 123–32.

Williams-Thorpe, O. and Thorpe, R.S. 1988   'The provenance of donkey mills from Roman Britain' *Archaeometry* 30 (2), 275–89.

Wilson, M. 1983   'Pottery from the apsed building' in S.S. Frere and S. Stow, 198–206.

Wilson, M. 1995   'Pottery from C.E.C. sites' in K. Blockley *et al.*, 674–81.

Worsfold, F.H. 1943   'A report on the Late Bronze Age Site excavated at Minnis Bay, Birchington, Kent, 1938–40', *P.P.S.* xi, 28–47.

Wymer, J. and Bonsall, C. (eds) 1977   *Gazetteer of Mesolithic Sites in England and Wales with a Gazetteer of Upper Palaeolithic sites in England and Wales*, C.B.A. Research Report 20, London.

Yates, D.T. 2001   'Bronze Age agricultural intensification in the Thames Valley and Estuary' in J. Brück (ed.), *Bronze Age landscapes: tradition and transformation*, Oxford, 65–82.

Young, C.J. 1977   *The Roman Pottery Industry of the Oxford Region*, B.A.R. British Series 43, Oxford.

INDEX

abandonment 12, 14, 34, 65, 78, 81, 99, 181, 281, 287
Acy-Romance (Ardennes), France
  Late Iron Age pottery 178
aerial photography xix, 11, 285, 289, 292, 293, 295
Aisne valley, France
  Late Bronze Age/Early Iron Age pottery 120, 129, 141, 150, 290
Aldermaston, Berkshire
  Late Bronze Age pottery 118, 119, 140, 307
amphora 39, 62, 71, 92, 95, 178, 179, 237, 242
animal bones (*see* bones, mammal)
antler xiv, 276, 278
Ardennes 118, 128, 129, 150, 178
Aulnay-aux-Planches (Marne), France 119, 143
awl 86, 270
axe 1, 24, 251, 254, 256, 257, 260, 288
Aylesford, Kent
  clay moulds 263
  Early Iron Age pottery 119, 120, 168
  Late Iron Age pottery 191

Baldock, Hertfordshire
  Roman brooch 274, 275
Barham Down, Kent
  Late Iron Age pottery 178, 179, 181
  round-houses 289
Beacon Hill, near Herne Bay, Kent 1, 16
Beaker pottery viii, xiv, 5, 15, 299, 300
Belgium 34, 39, 65, 118, 120, 121, 169, 170, 269, 295
Benwell, Tyne and Wear
  Roman pottery 250
Bigbury, near Canterbury, Kent
  Late Iron Age pottery 178, 179, 181, 189, 191, 194
  Middle Iron Age pottery 284

Birdoswald, Cumbria
  Roman pottery 250
Birgelen, Germany
  Late Bronze Age pottery 119, 121
bones
  bird 279
    duck 281
    fowl 280
    wader 281
  human 8, 33, 49, 78, 91, 279, 292, 300
  mammal 8, 78, 279
    cattle 63, 281
    deer 281
    dog 98, 99, 281
    horse 33, 78, 281
    ox 33, 78, 280, 281
    pig 63, 78, 281
    sheep 33, 63, 78, 281
Borden, Kent
  Late Iron Age pottery 191
Borlez (Hesbaye), Belgium
  Late Bronze Age pottery 119, 120
Borough Green, Kent
  Late Iron Age pottery 195
Bovenister (Liege), Belgium
  Late Bronze Age/Early Iron Age pottery 119, 121
  Late Iron Age pottery 130
Bridge, Canterbury, Kent 284
  Late Bronze Age pottery 118, 119, 120, 129
briquetage viii, 269, 270
bronze hoards 34, 120, 170, 284, 286, 289
brooches 77, 95, 274, 275
Broomfield, Herne Bay, Kent 167
  Bogshole Lane 286

Bucy-le-Long (Aisne), France
  Late Bronze Age/Early Iron Age pottery 119, 128
burial 91, 284, 291, 300
  coffin nails 91
  cremation 5, 12, 39, 49, 63, 89, 91, 216, 292
  inhumation 5, 15, 89, 93, 208, 292
Bury St Edmunds, Suffolk
  Early Bronze Age pottery 299
butchery 280, 281

Caerleon, Gwent
  Roman pottery 247
Canterbury, Kent
  Burgate Street
    Late Iron Age pottery 195, 197
  Canterbury Castle
    Late Iron Age pottery 179, 194, 201
    Roman pottery 214, 217, 218, 220, 221, 222, 223, 225, 227, 231
  Castle Street/Stour Street (Cakebread-Robey)
    Roman pottery 214, 217, 218, 221, 225, 227, 231
  Cranmer House, London Road
    Roman pottery 231
  East of Marlowe Theatre
    Roman pottery 225, 231
  Marlowe excavations
    Late Iron Age pottery 178, 179
    Roman pottery 214, 216, 217, 218, 220, 221, 222, 225, 227, 231
  Marlowe Theatre
    Late Iron Age pottery 214
    Roman pottery 220, 225, 227, 231
  Reed Avenue
    Roman pottery 214, 222
  Simon Langton Yard
    Roman pottery 225, 231
  St Augustine's College
    Roman pottery 227
  St George's Street
    Roman pottery 227, 231
  St Stephen's
    Roman pottery 221
  Whitehall Road
    Late Iron Age pottery 195, 201
Carshalton, Surrey 120
  Queen Mary's Hospital
    Late Bronze Age pottery 118, 119, 285
    perforated pottery slabs 268

Catenoy, 'Le Camp César' (Oise), France
  Late Bronze Age pottery 118, 119, 120, 132, 143
causeway 11, 14, 16, 18, 20, 25, 27, 32, 33, 35, 37, 39, 41, 71, 79, 81, 83, 295
cereal production (see farming)
cess-pit 35
Chamesson, 'Bouchot-Bouchard' (Côte d'Or), France
  Late Bronze Age/Early Iron Age pottery 156
Channel Tunnel 283, 284
Charente valley, France
  Late Bronze Age/Early Iron Age pottery 141
Charing, Kent
  Late Iron Age enclosure 291
Chassemy (Aisne), France
  Late Bronze Age/Early Iron Age pottery 119, 120, 150
  rectangular structure 290
Chichester, West Sussex
  Roman brooch 274
Chislet, Kent ix, xxi, 1, 167
Choisy au Bac (Oise), France
  Late Bronze Age pottery 119, 120, 121, 128, 143
clay moulds (see metalworking)
clay weight 59
Colchester, Essex
  Roman brooch 274, 275
  Roman pottery 233, 245, 250
Coldharbour Road (see Gravesend)
Corbridge, Northumberland
  Roman pottery 244, 247, 250
Cottington Hill, Thanet, Kent 300
Court St Etienne, Belgium
  Late Bronze Age pottery 118, 119, 120, 121, 150
cropmarks vii, xi, xv, xxi, 4, 5, 6, 11, 14, 15, 16, 24, 25, 31, 33, 39, 65, 67, 69, 71, 73, 75, 77, 78, 81, 83, 85, 86, 87, 89, 91, 92, 93, 95, 285, 292, 293

Destelbergen (East Flanders), Belgium
  Late Bronze Age/Early Iron Age pottery 128
Donk, Belgium
  Late Bronze Age pottery 118, 119, 150, 156
Dorking, Surrey
  Roman pottery 247
Dover, Kent
  Late Iron Age pottery 194
  Roman pottery 247
Durrington Walls, Wiltshire
  flint tools 257

Eastbourne, East Sussex
  Late Bronze Age pottery 119, 120, 129
Easton Maudit, Northamptonshire
  Roman brooch 275
Ebbsfleet, Kent
  Late Iron Age pottery 194
eclabousée (*see* rusticated pottery)
Eddington, Herne Bay, Kent
  Eddington Farm, enclosure 285
  Underdown Lane, round-houses 289, 313
Egham, Surrey
  Petters Sports Field, 118, 119, 286
Epple Bay, Birchington, Kent
  briquetage 269

farming
  arable 62, 93, 99, 292
  cereal production 63
  livestock 288, 292
  pastoral 63, 288, 292
Farnham Green, Surrey
  Late Bronze Age pottery 119, 140, 158
Faversham, Kent
  Late Iron Age enclosure 291
  Late Iron Age pottery 183
Fengate, Northamptonshire
  Late Bronze Age/Early Iron Age pottery 119, 141
  metallurgy 266
Fexhe (Liege), Belgium
  Late Bronze Age/Early Iron Age pottery 119
field system vi, 14, 15, 31, 65, 69, 78, 79, 81, 83, 85, 87, 89, 93, 95, 98, 292
Fishbourne, West Sussex
  Roman brooch 274
flint tools 1, 8, 251
  Late Neolithic 11, 15, 283, 292
  Mesolithic 1, 11, 15, 283, 292
food storage 295
Fooz (Liege), Belgium
  Late Bronze Age/Early Iron Age pottery 119, 121, 128
Ford, near Herne Bay, Kent 1
  archbishop's manor 5
Ford stream 62
Fort-Harrouard (Eure-et-Loire), France
  Late Bronze Age pottery 118, 119, 140, 143, 150
  pin moulds 258, 260, 263
France 34, 65, 120, 121, 122, 141, 168, 169, 170, 178, 258, 260, 284, 290, 291, 295, 296

Fresnes-sur-Marne (Marne), France
  Late Bronze Age/Early Iron Age pottery 119, 121

Geology
  Bullhead Bed 168
  Gault clay 15
  Head Brickearth 15, 167
  Head Gravel 1, 15
  Thanet Beds 1, 168
  Upper Chalk 167
glass viii, xiv, 75, 89, 265, 275, 276
glauconite 102, 103, 167, 168
Goirle (North Brabant), Belgium
  Late Bronze Age pottery 119, 120
granary 12, 39, 41, 45, 47, 52, 54, 57, 59, 65
Gravesend, Kent
  Coldharbour Road, pottery 284
  Hillside, Late Iron Age enclosure 291
Gravon (Seine-et-Marne), France
  Late Bronze Age pottery 119, 120
Greensand
  fabric 168, 218
  geology 285
  quern 78, 278
Grooved Ware 257
Gussage All Saints, Dorset
  crucible 266

Hacklinge, Worth, Kent
  briquetage 269, 270
haematite 118, 128, 141, 166, 237, 301
Hallstatt 118, 121, 122, 128, 129, 131, 156, 162
Hampiré (Ardenne), Belgium
  Late Bronze Age/Early Iron Age pottery 119, 120
Haneffe (Liege), Belgium
  Iron Age pottery 119, 130, 143
Haps, Netherlands
  Late Bronze Age/Early Iron Age pottery 119, 121, 128, 130
Harbour, John 1
  surface finds, Herne Bay Museum xix, 15, 251
Harpstedt, Germany
  urns 122
Harrietsham, Kent
  Late Iron Age enclosure 291
Hawkinge, Folkestone, Kent
  Late Iron Age pottery 189, 191, 194, 197
Heathery Burn, Co. Durham
  copper alloy pin 263

Heathrow, Middlesex
  Middle Iron Age enclosure 285
Herne Bay, Kent 1, 5, 285
Heybridge, Essex 195
  Heybridge Basin
    Late Bronze Age/Early Iron Age pottery 119, 120, 149
    Late Iron Age pottery 195
  Lofts Farm 285
    amber beads 289
    axe 288
    enclosure 286, 287, 293
    Late Bronze Age pottery 119, 150, 286
    perforated clay slab 288
Highsted, Sittingbourne, Kent
  burial 292
hillfort 33
Hillside (*see* Gravesend)
Hod Hill, Dorset
  Roman brooch 274
Holywell Coombe, Folkestone, Kent
  Early Bronze Age pottery 299
Hooidonksche Akkers, Netherlands
  Late Bronze Age/Early Iron Age pottery 119, 150, 156
Hoo St Werburgh, Kent
  pottery 284
Horion 'Distrigaz' (Hesbaye), Belgium
  Late Bronze Age/Early Iron Age pottery 119, 121, 128
horseshoe 77, 274
Houplin-Ancoisne (Nord Pas de Calais), France
  Late Bronze Age/Early Iron Age pottery 119, 122, 128
Hunsbury, Northamptonshire
  Late Bronze Age/Early Iron Age pottery 119, 141

industrial waste 49, 52, 64, 268, 286, 289
Inghem (Pas de Calais), France
  Late Bronze Age/Early Iron Age pottery 119, 170
ironworking 39, 52
  slag 41, 48, 52, 54, 67, 266, 290
iron oxide 102, 103, 166, 183, 184, 278, 301, 302
Ivinghoe Beacon, Buckinghamshire
  Late Bronze Age/Early Iron Age pottery 118, 119, 158

Julliberries Grave, Chilham, Kent 292
Juseret, Bercheux-la-Hutte, Belgium
  Late Bronze Age/Early Iron Age pottery 150

Kelvedon, Essex
  Late Iron Age pottery 193

Kemmelberg (Heuvelland), Belgium
  Late Bronze Age/Early Iron Age pottery 119, 120, 122, 128, 129, 150
Kew, Surrey
  Early Bronze Age pottery 299
knife xiv, 27, 79, 217, 256, 257, 260, 269, 270, 287

Lakenheath, Suffolk
  copper alloy pin 263
Lamine (Hesbaye), Belgium
  Late Bronze Age pottery 118, 119, 121, 150
latch lifter 87, 273
La Calotterie (Pas de Calais), France
  Late Iron Age pottery 178
La Tène 118, 120, 121, 122, 128, 129, 131, 132, 150, 156, 170, 284, 290, 291
La Varde, Guernsey
  Early Bronze Age pottery 299
Leicester
  Roman brooch 274
Lens St Servais, 'de Puydt' (Liege), Belgium
  Late Bronze Age pottery 119, 143
Les Rouliers (Ardenne), France
  Late Bronze Age/Early Iron Age pottery 119, 128, 150
Little Waltham, Essex
  rectangular building 290
London
  Hornchurch, Late Bronze Age enclosure 285
  Regis House, Roman pottery 243
  Roman pottery 247
loomweight 27, 276, 288, 291, 295
Loos (Pas de Calais), France
  Late Bronze Age/Early Iron Age pottery 119, 122
Lord of the Manor, Thanet
  Late Iron Age pottery 179
Lower Rhine 122, 170, 245
Low Countries 39, 65, 121, 122, 130, 170
Lydden Valley, Kent 270

Maidstone, Kent 168
Mancetter, Warwickshire
  Roman pottery 243
Manston, Kent
  Kent International Business Park 291
Margate, Kent
  Late Iron Age pottery 195, 197
Marne 65, 118, 119, 120, 121, 128, 150, 170
Marshside, near Herne Bay, Kent 1

Medway 34, 168
Mesolithic
   flints 1, 11, 15, 256, 258, 283, 295
metalworking xxii, 8, 11, 12, 16, 24, 28, 29, 33, 34, 35, 39, 51, 52, 63, 64, 115, 143, 258, 260, 266, 268, 270, 289, 290, 293, 295
   bronze pins 16, 24, 33, 258, 260, 263, 284, 286, 295
   burnt clay 8, 18, 20, 22, 24, 27, 28, 29, 30, 31, 32, 35, 37, 41, 45, 47, 48, 51, 52, 56, 57, 59, 61, 62, 67, 71, 73, 85, 92, 95, 268, 286, 288
   casting debris 34, 260, 286, 287
   clay moulds xxii, 16, 24, 33, 258–65, 266, 267, 286, 288, 295
   copper dross 20, 22, 24, 27, 28, 30, 31, 37, 52, 54, 286, 288, 290
   crucible xiv, 54, 64, 262, 265, 266, 289, 290
   debris 8, 16, 20, 25, 29, 52, 57, 64, 115, 143, 266, 286, 288, 289
Mill Hill, Deal, Kent
   clay mould 286, 288
   Late Bronze Age/Early Iron Age pottery 118, 119, 120, 284, 285
   Late Iron Age pottery 201, 292
Minnis Bay, Birchington, Kent
   briquetage 64, 269
   Late Bronze Age/Early Iron Age pottery 118, 119, 140
   Late Iron Age pottery 197
Momalle (Hesbaye), Belgium
   Late Bronze Age/Early Iron Age pottery 119, 121
Monkton Court Farm, Thanet, Kent
   pottery 283, 284
Mont Troté (Ardennes), France
   Late Bronze Age/Early Iron Age pottery 119, 120, 122, 128
Moxhe (Hesbaye), Belgium
   Late Bronze Age/Early Iron Age pottery 119, 121, 143
Much Hadham, Hertfordshire
   Roman pottery 245
Mucking, Essex xxi, 285, 287, 288, 289, 292
   flint tools 258
   Late Bronze Age/Early Iron Age pottery 119, 120, 158
   pottery slabs 268

nail 89, 91
needle 78, 270
Neolithic
   flints 1, 11, 15, 37, 254, 257, 258, 283, 295, 300
Netherlands 170

Neuwiedbekken, Netherlands
   Late Bronze Age pottery 118, 119, 122
Niedermendig (East Eifel), Germany 278, 279
Nijon, 'La Mottote' (Haute-Marne), France
   Late Bronze Age pottery 118
North Shoebury, Essex
   Late Bronze Age pottery 119, 120, 143

Oleye, Belgium
   Late Bronze Age pottery 118, 119
Owlesbury, Hampshire
   burial 292

Palaeolithic
   flints 1, 295
palisade 11, 16, 18, 20, 33, 78, 98, 99, 143
Paris Basin, France 128
perforated pottery slabs 18, 22, 24, 35, 41
periglacial features 5, 25
Pernant (Oise), France
   Late Bronze Age/Early Iron Age pottery 128
pins xxii, 24, 78, 85, 258, 260, 263, 266, 270, 274, 275, 286
Pitet (Liege), Belgium
   Late Bronze Age pottery 119, 143, 150
Plumpton Plain, East Sussex
   Late Bronze Age pottery 119, 143
Pont-sur-Yonne (Yonne), France
   Late Bronze Age pottery 118, 119
Prae Wood, Hertfordshire
   Late Iron Age pottery 194
probe 78, 270

quern 92
   Lower Greensand 78, 278
   Millstone Grit 79

radiocarbon (dating) 8, 156, 178, 284, 285, 299, 300
rampart 11, 16, 17, 18, 20, 33, 35
Ramsgate, Kent
   enclosure 285, 287, 293
Rathgall, Co. Wicklow, Ireland
   casting debris 260, 263
Reculver, near Herne Bay, Kent 1
Remicourt (Liege), Belgium
   Late Bronze Age/Early Iron Age pottery 119, 122
Remilly-Aillicourt (Ardennes), France
   Late Bronze Age pottery 118, 119

Richborough, Kent 1
  Roman brooch 274
  Roman pottery 214, 221, 242
ring 28, 270, 286, 287
Robert Brett and Sons Ltd xix, xxi
Roitzheim, Euskirchen, Germany
  Late Bronze Age pottery 118, 119
Roman
  bath-house 99, 291
  burial 89, 91, 208
  coin 97, 98, 99
  hypocaust xv, 98, 242, 244, 281
  opus signinum 97, 99
  painted plaster 99
  pottery
    'Brockley Hill' 216
    'Rhenish' 216, 245, 319
    'Stuppington Lane' 214, 217, 221
    Alice Holt ware 216, 231
    amphora 39, 62, 71, 92, 95, 178, 179, 237, 242
    Colchester 233
    Gallo-Belgic 79, 92, 93, 95, 191, 193, 201
    Hofheim flagon 178, 191, 194
    Mayen 216
    mortaria vii, 73, 79, 92, 98, 214, 216, 245, 247, 250
    Moselkeramik 216
    Nene Valley 216, 245
    North Kentish ware 93
    Oxfordshire 216, 231, 245
    Portchester 216
    samian vii, xiv, 54, 73, 75, 77, 79, 83, 85, 87, 91, 92, 95, 98, 99, 214, 216, 221, 242, 244
  tile 97, 291
Rosmeer, Belgium
  Early Iron Age pottery 119, 121
rusticated pottery (*eclabousée*) xv, 24, 35, 37, 39, 41, 43, 45, 48, 49, 52, 54, 55, 56, 57, 59, 61, 62, 65, 105, 109, 121, 122, 131, 132, 145, 166, 167, 169, 170, 178, 284, 290, 299

Saint-Georges (Liege), Belgium
  Late Bronze Age pottery 118, 119, 120, 128, 150
Saint-Sauveur, 'La Prévôtée' (Oise), France
  Late Bronze Age pottery 119, 150
salt 269
  salt processing 12
  salt production 8, 39, 52, 54, 57, 63, 64, 105, 158, 268, 269, 270, 288, 290, 295
  vessel 51, 54, 64, 156, 268, 288

samian ware (*see* Roman pottery)
saw 73, 273
Seine, river 128
Seine-Maritime, France 170
Sheepen, Hertfordshire
  Late Iron Age pottery 193, 317
Sheppey, Kent
  Kingsborough Farm 285, 287
Shoreham, West Sussex
  Early Bronze Age pottery 299
shrine 47, 63, 64
Silchester, Hampshire
  Roman brooch 274
Sint-Gillis-Waas (East Flanders), Belgium
  Late Bronze Age/Early Iron Age pottery 122
Somme, France 122, 170
South Shields, Tyne and Wear
  Roman pottery 250
Spain 169, 216, 237
spearhead 24, 27, 260, 273
Spiennes, Camp-à-Cayoux (Hainault), Belgium
  Late Bronze Age/Early Iron Age pottery 119, 122
spindlewhorl 49, 62, 78, 89, 91, 288
spoon 270
Springfield, Kent
  flint tools 258
  Late Bronze Age pottery 119
Springfield Lyons, Essex
  bronze casting 286, 289
  Late Bronze Age enclosure 285, 286, 287, 288, 289
  Late Bronze Age pottery 119, 120
Staple Howe, North Yorkshire
  copper alloy pin 263
  Late Bronze Age pottery 118, 119
Stourmouth, Kent 1
Streel (Hesbaye), Belgium
  Late Bronze Age/Early Iron Age pottery 119, 122, 128
stylus 85, 270, 273
St Mildred's Bay, Margate, Kent
  briquetage 64, 269
Sussex
  Late Iron Age pottery 189, 191
Swalecliffe, Kent
  briquetage 269, 270
Swarling near Canterbury, Kent
  Late Iron Age pottery 192
sword 24, 156, 260

Taverny, Le Camp de César (Val d'Oise), France
  Late Bronze Age pottery 119, 120
Thames Estuary xxi
Thames valley 11, 34, 65, 118, 120, 169, 268, 288, 289, 295
Thanet, Kent 1, 64, 168, 179, 269, 270, 283, 284, 292, 300
Thiverny (Oise), France
  Late Bronze Age pottery 119, 128
Thurnham, Kent 291
Tierceau, Orp-le-Grand (Brabant), Belgium
  Late Bronze Age/Early Iron Age pottery 130
Tinqueux (Marne), France
  Late Bronze Age/Early Iron Age pottery 119, 128, 150
toilet instruments 78, 270
trade 34, 168, 216, 231
tweezers 78, 83, 270

Underdown Lane (*see* Eddington)
Upchurch, Kent
  Roman pottery 83, 91, 215, 216, 221, 222, 227, 231, 247

Verberie, 'Le Buisson-Campin' (Oise), France
  Late Bronze Age pottery 119, 120, 150
Verlaine, 'Blanc Boise' (Hesbaye), Belgium
  Late Bronze Age pottery 118, 119
Verulamium, Hertfordshire
  Roman pottery 244, 245, 247
Vieux Moulin, 'Saint-Pierre en Chastre' (Oise), France
  Late Bronze Age pottery 119, 120
Villeneuve-Saint-Germain (Aisne), France
  Late Bronze Age/Early Iron Age pottery 119, 150
Vixian
  Late Bronze Age/Early Iron Age pottery 128

Vrigny (Marne), France
  Late Bronze Age/Early Iron Age pottery 119, 121, 150
Vron (Somme), France
  Late Bronze Age/Early Iron Age pottery 119, 122

Wallingford, Berkshire
  Late Bronze Age/Early Iron Age pottery 119, 141
Walney North End, Cumbria
  copper alloy pin 263
Wantsum channel 1, 11, 15, 20, 33, 34, 62, 64, 71, 81, 182, 270, 289
Warnant (Liege), Belgium
  Iron Age pottery 119, 130
weaving 276, 288
  comb 62, 63, 276, 278
Westbere, near Canterbury, Kent
  Late Iron Age pottery 192
Weybridge, Surrey
  Brooklands
    Late Bronze Age/Early Iron Age pottery 119, 122, 158
Whitfield-Eastry by-pass, Kent
  Late Iron Age pottery 191, 194
  rectangular structure 291
Winchester, Hampshire
  Roman brooch 275
Wollaston, Northamptonshire
  rectangular building 290
Wroxeter, Shropshire
  Roman pottery 247

York
  Roman pottery 243